MW01675118

The Windows 95 Textbook

Extended Edition

Stewart Venit

California State University
Los Angeles

Scott/Jones, Inc., Publishers

P. O. Box 696, El Granada, CA 94018
scotjones2@aol.com
(415) 726-2436 *or* Fax: (415) 726-4693
http://www.scottjonespub.com

The Windows 95 Textbook: Extended Edition
Stewart Venit

ISBN 1-57676-000-6

Book Production: The Canfield Bookworks
Book Manufacturing: Malloy Lithographing, Inc.
Composition: Stewart Venit
Text Design: V & J Enterprises

9 8 7 X Y Z

ADDITIONAL TITLES OF INTEREST FROM SCOTT/JONES

The Windows (3.1) Textbook
A Short Course in Windows 95
The Windows 95 Textbook: Standard Ed.
by Stewart Venit

Fortran for Scientists & Engineers, 2nd edition
by Gary Bronson

Visual Basic with Business Applications
by Mark Simkin

The DOS Primer and More, 2nd edition
by Dorothy Calvin

Problem Solving with C
by Jacqueline Jones and Keith Harrow

The DOS-6 Coursebook
Visual Basic Programming
The Visual Basic 4 Coursebook
by Forest Lin

C by Discovery, Second Edition
(emphasis on ANSI C)
by L. S. Foster

C Through Objects
by John Connely

A Short Course in Access 7
by Maggie Trigg and Phyllis Dobson

Assembly Language for the IBM PC Family (Second edition)
Quick Start in C++
by William Jones

FORTHCOMING TEXTS FROM SCOTT/JONES

Time to Excel
by Marvin Harris

A Short Course in MS Word 7
by Donna Madsen and Kay Forest

Principles of Programming using Visual Basic
by Gary Bronson

Contents

Preface *xi*

Introduction *I-1*

Personal Computers *I-2*
- What is a Computer? *I-2*
- The Central Processing Unit *I-3*
- Internal Memory *I-4*
- Mass Storage Devices *I-4*
- Input Devices *I-6*
- Output Devices *I-7*

Software, Operating Systems, and Windows *I-8*
- Applications Software *I-9*
- The Operating System *I-9*
- Microsoft Windows *I-11*

A Brief History of the Personal Computer *I-14*

Summary *I-17*
Review Exercises *I-18*

Chapter 1 **The Basics of Using Windows 95** *1*

1.1 The Windows 95 Desktop *2*

1.2 Of Mice and Menus *3*
- Using the Mouse *3*
- Using Menus *4*

Types of Menu Items *6*
1.3 Windows within Windows *9*
Operations on Windows *10*
Manipulating Windows *10*
Scroll Bars *13*
1.4 Conversing with Dialog Boxes *16*
A Typical Dialog Box *16*
Additional Dialog Box Features *19*
1.5 Shutting Down Windows 95 *21*
Chapter Summary *24*
Review Exercises *25*
Lab Exercises *29*
If You Want to Learn More ... *32*

Chapter 2 **Working with Applications and Documents** ***35***

2.1 Starting and Closing Applications *36*
Using the Start Menu *36*
Other Ways to Start Applications *39*
Closing an Application 39
2.2 Working with Documents *41*
An Introduction to WordPad *41*
Saving a Document *44*
Closing a Document *46*
Opening a Document *47*
Printing a Document *48*
2.3 Running Several Applications at Once *51*
Switching Among Applications *52*
Transferring Information between Documents *53*
An Example *54*
2.4 Getting On-screen Help *57*
Accessing Online Help *57*
Locating the Information You Need *58*
Using a Help Window *62*
Context-Sensitive Help *63*
Chapter Summary *66*
Review Exercises *68*
Lab Exercises *71*
If You Want to Learn More ... *75*

Chapter 3 **Managing Files, Folders, and Disks** *77*

3.1 The Windows 95 File System *78*
What are Files and Folders? *78*
Naming Files and Folders *79*
Path Names *81*

3.2 An Introduction to Windows Explorer *81*
The Explorer Window *81*
The Folder Tree Pane *82*
The Contents Pane *83*
Contents Pane View Options *85*

3.3 Moving and Copying Files and Folders *89*
Selecting Files and Folders *89*
Moving and Copying Objects *91*
The Send To Command *94*

3.4 Other Operations on Files and Folders *96*
Deleting Files and Folders *96*
Renaming Files and Folders *98*
Creating New Files and Folders *99*
Creating Shortcuts *101*

3.5 My Computer *103*
Starting My Computer *103*
Using My Computer to Browse Folders *104*
Using My Computer to Operate on Files and Folders *106*

3.6 Formatting and Copying Floppy Disks *110*
Formatting a Floppy Disk *110*
Copying an Entire Diskette *112*

Chapter Summary *114*
Review Exercises *115*
Lab Exercises *119*
If You Want to Learn More ... *123*

Chapter 4 **Using Windows Efficiently** *127*

4.1 Tricks with the Taskbar *128*
Changing the Way the Taskbar is Displayed *128*
Manipulating Application Windows from the Taskbar *131*

4.2 Customizing the Start Button Menus *135*
The What and Why of the Start Button Menus *135*

Adding Menu Items by Drag-and-Drop *136*
A More Flexible Way to Add Menu Items *137*
Removing Items from the Start Button Menus *140*
Other Ways to Add or Remove Menu Items *141*

4.3 The Windows Find Utility *143*
The Find Utility Window *143*
Performing a Simple Search *144*
Refining the Search Criteria *146*
Using the Results of a Search *148*

4.4 Associating File Types with Applications *150*
File Types *150*
Creating a New Registered File Type *152*
Removing or Modifying a Registered File Type *156*

4.5 Property Sheets *159*
The Property Sheet for a File or Folder *159*
The Property Sheet for a Shortcut *160*
Creating a "Project Folder" *162*

Chapter Summary *164*
Review Exercises *166*
Lab Exercises *170*
If You Want to Learn More ... *174*

Chapter 5 Control Panel: Customizing Windows *177*

5.1 An Introduction to Control Panel *178*
The Control Panel Window *178*
Control Panel Functions *180*
Closing Control Panel *181*

5.2 Changing the Desktop Background *182*
Choosing a Desktop Pattern *182*
Choosing Wallpaper *184*
Choosing a Screen Saver *185*

5.3 Changing the Appearance of a Window *188*
Choosing a Predefined Window Scheme *188*
Creating a Custom Window Scheme *190*

5.4 Adjusting the Feel of Keyboard and Mouse *193*
Changing the Speed of the Keyboard *193*
Changing the Action of the Mouse *195*

5.5 Other Basic Control Panel Options *198*
Setting the Computer's Clock *199*

Installing New Programs *200*
Viewing Your Fonts *202*

Chapter Summary *205*
Review Exercises *206*
Lab Exercises *209*
If You Want to Learn More ... *213*

Chapter 6 More About Control Panel *217*

6.1 Managing Printers *218*
The Printers Folder *218*
Changing the Printer Setup *219*
Managing Print Jobs *223*
Adding a New Printer *225*

6.2 Installing New Hardware *228*
Plug-and-Play *229*
The Add New Hardware Utility *230*

6.3 Sounds and Multimedia *234*
The Sounds Utility *234*
The Multimedia Utility *237*

6.4 Accessibility Options *240*
Keyboard Options *240*
Sound Options *242*
Display Options *243*
Mouse Options *244*
Other Accessibility Options *245*

6.5 Other Control Panel Options *247*
The Modems Utility *247*
The System Utility *250*
Other Control Panel Utilities *254*

Chapter Summary *255*
Review Exercises *256*
Lab Exercises *260*
If You Want to Learn More ... *264*

Chapter 7 Word Processing with WordPad *267*

7.1 WordPad Revisited *268*
The WordPad Window *268*

Editing a Document *269*

7.2 Using Fonts in WordPad *273*

Fonts Revisited *274*
Using the Font Dialog Box *275*
Using the Format Bar *276*

7.3 Formatting Text in WordPad *278*

Formatting the Document as a Whole *278*
Formatting Paragraphs *280*

7.4 Using Graphics in a WordPad Document *287*

Inserting a Graphic into a Document *287*
Editing a Graphic *290*
Deleting, Moving, and Resizing a Graphic *290*

7.5 Other Features of WordPad *294*

Find and Replace *294*
Print Preview *296*
Specifying a File Format *298*
And a Few Frills ... *301*

Chapter Summary *305*
Review Exercises *307*
Lab Exercises *310*
If You Want to Learn More ... *314*

Chapter 8 Creating Graphics with Paint *317*

8.1 An Introduction to Paint *318*

The Paint Window *318*
Drawing a Graphic *320*

8.2 Using the Drawing Tools *323*

Creating Lines, Curves, and Other Strokes *323*
Creating Geometric Shapes *326*
Inserting Text into a Graphic *329*

8.3 Editing a Graphic *334*

Erasing Mistakes *334*
Zooming In on the Graphic *335*
Selecting Part of a Graphic *338*

8.4 Manipulating Cutouts *341*

Basic Operations on Cutouts *341*
Moving, Copying, and Sweeping a Cutout *343*
Resizing a Cutout *345*
Other Operations on Cutouts *346*

8.5 Other Features of Paint 351
Setting Up the Page 351
Print Preview 353
Changing the Size of the Drawing Area 354
Creating Wallpaper 355
Chapter Summary 357
Review Exercises 358
Lab Exercises 362
If You Want to Learn More ... 365

Chapter 9 Using Other Windows Accessories 369

9.1 The Windows Calculators 370
The Standard Calculator 370
The Scientific Calculator 372
9.2 The Notepad Text Editor 377
Basic Features 378
Beyond the Basics 379
9.3 Backing Up Your Hard Disk 383
Starting the Backup Utility 383
The Backup Procedure 384
Restoring Backed Up Files 387
Some Options for the Backup Process 388
9.4 Using Other System Tools 391
ScanDisk 391
Disk Defragmenter 395
DriveSpace 398
9.5 Additional Accessories 402
Character Map 402
Multimedia Accessories 403
Communications Accessories 404
Chapter Summary 405
Review Exercises 407
Lab Exercises 410
If You Want to Learn More ... 414

Chapter 10 Networking with Windows 95 419

10.1 Networking 420
Types of Networks 420

Network Hardware *421*
Accessing a Network *423*
The Network Neighborhood *424*
The Network Control Utility *425*

10.2 Dial-Up Networking *427*
Installing the Dial-Up Networking Files *428*
Using the New Connection Wizard *429*

10.3 Using Microsoft Exchange *432*
How Exchange Works *432*
Installing Exchange *433*
Electronic Mail Terminology *436*
Sending Electronic Mail *437*
Receiving Electronic Mail *440*
Managing Mail Messages *440*
Using Mail-enabled Applications *441*

10.4 Just the Fax *442*
Sending a Fax *444*
Receiving a Fax *447*

10.5 HyperTerminal *451*
Some Communications Basics *451*
Using HyperTerminal *452*
Configuring HyperTerminal for the Connection *453*
Connecting to the Host Computer *457*
Using the Host Computer *458*
Transferring Files *459*
Terminating Your Session *461*

10.6 Portable Computing *461*
Docking Detection *462*
Direct Cable Connection *463*
The Briefcase Utility *466*
Deferred Printing *469*

Chapter Summary *471*
Review Exercises *474*
Lab Exercises *478*
If You Want to Learn More ... *482*

Chapter 11 **Windows and the Internet** ***483***

11.1 The Internet *484*
A Brief History of the Internet *485*

Internet Names and Addresses *485*
Connecting to the Internet *487*

11.2 Using Internet Explorer *489*
Navigating with Internet Explorer *489*
Performing Searches *495*
Disconnecting from the Internet *499*
Printing Internet Pages *500*
Sending and Receiving Internet Mail *502*
Downloading Files *505*

11.3 Configuring an ISP Internet Connection *506*
TCP/IP Transmission *506*
Configuring the Connection *507*

Chapter Summary *509*
Review Exercises *511*
Lab Exercises *513*
If You Want to Learn More ... *516*

Chapter 12 Additional Topics ***519***

12.1 Running DOS Programs *520*
Running DOS Applications under Windows *520*
Running a DOS Session *523*

12.2 Property Settings for DOS Programs *526*
Displaying a DOS Program's Property Sheets *526*
Basic Properties *528*
Types of Memory Used by DOS Programs *530*

12.3 Startup Options and Configuration Files *535*
The Boot Process *535*
Startup Options *536*
The Config.sys and Autoexec.bat Files *540*

12.4 The Windows Registry *543*
The Structure of the Registry *544*
Editing the Registry *545*
Backing Up and Restoring the Registry *550*

12.5 Object Linking and Embedding *556*
What is OLE? *556*
How to Embed or Link an Object *557*
Editing an Embedded or Linked Object *562*

Chapter Summary *567*
Review Exercises *569*

Lab Exercises *573*
If You Want to Learn More ... *577*

Appendix A General Shortcut Keys *A-1*

Appendix B Some Useful DOS Commands *A-5*

Appendix C Answers to Odd-Numbered Review Exercises *A-13*

Index *N-1*

Preface

The Windows 95 Textbook: Extended Edition is intended for use in a variety of courses that teach the Windows 95 operating system. It is expected that some readers will have had little or no experience with computers, whereas others will be familiar, to various degrees, with the workings of DOS or Windows 3.1. With this in mind, we have written the text for the novice user, but in such a way that those with more experience can easily skip over or quickly read the material with which they are familiar. For example, almost all the general information about computers has been placed in the Introduction. Other aids to quickly locating and moving through familiar topics are described under *Features of the Text*, later in this preface.

Organization of the Text

We have organized this text to provide flexibility in choosing topics and the order in which they are presented. A pictorial representation of the text's organization is shown in the Chapter Dependency Flowchart on the next page. Here is a more detailed description:

- An Introduction provides general information about computer hardware and software. It is intended primarily for those students who have little or no experience with computers, but may also be useful reading for others.
- Chapter 1, which covers the basics of using Windows 95, is the normal jumping-off point for students who have some familiarity with computers, but none with Windows 95. Most of the concepts

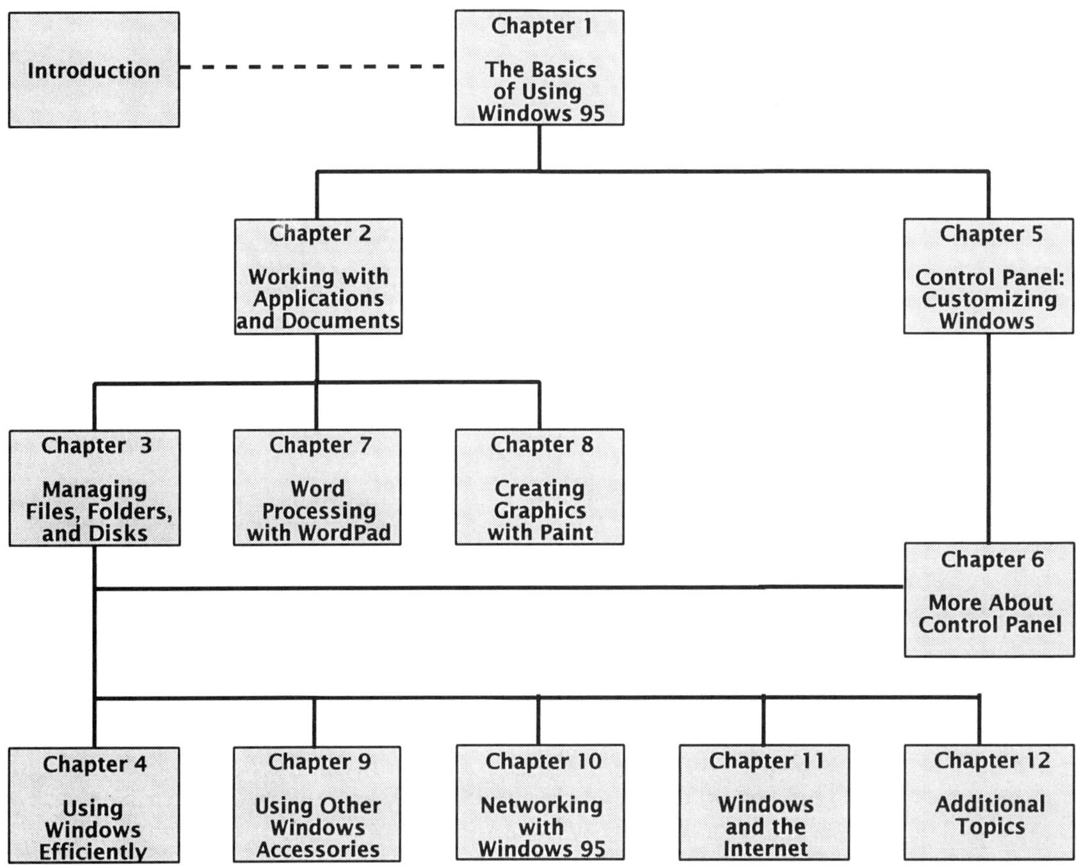

Chapter Dependency Flowchart

that are discussed here should seem fairly familiar to those who have used Windows 3.1. Be aware that the terminology and techniques discussed in Chapter 1 are used throughout the text.

- Chapter 2 presents some fundamental material on working with applications and documents, and would typically be covered next. However, those instructors who want to follow a more gentle path can instead jump to Chapter 5, which deals with some of the ways to customize Windows 95.
- After completing Chapter 2, Chapter 3, 5, 7 or 8 could be covered next. Chapter 3 is the most difficult of these, but also contains the most important material.

- After completing Chapter 3, almost all the remaining chapters are accessible to the reader. There is only one exception: It would be wise to cover the first chapter on Control Panel (Chapter 5) before tackling its more advanced aspects in Chapter 6.
- Chapters 4, 9, and 12 each deal with an assortment of related, but mostly independent topics. In each of these chapters, individual sections may usually be omitted, if so desired. Moreover, the first two sections of Chapters 4 and 9 and the first section of Chapter 12, cover relatively straightforward material that does not require the Chapter 3 prerequisite implied by the flowchart above.

Features of the Text

End-of-section Tutorials

1. Certainly, the best way to learn Windows 95 is to use Windows 95. With this in mind, we have written the text in a way that encourages students to follow along at the computer. Moreover, almost all sections end with a brief Tutorial that reviews the material by leading the student through a hands-on exercise.

No delay in starting up

2. The text introduces Windows' terminology and techniques immediately; we start up Windows on the first page of the first chapter. On the other hand, for those courses that require it, the Introduction provides general information on using personal computers.

Objectives and summaries

3. We have tried to integrate the material in each chapter as much as possible, so that it forms a cohesive whole. To help in this regard, every chapter (and the Introduction, as well) begins with a brief overview and statement of objectives, and ends with a fairly comprehensive summary.

Chapter exercises

4. The text contains two types of exercises at the end of every chapter:
   - Review Exercises (completion, true/false, and multiple choice) test the students' knowledge of facts presented in the chapter. Answers to the odd-numbered questions are provided in Appendix C.
   - The last Review Exercise in each chapter asks the student to "Build Your Own Glossary" — to provide definitions for a given list of important terms introduced in that chapter. (To make this task a little easier, the listed terms are boldfaced when they first appear within the chapter.)
   - Lab Exercises require the students to perform the kinds of tasks they will encounter in using Windows on an everyday basis.

If You Want to Learn More ...

5. For those students who want something extra, the very end of every chapter contains a section entitled "If You Want to Learn More ...". This section consists of a series of notes that delve more deeply into some of the chapter material and point, when possible, to future sections of the text that expand on this material.

TIPs

6. TIPs appear periodically throughout the text. These short notes provide insight into, or specialized knowledge about, the topic at hand. A fact or technique may be called a TIP because it is especially important or because it is interesting or unusual.

WARNINGs

7. Other specialized notes are designated as WARNINGs. They caution the reader against taking certain actions, which in some circumstances could lead to extreme regret.

Margin notes

8. Occasional brief phrases in the left margin of the text make it easy for the reader to locate subtopics and important procedures.

Supplements

9. The following ancillary material is available for this textbook:
   - A *Student Disk*, containing the files referenced in the Tutorials and Lab Exercises, accompanies the text.
   - The answers to the even-numbered Review Exercises are available to instructors directly from the publisher*.
   - A test bank of additional short-answer questions (prepared by Wesley Scruggs of Brazosport College), keyed to the material in the text, is also available to instructors directly from the publisher.

A Few Words about Homework

This text, through its end-of-chapter exercises, provides an ample supply of homework problems. The Review Exercises can usually be answered with a single word (or letter, in the case of the multiple choice problems), and the Lab Exercises contain frequent questions that require a brief answer or explanation. (The Lab Exercises also occasionally call for an optional screen capture.)

In a computer course, it is desirable to provide students, as quickly as possible, with the ability to use the computer for printing solutions to their homework problems. For this reason, we introduce, relatively early in the text, the basics of WordPad (Section 2.2) and the techniques for capturing windows and screens (Section 2.3). Once this

*The address and telephone numbers of the publisher appear on the back cover.

material has been completed, students will be able to hand in computer-printed homework.

Acknowledgments

I would like to thank the many people who helped bring this project to fruition. A textbook always benefits from varied points of view and I was lucky to have the following experienced instructors offer helpful suggestions for the developing manuscript:

Faculty reviewers

Lynn Aaron
Rockland College

Fred Clark
Peninsula College

Dineen Ebert
St. Louis CC — Meramec

Lew Garrett
Alvin Community College

Charles Fromme
Queensborough Community College

Wade Graves
Grayson Community College

Thomas Hodgson
St. Louis CC — Meramec

Anne Houck
Pima Community College

Kathy Jesiolowski
Milwaukee Area Technical College

Alex Kane
Western Iowa Tech CC

Paul Lecoq
Spokane Falls College

Jill Lombardo
Wenatchee Valley College

Ruby Loveless
Aims Community College

Gloria Nobles
American River College

Carol Paxton
Heywood Community College

Crystal Sloan
Roan College

Wesley Scruggs
Brazosport College

Glen Tatum
Southeast Community College

Kathryn Traxler
Louisiana State University

Don Voils
Palm Beach Junior College

Jin Wang
Alabama State University

Nancy Webb
City College of San Francisco

The following professors helped to shape the current text by sharing with me, over the past two years, classroom feedback from my original Windows (3.1) textbook:

Charles Christensen
Waubonsee Community College

Nina Edgmand
Salt Lake Community College

Norman Hahn
Thomas Nelson College

Alex Kane
Western Iowa Tech CC

Usha Jindal
Washtenaw Community College

Shirley Orsinelli
San Diego Mesa College

The text was class-tested by Tom Hodgson and Anne Houck. I would like to thank the following students, who submitted reviews upon completion of their course:

Student testers

Thomas Burns

Christy Chassere

Omar Fernandez

Ruth Hille

Joseph Kofron

Diane Lott

Angela Martin

Mark Mindu

Kathleen Nolte

Kathryn Young

My publisher, Richard Jones, gave enthusiastic and unwavering support for this text, and managed, as usual, to make criticism sound like praise. I am also grateful to Leslie Hardin of Oklahoma City Community College for her outstanding contribution to Chapters 10 and 11. Rich Marmon contributed to these chapters, as well.

I would like to thank my wife, Corinne, and my daughter, Tamara, for understanding that a project of this sort requires the author to spend countless hours glued to a computer monitor. Finally, special mention should be made of my dogs, Maggie and Abby, who often kept me company, sleeping peacefully next to the humming computer.

Introduction

We are living in a world that is becoming increasingly dependent on the electronic computer. Computers help run our businesses and institutions, design and build manufactured products, provide instantaneous worldwide communication, publish our newspapers, magazines, and books, and supply all sorts of educational and recreational activities. Many forms of employment now require some kind of **computer literacy** — an understanding of how to use a computer effectively.

In this introduction, we will describe, in general terms, the computer's *hardware* and *software* — the components and programs that make it work. Although this material is not essential for an understanding of Windows 95, it may help with certain topics and will probably increase your computer literacy. More specifically, you will learn about:

1. Computers in general and personal computers in particular.
2. The components of a computer: its central processing unit, internal memory, mass storage, and input and output devices.
3. Types of computer applications.
4. The function of an operating system.
5. Microsoft Windows — what it is and why it's important.
6. The history of the personal computer.

Personal Computers

Everyone who uses a computer on a daily basis becomes accustomed to dealing with special computer-related terminology. Yet, to a beginner, many of these terms can be confusing and even intimidating. There are floppy disks and hard disks, kilobytes and megabytes, mice and monitors, and much, much more. In this section, we will try to take some of the mystery out of computer terminology.

What is a Computer?

As with any evolving technology, precisely defining the term *computer* is not easy. Computers can take many different forms and their capabilities are constantly expanding. Yet, all computers do the same basic things. Every **computer** can input, store, manipulate, and output vast quantities of data at very high speed. Moreover, all computers are *programmable* — they can follow a list of instructions (a **program**) and act upon intermediate results without human intervention.

A **personal computer** (also called a **microcomputer** or a **PC**) is a relatively small type of computer, intended for use by one person at a time. (Larger machines — known as *minicomputers*, *mainframes*, and *supercomputers*, in order of increasing size and power — can be simultaneously shared by many users, connected to the computer by cables or telephone lines.) All personal computers are small enough to fit on a desktop; portable PCs are even smaller — usually no larger than a looseleaf binder. A drawing of a typical PC is shown in Figure 1.

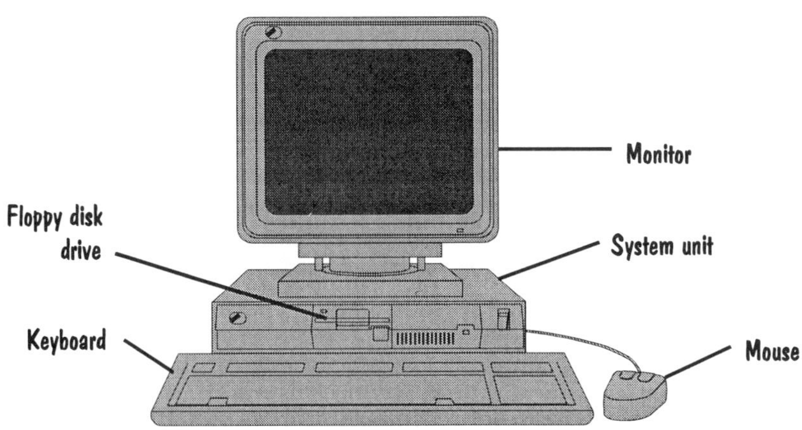

Figure 1 A Typical Personal Computer

Components of a computer

As the definition implies, a computer must have the ability to input, store, manipulate, and output data. These functions are carried out by the five main components of a computer system:

1. The central processing unit
2. Internal memory
3. Mass storage devices
4. Input devices
5. Output devices

In a personal computer, the first two of these components (and usually the third as well) are housed in the **system unit** (see Figure 1). The input devices, such as the keyboard and mouse, and output devices, such as the monitor, are housed in their own enclosures and are connected to the system unit by cables. Devices like these, that are used by a computer but located outside the system unit, are sometimes called **peripherals**. All the physical equipment that makes up the computer system is known as **hardware**.

The Central Processing Unit

The **central processing unit** (also called the **processor** or **CPU**) is the brain of the computer. It receives all program instructions, performs the arithmetic and logical operations necessary to execute them, and controls all the other computer components. In a personal computer, the processor consists of hundreds of thousands of transistors residing on a single *chip* the size of a large postage stamp and plugged into the computer's main circuit board, the *motherboard*.

More than any other component, the CPU distinguishes one computer from another. In the kind of computer you will be using, which is known as **IBM-compatible**, the processor is one of the following types (in order of increasing power): 386 (pronounced "three-86"), 486 ("four-86"), *Pentium*, or *Pentium Pro*.

The power of a processor is determined largely by two factors: its speed, measured in *megahertz* (MHz), and the amount, or number of *bits*, of data it can process at a time. (A **bit** is the smallest piece of information a computer can manipulate; its value is represented by either a 0 or 1.) For example, the Pentium is a 64-bit chip that comes in variations that run at speeds from 60 MHz to (as of this writing) 200 MHz. To use Windows 95, you need a computer with at least a 32-bit chip, and the more speed the better.

Internal Memory

A computer uses its **internal memory** to store the instructions and data to be processed by the CPU. In a personal computer, memory resides on a series of chips either plugged directly into the motherboard or into one or more smaller circuit boards connected to the motherboard.

ROM and RAM Internal memory is divided into two types: ROM and RAM. **ROM** stands for *Read-Only Memory.* It contains an unalterable set of instructions that the computer consults during its start-up process and during certain other basic operations. **RAM** (*Random Access Memory*), on the other hand, can be both read from and written to. (Think of ROM as a reference sheet, while RAM is a scratchpad — a very large scratchpad.) RAM is used by the computer to hold program instructions and data. Whereas ROM is a permanent form of memory storage, all the information stored in RAM is lost when the computer is turned off.

Memory is usually measured in *kilobytes* and *megabytes*, where one **byte** consists of eight bits and is the amount of memory used to store one character of information. (Loosely speaking, a *character* is any symbol you can type, such as a letter, a digit, or a punctuation mark.) One **kilobyte**, abbreviated *KB*, is 1,024 (= 2^{10}) bytes and one **megabyte** (*MB*) is 1,024 kilobytes. Thus, a computer with eight megabytes of RAM, a typical amount nowadays, can store 8,388,606 (= 8 × 1,024 × 1,024) characters of information.

Mass Storage Devices

In addition to ROM and RAM, a computer needs **mass storage**, another form of memory, which stores programs and data semi-permanently. (They remain in mass storage until you decide to erase them.) However, to make use of any information stored on a mass storage device, that information must first be *loaded* (copied) into RAM.

Disk drives On personal computers, the primary type of mass storage device is the **disk drive**. Most PCs contain a *hard disk drive* housed within the system unit and one or two *floppy disk drives*, also housed within the system unit but accessible from the outside (see Figure 1). To store information, the hard disk drive makes use of a constantly spinning magnetic platter — the **hard disk** — which is sealed within the drive. **Floppy disks** (or **diskettes**), on the other hand, are stored away from the computer and, when needed, are inserted into the diskette drive.

Floppy disks Floppy disks and their drives come in two sizes: 3½ or 5¼ inches in diameter (Figure 2). Surprisingly, the smaller 3½-inch disk has a greater storage capacity than the larger one. *High density* 3½-inch diskettes hold up to 1.44 MB of data; high density 5¼-inch diskettes hold up to 1.2 MB. *Low density* diskettes, which are used in older machines, store less information. Hard drives hold much more data than floppies. Nowadays, computers come with hard drives that often exceed 1,024 megabytes — one **gigabyte** (GB) — of storage.

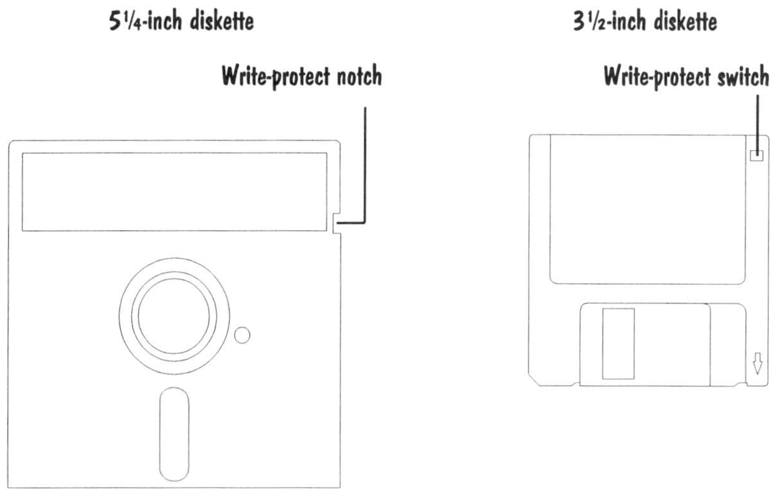

Figure 2 Floppy Disks

Write-protecting a diskette If you want to prevent the accidental erasure of data on a floppy disk, you can *write-protect* it. A write protected diskette can be read from, but not written to or erased. To write-protect a 5¼-inch floppy, cover its write-protect notch with a small piece of tape; to write-protect a 3½-inch diskette, throw its write-protect switch (see Figure 2).

You may be wondering why computers contain both hard and floppy drives. Typically, the hard drive is used to store most of the programs and data to be used by a PC. Floppy drives, which are much slower in operation, are typically used in the following ways:

- To transfer newly purchased programs from the distribution disks to the computer's hard disk.
- For *backup* purposes — to make copies of valuable hard disk data in the event that the hard disk becomes damaged.
- To help transfer information from one computer to another.

- For *archival* purposes — to move information from the hard disk to floppies when it is unlikely to be needed in the foreseeable future.

Other mass storage devices

Some personal computers are equipped with additional types of mass storage devices. A **tape drive**, which uses media that resemble audio cassettes, can be used to copy (back up) the entire contents of a hard disk. Should the hard disk become inoperable — should it *crash* — its data could then be retrieved from the backup tape. A tape drive works slowly, but this isn't too important considering its intended role.

A **CD-ROM drive** uses disks that are similar to audio compact discs (hence the "CD" in its name). These disks, like floppies, are removable and portable, but, unlike floppies, hold huge amounts of information — about 500 MB each. Because CD-ROM drives are read-only devices (hence the "ROM" in the name), they are used primarily:

- To distribute large applications to the computer user (instead of using dozens of floppies).
- To hold reference material such as encyclopedias, dictionaries, photographs, and the like.

Input Devices

The computer uses its **input devices** to receive data from the outside world. For this purpose, every computer includes a typewriter-like **keyboard** (see Figure 3). To enter information into the computer, you simply type it at the keyboard in the same way you would using an ordinary typewriter. The characters you type will simultaneously appear on the computer's display screen.

Special keys

Computer keyboards contain quite a few keys not found on a typewriter. (Figure 3 shows the most common keyboard layout for IBM-compatible machines.) These "extra" keys include:

- Twelve *function keys* labeled F1 through F12 are arrayed across the top of the keyboard. They perform special tasks that vary depending on the program you are using.
- Just to the right of the large block of typewriter-like keys are ten *cursor control keys*: the four *Arrow keys* (↑, ↓, ←, and →) plus Insert, Home, and so on. These keys allow you to move the *cursor*, which indicates the current typing position, around the screen.
- A *numeric keypad*, at the far right of the keyboard, allows you to enter numbers quickly. If the *Num Lock* light (above the keypad) is off, pressing one of these keys doesn't input a number; it per-

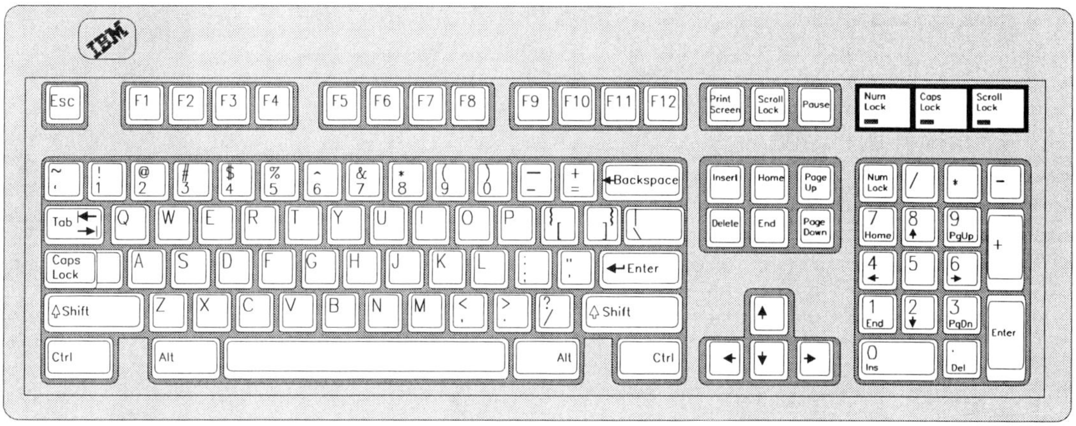

Figure 3 A Typical Keyboard Layout

forms the secondary function indicated on the key (for example, Home or ↑). To turn the Num Lock light on or off, press the Num Lock key.

You may notice a few other special keys (such as Esc and Print Screen) here and there on the keyboard. We will explain their function when appropriate, later in the text.

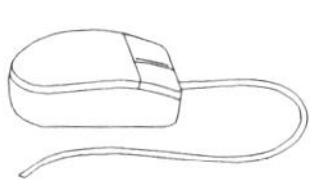

Another standard input device is the **mouse**, a hand-held object containing two or three buttons, which (together with the cable that connects it to the computer) vaguely resembles a long-tailed rodent. When you roll the mouse around on the desk top, a pointer moves correspondingly on the screen. For example, if you roll the mouse to the left, the pointer moves left. Once the pointer is positioned appropriately on the screen, pressing a mouse button (*clicking the mouse*) performs a program function. The mouse can speed up many Windows operations, but it lacks the versatility of the keyboard.

Output Devices

Whereas input devices allow us to communicate with the computer, **output devices** make it possible for the computer to "talk" to us. The most common output devices are *monitors* and *printers.*

A **monitor** is a high resolution television-like screen enclosed in a case and controlled by circuitry — the *video adapter* — within the computer. (The screens on portable computers use an entirely different technology; they are usually *LCD* — liquid crystal display — *panels.*)

As is the case with televisions, monitor size is measured along the screen's diagonal. The most common screen sizes for desktop computers are 14 and 15 inches, but larger screens are also available. Another characteristic that affects the quality and cost of a monitor is its *resolution* — the number of *pixels* (tiny dots of light) it uses to create images. Nowadays, screen resolutions of 1024 × 768 — 768 horizontal rows, each containing 1,024 pixels — are becoming increasingly common. This kind of resolution puts even the finest of televisions to shame.

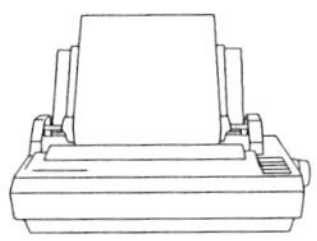

Unfortunately, output to the screen is both impermanent (it disappears when the power is turned off) and not terribly portable (you'd need a pretty long extension cord to take your screen output home from school). If you want to make a permanent copy of a program's output on paper, you need to use a **printer**.

The text and pictures produced by virtually all printers are composed of tiny dots of ink or an ink-like substance. The size of these dots and how closely they are packed together determines the quality of the output. Here are the most common types of printers in use today, in order of increasing price and quality of output:

- *Dot matrix printers* produce the "tiny dots" by rapidly striking an inked ribbon against the paper with a row of small pins. This kind of printer is relatively inexpensive and very reliable, but the quality of its output cannot match that produced by the other types. Its primary use nowadays is to print on multipart forms.
- *Ink jet printers* spray incredibly tiny drops of ink on the paper producing finer images than their dot matrix counterparts at a slightly higher speed and cost. Moreover, many ink jet printers can produce relatively good *color* output at a reasonable price. The main disadvantage of ink jets is their relatively high cost of operation.
- *Laser printers* produce the best output at the highest rate of speed, and are remarkably reliable. Although they are more expensive than other types of printers, lasers have become the standard for business use and are becoming increasingly common in the home, as well.

Software, Operating Systems, and Windows

The most powerful hardware cannot accomplish anything by itself. It needs **software** — computer programs — to bring it to life. Software provides instructions for the central processing unit and, in so doing, allows the computer user to write letters, calculate loan balances, draw pictures, play games, and perform countless other tasks.

Applications Software

Software is divided into two general categories: applications software and system software. **Applications** are programs you use to enhance your productivity, solve problems, supply information, or provide recreation. To be able to run programs like these is the reason one learns to use a computer.

The most commonly used applications include:

Types of applications

- *Word processors* help you create, edit, and print documents such as letters, reports, memos, and so on.
- *Database managers* allow you to enter, access, and modify large quantities of data. You might use a database program to create a personal phone directory. A business can use this kind of application to maintain customer lists and employee records.
- *Spreadsheet programs* simplify the manipulation and calculation of large amounts of tabular data (spreadsheets). These programs are often used by businesses to try to foresee the effect of different strategies on their bottom line.
- *Drawing and painting programs* allow one to use the computer to (as you may have guessed) draw or paint pictures — *graphics* — on the screen and print them on paper.
- *Multimedia applications* make extensive use of graphics, sound, and sometimes video images to provide information or entertainment.

Applications are developed and published by many different companies and are sold by retail stores and mail order firms. Each software package consists of a *user's guide* together with one or more diskettes or CDs that contain the application *files* — the programs, data, and documents needed by the application. Before you can use a software package, it must be *installed* — some of its files must be copied (by the computer) from the floppies or CDs to the hard disk.

The Operating System

The second general software type is **system software**, the programs used by the computer to control its hardware. The most important piece of system software is the **operating system** — the computer's master control program. The operating system has two general functions:

1. It helps the application you are using to communicate with the computer hardware. Applications are written to run under a specific operating system, which supplies easy ways for the programmers to access the computer's disk drives, memory, and so on.

2. It provides an *interface* — a link — between you and the computer that allows you to install and start up applications, manipulate disk files, and perform other very basic tasks.

DOS The central processing unit may be the brain of the computer, but the operating system gives the machine its personality. Most IBM-compatible computers use an operating system known as **DOS** (for *disk operating system*), which was developed by Microsoft Corporation for the original IBM Personal Computer introduced in 1981. Although major changes have been made to it over the years, DOS still retains much of the awkwardness of its distant past.

An immediate clue to an operating system's personality is its *start-up screen*, the one you see after you turn on the computer and it has gone through its preliminary functions. With pure, unadorned DOS, you are presented with a few lines of mysterious-looking text ending with the **DOS prompt** (most likely, `C:\>`) followed by a blinking underline (the *cursor*). This is DOS' way of asking you to enter a command. For example, if you want to start up your word processor, you might type the following two lines (pressing the Enter key at the end of each):

```
CD \WP51\DATA
\WP51\WP
```

This kind of **command line interface** is classic DOS. In order to direct DOS to perform a function, the computer user must memorize (or have a handy list of) a large number of arcane commands. This is certainly not a *user-friendly* system.

GUIs A vast improvement in user-friendliness is the **graphical user interface** (**GUI**, pronounced "gooey") popularized by the Apple Macintosh line of computers. In a GUI, the start-up screen contains a collection of small stylized pictures called **icons** (see Figure 4) together with a set of **menus** that supplies available options. (The menus in Figure 4 are entitled *File*, *Options*, *Window*, and *Help*.) With a graphical user interface, you can start up applications and perform other operating system functions as easily as moving the mouse pointer to the corresponding icon or menu item and pressing a mouse button. The keyboard can also be employed to carry out functions, but using a GUI is much easier with a mouse.

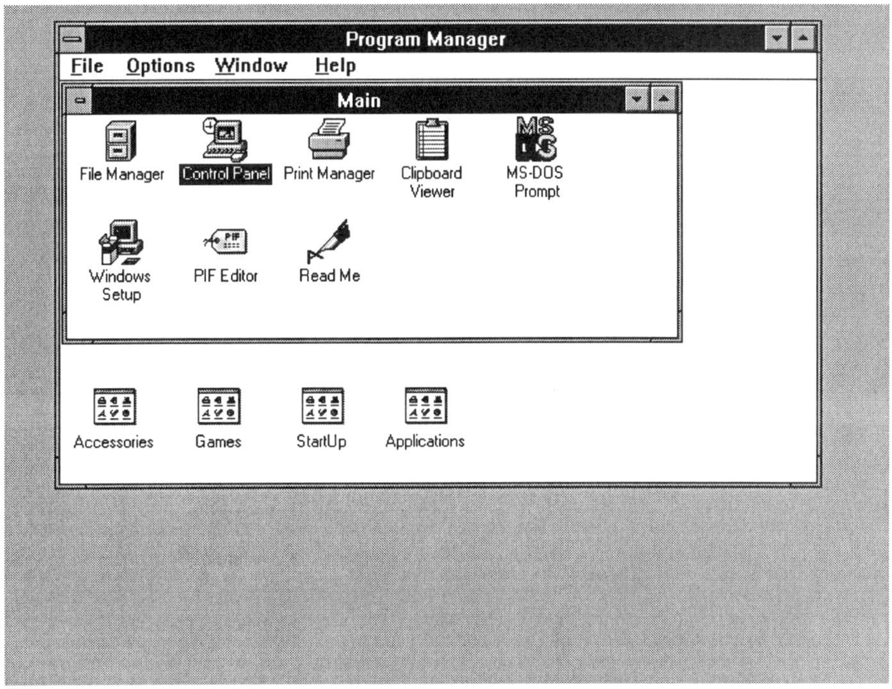

Figure 4 A Typical Windows 3.1 Start-up Screen

Microsoft Windows

Windows is a very sophisticated piece of software, originally developed in 1985 by Microsoft Corporation, that employs a graphical user interface to help make IBM-compatible computers easier to use. Although Windows sold slowly at first, version 3.0 (introduced in 1990) and especially version 3.1 (1992) were wildly popular. The latter version established Windows as the standard operating environment for IBM-compatible computers. (Figure 4 shows its start-up screen.)

Windows 95

However, Windows 3.1 is not an operating system in the true sense of the term; it will not run unless DOS is present in RAM. This limitation, in turn, leads to certain problems and inefficiencies in its use. In August 1995, Microsoft brought the long-awaited Windows 4.0 to market. Officially known as **Windows 95**, this new version no longer requires DOS in order to run. Windows 95 is a true operating system.

Advantages of Windows

Using Windows provides many advantages over plain old DOS:

- Its graphical user interface is much easier to use than DOS' command line interface.

- Windows has *multitasking* capabilities — you can run more than one application at a time, each occupying its own area on the screen. For example, you can start up a paint program to draw a picture without closing down the word processor that is already running.
- You can easily transfer data from one application to another. For example, the picture you've just completed in the paint program can be inserted by Windows into your word processing document.
- Windows provides uniform standards for the look and feel of applications developed to run under it. (Such programs are called *Windows applications*; those not designed specifically for Windows are called *DOS applications*.) This is of great benefit to the computer user, making it easier to learn and use new applications.
- The Windows user interface is highly customizable; you are given a great amount of control over the way that it looks and acts. For example, you can design your own start-up screen, choose your own screen colors, position and size the areas on the screen in which your applications are running, and much, much more.
- Windows supplies a large number of useful small and medium-sized applications. These include an on-screen calculator, a word processor, a paint program, an easy-to-use file manager, and even a couple of games.
- Windows provides modules that control a wide assortment of different monitors, printers, mice, and other peripherals. As a result, applications programmers don't have to worry about writing their own software to communicate with the huge variety of available input and output devices.

New features of Windows 95

Windows 95 generally improves on the advantages mentioned above and adds some new features as well:

1. The most noticeable change in Windows 95 is in the user interface. It is still a GUI, but with a much different look than Windows 3.1. Until you customize it, the start-up screen has the somewhat spartan look shown in Figure 5, but in many respects, the new interface is easier to use than that of Windows 3.1.
2. Windows 95 has added features that allow you to get work done faster and more easily. These include the Start button for easy startup of your programs, the Taskbar for quickly switching between applications, Desktop shortcuts for frequently used items, and the ability to give files more reasonable names than previously allowed.

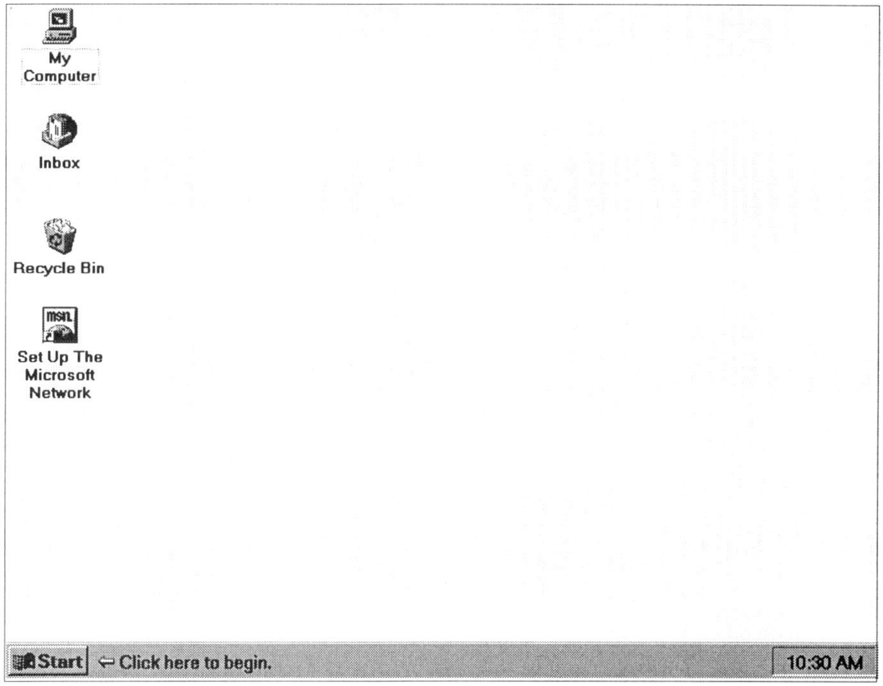

Figure 5 A Windows 95 Start-up Screen

3. Adding new hardware is easier under Windows 95; it provides a hardware "wizard" to guide the process and *Plug and Play* technology to prevent conflicts with other devices.
4. Windows 95 has new built-in programs, including improved communications, more sophisticated multimedia tools, and a few utilities for maintaining and better utilizing the hard disk.
5. Recognizing the growing importance of both networks and portable computers, Windows 95 has
   - Improved networking capabilities, including easier network setup and browsing; and
   - Provided better support for portable computers, including power management and file transfer between laptop and desktop.

Many of these features may make little sense to you now, but you will surely come to understand most of them as you progress through the text.

A Brief History of Personal Computers

Early computers

The electronic computer is a relatively modern invention; the first fully-operable computer was developed about 50 years ago, at the end of World War II, by a team at the University of Pennsylvania's Moore School of Engineering. This team was headed by John Mauchly and J. Presper Eckert, who named the new machine *ENIAC*, for Electronic Numerical Integrator and Calculator. ENIAC was hardly a *personal* computer, occupying a large room and weighing about 33 tons. By today's standards, ENIAC was also extremely slow, unreliable, and expensive to operate. In 1945, on the other hand, it was considered a marvel.

Over the next 30 years, computers became smaller, faster, and less expensive. However, most of these machines were kept isolated in their own air-conditioned rooms, tended by specially trained personnel. By 1975, computers were in great demand at universities, government agencies, and large businesses, but relatively few people had ever come face-to-face with an actual computer. This all began to change in the late 1970s.

To understand why, let's take a closer look at the early computers. ENIAC and its immediate successors were large, slow, and unreliable primarily because they used thousands of large, slow, and unreliable *vacuum tubes* in their electronic circuits. Vacuum tubes were glass cylinders, typically about four inches high and an inch in diameter, which generated a lot of heat and thus couldn't be placed very close together. Then, in 1947, a momentous event occurred at Bell Labs — William Shockley, John Bardeen, and Walter Brattain announced the invention of the *transistor*. Only about an inch long and a quarter inch across, a transistor did the same job as a vacuum tube but produced very little heat.

The downsizing of computers began in the 1950s as transistors replaced vacuum tubes, and continued into the 1960s with the introduction of the *integrated circuit* (IC) — an ice cube-sized package containing hundreds of transistors. By the late 1960s, *microchips*, consisting of thousands of electronic components residing on a piece of silicon the size of a postage stamp, had begun to replace ICs. At this time, a new breed of *minicomputers* appeared, costing less than $25,000 and occupying a space no larger than a small filing cabinet. Then, in 1970, Ted Hoff, Jr., working at Intel Corporation, invented the **microprocessor**, a central processing unit on a chip. The technological world was now ready for the personal computer.

The personal computer

The first personal computer to be successfully marketed to the public was built in 1974. It was designed by Micro Instrumentation and Telemetry Systems (MITS), a small electronics firm located in New

Mexico, which named it the Altair 8800. The Altair was a very primitive machine, about the size of a bread box; it contained 256 bytes (not kilobytes) of RAM, had no ROM, and its input and output devices consisted of rows of toggle switches and lights, respectively. It was also quite inexpensive — $395 in kit form. Sales of the Altair took off after an article about it appeared in the January, 1975 issue of *Popular Electronics* magazine.

Although add-on products for the Altair 8800 (such as memory boards and paper tape readers) gradually appeared over the next couple of years, it's questionable whether anyone ever did any useful work on this machine. Nevertheless, the Altair is of major historical significance because it inspired thousands of computer hobbyists and professionals to become interested in personal computers.

Two of the hobbyists inspired by the Altair were Paul Allen and Bill Gates, both about twenty years old and living in the Boston area at the time. They joined together to write and sell a version of the BASIC programming language for the new computer. With the easy-to-use BASIC available, Altair owners no longer had to write programs in low-level, mind-numbing machine language. Soon thereafter, Gates and Allen formed Microsoft Corporation, which is now the world's largest software company (and the publisher of Windows).

Another Altair aficionado was Stephen Wozniak, who joined forces with his friend and fellow Californian, Steven Jobs, to form Apple Computer, Inc. In 1977, they brought the now legendary Apple II personal computer to market. The Apple II was an instant hit and for the next few years, Apple was the fastest growing company in the United States.

The IBM PC

By 1980, there were dozens of companies manufacturing personal computers, but the major producers of the larger minicomputers and mainframes had not yet entered the fray. This changed dramatically in 1981, when IBM brought out its first personal computer (which was not so imaginatively named the *IBM Personal Computer*). Although it wasn't much more powerful than most other personal computers of the time, the IBM PC (Figure 6) was a milestone in the history of personal computers for two basic reasons:

1. For many businesses, especially the larger ones, it "legitimized" personal computers. If IBM was selling them, the reasoning went, then maybe PCs really could be useful business tools. As a result, the IBM PC became wildly popular; IBM could not produce them fast enough to keep up with the demand.

2. It was built with generic parts and used the PC-DOS operating system, which was developed by Microsoft and was virtually identical to MS-DOS, a Microsoft product. The IBM PC also used

open architecture — IBM published detailed specifications so that anyone could build circuit boards for it to expand its capabilities. These features enabled enterprising companies to "clone" the PC — to build their own "IBM-compatible" personal computers.

Figure 6 Two Historic Computers

The Apple Macintosh

For the next few years, the personal computer industry slowly evolved as a few IBM clones and dozens of non-IBM-compatible PCs were brought to market. Then, in 1984, Apple introduced the Macintosh (Figure 6), which it advertised, with a decidedly anti-IBM slant, as "the computer for the rest of us". With its small size and integral screen, the "Mac" certainly *looked* different, but what really made it stand out was its easy-to-use, mouse-driven, graphical user interface. (This GUI is similar, broadly speaking, to the Windows interface developed later by Microsoft. Both interfaces, and the mouse as well, trace their roots back to work done about 1980 at Xerox Corporation's Palo Alto Research Center.) The Apple Macintosh was not at all compatible with the IBM PC. Nevertheless, after a slow start, it became increasingly popular. Today, the Macintosh and its descendants are the only remaining popular alternative to IBM-compatible personal computers.

Recent developments

From this point on, the increased competition for the PC buyer's dollar brought forth new and more powerful computers at an ever-accelerating rate. This boom was fueled by Intel Corporation, which introduced a new generation of microprocessor every few years. Whenever they did, microcomputer manufacturers quickly brought out machines designed around the new chip and software developers used the greater speed to create more sophisticated applications.

Windows Microsoft Windows was one of the major beneficiaries of the more powerful computers. When it was first introduced in 1985, Windows ran sluggishly on the existing hardware (graphics-intensive programs require relatively fast computers), and it did not have much success. However, by the time the much improved version 3.0 was brought to market in 1990, hardware had caught up with the demands of the software and this version of Windows was an immediate hit. Then, when an even better version 3.1 was introduced in 1992 in the midst of a computer price war that made top-of-the-line machines affordable, Windows became the standard operating environment for IBM-compatible microcomputers. The current version of Windows, Windows 95, was rolled out in August, 1995 with the most publicized (and most costly) introduction for any computer product ever.

Summary

Components of a Computer	Central processing unit (CPU)	Receives and executes program instructions; controls the other computer components.
	Internal memory (RAM and ROM)	Stores instructions and data to be processed by the CPU; contents of RAM are lost when the computer's power is turned off.
	Mass storage devices	Store all applications and data used by the computer. Examples are hard and floppy disk drives, and CD-ROM and tape drives.
	Input devices	Transmit information from the user to the computer. Examples are the keyboard and mouse.
	Output devices	Transmit information from the computer to the user. Examples are monitors and printers.
Types of Software	Applications	Include word processors, database managers, spreadsheet programs, painting programs, and multimedia applications.
	System software	Includes the computer's operating system (for example, DOS or Windows 95).
Microsoft Windows	Advantages of Windows over DOS	Customizable graphical user interface (GUI), multitasking, easy transfer of data between programs, software tools and uniform standards for application development, and built-in utilities.

	Advantages of Windows 95 over Windows 3.1	Simplified user interface, added user-friendly features, easier installation of hardware devices, and improved support for multimedia devices, laptops, and networks.
History of the Personal Computer	1945	The first fully-operable electronic computer, ENIAC, is built.
	1947	The transistor is invented
	1970	The microprocessor, a CPU on a chip, is invented.
	1974	The first widely-marketed personal computer, the Altair 8800, is built.
	1977	The Apple II makes its debut.
	1981	The IBM PC is introduced.
	1984	The Apple Macintosh, with a user-friendly GUI, hits the market.
	1985	Microsoft rolls out the first version of Windows.
	1992	Windows 3.1 is brought to market.
	1995	Windows 95 is launched.

Review Exercises

Personal Computers

1. The physical components of a computer system are referred to as its ____________.
2. A computer's main circuit board is called its ____________.
3. One byte of memory consists of ____________ bits.
4. One kilobyte is equal to ____________ bytes.
5. Some examples of mass storage devices are floppy disk drives, hard disk drives, and ____________ drives.
6. Of the various types of printers, the highest quality output is produced by a ____________ printer.
7. True or false: Computer components housed outside the system unit are called peripherals.
8. True or false: A bit can be represented by a 0 or a 1.
9. True or false: The contents of a computer's ROM are lost when the power is turned off.
10. True or false: Floppy disk drives access data more slowly than hard disk drives.

11. True or false: A CD-ROM drive can be used for backup purposes.
12. True or false: Computer keyboards contain fewer keys than a standard typewriter.
13. True or false: Laser printers are especially good at printing on multipart forms.
14. Which of the following components is *not* contained within the system unit of a typical PC?
    a. The motherboard
    b. A floppy disk drive
    c. Random access memory (RAM)
    d. None of the above answers is correct.
15. The computer's central processing unit
    a. Processes program instructions.
    b. Performs arithmetic and logical operations.
    c. Controls the other components of the computer.
    d. Performs all the above functions.
16. Which of the following is an input device?
    a. A monitor
    b. A keyboard
    c. A printer
    d. Read-only memory (ROM)
17. One advantage of a floppy disk over a hard disk is that
    a. It can be used to transfer data between computers.
    b. It holds more data.
    c. Data can be retrieved from it more quickly.
    d. None of the above answers is correct.

Software and Operating Systems

18. Software is divided into two broad categories: ____________ software and system software.
19. The master control program that oversees the computer's operations is called its ____________.
20. The generic name for the operating system used by virtually all IBM-compatible computers until the advent of Windows 95 is ____________.
21. Windows makes use of a GUI, which stands for ____________.
22. True or false: Computer programs are also known as software.
23. True or false: Most computer users find it easier to use a command line interface than a graphical user interface.
24. True or false: One of the advantages of Windows over DOS is the

speed with which it runs applications.

25. True or false: Unlike Windows 3.1, Windows 95 is a true operating system.

26. Which of the following is an example of system software?

    a. The computer's RAM
    b. The computer's operating system
    c. A computer game
    d. A word processor

27. One advantage of DOS over Windows is that

    a. It can run several programs at once.
    b. It is easier to learn to use.
    c. It requires less powerful hardware.
    d. All of the above are correct.

28. Windows 95

    a. Requires DOS to be running before it can be started up.
    b. Can run most programs that were written for DOS and Windows 3.1.
    c. Runs on both IBM-compatibles and the Apple Macintosh.
    d. Was the first operating system to use a graphical user interface.

History

29. The first fully-operable electronic computer was known by the acronym ____________.

30. The ____________, a CPU residing on a single computer chip, was invented in 1970.

31. The first personal computer received national attention in the year ____________.

32. The first microcomputer built by International Business Machines Corporation was called the ____________.

33. The first widely-used computer to make use of a graphical user interface was the ____________.

34. True or false: The invention of the transistor led to smaller, cheaper, more reliable computers.

35. True or false: The first personal computer was manufactured by Apple Computer, Inc.

36. True or false: The Apple Macintosh makes use of the Windows 95 operating system.

37. True or false: Computers have not increased appreciably in speed and power in the last ten years.

38. The first *personal* computer was

    a. ENIAC.
    b. The Altair 8800.
    c. The Apple II.
    d. The IBM Personal Computer.

39. Microsoft Corporation was founded by

    a. Stephen Wozniak and Steven Jobs.
    b. Richard Rodgers and Oscar Hammerstein.
    c. J. Presper Eckert and John Mauchly.
    d. Paul Allen and William Gates.

40. In the 1990s

    a. Intel Corporation introduced its first computer chip.
    b. Microsoft Corporation brought out Windows.
    c. Apple Computer, Inc. introduced the Macintosh computer.
    d. None of the above is correct.

Build Your Own Glossary

41. The following words and phrases are important terms that were presented in this Introduction. (They appear within the text in boldface type.) Write a definition for each term. After you learn to use WordPad (in Section 2.2), you should enter these definitions into the Glossary file on the Student Disk.

Application
Bit
Byte
CD-ROM drive
Central processing unit (CPU)
Command line interface
Computer
Computer literacy
Disk drive
Diskette
DOS
DOS prompt
Floppy disk
Gigabyte (GB)
Graphical user interface (GUI)
Hard disk
Hardware
IBM-compatible computer
Icon
Input device
Internal memory
Keyboard
Kilobyte (KB)
Mass storage
Megabyte (MB)
Menu
Microcomputer
Monitor
Mouse
Operating system
Output device
Peripheral
Personal computer (PC)
Printer
Processor
Program
Random access memory (RAM)
Read-only memory (ROM)
Software
System software
System unit
Tape drive
Windows
Windows 95

CHAPTER 1

The Basics of Using Windows 95

In the introduction to this text, we discussed the *what* and *why* of Windows 95. Recall that the primary goal of this powerful operating system is to make computers easier to use. In this chapter, you will begin to see some of the things that Windows can do and how easily they are done. More specifically, you will learn to:

1. Recognize the elements of the Windows 95 Desktop.
2. Use the mouse to perform basic Windows operations.
3. Choose items from menus.
4. Move, resize, minimize, maximize, and close windows.
5. Scroll through the contents of a window.
6. Use dialog boxes to indicate preferences.
7. Shut down Windows 95.

1.1 The Windows 95 Desktop

If Windows 95 is installed on your computer, when you turn on the machine, you will soon see the words *Starting Windows 95 ...* and then the Windows logo will appear. After a while, the Windows 95 opening screen will be displayed. A simple opening screen is shown in Figure 1. Depending on how your computer has been set up, its opening screen might look quite different from the one pictured here.

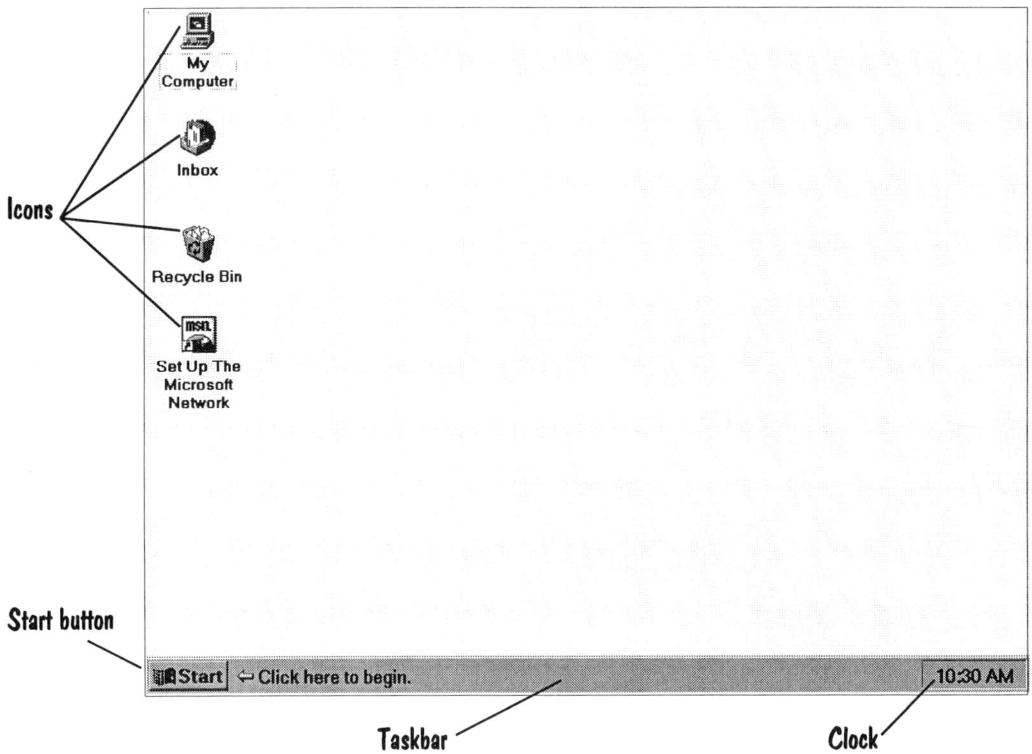

Figure 1 The Windows 95 Desktop

The entire screen area is referred to as the Windows **Desktop**. Just like a regular desk top, it's the place on which you will do your work. Currently (in Figure 1), there are only a few objects on the Desktop. After we begin working with a program or two, however, most of the Desktop will be covered by *windows* of various sorts and the objects you see here (except the Taskbar) will usually become obscured.

The **Start button**, located in the lower left corner of the screen in Figure 1, is, as the text "Click here to begin" suggests, the jumping off point for a typical Windows session. It provides access to all the applications (programs) installed on your computer. We will discuss the use of the Start button at the beginning of Chapter 2.

The labeled pictures along the left side of the screen are called **icons**. These icons (and others like them throughout the Windows environment) provide easy access to various aspects of Windows 95. For example, as you will see in Chapter 3, the icon labeled "My Computer" allows you to work with virtually every piece of hardware and software that is part of your computer system.

The **Taskbar** displays the applications and documents that you are currently using. The only item on the Taskbar in Figure 1 is the Clock utility, which not only provides the time of day but, as you will see later, can also be used to display the date and a month-by-month calendar.

1.2 Of Mice and Menus

As you know, one of the primary advantages of working with Windows 95 is that it is easy to use. It accomplishes this, in part, by the extensive use of the mouse and menus.

Using the Mouse

When a mouse is moved around on a flat surface, its pointer moves in a corresponding way on the screen. The shape of the mouse pointer depends on the application that is running and the use to which it is being put. The pointer may look like an arrow, a double-headed arrow, an I-beam, or a hand, among other things.

In Windows and its applications, the mouse can be used to select items displayed on the screen, initiate actions, and move and resize certain objects. Before we illustrate these uses, let's discuss some important mouse terminology.

Mouse terminology

- To *point at* an object means to move the mouse so that its on-screen pointer is positioned over the specified object and held in place for a few moments.
- To *click* the mouse means to press and release the left mouse button. To *right-click* is to press and release the right mouse button. To click (or right-click) *on* an object means to point at the

object and then click (or right-click).[*]

- To *double-click* on an object means to point at the object and click the left mouse button twice in rapid succession.
- To *drag* an object with the mouse means to point at the object, press (but not release) the left mouse button, move the mouse pointer to a new location, and then release the button. To *right-drag* an object is to perform the same actions using the right mouse button instead of the left.

To illustrate these operations, let's return to the computer screen shown in Figure 1. If we double-click on the My Computer icon, the **window** — boxed-in area on the screen — shown in Figure 2 appears. (Your My Computer window may look quite different from the one pictured here. Don't worry; for the purposes of the current discussion, it does not matter.)

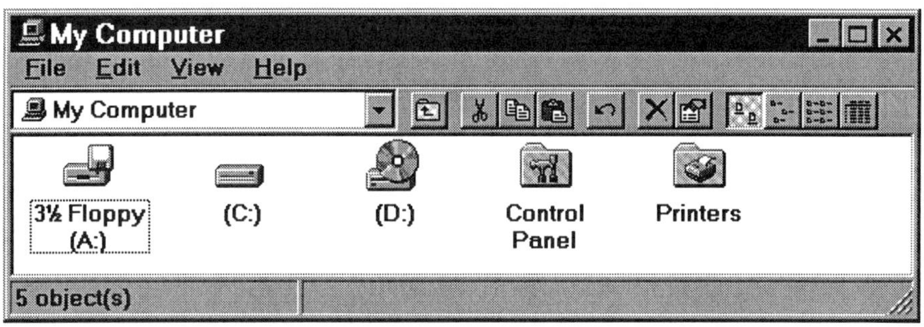

Figure 2 The My Computer Window

TIP

If you double-click on an object and it doesn't initiate an action, you may have moved the mouse slightly between clicks or perhaps you didn't follow the first click by the second quickly enough. Try double-clicking again.

Using Menus

The first line of the My Computer window (Figure 2) is called its **title bar**; it contains the name of the window together with some symbols

---

[*] If the functions of your left and right mouse buttons seem to be reversed, they can easily be restored to their "normal" settings. Either ask your lab coordinator to do this for you or see Section 5.4. (If you want to try it yourself, first finish reading Chapter 1.)

that we'll discuss in Section 1.3. Below the title bar is the My Computer **menu bar**:

Opening a menu

These words are the names of **menus** —lists of commands — that can be used to manipulate the contents of the My Computer window. To *open* (display) a menu, simply click on its name. For example, if you click on the word *View*, the menu pictured in Figure 3 appears. (Because this kind of menu looks as if it were pulled down, like a window shade unrolling from the word View, it is called a **pull-down menu**.)

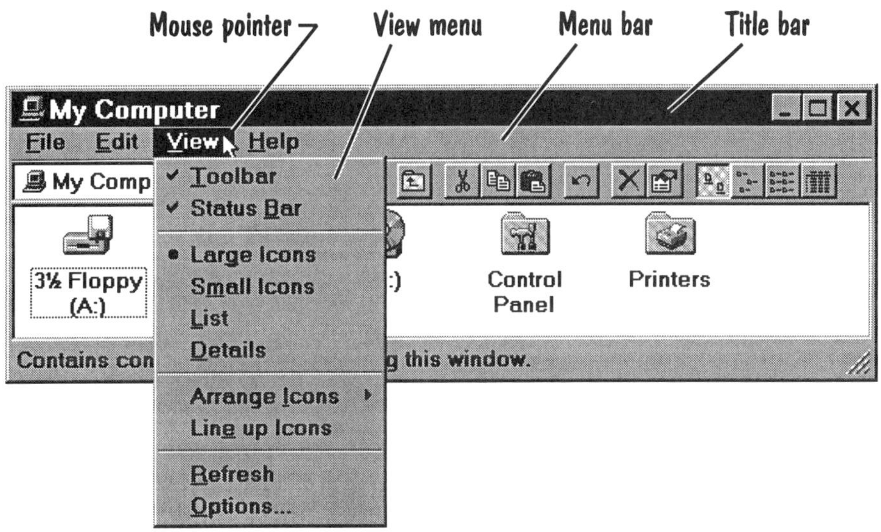

Figure 3 A Typical Pull-down Menu

Selecting a menu option

Once a menu has been opened, you can choose one of the options listed by clicking on that item. (Doing so will also close the menu.) For example, to choose the "Line up Icons" option from the View menu in Figure 3, move the mouse pointer straight down until it is positioned over this item (it will become highlighted) and click the left button.

NOTE

If you prefer, the options listed on a pull-down menu can be accessed using the keyboard. Notice that each name on the menu bar has one letter underlined; for example, the *V* in View. To display a pull-down menu, hold down either Alt key, press the key corresponding to the underlined letter, and then release the Alt key. (We will write this sequence of actions as — if the underlined letter is V — "press Alt+V".) Then, to select an option on that menu, either:

- Press the key corresponding to the underlined letter in the desired option.

or

- Press the Down Arrow key (↓) until the desired option is highlighted and then press the Enter key.

For example, to display the View menu as in Figure 3, hold down the Alt key, press the key labeled V, and release Alt. Then, to select the Line up Icons option, *either* press the E key *or* press the Down Arrow key several times until the option is highlighted and then press the Enter key.

Canceling a menu If you want to close a menu without selecting any of the options, just click on any other part of the screen. As an alternative, press the Escape key.

Types of Menu Items

Let's take a closer look at the View menu that is displayed in Figure 3. Notice that some options on this menu are preceded or followed by a special symbol, such as a check mark or bullet (see Figure 4).

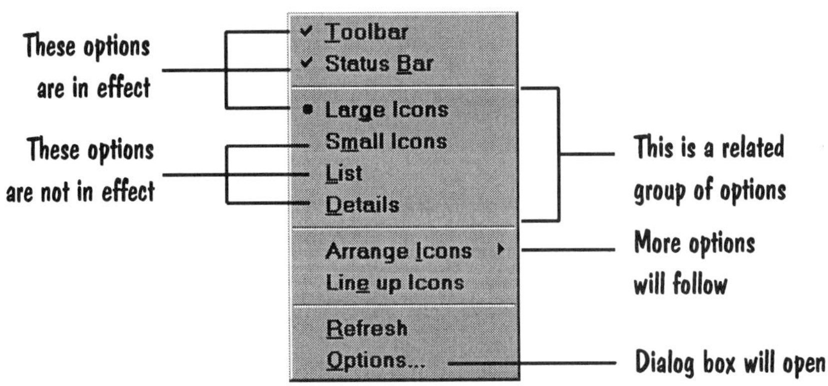

Figure 4 Special Symbols for Menu Options

These symbols have a consistent meaning in Windows and its applications:

Menu symbols

- If a *check mark* (✔) appears next to a menu option, it indicates that this item or characteristic is currently in effect. For example, in Figure 4, the check marks next to Toolbar and Status Bar indicate that both these objects are displayed in the My Computer window. If you click on Toolbar, the menu will close and the Toolbar will disappear from the window. (Try it!) Then, the next time you pull down the My Computer View menu, you'll notice that the check mark next to Toolbar has disappeared as well — this option is no longer in effect. To get it back, choose Toolbar again. We call this kind of option a *toggle*: if the Toolbar *is* currently displayed, choosing the menu option turns it off; if it is *not* displayed, choosing the option turns it on.
- A *bullet* (•) next to a menu option not only means that this option is in effect, but also indicates that the rest of a group of related items are *not* in effect. (The horizontal lines within a menu — see Figure 4 — divide it into these groups.) For example, the bullet on the Large Icons option in Figure 4 describes the contents of the My Computer window (see Figure 3). This window does *not* contain Small Icons, a List, or Details. Only one bulleted item within its group can be in effect at any given time.
- A *triangle symbol* (▸) next to a menu item indicates that a *submenu* of additional options will appear if you "point at" this item. For example, if you move the mouse pointer over the Arrange Icons option in Figure 4 and hold it steady for a few moments, the following submenu is displayed at its right:

- If you choose a menu name that is followed by an *ellipsis* (three consecutive periods), a *dialog box* will appear requesting additional information. (Dialog boxes are discussed in Section 1.4.) For example, choosing the Options item from the View menu of Figure 4 displays a dialog box presenting the available options. (If you open this dialog box, you can close it, removing it from the screen, by clicking on the button labeled Cancel or by pressing the Escape key.)

Before we close this section, let's pull down My Computer's Edit menu (by clicking on the word Edit on the menu bar) to illustrate a couple of additional points. This menu is shown in Figure 5.

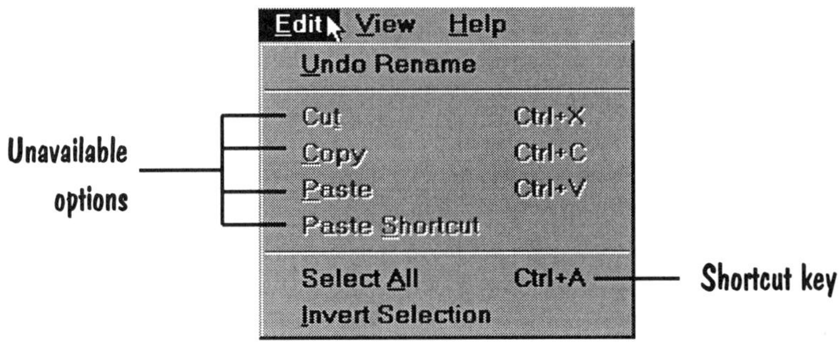

Figure 5 The My Computer Edit Menu

In Figure 5, notice that:

- The second group of options is *dimmed* — it appears to be "faded out". This indicates that these options are temporarily not available. If you click on one of these items, nothing will happen!
- Keystrokes (such as Ctrl+A) appear next to several menu items. These keystrokes are called **shortcut keys**. They provide a quick way of choosing the corresponding menu option *without displaying the menu itself.* For example, to select all the objects in the My Computer window without displaying the Edit menu, just press Ctrl+A; that is, hold down the Ctrl (Control) key, type A, and then release Ctrl.

NOTE

If you have been following along at the computer and you now want to close the My Computer window, click on the little box marked with an X in the upper-right corner of this window. To shut down Windows 95, which is wise to do before turning off your computer, follow the instructions in Section 1.5.

1-2 TUTORIAL

Try the following exercises on your own.

1. Turn on your computer (if it's not already on) to start Windows 95. If the My Computer window is open, close it by clicking (tapping the left mouse button) on the little box marked with an **X** in the upper-right corner of this window.
2. *Click* on the My Computer icon (by moving the mouse pointer — an arrow shape — over this icon, then tapping the left mouse button). The words *My Computer* should now be highlighted.
3. *Drag* the My Computer icon to another location on the Desktop. (Position the mouse pointer over the icon; press, but do not

release, the left mouse button; move the pointer to a new location on the screen, and release the mouse button.)

4. Drag the My Computer icon back to its original location.
5. *Double-click* on the My Computer icon (by clicking twice in rapid succession on this icon). The My Computer window should open. If not, try double-clicking again, being sure not to move the mouse as you do so.
6. Click on the word *View* on the menu bar. The View menu should open.
7. On the View menu, there will be a *bullet* next to one of the options in the second group (beginning with "Large Icons"). Click on one of the other three items in this group. The View menu should close. Notice the change in the My Computer window.
8. Open the View menu and *point at* Arrange Icons by moving the mouse pointer over these words and holding it still for a few moments. A submenu should appear. Note whether or not the option Auto Arrange is checked on this submenu.
9. Now click on the Auto Arrange option. The two menus will close. Reopen the View menu and the Arrange Icons submenu. If Auto Arrange had originally been "checked", it should now be "unchecked", and vice-versa.
10. Reopen the View menu and click on the "Options..." item. A new window — a dialog box — will open. Close it by pressing the Escape key or by clicking on the box marked with an **X** in the upper-right corner of this window.
11. If you want to quit, to shut down Windows 95 see the NOTE that precedes this tutorial.

1.3 Windows within Windows

While working at your desk (say, doing homework), you might have several documents open at once — perhaps a textbook, a reference book, and your notebook. This is often the case on the Windows Desktop as well. Here, the documents and other related objects are contained in *windows*. Depending on what you're doing at the moment, you might want to move some of these windows around, make one of them bigger, or perhaps take some of them off the Desktop. In this section, we will describe how to perform these actions —how to move, resize, and close windows.

Operations on Windows

Before we explain *how* to move or resize a window, let's look at a few reasons *why* you might want to perform these operations. For one thing, it's usually much easier to use the contents of a window when it occupies the entire screen; you can view more information and, in some cases, see more detail as well. Often, however, when a window opens, it just occupies part of the Desktop. (This was the case with our My Computer window in Section 1.2.) In such a case, you might want to increase the size of the window, perhaps **maximizing** it so that it uses as much screen real estate as possible.

The disadvantage of maximizing a window is that it then might obscure everything else on the Desktop. Even when not maximized, it might cover vital information in another window or on the Desktop itself. Thus, at times you will want to reduce the size of a window or even **close** it, which takes it off the Desktop. Instead of closing a window, it is sometimes possible to **minimize** it, which also removes it from the screen. The difference between closing and minimizing a window is a subtle one:

- *Closing a window* removes its contents from the computer's internal memory, RAM (see the Introduction).
- *Minimizing a window* keeps its contents in RAM and reduces the window to a button on the Taskbar, allowing us to restore the window quickly and easily.

Manipulating Windows

To illustrate the different ways in which we can manipulate a typical window, let's open the My Computer window by double-clicking on the My Computer icon, as we did in Section 1.2. Figure 6 shows the parts of the title bar that are involved in moving, minimizing, maximizing, and closing a window.

Moving a Window To *move* a window, drag its title bar to the new location. More specifically, position the mouse pointer over the title bar, press (but don't release) the left mouse button, and move the mouse in the direction you want the window to move.

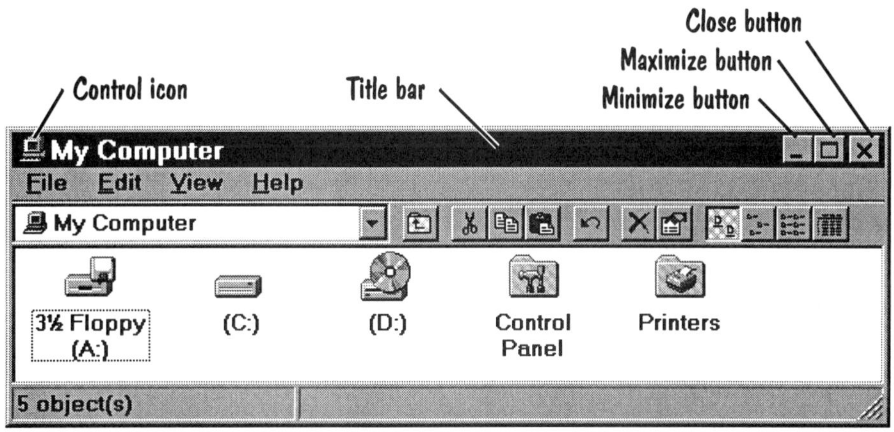

Figure 6 Parts of the Title Bar

As you do so, an outline of the moving window appears on the screen. When this outline is positioned to your liking, release the mouse button.

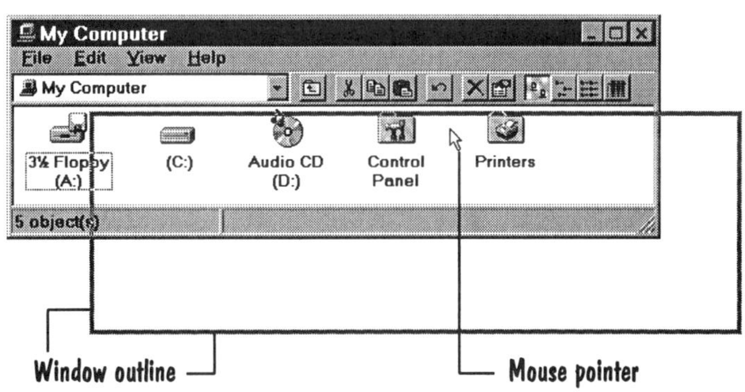

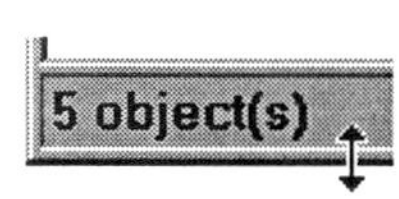

Resizing a Window To *resize* a window, drag its border or corner to a new position. For example, to increase the height of a window, position the mouse pointer on the bottom border (it becomes a two-headed arrow, as pictured above) and drag the border down. When the window outline indicates that you've achieved the desired height, release the mouse button; the window will redraw to its new size. (If you drag a window *corner*, both sides attached to that corner move at once.)

TIP

If you change your mind during the process of moving or resizing a window and want to cancel the operation, press the Escape key before releasing the mouse button.

Minimizing, Maximizing, or Closing a Window To *minimize*, *maximize*, or *close* a window, click on the **minimize button**, **maximize button**, or **close button**, respectively (on the right end of the title bar).

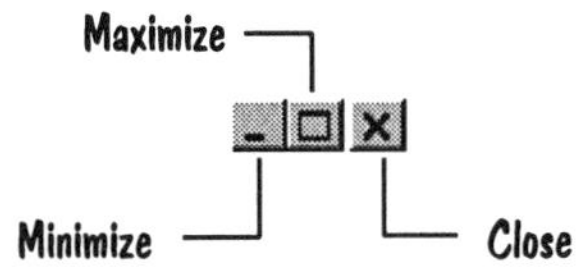

Note that:

- When a window is minimized, it is removed from the screen but its name and icon continue to appear on a button on the Taskbar. To reopen a minimized window, click on its Taskbar button.
- When a window is maximized, it expands to its largest possible size and the maximize button is replaced by a **restore button.** Clicking on the latter, **restores** the window, returning it to its former position and size. 
- When a window is closed, it disappears from the screen.

TIP

You can also *maximize* a window by double-clicking on its title bar. Once a window is maximized, the same operation —double-clicking on the title bar — restores it. A window can also be *closed* by double-clicking on its Control icon (see Figure 6), but since every Windows 95 window has a close button, this fact is useful for little more than impressing your friends, and it's not likely to do even that.

NOTE

Although using the mouse is easier, Windows 95 does allow you to use the keyboard to perform the move, resize, maximize, minimize, and close operations on a window. These operations (when available) are listed on the window's **Control menu**. To open the Control menu using the keyboard, press Alt+Spacebar or Alt+Hyphen, whichever works. (Remember: The notation "Alt+*keystroke*" means "hold down the Alt key, type the keystroke, and then release the Alt key.) The Control menu will appear in the upper left corner of the window, as shown in the following figure:

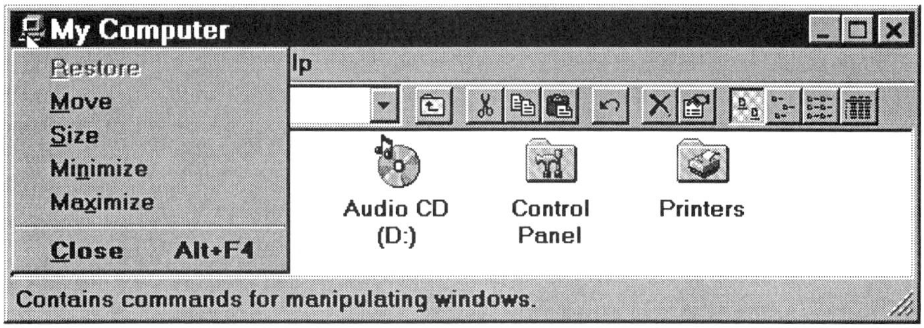

(You can also open its Control menu by right-clicking on the window's title bar or by clicking on its Control icon — see Figure 6 — if the window has one.) Choosing the Minimize, Maximize, Close, or Restore option performs the indicated task. Choosing Move or Size requires some maneuvering with the Arrow keys to complete the task; for these two operations, it's *a lot* easier to use the mouse!

Scroll Bars

When a window is not large enough to view all its contents at once, one or two **scroll bars** will be displayed to allow you to move through the contents without increasing the size of the window. For example, if we decrease the size of the My Computer window shown in Figure 6 so that the icons are partially or completely covered, the resulting window will look similar to the one in Figure 7.

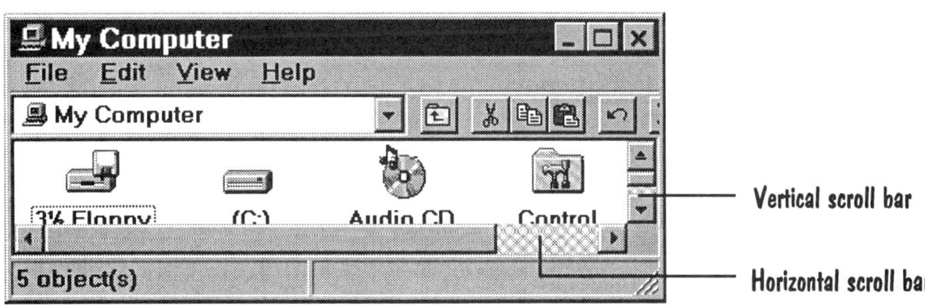

Figure 7 Scroll Bars Visible in a Window

Scrolling in a window

If the contents of a window — let's call it a *document*, even if it's just a collection of icons — is only partly visible, you have to **scroll** to see the rest of it. To understand how this works, imagine that the entire document is lying on the Desktop, but the window acts like a "cutout", allowing us to see only part of it. To see more (without increasing the window's size), we have to move the cutout around. For example, when you *scroll down*, imagine the cutout moving in a downward direction so that a lower part of the document comes into view. (In actuality, the window stays fixed on the screen and, figuratively speaking, the document itself moves around.)

You can use the mouse to scroll through the contents of a window by clicking on various parts of a scroll bar (see Figure 7): the *horizontal* scroll bar scrolls the window left or right; the *vertical* scroll bar scrolls it up or down. Let's take a closer look at a vertical scroll bar:

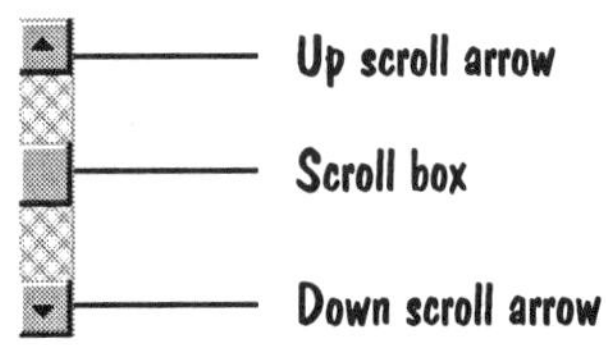

Here's how this scroll bar is used. (A horizontal scroll bar works in an analogous way.)

- Clicking the up or down scroll arrow scrolls the window up or down one "step". Holding down the mouse button while pointing at the up or down scroll arrow scrolls the window continuously in that direction until you release the button.
- Clicking on the scroll bar above or below the scroll box scrolls up or down one window's worth of information.
- Dragging the scroll box up or down scrolls the window proportionally within the document. For example, if you drag the scroll box to the middle of the scroll bar, the window will scroll about halfway through the document.

NOTE

The horizontal and vertical scroll bars also give visual clues to the size of the document in the window and your current location within it:

- The *length* of a scroll box is proportional to the amount of the document you are viewing. For example, the horizontal scroll box in Figure 7 is roughly 80% of the length of the corresponding scroll bar; we can deduce from this that we are seeing about 80% of the width of the underlying "document". The vertical scroll box in Figure 7 is about half the length of its scroll bar; we are viewing about half the height of the document.
- The *position* of a scroll box along its scroll bar gives your relative

location in the document. For example, in Figure 7, the horizontal scroll box is positioned at the left of its bar and the vertical scroll box is positioned at the top of its bar; we conclude that we are viewing the upper-left part of the underlying "document".

1·3 TUTORIAL

Try the following exercise on your own.

1. Start up your computer (if necessary) and open the My Computer window by double-clicking on its icon.
2. If the My Computer window is maximized (occupies the entire screen above the Taskbar), restore it by double-clicking on the title bar.
3. Minimize this window by clicking on its minimize button, toward the right end of the title bar. The title *My Computer* and its icon continue to appear on a button on the Taskbar.
4. Reopen the My Computer window by clicking on its Taskbar button.
5. Move the My Computer window to the upper-left corner of the screen by positioning the mouse pointer on the title bar and dragging the window outline to the appropriate place.
6. Make the window as small as possible in the horizontal direction. To do so, position the mouse pointer over the right window border (the pointer is placed properly when it turns into a "double arrow") and drag the outline of the border to the left as far as it will go. The horizontal scroll bar (and possibly the vertical one, as well) should appear.
7. Scroll across the window by positioning the mouse pointer over the right scroll arrow and holding down the left mouse button until the scroll box reaches the right end of the scroll bar. Now scroll back the other way by dragging the scroll box to the left end of the scroll bar. Increase the window to its former size.
8. Maximize the My Computer window by clicking on the maximize button, toward the right end of the title bar.
9. Pull down the Control menu by clicking on the Control icon (which looks like a computer) on the left end of the title bar (or by pressing Alt+Spacebar). Notice that the Maximize option is dimmed.
10. Restore the My Computer window by clicking on the Restore option on the Control menu.
11. Close the My Computer window by clicking on the close button on the right end of the title bar. (Should you now want to shut down your computer, see Section 1.5.)

1.4 Conversing with Dialog Boxes

As you may recall, choosing a menu item followed by an ellipsis (...) displays a dialog box. A **dialog box** is a special type of window that presents groups of related options from which you can make selections. As you work with Windows 95 and its applications, you will encounter a seemingly infinite variety of dialog boxes. Yet, all dialog boxes have certain things in common. In this section, we will discuss these common features.

A Typical Dialog Box

To illustrate the features of a dialog box, let's take a look at a very interesting one. (Although we will discuss the types of objects in this dialog box here, a description of its capabilities will come later, in Chapter 4.) If you right-click (click the right mouse button) on an empty area of the Desktop, the following menu appears:

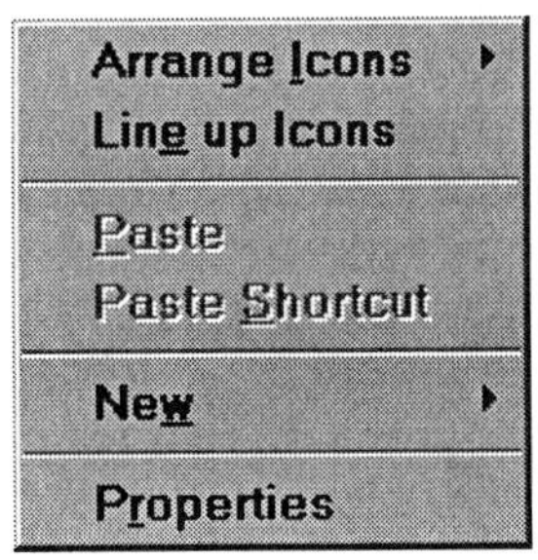

Choosing the Properties option from this menu opens the Display Properties dialog box shown in Figure 8. (Notice that there isn't any ellipsis next to the Properties option on the menu!)

At the top of this dialog box is the familiar title bar, which supplies the name of the window. It also contains a close button (marked with an X) and a help button (marked with a ?), but not a minimize or maximize button. In general, dialog boxes cannot be resized in any way; in particular, they cannot be minimized or maximized. Dialog boxes *can* be moved about the screen; as with any window, just drag its title bar to the desired location.

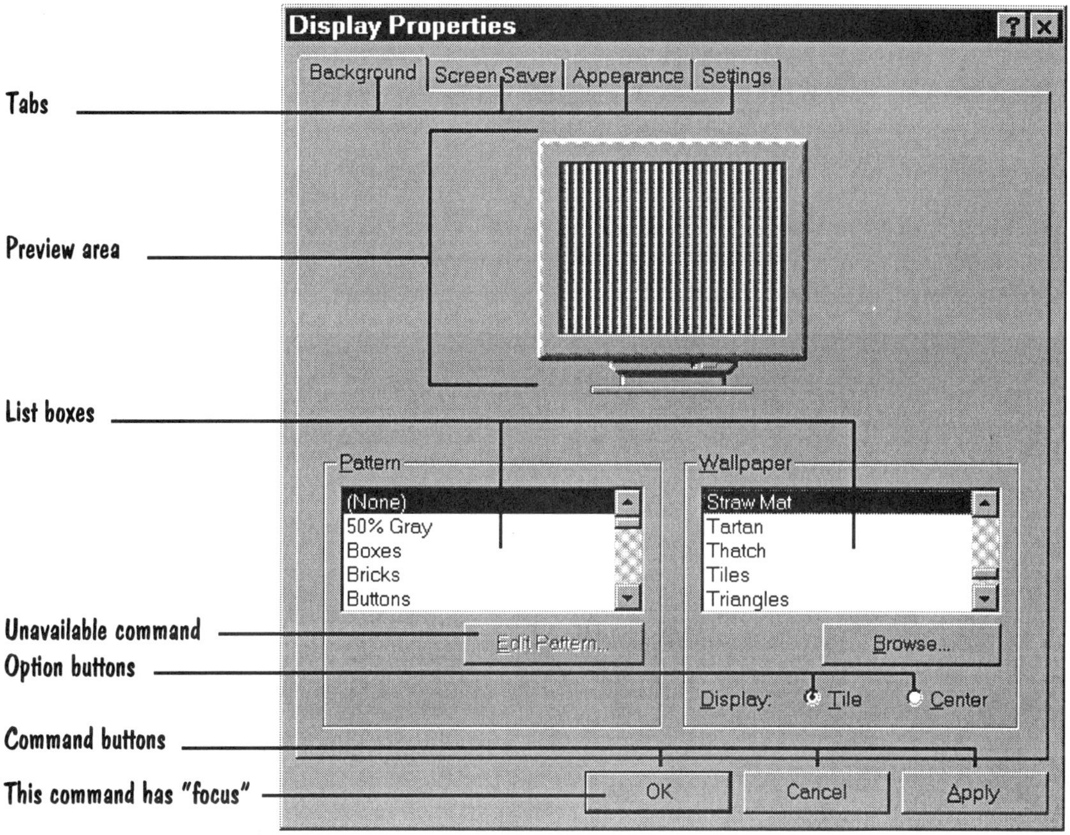

Figure 8 A Typical Dialog Box

Most objects in a dialog box allow the user (that's you!) to specify preferences or execute commands. These objects (for example, the tabs, command buttons, option buttons, and list boxes of Figure 8) are arranged in related groups and associated with easily recognized symbols. Each symbol indicates a different function, as described below.

Command buttons are represented by large labeled rectangles. When you click on a command button, it initiates an action. For example, clicking on the Browse button in Figure 8 opens another dialog box. (Notice the ellipsis following the word *Browse*.) Here are a few special features of command buttons:

- Exactly one command button in a dialog box is enclosed in a heavy outline. (In Figure 8, it's the OK button.) We say that this is "the default button" or that it "has the focus". As you select options in a dialog box, the focus sometimes moves to another button. Nevertheless, the button that currently has the focus can always be activated by pressing the Enter key (or by clicking on the button).

- Almost all dialog boxes have a button labeled "OK" or "Close". When this button is activated, the dialog box closes and the options you have selected go into effect.
- The Cancel button allows you to close a dialog box without putting any of your new selections into effect. (Pressing the Escape key has the same effect as clicking on the Cancel button.)
- If the label on a command button is dimmed (for example, the Edit Pattern button in Figure 8), this option is not available at this time. (In this particular case, there is no pattern to edit!)

Option buttons are represented by small circles. These buttons are sometimes called *radio buttons* because they work like the station selection push buttons on a radio — when you click on one of them, it is *selected* (turned on) and the others are automatically *deselected* (turned off). For this reason, in a group of these buttons, exactly one of the corresponding options is selected at any given time. The currently selected option button is indicated by a "bullet". For example, in Figure 8, the Tile option is currently selected. If you click on the Center button, it will acquire the bullet (indicating that this option has been selected), and the Tile option will be deselected.

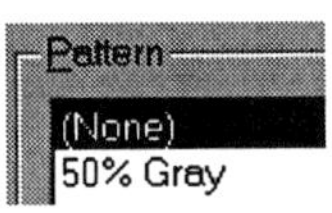

A **list box** is a rectangular box that contains a list of items from which you can choose. To select an item, click on its name. If the list is too long to fit in the box, a scroll bar will be displayed so that you can scroll through the entire list. The currently selected item in the list is highlighted. For example, in Figure 8, the selected item in the Pattern list box is "(None)" and the selected Wallpaper is "Straw Mat".

Tabs, which resemble file folder tabs, always appear at the top of a dialog box (if they appear at all). The currently selected tab (which is "Background" in Figure 8) appears to be in front of the others. The name on the tab provides a short description of the group of options currently visible in the dialog box. To select another tab, click on it; a new "page" of options will become available. Figure 9 shows the result of clicking on the Screen Saver tab in the dialog box of Figure 8.

NOTE

Some dialog boxes also display written or pictorial information for the user. For example, the dialog box in Figure 8 contains a *preview window* that shows the effect your selections will have on the Windows Desktop should you choose the OK (or Apply) command button.

Additional Dialog Box Features

If you click on the Screen Saver tab in the Display Properties dialog box of Figure 8, most of the contents of this window change, providing a new set (*page*) of options from which to choose. The result is shown in Figure 9, which illustrates additional features of a dialog box.

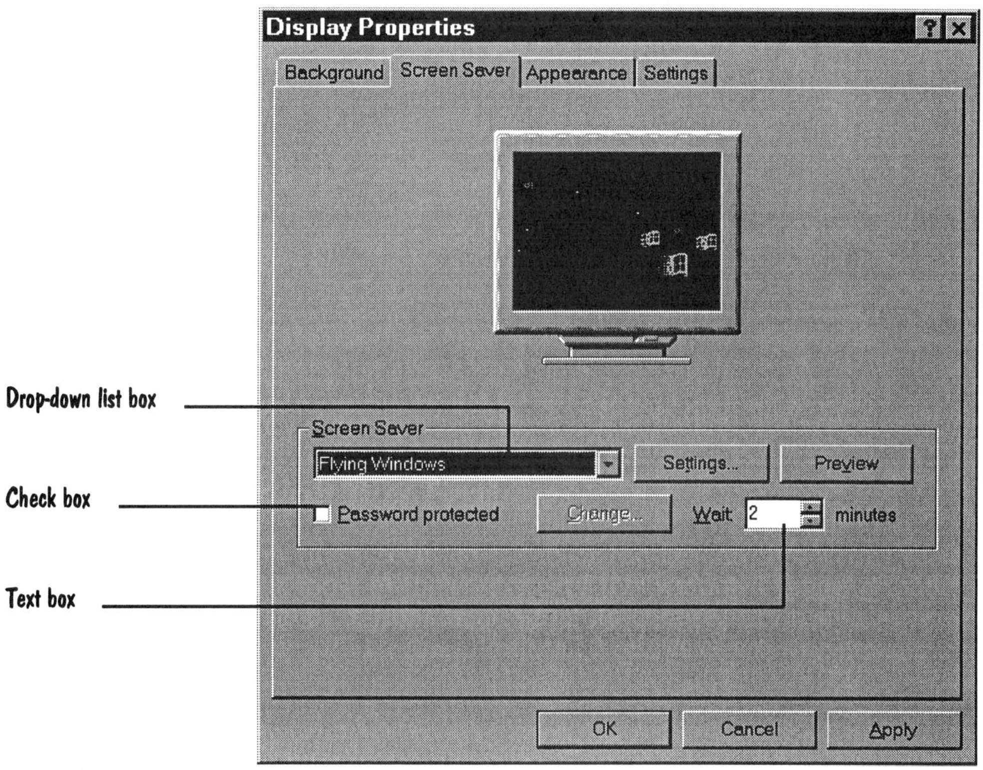

Figure 9 Additional Features of a Dialog Box

A **check box** is represented by a small square, which may or may not contain a check mark. When the check box is selected, the check mark is present; when it is deselected, the check mark does not appear. For example, the deselected check box in Figure 9 indicates that this screen saver is not "password protected". A check box is a toggle:

- If you click on it when it's deselected, then it becomes selected (and a check mark appears).
- If you click on it when it's selected, then it becomes deselected (and the check mark disappears).

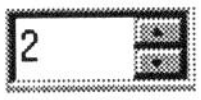

A **text box** allows you to input a number or name into a dialog box. It is symbolized by a rectangle that contains the *current value* for that option — the number or name that is used if you don't change it. For example, in Figure 9, 2 is the current value for the Wait text box. To change it, click on the text box, press the Backspace key to erase the current value, and then type a new one. (Do not press the Enter key after typing unless you want to activate the command button that has the focus!) Some text boxes, like the one in Figure 9, contain up and down arrows which provide an alternate way to change the current value. Here, each click on the appropriate arrow moves the time up or down one minute.

A **drop-down list box** is a special type of list box. Here, only one of the listed items (the current value) is initially visible. To see the rest of the list, click on the downward-facing triangle at the right end of the box. Then, to select an item from the list, click on that item. The list will close and the new item will be the one displayed.

TUTORIAL

Try the following exercise on your own.

1. Start up your computer (if necessary) and/or close any open windows by clicking on their close buttons.
2. Open the Display Properties dialog box by right-clicking on (an empty area of) the Desktop and then selecting Properties from the resulting menu.
3. If the Tile option button is not selected (if it doesn't have a darkened center), select it by clicking on it.
4. From the Wallpaper text box, select the Straw Mat wallpaper. To do so, scroll down the list until Straw Mat appears and then click on this item. The "screen" in the preview window should look like the one shown in Figure 8.
5. Select the Center option button. You should see a dramatic difference in the preview window.
6. Click on the Screen Saver tab to view a new page in the dialog box. It should look similar to the one in Figure 9.
7. Open the Screen Saver drop-down list by clicking on the down triangle in this box.

8. Select Mystify from this list (by clicking on it) and then choose the Preview button (by clicking on it) to view the Mystify screen saver. To return to the Display Properties dialog box, click the mouse.
9. Change the time in the Wait text box to 5 minutes by clicking on this box and then on its up or down arrow until "5" appears in the text box.
10. Choose Cancel by clicking on the Cancel command button or by pressing the Escape key. If you now want to shut down your computer, follow the instructions in Section 1.5.

1.5 Shutting Down Windows 95

All good things (in fact, all things in general) must come to an end. At some point, you're going to want to quit working with Windows 95 and turn off your computer. To do so, you should:

1. Close all applications that are currently running. If an application's window is open on the Desktop, click on its close button (see Section 1.3); if the application has been minimized, right-click on its Taskbar button and then choose Close from the resulting menu. If you have used an application to modify a document and have not saved these changes to disk, Windows will display a message warning you of this fact. (We will discuss closing applications and saving documents in Section 2.2.)

2. Click on the Start button, which can normally be found in the lower-left corner of the Desktop. This action opens the **Start menu**:

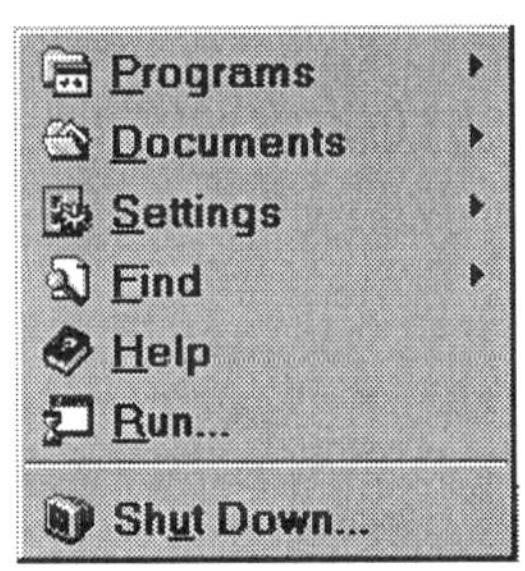

NOTE If the Start button is not visible anywhere on the Desktop, you can open the Start menu by pressing Ctrl+Esc; that is, hold down the Ctrl (Control) key, press the Esc (Escape) key, and then release Ctrl.

3. Click on the Shut Down option on the Start menu. The dialog box shown in Figure 10 will open.

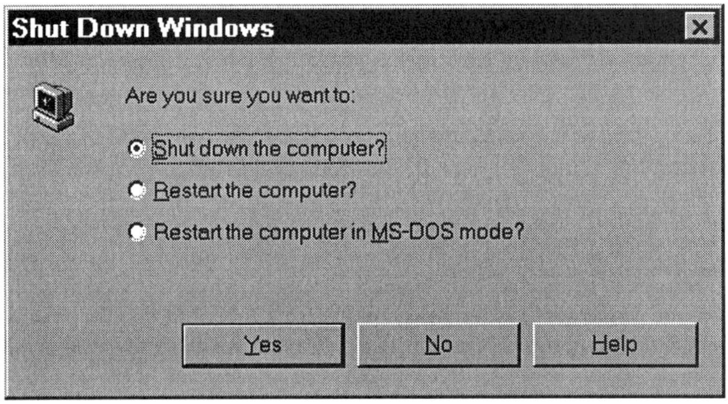

Figure 10 The Shut Down Windows Dialog Box

4. Now select an option* by clicking, if necessary, on the appropriate option button and choosing the Yes command button. Or, close this dialog box and return to Windows 95 by choosing No (or by pressing the Escape key).

   - The first option, "Shut down the computer?", should be selected when you want to turn off your computer. Activating this option eventually brings up the message: "It's now safe to turn off your computer."

WARNING

If you want to turn off your computer, you should first shut down Windows 95. Doing so ensures that all open files will be properly closed. As a result, you are much less likely to inadvertently lose data or your preferred Windows settings.

   - Activating the second option, "Restart the computer?", restarts Windows 95, reinitializing all its settings. This option is usually used after a program *crashes* (terminates abruptly) and/or Windows itself does not seem to be responding properly to your commands.
   - The third option, "Restart the computer in MS-DOS mode?",

*If your computer is connected to a network, there may be a fourth available option listed in this dialog box.

shuts down Windows 95 and starts **DOS**, Microsoft's plain vanilla operating system (see the Introduction). Once in DOS, you can safely turn off the computer when you see the DOS prompt (probably, `C:\WINDOWS>`). You can also start Windows 95 at the DOS prompt by typing `WIN` and pressing the Enter key.

TIP

Here are a couple of shortcuts for shutting down Windows:

- You can display the Shut Down Windows dialog box after closing down all applications by pressing the Alt+F4 keystroke combination.
- You can activate the "Shut down the computer?" option in the Shut Down Windows dialog box even if there are applications running. In this case, Windows will attempt to close these applications and, if successful, shut down your computer. (If you try this approach, you may see a message prompting you to save changes in a document or requesting that you close certain applications yourself.)

1.5 TUTORIAL

Try the following exercise on your own.

1. Turn on your computer, if necessary, to start Windows 95. If Windows is already running, close all windows by clicking on their close buttons.
2. Restart Windows 95: Open the Start menu by clicking on the Start button (if you can't find this button, press Ctrl+Esc to open the Start menu); choose Shut Down from the menu; select the "Restart the computer?" option button in the resulting dialog box; and choose the Yes command button.
3. When Windows 95 starts again, press Alt+F4 to open the Shut Down Windows dialog box. This time, select the "Restart the computer in MS-DOS mode?" option button and choose Yes. After a few seconds, you should see a mostly blank screen displaying the DOS prompt, probably `C:\WINDOWS>`.
4. Type `WIN` and press the Enter key to start Windows 95.
5. This time, open the Shut Down Windows dialog box, select the "Shut down the computer?" option button, and choose Yes. When the message "It's now safe to turn off your computer." appears, do just that.

Chapter Summary

Objects on the Desktop	Icons	Small stylized pictures representing Windows' objects
	Start button	Opens the Start menu when clicked
	Taskbar	Contains the Clock and buttons for applications that are currently running
	Windows	Boxed-in areas of the screen that contain applications, documents, dialog boxes, and other items
Mouse Terminology	Point at an object	Move the mouse so that its pointer is positioned over the object.
	Click	Press and release the left mouse button.
	Right-click	Press and release the right mouse button.
	Click/right-click *on* an object	Point at the object and click the left/right mouse button.
	Drag/right-drag an object	Point at the object, press (but don't release) the left/right mouse button, move the pointer to another position, and release the button.
Working with Menus	To open a menu	Click on its name (or press Alt+*underlined letter*).
	To choose an item from a menu	Click on it or, if ▸ is present, point at the item (*or*, in either case, type the letter that is underlined in the item's name).
Working with Windows	To move a window	Drag its title bar to a new location.
	To resize a window	Drag a window border or corner to a new location.
	To maximize/minimize/restore a window	Click the appropriate button at the right end of the title bar; for maximize or restore, double-click on the title bar.
	To close a window	Click on its close button.
	To scroll in a window	Click on the scroll bar arrows; drag the scroll box; *or* click on the scroll bar between an

		arrow and the box.
	To open a window's Control menu	Click on the Control icon; right-click on the title bar; *or* press Alt+Spacebar or Alt+Hyphen.
Parts of a Dialog Box	Command buttons	Initiate actions such as close, cancel, etc.
	Option (radio) buttons	Allow one of several related options to be selected
	List boxes	Allow an item to be selected from a list
	Tabs	Display a "page" of related options
	Check boxes	Turn a particular option on or off
	Text boxes	Allow text or numbers to be input by the user
Shutting down Windows 95	To open the Start menu	Click on the Start button *or* press Ctrl+Esc.
	To open the Shut Down Windows dialog box	Close all running applications, and choose Shut Down from the Start menu *or* press Alt+F4.
	To choose a shut down option	Select the corresponding option button in the Shut Down Windows dialog box and activate the Yes command button. (Activating the No button cancels the dialog box.)

Review Exercises

Section 1.1

1. A(n) ____________ is a small stylized picture used to represent a Windows 95 object.
2. The ____________ button is positioned to the left of the Taskbar.
3. True or false: To start Windows 95, you must type the proper command after turning on your computer.
4. The Windows *Desktop* refers to:

   a. The area occupied by your computer, keyboard, and mouse.
   b. The windows that are currently open.

c. The application that is currently running, including its menus, toolbars, and so on.
d. None of the above is the Windows Desktop.

Section 1.2

5. To click on an object on the screen, move the mouse pointer over that object and press the ___________.
6. To open an application's View menu, you can click on the word ___________ on the menu bar.
7. If the name of a menu item is followed by an ellipsis (...), then choosing that menu item opens a(n) ___________.
8. True or false: When double-clicking the mouse, you should pause for a second or two between clicks.
9. True or false: To use a shortcut key to perform a task, open the menu that lists that task, and then press the shortcut key.
10. True or false: To right-drag an object, move the mouse pointer over it and click the right button.
11. When you position the mouse pointer over an object, hold down the left button, and move the pointer to a new location, it is called
    a. Clicking on the object.
    b. Double-clicking on the object.
    c. Dragging the object.
    d. Pointing at the object.
12. If an item on a menu is dimmed, clicking on that item
    a. Opens a dialog box.
    b. Opens a submenu.
    c. Closes the menu.
    d. Does nothing at all.

Section 1.3

13. To move a window, drag its ___________ to the desired location on the screen.
14. Clicking on a window's __________ increases the window's size as much as possible.
15. To increase the width of a window without increasing its height, drag its ___________ to the right or its ___________ to the left.
16. True or false: You can close a window by clicking on its title bar.
17. True or false: When a window is minimized, the window disappears from the screen.
18. True or false: When a window opens, horizontal and vertical scroll bars are always displayed.
19. Which part of a window contains its maximize, minimize, and

close buttons?

a. Its title bar.
b. Its menu bar.
c. Its toolbar.
d. Its status bar.

20. If an application is maximized, from its Control menu, you *cannot*

a. Open the application's window.
b. Close the application's window.
c. Minimize the application's window.
d. Restore the application's window.

In Exercises 21 and 22, identify the indicated parts of the window shown in Figure 11. Your answers should come from the following list:

Close button	Control icon
Horizontal scroll bar	Maximize button
Menu bar	Minimize button
Title bar	Vertical scroll bar

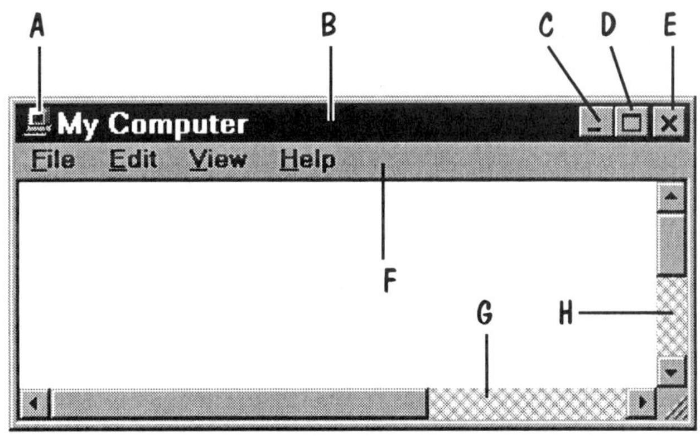

Figure 11 Window for Exercises 21 and 22

21. Identify the components of the window in Figure 11 that are marked A, B, C, and D.

22. Identify the components of the window in Figure 11 that are marked E, F, G, and H.

Section 1.4 23. When you click on the command button labeled ____________ in a dialog box, the box closes and the selected options go into effect.

24. In a dialog box, instead of clicking on the Cancel button, you can press the ____________ key.

25. In a dialog box, a ____________ allows the user to turn an option on or off without affecting other options.

26. True or false: Dialog boxes can be moved around the screen.

27. True or false: A drop-down list box only displays a single item until you click on the appropriate symbol to "open" it.

28. True or false: In a group of related option buttons, only one button can be selected at any given time.

29. Which of the following objects appears on the title bar of a dialog box?

    a. A minimize button.
    b. A maximize button.
    c. A close button.
    d. A Control icon.

30. Dialog boxes never contain:

    a. Command buttons.
    b. Restore buttons.
    c. Option buttons.
    d. Tabs.

Section 1.5

31. The Shut Down option, which allows us to shut down Windows 95, appears on the ____________ menu.

32. The Shut Down Windows dialog box gives us the option of shutting down or ____________ Windows 95.

33. True or false: It is a good idea to shut down Windows 95 before turning off your computer.

34. True or false: To display the Start menu, even if the Start button is not visible on the screen, press Ctrl+Esc.

35. You can display the Shut Down Windows dialog box after closing all applications by pressing the keystroke combination:

    a. Alt+Spacebar
    b. Alt+Hyphen
    c. Alt+F4.
    d. None of these keystrokes works.

Build Your Own Glossary

36. The following words and phrases are important terms that were introduced in this chapter. (They appear within the text in boldface type.) Write a definition for each term. After you learn to use WordPad (in Section 2.2), you should enter these definitions into the Glossary file on the Student Disk.

Check box	Close button	Control icon
Close a window	Command button	Control menu

Desktop	Menu bar	Scroll bar
Dialog box	Minimize a window	Shortcut key
Drop-down list box	Minimize button	Start button
Icon	Option button	Start menu
List box	Pull-down menu	Tab (in a dialog box)
Maximize a window	Restore a window	Taskbar
Maximize button	Restore button	Title bar
Menu	Scroll	Window

Lab Exercises

Work each of the following exercises at your computer. Begin by turning the machine on (if necessary) to start Windows 95. Then, close all open windows by clicking on the button labeled with an X on the title bar of each window. If you want to shut down the computer after completing an exercise, follow the instructions in Section 1.5.

Lab Exercise 1 (Section 1.2)

a. *Right*-click (click with the right mouse button) on an empty part of the Desktop. On the resulting menu:

   Which options (if any) are dimmed?
   Which options (if any) will open a dialog box when selected?
   Does a bullet appear next to any option?

b. Point at the Arrange Icons option to open its submenu. Notice that there is an Auto Arrange item on the submenu. (Don't click on it!) The Auto Arrange item is a toggle. Is it selected? How do you know?

c. Point at the New option on the original menu. In the submenu that appears, click on Folder. What is the name of the new icon that has appeared on the Desktop?

d. Click on an empty part of the Desktop. Then *right*-drag the new icon to another empty part of the Desktop. How many items are listed on the menu that appears when you release the mouse button?

e. Select the Copy Here option. How many copies of the new icon now appear on the Desktop?

f. Drag each copy of the new icon on top of the Recycle Bin icon. What happens each time?

Lab Exercise 2 (Section 1.2)

a. Double-click on the Recycle Bin icon to open its window. List the names of the menus that appear on the menu bar.

b. Open the Edit menu. What is the shortcut key for the Cut option? Is this option dimmed?

c. Press Ctrl+A, the shortcut key for the Select All option. Why didn't anything happen?

d. Cancel the Edit menu (close it without choosing any item). What mouse action or keystroke did you use?

e. Open the View menu. How many items have bullets next to them? How many items have submenus?

f. The Toolbar menu item is a toggle; is there a check mark next to it? Choose the Toolbar item. The View menu will close. What else happened?

g. Reopen the View menu. Is the Toolbar menu item "checked" now?

h. *Right*-click (click with the right button) on the Status Bar item. What, if anything, happened?

i. Click on the word *View* to close this menu. Then, click on the button labeled with an X in the upper-right corner of the Recycle Bin window to close it.

Lab Exercise 3 (Section 1.3)

a. Click on an empty part of the Desktop, then press the F3 function key to open the Find window. Does this window have a Control icon on its title bar?

b. If the Find window is maximized, restore it. Then, decrease its width as much as possible. Is the entire window title visible now? Did any scroll bars appear?

c. Try to increase or decrease the height of this window. Was it possible to do either?

d. Maximize the Find window. Does it occupy the entire screen?

e. Right-click the title bar to display the Control menu. List the items that appear on this menu. Cancel the Control menu by clicking elsewhere in the window.

f. Move the window in a *horizontal* direction. Was the restore button replaced by a maximize button? If not, click on the restore button.

g. Minimize the window to a button on the Taskbar; then restore it to a window. Is it the same size as it was before being minimized?

h. Resize the Find window to the approximate size it had when you began this exercise and close this window.

Lab Exercise 4 (Section 1.3)

a. Right-click on an empty part of the Desktop; then select Properties from the resulting menu to open the Display Properties window.

b. Notice that this window (a *dialog box*) does not contain a minimize or maximize, button or a Control icon. Try to maximize the window by double-clicking on its title bar. Did this work?

c. Can this dialog box be: Moved? Resized? Minimized?

d. Open the window's Control menu. What mouse action or keystroke combination did you use? What items are listed on the Control menu? Cancel this menu.

e. In the small window entitled *Pattern*, use the vertical scroll bar to scroll to the bottom of the list. What name appears there? Why isn't a *horizontal* scroll bar displayed?

f. Try closing the Display Properties window by pressing Alt+F4. Did it work? If not, close it by clicking on the close button.

Lab Exercise 5 (Section 1.4)

a. Double-click on the Clock on the Taskbar to open the Date/Time Properties dialog box. (If you can't find the Taskbar, press Ctrl+ Esc to display it.)

b. Try to change the year displayed in the Date text box to 1800. Were you able to do this?

c. Using the up and down arrows in the Date text box, determine the allowable range of years. What is it?

d. Click on the Time Zone tab to change to this set of options.

e. Open the drop-down list and scroll to the bottom. What place is given for the "GMT+12:00" entry? Close the drop-down list.

f. Click on the ? button on the title bar; then click on the text to the right of the check box. What happened?

g. Close this dialog box by clicking on Cancel or by pressing the Escape key.

Lab Exercise 6 (Section 1.4)

a. Click on an empty part of the Desktop; then press the F3 function key to open the Find window.

b. Deselect the *Include subfolders* check box. Did the text in the *Look in* drop-down list box change?

c. Click on the Date Modified tab. Notice that the *All files* option button is selected.

d. Select the *between* option button. What happened to the *All files* button?

e. Select one of the *previous* option buttons. Try to enter the number 0 in the corresponding text box. Could you do this?

f. Click on the Advanced tab and open the drop-down list. Why is a vertical scroll bar necessary here? What name is at the bottom of the list?

g. Close the Find window by clicking on its close button.

Lab Exercise 7 (Section 1.5)

a. Open the Shut Down Windows dialog box; then close it without shutting down or restarting the computer. How did you do this?

b. Reopen the Shut Down Windows dialog box and activate the "Restart the computer in MS-DOS mode?" option. What text eventually appears on the screen?

c. Insert the Student Disk that accompanies this text into its drive; then type `a:dosprog` and press the Enter key. Does the application you just started appear in a *window*?

d. Follow the on-screen instructions to exit this application. What did you do to exit?

e. Restart Windows 95 by typing `win` and pressing the Enter key. Was the Windows 95 logo displayed before Windows started?

f. Open the Shut Down Windows dialog box and activate the "Shut down the computer?" option. What message is displayed prior to "It's now safe to turn off your computer"?

g. Turn off your computer.

If You Want to Learn More ...

This section, and others like it throughout the text, present some notes that allow you to delve more deeply into the material in the current chapter. Most of the notes found here deal with esoteric or advanced topics, so there is no need for you to spend an undue amount of time reading them now. On the other hand, you may find some of these comments interesting and, on occasion, they may help you work through a potentially frustrating situation.

More on the Taskbar Clock

The Taskbar Clock gives not only the time but also the current day and date. To view the latter, position the mouse pointer over the clock and hold it steady for a few moments. Here are a couple of more tips on using the Clock:

- If the Clock does not appear on the Taskbar, right-click on an empty part of the Taskbar, and choose the Properties option from the pop-up menu. Then select the Show Clock check box in the resulting dialog box and choose the OK command button.
- If the Clock is not showing the correct time or date, double-click on it. The Date/Time Properties dialog box will open, and the date and time can be adjusted, as described in Section 5.5.

Quicker restarts

To decrease the amount of time it takes the computer to restart (see Section 1.5), proceed as follows:

1. Open the Shut Down Windows dialog box from the Start menu and select the "Restart the computer?" option.
2. Hold down the Shift key as you click on the Yes command button.

Windows will shortcut part of the usual restart process, and the Desktop will reappear considerably more quickly.

Navigating with the keyboard

Certainly, the easiest way to select items on the Desktop or in a dialog box is to use the mouse. But Windows supplies keyboard alternatives for most mouse operations, including these. For example:

- To select a particular Desktop icon (when no window is active), press the appropriate Arrow keys until the icon is highlighted. (If nothing seems to happen when you press an Arrow key, press the Tab key until one of the Desktop icons becomes "boxed-in".) Once an icon is highlighted, pressing the Enter key has the same effect as double-clicking on that icon.
- You can move the focus (see Section 1.4) from one item to another in an active dialog box by pressing the Tab key. To cycle through a set of option buttons when they have the focus, repeatedly press an Arrow key. To select or deselect the check box that has the focus, press the Spacebar.

For a more complete list of keyboard alternatives, see Appendix A.

Displaying an off-screen title bar

If part of a window is located beyond the screen boundary, you can usually move the entire window on-screen by dragging its title bar. However, this technique does not work if the title bar itself is "off the screen". In this situation, there are two basic ways to get the title bar back on-screen. First, click on any part of the window to make it the active window. Now, either press Alt+Spacebar to open the window's Control menu or right-click on the window's Taskbar button to open a pop-up menu. Then:

- Maximize the window (if it *can* be maximized) by choosing the Maximize command from either of these two menus.

or

- Choose the Move command from either of these two menus and then use the Arrow keys to move the window in the appropriate direction. When the moving window outline is positioned where you want, press the Enter key to complete the process.

Where to go from here

Here's where to find more information about some of the topics discussed in this chapter.

- Adding and removing Desktop icons (*shortcuts*) — Section 3.4
- Changing the Desktop background — Section 5.2
- Using the Taskbar — Sections 2.3 and 4.1
- Using the other Start menu options:

  Programs, Documents, and Run — Section 2.1
  Settings — Sections 4.1, 5.1, and 6.1
  Find — Section 4.3
  Help — Section 2.4

- Changing the appearance of various Desktop and window elements (such as the title bar color or icon text) — Section 5.3

CHAPTER 2

Working with Applications and Documents

In Chapter 1 we discussed the structure and general use of some basic Windows 95 objects — the Desktop, menus, windows, and dialog boxes. In this chapter, we will concentrate on how to use Windows 95 to run your **applications** (programs) and manipulate your **documents** (the work created by an application). To be more specific, you will learn:

1. Various ways to start and close applications.
2. How to use the WordPad application to create simple word processing documents.
3. How to open, save, print, and close documents.
4. How to switch among the applications that are running.
5. How to transfer information from one document to another.
6. How to "capture" windows and screens.
7. How to use the online Windows 95 Help system to locate information about a desired topic.
8. How to obtain online context-sensitive help.

After completing this chapter, you should be able to use Windows 95 to print a copy of your homework!

2.1 Starting and Closing Applications

Windows 95 supplies a myriad of ways to start (or *open*) and exit (or *close*) applications. In this section we will describe most of these techniques.

Using the Start Menu

Recall that if you click on the Start button to the left of the Taskbar or press the Ctrl+Esc keystroke combination, the Windows 95 Start menu opens (Figure 1). In Section 1.5, we discussed how to use the last item on this menu to shut down or restart Windows 95. Here, we will describe how to use the Start menu to open the applications available on your computer.

Figure 1
The Start Menu

The Programs option

Usually, the most straightforward way to open a program is to select the **Programs option** from the Start menu. When you point at this item (holding the arrow-shaped mouse pointer steady for a moment or two), a submenu listing specific applications and groups of applications will be displayed, as shown in Figure 2. (Your list of programs will undoubtedly be different from the one that appears here.)

On the submenu, the items followed by a right-facing triangle (such as Accessories, at the top in Figure 2) represent *groups* of applications; if you point at one of these items, another submenu will open, presenting further applications and possibly groups of applications. A submenu item that is not followed by a right triangle (such as Windows Explorer at the bottom of the list) represents a program. To start a program, just click on it! The Start menu will close and the program will begin running.

For example, suppose you want to open WordPad, a word processor that is included with the Windows 95 software package. To do so, click on the Start button to open the Start menu and point at the Programs option to open its submenu (Figure 2). Then, point at the Accessories option, which opens another submenu, and finally click on the WordPad item at the bottom of the latter. After a few moments, the WordPad opening screen will be displayed.

Figure 2
Pointing at the Programs Option on the Start Menu

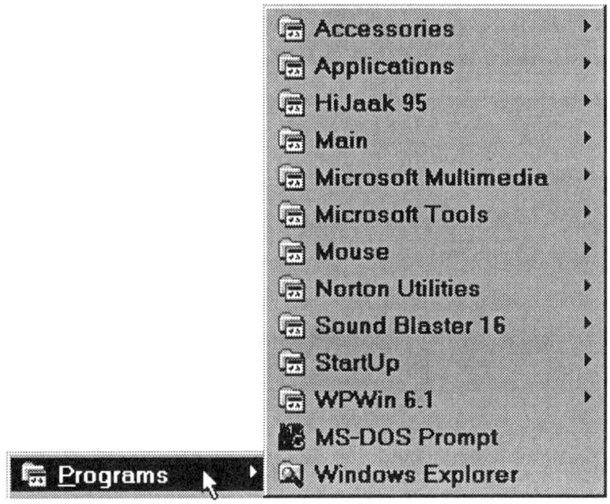

The Documents option

Using the **Documents option** on the Start menu can sometimes be a real time-saver. Pointing at this item (see Figure 3) displays a submenu containing a list of the last 15 documents you saved to disk while running programs designed for Windows 95. (We will discuss saving documents in Section 2.2.) Clicking on one of the listed documents starts the application that created it and also displays (*opens*) the designated document within it.

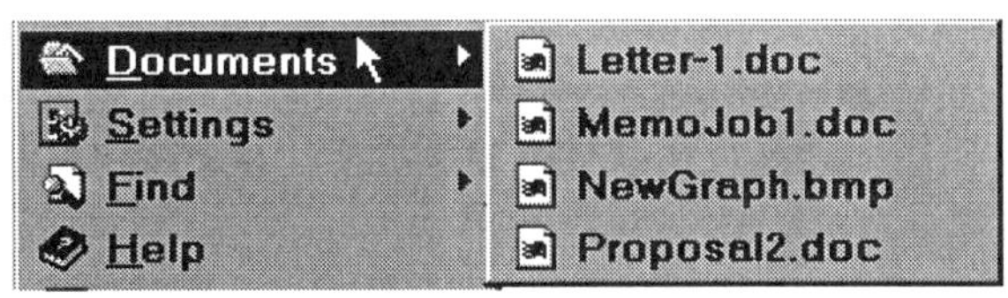

Figure 3 Pointing at the Documents Option

The Run option

The techniques we have just described for starting an application are quick and easy, but require that the program, or a document created by it, appear on one of the Start submenus. The **Run option**, which appears near the bottom of the Start menu, can be used to open *any* application on your hard or floppy disks.

When you click on the Run command, the following dialog box is displayed:

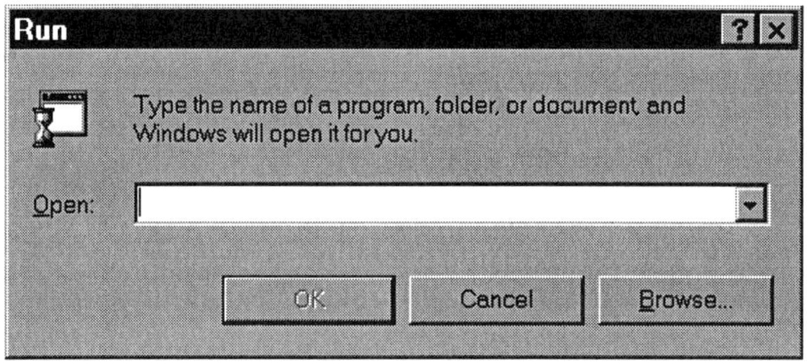

To start a program from this dialog box, you must know its file name, and possibly the folder in which that file is located — this is the major drawback of using the Run option. (We will discuss files and folders in Section 3.1.) If you have this required information, you can open the desired application by performing any of the following actions:

- Type the appropriate folder and file names (the program's *path name*) in the Open text box. (If a highlighted name already appears there, just type over it!) Then, click on the OK button or press the Enter key.
- If you have previously started the desired application from the Run dialog box, its name may appear on the Open drop-down list. Display this list (by clicking on the down-triangle), select the program's file name, and activate the OK button.
- Click on the Browse command button to open the Browse dialog box and use it to help you locate the program's file name; then activate the OK button. (This technique requires some familiarity with the Windows 95 folder system, which we will discuss in Chapter 3.)

In any case, the Run dialog box will close and the program will start.

As you can see, using the Run option is usually not the easiest way to start a program. However, there is one case in which Run is especially useful: when the program you want to start is on a floppy disk (diskette). To start a program from a floppy:

1. Insert the diskette in its drive.
2. Select the Run option from the Start menu.
3. Type the characters a: (assuming that the diskette is in this drive) followed by the program's file name in the text box; for example, a:big-game.

4. Press the Enter key or click on the OK button. The Run dialog box will close and the program will start.

Other Ways to Start Applications

Typically, Windows 95 provides a variety of ways of performing just about any task, and opening applications is no exception. You have already seen several ways in which the Start menu can be used for this purpose. Here are a few additional important techniques for starting programs:

The easiest way

If an icon representing an application or document appears on the Desktop, just *double*-click on it to open that application or document. (In Chapter 1, we used this technique to open the My Computer application.) If you use a particular application frequently, it makes a lot of sense to place an icon (*shortcut*) for it on the Desktop. We will discuss how to do this in Section 3.4.

Using Windows Explorer or My Computer

Just about every aspect of your computer system can be accessed using either Windows Explorer (on the Programs submenu) or My Computer (which is represented by an icon on the Desktop). Both of these applications can locate and start any program on your hard or floppy disks. We will discuss Windows Explorer and My Computer in Chapter 3.

Closing an Application

If you read Chapter 1 carefully (or worked its tutorials), you already know how to close a Windows-based application — just close its window. As usual, this task can be done in several ways. The following techniques are listed (more or less) in order of likely use; take your pick:

Ways to close Windows-based applications

- Click on the application window's close button (on the right end of the title bar). 
- Choose Exit from the application's File menu.
- Right-click on the application's Taskbar button and choose Close from the resulting menu.
- Press Alt+F4 (hold down the Alt key, tap the F4 key, and release Alt).
- Double-click on the application's Control icon (on the left end of the title bar).
- Open the application's Control menu by clicking on its Control

icon (right-clicking the title bar may also work) and choose the Close option.

NOTE

If you have used the application to make changes to a document and did not subsequently save the document to disk, Windows will display a warning message before closing the application. We will discuss this further in Section 2.2.

Closing DOS applications

As we mentioned in the Introduction, Windows 95 not only runs applications specifically designed for itself and Windows 3.1, but it also runs *DOS applications*. Although some DOS applications can be closed by selecting Exit from their File menus (if they have one!), none of the other techniques listed above is likely to work. If you try one of them, you'll probably just get a message that "Windows cannot shut down this program automatically."

Unfortunately, DOS applications, especially older ones, are notorious for performing common tasks in their own peculiar ways. So, you'll just have to learn the keystrokes or mouse clicks necessary to exit each DOS application you use. After exiting the program, its window may still remain on the screen, with the word *Finished* displayed at the left end of the title bar. To close the window, use any of the usual techniques (such as clicking on the close button).

TIP

There is another way to exit *any* application, but it should only be used in an emergency; for example, if the application has "locked up", and no longer responds to the keyboard or mouse. In this case, hold down the Ctrl and Alt keys, tap the Del key, and then release Ctrl and Alt. A dialog box will open, listing all programs that are currently running. The offending application should be highlighted in this list. (If it isn't, click on it.) Now activate the End Task command button and follow the on-screen instructions. Using this procedure, you will probably lose all unsaved work in the application that has locked up, but other open programs should survive unscathed.

2-1 TUTORIAL

Try the following exercises on your own.

1. Turn on your computer, if necessary, to start up Windows 95.
2. Open the WordPad application from the Start menu:
   - Click on the Start button to open the Start menu.
   - Point at the Programs option (and keep the mouse pointer stationary for a few moments) to open this submenu.

- Now, point at the Accessories item at the top, to display another submenu.
- Finally, click on the WordPad item to start this application.

3. Close the WordPad application by clicking on its close button.
4. Open the Start menu and point at the Documents option to open this submenu.
5. If any documents are listed, click on one of them, which should open that document within the application that created it. Close this application by choosing Exit from its File menu.
6. Place the Student Disk in its drive.
7. Start the DOSPROG application on this diskette:
   - Open the Start menu and click on the Run option to open the Run dialog box.
   - Type `a:dosprog` in the Open text box and press the Enter key. The Run dialog box will close and the program will start.
8. Exit the DOSPROG application by following the on-screen instructions. If the application window remains on the screen, close it by pressing Alt+F4.

2.2 Working with Documents

In Windows, the word *document* is used to refer to any collection of data that is created by an application. Thus, a document could be a letter written using a word processor, a picture created by a painting program, or a collection of numbers produced by a spreadsheet program. Nevertheless, there are certain operations that are common to almost all documents: they must be created, saved, opened, printed, and closed. The way in which a document is created *does* vary considerably from application to application. However, all Windows documents are opened, saved, printed, and closed in a uniform way. (This is one of the beauties of using Windows!) In this section, we will use the WordPad application to illustrate these operations.

An Introduction to WordPad

WordPad is one of the small applications (sometimes called *applets* or *accessories*) that is included as part of the Windows 95 package. WordPad is a *word processor* — an application used to create text-based documents such as memos, letters, reports, and so on. In this section, we will be viewing WordPad as an example of a typical Windows 95 application, but in the process you will learn enough to use it to produce very simple documents. WordPad's features will be discussed in more detail in Chapter 7.

To start WordPad, select Programs from the Start menu and Accessories from the resulting submenu. Then, click on the WordPad item on the Accessories submenu. This action starts WordPad and opens a window similar to the one in Figure 4. (The Toolbar, Format Bar, Ruler, and Status Bar may or may not be displayed.)

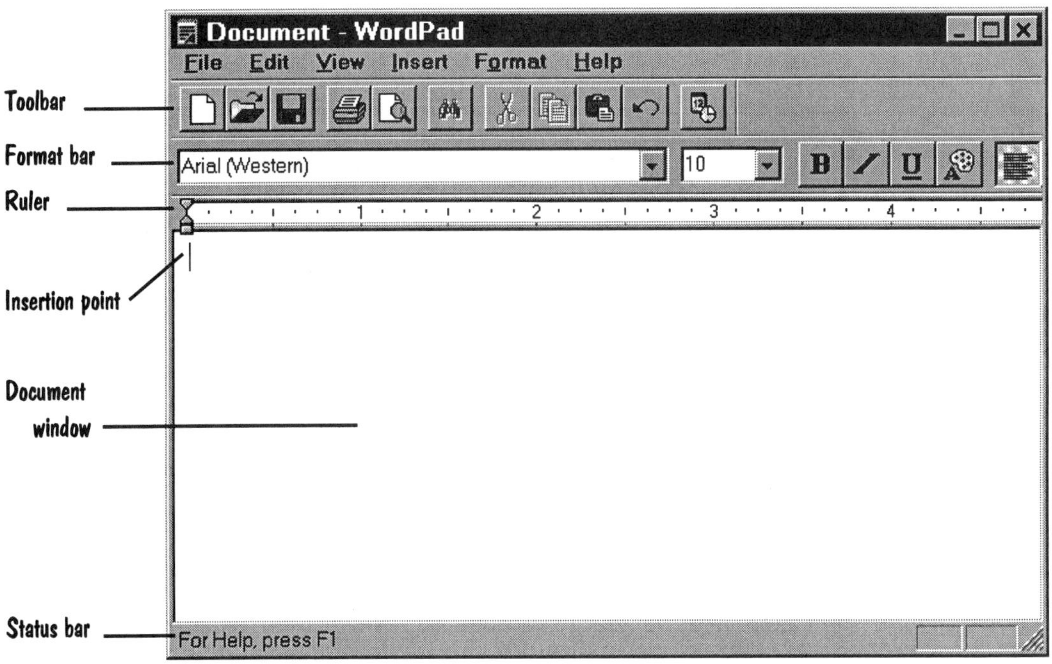

Figure 4 The WordPad Window

Entering text Once you have started WordPad, type whatever you want at the keyboard; the corresponding text will appear in the *document window* and be stored in the computer's internal memory, RAM. The *insertion point*, the blinking vertical bar, indicates where the next character you type will appear on the screen.

When you reach the end of a line, just keep typing; WordPad's *word wrap* feature will automatically continue the text at the beginning of the next line. To start a new line manually, press the Enter key and the insertion point will also move to the beginning of the next line. To skip a line, press Enter again. (When you reach the bottom of the window, moving to the next line will scroll the window down.)

For example, if you type your name, your class, and the date, pressing the Enter key after your name and class, the three entries will appear on separate lines. Moreover, if you press Enter *twice* after the date and then type Homework 1, the screen will look like the one shown in Figure 5.

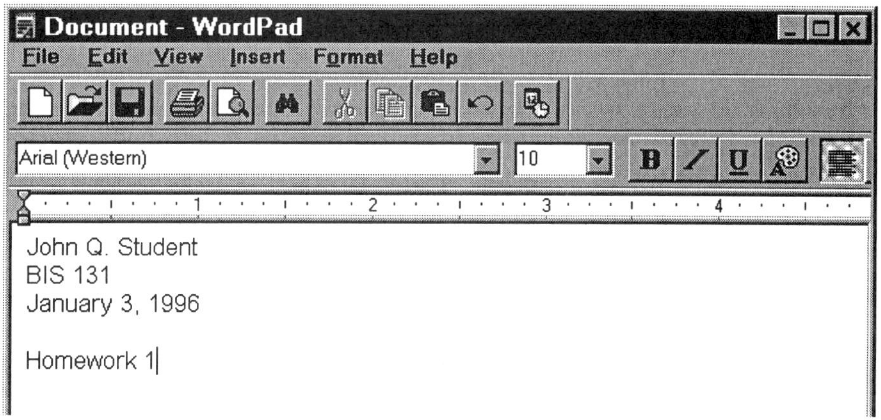

Figure 5 Entering Text into the WordPad Window

Correcting mistakes

It is very easy to correct typing errors. To erase the character just to the *left* of the insertion point, press the Backspace key (which may be labeled ←); to delete the character just to the *right* of the insertion point, press the Delete (Del) key. Holding down either key erases a succession of characters. You can use the mouse or the keyboard to move the insertion point to a mistake anywhere in the document:

- To use the mouse, scroll the document window (Section 1.3), if necessary, until the desired location is visible on the screen. Then, click on this location to move the insertion point there.
- You can also use the Arrow keys (←, →. ↑, ↓) to move the insertion point left, right, up, or down and to scroll the window.

For example, suppose your screen looks like the one in Figure 5, and you realize you've made a mistake: your middle initial is "X", not "Q". To correct the error:

1. Move the insertion point just before the Q by either mouse-clicking on this location or pressing the Up Arrow key four times and the Left Arrow key six times.

2. Press the Delete key to erase the Q.
3. Type an X.

Saving a Document

The short document we just created (Figure 5) is not only displayed on the screen, but also stored in RAM. If we start a new document, close WordPad, or shut down Windows, the document will be removed from both the screen and RAM. Thus, if we want to retrieve this document in the future, we must store a copy of it on a more permanent medium — we must **save** the document to disk! The save operation, with your help, also provides a name for the document. In this section, we will only discuss how to save a document to a floppy disk (diskette), but once you learn to navigate the Windows 95 folder system (Chapter 3), you will see how to save it to a specified location on a hard disk.

The Save command

To save the document that is currently displayed to a floppy disk:

1. Insert the diskette into its drive.
2. Choose Save from the File menu.
   - If this document has been saved before, the current version will be saved under the same name, *replacing the former version on disk.* The File menu will close and you will be returned to the document window.
   - If this document has *not* been saved before, the Save As dialog box (Figure 6) opens and you must carry out all the remaining steps of this procedure.
3. If the *Save in* box does not contain "3½ Floppy" or "5¼ Floppy", then display its drop-down list (like the one at the right) by clicking on the down-triangle. Now select the appropriate floppy drive by clicking on it.

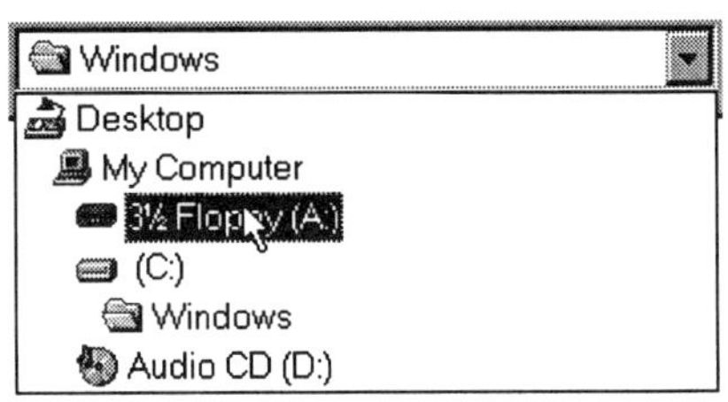

4. Erase the name in the File name text box (click in the box and then use the Delete or Backspace key) and type a name* for the

---

*If you're using WordPad or another application designed to run under Windows 95, you may choose almost any name up to 255 characters in length. If you're using any other application, the name should be no longer than 8 characters and there are restrictions on the characters you can use. (See Section 3.1 for more information.)

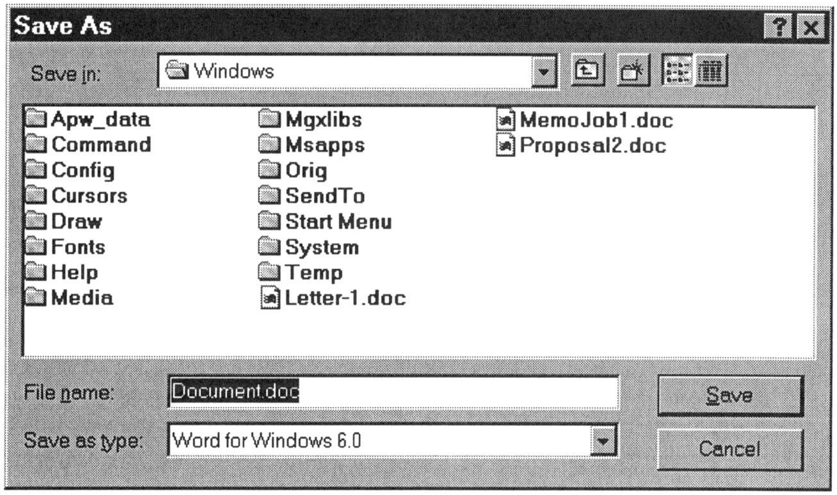

Figure 6 The Save As Dialog Box

document. For example, in saving the document displayed in Figure 5, we might use the name Homework 1.

5. To complete the save operation (and close the dialog box), press the Enter key or click on the Save command button.

NOTE

A simpler way to save a document in WordPad and many other Windows 95 applications is to use its **Toolbar**, which sits just under the menu bar, as shown in Figure 4. (If the Toolbar is not visible on the screen, choose the Toolbar item from the View menu to display it.) The icons on the Toolbar provide quick access to certain menu commands. When you mouse-point at one of the icons, a **tool tip** appears, indicating the icon's function:

To activate a Toolbar function, just click on it. For example, clicking on the floppy disk icon has the same effect as choosing Save from the File menu!

TIP

The Save As command

On occasion, you may make changes to a document, but want to keep both the old and new versions. In this case, you cannot use the Save command; it will automatically erase the old version while saving the new one. Instead, you should choose the Save As item from the File menu, which displays the Save As dialog box even though the current document has been previously saved. Now, just save the new (current) version under a name different from the old one, and both versions are safely stored on disk.

Closing a Document

To **close** a document means to remove it from both the screen and RAM. When you exit a Windows application, any open documents are closed automatically. You may, however, wish to close a document before exiting your application, perhaps to begin working on another document. To accomplish this in WordPad:

The New command

1. Choose New from the File menu or click on the New icon on the Toolbar. The New dialog box will be displayed.

2. Activate the OK command button to accept the default document type. If you have not saved the latest changes to this document, a message similar to the following one will appear:

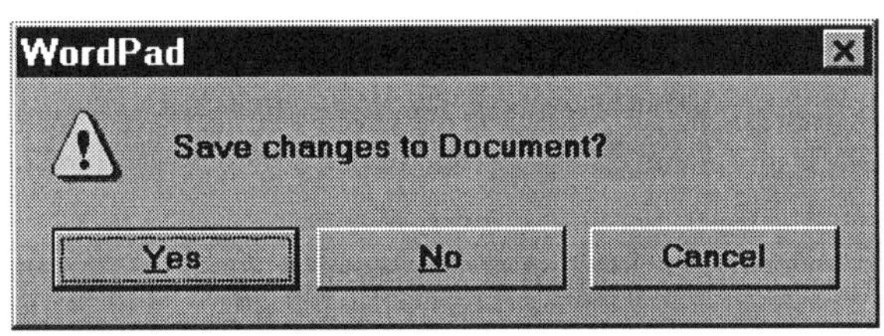

3. Choose the Yes command button and Windows will give you the opportunity to save your changes; choose No and the document will close, but your changes will not be saved to disk. Clicking on the Cancel button (or pressing the Escape key) returns you to the document; it will not close.

NOTE

WordPad only allows one document window to be open at any time. Certain other Windows applications allow multiple open document windows. Choosing New in such a case does not close the current document; it just clears it from the screen. To close a document when multiple open windows are allowed, choose Close from the File menu.

Opening a Document

When you save a document, it is stored on disk under the name you have chosen for it. Saving it does not remove it from the screen or the computer's RAM, so you *can* continue to work on it. However, after the document has been closed, to work on it again you must have Windows copy it from disk into RAM and display it on the screen. In other words, you must **open** the document. Just as there are many ways to open an application, Windows 95 provides many ways to open a document.

The Open command

To open a document within an application that is already running, one normally uses the Open command. We will demonstrate here how to use this command to open a document that is stored on a floppy disk, but once you learn to navigate the Windows 95 folder system, it will be just as easy to open any document. To open a document stored on a diskette:

1. Start (if necessary) the application that created the document.
2. Insert the diskette containing the document into its drive.
3. Choose Open from the File menu or click on the Open icon on the Toolbar. The Open dialog box, like the one in Figure 7, will be displayed. If the floppy drive does not appear in the *Look in* text box, click on the down-triangle and select the floppy drive from the drop-down list.

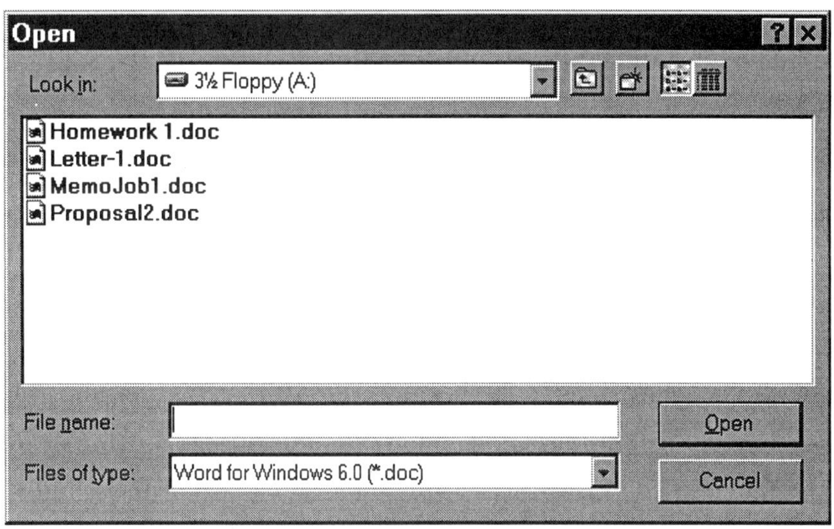

Figure 7 The Open Dialog Box

4. If the name of the document you want to open isn't listed, display the *Files of type* drop-down list and select the entry labeled "All Documents (*.*)". A new, probably longer, list of names will be displayed and the document you are seeking may be one of them.
5. Select the document you want to open from the list. It will become highlighted.
6. Activate the Open command button. The dialog box will close and the specified document will open.

Open programs and documents simultaneously

The Open command works well if the relevant application is already running. If it isn't, you may be able to open a document and the application that created it at the same time using one of the following simple techniques:

- If the document to be opened is represented by an icon (a *shortcut*) on the Desktop, just double-click on this icon. The application associated with the document will start running and the document will open within it. (We will discuss how to create shortcuts in Section 3.4.)

The Documents option

- If the document was created by a Windows 95-based application and was saved recently, then to open it:
    1. Select the Documents option from the Start menu (by clicking on the Start button and pointing at *Documents*). A submenu of the last 15 documents that were saved will be displayed.
    2. Click on the desired document. The application associated with it will start and open the document, as well.

NOTE

These simple techniques may not always work as planned. When you double-click on a document's icon or select an item from the Documents submenu, Windows 95 sometimes starts an application other than the one that created the specified document.

For example, on our Documents submenu, there is a file named "Homework 1.doc". This document was created by WordPad and saved earlier in this section. (The ".doc" *extension* in the name was added automatically by Windows when the document was saved.) But, when we click on Homework 1.doc in the list of documents, Windows interprets the extension as that of a document created by the Microsoft Word word processor, and starts this application instead of WordPad.

Printing a Document

When you **print** a document, you send a copy of it to a printer. Here is the most straightforward way to print a document:

1. Open the document if it is not already on screen.
2. Choose the Print command from the File menu. The Print dialog box will open, as shown in Figure 8.

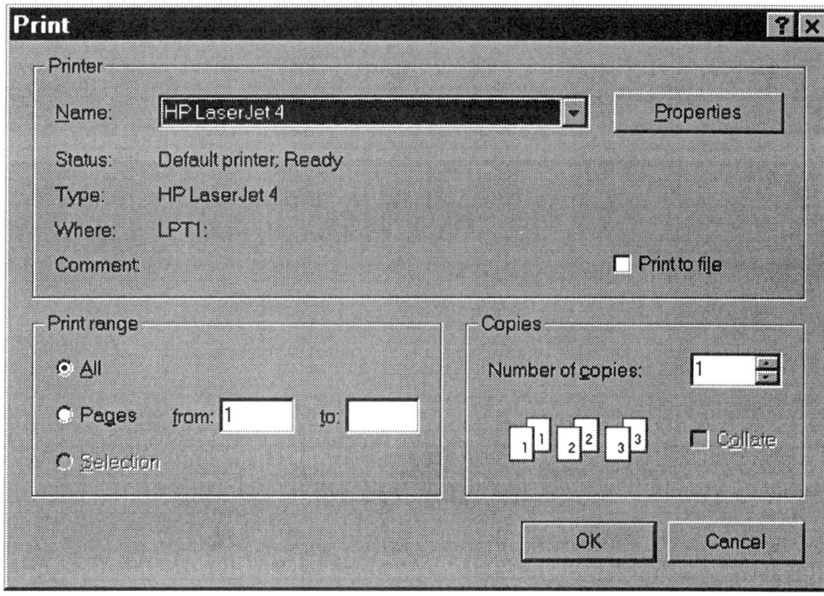

Figure 8 The Print Dialog Box

3. Make the desired selections from this dialog box:
   - If your computer is connected to more than one printer, you can select the one you want to use from the Printer Name drop-down list.
   - If you don't want to print the entire document (indicated by the *All* option button), you can print a range of pages by clicking on the *Pages* option button and then filling in the *from* and *to* text boxes. You can also *select* a portion of your document (as described in Section 2.3) prior to opening the Print dialog box and then print just the selected text by clicking on the Selection option button.
   - If you want to print more than one copy, change the number that appears in the *Number of copies* text box. To collate (sort) the copies, select this check box.
4. Make sure that the selected printer is ready to receive information.

5. Activate the OK command button. The document (or the selected portion of the document) will be printed.

TIP

If you want to print a document using the default information in the Print dialog box (for example, all pages and one copy), you need not open this dialog box. Just click on the Print icon on the Toolbar. The dialog box will not be displayed and the print process will begin immediately.

2.2 TUTORIAL

Try the following exercises on your own.

1. Turn on your computer (if it's not already on) to start up Windows 95.
2. Start the WordPad word processor: Click on the Start button, point at Programs to open this submenu, point at Accessories to open a second submenu, and then click on WordPad on the latter.
3. Insert the Student Disk in its drive and open the `Homework 1` document that is stored on it: Choose the Open command from the File menu, select the floppy drive from the *Look in* drop-down list, click on the name "Homework 1", and activate the Open command button.
4. Edit the Homework 1 document so that it gives *your* name and class and the current date. To do so:
   - Repeatedly press the Delete key until the current name is erased.
   - Type in your name.
   - Click the mouse pointer (an "I-beam" symbol) at the beginning of the next line (or press the Right Arrow key once) to move the insertion point to this location.
   - Repeat these steps to correct the class and date.
5. Save the new document under the new name `My Homework 1`: Choose the Save As (*not* Save) command from the File menu, select the floppy drive from the *Save in* drop-down list, type the new name in the *File name* text box, and activate the Save command button.
6. Print the current document: Either
   - Choose Print from the File menu and activate the OK button.

   or
   - Click on the printer icon on the Toolbar. (If it is currently not visible, choose Toolbar from the View menu to display it.)
7. Clear the current document from the screen: Select New from the

File menu (or click on the "page" icon on the Toolbar) and then activate the OK command button in the dialog box.

8. Exit WordPad: Choose Exit from its File menu or click on the close button on the title bar.

2.3 *Running Several Applications at Once*

As you know, Windows allows you to run several applications at the same time, each of which is instantly available. To see how this can be useful, suppose that you are using the WordPad word processor to write a report and you realize that a picture will illustrate your point better than the proverbial thousand words. To create the picture, you start Paint, the painting program supplied with Windows 95 and which (like WordPad) is found on the Accessories submenu of the Start menu's Programs option.

Starting Paint does not close WordPad, so these two applications are now both running at the same time (see Figure 9). After completing

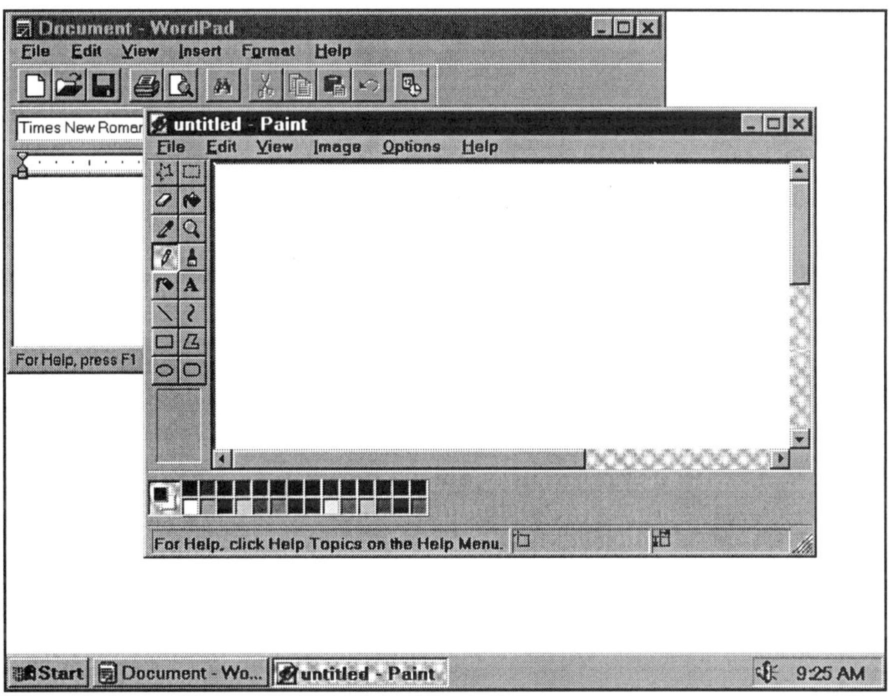

Figure 9 WordPad and Paint Open on the Desktop

your picture, you switch back to WordPad, copy the picture into the word processing document, and continue writing. Before you finish this Windows session, you might use other applications as well, perhaps to make a backup copy of your documents or just to take a break with a computer game.

To make use of the kind of flexibility illustrated in this scenario, you have to be able to quickly and easily switch among several running applications and to transfer information between them. We will discuss these techniques in the remainder of this section.

Switching Among Applications

Each application that is currently running is represented by a button on the Taskbar. The program in which you are currently working is called the **active application.** Its Taskbar button appears to be "brighter" than the others and its title bar is highlighted (see the Paint button and title bar in Figure 9).

Ways to switch applications

To switch from the active application to an inactive one, perform any of the following actions:

- If any portion of the inactive program's window is visible, just click within that window. It becomes the active one and moves to the front.
- Click on the inactive program's Taskbar button. (Remember: If the Taskbar is not visible on the screen, it can be displayed by pressing the Ctrl+Esc keystroke combination.) This application becomes the active one and its window is displayed on the screen.
- Hold down the Alt key and press the Tab key. A window similar to the following one will appear on the screen:

In this window, each icon represents a currently running program. The application corresponding to the "boxed in" icon has its name displayed on the line below. To cycle through your running applications, continue to hold down the Alt key, and repeatedly press the Tab key; the "box" will move from icon to icon. When the name of the desired application appears in the window, release the Alt key. Windows makes this application the active one and displays it on the screen.

Transferring Information between Documents

The process of transferring information — for example, a block of text or a picture — from one document (the *source*) to another (the *target*) usually involves the following steps:

1. In the source document, *select the information* to be transferred. Here's how to select a *block of text* while running any Windows application. Either

   - Position the mouse pointer in front of the first character in the desired block of text and drag the insertion point to the end of the block.

   or

   - Position the insertion point in front of the first character in the desired block of text, hold down the Shift key, move the insertion point to the end of the block (for example, using the Arrow keys), and then release Shift.

   In either case, the selected text will be highlighted. (If you want to *deselect* the text, just click the mouse anywhere else in the document or press an Arrow key.)

2. *Cut* or *copy* the selected information to the Windows **Clipboard**, a temporary storage location in RAM set aside for this purpose. When information is **cut**, it is deleted from the source document and moved to the Clipboard; when information is **copied**, it is also transferred to the Clipboard, but the source document remains unchanged. To perform the cut or copy operation, choose the Cut or Copy command from the source application's Edit menu.

WARNING

The Clipboard can only hold one block of information at a time. Thus, when you cut or copy something to the Clipboard, Windows automatically erases the previous contents (if any). No warning message will be issued!

You can examine the current contents of the Clipboard by opening the **Clipboard Viewer** utility. (Some configurations of Windows 95 contain **Clip*book* Viewer** instead.) To start Clipboard Viewer, choose this item from the Accessories submenu of the Start button. The current Clipboard contents will be displayed in the Clipboard Viewer window. (Clipbook is also started from the Accessories submenu, but the contents of the Clipboard are not displayed automatically; you have to choose the Clipboard command from the Window menu.)

3. Start, or switch to, the target application (unless the source and target are the same) and open the target document, if necessary.
4. In the target document, position the cursor where you want to insert the information.
5. **Paste** (insert) the information on the Clipboard into the target document at the cursor position by choosing the Paste command from the target application's Edit menu.

   Pictorially, the process looks like this:

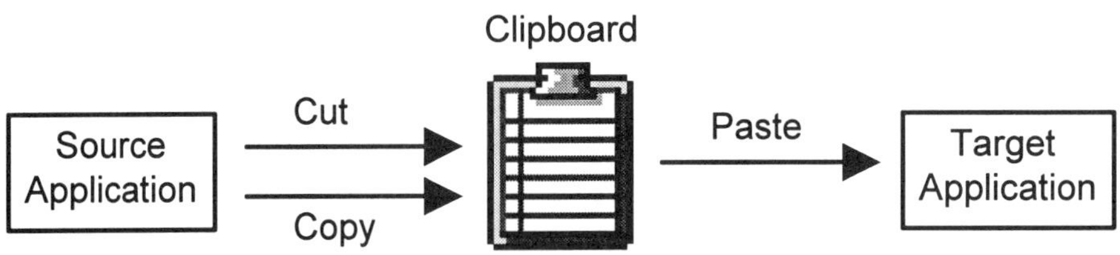

TIP

Here are a couple of other ways to issue the cut/copy or paste commands that work with many Windows applications. After selecting the text to be transferred to the Clipboard, you can *cut or copy* it by either

- Pressing Ctrl+X for cut or Ctrl+C for copy.

or

- Positioning the mouse pointer over the selected text, right-clicking, and choosing Cut or Copy from the resulting menu.

To *paste* text from the Clipboard, position the cursor where you want to insert the text and then, either press Ctrl+V or right-click the mouse and choose Paste from the resulting menu.

NOTE

If you want to copy the *entire current screen* to the Clipboard, press the Print Screen key. To copy the *active window* to the Clipboard, press Alt+Print Screen. In both cases, you can paste these graphics into the target document in the usual way, as described in steps 4 and 5 of the procedure given above.

An Example

Now let's take a look at a specific example of the cut/copy and paste process. We will copy some text from a WordPad document into a Notepad document. (Notepad is a very simple word processor, a *text editor*, supplied with Windows 95.) First we start WordPad and open the Homework 1 document, which can be found on the Student Disk. The resulting WordPad window is shown in Figure 10.

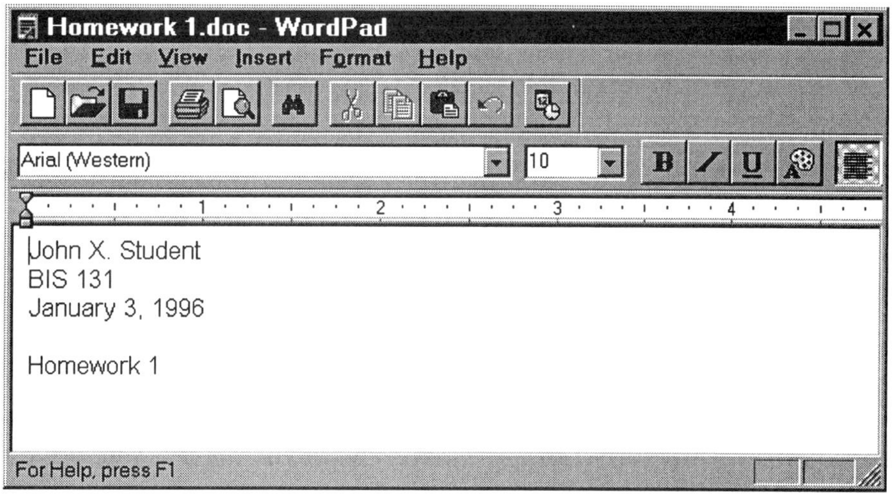

Figure 10 The Text to be Copied

Suppose we want to copy the first three lines (the student's name, his class, and the date). To do so, we must first select the text. Notice that the insertion point in Figure 10 is already positioned at the beginning of this block of text. So, all we need do to select it is

- Hold down the Shift key, tap the Down Arrow key three times, and release Shift.

or

- Position the mouse pointer at the insertion point and drag it down until the first three lines are highlighted.

in either case, the text in the window will look like this:

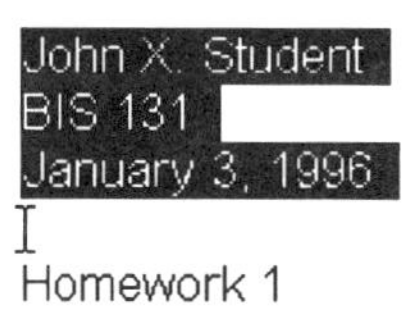

Now, we copy the selected text to the Clipboard by choosing the Copy command from WordPad's Edit menu.

To paste the contents of the Clipboard into Notepad, we start this application by clicking on its name on the Accessories submenu of the

Start menu's Programs option. (Or, if Notepad is already running, we switch to it by clicking on its Taskbar button.) Then, we choose the Paste command from Notepad's Edit menu. The selected text will be transferred to the beginning of the Notepad document, as pictured in Figure 11. (Notice that the pasted text has a somewhat different appearance from the original. This occurs because Notepad only displays text in the font — typeface — shown in the figure.)

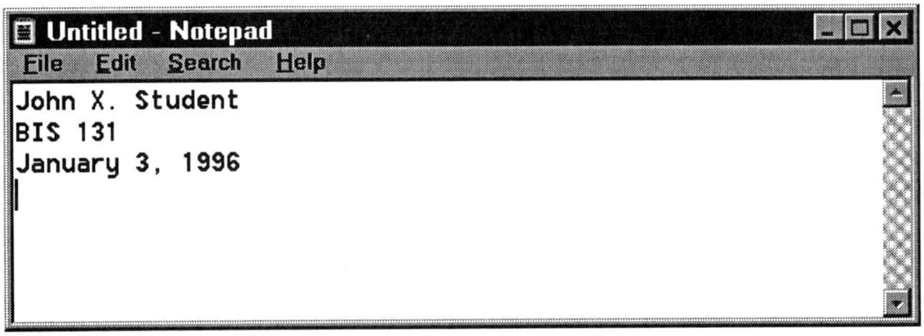

Figure 11 The Original Text Pasted into Notepad

2-3 TUTORIAL

Try the following exercises on your own.

1. Turn on your computer (if it's not already on) to start up Windows 95. Close any open windows.
2. Start the WordPad word processor (from the Accessories submenu of the Start menu's Programs option).
3. Type the text: `This is a test.`
4. Select this block of text by either:
   - Dragging the insertion point to the beginning of the sentence.

   or
   - Holding down the Shift key, tapping the Left Arrow key until the insertion point is at the beginning of the sentence, and releasing Shift.

   In either case, the sentence should now be highlighted.
5. *Cut* the selected text to the Clipboard by choosing Cut from WordPad's Edit menu or by pressing Ctrl+X.
6. Start the Notepad application by clicking on its name on the Accessories submenu of the Start menu's Programs option.

7. *Paste* the text from the Clipboard into Notepad by choosing Paste from its Edit menu or by pressing Ctrl+V.
8. Switch to WordPad by clicking on its Taskbar button. (If the Taskbar isn't visible, press Ctrl+Esc to display it.)
9. Paste the sentence into the WordPad document by right-clicking the mouse and selecting Paste from the resulting menu.
10. Close WordPad and then close Notepad, answering No to the "Save changes?" warning message in both cases.

2.4 Getting On-screen Help

No matter how experienced you become at using Windows and its applications, there will be times when you'll need some help in performing a particular task. At such a time, you might find the answer to your questions in this book, but it may be more convenient to use the Windows 95 **online help** system. This powerful feature provides immediate on-screen information about Windows itself or the Windows application that is currently active on your Desktop.

Accessing Online Help

Types of help available

The Windows 95 Help system provides access to several kinds of online help:

1. Extensive help is available for Windows itself and can be accessed at any time. This kind of help includes general information about using Windows, procedures for performing specific tasks, and troubleshooting advice when things go wrong.
2. Application-specific help is provided by the publisher of each program you use. This help can be accessed while that application is running.
3. *Context-sensitive* help provides help with the task at hand. It is available for Windows 95 itself and for most Windows-based applications.

Starting the Help system

How you enter the Windows Help system depends on the kind of help you need:

- To access help with Windows 95, click on the Start button and then click on the Help option on the Start menu. The dialog box shown in Figure 12 will open.

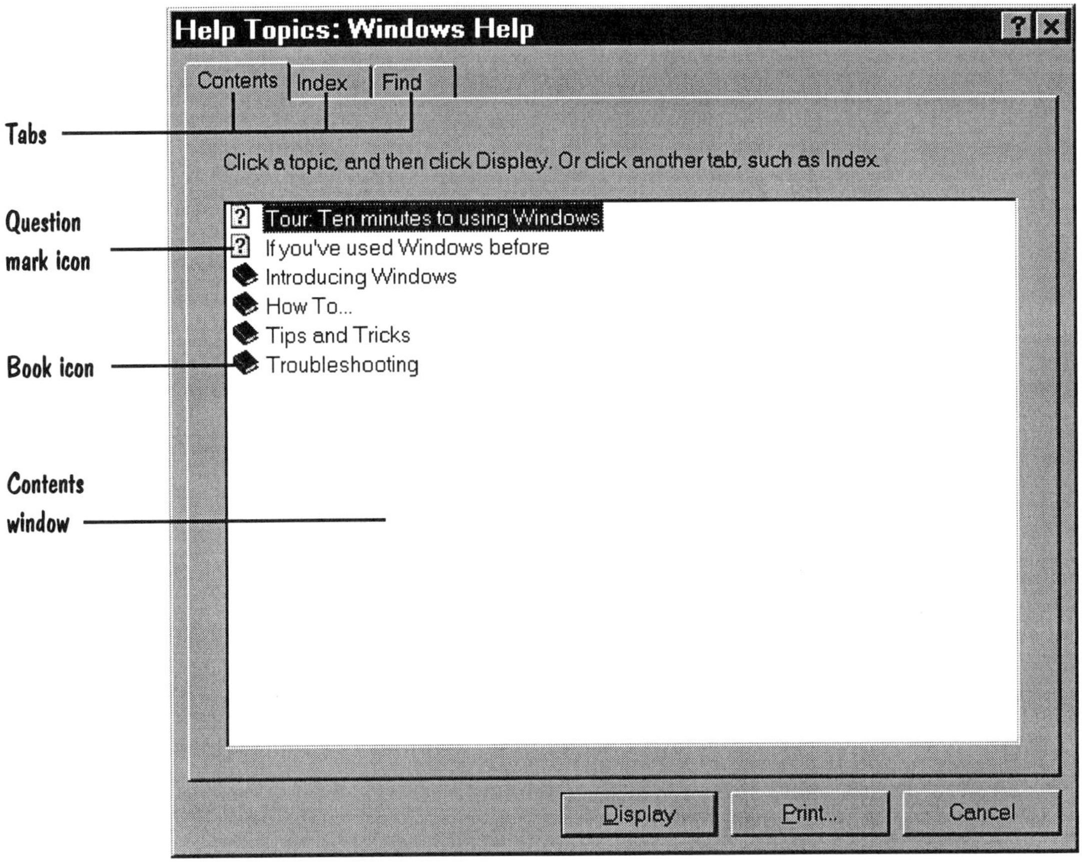

Figure 12 The Windows Help Topics Dialog Box

- Help for the active Windows application can be accessed by displaying that program's Help menu and choosing the option entitled Help Topics or Help Contents. If this application was designed to run under Windows 95, a dialog box similar to the one in Figure 12 will open; if not, a Help dialog box will open, but it may look considerably different from the one in Figure 12.
- There are a couple of ways to access context-sensitive help. We will discuss them at the end of this section.

Locating the Information You Need

Notice that the Help Topics dialog box in Figure 12 has three tabs: Contents, Index, and Find. The corresponding pages of this dialog box provide different ways to locate the information you need.

The Contents Page Clicking on the Contents tab (if this page is not already displayed) provides access to information of a general nature. For example, as you can see in Figure 12, the Windows Help Contents topics include a brief "tour" of Windows, procedures for performing some common tasks, and help with troubleshooting.

If a topic in the Contents window is preceded by a book icon (such as "Introducing Windows" in Figure 12), double-clicking on this topic will "open the book" and display a list of subtopics. For example, Figure 13 shows the Contents window after double-clicking on Introducing Windows and then double-clicking on Welcome.

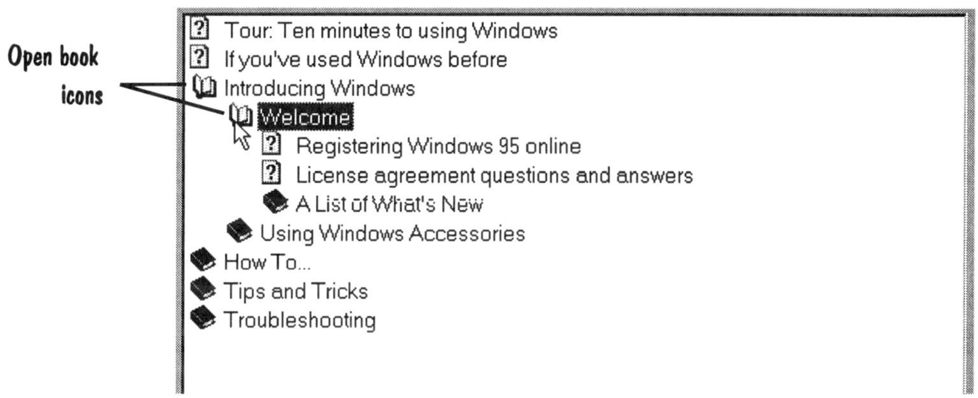

Figure 13 Displaying Subtopics in the Contents Window

If a topic on the Contents list is preceded by a question-mark icon (such as "If you've used Windows before" in Figure 13), double-clicking on that topic will open a Help window supplying information about it. (You can also open the topic's Help window by clicking on the topic, which highlights it, and then activating the Display command button.) We will discuss these Help windows later in this section.

Instead of viewing information about a topic on-screen, you can print this material by clicking on the desired topic and activating the Print command button. The Print dialog box, like the one shown in Figure 8 of Section 2.2, will appear on the screen. To begin printing, activate the OK command button.

The Index Page Clicking on the Index tab of the Help Topics dialog box displays a much more detailed list of items than Contents (see Figure 14).

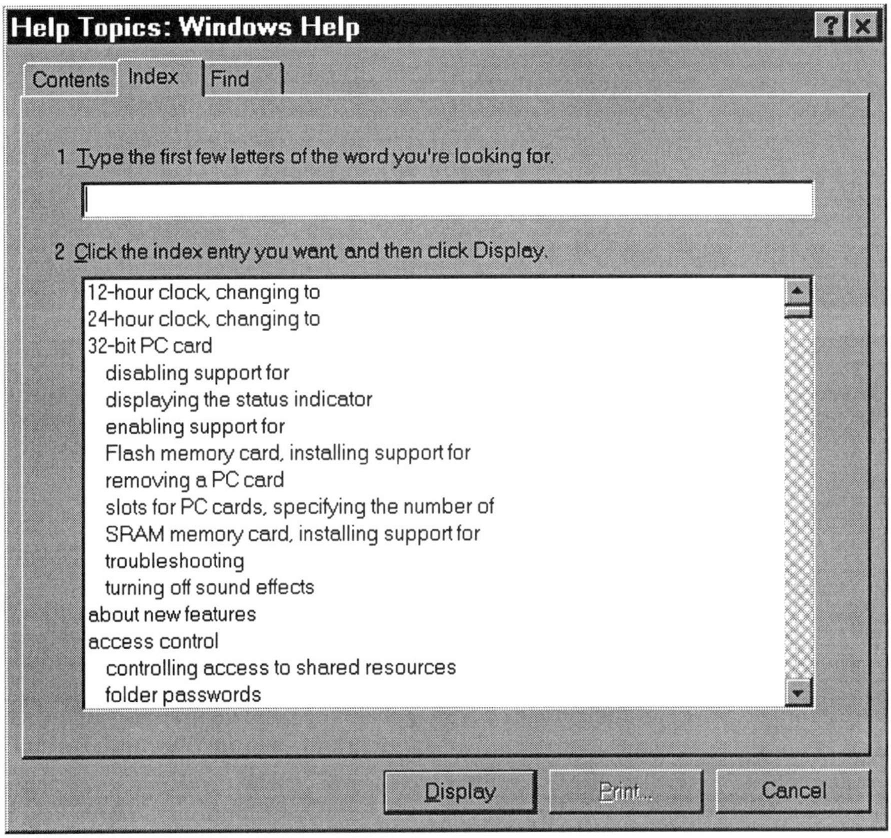

Figure 14 The Index Page of the Help Topics Dialog Box

To use Index to open a Help window for a particular topic:

1. Double-click on the desired item, or click on it and then click on the Display button. (To move quickly through the list of items, type the first few letters of the topic you're seeking in the text box; the first topic beginning with these letters is highlighted.)
2. If there is more than one topic associated with the item you have chosen in step 1, a Topics Found dialog box will open, displaying a list of subtopics. Double-click on the desired topic (or click on it and then on Display).

The Find Page Windows 95 and applications designed for it contain a *Find utility* that enables you to search Help for a specific word or phrase. When the Find utility is first accessed for Windows or an application, it searches the relevant Help files and creates a database of the words it finds. Once the database is set up, you can use Find by clicking on its tab in the Help Topics dialog box (the result is shown in Figure 15) and carrying out these three steps:

1. Type a key word in the text box at the top of the Find page. For example, if you are trying to determine how to use your modem with Windows to place a phone call, you might type *phone.* Now click on the Find Now command button, and a list of words in the Find database that match your key word will appear in the middle window. (If Find Now is dimmed, the list of words will appear as you type.)
2. From the list in the middle window, select the words in which you are interested. To select words, click on the first, then hold down the Ctrl key as you click on the others. For example, if you're interested in phone calls, select *phone*, *Phone*, and *telephone* in

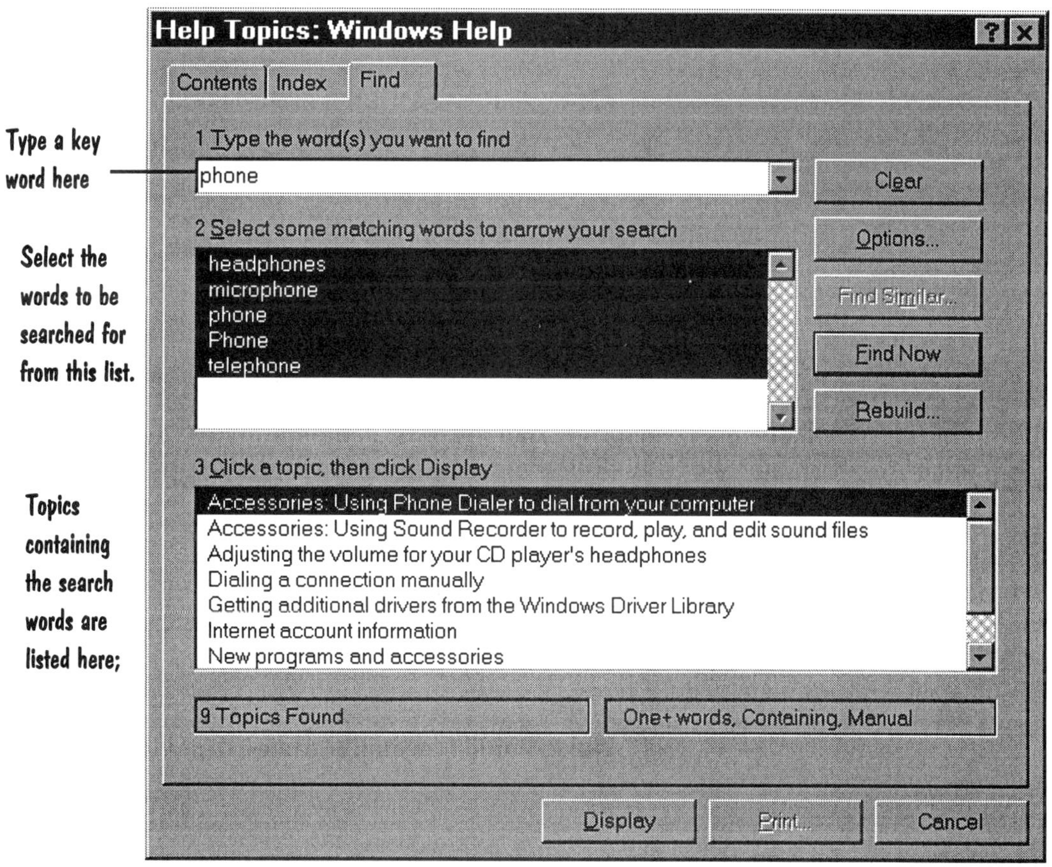

Figure 15 The Find Page of the Help Topics Dialog Box

this manner. The topics that contain these words then appear in the bottom window.

3. Select a topic from the bottom window by clicking on it and then activating the Display button (or just double-clicking on the topic). The Help window for this topic will open.

TIP

You can use any of the three Help Topics pages — Contents, Index, or Find — to display the Help window for a specific topic. The Contents option (like the table of contents for a book) usually contains just a few relatively broad topics. This option is useful if you want to browse through general information. The Index option (like the index of a book) contains a much more detailed list of topics. This is usually the first place you would go for help with a specific task. The Find utility is a little less convenient to use than the Contents or Index, but it will locate information that the other two cannot.

Using a Help Window

Activating the Display command button in the Help Topics dialog box opens a **Help window** displaying information about the selected topic. For example, Figure 16 shows the Help window containing information about using the Windows 95 Phone Dialer accessory.

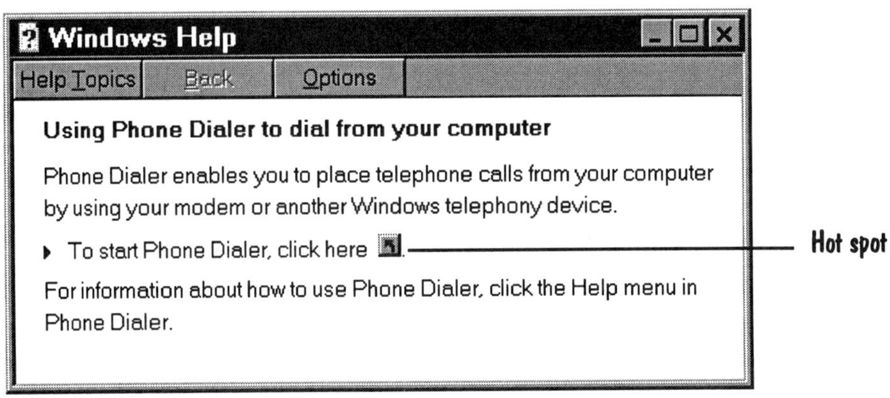

Figure 16 A Typical Help Window

Features of a Help window

Here are some features of the Help window:

- You can return to the Help Topics dialog box by clicking on the

Help Topics command button.

- You can return to a previous Help window by clicking on the Back command button.
- If you click on the Options command button (or right-click in the window) a menu is displayed that allows you to

  Annotate the topic; that is, associate additional information with it. Once the topic is annotated, a paper clip icon appears next to its title; clicking on this icon opens a dialog box that displays your annotation.

  Copy the contents of the Help window to the Clipboard.

  Print the contents of the Help window on a printer.

  Choose from three *font* sizes for the Help window's text.

  Choose to keep the Help window *on top* so that it doesn't disappear from view when you switch to an application.

- Some windows contain **hot spots**, represented by small square buttons. If you mouse point at one of these, the pointer becomes a hand icon. Clicking on a hot spot opens a new window with related information or, if the hot spot contains an arrow, clicking on it opens an application.

Context-Sensitive Help

Context-sensitive help provides information about some aspect of the task at hand. For example, suppose you've opened the Run dialog box (see Section 2.1) but have forgotten the purpose of the Browse command button. You can use Windows 95 online context-sensitive help to explain its function without bringing up the entire Help system. Context-sensitive help, when it's available, can be accessed in several ways:

- If the active window contains a question-mark button on thc title bar, click on this button. The cursor will become an arrow with the question-mark attached, as shown at the right. Now click on the item for which you want help, and a small window will pop up, displaying information about this object. For example, if you click on the question-mark icon in the Run dialog box and then click on the Browse command button, the pop-up window shown at the top of the next page will appear.

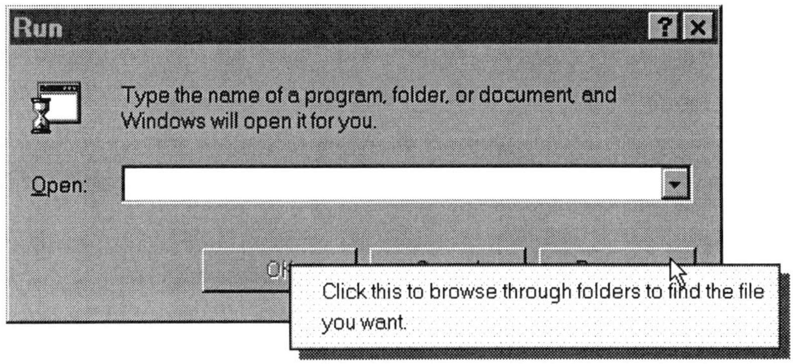

To close the pop up window, click anywhere on the screen.

- With Windows 95 and most applications designed for it, you can right-click on an object to access context-sensitive help. Right-clicking displays a one-item *What's This?* menu:

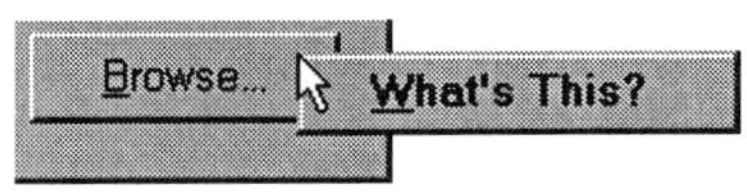

Click on this command to open an explanatory pop-up window.

- When using an older Windows application, you probably won't see a question-mark button and right-clicking on an object probably won't work either. However, the application's dialog boxes may contain a Help command that gives information about using that dialog box. If not, try pressing the Shift+F1 keystroke combination or just the F1 function key to get help with the dialog box.

2-4 TUTORIAL

Try the following exercises on your own.

1. Turn on your computer (if necessary) to start Windows 95.
2. Start Windows 95 Help by clicking on the Start button and then clicking on the Start menu's Help option. The Windows Help Topics dialog box will open.
3. Let's locate information about the Calculator accessory that is supplied with Windows 95:
   - Click on the Index tab to display the Index page.
   - Type the word *calculator* in the text box.
   - In the topics window, double-click on the word *starting* a couple of lines below the "Calculator" entry.

A Help window entitled "Using Calculator to make calculations" will open.

4. Click on the *hot spot* — the small gray button with a curved arrow on it — to start Calculator. Its window will appear on the screen.
5. Now let's get some general information about Calculator:
   - Choose Help Topics from the Help menu. The Calculator Help Topics window will open.
   - Click on the Contents tab (if necessary) to display this page.
   - Display the list of subtopics under *Performing Calculations* by double-clicking on its "book" icon. Then, click on *Performing a simple calculation* and click on the Display command button. A Help window with information about this topic will open.
6. Click on the Options command button to display the Options menu and successively choose each option to see what it does.
7. Click on the Help Topics command button to return to the Calculator Help Topics dialog box.
8. Click on the Find tab to display the Find page. (If the Find Setup Wizard dialog box appears, click on the Next command button, then on the Finish button.)
9. Let's search for information on clearing the calculator's memory:
   - Type *clear* in the text box. One or two words will appear in the middle window and one or two topics in the bottom window.
   - Select (click on) the topic "Working with numbers stored in memory" and activate the Display command button. A Help window with information on this topic will open.
10. Click on the Back command button to return to the first Calculator Help window. Close this window. Calculator will become active.
11. Notice that one of the calculator keys is labeled *Back*. To determine the function of this key:
    - Right-click on it. The one-item *What's This?* menu will be displayed.
    - Click on the *What's This?* command. A window will pop up explaining the function of the Back key. Click anywhere in the Calculator window to close the pop-up window.
12. Close the Calculator application.

Chapter Summary

Starting an Application	From the Start menu	Click on the Start button (or press Ctrl+Esc) to open the Start menu and then use either the Programs, Documents, or Run option.
	From the Desktop	Double-click on the application's icon.
	From Explorer, My Computer, or the Find utility	See Section 3.2, 3.5, or 4.3.
Closing an Application	To close a Windows application, take any of these actions	Click on its close button; *or* select Exit from its File menu; *or* press Alt+F4; *or* right-click on its Taskbar button and choose Close from the resulting submenu.
	To close a DOS application	Use the procedure appropriate for that application and then close its window (if necessary) by clicking on the close button.
Basic WordPad Operations	To start WordPad	Open the Start menu and click on WordPad on the Accessories submenu of the Programs option.
	To enter text	Type it at the keyboard.
	To delete text	Move the insertion point to the desired place using the mouse or Arrow keys, then press the Delete (or Backspace) key to delete the character in front of (or behind) the insertion point.
Operations on Documents	To open a document	Point at the Documents option on the Start menu and click on the desired document; *or* start the application that created the document and choose Open from its File menu.
	To save a document	Choose Save or Save As from the File menu.
	To print a document	Choose Print from the File menu.
	To close a document without closing the application	Choose New from the File menu (or, if the application allows multiple open document windows, choose Close from the File menu).

Running Several Applications at Once	To switch to another running application	Click on any part of its window; *or* click on its Taskbar button; *or* hold down the Alt key while repeatedly pressing Tab until the name of the desired application appears, then release both keys.
	To select a block of text in a document	Position the insertion point at the beginning of the block and then either: mouse-drag it to the end of the block; *or* hold down the Shift key and move the insertion point to the end of the block.
	To cut/copy selected information to the Clipboard	Choose Cut/Copy from the Edit menu; *or* right-click and select Cut/Copy from the resulting menu.
	To paste information from the Clipboard	Position the cursor in the proper place and select Paste from either the Edit menu or the right-click menu.
	To copy the entire screen/active window to the Clipboard	Press Print Screen/Alt+Print Screen.
Using Help	To start Help	Choose Help from the Start menu for help with Windows; *or* choose Help Topics from an application's Help menu.
	To locate information	Use the Contents, Index, or Find pages of the Help Topics dialog box to locate and display the desired topic in a Help window.
	In a Help window	Choose Help Topics to return to the Help Topics dialog box; choose Back to return to the previous Help window; choose Options (or right-click in the window) to annotate, copy, or print the contents of the Help window.
	To obtain context-sensitive help	Click on the question-mark button on the title bar and then click on the desired item; *or* right-click on the desired item and then on the *What's This?* command.

Review Exercises

Section 2.1

1. You can open the Start menu by clicking on the Start button or by pressing the ____________ keystroke combination.
2. Positioning the mouse pointer over the ____________ item on the Start menu displays a menu of programs and groups of programs.
3. To close an application, you can choose ____________ from the File menu.
4. True or false: You can start an application that is represented by an icon on the Desktop by double-clicking on that icon.
5. True or false: To start a program named MyProg that is located on the floppy disk in the A: drive, choose Run from the Start menu, type A:MyProg in the dialog box, and press the Enter key.
6. True or false: All DOS applications are exited in the same way as a Windows application.
7. Which of the following items on the Start menu cannot be used to open an application?
   a. Programs
   b. Documents
   c. Settings
   d. Run
8. Which of the following will not close a Windows application?
   a. Clicking on its close button.
   b. Clicking on its minimize button.
   c. Right-clicking on its Taskbar button and choosing Close from the resulting menu.
   d. Pressing the Alt+F4 keystroke combination.

Section 2.2

9. WordPad is listed on the ____________ submenu, which contains a group of small applications built into Windows 95.
10. To ____________ a document means to copy it from the computer's RAM onto disk.
11. To ____________ a document means to copy it from disk into RAM and simultaneously display it on the screen.
12. The ____________ option on the Start menu displays a list of documents that were recently saved by Windows 95 applications.
13. True or false: Choosing New from WordPad's File menu closes the current document and clears the document window.
14. True or false: If you create but never save a document, you will

not be able to open it once it has been closed.

15. True or false: You can open, close, save, and print a WordPad document by using its Toolbar.
16. True or false: If you click on the print icon on the WordPad Toolbar, one copy of the entire on-screen document will be printed.
17. WordPad's File menu contains two different commands for
    a. Saving a document.
    b. Opening a document.
    c. Printing a document.
    d. Exiting the application.
18. To save a document that is not yet named:
    a. You can use the Open command.
    b. You can use the Save command.
    c. You can use the New command.
    d. None of the above commands can do the job.

Section 2.3

19. To switch to an inactive application, you can click on its button located on the ____________.
20. You can select a block of text by positioning the insertion point at the beginning of the block and holding down the ____________ key as you move the insertion point to the end of the block.
21. When information is cut or copied from a document, it is transferred to the Windows ____________.
22. True or false: Windows 95 allows you to have more than one application window open on the screen.
23. True or false: When information is transferred to the Clipboard, its previous contents (if any) are erased.
24. True or false: Pressing the Print Screen key copies the entire screen to the Clipboard.
25. Which of the following techniques cannot be used to switch to an inactive application?
    a. Click on the inactive application's window.
    b. Click on the inactive application's Taskbar button.
    c. Press the Ctrl+Esc keystroke combination.
    d. Press the Alt+Tab keystroke combination.
26. To transfer selected information to the Clipboard and simultaneously delete it from a document:
    a. Choose Cut from the application's Edit menu.
    b. Choose Copy from the application's Edit menu.

c. Choose Paste from the application's Edit menu.
d. Choose Delete from the application's Edit menu.

Section 2.4

27. To obtain online help for Windows itself, click on the Help item on the ____________ menu.

28. To obtain online help for the active application, click on Help Topics on the ____________ menu.

29. If a topic on the Contents page of the Help Topics dialog box is preceded by a ____________ icon, it contains a list of subtopics.

30. If you would like to change the font size of the text in a Help window, begin by clicking on the ____________ command button.

31. True or false: If a window has a question-mark button on the title bar, you can click on this button to access context-sensitive help.

32. True or false: Clicking on a hot spot in a Help window displays a new window or starts an application.

33. True or false: If you can't locate the topic you're seeking in the Help Topics Index, you should try the Help Topics Find utility.

34. Which of the following is not a tab in a Help Topics dialog box:

    a. Contents
    b. Glossary
    c. Index
    d. Find

35. The Options menu in a Help window allows you to

    a. Return to the Help Topics dialog box.
    b. Return to a previous Help window.
    c. Print the contents of the window.
    d. Change the size of the Help window.

36. To obtain context-sensitive help in a Windows 95 dialog box:

    a. Click on an object in the box.
    b Double-click on an object in the box.
    c. Right-click on an object in the box.
    d. Drag the *What's This?* button onto an object.

Build Your Own Glossary

37. The following words and phrases are important terms that were introduced in this chapter. (They appear within the text in bold-face type.) Use WordPad (see Section 2.2) to enter a definition for each term, preserving alphabetical order, into the Glossary file on the Student Disk.

Active application	Clipboard Viewer	Context-sensitive help
Application	Clipbook Viewer	Copy to Clipboard
Clipboard	Close a document	

Cut to Clipboard
Document
Documents option (on Start menu)
Help window
Hot spot
Online help
Open a document
Paste from Clipboard
Print a document
Programs option (on Start menu)
Run option (on Start menu)
Save a document
Toolbar
Tool tip
WordPad

Lab Exercises

Work each of the following exercises at your computer. Begin by turning the machine on (if necessary) to start Windows 95. Then, close all open windows.

Lab Exercise 1 (Section 2.1)

a. Start MS-DOS Prompt, which is a DOS application that appears on the Programs submenu of the Start menu. If, once MS-DOS Prompt is open, you don't see a title bar, press Alt+Enter to run MS-DOS Prompt in a window.

b. Try to close MS-DOS Prompt by pressing Alt+F4. Does this work? If not, try to close its window by clicking on the close button. If this doesn't work, type Exit and press the Enter key.

c. Insert the Student Disk in its drive and start the Dosprog program on this disk by using the Start menu's Run command. What did you type in the text box to get Dosprog to open?

d. If Dosprog is not running in a window, press Alt+Enter. Try to close this application by clicking on its close button. What does the resulting dialog box tell you? (Click on the No button.)

e. Exit Dosprog by pressing the Enter key. Notice that its window remains on the screen, but the title bar has changed. What word now appears on it?

f. Click on the close button again to close the Dosprog window, and remove the Student Disk from its drive.

g. Repeatedly open and close the Windows Explorer application, which can be found on the Programs submenu of the Start menu. Try the following methods for closing it:

Click on its close button.
Right-click on its Taskbar button and choose Close from the resulting menu, if one appears.
Press Alt+F4.

Right-click the title bar and choose Close from the resulting menu, if one appears.

Which techniques worked?

Lab Exercise 2 (Section 2.2)

a. Start the WordPad word processor.

b. Type your name, your class, and the date on separate lines. Then, skip a line and type: Chapter 2, Lab Exercise 2

c. Insert the Student Disk in its drive.

d. Save your document to this diskette; use the name Ch 2, LabEx 1. What name appears on the title bar?

e. Print the document.

f. Type the current time on the same line as the date.

g. Save the revised document using the Save command on the File menu. Did the name on the title bar change?

h. Print the revised document.

i. Exit WordPad and remove the diskette from its drive.

Lab Exercise 3 (Section 2.2)

a. Start the WordPad word processor and insert the Student Disk in its drive.

b. Open the document named Memo on this diskette.

c. Change the date to the current date, the *From* entry to your name, and the *Re* entry to Windows 95.

d. Move the insertion point to the end of the document (two lines below *Re*) and type a short description of Windows 95.

e. Save the document to the floppy disk under the new name Win95 Memo (using the Save *As* command).

f. Print the revised document.

g. Exit WordPad and remove the diskette from its drive.

Lab Exercise 4 (Section 2.3)

a. Start the WordPad word processor and insert the Student Disk in its drive.

b. Open the document named Preamble on this diskette.

c. Select all the text in this document except for the title.

d. Copy the selected text to the Clipboard.

e. Move the insertion point to the end of the document (deselecting the block of text in the process) and then move the insertion point down two lines by pressing the Enter key twice.

f. Paste the contents of the Clipboard into the document.

g. Repeat steps *e* and *f*. (The Preamble should now appear three times.)

h. Print the current document.

i. Exit WordPad, answering No to the "Save changes" message, and remove the diskette from its drive.

Lab Exercise 5 (Section 2.3)

a. Start the WordPad word processor and then start the Calculator application by clicking on Calculator on the Accessories submenu of the Start menu's Programs option.

b. Open Calculator's View menu. If Standard is not checked, choose this item; otherwise, press the Escape key to close the View menu.

c. Click successively on the 1, 2, and 3 calculator keys (which enters the number 123 into the calculator's "display").

d. Copy the contents of the display to the Clipboard by choosing Copy from the Edit menu. (Notice that in the Calculator application, you need not select the number before copying it.)

e. Switch to WordPad and paste the Clipboard contents into the document.

f. Switch back to Calculator and copy its window to the Clipboard (using *Alt*+Print Screen, not Print Screen).

g. Exit Calculator, which makes WordPad active.

h. Skip a couple of lines and paste the contents of the Clipboard (the captured window) into the WordPad document.

i. Print the document and exit WordPad (saving the document to a floppy disk if you want).

Lab Exercise 6 (Section 2.4)

a. Start Windows 95 Help by choosing Help from the Start menu (which opens the Windows Help Topics dialog box).

b. If the Contents page is not displayed, click on its tab.

c. Right-click within the Contents topics window and click on the *What's This?* command. What is the subject of this context-sensitive help? Close the pop-up window.

d. Click on the question-mark button on the title bar; then on the

Contents tab. What message is displayed? Close the pop-up window.

e. Display the topic entitled "If you've used Windows before". What is the title of the resulting Help window?

f. In the Help window, click on the "How to start programs" hot spot. Which technique for starting programs is described?

g. Open the Options menu for this Help window and point at the Font item. What choices do you have for font size?

h. Close the Help window to exit Help.

Lab Exercise 7 (Section 2.4)

a. Start WordPad and choose Help Topics from the Help menu to open the WordPad Help Topics dialog box.

b. Let's try to determine the function of the WordPad Ruler. Click on the Index tab (if this page is currently not displayed).

c. Type *ruler* in the text box. What is the name of the topic that is highlighted?

d. Activate the Display command button to open the Help window corresponding to the highlighted topic. According to the "Tip", what is the apparent function of the Ruler?

e. Return to the Help Topics dialog box and click on the Find tab. (If the Find Setup Wizard dialog box appears, click on Next, then on Finish.)

f. Type *ruler* in the text box. How many topics are listed in the bottom window?

g. Display the topic entitled "Setting tabs". On which WordPad menu is the Tabs command located?

h. Choose the Tabs command from the appropriate WordPad menu. The Tabs dialog box will open. Now, using either the *Setting tabs* Help window or context-sensitive help in the Tabs dialog box, answer the following questions:

- What is the difference between the Clear and Clear All commands?
- What is the purpose of the Set command button in the Tabs dialog box?
- How does one delete a tab using the Ruler?

i. Close the Help window and exit WordPad.

If You Want to Learn More ...

The notes presented here allow you to delve more deeply into some of the topics covered in this chapter.

Redisplaying the Taskbar

As you know, if the Taskbar is hidden from view, you can temporarily redisplay it by pressing Ctrl+Esc. To permanently redisplay the Taskbar:

1. Choose the Taskbar item from the Settings submenu of the Start menu. The Taskbar Properties dialog box will be displayed.
2. Select the *Always on top* check box and deselect the *Auto hide* check box.
3. Choose the OK command button.

(To hide the Taskbar, select the *Auto hide* option in the Taskbar Properties dialog box.)

Accessing the Taskbar from the keyboard

If you are a confirmed mouse-hater, here's a way (albeit an awkward one) to access the Taskbar buttons using the keyboard:

1. Press Ctrl+Esc to open the Start menu (and display the Taskbar, if it's hidden).
2. Press the Esc key to close the Start menu and place the "focus" on the Start button.
3. Press the Tab key to move the focus to the Taskbar.

You can now cycle through the Taskbar buttons by repeatedly pressing the Arrow keys. To activate the selected button, press the Enter key.

Dealing with some WordPad "problems"

In using WordPad, you may encounter some difficulties simply because we did not discuss it in very much detail in Section 2.2. Here's how to handle a few common problems:

- If word wrap is not in effect (the insertion point doesn't move to a new line unless you press the Enter key), choose the Options item from the View menu, select the *Wrap to ruler* option button in the resulting dialog box, and choose the OK command button.
- If, when you print a document, the page margins are not to your liking, choose the Page Setup command from the File menu, enter the desired margins in the resulting dialog box, and choose the OK command button.

- If, when you print a document, the text runs parallel to the long side of the page, choose the Page Setup command from the File menu, select the *Portrait* option button in the resulting dialog box, and choose the OK command button.

For a complete discussion of WordPad, see Chapter 7.

Browsing in online help

If you need help with a specific topic, as you know, the Contents page of the Help Topics dialog box is not very useful. Nevertheless, when you have some time free, you might enjoy browsing through some of the topics found there. Although many of these discussions will be difficult to follow until you read further in this textbook, here are a couple of topics that you might find interesting now:

- *Tour: Ten minutes to using Windows* doesn't supply much information, but it will reinforce some of the material you've learned in the first two chapters of this text. (You may have to insert the Windows CD-ROM in its drive to run the Tour.)
- *If you've used Windows before* compares Windows 95 to Windows 3.1. This topic may be of interest if you are familiar with Windows 3.1. If this is the case, you should also check out *A List of What's New*, which can be found under the *Welcome* subtopic of the *Introducing Windows* topic.

Where to go from here

Here's where to find more information about some of the topics discussed in this chapter.

- Starting applications — Sections 3.2 (using Explorer) and 4.3 (using the Find utility)
- Adding and removing items from the Programs option submenus — Section 4.2
- Associating document types with applications — Section 4.4
- Using WordPad — Chapter 7
- Changing printer settings — Section 6.1
- Transferring information between applications — Sections 7.4, 8.3, and 12.5

CHAPTER 3

Managing Files, Folders, and Disks

In Chapter 2 we discussed, in a general way, how to use applications (programs) and documents. Both applications and documents are stored in files, which in turn are located in folders on a disk. This chapter describes how to use Windows Explorer and My Computer to perform basic operations on files, folders, and disks. To be more specific, you will learn:

1. How the Windows 95 file system is organized.
2. The rules for creating valid file and folder names.
3. How to select files and folders in Explorer.
4. How to use Explorer to
   - Move or copy files and folders.
   - Create, rename, and delete files and folders.
   - Create shortcuts.
5. How to use My Computer to locate and manipulate files and folders.
6. How to use Explorer or My Computer to format and copy floppy disks.

3.1 The Windows 95 File System

Computer disks are capable of storing a lot of information — both data and programs. In order to facilitate access to this information, Windows 95, with your help, organizes it into files and folders. In this section, we will provide some useful information about these concepts.

What are Files and Folders?

Files A **file** is a collection of information that has been generated by the computer and stored (saved) on disk. A file may contain an application, in which case it's called a *program file*, or data created by an application, which is a *data file*. For example, recall that when you save a document for the first time in the WordPad word processor (itself a collection of files stored on your hard disk), you choose a name for that document. When you issue the Save (or Save As) command, Windows creates a file by copying the document from internal memory (RAM) to disk and assigning the name you chose to it.

Folders Since a hard disk can contain thousands of files, it is necessary to organize them into **folders** (or **directories***). Each folder is a collection of related files that you (or a program) have grouped together and given a name. For example, you might place all the letters you've written in one folder called Letters and all your reports in another folder (uncreatively) called Reports.

Sometimes it makes sense to place a related group of folders within a larger folder. In this case, the bigger folder is called the **parent folder** and each of the folders within it is a **subfolder** (or *child folder*) of the parent. For example, your disk might have several folders that contain word processing data files: Letters, Reports, and so on. To better organize the disk, you could place all of these in a (parent) folder called, say, Word Processing. (A parent folder can contain files as well as subfolders. For example, on a hard disk, the Word Processing folder might hold the *program* files for your word processing application.)

The folders on a disk form a tree-like structure with subfolders branching out from their parents, which in turn may be subfolders themselves. On each disk there is one folder, called the **root folder**, that contains all the others. Figure 1 shows a *folder tree* — a graphical

*The Windows 95 documentation uses the term *folder* instead of *directory*. If you are familiar with DOS or Windows 3.1, just think *directory* whenever you see *folder*. Don't worry; you'll soon get used to the new terminology.

way of representing the folder structure of a disk. It may take a little imagination to see this structure as a tree; in particular, notice that the root is at the top!

In Figure 1, the root folder is designated by "3½ Floppy (A:)" and its three subfolders (Drawing Files, Word Processing, and Zingers) are shown connected to it by dotted lines. Notice that the Drawing Files and Word Processing folders have subfolders of their own (each connected to its parent by dotted lines), and one of these subfolders (Letters) also has subfolders. Each folder, including the root, may contain files as well.

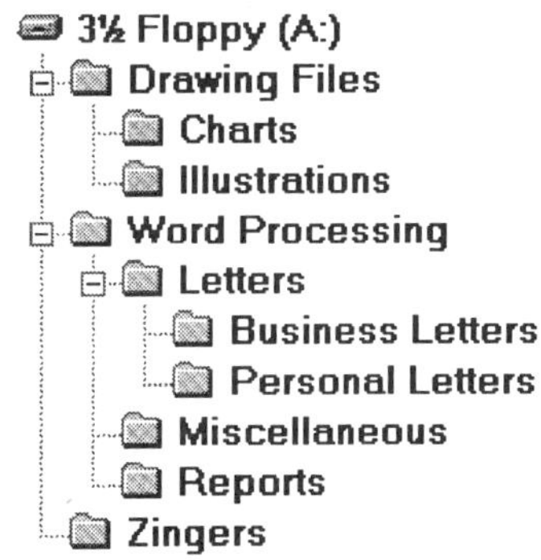

Figure 1 A Folder Tree

Naming Files and Folders

Disk drive designations

Every drive, folder, and file used by your computer must have a name. Drive designations (for hard and floppy disk drives, CD-ROM drives, network drives, and the like) are assigned by the operating system. They consist of a single letter followed by a colon; for example, A: and B: are reserved for the computer's floppy drives and its primary hard disk is designated C:, even if there is only one floppy drive. Other drives (D:, E:, etc.) may be present as well.

DOS file names

Naming files can get complicated. There are different rules for what constitutes a valid file name depending on whether the program that created the file was designed to run under DOS or Windows 3.1 on the one hand, or under Windows 95 on the other. If the program that created the file is a DOS or Windows 3.1 application, the resulting name is known as a **DOS file name**, and must follow these rules:

- The name may consist of two parts: A required *filename* containing from one to eight characters, possibly followed by an *extension* consisting of up to three characters. If the extension is present, it must be separated from the filename by a period (.). For example, for the file Joe.Ltr, Joe is the filename and Ltr is the extension.
- The filename and extension may contain any characters *except*

period (.)	comma (,)	colon (:)
semicolon (;)	quotation mark (")	brackets ([ ])
slash (/)	backslash (\)	equals sign (=)
vertical bar (|)	question mark (?)	asterisk (*)

Moreover, *no spaces* are permitted in a DOS file name.

- Lowercase letters are not distinguished from uppercase letters. So, the names MyFile, myfile, and MYFILE are considered identical.

For example, the following names are all valid:

Ch1 Ch1.Txt Ch-1.{ history.rpt X 1(#$%).n1

However, the following names are *invalid* DOS file names:

inventory.dat	(Filename is too long.)
Top Gun	(Spaces are not allowed.)
File:1	(The colon is an illegal character.)

Windows 95 file and folder names

Windows 95 frees us from many of the restrictions imposed by DOS file names. Most importantly, in naming a file created by a Windows 95-based application or *any* Windows 95 folder, you may use up to 255 characters, including spaces. (For this reason, these names are called **long file names.**) Moreover, all punctuation marks *except* for the following ones are permitted in long file names:

colon (:)	vertical bar (|)	quotation mark (")
slash (/)	backslash (\)	question mark (?)
asterisk (*)		

As a result, the following names are valid for a folder or for a file created by an application designed to run under Windows 95:

J. Gomez - Letter 1	(but *not* J. Gomez: Letter 1)
BIS HW #7 1-5-96	(but *not* BIS HW #7 1/5/96)
Annual Report - 1995	(but *not* "Annual Report - 1995")

Long file names may have extensions, but they are usually assigned by Windows, not the user.

NOTE

Long file names can only be created and used by Windows 95 itself and Windows 95-based applications. So, when you are running a DOS or Windows 3.1 program, you have to follow the stricter rules for DOS file names.

This situation raises an interesting question: What happens if you try to open a document with a long file name in an application that doesn't support long file names? In this case, Windows 95 supplies a "DOS alias", a related DOS file name, for use in this application. To form the alias, Windows truncates the original file name to six characters and inserts two special symbols followed by the file's extension. In addition, any blank spaces are deleted and illegal characters are replaced by underscores. For example, suppose you create documents named `Assignment #5`, `Assignment #6`, and `Asg [7]` in WordPad and then open each of these documents in a Windows 3.1-based word processor. Here, the document file names become assign~1.doc, assign~2.doc, and asg_7_~1.doc.

Path Names

When you start an application, Windows automatically specifies a certain folder as the current (or default) folder for that application. (To see which folder is the current one, just open the Save As or Open dialog box; it will be displayed in the *Save in* or *Look in* text box.) If you want to refer to any file in the current folder, you need only give its file name. For example, if you save a file, naming it Sam.doc, it is automatically placed in the current folder.

To refer to a file that is not in the current folder, you must change folders or give the file's **path name**, a kind of road map that tells Windows how to find the file. The path name for a file begins with the drive designation (for example, C:), followed by the names of the root folder (which is \, a backslash) and all subfolders (from largest to smallest) that contain the file, and ends with the name of the file itself. All subfolder names must be followed by backslashes. Thus, the complete path name for a file called Sam.doc in the Personal Letters folder in the folder tree shown in Figure 1 is:

A:\Word Processing\Letters\Personal Letters\Sam.doc

3.2 An Introduction to Windows Explorer

When you use Windows on a regular basis, you will frequently find it convenient to delete, move, copy, or rename files and folders. Windows' primary tool for performing these kinds of operations is the **Explorer** application. In this section, we will provide some basic information about Explorer; its capabilities will be discussed in more detail in Sections 3.3 and 3.4.

The Explorer Window

To start Explorer, click on the Start button (or press Ctrl+Esc) to open the Start menu. Then, point at the Programs option and click on Windows Explorer on the resulting submenu. When you do, a window similar to the one in Figure 2 will open.

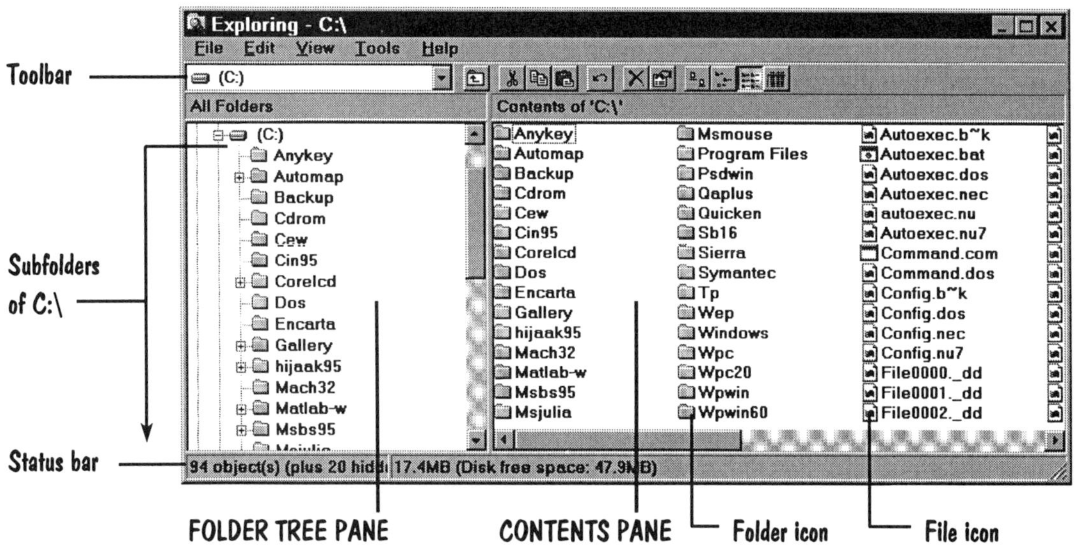

Figure 2 The Explorer Window

The Explorer window has a title bar, menu bar, and Toolbar at the top and a status bar at the bottom. The Toolbar and status bar can be hidden. To hide either bar (or display it if it's currently hidden), choose the item bearing its name from the View menu. Most of the Explorer window is divided into two large subwindows or *panes*: the *folder tree* pane on the left and the *contents* pane on the right.

The Folder Tree Pane

The **folder tree pane** lists all folders on all drives connected to your computer and also provides access to other objects on the Desktop, such as My Computer and the Recycle Bin. In fact, if you scroll up the folder tree pane, you'll see that all objects listed in this window, including drives, are considered subfolders of the Desktop folder!

When you start Explorer, the drive containing the Windows folder is displayed at the top of the folder tree pane and all immediate (*child*) subfolders are listed in alphabetical order beneath it. The files and folders contained within the current (or *open*) folder are shown in the contents pane. For example, in Figure 2, the contents pane displays the subfolders and some of the files in the C:\ folder. If you want to view the contents of another object in the folder tree pane, just scroll the folder tree up or down until that object is visible and click on it. Its name will become highlighted and, if it is represented by a folder icon, that icon will "open", as shown at the right.

NOTE

Opening a folder displays an up-to-the-moment list of its contents, even if they have changed in the current session. You should be aware, however, that there are situations in which the contents pane does not accurately reflect the contents of the open folder. The most common of these occurs if you change the disk in a floppy drive when its folder is open; in this case, Windows will continue to display the contents of the previous disk. To view the contents of the new disk, either click again on the floppy drive icon in the folder tree pane or choose the Refresh command from the View menu.

Expanding the folder tree

To see subfolders that are hidden from view (even after scrolling), you have to *expand* a branch of the folder tree. When a folder contains hidden subfolders, its name and icon are preceded by a plus (+) symbol (see, for example, the Automap folder in Figure 2). To view these subfolders, expanding this branch of the folder tree, either

- Click on the plus symbol.

or

- Double-click on the folder name or icon.

In either case, the subfolders will be displayed and the plus symbol will become a minus (-) symbol. (If you double-click on the folder's name, that folder also becomes the current folder and its contents are displayed in the contents pane.) Clicking on the minus symbol *collapses* the branch, hiding the subfolders.

For example, if we click on the plus symbol next to the Automap folder icon, a list of subfolders will be displayed, as shown at the right. Notice that there is a plus symbol attached to the Userdata subfolder, indicating that this folder has subfolders of its own. Now, if we click on the minus sign preceding Automap, this branch collapses, returning the folder tree to its original look, as in Figure 2.

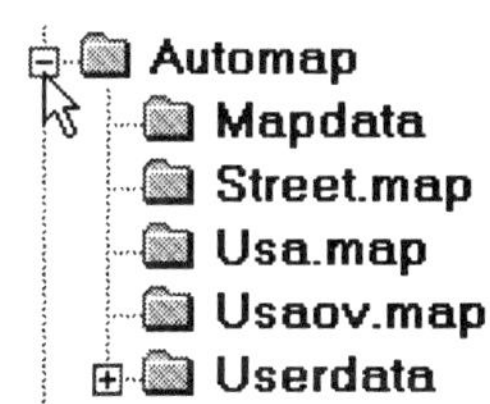

The Contents Pane

As you know, the **contents pane** of the Explorer window lists all folders and files contained in the current folder. The word *folder* in this context refers to any folder, drive, or other object (such as My

Computer) that can be accessed through Explorer.

Just as in the folder tree pane, clicking on an object in the contents pane selects that object, highlighting its name and icon. (We will have more to say about selecting objects in Section 3.3.) If you *double*-click on an object, what happens next depends on the nature of the object:

Double-clicking an object in the contents pane

- Double-clicking on a folder icon opens that folder, displaying its contents in the contents pane. (In other words, double-clicking on a folder icon in the contents pane has the same effect as clicking on the corresponding icon in the folder tree pane.)
- Double-clicking on a program file icon opens the corresponding application. This technique provides an effective way to start any application on your hard or floppy disks.
- Double-clicking on a document file that is associated with an application starts that application and opens the given document within it. (We will discuss the process of associating documents with a particular application in Section 4.4.)
- Double-clicking on any other kind of file icon displays the Open With dialog box. This dialog box allows you to select an application to be used with the given file. Choosing the OK command button starts that application and opens the file within it.

TIP

The Tools menu

On a well-used hard disk, there may be hundreds of folders, with a correspondingly intricate folder tree. It's not surprising that finding a particular folder may be difficult. To help you in this regard, Explorer provides easy access to the Windows Find utility. You can open this utility by pointing at the Find item on the Tools menu and then choosing Files and Folders from the submenu. (We will discuss Find in Section 4.3.)

The other Tools menu item, Go To, is less helpful but easier to use. If you know the path name of the desired folder, choose the Go To command; the following dialog box will be displayed:

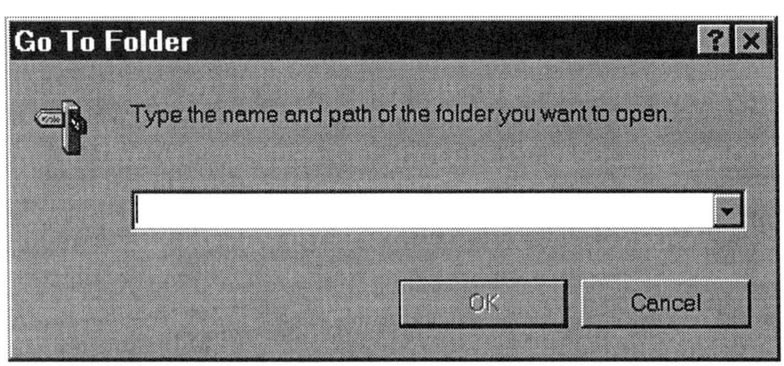

As the instructions suggest, type the path name of the desired folder in the text box; then choose the OK command button. The dialog box will close, returning you to Explorer. The selected folder will be highlighted in the folder tree pane and its contents will be displayed in the contents pane.

Contents Pane View Options

Explorer displays the contents pane in one of four ways, depending on your preference. These options are described below; to select one of them, choose the corresponding item from the View menu. The selected view option will remain in effect, even in future Windows sessions, until you change it again.

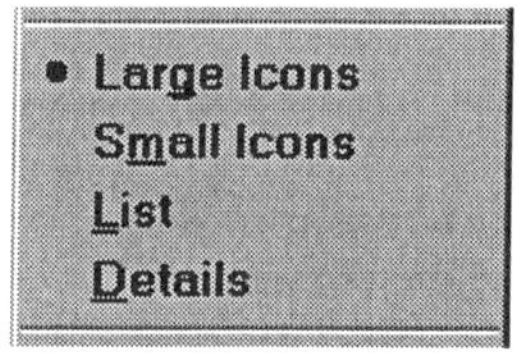

The Large Icons and Small Icons View Options Here, each object in the contents pane is represented by an icon (either large or small) labeled with the name of the object (Figures 3 and 4). You can move these icons one by one to a prominent position in the window (say, the upper left corner) by dragging them with the mouse. To be more specific:

Moving icons

1. Select the icon that you want to move by clicking on it.
2. Position the mouse pointer over this icon, hold down the left mouse button, and move the pointer to the icon's new location. An outline of the icon (and its label) will move with the pointer, as shown at the right.

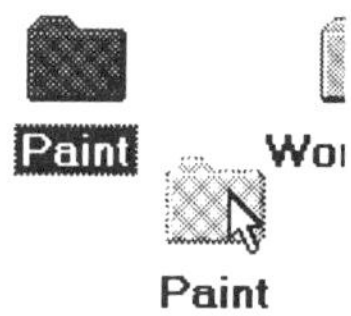

3. When the icon is positioned where you want it, release the mouse button.

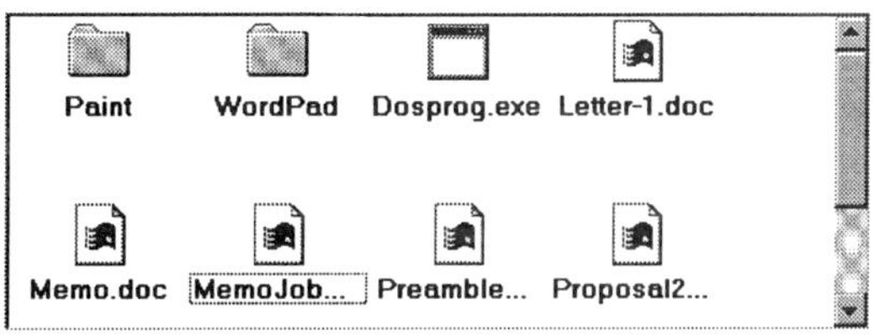

Figure 3 Contents Pane — Large Icons

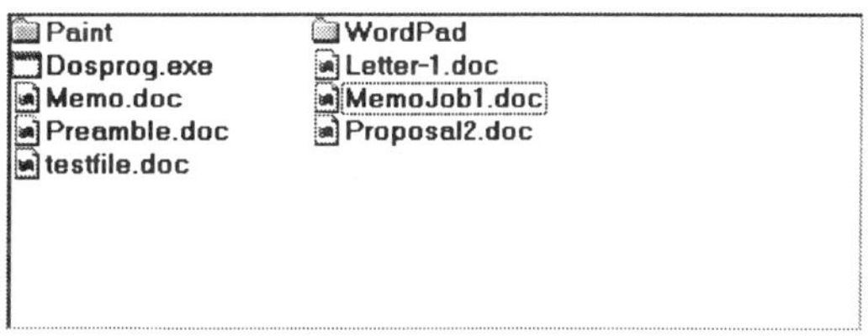

Figure 4 Contents Pane — Small Icons

Lining up the icons

To display the new arrangement of icons in neatly ordered rows and columns (as illustrated in Figures 3 and 4), choose Line Up Icons from the View menu. Or, to have Windows automatically line up the icons whenever they are moved, turn on the Auto Arrange option from the Arrange Icons submenu of the View menu. (Turning *off* this option before rearranging icons may make it easier to carry out the process.)

The List and Details View Options Choosing the List option (Figure 5) from the View menu displays the icons and names in the contents pane in a similar way to that of the Small Icons option. (With the List option, the icons are displayed in columns instead of rows and cannot be individually moved about.) The Details option (Figure 6) lists the objects in the contents pane, one per line, together with the information specified on the buttons at the top if this pane:

- *Size* refers to the size of a file in kilobytes (KB) or megabytes (MB).
- *Type* refers to the kind of object; for a file, Windows determines its type (for example, *application*) from the file name extension.
- *Modified* provides the most recent date and time that a file was saved; for folders, it is the time it was created.

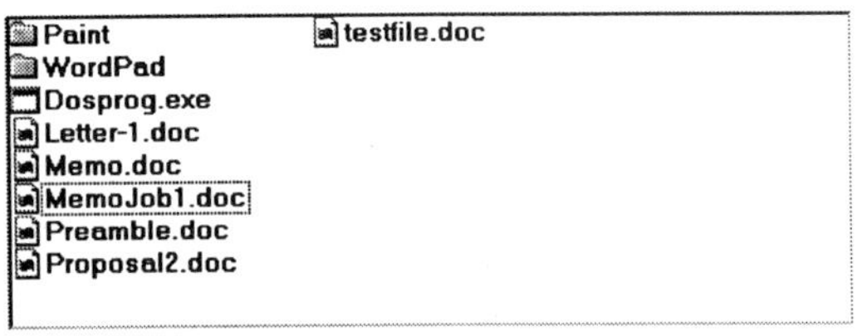

Figure 5 Contents Pane — List Option

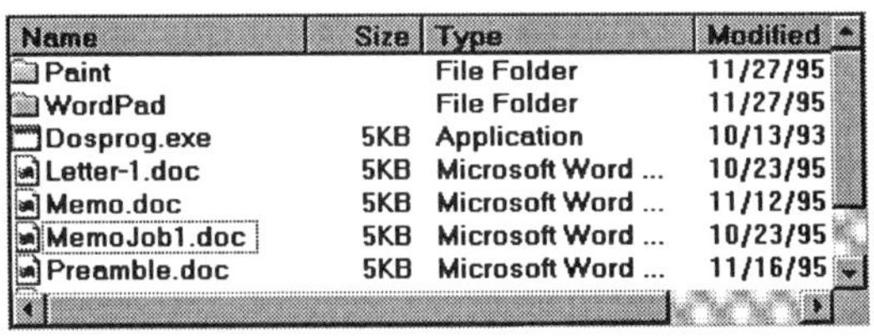

Figure 6 Contents Pane — Details

Ordering files in the Details view

By default, the Details view displays the files in the contents pane in the alphabetical order of their names. (Folders in the contents pane are always displayed at the top of the list.) You can list files in other orders, as well. To do so, click on the appropriate button at the top of the contents pane; that is:

- Click on the Size button to list files in order of increasing size; click again on this button to list them in decreasing size order.
- Click on the Type button to list files in alphabetical order by type; click again on this button to list them in reverse alphabetical order by type.
- Click on the Modified button to list files in order of their last modification date; most recently modified files are listed first.

Clicking again on this button lists recently modified files last.

- Click on the Name button to restore alphabetical order by name; clicking again on this button lists files in reverse alphabetical order.

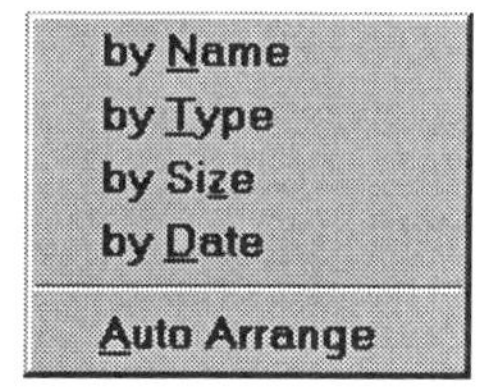

The icons in *all* the view options (Large Icons, Small Icons, List, and Details) can be ordered by either name, file size, type, or modification date. Just choose the appropriate item from the Arrange Icons submenu of the View menu. However, "reverse orders" are not possible using the Arrange Icons submenu. For example, selecting *by Size* from this menu lists the icons in order of increasing file size; icons cannot be listed in order of *decreasing* size using the Arrange Icons menu.

TIP

You can use Explorer's Toolbar to quickly select a different contents pane view option. Just click on the appropriate button, as indicated below. (The "List" button is shown selected.)

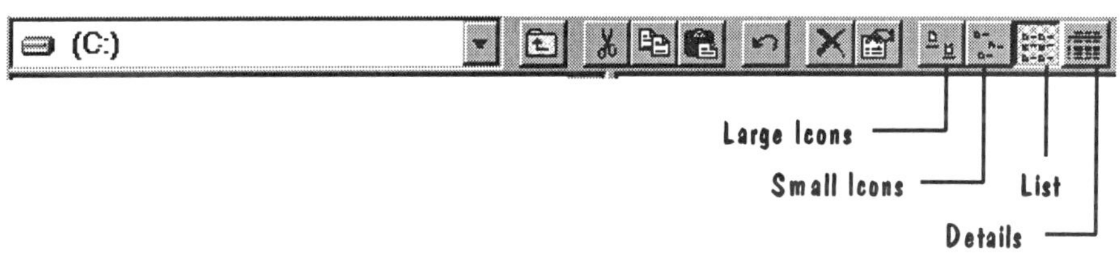

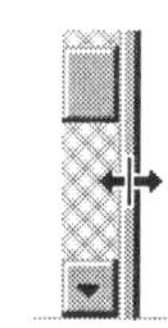

In any view, you may want to make the contents pane as large as possible. To do so, first maximize the Explorer window. Then, move the mouse pointer over the vertical bar separating the folder tree and contents panes (the pointer becomes a double-headed arrow, as pictured at the right). Now, drag the bar to the left, and the contents pane will expand accordingly.

NOTE

As you can see, the Toolbar contains several other buttons and a drop-down list, as well. The drop-down list and the Up One Level button next to it provide alternate ways to navigate the Windows folder system. They are of more benefit in My Computer than in Explorer, and will be described when we discuss the former in Section 3.5. Some of the other buttons on the Toolbar are helpful in performing operations on files and folders; they will be discussed in Sections 3.3 and 3.4.

3-2 TUTORIAL

Try the following exercises on your own.

1. Turn on your computer, if necessary, to start up Windows 95 and close any open windows.
2. Start Explorer: Click on the Start button, then point at the Programs option on the Start menu, and finally click on Windows Explorer on the resulting submenu. The Explorer window will open. Maximize this window.
3. Insert the Student Disk in its drive and select this drive in the folder tree (left) pane of the Explorer window. For example, if the Student Disk is in the A: drive, scroll the folder tree pane up until the "3½ Floppy (A:)" folder appears; then, click on this item. The files and folders in the root folder of the disk will be displayed in the contents (right) pane of the window.
4. Expand the "3½ Floppy (A:)" branch of the folder tree by clicking on the plus symbol to the left of this item. (You can also do this by double-clicking on the name "3½ Floppy (A:)".)
5. Choose the Large Icons option from the View menu. Now, drag the Paint folder icon to a new position in the contents pane: Position the mouse pointer over it, then hold down the left mouse button while moving the pointer (and icon) to a new location in the contents pane, and finally release the mouse button.
6. Arrange the icons in the contents pane neatly by choosing Line Up Icons from the View menu.
7. Point at the Arrange Icons item on the View menu and then choose *by Size* from the submenu to sort the files in order of increasing size. Take note of the other sorting options available on the submenu!
8. If the Toolbar is not visible in the Explorer window, choose Toolbar from the View menu to display it.
9. Successively click on the Small Icons, List, and Details Toolbar buttons. (To determine which ones they are, hold the mouse over each Toolbar button until the identifying *Tool Tip* appears.) Notice the effect of each view option.
10. With the Details view in effect, sort the files in order of the last date they were saved by clicking on the button labeled *Modified* at the top of the contents pane. Click on this button again to reverse the order. Also try the other buttons (Name, Size, and Type) to see their effect.
11. Exit Explorer (as you would any application) and remove the Student Disk from its drive.

3.3 Moving and Copying Files and Folders

An application like WordPad allows you to modify the content of *files*; Explorer, on the other hand, allows you to manipulate the contents of *folders*. Using Explorer, you can move, copy, rename, delete, and create files and subfolders. In Sections 3.3 and 3.4, we will describe how to accomplish each of these tasks.

Selecting Files and Folders

The first step in using Explorer to manipulate a file, a folder, or a group of files or folders is to identify or *select* the objects* in which you are interested. A selected object is displayed with a highlighted name and icon, as illustrated below.

Selected object

Object not selected

How to select an object

To select an object from the *folder tree pane*:

1. If necessary, scroll the pane or expand the tree (see Section 3.2) until the name of the object appears.
2. Click on the object to select it. (The selected folder will open, displaying its contents in the contents pane.)

To select an object from the *contents pane*.

1. Scroll the pane, if necessary, until the name of the object appears.
2. Click on the object to select it. (If the selected object is a folder, it will *not* open; the current folder remains unchanged. However, *double*-clicking on a folder in the contents pane *does* open it, making it the current folder.)

Selecting multiple objects

To save time in performing operations on files and folders, it is often useful to manipulate several of them at once. For example, if you want to delete ten files from disk, it is faster to select all ten and then perform the delete operation, rather than selecting and deleting them one at a time. Selecting *multiple* (more than one) objects can only be done in the contents pane, but it can be done in several ways:

---

*Recall that, in this context, an *object* is any item listed in Explorer's folder tree or contents pane. Any Explorer object (including My Computer, a floppy drive, and the Desktop itself!) that is not a file is considered to be a *folder*.

- Click on one of the objects to be selected; then, hold down the Ctrl key and click on the others; finally, release Ctrl.
- If the objects to be selected are *in consecutive order*: click on the first object; then, hold down the Shift key and click on the last object in the group; finally, release Shift.
- If the objects to be selected are *adjacent to one another*, drag a box around them, as illustrated at the right. To be more specific, position the mouse pointer to the upper left of the objects to be selected, hold down the left mouse button, move the pointer to the lower right of the desired objects, and release the button.

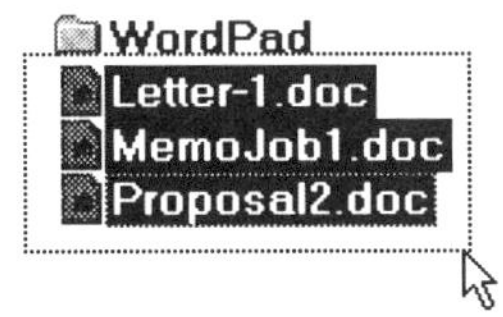

- To select *all* objects in the contents pane, choose Select All from Explorer's Edit menu. To select *almost all* the objects in the contents pane, select those objects you do *not* want and choose Invert Selection from the Edit menu.

As an example of the selection process, here's one way to select the objects shown highlighted in Figure 7:

1. The files Memo.doc, MemoJob1.doc, and Preamble.doc are in consecutive order, so we click on the first, hold down the Shift key, click on the last, and release Shift.
2. To select the remaining files, Dosprog.exe and testfile.doc, we hold down the Ctrl key, click on each file, and release Ctrl.

Figure 7 Selection Process Example

TIP

To select additional objects after at least one has been selected, be sure to hold down the Ctrl key while clicking. If you forget to press this key, all previously selected objects will be deselected!

If you want to deselect an object after some have been selected, hold down the Ctrl key while clicking on the object. Here, too, don't forget to hold down Ctrl. Otherwise, all objects *except* the one you click on will be deselected!

Moving and Copying Objects

When you **move** an object, it is deleted from its original location and placed in a new location. When you **copy** an object, a duplicate of that object is placed in the new location, but it is not deleted from the original. If the object being moved or copied is a folder, then it and all its contents (files and subfolders alike) are moved or copied to the new location. With one exception (which we will mention later), the move and copy operations are performed in analogous ways, so we will discuss them together.

You can move or copy an object from one folder (the *source*) to another (the *destination*) in two fundamental ways:

1. Drag the object from the source and drop it onto the destination.
2. Cut or copy the object from the source and paste it into the destination.

Drag-and-Drop Move or Copy To move or copy objects using the **drag-and-drop** method sometimes takes a little preparation, but the actual operation is very simple. It involves the following steps:

1. Select the objects to be moved or copied.
2. Arrange the Explorer window so that at least one of the selected objects as well as the destination folder are both visible. To do this, you may have to scroll or expand the folder tree to display the destination folder.
3. Position the mouse pointer over any selected object and:
   - If you want to *move* the object, hold down the Shift key and drag the pointer to the destination.
   - If you want to *copy* the object, hold down the Ctrl key and drag the pointer to the destination.

   As you drag the mouse pointer, it seems to pull the objects' icons and names with it (see Figure 8, on the next page). The plus symbol below the pointer arrow in Figure 8 indicates that this is a copy operation. When *moving* objects, the plus symbol will not appear.
4. As the mouse pointer approaches the destination folder, the latter will become highlighted (see the Windows folder in Figure 8) to let you know that you're on target. Now, release the mouse button (and the Ctrl or Shift key) and the *Moving...* or *Copying...* animated dialog box will appear, confirming that the operation is taking place. (If you change your mind and want to abort the process, press the Escape key before releasing the mouse button.)

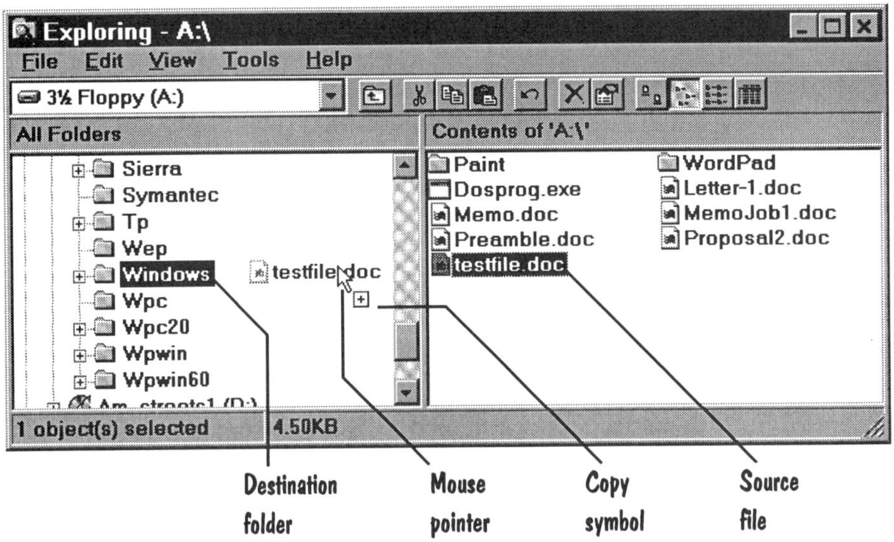

Figure 8 Drag-and-Drop Copying

If you try to move or copy an object into a folder that already contains an object with the same name, the Confirm File Replace (or Confirm Folder Replace) dialog box (Figure 9) will appear. Choose the Yes command button if you want the source file to replace the destination file in this folder, *deleting the destination file* in the process. Otherwise, click on the No button. (If you are moving or copying multiple

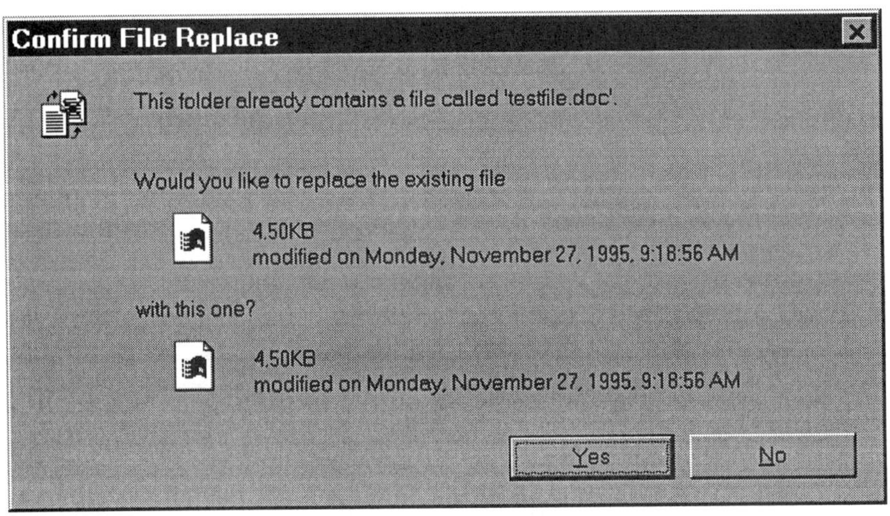

Figure 9 The Confirm File Replace Dialog Box

objects, this dialog box will also contain Yes to All and Cancel buttons. Choosing Yes to All indicates that you want to replace all destination files that have the same name as a source file; choosing Cancel aborts the Move or Copy operation.)

TIP

When *moving* objects between folders on the *same drive*, you do not have to hold down the Shift key while performing the drag-and-drop. When *copying* objects between folders on *different drives*, you do not have to hold down the Ctrl key.

If you don't want to memorize the Shift/Ctrl rules, Windows 95 provides an alternative: just *right-drag* a selected object from the source to the destination. In this case, when you release the mouse button, the menu shown here will appear. To *move* the file to the destination, choose the Move Here command; to *copy* the file, choose the Copy Here command.

Both the left-drag and right-drag techniques work when the destination is an icon on the Desktop or the Desktop itself. For example, to copy a file to the My Computer folder, select the file in Explorer and either

- Drag it onto the My Computer icon on the Desktop (you need not hold down the Ctrl key).

or

- Right-drag it onto the My Computer icon and choose Copy Here from the menu that pops up when you release the mouse button.

Cut/Copy and Paste Move or Copy The second basic method for moving or copying objects resembles the process for transferring information from one document to another (see Section 2.3). It involves the following steps:

1. Select the objects to be moved or copied.
2. Choose Cut (if you're moving the objects) or Copy (if you're copying the objects) from any of the following:
   - Explorer's Edit menu.
   - Explorer's Toolbar.

- The menu (pictured at the right) that pops up when you right-click on one of the selected files.

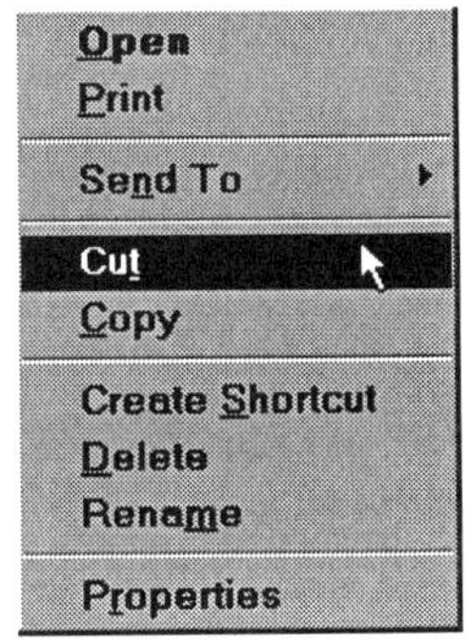

3. Select the destination folder in the folder tree pane.
4. Choose Paste from Explorer's Edit menu, Toolbar, or the menu that pops up when you right-click the destination folder.

If there is an object in the destination folder with the same name as one of the objects being moved or copied, a Confirm File Replace or Confirm Folder Replace dialog box will be displayed (see Figure 9). Choose the Yes or No command buttons, as you wish.

TIP

Suppose you move or copy an object (using any method) and then decide that this wasn't such a good idea. You could move the object back to the source folder or delete it from the destination, but there is an easier way. Windows supplies an Undo command that cancels the last move or copy. This command is located on Explorer's Edit menu. It can also be executed by clicking on the Undo Toolbar button (shown at the right).

The Send To Command

Perhaps the most common use of the copy operation in Windows is to copy a file or group of files to a floppy disk. This action is usually taken for one of two reasons:

- To *back up* files on the hard disk (to make copies in case the hard disk becomes damaged or its files cannot be accessed for some other reason).
- To transfer files to another computer.

Windows 95 makes it very easy to copy files or entire folders to a floppy disk. To do so:

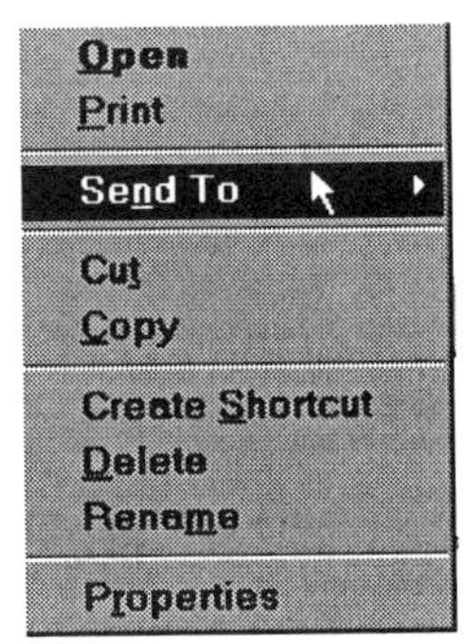

1. Select the objects you want to copy.
2. Right-click on one of them, which opens the menu shown at the right.
3. Point at the Send To command on this menu.

4. Choose the appropriate floppy disk drive from the resulting submenu.

3.3 TUTORIAL

Try the following exercises on your own.

1. Turn on your computer, if necessary, to start up Windows 95, and close any open windows.
2. Start Explorer, maximize its window, and select the List view option from the View menu or Toolbar.
3. Insert the Student Disk in its drive and select this drive (for example, "3½ Floppy (A:)") in the folder tree pane.
4. Select the last five (consecutive) files listed by clicking on the first of them, then holding down the Shift key while clicking on the last.
5. Deselect the selected files by clicking on an empty part of the contents pane.
6. Select the files Fonts, Preamble, and Testfile by clicking on the first of these, then holding down the Ctrl key as you click on the other two.
7. Deselect the Fonts file by holding down the Ctrl key while clicking on it.
8. Move the two remaining selected files to the Paint subfolder using the (right-) drag-and-drop method:
   - Move the mouse pointer over either file name and press, but do not release, the *right* mouse button.
   - Reposition the pointer so that the Paint folder name and icon become highlighted and release the mouse button.
   - Choose Move Here from the resulting pop-up menu.
9. Move the Testfile and Preamble files back to the root folder of the Student Disk using the cut and paste method:
   - Open the Paint folder by double-clicking on its icon in the contents pane.
   - Select Testfile and Preamble.
   - Choose Cut from Explorer's Edit menu or click on the Cut Toolbar button.
   - Open the diskette's root folder by clicking on its drive icon (for example, "3½ Floppy (A:)") in the folder tree pane.
   - Choose Paste from Explorer's Edit menu or click on the Paste Toolbar button.
10. Copy the Fonts file from the root folder to the Paint subfolder

using (left-) drag-and-drop:

- Select the Fonts file.
- Position the mouse pointer over the selected file name, hold down the left mouse button and the Ctrl key (Ctrl is for *copy*, Shift is for *move*).
- Reposition the pointer so that the Paint folder name and icon become highlighted, and release the mouse button and Ctrl key.

11. Undo the last copy operation by choosing Undo Copy from the Edit menu or clicking on the Undo Toolbar button. 
12. Exit Explorer and remove the Student Disk from its drive.

3.4 Other Operations on Files and Folders

In Section 3.3, we described how to select, move, and copy objects (files and folders). In this section we will continue this discussion, describing how to use Explorer to delete, rename, and create files and folders. We will also introduce the concept of a *shortcut*.

Deleting Files and Folders

Deleting objects from disk is a common operation, often used to create additional free disk space or just to reduce clutter. In the usual sense of the word, to **delete** a file or folder means to remove it and all its contents from disk. When you use Explorer to delete an object, however, that object is normally (but not necessarily always) just copied to a special folder called the **Recycle Bin.** To remove the object from disk, you then have to delete it from the Recycle Bin.

Ways to delete objects

To delete files or folders, start Explorer and select the objects to be deleted (see Section 3.3). Then, perform any of the following actions:

- Press the Delete (Del) key.
- Drag any of the selected objects onto the Recycle Bin icon on the Desktop. 
- Click on the Delete button (shown at the right) on Explorer's Toolbar. 

- Choose the Delete command from Explorer's File menu.
- Right-click on any of the selected objects and choose the Delete command from the resulting pop-up menu.

After performing one of these actions, the Confirm File Delete or Confirm Folder Delete dialog box shown in Figure 10 may appear. Choose the Yes or No command button, as appropriate.

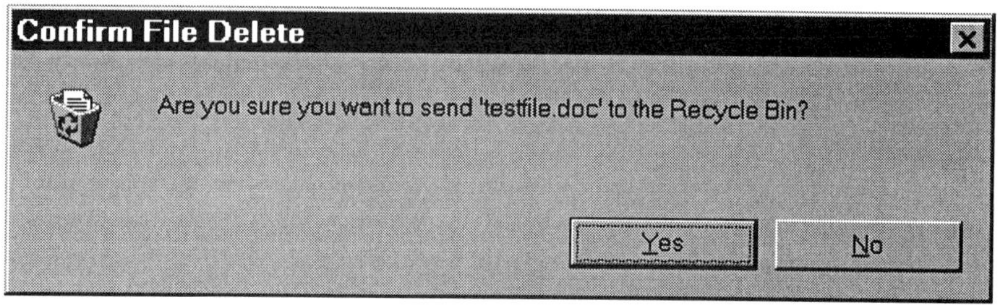

Figure 10 The Confirm File Delete Dialog Box

WARNING

By default, Windows 95 does not send files deleted from floppy disks to the Recycle Bin. In this case, the message in the Confirm Delete dialog box will read "Are you sure you want to delete ..." and, if you activate the Yes button, the selected objects will immediately be removed from disk. If one of these objects is a folder, all its contents — files and subfolders alike — will be removed from disk. So, before you give the command to delete files or folders, think about what you are doing and whether you really want to do it!

The Recycle Bin The Recycle Bin is simply a Windows 95 folder. When files or folders are "deleted" by sending them to the Recycle Bin, these objects still take up disk space and can still be retrieved (or *restored*). If you are sure you no longer need an object in the Recycle Bin, you should delete that object to increase your free disk space. The safest way to accomplish this is to:

1. Open the Recycle Bin by double-clicking on its Desktop icon. The Recycle Bin window will be displayed (see Figure 11 on the next page).
2. Select the objects you want to delete.
3. Delete the selected objects: Press the Delete key, or choose Delete from the File menu, or click on the Toolbar's Delete button, or right-click on a selected object and choose Delete from the pop-up menu.
4. If a Confirm Delete dialog box appears, asking whether you're sure you want to delete the objects, choose the Yes button (unless

you've changed your mind). The selected objects are now removed from disk.

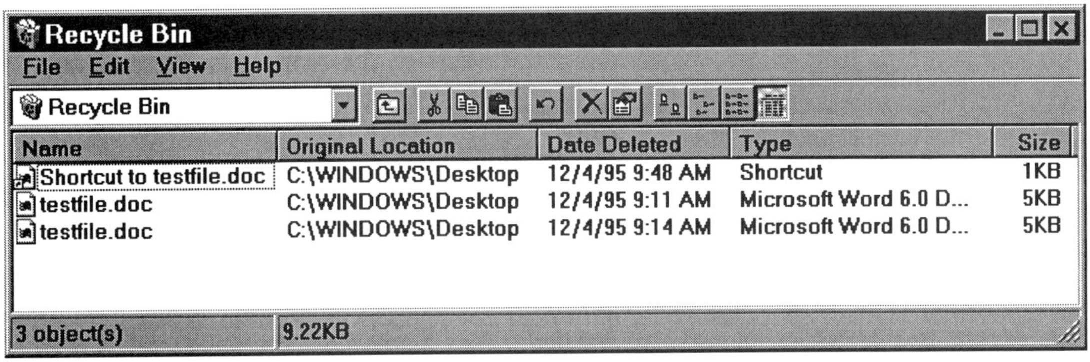

Figure 11 The Recycle Bin Window

NOTE

As you can see in Figure 11, the Recycle Bin window strongly resembles the Explorer window. In fact, the Recycle Bin window is just Explorer's view of the Recycle Bin folder without the folder tree pane. There are, however, two menu options available for the Recycle Bin that are not available for a typical folder:

1. You can choose Empty Recycle Bin from the File menu to delete *all* objects in the Recycle Bin. (You can also accomplish this task by right-clicking on the Recycle Bin's Desktop icon and then choosing Empty Recycle Bin from the pop-up menu.)
2. You can choose Restore from the File menu to move selected objects back to their original location.

Renaming Files and Folders

To **rename** (change the name of) a file or folder:

1. Start Explorer and select the object to be renamed.
2. Perform any of the following actions:
   - Choose Rename from Explorer's File menu.
   - Right-click on the selected object and choose Rename from the pop-up menu.
   - Click again on the selected object.

In any case, Windows places a box around the selected object's name (as shown at the right) to let you know that this object can now be renamed.

3. Type a new name for the object and press the Enter key.

If an object in the current folder has the same name as the one you are trying to assign to the selected object, the following dialog box will be displayed:

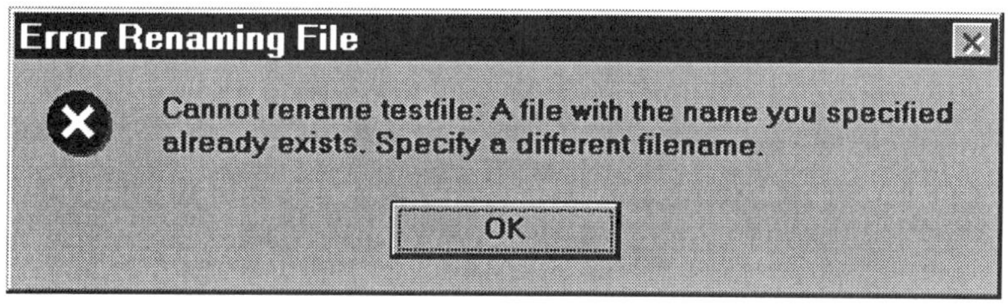

Click on the OK button (or press the Enter key) and this message will be cleared from the screen. If you want to give the selected object the same name as an existing object in that folder, you have to first rename or delete the existing one.

NOTE

You can rename objects on the Desktop in a similar way:

1. Select the object to be renamed by clicking on it.
2. Either click on the object again; or right-click on the object and choose Rename from the pop-up menu. Windows will place a box around the object's name.
3. Type a new name and press the Enter key.

Creating New Files and Folders

As you know, data files (documents) are normally created within a specific application. For example, if you start WordPad, type some text, and save the resulting document (assigning it a name in the process), a file with that name is created on disk. Most of the folders on your hard disk were also created "automatically"— usually when Windows 95 or an application was installed.

You can also use Explorer to create both files and folders. (Creating a file this way is not terribly useful, but creating a new folder — say, to hold certain related documents — is an important operation.) To create a file or folder:

1. Start Explorer and select (in the folder tree pane) the folder in which you want the new object to reside.
2. Take either of the following actions:
   - Point at the New item on the File menu.

   or
   - Right-click on an empty part of the contents pane and point at the New item on the resulting pop-up menu.

   In either case, a submenu, similar to the one in Figure 12, will be displayed.

Figure 12 The New Menu

3. Choose either Folder or one of the file types listed at the bottom of this menu. A new object will appear in the contents pane named, for example, New Folder, New Text Document, or New Bitmap Image. The name of the object will be highlighted and boxed-in, ready for renaming.
4. Rename the object whatever you want by typing a new name and pressing the Enter key.

As an example, we will create a new subfolder of the Windows folder and name it Data Files. To do so, we:

1. Start Explorer.
2. Scroll the Folder tree pane until the Windows folder comes into view.
3. Click on the Windows folder to select it. (The word *Windows* becomes highlighted.)
4. Point at the New command on Explorer's File menu and choose Folder from the resulting submenu. (A highlighted object called *New Folder* appears in the contents pane; the "box" around its name indicates that it's ready to be renamed.)
5. To rename the folder, type Data Files and press the Enter key.

Creating Shortcuts

Recall (from Section 2.1) that one of the easiest ways to start an application is to double-click on its Desktop icon. Consequently, it would certainly be convenient to have an icon on the Desktop for each of your favorite programs. As you will see, Windows makes this easy to do.

What's a shortcut?

Some Desktop icons actually represent **shortcuts** to objects (files or folders); when you double-click on such an icon, the shortcut provides Windows 95 with the location and name (the path name) of the corresponding object. Thus, a shortcut is not a copy of an object, just a small file called a *pointer* (or *link*) that tells Windows where to find the relevant file or folder. For this reason, you can create shortcuts to your heart's content with very little adverse effect on your free disk space.

There are several ways to create a shortcut and place it on the Desktop. Here's one way to use Explorer to accomplish this task. (Another technique is given in Section 3.5.)

1. Start Explorer and open the folder that contains the object for which you want to create a shortcut.
2. Right-click on the object, selecting it and also opening a menu similar to the one shown at the right.

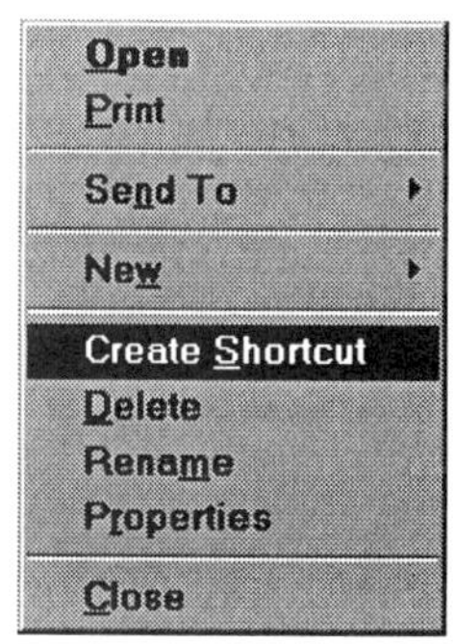

3. Choose Create Shortcut form the pop-up menu. A new object entitled "Shortcut to ..." will appear in the contents pane.
4. To move the shortcut to the Desktop, either
   - Drag it onto the Desktop (you may have to reduce the size of the Explorer window to accomplish this).

   or
   - Cut the object to the Clipboard (by clicking on the Cut Edit menu command or Toolbar button) and paste it onto the Desktop (by right-clicking on the Desktop and choosing Paste from the pop-up menu).
5. The shortcut will now appear on the Desktop as an icon. (Icons for shortcuts contain a small arrow in the lower left corner, as shown here for the WordPad shortcut icon.) Once on the Desktop, you can:

Shortcut "arrow"

   - Move the shortcut to a new location by dragging it with the mouse.

- Rename the shortcut by clicking on its highlighted icon or right-clicking on it and choosing Rename from the pop-up menu. In either case, a "box" will appear around the shortcut's name. Now, type a new name and press the Enter key.

TIP

You can also create shortcuts directly on the Desktop without starting up Explorer. To do so:

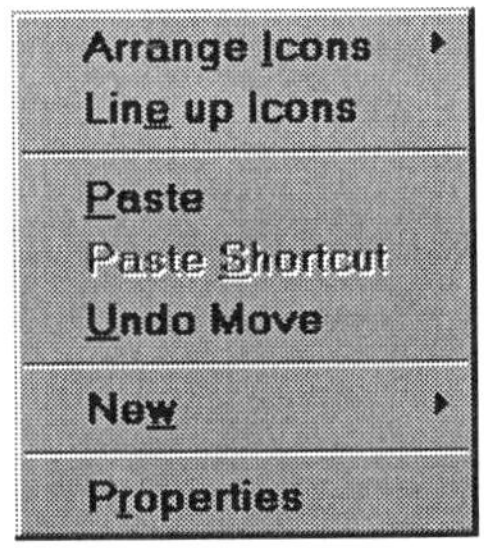

1. Right-click on an empty part of the Desktop. The menu shown at the right will pop up.
2. Point at New on this menu and then choose the Shortcut option on the resulting submenu. This action starts the Create Shortcut "wizard".
3. Either type the path name of the desired file in the *Command line* text box or click on the Browse button to have Windows help you locate this file. (We will discuss *browsing* in Section 3.5.)
4. Choose the Next command button and you will be asked if you want to rename the shortcut.
5. Type a new name, if you want, and then choose the Finish command button. The new shortcut will appear on the Desktop.

This technique works from within Explorer, as well — the New command can be accessed from the File menu or the menu that pops up when you right-click on a selected object (see Figure 12). However, from within Explorer, you'll have to move the new shortcut to the Desktop "manually".

3-4 TUTORIAL

Try the following exercises on your own.

1. Turn on your computer, if necessary, to start up Windows 95, and close any open windows.
2. Start Explorer and select the List view option from the View menu or Toolbar.
3. Insert the Student Disk in its drive and select this drive (for example, "3½ Floppy (A:)") in the folder tree pane.
4. Select the file named DeleteFile from the contents pane.
5. Size and move the Explorer window so that the selected file, the Recycle Bin Desktop icon, and an empty part of the Desktop are all visible.

6. Create a shortcut for the selected file and place it on the Desktop:
   - Right-drag the file onto an empty part of the Desktop.
   - Choose Create Shortcut(s) Here from the menu that pops up when you release the mouse button.
   - Rename the shortcut icon "DelFile" by clicking on it, typing the new name, and pressing the Enter key.
7. Delete the new DelFile icon by dragging it (using the left mouse button) onto the Recycle Bin icon.
8. Restore the DelFile shortcut: Open the Recycle Bin (by double-clicking on its icon), select the DelFile shortcut, and choose the Restore command from the File menu. Now, close the Recycle Bin.
9. Delete the DelFile shortcut again, this time by selecting it and pressing the Del key. Answer Yes to the Confirm Delete query.
10. Rename the DeleteFile object in the root folder of the floppy disk by selecting this file in Explorer's contents pane, right-clicking on it, choosing Rename from the pop-up menu, typing a new name of your choosing, and pressing the Enter key.
11. Delete this newly-renamed file by choosing Delete from Explorer's File menu. Answer Yes to the Confirm Delete query.
12. Exit Explorer and remove the Student Disk from its drive.

3.5 My Computer

As you saw in Chapter 1, the Desktop contains an icon called **My Computer** that provides access to virtually all aspects of your computer system. In particular, from the My Computer window you can carry out all the operations on files and folders that we have discussed in this chapter. This is not surprising once you realize that the My Computer icon is simply a built-in shortcut to Explorer's My Computer folder! If you keep this fact in mind, it will be easier to understand the workings of My Computer.

Starting My Computer

My Computer

As you know, you can open the My Computer window, which is shown in Figure 13 on the next page, by double-clicking on its Desktop icon. Notice that this window is similar in appearance to the Explorer window, but My Computer lacks a folder tree pane; it uses a single subwindow, a contents pane, to display information.

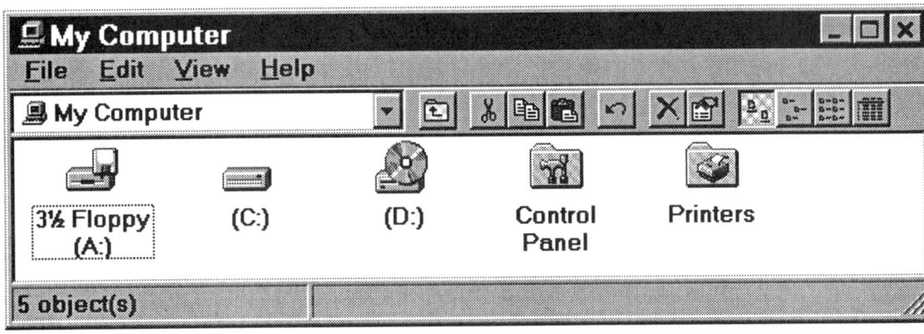

Figure 13 The My Computer Window — Large Icons View

NOTE

You can also start My Computer by right-clicking on its icon and choosing Open from the resulting pop-up menu. Interestingly enough, if you choose Explore instead of Open from this menu, Explorer will start and display a dual-pane view of the My Computer folder.

The fact that the My Computer window lacks a tree pane results in two basic differences between the way My Computer and Explorer are used to locate and manipulate objects:

1. My Computer provides less flexibility than Explorer in navigating (or **browsing**) the Windows file system. For example, it is often more difficult to locate a particular folder in My Computer.
2. Certain drag-and-drop operations are not carried out as easily in My Computer as in Explorer. For example, it is usually more difficult to drag a given file onto a certain folder in My Computer.*

We will now examine the consequences of each of these differences.

Using My Computer to Browse Folders

Opening a subfolder

Once you have started My Computer, you can easily access its subfolders: your computer's drives, the Printers folder, and so on (see Figure 13). Just double-click on an icon to open one of these folders, and its contents will be displayed in a new window. For example, if you double-click on the "(C:)" icon, a window will open displaying all the

*In light of these deficiencies, you might be wondering why Microsoft chose to give My Computer such prominence in the Windows 95 interface. One reason for this approach is to provide easy access, especially for the novice user, to all aspects of the computer system — its drives, files, printers, settings, and so on.

files and subfolders in the root folder of the C: drive. A subfolder of *any* folder is opened in the same way — by double-clicking on its icon.

NOTE The previous My Computer window may or may not close when a new one opens. You can control whether or not a separate window opens whenever you change folders by choosing the Options command from the View menu, selecting the appropriate option button in the resulting dialog box, and choosing the OK command button. We will further discuss this feature later in this section.

Opening a parent folder

If you want to open the parent folder of the current folder (going up one level in the folder tree), take any of the following actions:

- Press the Backspace key.
- Click on the Up One Level button on the current window's Toolbar (Figure 14). Remember: If the Toolbar is not displayed, choose Toolbar from the View menu to display it.
- If the parent window is visible on the screen, click on it; or, if the parent window's button appears on the Taskbar, click on that.

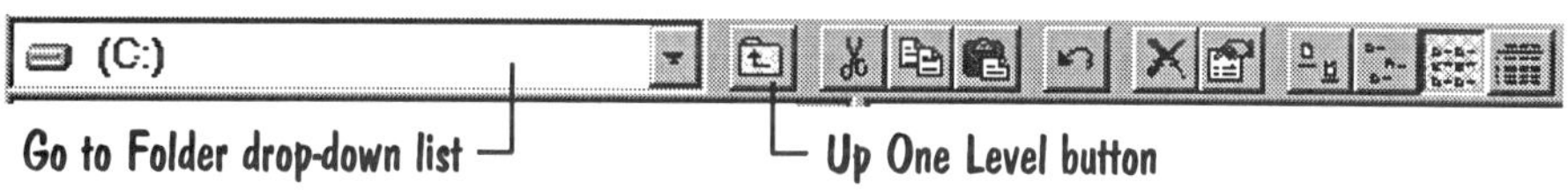

Figure 14 The My Computer Toolbar

Using the Go to Folder drop-down list

The Go to Folder drop-down list on the Toolbar (see Figure 14) provides a way to change folders more quickly in certain situations. When you open this drop-down list (by clicking on the down-triangle), a "mini-tree" is displayed, showing the immediate (child) subfolders of the Desktop and My Computer, as well as the chain of subfolders forming the path to the current folder (Figure 15). The current folder is shown in the text box at the top of the list.

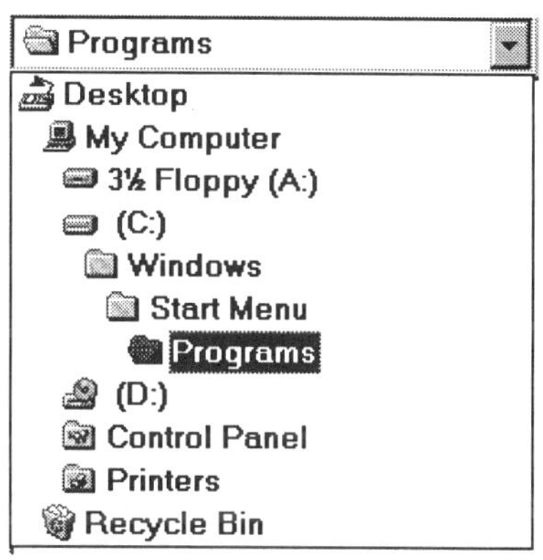

Figure 15 A Typical Go to Folder Drop-down List

To display the contents of one of the listed folders, just click on it.

The Go to Folder drop-down list can be a great time-saving convenience. For example, suppose the current folder is Programs, as in Figure 15. To display the contents of the disk in the 3½" floppy drive, just open the drop-down list and click on the "3½ Floppy (A:)" object.

TIP

The following tips make it easier to use My Computer to browse folders:

- The default view option for My Computer is Large Icons. It's much easier to see what's in the current folder if you use the View menu or the Toolbar buttons to switch to the Small Icons or List view option (see Section 3.2).
- Display the *path* of the current folder on its window's title bar (if it is not already displayed there) by choosing the Options command from the View menu, clicking on the View tab in the resulting dialog box, selecting the *Display the full MS-DOS path in the title bar* check box, and choosing the OK command button.
- If each change of folder has opened a separate window, you can close all these windows at the same time by holding down the Shift key while clicking on the last window's close button.

NOTE

Some Windows dialog boxes (such as Run, Save As, and Open) allow you to browse folders as you do in My Computer. For example, if you activate the Browse command button in the Run dialog box (see Section 2.1), a dialog box like the one in Figure 16 will open. Using the Toolbar buttons, you can select a List or Details view option or go Up One Level. You can also Go to Folder via the Toolbar drop-down list. In addition, if you're looking for a file of a particular type, you can restrict the kinds of files that are displayed by using the *Files of type* drop-down list.

Using My Computer to Operate on Files and Folders

Objects — files, folders and shortcuts — are manipulated from within a My Computer window in essentially the same way as in Explorer (see Sections 3.3 and 3.4). For example, you can copy a file from one folder to another using the Copy and Paste commands, as follows:

1. Open the folder containing the file to be copied.
2. Right-click on the desired file, which selects it and displays a pop-up menu.

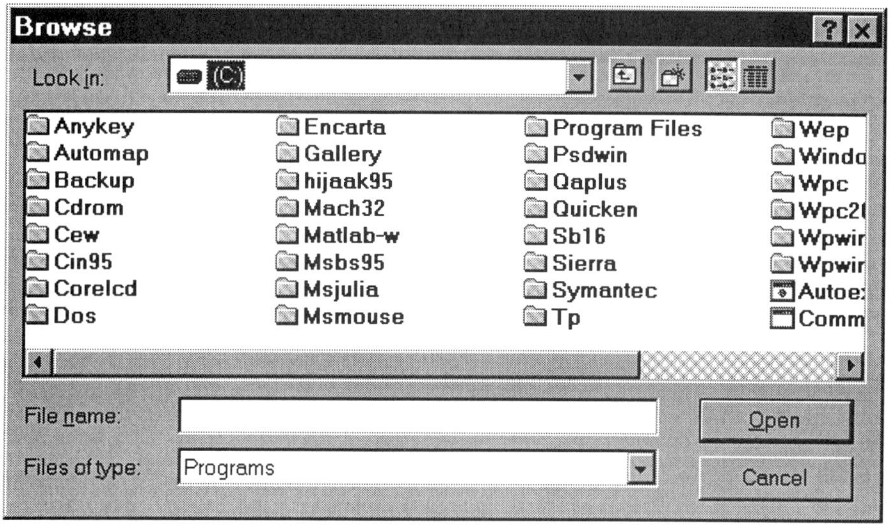

Figure 16 A Browse Dialog Box

3. Choose the Copy command from the pop-up menu.
4. Right-click on the destination folder's name, which displays a pop-up menu.
5. Choose the Paste command from this pop-up menu and the process is complete.

Notice that this procedure could be used without change in Explorer, but there is one subtle difference in its execution here. To carry out steps 1 and 4 in Explorer, you would most likely just scroll and expand the folder tree pane (if necessary) until the name of the desired folder appeared; then click on it. In My Computer, on the other hand, you might have to open several windows in each of steps 1 and 4 before the desired folder became visible!

Drag-and-drop in My Computer

The difference just described causes the greatest trouble if you want to perform a drag-and-drop move or copy (see Section 3.3). The problem here is that the object to be moved or copied *and* the destination folder must be visible at the same time. This is not much of a problem in Explorer, but requires some preparation in My Computer.

The trick to drag-and-drop moving or copying in My Computer is to open both the source and destination folders and arrange them so that both are visible on the screen. For example, suppose we want to copy a file named Testfile.doc from a floppy disk to the Windows folder on the C: drive. To do this using drag-and-drop in My Computer:

1. Insert the floppy disk into its drive and start My Computer.
2. Ensure that a separate window will open for each new folder by choosing the Options command from the View menu and (if necessary) selecting the *Browse folders using a separate window for each folder* option button in the resulting dialog box before activating the OK command button.
3. Back in My Computer, double-click on the (C:) icon to open the root folder of the C: drive, C:\.
4. Scroll the C:\ window until the Windows folder's name appears.
5. Switch back to the My Computer window by clicking on it or its Taskbar button.
6. Double-click on the appropriate floppy drive icon to open its window.
7. Scroll this window (if necessary) until Testfile.doc appears and click on it to select this file. The current arrangement of windows is shown in Figure 17.

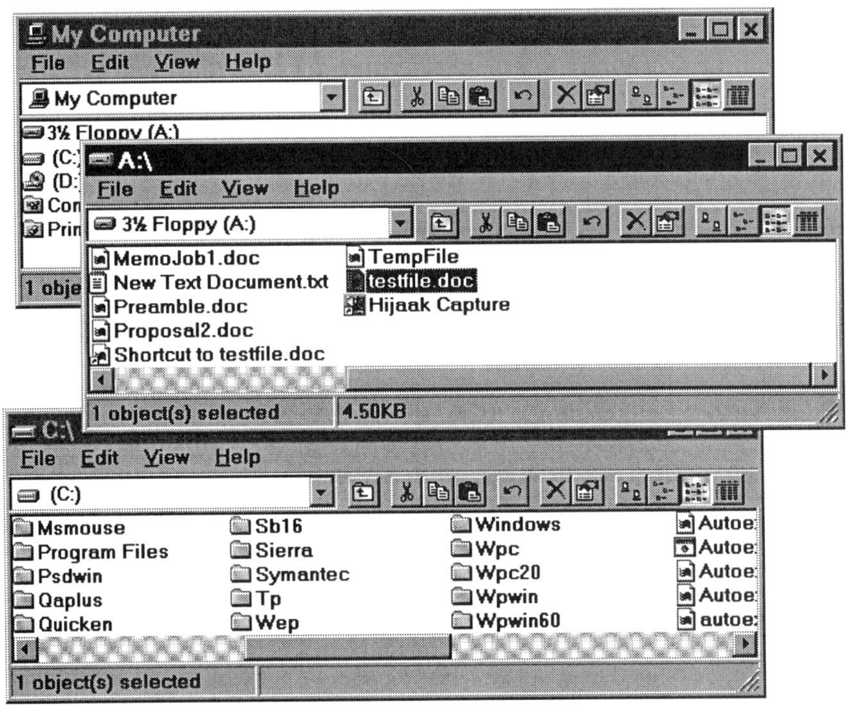

Figure 17 Preparing to Copy with My Computer

8. If necessary, resize or move the floppy drive window and the C:\ window so that the names Testfile.doc and Windows are both visible.

9. Drag the Testfile.doc file onto the Windows folder. The Copying animated dialog box will confirm that the copy operation is taking place.

3.5 TUTORIAL

Try the following exercises on your own.

1. Turn on your computer, if necessary, to start up Windows 95, and close any open windows.
2. Start My Computer by double-clicking on its Desktop icon.
3. Elect to use a single My Computer window to display all folders:
   - Choose Options from the View menu to open the Options dialog box.
   - Select the "Browse folders by using a single window that changes as you open each folder." option button.
   - Choose the OK command button.
4. Insert the Student Disk in its drive and then select this drive by double-clicking on the appropriate icon (for example, "3½ Floppy (A:)").
5. Open the WordPad subfolder by double-clicking on it.
6. Right-click on the Fonts file in the WordPad subfolder and copy it to the Clipboard by choosing the Copy command from the pop-up menu.
7. Open the root folder on the A: drive (A:\), the parent of the WordPad folder, by either clicking on the Up One Level Toolbar button or pressing the Backspace key.

8. Paste the Fonts file into the A:\ folder by choosing the Paste command from the Edit menu. If the Confirm File Replace dialog box appears, choose the No command button.
9. If the Toolbar is not visible in the My Computer window, display it by choosing Toolbar from the View menu. Open the root folder on the C: drive:
   - Open the Toolbar's Go to Folder drop-down list (see Figure 14 on page 105).
   - Click on the "(C:)" item in the drop-down list.
10. Close the My Computer window and remove the Student Disk from its drive.

3.6 *Formatting and Copying Floppy Disks*

All the procedures we have discussed in this chapter apply to files and folders on floppy disks (diskettes) as well as hard disks. Two additional operations are useful with floppies: formatting and copying disks. In this section, we will discuss these procedures.

Formatting a Floppy Disk

Before information can be stored on a disk, the disk must be **formatted**. This process prepares the disk to store information, dividing it into sectors and creating a file allocation table on it, and also erases any data that had been stored on the disk prior to formatting. Hard disks are usually formatted by the manufacturer or dealer, and most floppies are also sold already formatted. (In the latter case, the word "formatted" will appear on the box and on each individual disk.) Nevertheless, from time to time, you will have to format a diskette for one of the following reasons:

- To prepare an unformatted diskette for use.
- To reformat a Macintosh disk for use on your IBM-compatible computer.
- To quickly erase all files on a disk.

WARNING

Keep in mind that the format procedure erases all information on the disk being formatted! So, never format a disk unless you are sure there is nothing stored on it or (if there is data on the disk) that you no longer need its contents. Unless the disk is fresh out of the box, it's wise to check its contents before formatting it. To do so, insert the diskette in its drive, start Explorer, and select the appropriate floppy drive (3½ or 5¼) in the folder tree pane. If a message is displayed informing you that the disk is not formatted, fine. Otherwise, check each file listed in the contents pane. If you see a file that you're not sure you want erased, open it to view its contents before proceeding.

If you format a disk and then realize you made a mistake — it did contain some information you need — immediately inform your instructor or lab coordinator. It *might* be possible to recover the desired files if you have not yet used the newly-formatted diskette.

To format a floppy disk:

1. Insert the diskette to be formatted in its drive.

2. Start My Computer or Explorer and select this drive.
3. Right-click on the selected drive and choose Format from the resulting pop-up menu (Figure 18). Or, in My Computer, choose Format from the File menu. A Format dialog box, like the one in Figure 19, will be displayed.
4. Select the proper Capacity for the diskette from the drop-down list:
   - For 3.5" disks, select *1.44 Mb* if the disk is a high density one (with an "HD" on its label); select *720 Kb*, otherwise.
   - For 5.25" disks, select *1.2 Mb* if the disk is a high density one (with an "HD" on its label); select *360 Kb*, otherwise.

Figure 18
Floppy Disk Menu

5. Select a "Format type" option from the option buttons:

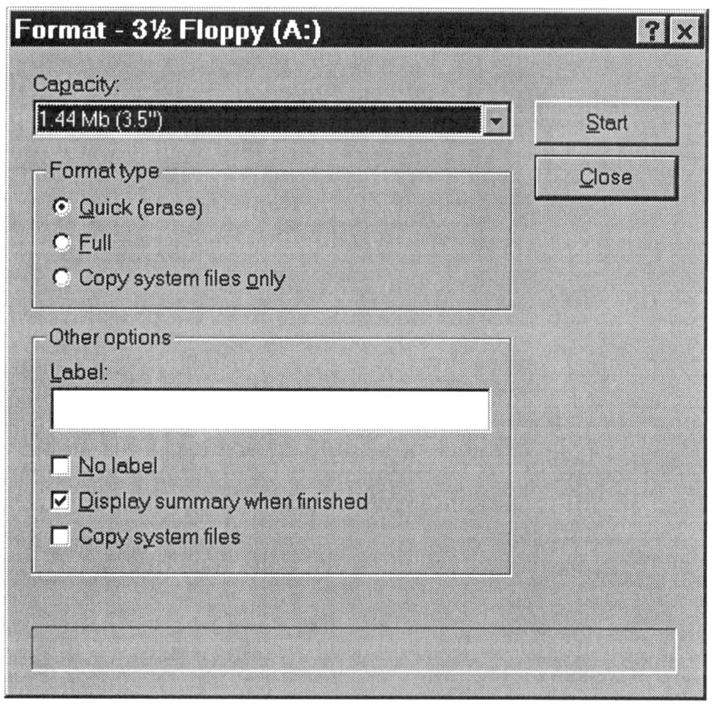

Figure 19 The Format Dialog Box

- *Quick (erase)* can only be used with diskettes that have already been formatted. It "erases" all information on the disk (by removing the file allocation table and other system information). This option provides a convenient way to erase old, unneeded disks so they can be used again. Quick format is much faster than the normal (or *full*) format process.
- *Full* is the option used to format a diskette which has not yet been formatted for an IBM-compatible computer.
- *Copy system files only* is used with formatted diskettes. It creates a *bootable* diskette — if placed in the computer's A: drive at startup, the computer will access the information on this disk, instead of the hard disk, and start DOS. A bootable diskette is useful if your hard disk has become damaged.

6. Type a name for the diskette in the Label text box if you want to associate a name with this diskette. The label (or *volume label*) for a diskette is displayed by certain programs. Select the *No label* check box if you want to delete a previous label for the diskette.
7. Select the *Display summary when finished* check box to display information about the free space on the disk when the formatting process is complete.
8. Select the *Copy system files* check box to create a bootable diskette during the formatting process.
9. Choose the Start command button to begin the formatting process. The message "Formatting" and a bar graph showing the percentage of the process completed will appear at the bottom of the Format dialog box.

Copying an Entire Diskette

If your computer has two floppy disk drives, you can use the copy procedure, described in Section 3.3, to copy all files from one diskette to another. Windows provides a simpler way to copy all the contents of one diskette to another, even if your machine only has one floppy disk drive, as long as the diskettes have the *same size and capacity*. Here's how it works:

1. Insert the diskette to be copied (the *source disk*) in its drive. If you have two drives of the same capacity, insert the disk to be copied to (the *destination disk*) in the other drive.
2. Start My Computer or Explorer and select the source drive.
3. Right-click on this drive and choose Copy Disk from the pop-up menu (see Figure 18). Or, in My Computer, choose Copy Disk from

the File menu. A Copy Disk dialog box, similar to the one in Figure 20, will be displayed.

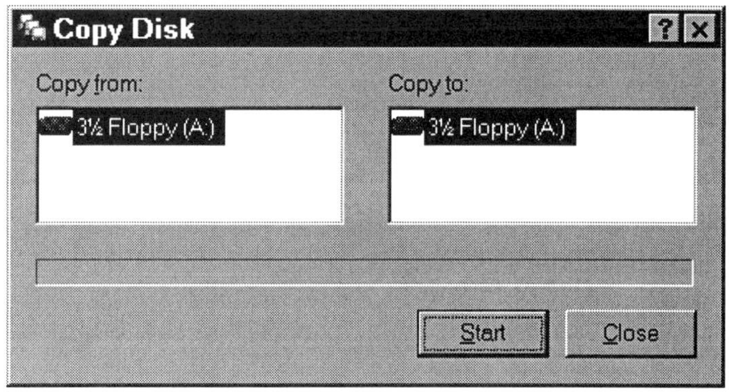

Figure 20 The Copy Disk Dialog Box

4. Choose the Start command button to begin the copying process. Messages and a bar graph at the bottom of the Copy Disk dialog box will indicate the progress of the operation.
5. If you have only one floppy drive, the following dialog box will appear halfway through the copy process:

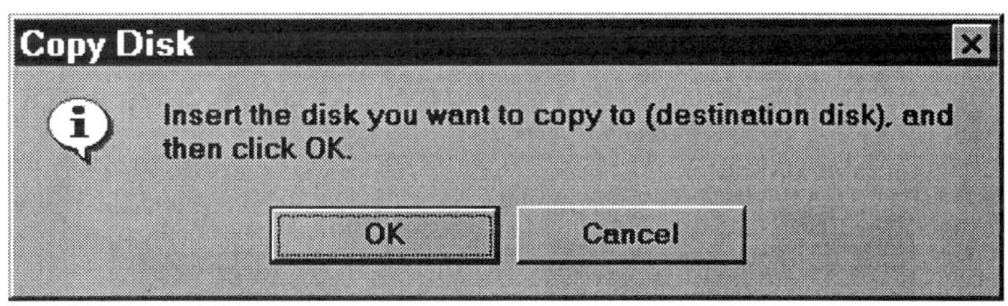

   Insert the destination disk in its drive. Be aware that the copy process will *erase all information* on this disk!

6. When the copy process is complete, a message to this effect will appear at the bottom of the Copy Disk dialog box. When it does, choose the Close command button.

WARNING When you carry out the copy disk process, all existing information on the destination disk is erased and replaced with a copy of the source disk. Consequently, before beginning the process, be sure that there are no files of any value on the destination disk.

Chapter Summary

File Names	Long file name (for folders and Windows 95 applications)	Maximum length is 255 characters; all characters are allowed *except*: | : " / \ * ?
	DOS file name (for Windows 3.1 and DOS applications)	Consists of a *filename* made up of one to eight characters followed by an optional extension (up to three characters), separated from the filename by a period. Forbidden characters are the space (blank) and: . , : ; " [ ] / \ = | * ?
Basic Operations in Explorer	To start Explorer	Open the Start menu, point at the Programs option, and choose the Explorer item from the submenu.
	To expand a branch of the folder tree	In the folder tree pane, either click on the plus symbol next to the desired folder or double-click on the desired folder's name.
	To open a folder	Click on the folder in the folder tree pane or double-click on the folder in the contents pane.
	To open a file	Double-click on the file in the contents pane.
	To select a view option (Large Icons, Small Icons, etc.)	Click on the appropriate Toolbar icon or choose the appropriate option from the View menu.
	To sort the objects in the contents pane	Choose the appropriate item from the Arrange Icons submenu of the View menu or, in Details view, click on the appropriate button at the top of the contents pane.
Selecting Files and Folders	A single object	Click on it.
	Objects in sequence	Click on the first, then hold down the Shift key while clicking on the last.
	Additional objects	Hold down the Ctrl key while clicking on them.
	All objects in the contents pane	Choose Select All from the Edit menu or press Ctrl+A.
Operations on Files or Folders (in Explorer or My Computer)	To move or copy selected objects	Hold down the Shift (for *move*) or Ctrl (for *copy*) key while dragging the objects onto the target; *or* right-drag the objects onto the target and choose either Move or Copy from the pop-up menu; *or* Cut (for *move*) or Copy

		the objects to the Clipboard and Paste them onto the target.
	To copy selected objects to a floppy disk	Right-click on one of the objects, point at Send To on the pop-up menu, and choose the floppy drive from the resulting submenu.
	To delete the selected objects	Press the Del key; *or* drag the objects onto the Recycle Bin; *or* choose Delete from the File menu or the right-click menu.
	To rename a selected object	First, click on the object again, *or* choose Rename from the File menu or the right-click menu, *or* press the F2 key. Then, type the new name and press the Enter key.
	To create a new file or folder	Point at the New item on either the File menu or the right-click menu, then choose the appropriate item from the submenu.
	To create a shortcut to a selected object	Right-drag the object to the desired location and choose Create Shortcut(s) Here from the pop-up menu; *or* right-click on the object and choose Create Shortcut from the pop-up menu; *or* right-click on an empty part of the Desktop, point at the New item on the pop-up menu, choose Create Shortcut from the submenu, and follow the instructions in the Create Shortcut wizard.
Operations on Floppy Disks (in Explorer or My Computer)	To format a floppy disk	First, insert the disk in its drive, right-click on that drive's folder icon, and choose Format from the pop-up menu. Then, in the resulting dialog box, select options and choose the Start command button.
	To copy an entire floppy disk	First, insert the disk to be copied in its drive, right-click on that drive's folder icon, and choose Copy Disk from the pop-up menu. Then, choose the Start command in the resulting dialog box and follow the on-screen instructions.

Review Exercises

Section 3.1

1. A ___________ is a collection of information generated by a program and saved on disk.

2. A ____________ is a collection of files that have been grouped together and given a name.
3. True or false: A folder may contain files and/or subfolders.
4. True or false: If the path name for a file is A:\Paint\Truck.bmp, then it is located in the Paint folder on the disk in the A: drive.
5. Which of the following is a valid DOS file name?
    a. `Homework 1`
    b. `Homework.1`
    c. `HomeworkOne`
    d. All of these names are valid DOS file names.
6. Which of the following is a valid long file name?
    a. `Homework 1`
    b. `Homework.1`
    c. `HomeworkOne`
    d. All of these names are valid long file names.

Section 3.2

7. In the Explorer window, the ____________ pane can contain both files and folders.
8. To see the subfolders of a given folder in Explorer's left pane (if they are not currently displayed), click on the ____________ symbol that precedes the name of the folder.
9. If you want to display the size of a file shown in Explorer's contents pane, click on the ____________ item on the View menu.
10. True or false: Explorer's left pane only shows the folders present on the C: drive.
11. True or false: In Explorer, you can use the Toolbar to select one of four view options (Large Icons, Small Icons, List, or Details).
12. True or false: In Small Icons view in Explorer, it is possible to order the icons in alphabetical order by file type.
13. The only Explorer view option in which you can display files in decreasing size order is:
    a. Large Icons
    b. Small Icons
    c. List
    d. Details
14. In which of the following view options can file names and icons be moved, one by one, around Explorer's contents pane?
    a. Large Icons only
    b. Small icons only

c. Both Large Icons and Small Icons
d. Neither Large Icons nor Small Icons

Section 3.3

15. To select two nonconsecutive files in Explorer, click on the first and hold down the ____________ key while clicking on the second.
16. To copy a file from one folder to another on the C: drive, hold down the ____________ key and drag the file to its destination.
17. A simple way to copy a selected file to the disk in the A: drive is to right-click on the file, point at the ____________ command on the pop-up menu, and choose 3½ Floppy (A) from the submenu.
18. True or false: To select a group of objects that are in consecutive order in Explorer's contents pane, click on the first and then hold down the Shift key while clicking on the last.
19. True or false: When you right-drag an object in Explorer and release the mouse button, the pop-up menu allows you to move *or* copy it to the new location.
20. True or false: The Cut and Copy buttons on Explorer's Toolbar can be used to move text, but not files.
21. If one object in Explorer's contents pane is selected and you click on another (without holding down any key), then
    a. The first object is deselected; the second is selected.
    b. The first object remains selected; the second is not selected.
    c. Both objects are selected.
    d. Neither object is selected.
22. To *move* a file from the Windows folder to the disk in the A: drive, you can
    a. Use the Cut and Paste commands on Explorer's Edit menu.
    b. Drag the file from the Windows folder and drop it on the A: drive icon.
    c. Use the Send To command.
    d. None of these techniques can be used to move the file.

Section 3.4

23. If you select an object in Explorer and press the Delete key, that object is normally moved to a folder called the ____________.
24. To create a subfolder of the Windows folder using Explorer, right-click in the contents pane and point at the ____________ command on the resulting pop-up menu.
25. Windows places a ____________ around an object's name to let you know that this object can now be renamed.
26. True or false: If you choose the Empty Recycle Bin command from its File menu, all objects in the Recycle Bin are removed from disk.

27. True or false: Shortcuts on the Desktop cannot be renamed.

28. True or false: A shortcut to a file is actually a copy of that file.

29. In Explorer, to delete the currently selected object, you can

    a. Press the Delete key.
    b. Choose the Delete command from the File menu.
    c. Click on the Toolbar's Delete button.
    d. Perform any of the above actions.

30. Suppose you have just created a shortcut in Explorer. To place this shortcut on the Desktop, you can

    a. Drag it onto the Desktop.
    b. Cut it to the Clipboard and Paste in onto the Desktop.
    c. Copy it onto the Clipboard and Paste it onto the Desktop.
    d. Perform any of the above actions.

Section 3.5

31. To start My Computer, ____________ on its Desktop icon.

32. In My Computer, to open the parent folder of the one currently open, press the ____________ key on the keyboard.

33. True or false: In My Computer, you can control whether or not a separate window is displayed when you open a new folder.

34. True or false: You can use My Computer to move, copy, delete, rename, and create files, but not folders.

35. Suppose My Computer is displaying the contents of the Windows folder, which is a subfolder of the root folder on the C: drive. Opening the Go to Folder drop-down list, you will see

    a. Every subfolder of the Windows folder.
    b. Every subfolder of the root folder on the A: drive.
    c. Every subfolder of the My Computer folder.
    d. None of the above folders.

36. In My Computer, which view options are available?

    a. Large Icons and Small Icons, but not List or Details.
    b. List and Details, but not Large Icons or Small Icons.
    c. Large Icons, Small Icons, List, and Details.
    d. Only the default view is available.

Section 3.6

37. To format a floppy disk using Explorer, begin by ____________ on the appropriate drive icon in the folder tree pane.

38. The Copy Disk command can only be used with floppy disks of the same ____________ and ____________.

39. True or false: After formatting a disk, you will not be able to access the information that had previously been stored on it.

40. True or false: When you use the Copy Disk command, all information on the source disk is erased.

41. Which option button should you select in the Format dialog box to format an unformatted diskette?

    a. Quick
    b. Full
    c. Copy system files only
    d. None of these options will format an unformatted diskette.

42. To create a bootable diskette without erasing the data on it, in the Format dialog box

    a. Select the *Quick* option button.
    b. Select the *Full* option button.
    c. Select the *Copy system files only* option button.
    d. Select the *Copy system files* check box.

Build Your Own Glossary

43. The following words and phrases are important terms that were introduced in this chapter. (They appear within the text in boldface type.) Use WordPad (see Section 2.2) to enter a definition for each term, preserving alphabetical order, into the Glossary file on the Student Disk.

Browse folders	File	Parent folder
Contents pane	Folder	Path name
Copy file or folder	Folder tree pane	Recycle Bin
Delete file or folder	Format a diskette	Rename file or folder
Directory	Long file name	Root folder
DOS file name	Move file or folder	Shortcut
Drag-and-drop	My Computer	Subfolder
Explorer		

Lab Exercises

Work each of the following exercises at your computer. Begin by turning the machine on (if necessary) to start Windows 95. If you want to produce a written record of your answers, review the material on WordPad and capturing screens in Sections 2.2 and 2.3.

Lab Exercise 1 (Section 3.2)

a. Start Windows Explorer and maximize its window.
b. Insert the Student Disk in its drive and select this drive in the folder tree pane.

c. Display, *in the folder tree pane*, the subfolders of the floppy disk drive's (root) folder. How did you do this?

d. Select the Details view option. In what year was the Dosprog application created?

e. Sort the files by modification date. Which *object* is at the top of the list? Which *file* is highest on the list?

f. Select the Large Icons view.

g. Interchange the positions of the Paint and Memo icons. Use the View menu to line up the icons. Did the icons return to their original positions?

h. Restore the Explorer window and resize it so that the Paint and Memo icons are visible, but the window is as small as possible. Which scroll bars appeared? *Optional*: Capture this Explorer window.

i. Close Explorer and remove the diskette from its drive.

Lab Exercise 2 (Section 3.3)

a. Start Explorer and maximize its window.

b. Insert the Student Disk in its drive and select this drive in the folder tree pane.

c. Select Small Icons view. In what order are the files listed?

d. Select all files (but no folders). How did you do this?

e. *Copy* the selected files to the Paint folder on the floppy disk by dragging them onto the Paint icon. Is it *necessary* to hold down the Ctrl key while dragging the files?

f. Open the Paint folder and select the Details option. How many of the listed files are *not* of the "Bitmap Image" type?

g. *Move* (by drag-and-drop) the copied files back to the root folder of the floppy disk. (Answer "Yes to All" to the Confirm Replace message.) Is it *necessary* to hold down the Shift key while dragging the files?

h. Close Explorer and remove the diskette from its drive.

Lab Exercise 3 (Section 3.3)

a. Start Explorer, maximize its window, and select the Small Icons view option.

b. Insert the Student Disk in its drive and select this drive in the folder tree pane.

c. Select the file MemoJob1 and *cut* it to the Clipboard. Then, select the file Memo and *copy* it to the Clipboard. Was either file deleted from the contents pane?

d. Minimize Explorer and any other open windows.

e. Right-click on the Desktop and choose Paste from the pop-up menu. Which file has appeared on the Desktop?

f. Restore the Explorer window and resize and move it so that the copied file is visible on the Desktop. Now, using the right-drag technique, *move* the file back to the contents pane. (Answer "Yes" to the Confirm File Replace message.) Where in the contents pane were the file name and icon placed?

g. Close Explorer and remove the diskette from its drive.

Lab Exercise 4 (Section 3.4)

a. Start Explorer, maximize its window, and select the Small Icons view option.

b. Insert the Student Disk in its drive and select this drive in the folder tree pane.

c. Create a new subfolder of the (root) floppy drive folder. It appears highlighted in the contents pane. What is it called?

d. Rename the new folder My Folder. How did you accomplish this?

e. Size the Explorer window so that an empty part of the Desktop is visible. Then, right-drag My Folder to the Desktop, release the mouse button, and choose Create Shortcut(s) Here from the pop-up menu. How would one know, just by looking at the *icon*, that it represents a shortcut?

f. Open My Folder by double-clicking on its Desktop shortcut. Does its window have both a left and right pane? *Optional*: Reduce the window to a small size and capture it.

g. Delete the My Folder *folder* from the floppy drive. Did the My Folder *window* close when the folder was deleted?

h. Close the My Folder window, if necessary, and delete its shortcut.

i. Open the Recycle Bin and delete any references to My Folder. Was a Confirm Delete message displayed?

j. Close Explorer and remove the diskette from its drive.

Lab Exercise 5 (Section 3.5)

a. Start My Computer, maximize its window, and select the List view option.

b. Choose the Options command from the View menu. In the resulting dialog box, select the lower of the two option buttons and choose OK. What is the selected option called?

c. Select the drive that contains the Windows folder by double-clicking on it. Try C: first, then others. On which drive is the Windows folder located?

d. Open the Windows folder. How many subfolders does it have?

e. Successively open the following subfolders: Start Menu, Programs, and Accessories. What are the subfolders of Accessories?

f. Display the Go to Folder drop-down list. Are all the folders you've opened in this exercise listed there? *Optional*: Close the drop-down list and size the current window so that it's not much larger than this list. Then, capture the active window and reopen the drop-down list.

g. Select Recycle Bin from the Go to Folder list. In the new window, open the Go to Folder list again. Is the Accessories folder still listed there?

h. Close the Recycle Bin window.

Lab Exercise 6 (Section 3.5) Repeat Exercise 2, replacing every occurrence of *Explorer* by *My Computer* and *folder tree pane* or *contents pane* by *My Computer window.*

Lab Exercise 7 (Section 3.6) [This exercise requires a blank floppy disk.]

a. Start Windows Explorer and insert a blank diskette in its drive.

b. Check the contents of the diskette by selecting the appropriate drive from the folder tree. What is displayed in the contents pane?

c. If the diskette contains any files or folders, do *not* continue this exercise! Otherwise, format the diskette, selecting the *Full* option and deselecting all check boxes in the Format dialog box. When you choose the Start command button, what message appears at the bottom of the dialog box?

d. Again use Explorer to check the contents of the diskette. Are any files or folders listed now?

e. Open the Format dialog box again. This time, select the *Copy system files only* option button (*not* the check box), and choose Start. What message is displayed in the dialog box?

f. One more time, check the diskette's contents. What are they?

g. Close Explorer and remove the diskette from its drive.

If You Want to Learn More ...

The notes presented here allow you to delve more deeply into some of the topics covered in this chapter.

Other ways to start Explorer

When you start Explorer from the Start menu's Programs submenu, this action also opens the root folder of the drive that contains the Windows files. You can also start Explorer in the following ways:

- Right-click on the Start button and then choose Explore from the pop-up menu. In this case, the Start Menu subfolder of the Windows folder will be opened.
- Right-click on the My Computer icon (or any folder icon) and then choose Explore from the pop-up menu. Here, the My Computer window (or the folder's window) will be opened in the process.

Of course, you can also put a shortcut to Explorer on the Desktop and start Explorer by double-clicking on this icon. An even better idea is to put several Explorer shortcuts on the Desktop and configure them to automatically open your favorite folders. Here's how:

1. Create a shortcut to Explorer as described in Section 3.4. (Its file is located in the Windows folder.)
2. Right-click on the Explorer shortcut's icon and choose Properties from the pop-up menu.
3. Click on the Shortcut tab in the Properties dialog box.
4. In the Target text box, type C:\EXPLORER.EXE /E, immediately followed by the path name for the folder you want to be opened when Explorer starts. For example, to automatically open the Windows folder, type: C:\EXPLORER.EXE /E,C:\WINDOWS
5. Choose the OK command button.
6. Rename the shortcut appropriately.

Starting up with Explorer running

If Explorer, My Computer, or any folder window is open when you shut down Windows, that window will open automatically the next time Windows is started. If you do not want the window to open in this situation, hold down the Shift key when you hear the "start-up sound" — just as the Desktop icons begin to appear on the screen. Holding down the Shift key also causes Windows to ignore the applications present in your StartUp folder (see Section 4.2); they, too, will not open when Windows starts.

Keyboard alternatives in Explorer

There are many keyboard shortcuts that work with Explorer (most also work with My Computer). Here are a few that you might find useful:

- Asterisk (on the numeric keypad) expands all folders in the folder tree pane.
- Backspace opens the parent of the current folder.
- Ctrl+A selects all objects in the contents pane.
- Ctrl+C or Ctrl+X copies or cuts, respectively, all selected objects to the Clipboard; Ctrl+V pastes objects from the Clipboard.
- Plus or Minus (on the numeric keypad) respectively expands or collapses the folder selected in the folder tree pane.
- Shift+Del deletes the selected objects without sending them to the Recycle Bin.

For a complete list of shortcut keys, see Appendix A.

Recycle Bin properties

As you know, when you "delete" a file, folder, or shortcut that resides on a hard drive or the Desktop, it is normally sent to the Recycle Bin after you respond Yes to a confirmation message. (Objects deleted from floppy disks or cut to the Clipboard are not placed in the Recycle Bin; they are immediately deleted.) To change the way the Recycle Bin works:

1. Right-click on the Recycle Bin icon and choose Properties from the resulting pop-up menu. The Recycle Bin Properties dialog box will be displayed.
2. If you want objects removed immediately when you delete them, select the *Do not send files to Recycle Bin* check box.
3. If you don't want a confirmation message displayed when you delete objects, deselect the *Display delete confirmation dialog* check box.

The Recycle Bin Properties dialog box offers additional options that you might want to explore on your own.

More on double-clicking files and folders

As you know, when you double-click a file or folder in Explorer, My Computer, or any folder window, that object is opened. Here are a couple of other things you should know about this concept (still more will be said in Section 4.4):

- If you want to open several objects at once, select them and hold down the Ctrl key while double-clicking on one of them. (If you just double-click on one of the selected objects, only that object will open.)

- In My Computer or any folder window, double-clicking on a folder icon opens a folder window with a single-pane view of its contents. If you want an Explorer-like, dual-pane view instead, right-click on the folder icon and choose Explore from the pop-up menu.

Where to go from here

Here's where to find more information about some of the topics discussed in this chapter.

- Copying, moving, deleting, and renaming files and folders (using the Find utility) — Section 4.3
- Creating shortcuts:

  On the Start menu and Programs submenu — Section 4.2
  Using the Find utility — Section 4.3
- Properties of shortcuts — Section 4.5

CHAPTER 4

Using Windows Efficiently

In Chapters 2 and 3, we presented basic information about working with applications, documents, files, folders, and disks. You will probably make use of some of this material every time you use Windows. In this chapter, we present additional information about these topics. Although none of this new material is critical, it should help you to use Windows more productively. You will learn:

1. To move the Taskbar to another location, increase its size, and hide it from view.
2. To rearrange (tile or cascade) open application windows, or minimize them all at once, if so desired.
3. To customize the Start button menus by adding or deleting items from them.
4. To use the Windows Find utility to search for files and folders on your hard disk.
5. To manipulate (for example, move or copy) the files or folders found by the Find utility.
6. To associate a file type (extension) with a specific application so that certain actions (such as open or print) can be performed on a document without first starting the corresponding application.
7. To display the property sheet for a file, folder, or shortcut, and interpret the information provided on it.

4.1 *Tricks with the Taskbar*

The **Taskbar** (Figure 1) is a key element in the Windows 95 interface. As you know, it contains the Start button, which makes it easy to open certain programs and documents (see Section 2.1) and a button for each open application, which makes it easy to switch from one to another (see Section 2.3). Your Taskbar may contain other items as well: perhaps a digital clock or a few small icons for, say, adjusting speaker volume or monitoring print jobs. In this section, we will discuss additional features of the Taskbar.

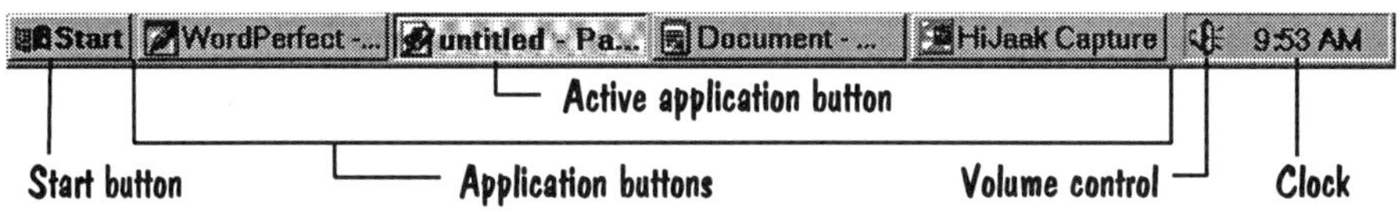

Figure 1 A Typical Taskbar

Changing the Way the Taskbar is Displayed

By default, the Taskbar is positioned at the bottom of the screen and is always visible, even when application windows are maximized. If you wish, you can:

- Increase the size of the Taskbar.
- Reposition the Taskbar at the left, right, or top edge of the screen.
- Hide the Taskbar from view.
- Remove the clock from the Taskbar.

We will now describe how to perform each of these tasks.

Increasing the Size of the Taskbar If several applications are running, their Taskbar buttons will be reduced in size to fit on the Taskbar. This, in turn, limits the amount of text that can be displayed on each. For example, in Figure 1, notice how the text on the first three application buttons has been truncated, as indicated by the ellipses (...). To increase the size of the Taskbar, and restore its buttons to their normal size:

1. Move the mouse cursor over the top edge of the Taskbar. It will become a double-headed arrow when positioned properly.
2. Drag the cursor up until the Taskbar is the desired height, as indicated by the moving outline. The Taskbar buttons will be

resized and repositioned when you release the mouse button.

A two-row high Taskbar is shown here:

The size and style of the text on the Taskbar buttons is determined by the font selected for the active window's title bar. You can change this font and, in so doing, the button font as well, from within the Display Properties dialog box. See Section 5.3 for the details of this procedure.

Repositioning the Taskbar The Taskbar can be positioned at any of the four edges of the screen. To move the Taskbar from its current location to another edge of the screen:

1. Position the mouse cursor over an empty part of the Taskbar.
2. Hold down the left mouse button and drag the cursor toward one of the other screen edges. As you approach this edge, an outline will appear indicating where the Taskbar will be repositioned.
3. Release the mouse button; the Taskbar will be displayed in the new location. The following figure shows it at the left screen edge.

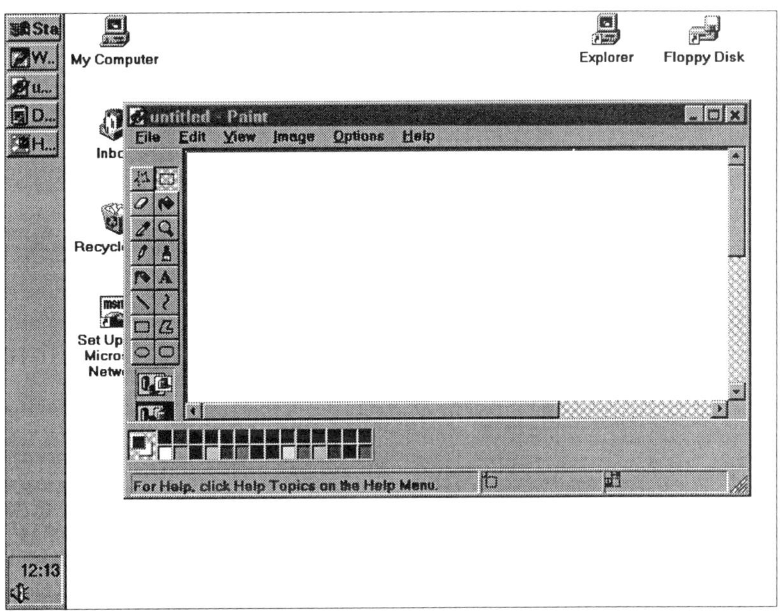

Hiding the Taskbar The Taskbar is convenient to have around, but it does take up space on the Desktop. At times, you may want to hide the Taskbar so that application windows can use the entire screen. To hide the Taskbar (or redisplay it if it is currently hidden):

1. Click on the Start button to open the Start menu, point at the Settings option, and choose the Taskbar item on the resulting submenu. The Taskbar Properties dialog box, shown in Figure 2, will be displayed. (You can also open the Taskbar Properties dialog box by right-clicking on an empty part of the Taskbar and choosing Properties from the resulting pop-up menu.)

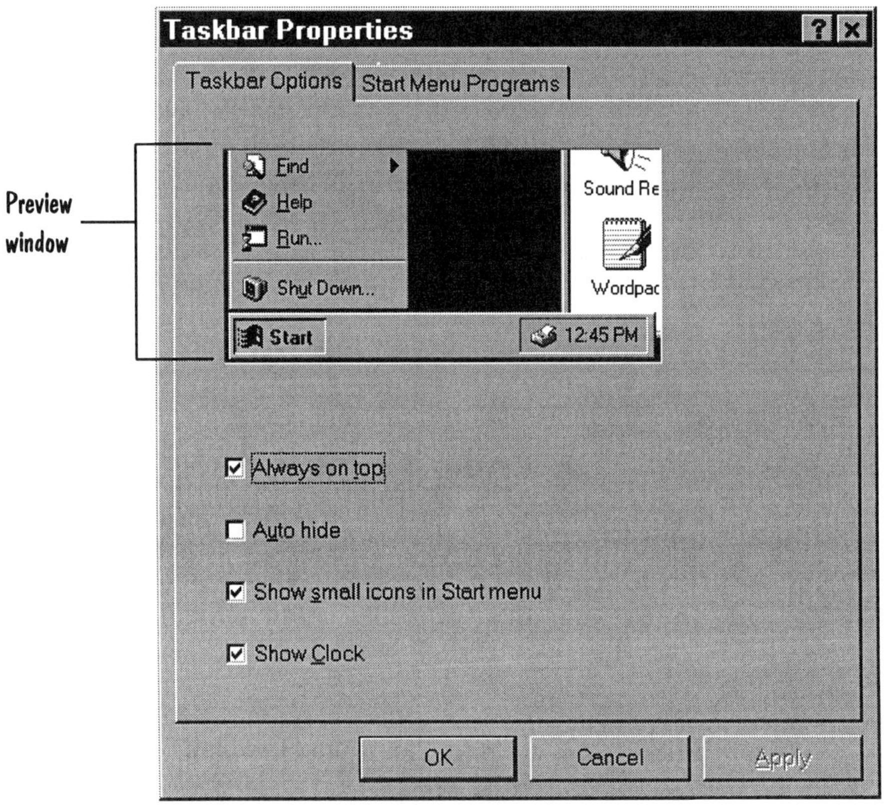

Figure 2 The Taskbar Properties Dialog Box

2. Select the *Always on top* check box to prevent the Taskbar from being obscured by windows that might otherwise cover it.
3. Select the *Auto hide* check box to hide the Taskbar. When Auto hide is selected, the Taskbar is reduced to a thin line at the edge

of the screen. To temporarily redisplay the Taskbar, point the mouse at this thin line. Moving the mouse pointer away from that edge of the screen will cause the Taskbar to disappear again.

4. Choose the OK command button to put your changes into effect and close the dialog box, or choose the Apply button to put your changes into effect without closing the dialog box.

NOTE

Selecting the "auto hide" feature is a convenient way to increase the amount of screen real estate available to your running applications. Be aware, however, that if *Always on top* is not selected and an application is running full-screen, pointing at the Taskbar "line" will not display the Taskbar; it will still be obscured by the application window! Also keep in mind that you can *always* display the Taskbar (and simultaneously open the Start menu) by pressing the Ctrl+Esc keystroke combination.

Hiding the Clock To hide the Taskbar clock (which provides a little more room for application buttons):

1. Open the Taskbar Properties dialog box (Figure 2), as described above.
2. Deselect the *Show clock* check box. (Reselecting this check box will, of course, redisplay the clock if it is currently hidden.)
3. Choose the OK command button.

Manipulating Application Windows from the Taskbar

Using the Taskbar, you can also:

- Minimize all open windows simultaneously, or restore all windows that have been minimized in this way.
- Rearrange windows by **cascading** or **tiling** them on the Desktop.

These operations are carried out by:

1. Right-clicking on an empty part of the Taskbar, which opens the menu shown in Figure 3.
2. Choosing the desired option from this menu. (Recall that choosing the Properties item displays the Taskbar Properties dialog box.)

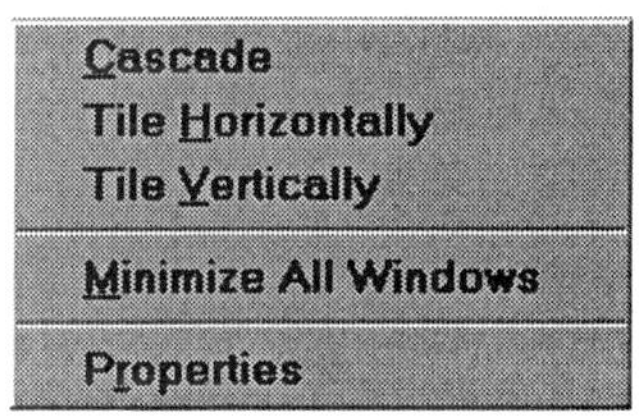

Figure 3 The Pop-up Taskbar Menu

Arranging Windows on the Desktop The first three items on the pop-up menu shown in Figure 3 affect the way open application windows are grouped on the Desktop:

- Choosing the Cascade command overlaps the windows in such a way that little more than the title bars of the back windows can be seen (Figure 4). The window that was active when this command was issued becomes the one in front. To bring another window to the front, just switch to the corresponding application.
- Choosing the Tile Horizontally command arranges the windows in a non-overlapping fashion, one above the other. The effect is shown in Figure 5.
- Choosing the Tile Vertically command arranges the windows side-by-side in a non-overlapping fashion. See Figure 6.

NOTE

The Cascade and Tile commands only apply to the windows that are open when the command is issued. If another window is opened or restored later on, it will not be included in the grouping. However, if you maximize or minimize one of the grouped windows and then restore it, the original cascading or tiling will also be restored.

Minimizing All Open Windows The Minimize All Windows command on the pop-up Taskbar menu (shown in Figure 3) does just

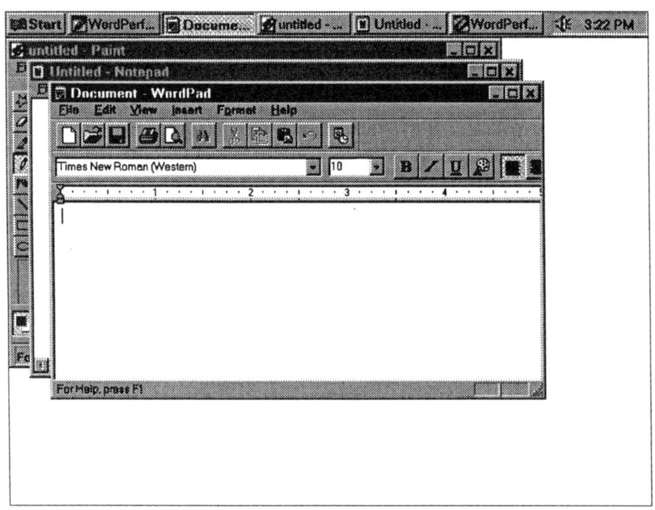

Figure 4 Cascading Windows

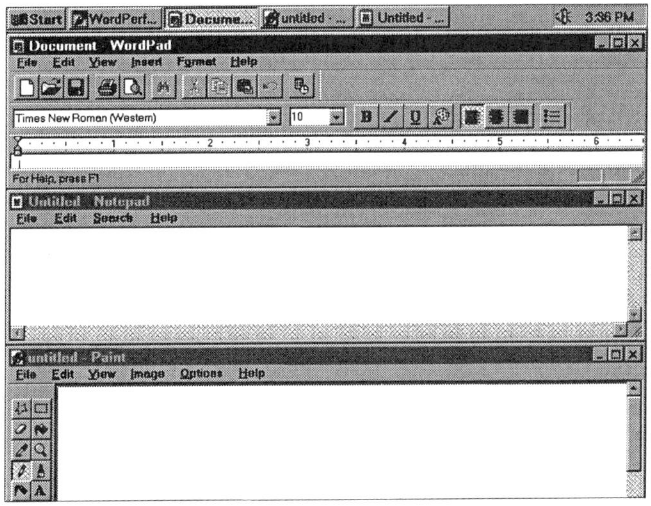

Figure 5 Windows Tiled Horizontally

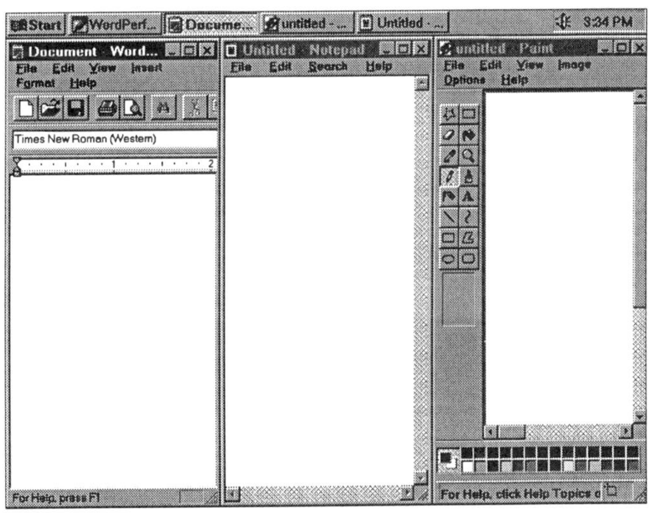

Figure 6 Windows Tiled Vertically

that — it minimizes all open windows. When you reopen the pop-up Taskbar menu after issuing this command, you will notice another available option — Undo Minimize All. As you might guess, choosing this command restores all windows that were reduced to Taskbar buttons by the previous Minimize All Windows command.

4-1 TUTORIAL

Try the following exercises on your own.

1. Turn on your computer, if necessary, to start Windows 95 and close any open windows.
2. If the Taskbar is not visible on the screen, press Ctrl+Esc to display it and the Start menu; then press Esc to close the latter.
3. Reposition the Taskbar at another edge of the screen by dragging it there; that is, position the mouse pointer over an empty part of the Taskbar, press (and hold down) the mouse button, move the pointer to the desired edge of the screen, and release the button.
4. Position the Taskbar at the bottom edge of the screen.
5. Change the size of the Taskbar: Position the mouse pointer over the top edge of the Taskbar (the pointer will become a double-headed arrow), drag the pointer upward (the Taskbar will grow in size), and release the mouse button. Now, return the Taskbar to its former size by a similar process.
6. Open the Taskbar Properties dialog box by clicking on the Start button, pointing at the Settings option, and choosing the Taskbar command from the resulting submenu.
7. Select the *Auto-hide* check box and choose the Apply command button. The Taskbar will disappear from the screen. To redisplay it, move the mouse pointer past the bottom edge of the screen. Move the pointer away from the bottom edge of the screen, and the Taskbar will disappear again.
8. Deselect Auto-hide and choose the OK command button to close the dialog box.
9. Open the WordPad application (from the Accessories submenu of the Start menu's Programs option) and maximize it. Then, open the Paint application (also on the Accessories submenu) and maximize it.
10. Right-click on an empty part of the Taskbar, successively choose each of the following commands from the resulting pop-up menu, and notice the effect. (You will have to reopen this menu before issuing a new command.)
    - Cascade
    - Tile Horizontally
    - Tile Vertically
    - Minimize All Windows
    - Undo Minimize All
    - Properties
11. Close all open windows.

4.2 Customizing the Start Button Menus

When Windows 95 was installed on your computer, it automatically created several Start menu submenus and placed various items on them. Moreover, if a Windows application was installed later on, it created additional items on one of the submenus. In this section, we will demonstrate how you can "manually" add items to, or remove them from, the Start menu or one of its Programs option's submenus[*].

The What and Why of the Start Button Menus

Each item on a Start button menu is actually a *shortcut* (see Section 3.4) to a file or folder. The shortcuts on the Start button menus are themselves small files stored in various related folders. The shortcuts on the Start menu itself are located in the Start Menu subfolder of the Windows folder, and those in the Programs option submenu are located in the Programs subfolder of the Start Menu folder. Similarly, each submenu of the Programs option corresponds to a subfolder of the Programs folder. Part of the folder tree is shown above.

The shortcuts on the Start button menus may represent applications, documents, or folders. In fact, any file or folder listed in Explorer can be placed on these menus. Clicking on a menu item (shortcut) opens the corresponding file or folder. To be more specific, clicking on

- A shortcut to a program file starts the corresponding application.
- A shortcut to a document starts the application associated with it and then opens the document within that application.
- A shortcut to a folder opens the corresponding folder, displaying its contents in a window.

Thus, the Start button menus can be configured to provide easy access to your most-used applications, documents, and folders. The Start menu itself is an especially convenient location for shortcuts to your favorite things. Although Desktop icons can be used for the same purpose, they are often buried beneath an open window or two. The Start menu, on the other hand, is always a mouse click (or, at worst, the Ctrl+Esc keystroke) away from the task at hand.

[*]For simplicity's sake, we will refer to the Start menu itself or any of its Programs option's submenus as a **Start button menu**.

Adding Menu Items by Drag-and-Drop

If you want to add an item to the Start menu itself, the easiest way to do it is by dragging the relevant file or folder (or a shortcut to it) onto the Start button. To be more specific:

1. Locate the file or folder you want to add to the Start menu:
   - If you are seeking a particular folder, it's usually easiest to start Explorer and find it by "brute force" — scroll down the folder tree pane, expanding the various branches if necessary, until you spot the folder you want.
   - If you are seeking a document, a relatively easy way to determine its location is to start the application that created it and display the Open dialog box. You will either see the desired file listed there or be able to find it with a little browsing.
   - If you are seeking a particular program file, you should be able to discover its name and the folder containing it by checking the application's documentation.
2. Drag its icon onto the Start button and release the mouse button.

TIP

Often, the easiest way to locate a particular file or folder is to use the Windows Find utility, which is described in Section 4.3. Find will search your entire hard disk, if necessary, for the desired object while you sit back and relax.

The next time you click on the Start button, you will see the new item displayed near the top of the Start menu. In fact, if you add several items to the Start menu, they will be grouped, in alphabetical order, in a section at the top of this menu. A typical example is shown at the right.

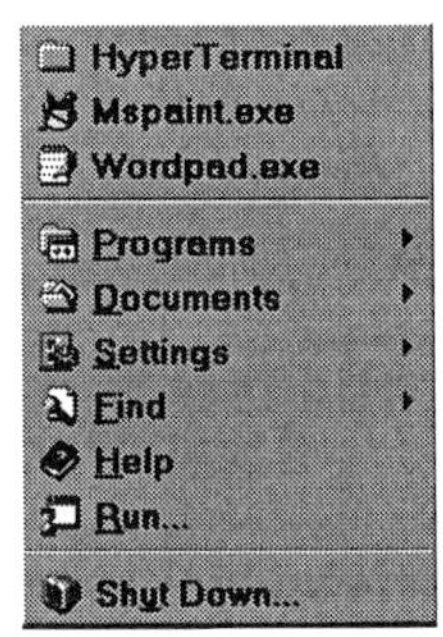

NOTE

After adding a shortcut to the Start menu, you may want to rename it. Unfortunately, this takes some work. To rename the new shortcut, start Explorer or My Computer and open the folder in which all Start menu shortcuts are stored — the Start Menu subfolder of the Windows folder. Locate the desired shortcut and rename it using one of the techniques described in Section 3.4.

A More Flexible Way to Add Menu Items

Although the drag-and-drop technique that was just described is easy to carry out, it can only be used to add items to the Start menu itself. At times, you will want to add an item to a specific submenu of the Start menu's Programs option. In this case, you cannot use drag-and-drop. Instead, proceed as follows:

1. Open the Taskbar Properties dialog box by either:
   - Pointing at the Settings option on the Start menu and choosing Taskbar from the resulting submenu.

   or
   - Right-clicking on an empty part of the Taskbar and choosing Properties from the resulting pop-up menu.
2. Click on the Start Menu Programs tab. The corresponding page of dialog box will be displayed, as shown in Figure 7.

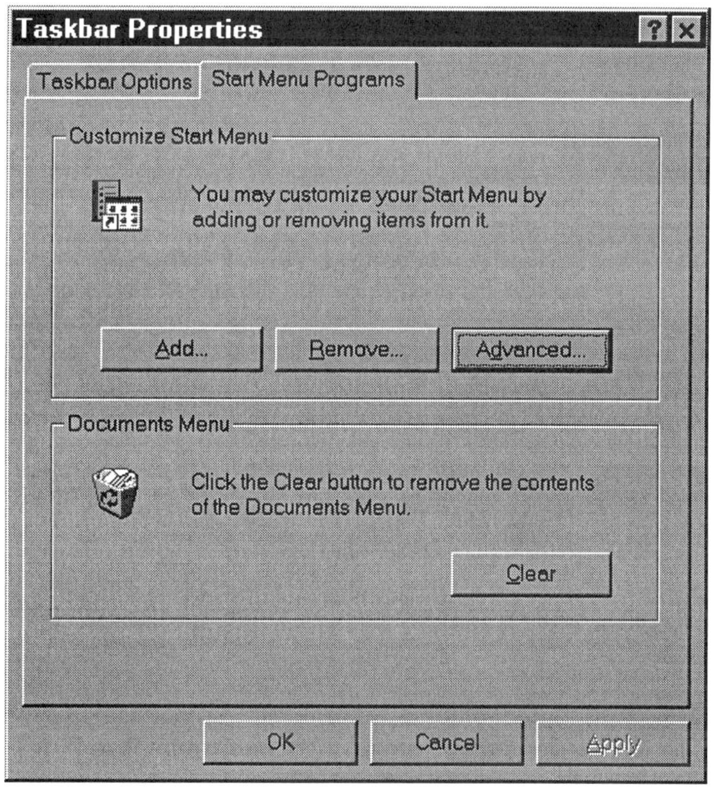

Figure 7 Clicking on the Start Menu Programs Tab

3. Choose the Add command button. This action starts a Create Shortcut "wizard" and opens the corresponding dialog box.
4. If you know the path name (see Section 3.1) of the file or folder for which you want to create a shortcut, type it in the Command line text box and skip to step 6.
5. If you don't know the desired object's path name, choose the Browse command button, which opens a Browse dialog box (Figure 8) to help you locate the file or folder. (Browsing folders is discussed in Section 3.5.)

   By default, this Browse dialog box lists only folders and program files. If you are looking for a document, select the "All files" item from the *Files of type* drop-down list to display all files contained in the current folder.

   When you locate the file or folder you are seeking, double-click on it or select it and activate the Open command button. The Browse dialog box will close and the path name of the object you have selected will appear in the Command line text box of the Create Shortcut dialog box.
6. Click on the Next command button. The Select Program Folder dialog box will open (Figure 9) and display a folder tree showing the Start Menu folder (which contains the shortcuts on the Start menu) and its subfolders (which correspond to the Programs option menu and its submenus).

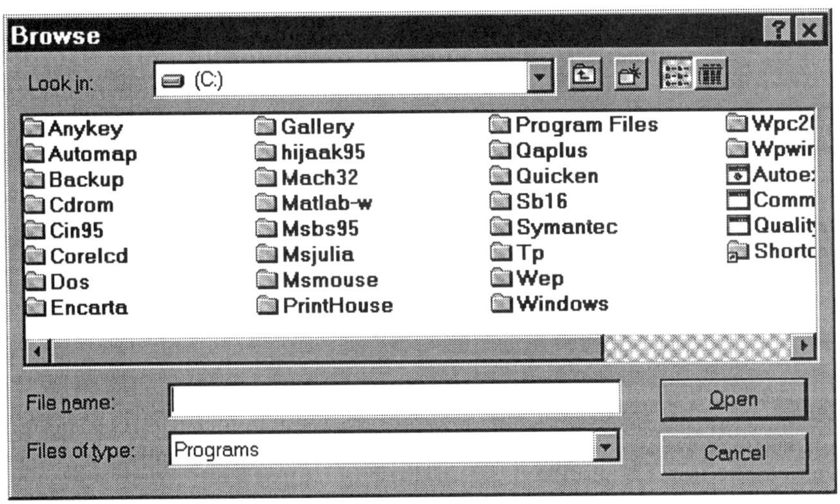

Figure 8 A Browse Dialog Box

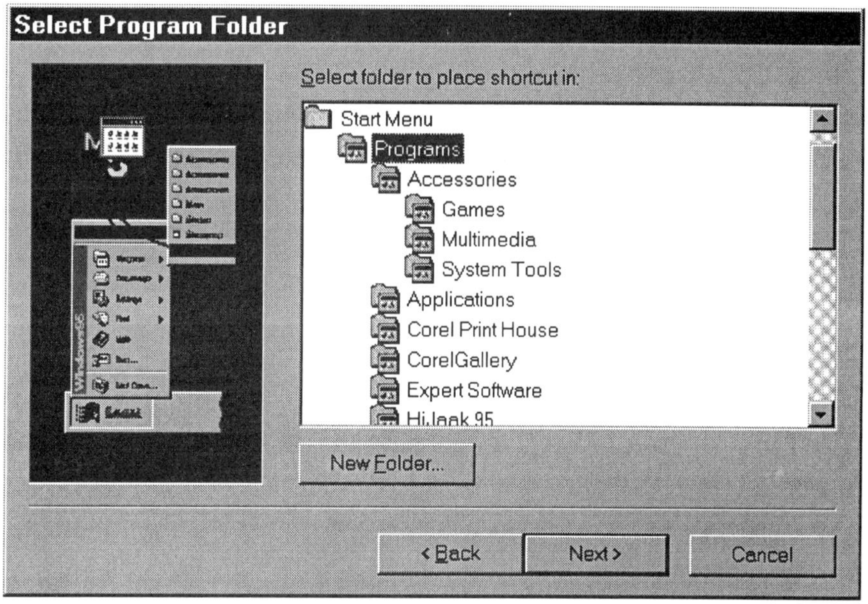

Figure 9 The Select Program Folder Dialog Box

7. If you want to create a new submenu, select the folder corresponding to the menu on which you want your new submenu to appear, and activate the New Folder command button. (At the right, we show the result of selecting Accessories and then choosing New Folder.) A new subfolder will be displayed. To rename it, just type a new name.

8. Select (click on) the folder that corresponds to the menu in which you want the new shortcut to appear.
9. Choose the Next command button. A new dialog box will appear allowing you to select a name for the new shortcut. If you don't want to use the default name, type a new name in the text box.
10. Choose the Finish command button, which returns you to the Taskbar Properties dialog box.
11. Choose the OK command button to close this dialog box.

TIP

The Windows\Start Menu\Programs folder contains a special subfolder called StartUp. Each application, document, and folder contained in the StartUp folder automatically opens every time you start Windows.

Thus, if you run certain applications whenever you use Windows, you might consider adding their shortcuts to the StartUp folder.

Removing Items from the Start Button Menus

A menu item can be removed from a Start button menu in the following way:

1. Open the Taskbar Properties dialog box as described above.
2. Click on the Start Menu Programs tab. The dialog box page shown in Figure 7 (on page 137) will be displayed.
3. Choose the Remove command button. This action opens the Remove Shortcuts/Folders dialog box shown in Figure 10.

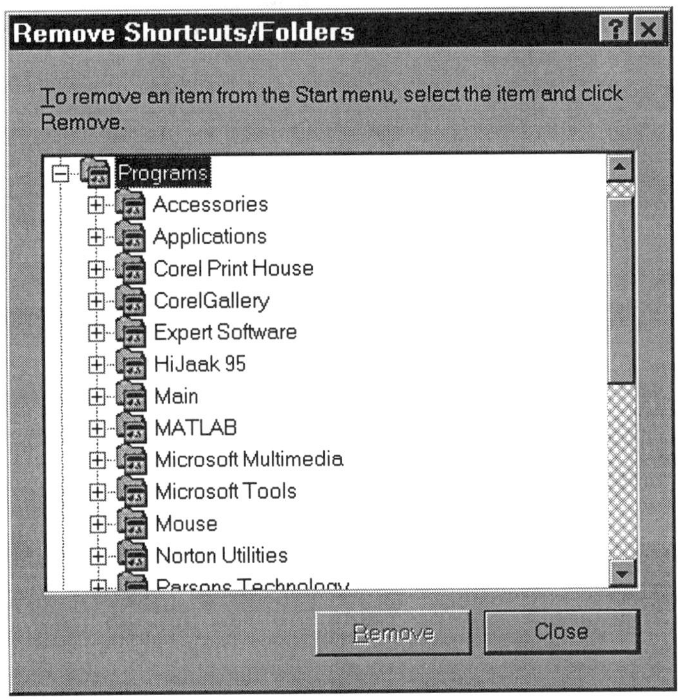

Figure 10 Remove Shortcuts/Folders Dialog Box

4. Select (click on) the folder corresponding to the menu on which the desired item is located. (You may have to expand a branch of the tree to display a particular subfolder.)

5. Choose the Remove command button. Be aware that when you remove a folder, all shortcuts within it are removed as well! (You may see a warning message at this point.)
6. Choose the Close command button. The Remove Shortcuts/Folders dialog box will close and you will be returned to the Taskbar Properties dialog box.
7. Choose the OK command button to close the Taskbar Properties dialog box, completing the process.

Other Ways to Add or Remove Menu Items

If you examine the Start Menu Programs page of the Taskbar Properties dialog box (Figure 7), you will notice two additional command buttons: Advanced and Clear.

The Advanced command button

Choosing the Advanced button starts Explorer, displaying a folder tree with the Start Menu folder at its root. Then, using the techniques described in Sections 3.3 and 3.4, you can:

- Place a shortcut in the Start Menu folder or any of its subfolders. This action adds an item to the corresponding menu.
- Delete an existing shortcut from a folder, which removes the corresponding item from its menu.
- Move or copy a shortcut from one folder to another, thus moving or copying the corresponding item from one menu to another.

If you are especially comfortable with Explorer and the way it works, you may find that using the Advanced button is preferable to the other methods for customizing the Start button menus.

NOTE

Since the Advanced button does nothing more than start Explorer, the techniques just described for adding, removing, or moving menu items can be accomplished without opening the Taskbar Properties dialog box. Just start Explorer in the usual way, or right-click on the Start button and choose Explore from the pop-up menu, which starts Explorer and opens the Start Menu folder.

The Clear command button

Choosing the Clear command button in the Taskbar Properties dialog box removes all items from the Documents submenu of the Start menu. No warning message is given.

TIP

If you would like to remove *selected items* from the Documents menu, start Explorer and open the Recent subfolder of the Windows folder. This folder contains the shortcuts on the Documents submenu. To selectively delete items from this submenu, just delete the corresponding shortcuts from the Recent folder!

TUTORIAL

Try the following exercises on your own.

1. Turn on your computer, if necessary, to start Windows 95 and close any open windows.
2. Start Explorer (from the Programs option submenu of the Start menu) and open the Accessories subfolder of the Program Files folder.
3. Add a shortcut for the WordPad application to the Start menu by dragging the Wordpad file name from the contents pane onto the Start button. (If you now click on the latter, you will see "Wordpad" listed toward the top of the Start menu.)
4. Now, add a shortcut for the Paint application to the Programs option submenu of the Start menu:
   - Open the Taskbar Properties dialog box by right-clicking on an empty part of the Taskbar and choosing Properties from the resulting submenu.
   - Click on the Start Menu Programs tab in this dialog box.
   - Choose the Add command button, which starts the Create Shortcut wizard.
   - Now enter the path name for Paint in the *Command line* text box by choosing the Browse command button, opening the Accessories subfolder of the Program Files folder, selecting "Mspaint", and pressing the Enter key.
   - Choose the Next command button, which opens the Select Program Folder dialog box.
   - To tell Windows that you want the shortcut on the Programs submenu, select the Programs folder in the tree and choose the Next command button, which opens another dialog box.
   - Finally, select a name for the new menu item: Type *Paint* in the text box and choose the Finish command button. (You can check, if you want, that a Paint item now appears on the Programs submenu of the Start menu.)
5. Remove the WordPad item from the Start menu:
   - On the Start Menu Programs page of the Taskbar Properties dialog box, choose the Remove command button.
   - In the resulting folder tree, select Wordpad (which is listed as a subfolder of Start Menu, toward the bottom of the tree).

- Choose the Remove command button; then choose Close.

6. Now remove the Paint item from the Programs submenu in another way:
   - On the Start Menu Programs page of the Taskbar Properties dialog box, choose the Advanced command button. Explorer will start, opening the Start Menu folder.
   - Open the Programs subfolder (by clicking on it) in the left pane; then select the Paint shortcut in the right pane.
   - Press the Delete key (or choose Delete from the right-click pop-up menu), answer Yes to the query in the resulting dialog box, and the process is complete.
7. Close all open windows.

4.3 The Windows Find Utility

A typical hard disk contains thousands of files spread across dozens of folders. As a result, locating a particular file or folder (say, to create a shortcut for it) can be a daunting task. Fortunately, Windows provides a powerful utility, called **Find**, that helps you with the search. In this section, we will discuss how to use Find to locate files and folders. (If your computer is connected to a network, Find can also help you search for computers on the network.)

The Find Utility Window

There are several ways to start the Find utility:

- Click on the Start button, point at the Find option, and choose Files or Folders from the resulting submenu.
- Right-click on the Start button, the My Computer icon, or any folder icon, and choose the Find command from the pop-up menu.
- Click on an empty part of the Desktop and then press the F3 function key.
- In Explorer, either press the F3 function key, or point at the Find command on the Tools menu and choose Files or Folders from the resulting submenu.

In any case, the Find window (Figure 11, on the next page) will open.

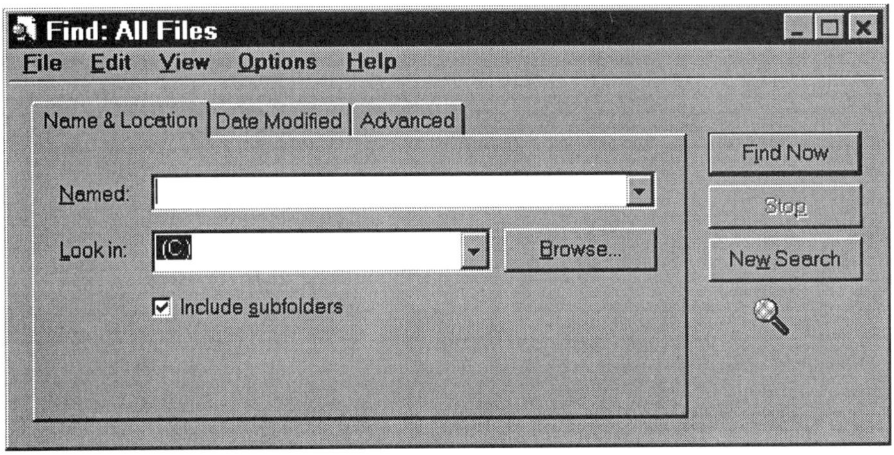

Figure 11 The Find Window

Since Find is an application, its window can be resized, minimized, or maximized. Notice (in Figure 11) that the Find window contains both pull-down menus and tabs. The menus provide capabilities that are similar to those of Explorer; the tabs supply options that help narrow the search for a particular file or folder.

Performing a Simple Search

Typically, we use the Find utility to locate a file or folder because:

- We have forgotten its name.

or

- We don't know in which folder it is located.

If you know the name of the file or folder ...

If you know the name (or at least part of the name) of the file or folder you are seeking, proceed as follows:

1. Start the Find utility, as described above.
2. Type the name (or partial name) of the file or folder in the *Named* text box. (The *Named* drop-down list contains the entries for recent searches.)
3. If you know the folder that contains the object you are seeking, enter that folder in the *Look in* text box. As an alternative, you can choose the Browse button and then select the desired folder from the folder tree. If you don't know in which folder to look, enter the drive designation of the disk you are searching — for example, C: — in the *Look in* text box.

4. Select the *Include subfolders* check box if you want to search, not only the *Look in* folder, but all its subfolders as well.
5. Choose the Find Now command button to start the search. All files and folders in the specified folders whose names contain the text entered in the *Named* text box will be displayed in a Search Results window in the lower part of the Find window; the Status bar indicates the number of files found (Figure 12).

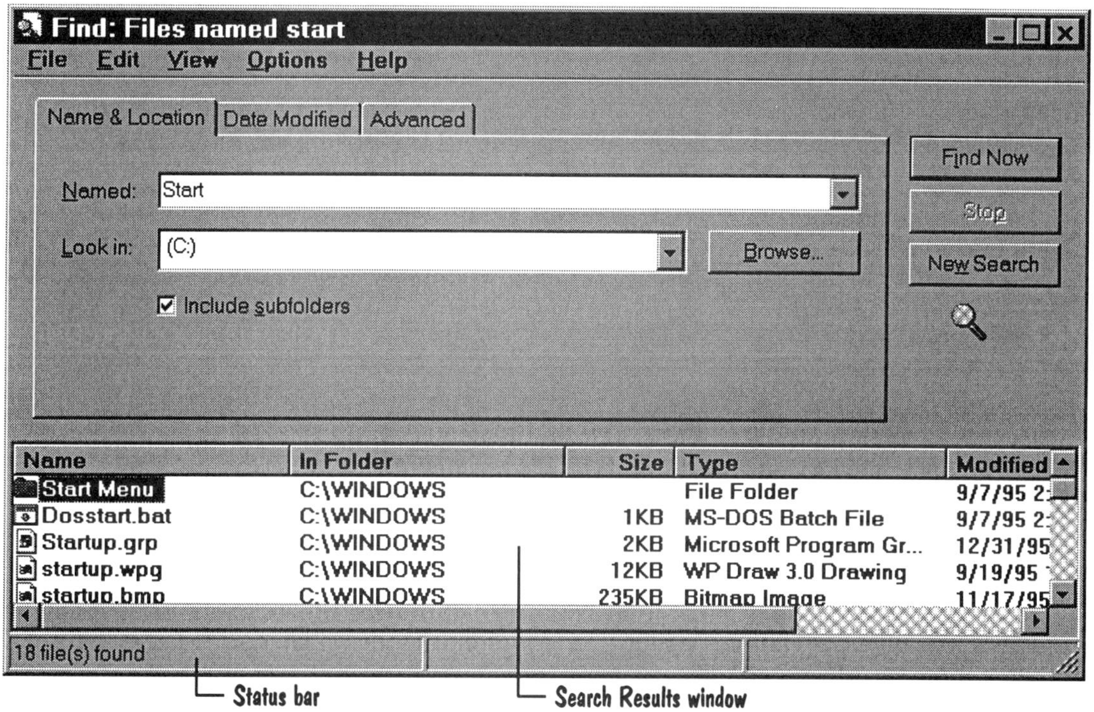

Figure 12 The Find Window After a Search

TIP

You can use *wildcards* in the *Named* text box to narrow the search. A **wildcard** is a symbol that represents one or more characters of any kind. Windows uses two wildcards:

- The symbol * represents any number of consecutive characters.
- The symbol ? represents any single character.

For example, in the *Named* text box, entering

.	displays all files and folders.
*.exe	displays all files with extension *exe*.

start??.*	displays all files with names that contain *start*, followed by two characters and any extension.
?s?	displays all files and folders with *s* somewhere in the name from the second to the next-to-last character.
?s?.*	displays all files with a three-letter name and *s* as the second letter.

Refining the Search Criteria

If you do not know the name of the file you are seeking or just want to narrow the search (so that fewer files will be found), use the Date Modified and/or Advanced pages of the Find window.

The Find windows's Date Modified tab

The Date Modified page is most useful in finding a *document* when:

- You know the approximate date that the file was last saved (perhaps because you have a dated paper copy of the document).

or

- The document was created or modified recently.

To start a search in one of these cases:

1. Start the Find utility, if necessary.
2. Fill in information on the Name & Location page, as described above. If you do not know certain information, leave the corresponding text box blank.
3. Click on the Date Modified tab to display the options shown in Figure 13.

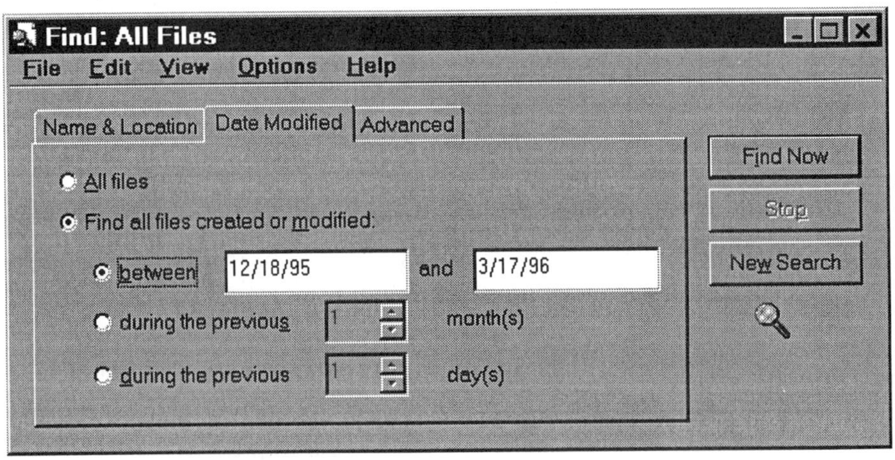

Figure 13 The Date Modified Page of the Find Window

4. Select the *Find all files created or modified* option button.
5. If you know the approximate date that the file was last saved, select the *between* option button and, in the two text boxes, enter dates that bracket the date the document was last saved.

   If the document was modified recently, you could select either the *during the previous days* or the *during the previous months* option button (depending on how recently the document was modified); then enter an appropriate number in the corresponding text box.
6. Begin the search by choosing the Find Now button. All files that match the search criteria will be displayed in the Search Results window, as shown in Figure 12.

The Find window's Advanced tab

The Advanced page of the Find window allows you to refine a search in a few additional ways. After providing as much information as possible on the Name & Location and Date Modified pages, click on the Advanced tab to display the options shown in Figure 14. Then:

- You can restrict the search to files of a specified type by selecting it from the *Of type* drop-down list.
- You can search for a piece (*string*) of text in a document by entering that string in the *Containing text* box. (This is an extremely useful option for locating a document. Just supply any piece of text that is unique to that document!)
- You can specify the minimum or maximum sizes for the files to be included in the search by using the *Size is* drop-down list and text box.

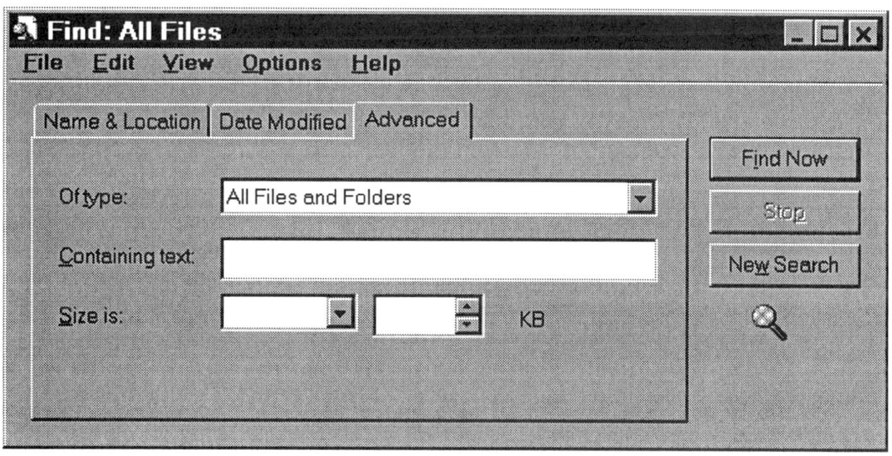

Figure 14 The Advanced Page of the Find Window

NOTE

In addition to Find Now, there are two other command buttons in the Find window:

- While a search is taking place, choosing the Stop button discontinues the search.
- Choosing the New Search button resets all search criteria to their defaults and clears all files and folders (if any) from the Search Results window.

Using the Results of a Search

As you know, when a search is complete, the files and folders found are displayed in the Search Results window at the bottom of the Find window (see Figure 12). For all practical purposes, this window can be used as if it were a My Computer window or the contents pane of an Explorer window. To be more specific:

- You can display the files in the Search Results window in different ways by choosing Large Icons, Small Icons, List, or Details from the View menu. The advantages of each view option are discussed in Section 3.2. (In Figure 12, the Details option is turned on.)
- You can select objects in the Search Results window using the techniques described in Section 3.3.
- Selected objects can be cut or copied to the Clipboard (so they can be pasted into other folders or onto the Desktop) by choosing Cut or Copy from the Edit menu, or by right-clicking on a selected object and choosing Cut or Copy from the resulting pop-up menu.
- You can drag-and-drop objects from the Search Results window to another folder, onto the Desktop, or onto the Recycle Bin.
- You can create a shortcut for an object in the Search Results window using the techniques described in Section 3.4.
- You can delete, rename, or open a selected object by choosing the corresponding command from either the File menu or the menu that pops up when you right-click the object. (An object can also be opened by double-clicking on it.)
- You can print selected documents by choosing Print from the File menu or the right-click pop-up menu.

4·3 TUTORIAL

Try the following exercises on your own.

1. Turn on your computer, if necessary, to start Windows 95 and close any open windows.

2. Start the Find utility by clicking on the Start button, pointing at the Find command, and clicking on Files or Folders.
3. Try to find the file that starts the Paint application. It is located somewhere on the drive that contains the Windows folder.
   - Enter this drive (for example, C:) in the *Look in* text box and type `Paint` in the *Named* text box.
   - Select (if necessary) the *Include subfolders* check box.
   - Choose the Find Now command button. After a few moments a list of files will appear in the lower part of the Find window, all of which include "paint" as part of their names. The file that you are seeking is called `Mspaint` and is of type "Application".
4. Start Paint by double-clicking on its file name. (Other operations, such as move and copy, can also be performed on any file listed in the Find window.) Now, close the Paint application.
5. Close the Find utility as you would any application.
6. Start Find again, this time by right-clicking on the Start button and choosing the Find command from the resulting pop-up menu.
7. Determine if any files were saved to the C: drive today:
   - Enter `C:` in the *Look in* text box, click on the Date Modified tab, and select the *Find all files created or modified* option button.
   - Click on the *between* option button and enter today's date in both of the corresponding text boxes.
   - Choose the Find Now command button. All files saved today to the C: drive will be listed at the bottom of the Find window.
8. Determine if there is a document on the Student Disk that contains the word *people*.
   - In the Find window, choose the New Search command button to reset the search parameters. (Click on OK when the warning message appears.)
   - Insert the Student Disk in its drive.
   - Click on the Name & Location tab and enter the appropriate drive designation (for example, A:) in the *Look in* text box.
   - Click on the Advanced tab and type `people` in the *Containing text* box.
   - Choose the Find Now command button. After the search, the file Preamble should be displayed (twice) in the Find window.
9. Remove the Student Disk from its drive and close the Find utility.

4.4 Associating File Types with Applications

To a certain extent, Windows 95 is a document-oriented operating system. For example, as you know, you can open certain documents by double-clicking on their icons (on the Desktop or in Explorer, My Computer, or any folder window). When you double-click on such an icon, the associated application starts and the document opens within it. In this section, we will discuss how a document becomes associated with an application and how you can create or modify such an association.

File Types

Windows assigns a **file type**, based on the file's extension, to every file stored on your disks. File types are displayed in the Type column of Details view in Explorer or any folder window (see Figure 15).

- If the file extension is *registered* (as described below), and is thus recognized by Windows, the corresponding file type is displayed (see, for example, "Bitmap Image" in Figure 15).
- If the file has an extension but it is not registered, its type is the extension itself (see "LOG File" in Figure 15).
- If the file has no extension, then it is typed as simply "File".

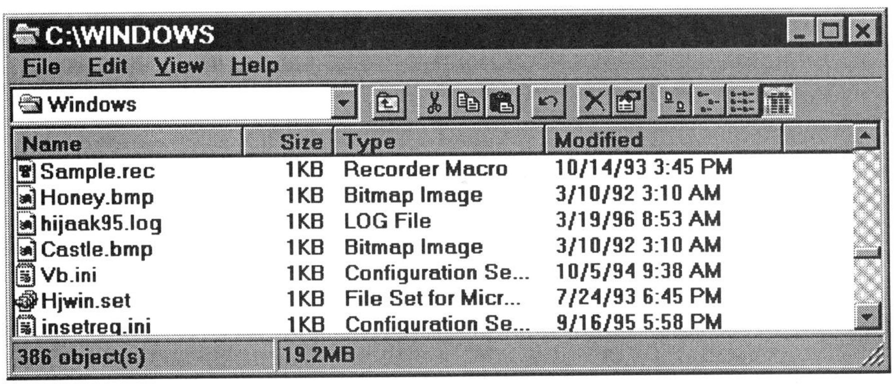

Figure 15 Some File Types

How extensions are registered

When a file extension is **registered** with Windows, it is associated with a particular application. These associations can occur in several ways:

- When Windows 95 was installed, it set up certain associations; for example, the extensions BMP and TXT are normally associated with Paint and Notepad, respectively. (The corresponding file type descriptions are "Bitmap Image" and "Text Document".) Moreover, if Windows 3.1 was present on the machine at the time Windows 95 was installed, any existing associations were carried over to Windows 95.

- Most Windows applications register at least one extension as part of their installation process.
- You can "manually" register an extension that is not yet associated with a particular application. We will discuss how to carry out this process, and how to modify or remove existing associations, later in this section.

NOTE

When an extension is registered, it is normally associated with a distinctive icon, often the icon of the corresponding application. All documents with that extension inherit this icon, which makes them easy to spot in Explorer and My Computer windows, especially in Large Icons view. In the figure below, the files `Charmap.hlp` and `Chimes.wav` have registered extensions, whereas `charmap.GID` does not; the latter has a generic icon.

charmap.GID Charmap.hlp Chimes.wav

Why register an extension?

Once an extension is registered with Windows, all documents with that extension become associated with a particular application. As a result, you can perform certain actions directly on these documents. For example, double-clicking on the document's icon (normally) opens the associated application, as well as the document. Moreover, additional actions can be specified on the menu that pops up when you right-click on the document's icon. From the right-click menu, you might be able to:

- Open the document within another specified application.
- View the document without opening its application.
- Print the document.
- Play the document, if it represents a sound file.

As you will see, some of the options that are available on a particular right-click menu depend on how the association between the file extension and the application was set up.

NOTE

The extension of a file having a registered file type may or may not be displayed as part of its file name in Explorer or a folder window. For example, since bmp is a registered extension, the file Arcade.bmp may be listed in the \Windows folder as `Arcade.bmp` or simply as `Arcade`. To display registered extensions (or hide them if they're currently displayed), choose Options from the View menu and click on the View tab in the resulting dialog box. Then, either select or deselect the *Hide MS-DOS file extensions for file types that are registered* check box.

Creating a New Registered File Type

Windows allows you to create new file types by registering extensions that are currently unregistered. In doing so, you associate an extension with a particular application and also define some of the options that will be available on the menu that pops up when you right-click on a file with that extension. Here's how it's done:

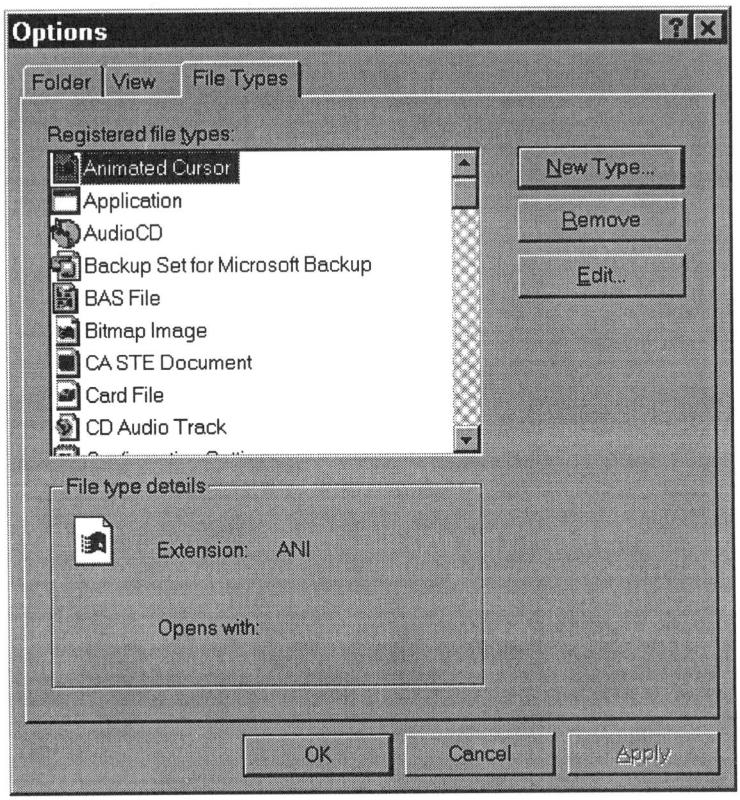

Figure 16 File Types Page of View Options Dialog Box

1. Start Explorer or My Computer.
2. Choose the Options item from the View menu and click on the File Types tab in the resulting dialog box. A list of registered file types is displayed, as shown in Figure 16. Notice that the extension corresponding to the highlighted type and the application that opens these files (if any) is displayed below the list box.
3. Choose the New Type command button to display the Add New File Type dialog box, which is shown in Figure 17.

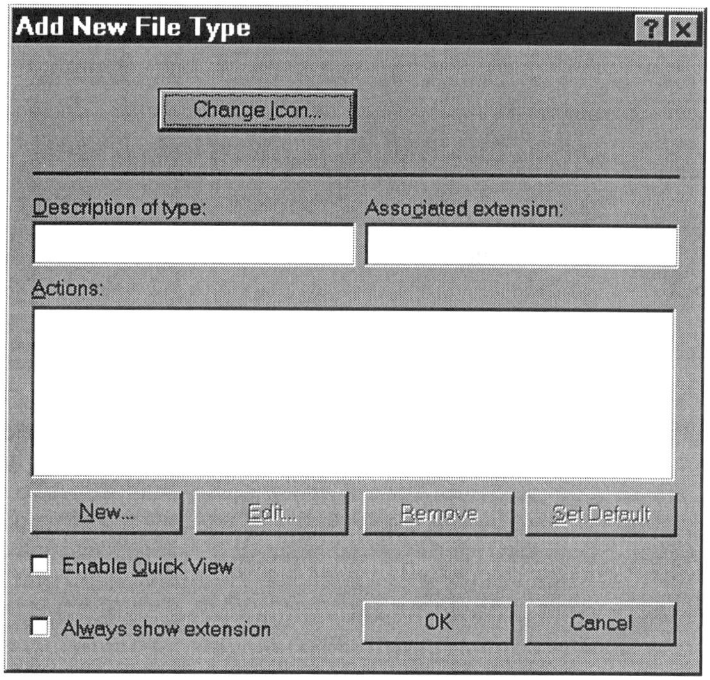

Figure 17 The Add New File Type Dialog Box

4. Type the extension you wish to register in the *Associated extension* text box and its description in the *Description of type* text box. (The description will appear in the Type column of a folder's Details view.) For example, if you use the extension LTR for all letters you write using WordPerfect for Windows, you might use *Letters* for the description of this extension.
5. Now, you have to define *actions* (such as Open or Print) for this association. These actions will appear on the menu that pops up when you right-click on a file with the specified extension. To

specify an action, choose the New command button, which opens the New Action dialog box (Figure 18).

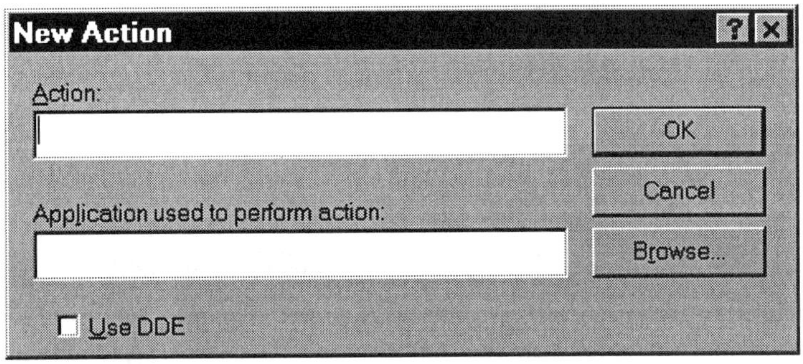

Figure 18 The New Action Dialog Box

Defining an action

6. In the *Action* text box, type a name for the action. This name will appear on the right-click pop-up menu. For example, if you want to be able to open the document from the right-click menu, use "Open" or, perhaps, "Open with WPWin".
7. Now type the command that will perform the action specified in step 6 in the *Application used to perform action* text box. If you want to *open* the application, give the appropriate program file's path name (which can usually be found in the application's documentation); for example, C:\WPWin60\WPWin.exe. If you can't determine the appropriate path name, choose the Browse command button, and then try to track down the relevant exe file. (If you want to perform an action other than opening the file, you'll have to check the application's documentation for the appropriate start-up command.)
8. Choose the OK button to return to the Add New File Type dialog box; the description of the action you have just defined appears in the *Actions* box.
9. If you want to define another action for the current file type, click on the New command button and repeat steps 6 through 8.

Selecting other options for the association

10. Select the *Enable Quick View* check box (when this option is available) if you want to be able to view the contents of a document without starting its associated application. (A *Quick View* item will appear on the right-click pop-up menu.)
11. Select the *Always show extension* check box if you want the extension for files of this type to be displayed when they are listed in Explorer or a folder window, regardless of whether or not other

registered extensions are hidden.

12. Choose the OK command button to complete the file type creation process. The Add New File Type dialog box will close and you will be returned to the Options dialog box.

The right-click pop-up menu

When you right-click on a file name that has an extension you have registered, a menu will pop up listing (among other standard items) the actions you defined when that file type was created. The menu item displayed in bold type (which is "Open with WPWin" in the menu shown at the right) is the *default* action; double-clicking on the file's icon (say, in Explorer) causes the default action to be executed.

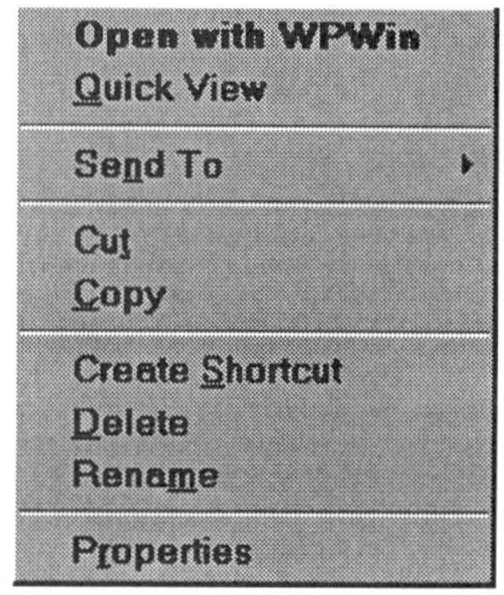

TIP

Here is a quick way to register a file type if the only action you want to associate with this type is opening the file:

1. Right-click on any file having the extension you want to register and choose the Open With command from the resulting pop-up menu. The Open With dialog box, shown below, will appear.

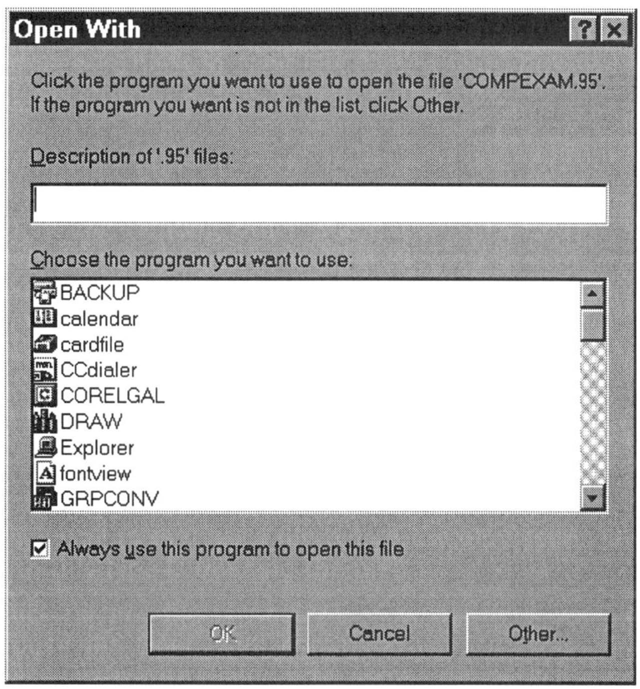

2. In the text box, provide a description of the file type; it will appear in the Type column of the Details view in Explorer or any folder window.
3. Select, from the list, the application you want to use to open files that have this extension, or choose the Other command button to browse for the desired application.
4. Be sure that the *Always use this program to open this file* check box is selected.
5. Choose the OK command button. (The selected application will start and the selected file will open within it.) The creation of the new file type is now complete.

Removing or Modifying a Registered File Type

Windows allows you to remove or modify an existing registered file type; you can, for example, change the application associated with it or add a new action to its right-click menu. To remove or modify an existing registered file type:

1. Start Explorer or My Computer.
2. Choose the Options item from the View menu, and click on the File Types tab in the resulting dialog box. The dialog box page shown in Figure 16 (on page 152) will be displayed.
3. In the list of registered file types, select the one with which you want to work; it will become highlighted.
4. If you want to remove the registration of the highlighted file type (ending the association between the corresponding extension and application):
   - Choose the Remove command button.
   - Choose the Yes button in the resulting warning message box.
   - Choose the OK command button.
5. If you want to modify the properties of the highlighted file type, choose the Edit command button (which opens an Edit File Type dialog box, like the one shown in Figure 19), and follow the rest of the steps of this procedure.
6. To change the icon for all files of this type:
   - Choose the Change Icon command button. The Change Icon dialog box will open.

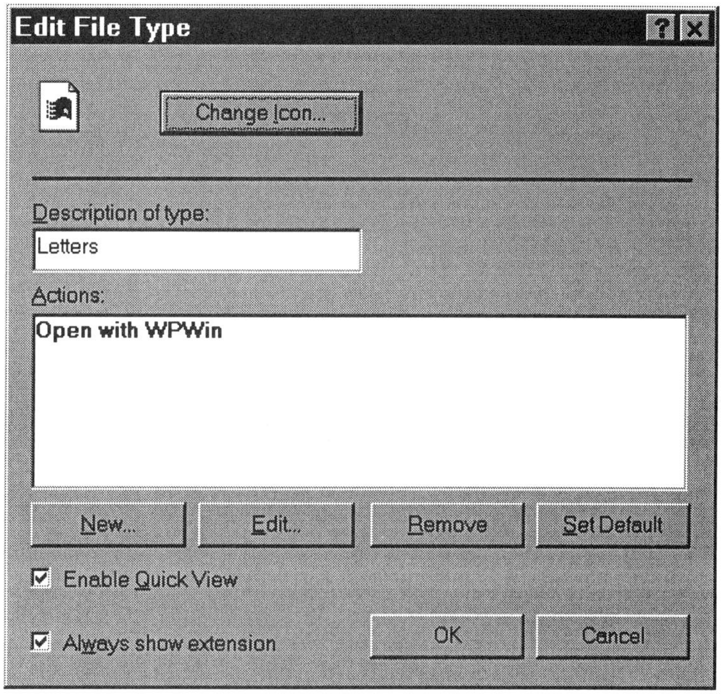

Figure 19 The Edit File Type Dialog Box

- Type the path name of a file that contains icons in the text box, or choose the Browse button to locate such a file. (The file \Windows\System\Shell32.dll contains an extensive collection of icons.)
- Click on the icon you want and choose the OK button.

7. To add an action to the right-click menu for this type, choose the New command button and proceed as described earlier in this section, under the heading "Creating a New Registered File Type".
8. To edit an existing action, select it and choose the Edit command button. Then, proceed as you would for a "new" action.
9. To remove an action from the right-click menu for this type, select the desired action and choose the Remove command button.
10. To return the set of actions to the default list for this file type, choose the Set Default command button.

11. Choose the OK command button when you're done with your modifications, and you will be returned to the Options dialog box.

4.4 TUTORIAL

Try the following exercises on your own.

1. Turn on your computer, if necessary, to start Windows 95 and close any open windows.
2. Start Explorer, choose the Options command on the View menu, and click on the File Types tab.
3. Associate the extension NOT with the Notepad application:
   - Choose the New Type command button, which opens the Add New File Type dialog box.
   - In the *Description of type* text box, enter Notepad Document; in the *Associated extension* text box, enter NOT.
   - Select the *Enable Quick View* check box (if available) so that a Quick View item will appear on the menu that pops up when you right-click on a file name with extension NOT.
   - Choose the New command button, which opens the New Action dialog box.
   - In the *Action* text box, type `Open with Notepad`; in the *Application used to perform action* text box, type the path name for Notepad: `\windows\notepad.exe` Now, if you double-click on a file name with extension NOT (or right-click on it and choose Open with Notepad from the pop-up menu), Notepad will start and open the file within it.
   - Choose the OK command button to close the New Action dialog box; then choose the Close command button to exit the Add New File Type dialog box.
4. In the Options dialog box, choose the Edit command button to open the Edit File Type dialog box.
5. Change the current icon for the Notepad Document file type:
   - Choose the Change Icon command button, which opens the Change Icon dialog box.
   - Select another icon from the *Current icon* box and choose the OK command button.
6. In the Edit File Type dialog box, choose the Close command button to return to the Options dialog box.
7. With the Notepad Document file type still highlighted, choose the Remove command button and answer Yes to the query.
8. Close the Options dialog box and then close Explorer.

4.5 *Property Sheets*

Just about everything in Windows, or that interacts with Windows, has "properties" — files, folders, disks, and even hardware, like printers and the mouse. When you right-click on an icon representing one of these objects, the last item listed on the resulting right-click menu is Properties. Choosing this menu item opens the object's Properties dialog box, which is commonly known as its **property sheet**. In this section, we will discuss property sheets for files, folders, and shortcuts.

The Property Sheet for a File or Folder

Figure 20 shows a typical file (or folder) property sheet. This particular dialog box was displayed by starting Explorer, right-clicking on the file name Internet.txt, and choosing Properties from the pop-up menu.

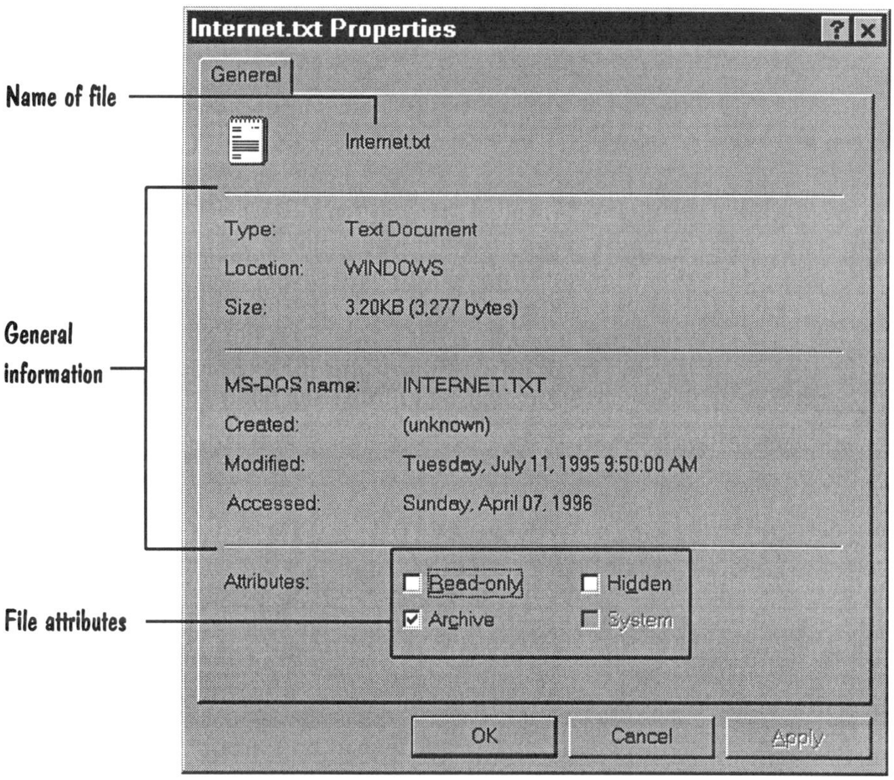

Figure 20 A Typical Property Sheet

The contents of a property sheet varies depending on the type of object it represents, but always includes general information about the object. The property sheets for files and folders also allow you to change their **attributes** (see Figure 20). A check mark next to an attribute indicates that the attribute is *set* — it is currently in effect; otherwise, we say that the attribute is *clear* — it is not in effect.

File Attributes

- Putting the *Read-only* attribute into effect makes it harder to accidentally erase or modify the file. Setting this attribute for a file is analogous to write-protecting a floppy disk (see the Introduction); it reduces the likelihood of accidental erasure or modification of the contents.
- The *Archive* bit is used in conjunction with backup software (see Section 9.3). The Archive bit is normally set for a file that has never been backed up or that has been modified since the last backup.
- When the *Hidden* attribute is set, the given file's name is not normally displayed in Explorer or a folder window.
- Windows attaches the *System* attribute to certain files, called *system files*, that it uses to perform basic functions. This attribute cannot normally be set or cleared by the user. (Notice that *System* is dimmed in Figure 20, indicating that this option is not available.)

Some Properties dialog boxes have more than one tab, providing additional pages of information and possibly additional available options. For example, all documents created in the Microsoft Word word processor have property sheets with three tabs: one for general information, a second that displays an optional user-generated summary of the document, and a third that provides additional statistics about the file.

The Property Sheet for a Shortcut

As you know, a shortcut is a small file that tells Windows where to find the associated (or *target*) object. When you right-click on a shortcut to a file or folder and choose Properties from the resulting pop-up menu, the property sheet for the shortcut (not for the target object) is displayed.

The property sheet for a shortcut normally contains two pages. The first page, which is displayed by clicking on the *General* tab, supplies information about the file in which the shortcut is defined; it provides the same information as the page shown in Figure 20. The second page, triggered from the *Shortcut* tab, supplies additional information and options. For example, if we display the Properties dialog box for a shortcut to the WordPad word processor and then click on the Shortcut tab, the resulting dialog box looks like the one in Figure 21.

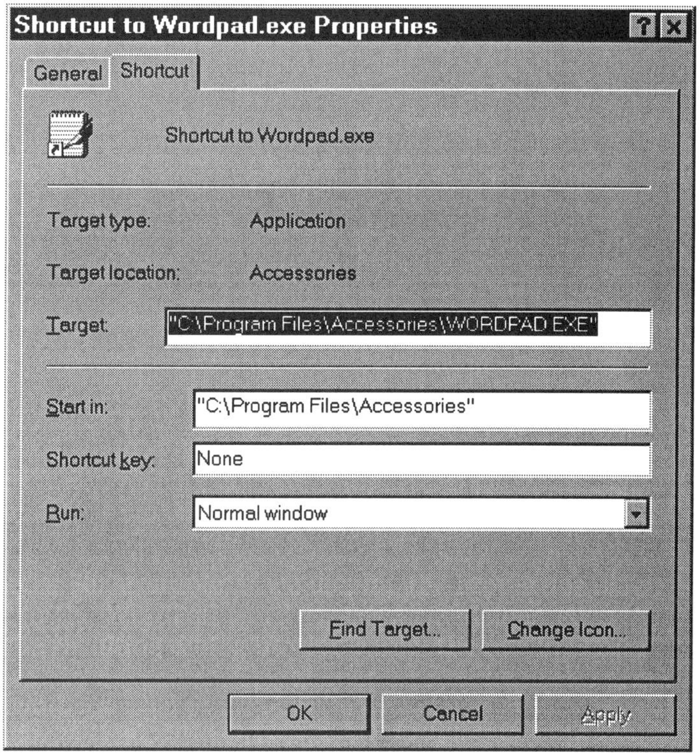

Figure 21 The Shortcut Page of a Property Sheet

The shortcut's name and icon are displayed at the top of the Shortcut page, followed by the target's type and the folder in which it resides. The text boxes and drop-down list on this page allow the user to alter certain properties of the shortcut. To be more specific:

Shortcut properties

- The *Target* text box contains the full path name for the target. The path is defined at the time the shortcut is created and would normally only need to be changed if the target file or folder were subsequently moved to another location. In this case, you would want to supply the new path name in this text box so that the shortcut would continue to work.
- The *Start in* text box shows the folder that will be opened by default after the shortcut is used to start an application. For

example, if WordPad is started using the shortcut of Figure 21, and you choose Open or Save As from the File menu, the contents of the Accessories folder will be displayed in the corresponding dialog box.

Shortcut keys

- The *Shortcut key* text box allows you to define a keystroke combination to open the file or folder. The shortcut keystrokes must begin with Ctrl+Alt and be followed by a single character. For example, to define the shortcut key Ctrl+Alt+W to start WordPad:

  1. Display the property sheet for a WordPad shortcut and click on the Shortcut tab (see Figure 21).
  2. Click in the Shortcut key text box.
  3. Press the W key (Windows automatically inserts Ctrl+Alt in front of the W).
  4. Choose the OK command button.

  Now, when you press Ctrl+Alt+W from anywhere within Windows or one of its applications, WordPad will start.

- The *Run* drop-down list supplies three options for displaying the file or folder window when you use this shortcut to open it:

  1. *Normal* means that the initial window will be the same size it was when the target file or folder was last closed.
  2. *Maximized* means that the target file or folder window will automatically be maximized when it is opened.
  3. *Minimized* means that the target file or folder, when opened, will automatically be reduced to a button on the Taskbar.

NOTE

The Shortcut page also contains two command buttons:

- Activating Find Target opens the folder window that contains the target and highlights the latter.
- Change Icon opens the Change Icon dialog box. (See Section 4.4 for information about changing an icon.)

Creating a "Project Folder"

Often, we use a computer to help us work on a project over an extended period of time. In this case, you can work more productively if you create a folder to house the tools and documents you need in working on the project. As you will see, shortcut properties are useful in this endeavor.

A project folder typically contains shortcuts to applications (and perhaps a few other objects) and subfolders containing data files. To illustrate the creation of a project folder, let's make some assumptions concerning the nature of our project:

- We anticipate needing to use the WordPad word processor and Paint graphics program.
- All the data files generated by the project will be stored in a single subfolder of the project folder called Data.
- We will frequently be printing documents and want to make this process as easy as possible.

Let's go through the steps in creating the appropriate project folder.

1. Create the project folder as a subfolder of the Desktop:
   - Right-click on the Desktop, point at the New command on the pop-up menu, and choose Folder from the submenu.
   - Rename the new folder *Project*.
2. Create shortcuts for WordPad and Paint:
   - Start Explorer and open the Accessories subfolder of the Program Files folder.
   - Select WordPad and Mspaint in the contents pane.
   - Right-drag these files onto the Project folder icon and choose Create Shortcuts(s) Here from the menu that appears when you release the mouse button.
3. Open the Project folder by double-clicking on its icon.
4. Rename the shortcuts in the Project folder *WordPad* and *Paint*.
5. Create a shortcut for the default printer:
   - In Explorer, open the My Computer folder, then double-click on the Printers icon, and select the appropriate printer.
   - Right-drag this printer's icon into the Project folder and choose Create Shortcut(s) Here from the pop-up menu.
   - Rename the new shortcut *Printer*.
6. Create a data folder as a subfolder of Project:
   - Right-click on an empty part of the Project folder, point at the New item on the pop-up menu, and choose Folder on the submenu.
   - Rename the new folder *Data*.
7. Change the default folder for the WordPad and Paint shortcuts to

the Data subfolder (so that all files will automatically be saved to this folder):

- Right-click on the WordPad shortcut, choose Properties from the pop-up menu, and click on the Shortcut tab in the resulting dialog box (see Figure 21).
- In the *Start in* text box, enter Desktop\Project\Data, and choose the OK command button.
- Repeat this process for the Paint shortcut.

8. Choose Large Icons view, remove the Toolbar (by choosing Toolbar from the View menu), and resize the Project folder window so that there is no unnecessary "white space". The resulting folder window is shown below.

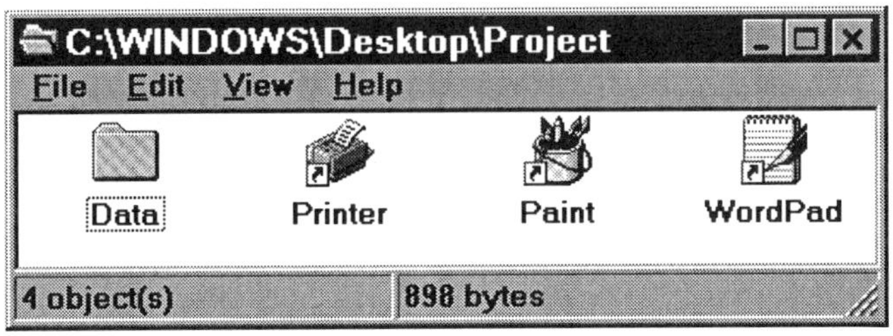

Now, all the tools and documents we need for our project are contained in one location. By opening the project window, we can start Paint or Wordpad, and all files created by these applications will be saved, by default, to the Data folder. Moreover, to print a Paint or WordPad file, all we need do is drag it from the Data folder onto the Printer icon.

TIP

If you want the Project folder to open whenever you start Windows:

- In Explorer, right-drag the Project folder onto the StartUp folder, which is a subfolder of \Windows\Start Menu\Programs.
- Choose Create Shortcut(s) Here from the pop-up menu.

Chapter Summary

Customizing the Taskbar	To reposition the Taskbar	Drag it to any other edge of the screen.

	To change the size of the Taskbar	Drag its outer edge away from the edge of the screen.
	To open the Taskbar Properties dialog box	Point at the Settings option on the Start menu and choose Taskbar from the submenu; *or* right-click on an empty part of the Taskbar and choose Properties from the pop-up menu.
	To turn on or off the Always on top, Auto hide, or Show Clock Taskbar options	Open the Taskbar Properties dialog box, select or deselect the appropriate check box, and choose OK.
Manipulating Windows from the Taskbar	To tile or cascade application windows	Right-click on the Taskbar and choose Cascade, Tile Horizontally, or Tile Vertically from the pop-up menu.
	To minimize all open application windows	Right-click on the Taskbar and choose Minimize All Windows from the pop-up menu.
Customizing the Start Button Menus	To add an item using drag-and-drop	Drag a file, folder, or shortcut onto the Start button; that item will be added to the Start menu.
	To display the Start Menu Programs page of the Taskbar Properties dialog box	Open the Taskbar Properties dialog box (see above) and click on the Start Menu Programs tab.
	To add items to any Start button menu	Choose the Add or Advanced command button on the Start Menu Programs page.
	To delete items from a Start button menu	Choose the Remove or Advanced command button on the Start Menu Programs page.
	To remove all items from the Documents submenu	Choose the Clear command button on the Start Menu Programs page.
Using the Find Utility	To start Find	Point at the Find option on the Start menu and choose Files or Folders from the submenu; *or* right-click on the Start button, My Computer icon, or any folder icon and choose Find; *or* in Explorer, point at Find on the Tools menu and choose Files or Folders from the submenu.
	Selecting the search criteria	In the Find window: use the Name & Location page to enter files and/or folders; use the Date Modified page to limit the search to

		certain dates; use the Advanced page to search for a piece of text or files of a certain size or type.
	Using the Search Results window	In the Search Results window, files or folders can be selected, cut, copied, deleted, renamed, opened, or printed.
File Types	To create, remove, or modify a file type	In Explorer or My Computer, choose Options from the View menu and click on the File Types tab in the resulting dialog box.
	To create a new registered file type	On the File Types page, choose the New Type button; then specify the extension to be registered and its description, and define the actions associated with this type.
	To remove an existing registered file type	On the File Types page, select the file type and choose the Remove button.
	To modify an existing registered file type	On the File Types page, select the file type and choose the Edit button.
Property Sheets	To display an object's property sheet	Right-click on the object's icon and choose Properties from the pop-up menu.
	Shortcut property sheets	Allow the user to change, for the target application, its path name, default folder, shortcut key, and initial window type.
File Attributes	Read-only	When set, the file cannot be modified or deleted.
	Archive	When set, indicates that the file needs to be backed up.
	Hidden	When set, the file's name is not normally displayed in Explorer or a folder window.
	System	When set, indicates that the file is a system file.

Review Exercises

Section 4.1

1. To increase the size of the Taskbar when it is located at the bottom of the screen, position the mouse cursor over its ___________ edge and drag it in an upward direction.

2. You can open the Taskbar Properties dialog box by right-clicking on the Taskbar and choosing ____________ from the pop-up menu.
3. When three windows are ____________ on the screen, each window occupies one-third of the available space.
4. True or false: When the auto-hide feature is in effect, the only way to display the Taskbar is to press Ctrl+Esc.
5. True or false: The Taskbar can be repositioned along any of the four edges of the screen.
6. True or false: To minimize all application windows simultaneously, right-click on the Taskbar and choose the Properties command.
7. Which of the following tasks cannot be accomplished using the Taskbar Properties dialog box?
   a. Ensuring that the Taskbar is "always on top".
   b. Hiding the Taskbar from view.
   c. Removing the Clock from the Taskbar.
   d. Repositioning the Taskbar at another edge of the screen.
8. Which of the following tasks cannot be accomplished by right-clicking on the Taskbar and choosing a command from the pop-up menu?
   a. Cascading the open application windows.
   b, Tiling the open application windows.
   c. Maximizing all open application windows.
   d. Minimizing all open application windows.

Section 4.2

9. The Windows Explorer item on the Programs submenu of the Start menu is actually a ____________ to a program file.
10. If you drag a file onto the Start button, a corresponding item is added to the ____________.
11. You can add items to the Programs submenu of the Start menu by using the ____________ page of the Taskbar Properties dialog box.
12. True or false: Choosing the Advanced command button in the Taskbar Properties dialog box starts Explorer.
13. True or false: The Clear command button in the Taskbar Properties dialog box removes all items from the Programs submenu.
14. True or false: If the `\Windows\Start Menu\Programs\StartUp` folder contains a shortcut to an application, that application will open every time Windows is started.

15. To add an item to the Programs submenu of the Start menu:
    a. Drop its shortcut onto the Start button.
    b. Drop its shortcut onto the Programs submenu of the Start button.
    c. Copy its shortcut into the \Windows\Start Menu folder.
    d. Copy its shortcut into the \Windows\Start Menu\Programs folder.
16. To delete one of the items on the Documents submenu of the Start menu
    a. Choose the Remove command button in the Taskbar Properties dialog box.
    b. Choose the Clear command button in the Taskbar Properties dialog box.
    c. Open the Recent subfolder of the Windows folder and delete the item from it.
    d. Open the Documents menu and drag the item onto the Recycle Bin.

Section 4.3

17. To use the Windows Find utility to locate a file, type its name in the ___________ text box on the Name & Location page.
18. After the Find utility completes a search, all files and folders found are displayed in the ___________ subwindow.
19. To open a folder located in a Find search, ___________ on its name in the Find window.
20. True or false: The Find utility can be used to locate all files and folders whose names contain the word *start*.
21. True or false: If the *Look in* text box contains C: and the *Include subfolders* check box is selected, the Find utility will search the entire C: drive for the specified file or folder.
22. True or false: You can copy a file from Find's Search Results window to the Clipboard by highlighting its name and choosing Copy from the Edit menu.
23. If you have forgotten a file's name but you know it contains the text "Dear Bob", you should enter this information on
    a. The Name & Location page of the Find window.
    b. The Date Modified page of the Find window.
    c. The Advanced page of the Find window.
    d. The Text page of the Find window.
24. If you have forgotten a file's name but you know that it was created in the last three days, enter this information on
    a. The Name & Location page of the Find window.

b. The Date Modified page of the Find window.
c. The Advanced page of the Find window.
d. The Recent page of the Find window.

Section 4.4

25. If double-clicking on a file's icon opens the file, then the corresponding file type is ____________ with Windows.

26. To associate an extension with an application, begin by choosing the ____________ command from Explorer's View menu.

27. True or false: An application cannot be associated with two different extensions.

28. True or false: The menu that pops up when you right-click on a file icon always contains a Print command.

29. The File Types page of the Options dialog box allows you to

    a. Create a new registered file type.
    b. Remove an existing registered file type.
    c. Edit an existing registered file type.
    d. Perform all of the above tasks.

30. Which characteristic of a file type registration cannot be changed in the Edit File Type dialog box?

    a. The icon associated with this file type.
    b. The extension associated with this file type.
    c. The actions associated with this file type.
    d. Whether or not Quick View is enabled for this file type.

Section 4.5

31. The Properties dialog box for an object is commonly known as its property ____________.

32. To open the Properties dialog box for an object, right-click on its icon and choose ____________ from the pop-up menu.

33. True or false: When a file's read-only attribute is set, that file cannot be modified.

34. True or false: The shortcut key assigned to a shortcut must begin with the Ctrl+Alt keystroke combination.

35. Which file attribute is cleared when the file is backed up using backup software?

    a. Archive
    b. Backup
    c. Hidden
    d. System

36. On the Shortcut page of the Properties dialog box for a shortcut to a folder, the word *target* refers to

a. The folder in which the shortcut resides.
b. The folder that opens when the shortcut is double-clicked.
c. The file that defines the shortcut.
d. None of the above is the target for a shortcut.

Build Your Own Glossary

37. The following words and phrases are important terms that were introduced in this chapter. (They appear within the text in boldface type.) Use WordPad (see Section 2.2) to enter a definition for each term, preserving alphabetical order, into the Glossary file on the Student Disk.

Attributes for a file or folder	Find utility	Taskbar
Cascade windows	Property sheet	Tile windows
File types	Registered file type	Wildcard
	Start button menu	

Lab Exercises

Work each of the following exercises at your computer. Begin by turning the machine on (if necessary) to start Windows 95 and closing any open windows. If you want to produce a written record of your answers, review the material on WordPad and capturing screens in Sections 2.2 and 2.3.

Lab Exercise 1 (Section 4.1)

a. If the Taskbar is hidden, display it. Position the Taskbar at the left edge of the screen. Is the Start button at its top or bottom?

b. Increase the size of the Taskbar as much as possible. What percentage (roughly) of the entire screen does it occupy?

c. Remove the Clock from the Taskbar or, if it's currently hidden, redisplay it. Also, ensure that the *Always on top* check box is selected. What dialog box did you open to accomplish these tasks?

d. Start My Computer and maximize its window. Does it cover part or all of the Taskbar?

e. Hide the Taskbar. Does the My Computer window expand to fill the entire screen?

f. Temporarily redisplay the Taskbar by moving the mouse pointer to the left edge of the screen. Does the Taskbar cover part of the My Computer window?

g. Close My Computer, "unhide" the Taskbar and Clock (if necessary), move the Taskbar to the bottom of the screen, and reduce it to normal size.

Lab Exercise 2 (Section 4.1)

a. Start WordPad and maximize it; then start Paint (which is also on the Accessories submenu of the Start button) and maximize it.

b. Cascade the WordPad and Paint windows. Which one is in front?

c. Tile the two windows horizontally. Which is on top?

d. Tile the windows vertically. Which is on the left?

e. Issue the Minimize All Windows command (from the Taskbar's right-click menu), reducing WordPad and Paint to buttons on the Taskbar. Which button is highlighted?

f. Restore the WordPad window; then close it.

g. Issue the Undo Minimize All command (from the Taskbar's right-click menu). Does the Paint window occupy the entire Desktop?

h. Close the Paint window.

Lab Exercise 3 (Section 4.2)

a. Start Explorer and open the Windows folder.

b. Use drag-and-drop to add Calc and Charmap items to the Start menu. Which item is positioned higher on this menu?

c. Close Explorer.

d. Use the Add command button in the Taskbar Properties dialog box to add a Charmap shortcut to the Programs submenu of the Start menu. Name this shortcut CHARMAP (all capital letters). Does it appear on this menu in capital letters?

e. Choose the Advanced command button in the Taskbar Properties dialog box and open the Programs subfolder in the resulting folder tree. Move the CHARMAP shortcut from the Programs subfolder to the Start Menu folder. Did Windows allow you to do this? Do both Charmap and CHARMAP appear on the Start menu?

f. Close the folder window.

g. Use the Remove command button in the Taskbar Properties dialog box to delete the Calc, Charmap, and (if it exists) CHARMAP items from the Start menu. Was a warning message displayed at any time?

h. Close any open windows.

Lab Exercise 4 (Section 4.3)

a. Start the Find utility. What steps did you take to accomplish this?

b. Locate all files and folders in the Windows folder, but *not* in any of its subfolders, with names that contain the word *start*. How many are there?

c. Clear the Search Results window without closing Find. How did you accomplish this?

d. Now locate all files and folders in the \Windows\Start Menu folder and its subfolders that contain the letters *ter*. How many were found?

e. Create a shortcut for the file Character Map (displayed in the Search Results window) and place it on the Desktop. Can this be done by both copy-and-paste and drag-and-drop?

f. Delete the new shortcut.

g. Open the file Character Map (displayed in the Search Results window). Can this be done by

    Double clicking on it?
    Right-clicking on it and choosing a command from the pop-up menu?
    Choosing the appropriate command from Find's File menu?

h. Close the Find utility.

Lab Exercise 5 (Section 4.3)

a. Insert the Student Disk in its drive and start the Find utility.

b. Use Find to locate all files in the root folder of this disk which satisfy each of the following criteria. (Be sure to clear the Search Results window after each search is complete.)

    - Files that were last saved in the year 1995
    - Files of type Application
    - Files that are at most 10 KB in size

    In each case, how many files were found?

c. In the WordPad folder of the Student Disk, locate all files that contain the word *this*. Which files, if any, were found?

d. Use Find to determine all files on the entire Student Disk that satisfy *all* of the following criteria:

    - Their names contain the letters *file*.
    - They were saved between 1/1/95 and 12/31/96.
    - They are larger than one KB in size.

e. Close the Find utility and remove the Student Disk from its drive.

Lab Exercise 6 (Section 4.4)

a. Start Explorer and display the File Types page of the Options dialog box. How many pages are there in this dialog box?

b. Create a new registered file type with extension NOT and description *Notepad Document.* What is the name of the dialog box in which this information is entered?

c. Define the following two actions for the new file type:

   1. Open with Notepad (The path name for Notepad is \Windows\Notepad.exe.)
   2. Print (Add " /p" — without the quotes, but with the space — after Notepad's path name to define this command.)

d. Choose the OK command button twice to return to the Options dialog box, and close the latter. Were any warning messages issued?

e. Insert the Student Disk in its drive and select this drive in Explorer's folder tree.

f. Check that your printer is ready, right-click on the NoteDoc file, and choose Print from the pop-up menu. Does Notepad close after printing is complete? If not, close Notepad.

g. Use the Options dialog box to remove the registered file type NOT. Were any warning messages issued in the process?

h. Close Explorer and remove the Student Disk from its drive.

Lab Exercise 7 (Section 4.5)

a. Insert the Student Disk in its drive.

b. Start Explorer and open the root folder of this drive.

c. Display the property sheet for the Shortcut to WordPad file. How did you accomplish this?

d. Set the Read-only attribute for this file. Is the System attribute available (can it be set)?

e. Try to delete the Shortcut to WordPad file. What message is displayed?

f. Using the Shortcut page of this property sheet:

   - Set the default folder ("Start in") to A:\.
   - Set the shortcut key to Ctrl+Alt+W.
   - Set the Run type to Minimized.

g. Press Ctrl+Alt+W. Does the WordPad window open? If not, open it.

h. Choose Open from the File menu. What is the current (active) folder in the Open dialog box?

i. Cancel the Open dialog box, close WordPad and Explorer, and remove the Student Disk from its drive.

If You Want to Learn More ...

The notes presented here allow you to delve more deeply into some of the topics covered in this chapter.

Get to the Desktop quickly

As you know, if you want to access a Desktop shortcut that is covered by open windows, you could do so by choosing the Minimize All Windows command from the Taskbar's right-click menu. Here are a couple of other ways to quickly access the Desktop shortcuts. Both of these techniques are based on the fact that the Desktop appears as a subfolder of the Windows folder in Explorer or My Computer. (The Desktop also appears at the top of the Explorer folder tree pane, but that doesn't help us here.)

- *Place the Desktop on the Start menu* In Explorer or My Computer, drag the Desktop subfolder of the Windows folder onto the Start button. It will now appear as a shortcut on the Start menu. When you click on this menu item, the Desktop folder will open, displaying all the shortcuts you normally see as icons on the actual Desktop. You can now double-click on one of these icons to open the corresponding file or folder.
- *Place the Desktop on the Taskbar* This technique is a little more complicated:
    1. In Explorer, right-drag the Desktop folder onto the StartUp subfolder of the Windows\Start Menu\Programs folder.
    2. Choose the Create Shortcut(s) Here item from the menu that pops up when you release the mouse button.
    3. Open the StartUp folder, right-click on the new shortcut, and choose Properties from the resulting menu.
    4. Click on the Shortcut tab in the Properties dialog box and select Minimized from the Run drop-down list.
    5. Choose the OK command button.

    Now, every time you start Windows, the Desktop folder will appear as a button on the Taskbar. Click on this button to open the Desktop folder and view its contents.

Using wildcards If you're an experienced DOS user, you have probably used wildcards (Section 4.3) quite a bit in copying, moving, or deleting files, or displaying directory lists. In Windows 95, wildcards can only be used in Open and Save As dialog boxes and in the Find utility (and, here, only in searching for files). However, if you wish to return to your wildcard ways while running Windows 95, there is a work-around: Choose the MS-DOS Prompt item from the Programs option on the Start menu; a window will open displaying the DOS prompt. Within this window, you can issue any available DOS command and include wildcards within it. (For more information about MS-DOS Prompt, see Section 12.1.)

File types and extensions There is little difference between file types and file extensions. As you know, in the Details view in Explorer or any folder window, Windows displays a "type" for each file listed. If a file's extension is not registered, then the listed file type is the same as the extension; if the file type *is* registered, then Windows displays a name of its own choosing for the file type. For example, all files with an exe extension are typed as "Application".

If a file type is registered, files of this type may be listed without the corresponding extension in Explorer and folder windows. To force Windows to display extensions for these files:

1. Choose the Options item from the View menu in Explorer or any folder window.
2. Click on the View tab in the resulting Options dialog box.
3. Deselect the check box called *Hide MS-DOS file extensions for file types that are registered.*
4. Choose the OK command button.

To keep Windows from appending an extension You should be aware that when you save a file within certain applications, Windows automatically types the file and appends the appropriate extension. For example, when you save a WordPad document, Windows will, by default, type it as a "Microsoft Word Document" and add the extension doc. This extension will be added even if you assign an extension of your own; for example, if you save a WordPad file as John.Ltr, it will be listed in Explorer (assuming MS-DOS extensions are displayed) as John.Ltr.doc.

If you do not want Windows to append the extension for a registered file type, when you save the file, enclose its name in quotations marks. For example, if you save a WordPad document as "John.Ltr", Windows will type it as Ltr File and no additional extension will be appended!

Other property sheets

In Section 4.5, we discussed the property sheets for files, folders, and shortcuts. Yet, just about everything in Windows has "properties". For example, if you start My Computer and right-click on any disk icon, the resulting pop-up menu will display a Properties command; choosing this command displays information about the selected disk. In fact, right-clicking on almost *any* icon displays a pop-up menu whose last item is Properties!

In later sections of the text, we will discuss the property sheets for other objects. These include:

Display properties for the Desktop (Sections 5.2 and 5.3).
Keyboard and mouse properties (Section 5.4).
Printer properties (Section 6.1).
Multimedia properties (Section 6.3).
Modem properties (Section 6.5).
Properties for the computer system as a whole (Section 6.5).
Properties for DOS applications (Section 12.2).

CHAPTER 5

Control Panel: Customizing Windows

People use computers in different ways and for different reasons. With this in mind, the designers of Windows 95 provided many ways to customize its user interface. When this capability is used properly, the result is a more pleasant and productive environment. In Section 3.4, we described one way that Windows can be customized — by placing shortcuts for frequently used applications, documents, or folders right on the Desktop. In this chapter, we will discuss how to use the Control Panel utility to further customize windows. To be more specific, you will learn:

1. How to start, use, and close Control Panel.
2. How to choose a repeating pattern or wallpaper to decorate the Desktop.
3. How to select a screen saver.
4. How to change the color and size of various objects in the Windows 95 interface.
5. How to adjust the keyboard repeat rate and delay.
6. How to modify the operation of the mouse.
7. About setting the computer's clock, installing new software, and viewing fonts.

5.1 An Introduction to Control Panel

Control Panel is a collection of small programs (*utilities*) that help you customize the Windows user interface — its colors, sounds, mouse operation, etc. — so that it looks and acts the way you want. In this section, we will provide an overview of the workings of Control Panel.

The Control Panel Window

To open the Control Panel window:

Starting Control Panel

1. Click on the Start button (or press Ctrl+Esc) to open the Start menu.
2. Point at the Settings option and hold the mouse steady for a second or two; the Settings submenu will open.

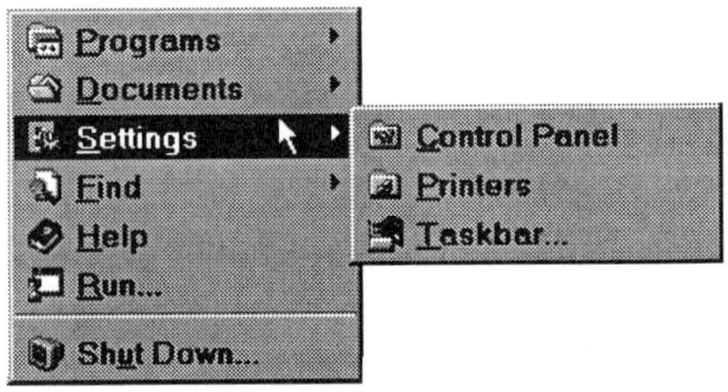

3. Click on the Control Panel item on this submenu. A window, similar to the one shown in Figure 1, will open.

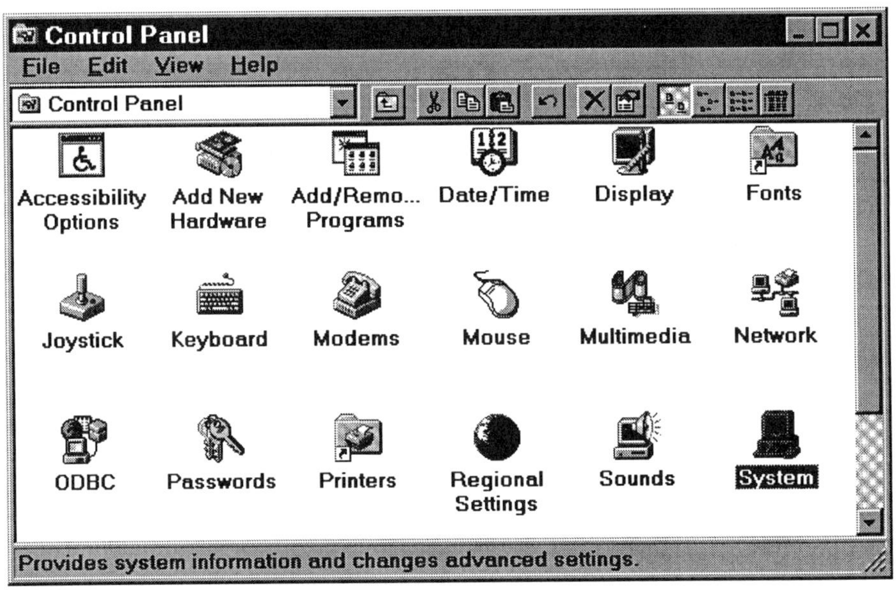

Figure 1 The Control Panel Window

At the top of the window are the usual title and menu bars. Directly below the menu bar is a Toolbar, which, as you will see, allows us to quickly access some Control Panel features. (If the Toolbar does not appear in your Control Panel window, choose the Toolbar command from the View menu; this command toggles the Toolbar on or off.) At the bottom of the window is a Status Bar (which can also be turned on or off from the View menu). The Status Bar provides a brief description of the currently selected icon (which, in Figure 1, is *System*).

Control Panel display options

The window shown in Figure 1 represents each of the Control Panel functions as a "large icon". If you want, you can display the various functions in several other ways. For example, if we choose the List option from the View menu, the window will look like this:

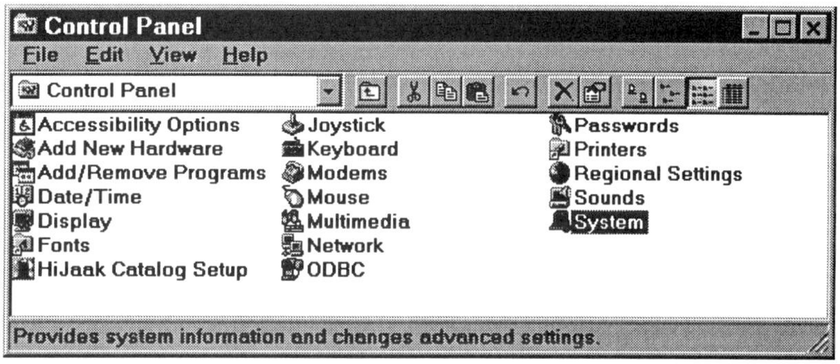

Two other display options are available on the View menu:

- Small Icons view looks similar to List view, but the icons are arranged in a different order.
- Details view lists each function on a separate line, which also contains a brief description of that function.

NOTE

The four display options (Large Icons, Small Icons, List, and Details) can also be accessed from the Toolbar. Just click on the appropriate button, as illustrated below:

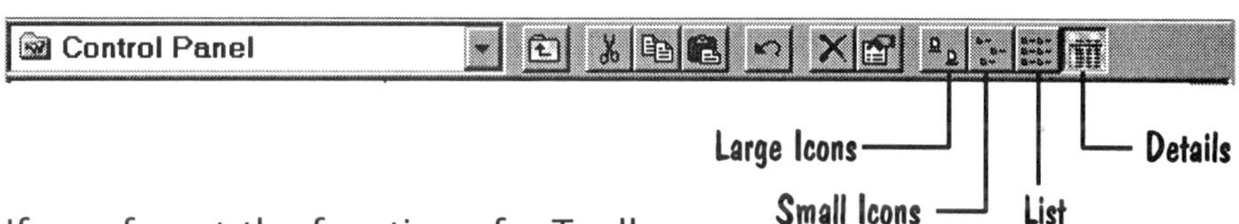

If you forget the function of a Toolbar button, point at it with the mouse; a *tool tip* will appear, as shown at the left, identifying it!

Control Panel Functions

Each of the icons displayed in the Control Panel window represents a utility that allows you to customize one aspect of Windows. The number, the type, and sometimes even the names of the available Control Panel functions depend on your system's configuration. The following table describes the most common functions.

Name	Description
Accessibility Options	Changes the way the keyboard, sounds, display, or mouse behave to make Windows more accessible to people with disabilities.
Add New Hardware	Aids you in installing new hardware such as modems, sound boards, and CD-ROM drives on your system.
Add/Remove Programs	Aids you in installing and removing software on your system.
Date/Time	Changes the date and time on your computer's clock.
Display	Changes screen colors, type appearance, the Desktop background, the size of objects, and screen resolution; installs screen savers.
Fonts	Adds, removes, and allows you to view the fonts on your system.
Joystick	Selects, calibrates, and tests joystick devices.
Keyboard	Changes the keyboard type, layout, and repeat rate and delay; changes the cursor blink rate.
Modems	Installs a new modem and changes a modem's properties.
Mouse	Changes the mouse type and allows you to modify aspects of its operation such as double-click speed and pointer shape and speed.
Multimedia	Changes properties for audio, video, and MIDI (Musical Instrument Digital Interface) devices, and the playing of audio compact discs.
Network	Adds, removes, and configures network connections; aids you in accessing an installed network.
Passwords	Sets up user passwords and preferences (profiles).
Printers	Adds, removes, and changes settings (such as resolution and paper type) for printers.

Regional Settings	Changes international settings such as the format of numbers, currencies, dates, and times.
Sounds	Changes Windows and system sounds, such as the sounds heard when Windows is started and exited.
System	Provides system information and allows you to change settings that affect system performance.

Choosing a function

To choose one of the available Control Panel utilities, perform any of the following actions:

- Double-click on the appropriate icon.
- Click on the appropriate icon to select it and choose the Open command from the File menu.
- Right-click on the appropriate icon, which selects it and pops up a menu, and choose Open from this menu.

When you use a Control Panel utility to modify a setting, the new setting remains in effect every time you use Windows until that setting is changed again.

Closing Control Panel

You can close (or exit) Control Panel in any of the following ways:

- Click on the close button on the right end of the title bar.
- Choose Close from the File menu.
- Press the Alt+F4 keystroke combination.

5-1 TUTORIAL

Try the following exercises on your own.

1. Turn on your computer, if necessary, to start up Windows 95 and close any open windows.
2. Start Control Panel:
   - Click on the Start button (or press Ctrl+Esc) to display the Start menu.
   - Point at the Settings option to open its submenu.
   - Click on the Control Panel item.
3. Maximize the Control Panel window.

4. If the Status Bar is not visible at the bottom of the Control Panel window, choose Status Bar from the View menu. Then, successively select (click on) each item in the window and take note of its function, which is displayed on the Status Bar.
5. If the Toolbar is not visible in the Control Panel window, choose Toolbar from the View menu. Click on each of the four view option buttons on the Toolbar and note its effect on the window.

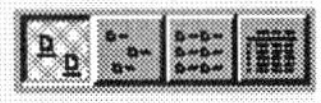

6. Close the Control Panel window by clicking on its close button or choosing the Close command on the File menu.

5.2 *Changing the Desktop Background*

The default Windows 95 Desktop has a solid, dark-colored background. In Section 5.3, we will describe how you can change the background color. This section discusses how to change the look of the Desktop in another way: by decorating it with a picture (graphic) and/or a repeating pattern. We will also describe how to have Windows display an animated image — a *screen saver* — when your system has been idle for a specified period of time.

Display

All the changes just described are accomplished using Control Panel's **Display** function. To start the Display utility, open Control Panel and choose the Display icon from its window (as described in Section 5.1). The Display Properties dialog box, shown in Figure 2, will then open.

You can also open the Display Properties dialog box without starting Control Panel. First, right-click on an empty part of the Desktop, which pops up the menu shown at the right. Then, choose the Properties item from this menu. The Display Properties dialog box will now appear on the screen.

Choosing a Desktop Pattern

As you can see in Figure 2, the Display Properties dialog box contains four tabs. The first of these, *Background*, allows you to decorate the Desktop with a repeating pattern or a graphic image (*wallpaper*). To use one of the supplied Desktop patterns:

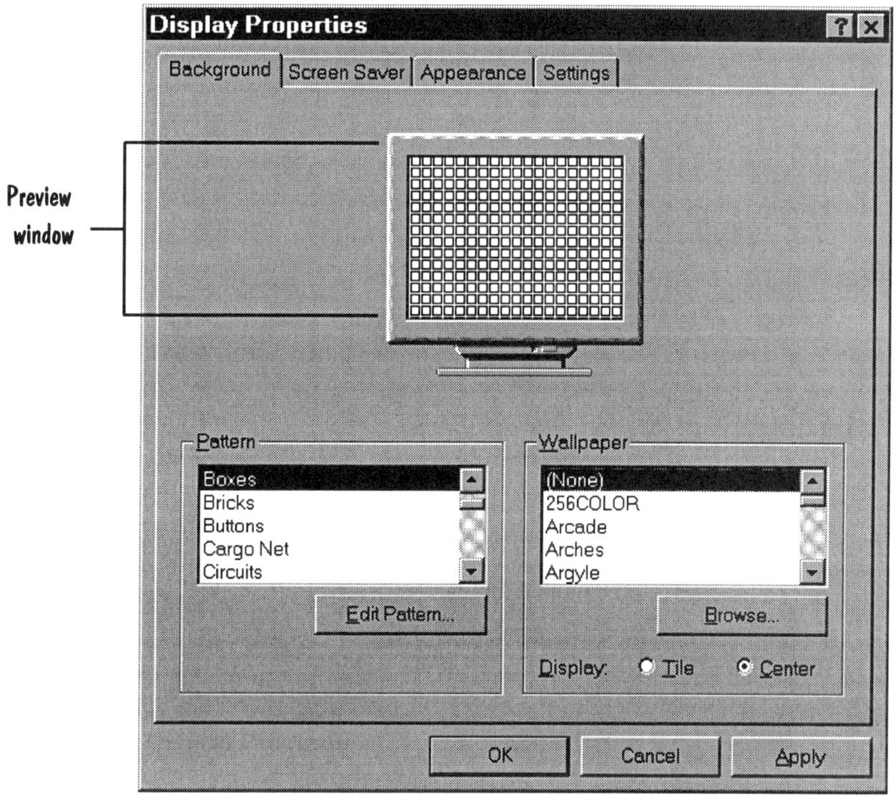

Figure 2 The Display Properties Dialog Box — Background Page

1. Open the Display Properties dialog box (Figure 2) as described above.
2. Select a pattern by clicking on its name in the Pattern list box. If you don't want to use a Desktop pattern, select "(None)" from the top of the list. The preview window will display a sample of that pattern. (The Boxes pattern is shown in the preview window of Figure 2.)

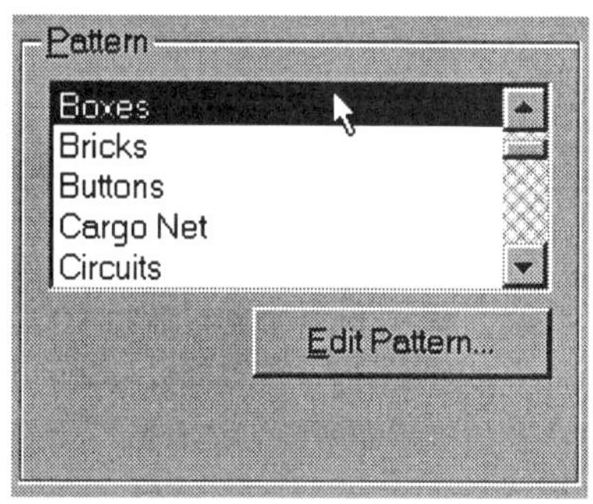

3. Choose the OK command button to put the pattern into effect and close the dialog box, or choose the Apply button to put the pattern into effect without closing the dialog box.

To see the selected pattern in all its glory, minimize all applications, including Control Panel, and close the Display Properties dialog box, if you haven't done so already.

NOTE

You can create Desktop patterns of your own design by selecting an existing pattern as described above and then choosing the Edit Pattern command button. The Pattern Editor dialog box will open, allowing you to change the current pattern or create a new one. The Pattern Editor is fun to play with; if you try it out, click on the close button to close its window when you're done.

Choosing Wallpaper

Instead of using a solid color or patterned Desktop, you can decorate it with a graphic image, commonly known as **wallpaper**. (Yes, using wallpaper to decorate a desktop does sound a little strange!) Choosing wallpaper is easy:

1. Open the Display Properties dialog box (Figure 2).
2. Select a particular wallpaper by clicking on its name in the Wallpaper list box. If you don't want to use wallpaper, select "(None)" from the top of the list. The preview window shows how the wallpaper will look on your Desktop.

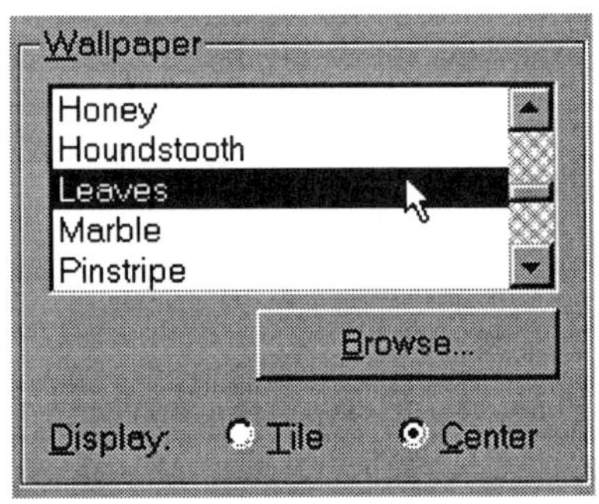

3. Select either the Center or Tile option button.
   - Selecting Center positions the graphic in the center of the screen. If it does not cover the entire screen, the solid or patterned Desktop will be visible around it (see Figure 3a).
   - Selecting Tile repeats the graphic as many times as necessary to cover the entire screen (as in Figure 3b). With small graphics, including most of those supplied with Windows, you will probably want to choose the Tile option.
4. Choose the OK command button to put the selected wallpaper into effect and close the dialog box, or choose the Apply button to put the wallpaper into effect without closing the dialog box.

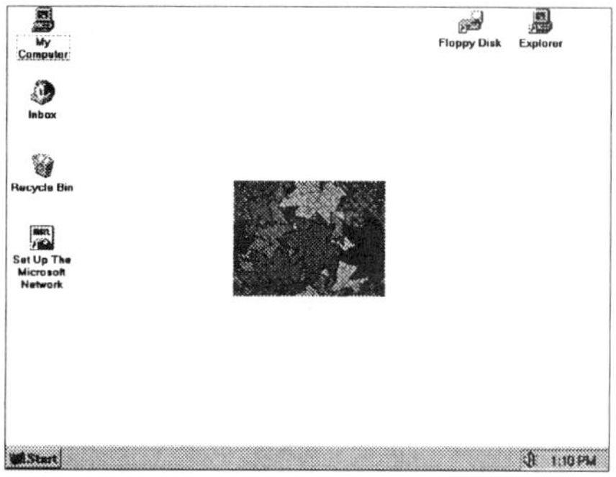

Figure 3a Centered Wallpaper

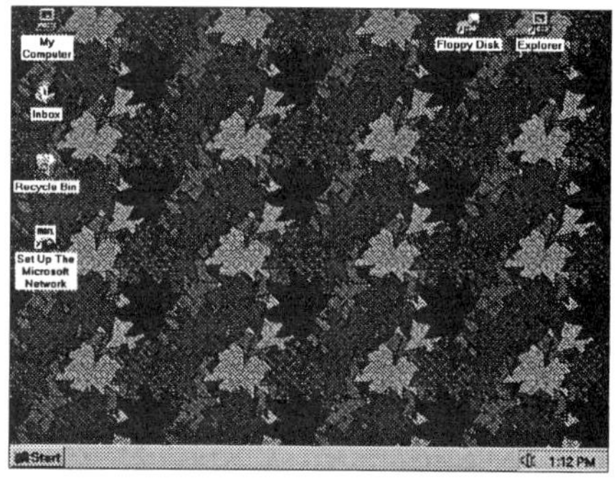

Figure 3b Tiled Wallpaper

Choosing a Screen Saver

When a **screen saver** is in effect and neither the mouse nor the keyboard is used for a specified period of time, the screen will go blank or an animated graphic will be displayed. Screen savers are used just for fun or to deter others from viewing your work while you are away from the computer. They may also prevent damage to the screen from an unchanging image being "burned" into it over time.

Using the Display Properties dialog box, you can choose from among several Windows-supplied screen savers, or choose not to use a screen saver. You can also customize existing screen savers and set the *delay time* — how long the system must be inactive before the screen saver appears.

To select a screen saver:

1. Open the Display Properties dialog box (Figure 2).
2. Click on the Screen Saver tab to display the corresponding page of the dialog box, shown in Figure 4 on the next page.
3. Select a screen saver by clicking on its name in the Screen Saver drop-down list. Select "(None)" if you don't want to use a screen saver. With some screen savers, you will then see a simulation of their action in the preview window.

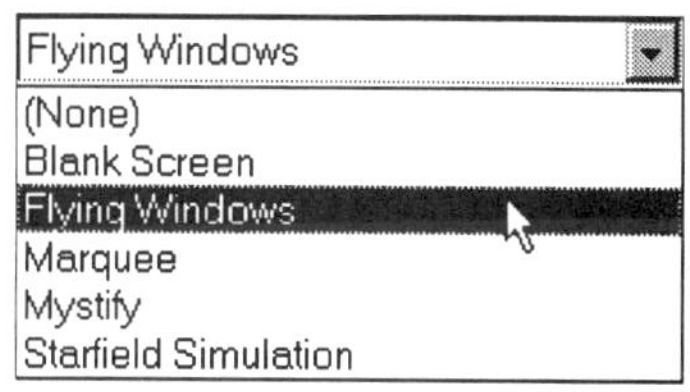

4. To customize the selected screen saver, click on the Settings command button. A dialog box will open allowing you to make certain changes in the way that screen saver works.

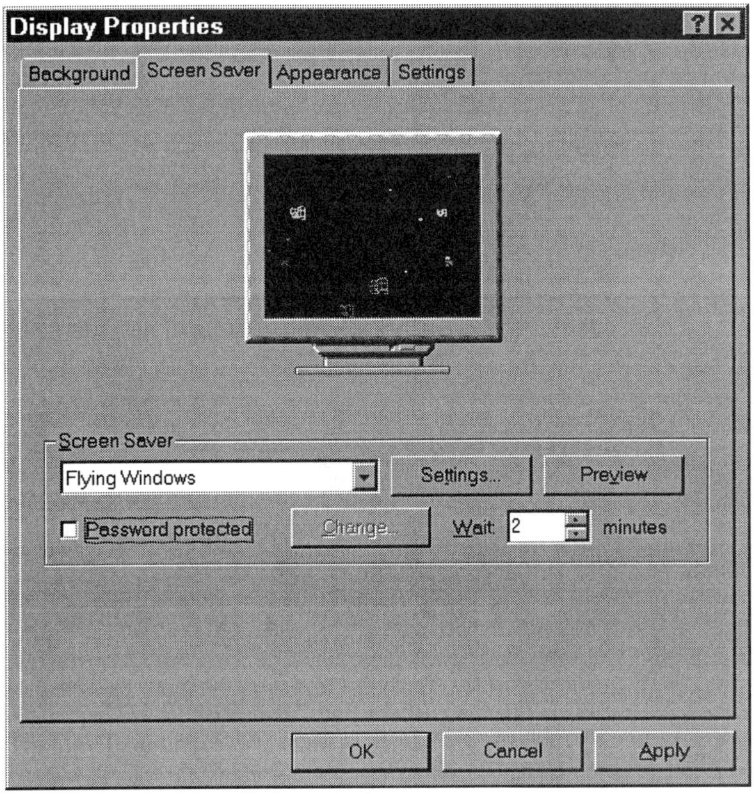

Figure 4 Display Properties — Screen Saver Page

5. To see what the screen saver looks like full-screen, click on the Preview command button. The selected screen saver will be activated for a few seconds. (You may have to click the mouse to deactivate it.)
6. To set the delay time, type a number in the Wait text box (or make use of the up and down arrows in this box to set the time).
7. Choose the OK command button to complete the process and close the dialog box, or choose the Apply button to record your changes without closing the dialog box.

If a screen saver has been selected, it will be activated after the specified delay time. To have the active application reappear on the screen, press any key or move or click the mouse.

NOTE

You can set up certain screen savers so that a password of your choice must be entered to remove the screen saver's image from the screen once it has been activated. To enable password protection, select the *Password protected* check box (see Figure 4), then choose the Change command button and enter your password in the resulting dialog box. (If password protection is not available for the selected screen saver, its check box will be "grayed out".)

5-2 TUTORIAL

Try the following exercises on your own.

1. Turn on your computer, if necessary, to start up Windows 95 and close any open windows.
2. Start Control Panel and open the Display utility by double-clicking on its icon.
3. Select several successive Desktop patterns from the Pattern drop-down list and notice their effect in the preview window of the Display Properties dialog box.
4. Select a wallpaper (your choice) from the Wallpaper drop-down list and select the Tile option button. Notice the effect in the preview window. Now, select the Center option button and notice the change in the preview window.
5. Choose the OK command button to close the Display Properties dialog box and put the pattern and wallpaper into effect.
6. Close the Control Panel window to see the full effect of the changes you have made.
7. Right-click on the Desktop and choose Properties from the pop-up menu to reopen the Display Properties dialog box.
8. Return the Pattern and Wallpaper to their original settings.
9. Click on the Screen Saver tab to open a new page of the Display Properties dialog box.
10. Select Flying Windows from the Screen Saver drop-down list and notice the effect on the preview window.
11. Choose the Preview command button to activate the screen saver (full-screen). Click the mouse to deactivate it.
12. Click on the Wait text box, erase the current number, type `1`, and choose the Apply button. This puts the screen saver into effect without closing the Display Properties dialog box.
13. Do not use the mouse or keyboard for one minute. The screen saver will then be activated. Deactivate it by clicking the mouse or pressing a key.

14. Return the Screen Saver drop-down list and Wait time to their original settings and choose the OK command button to close the Display Properties dialog box.

5.3 Changing the Appearance of a Window

In Windows 95, a typical window contains a number of different elements: a title and menu bar, buttons of various sorts, text, icons, scroll bars, and so on. Through Control Panel's Display utility, Windows allows you to create a **window scheme** — to choose the color and size of such elements. This feature is not only fun to play with, but can also make for a more pleasant working environment.

Windows supplies you with two basic levels of control in customizing the appearance of a window:

1. You can choose a *predefined* (built-in) window scheme.
2. You can create a *custom* window scheme (one of your own design) by:
   - Choosing a color for each of the window elements.
   - Choosing a size for certain elements, such as title, menu, and scroll bars.
   - Choosing a *font* (a type style and size) for identifying text within the window, such as titles and button captions.

All these operations are carried out from the Appearance Page of the Display Properties dialog box. To open this dialog box, either

- Start Control Panel (if it's not already open) and choose the Display icon from its window, as described in Section 5.1.

or

- Right-click on an empty part of the Desktop and choose the Properties option from the resulting pop-up menu.

Then, to display the Appearance page of this dialog box, click on the Appearance tab. The resulting window is shown in Figure 5.

Choosing a Predefined Window Scheme

Windows comes with a wide variety of built-in schemes that consist of a combination of colors, sizes, and/or fonts for the various window elements. To select one of these predefined schemes:

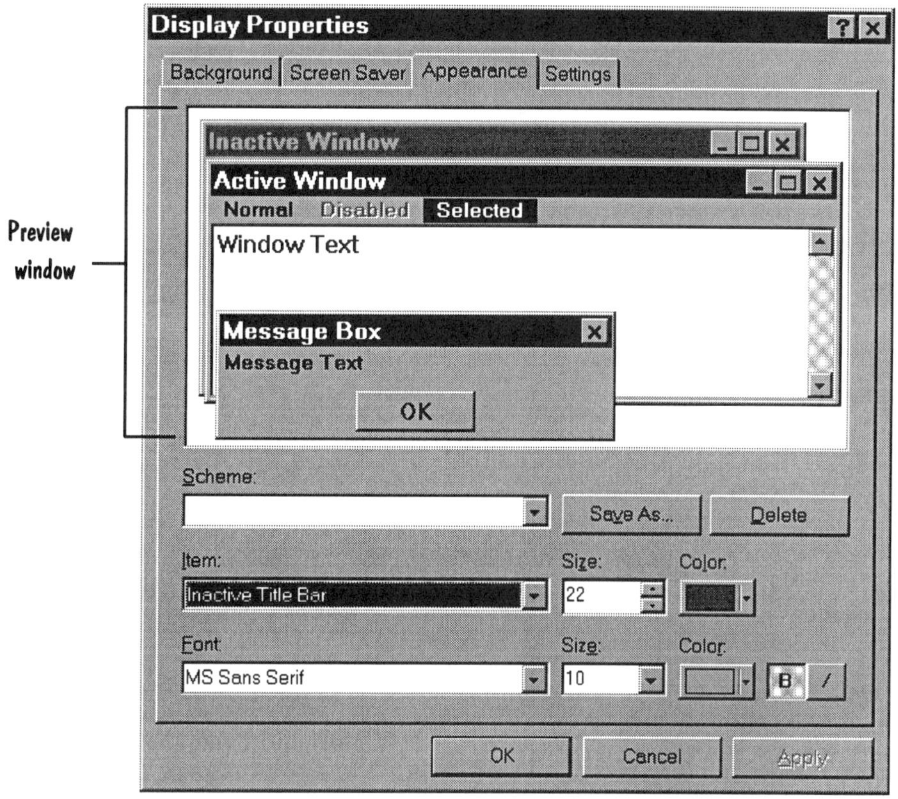

Figure 5 Display Properties Dialog Box — Appearance Page

1. Open the Display Properties dialog box and select the Appearance page as described above.
2. Open the Scheme drop-down list (by clicking on its down triangle). A list of the available schemes will be displayed.
3. Select a scheme from the list. The preview window in the dialog box (see Figure 5) will show the way various screen elements (active and inactive title bars, command buttons, text, and so on) will look under this scheme.

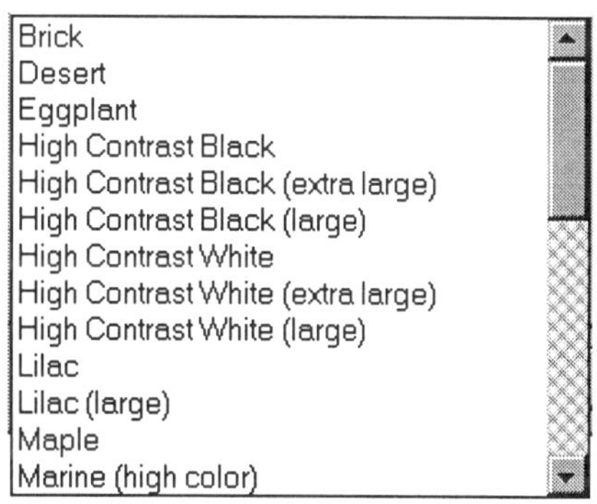

4. Choose the OK command button to put the new scheme into effect and close the dialog box, or choose the Apply button to put the scheme into effect without closing the dialog box. (If you'd rather keep the previous scheme, choose the Cancel command button.)

Creating a Custom Window Scheme

It is likely that you will want to change certain aspects of your favorite predefined window scheme or even create one that is completely different from any built-in scheme. Windows provides you with the tools to fine-tune a scheme as much as you like. Here's how to do it:

1. Open the Display Properties dialog box and select the Appearance page as described at the beginning of this section.
2. Select the predefined scheme that is closest to what you want from the Scheme drop-down list.
3. Select a screen element to be modified by either

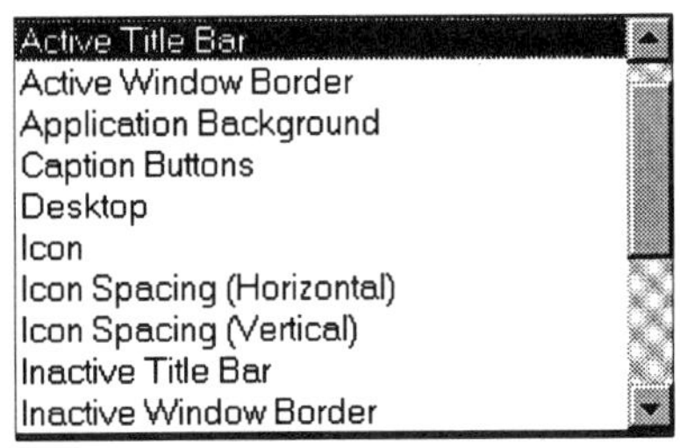

   - Clicking on that element on the Item drop-down list (see Figure 6).

   or

   - Clicking on that element in the preview window area.

   For example, if you want to change the look of the active title bar or the text that appears on it, either select Active Title Bar from the Item drop-down list or click on "Active Window" in the preview window.

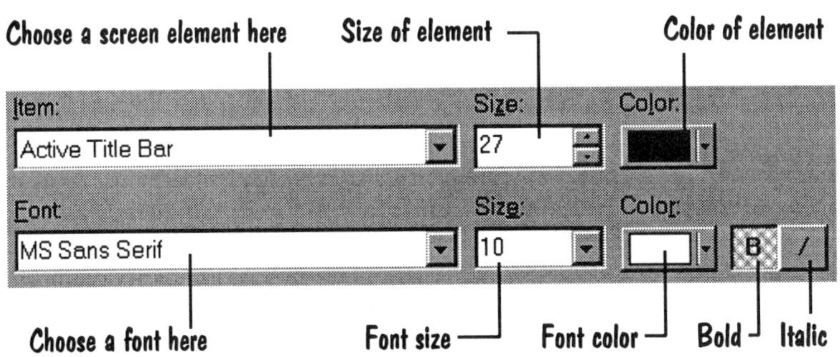

Figure 6 Selecting a Screen Element and its Size, Color, and Font

4. To choose a size for the selected screen element (if this option is available), click on the Size box next to the Item text box, as shown in Figure 6. The number in the Size box gives the height (or sometimes, width) of the object in *points*. There are 72 points per inch, so the height of the Active Title Bar of Figure 6 is 27/72 of an inch, or 3/8".

5. To choose a color for the selected screen element, click on the Color box to the right of the Item text box (Figure 6). A palette of 20 colors will be displayed, as shown at the right. Now, just click on the desired color or, if you want to view additional colors, click on the Other command button, which opens a dialog box with more color choices. (This dialog box also allows you to create your own colors.)

6. If the selected screen element contains text, you can choose the *typeface*, *font size*, *font color*, and elect to use *bold* or *italic* attributes for this text. As you make your selections, the text for the given screen element will change accordingly in the preview window.

   - To select a typeface (the font style), open the Font drop-down list (Figure 6) and select from the available choices.
   - To select a font size, enter a new number in the Size box to the right of the Font text box. The number displayed here represents the height of the font in *points*. (Remember: There are 72 points to the inch.)
   - To select a font color, click on the Color box to the right of the Font text box and select a color from the resulting palette. (See step 5 for more information on selecting a color.)
   - If you want, you can select boldface (thicker) or italic (slanted) type for the text by clicking on the appropriate button (see Figure 6).

7. Save your new window scheme, if so desired, by choosing the Save As command button (see Figure 5) and typing a name for the scheme in the resulting dialog box. This scheme will then be added to the list of available schemes on the Scheme drop-down list.

   If you don't save your scheme, but choose OK or Apply in step 8, the scheme will still be put into effect and used in all Windows sessions until another scheme is selected. After that, however, the only way to retrieve the scheme is to recreate it step-by-step.

8. After you have made all the changes you want, choose the OK

command button to put them into effect and close the dialog box, or choose the Apply button to put the changes into effect without closing the dialog box. (To leave the previous settings in effect, choose the Cancel command button.)

TIP

Modifying certain screen elements also affects other aspects of the Windows interface. For example:

- The settings for the Menu screen element are used for all Windows menus, including the Start menu.
- The font specified for the Icon screen element is also used in the Explorer folder tree and contents panes (see Section 3.2).
- The font specified for the Active Title Bar screen element is also used for the Taskbar.

NOTE

The Settings page of the Display Properties dialog box provides ways to *globally* change the size of objects on the screen; these settings change the size of *everything* by the same scale factor. We will not discuss these features of the Display Properties dialog box in this text.

5.3 TUTORIAL

Try the following exercises on your own.

1. Turn on your computer, if necessary, to start up Windows 95 and close any open windows.
2. Open the Display Properties dialog box: Right-click on an empty part of the Desktop and choose Properties from the pop-up menu.
3. Click on the Appearance tab to open this page of the dialog box.
4. Successively select several window schemes from the Scheme drop-down list and notice their effect on the preview window.
5. Select the Windows Standard scheme.
6. Change the Desktop color to white: Select the Desktop entry in the Item drop-down list, then click on the Color box, and finally, click on the white box in the pop-up palette.
7. Alter the size, color, and text of the active window's title bar:
   - Click on the Active Window title bar *in the preview window.* "Active Title Bar" will appear in the Item text box.
   - Change the height of the title bar to 25 points by clicking on the up-arrow in the Size text box (next to the Item box) until

the entry reads “25".

- Change the color of the active window’s title bar to red by clicking on the Color box (to the right of the Item box) and then clicking on the red-colored square in the pop-up palette.
- Change the active window’s title bar font by opening the Font drop-down list and selecting Arial from it.
- Increase the size of the active window’s title bar font to 10 points by clicking on the Size text box (next to the Font box), deleting the current number, and typing `10`.
- Add italics to the active window’s title bar text by clicking on the Italic button. 

8. Choose the Apply command button to put the new scheme into effect without closing the Display Properties dialog box. (Notice that the font used for the Taskbar buttons has changed.)
9. Select the original window scheme from the Scheme drop-down list (or select Windows Standard, if you’re not sure what that scheme was).
10. Choose the OK command button to close the Display Properties dialog box and put the scheme just selected into effect.

5.4 Adjusting the Feel of Keyboard and Mouse

In terms of your physical comfort while using a computer, some of the most important factors are the look of the screen display, and the operation of the keyboard and mouse. (Another important factor, the chair you sit on, is beyond our control.) In this section, we will discuss how to alter the operation of the keyboard and mouse so they are easier and more pleasant to use.

Changing the Speed of the Keyboard

Most keys on the keyboard have a *repeat feature*; when you press such a key and hold it down, the character or action corresponding to it is repeated until the key is released. For example, if you press the B key and hold it down for a few seconds, a sequence of Bs will appear on the screen.

The number of times a key repeats in a given period of time depends on two factors:

- The *repeat delay* — how long it takes for a key to start repeating once it is pressed.
- The *repeat rate* —how fast the key repeats after the delay time has elapsed.

To change these parameters:

Keyboard

1. Start Control Panel (if it's not already open) and choose the **Keyboard** icon, as described in Section 5.1. The Keyboard Properties dialog box, shown in Figure 7, will be displayed.
2. To decrease the repeat delay, drag the *Repeat delay* slider toward the word *Short* or click to the

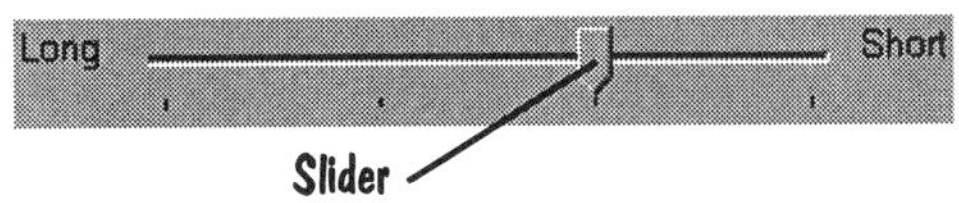

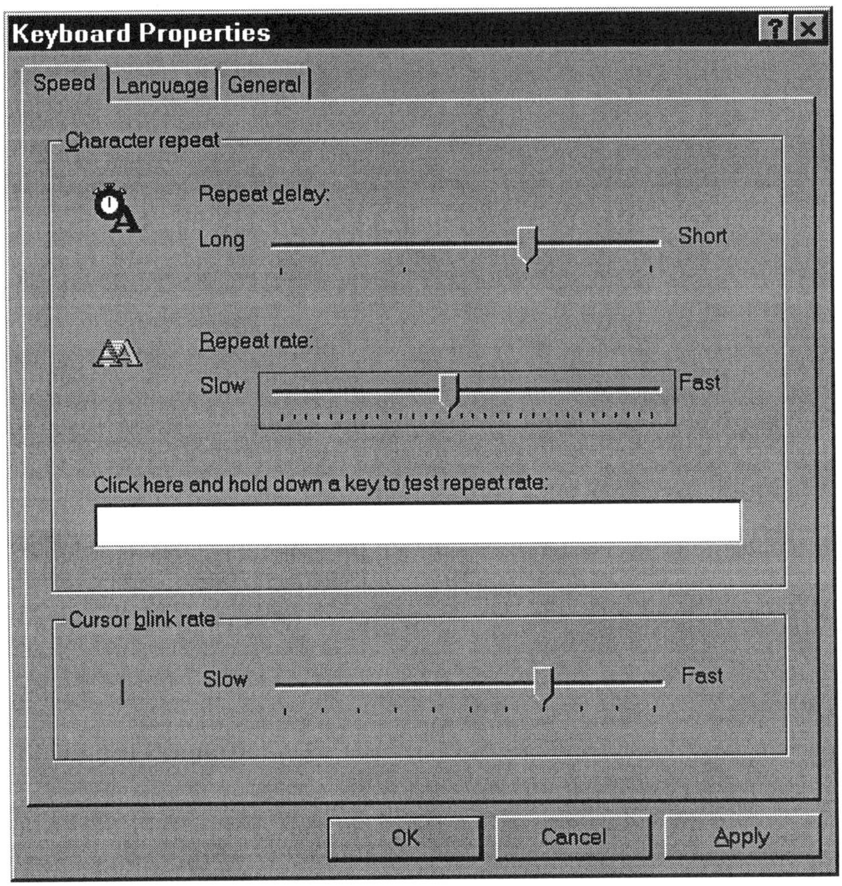

Figure 7 The Keyboard Properties Dialog Box

right of the slider; to increase the delay, drag the slider toward the word *Long* or click to the left of the slider.

3. To decrease or increase the repeat rate, drag the *repeat rate* slider toward *Slow* or *Fast*, respectively, or click to the left or right of the slider.
4. To see the effect of your changes without closing the Keyboard Properties dialog box, click in the text box; then, observe what happens when you hold down a character key such as B.
5. Choose the OK command button to put your changes into effect, or choose the Cancel button to leave things as they formerly were.

NOTE

As you can see in Figure 7, the Keyboard Properties dialog box can also be used to adjust the cursor blink rate. To do so, just drag the slider toward the left (*Slow*) or right (*Fast*), or click to the left or right of the slider.

Changing the Action of the Mouse

Different people have different preferences for the way the mouse "feels" when you move or click it. The feel of the mouse affects the ease with which you can choose menu items, double-click icons, move windows, and perform many other tasks.

To change the mouse settings:

Mouse

1. Start Control Panel (if it's not already open) and choose the **Mouse** icon, as described in Section 5.1. The Mouse Properties dialog box, shown in Figure 8 on the next page, will be displayed.
2. On the Buttons page of this dialog box (which is shown in Figure 8), you can:
   - Swap the functions of the left and right mouse buttons. By default, the left mouse button is the *primary button* — it is used to choose menu items, select icons, and so on; the right button performs the functions we have referred to as right-clicking and right-dragging. If you want to make the right mouse button the primary one, select the *Left-handed* option button (so-named because it usually makes the mouse easier to use for left-handed people). To return to the default configuration, select the *Right-handed* option button.

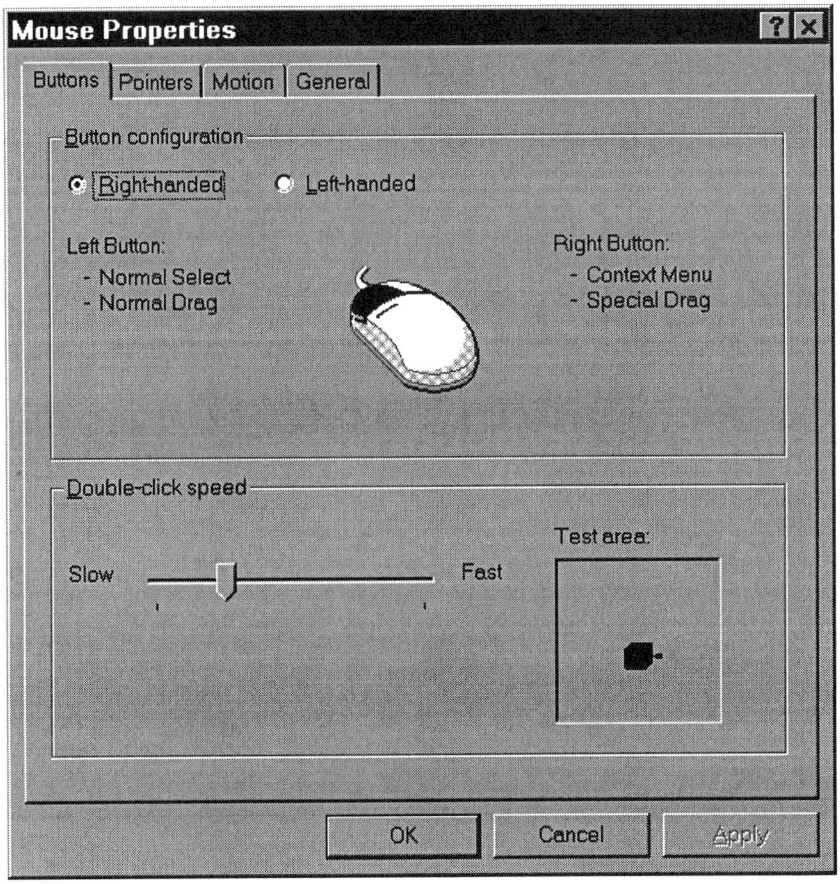

Figure 8 The Mouse Properties Dialog Box

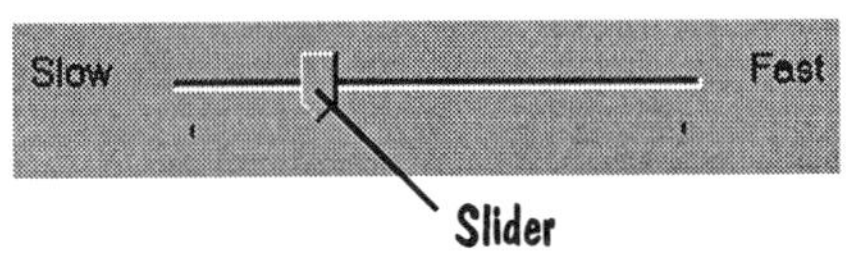

- Change the double-click speed — the amount of time that elapses before Windows 95 interprets a double-click as two separate clicks. Drag the *slider* to the left (toward *Slow*) or click to the left of the slider to allow yourself more time between clicks. You can test the results by double-clicking on the box in the *Test area*; if Windows interprets your two clicks as a double-click, a "jack-in-the-box" pops out.

3. Click on the Pointers tab to provide options that allow you to change the shapes of the various Windows pointers.

4. Click on the Motion tab to provide options that:
   - Change the *pointer speed* — the speed with which the pointer moves across the screen when you move the mouse on the desk top. To increase or decrease the speed, drag the slider in the appropriate direction:

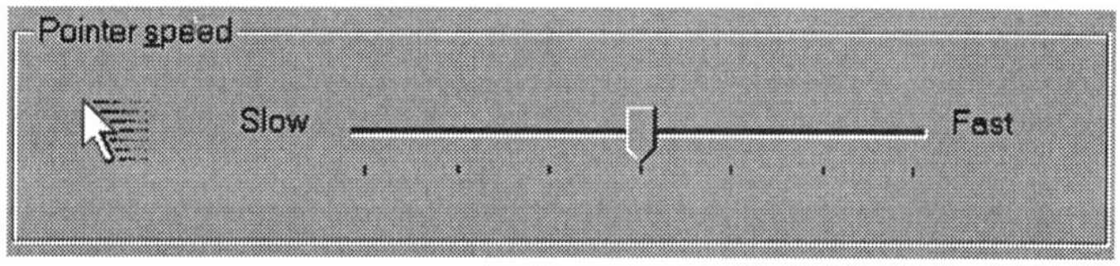

   - Show *mouse trails* — a sequence of pointer icons that follows the path of the mouse across the screen. To turn mouse trails on or off, select or deselect the check box on the Motion page. To increase or decrease the length of the trails, move the slider in the appropriate direction:

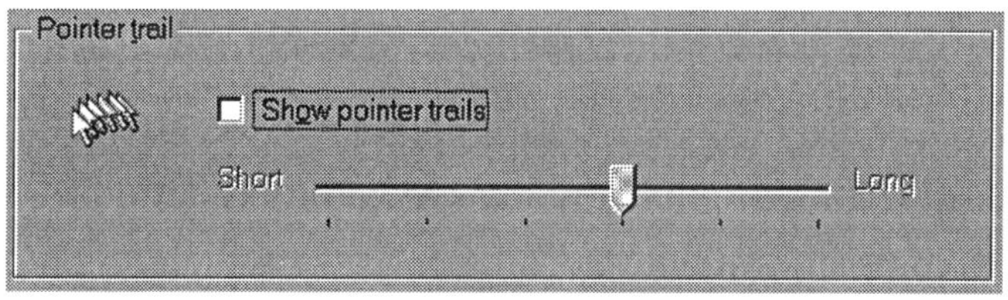

   If the *Show pointer trails* check box is selected, moving the mouse pointer in the dialog box demonstrates the effect. (Most people find pointer trails annoying on a regular monitor, but useful on some portable PC's LCD screens.)

5. Click on the General tab to specify the type of mouse you are using and to see options that are specific to that kind of mouse.
6. Choose the OK command button to put your changes into effect and close the Mouse Properties dialog box, or choose the Apply button to put the changes into effect without closing the dialog box.

5.4 TUTORIAL

Try the following exercises on your own.

1. Turn on your computer, if necessary, to start up Windows 95 and close any open windows.
2. Start Control Panel from the Settings option on the Start menu.

3. Open the Keyboard Properties dialog box by double-clicking on the Keyboard icon in the Control Panel window.
4. Set the *Repeat delay* to Long and the *Repeat rate* to Fast by dragging the sliders to the far left and far right, respectively. With these settings, a key must be held down "a long time" before it starts to repeat, but then repeats rapidly. Click on the test box and hold down a character key (such as A) to see the effect.
5. Set the *Repeat delay* to Short and the *Repeat rate* to Slow by dragging the sliders to the appropriate positions. Click on the test box and hold down a character key (such as A) to see the effect.
6. Set the *Cursor blink rate* slider to Slow; then set it to Fast. Notice the effect of each on the "insertion point" to the left of the slider.
7. Choose the Cancel command button to close the Keyboard Properties dialog box without putting your changes into effect.
8. Open the Mouse Properties dialog box by double-clicking on the Mouse icon in the Control Panel window.
9. Select the *Left-handed* option button and activate the Apply command button. Now, click the left mouse button on the *Right-handed* option button and notice the result. Then, right-click on the *Right-handed* option button and choose Apply again to return the mouse to "right-handed" use.
10. Set the *Double click speed* slider to Fast and then to Slow. In each case, double-click at a few different speeds on the "jack-in-the-box" to see the effect. Jack will pop up or go down if Windows interprets your two clicks as a double-click.
11. Click on the Motion tab to open the corresponding page.
12. Select the *Show pointer trails* check box and drag its slider from Slow to Fast. Notice the effect on the mouse pointer.
13. Click on the General tab and choose the Options command button on the resulting "page". Note the options available for your mouse and then close this dialog box.
14. Choose the Cancel command button in the Mouse Properties dialog box and then close the Control Panel window.

5.5 Other Basic Control Panel Options

In this section, we will discuss a few other basic Control Panel functions; they allow you to:

1. Set the computer's internal clock.
2. Install new programs.
3. View the fonts present on your hard disk.

Setting the Computer's Clock

Your computer contains an internal clock powered by a battery that keeps track of the date and time for the computer system. These settings are used by the Taskbar Clock, Explorer, and numerous other applications for various purposes.

The internal clock normally keeps fairly accurate time, but it may need to be adjusted every once in a while. To change the system date and time:

Date/Time

1. Start Control Panel (if it's not already open) and choose the **Date/Time** icon, as described in Section 5.1. The Date/Time Properties dialog box, shown in Figure 9, will be displayed.

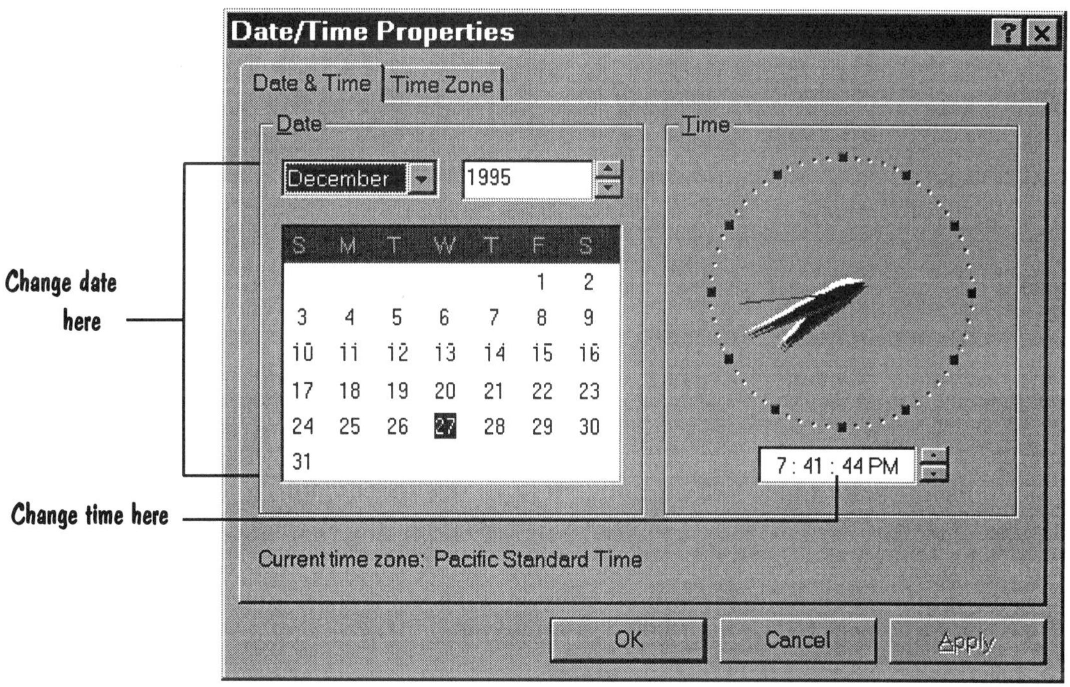

Figure 9 Date/Time Properties Dialog Box

2. Change the time with the aid of the digital clock in the lower right part of this dialog box. The hours, minutes, seconds and AM/PM areas are set separately. To change any of these areas, click on it, use the Backspace or Delete key to delete the current setting, and type in the new one (or click on the up or down arrow button until the correct setting appears).

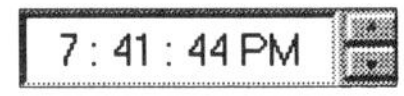

3. To change the date, use the left side of the dialog box. Select the correct month from the drop-down list and type in the correct year in the text box (or click on the up or down arrow button until the correct year appears). The correct day is set by clicking on the appropriate number on the calendar.
4. Choose the OK command button to put your changes into effect and close the Date/Time Properties dialog box, or choose the Apply button to put the changes into effect without closing the dialog box. (The Cancel button cancels all changes and closes the dialog box.)

TIP

Here are a couple of easier ways to open the Date/Time Properties dialog box shown in Figure 9:

- Double-click on the Clock on the Taskbar.

or

- Right-click on the Taskbar Clock and choose the Adjust Date/Time command from the resulting pop-up menu.

Installing New Programs

When you buy application software for use on your computer, it comes on a CD-ROM or a set of floppy disks. Before you can use the application, it must be **installed** on your hard disk. The installation process copies files from the distribution disks to the hard disk and supplies Windows with information about how the program operates. The mechanics of the process differ somewhat from application to application depending on the media (floppy disk or CD-ROM) used and whether or not the software was designed for Windows 95.

Windows 95 CD-ROMs

If your new application is designed for Windows 95 and comes on a CD-ROM, the installation process is very simple. Here's all there is to it:

1. Start Windows and insert the CD in its drive. A dialog box, typically entitled "Install New Program Wizard", will appear on the screen.
2. You will then be presented with a sequence of "pages" that pro-

vide information or ask you to state your preferences concerning various aspects of the installation process. To move to the next page, activate the Next command button.

3. When the process is complete, activate the Finish button.

Installing other applications

For applications that come on floppy disks or those that are not designed for Windows 95, the installation process is usually almost as easy:

1. Start Windows and insert the floppy disk labeled “Install” or “Setup” or the CD-ROM in its drive.

Add/Remove Programs

2. Start Control Panel (if necessary) and choose the **Add/Remove Programs** icon, as described in Section 5.1. The Add/Remove Programs Properties dialog box, shown in Figure 10, will appear.

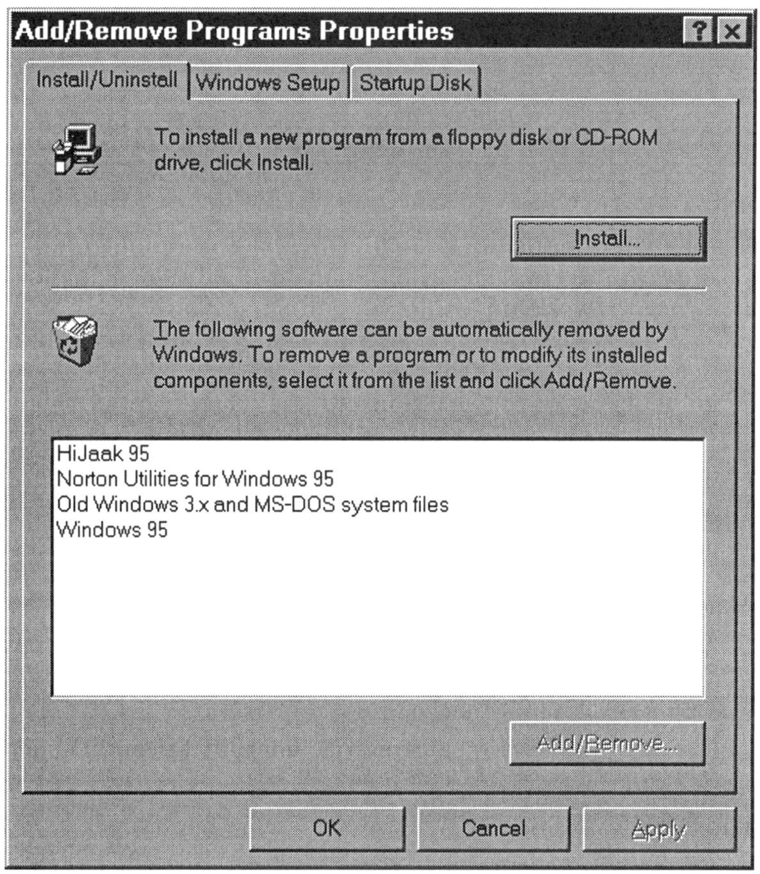

Figure 10 Add/Remove Programs Properties Dialog Box

3. Choose the Install command button. The Install Program dialog box will appear.
4. Choose the Next command button. Windows will automatically search the floppy disk or CD for an installation program and, if found, display its name.
5. If Windows is unable to locate the installation program (or if you are certain it has not found the right one), type its name in the text box. (You will find this information in the documentation that came with your program or on the installation disk itself.)
6. Choose the Finish command button. The new application's installation program will then begin to run.
7. Respond to any on-screen queries until the installation process is complete. A menu item for the new program is usually placed on one of the Start button's submenus during the process to make it easy to run the newly-installed software.

NOTE

The Add/Remove Programs Properties dialog box also allows you to:

- Remove all remnants of (that is, *uninstall*) an application designed for Windows 95, or Windows 95 itself, from your hard disk. The programs that can be uninstalled are listed on the Install/Uninstall page of the dialog box (see Figure 10).
- Remove old versions of DOS and Windows from your hard disk (which is also done from the Install/Uninstall page).
- Add or remove certain Windows 95 components, such as accessories, disk tools, and the Microsoft Network. (This option appears on the Windows Setup page of the dialog box.)
- Create a *startup disk* (bootable disk) — a floppy disk that can be used to start your system should the hard disk, or key information on it, become inaccessible. (This feature is located on the Startup Disk page of the dialog box.)

Viewing Your Fonts

A **font** is a collection of characters — letters, numerals, and other symbols — of a given design, size, and style. Examples of fonts are "12-point Times New Roman" and "10-point Arial bold"; these fonts look like this:

12-point Times New Roman **10-point Arial bold**

The design or *typeface* of a font determines the overall look of the characters; the fonts shown above are examples of the Times New Roman and Arial typefaces. The *size* of a font is its height, measured in points; a *point* is 1/72 of an inch. Thus, 12-point type is roughly 1/6-inch high. Fonts are also distinguished by their *attributes*; for example: regular, **bold**, or *italic*.

Some fonts are available in discrete sizes, such as 8-point, 10-point, etc. Others, known as **scalable fonts**, can be used in any size. Times New Roman and Arial are examples of a kind of scalable font called **TrueType**, which is included with the Windows software. TrueType fonts are available from many other sources, as well. (So are scalable fonts of other kinds, notably the widely used *Postscript* typefaces, developed by Adobe Systems, Inc.)

We will show how to make use of fonts in applications in Chapter 7. Here, we describe how to employ Control Panel to view or print samples of the fonts stored on your hard disk. (Control Panel also allows you to add or remove fonts from your disk, but we won't discuss this feature.) To view or print font samples:

Fonts

1. Start Control Panel and choose the **Fonts** icon, as described in Section 5.1. The Fonts subfolder of the Windows folder, shown in Figure 11, will open. (The "TT" icon indicates a TrueType font.)

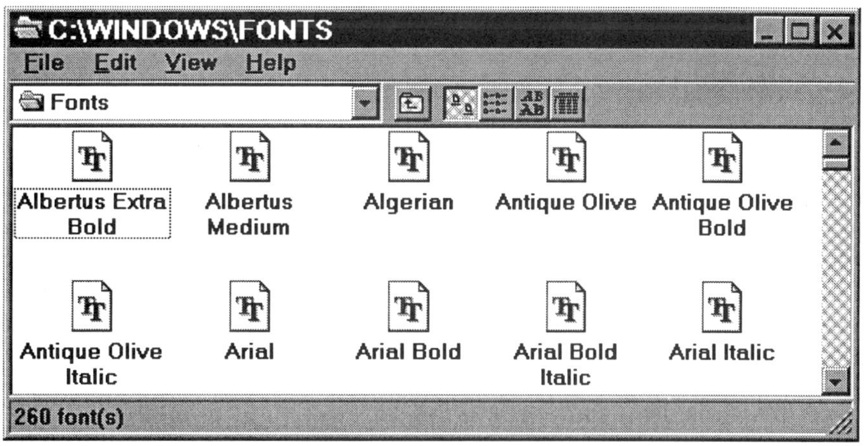

Figure 11 The Fonts Folder (Large Icons View)

2. Select the font in which you are interested by clicking on its name.
3. To view a sample of the selected font, perform any of the following actions:
   - Choose the Open command from the File menu.

- Double-click on the desired font.
- Right-click on the desired font and choose the Open command from the resulting pop-up menu.

In any case, a dialog box similar to the following one will be displayed:

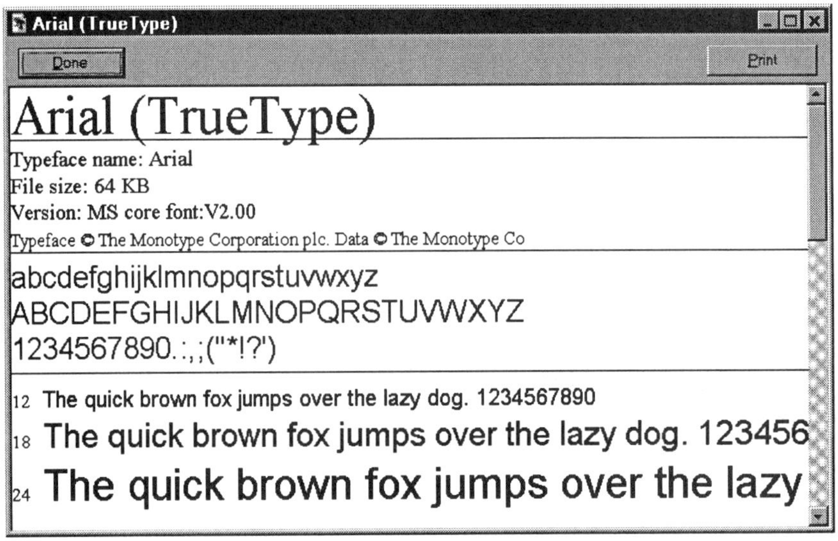

4. To print the displayed font sample, choose the Print command button from this dialog box and then choose OK in the resulting Print dialog box. (A sample of the selected font can also be printed directly from the Fonts folder window — Figure 11 — by choosing the Print command from either the File menu or the right-click pop-up menu.)
5. To close the dialog box and return to the Fonts folder window, click on the close button or choose the Done command button.

Figure 11 shows the default "Large Icons" view of the Fonts folder. Even when this window is maximized, it will probably only show a small portion of your available fonts without scrolling. To display more font names and icons:

- Choose the *Hide Variations (Bold, Italic, etc.)* command from the View menu if it's not already checked. Then, instead of seeing (for example) "Albertus Extra Bold" and "Albertus Medium", only "Albertus" will be displayed.
- Choose either List, Similarity, or Details from the View menu, or

by clicking a Toolbar button as indicated below. (If the Toolbar is not currently visible in the Fonts folder window, choose the Toolbar command from the View menu.)

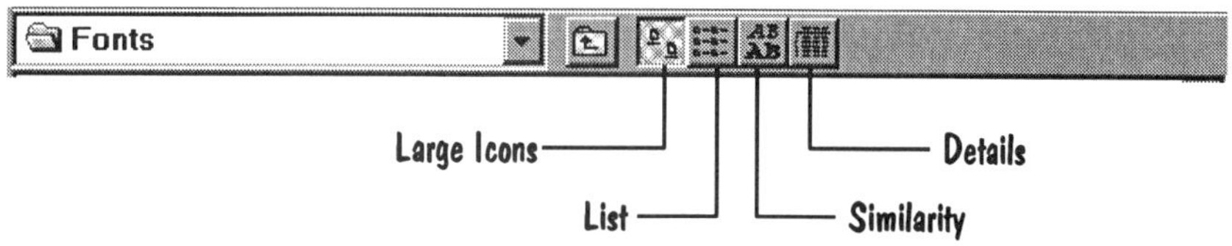

The List option displays the most font names at once; Similarity lists the fonts and describes their degree of similarity to the selected font; Details provides, for each font, the name, size, and creation date of the file that contains it. You will probably find the List view option to be the most useful.

Chapter Summary

Control Panel Basics	To start Control Panel	Click on the Start button to open the Start menu, point at the Settings option, and choose Control Panel from the submenu.
	To change views in the Control Panel window	Choose Large Icons, Small Icons, List, or Details from the View menu; *or* click on the appropriate Toolbar button.
	To select a Control Panel function (utility)	Double-click on its icon in the Control Panel window; *or* click on its icon and choose Open from the File menu.
Control Panel Utilities and their Functions	Display	Select and customize a Desktop pattern (Background page). Select wallpaper (Background page). Select and customize a screen saver (Screen Saver page). Select a built-in window scheme or modify an existing scheme (Appearance page). Change the screen resolution (Settings page).
	Keyboard	Change the repeat rate and delay. Change the cursor blink rate.
	Mouse	Select primary mouse button (Buttons page). Change double-click speed (Buttons page).

	Change mouse pointer icons (Pointers page). Change mouse pointer speed (Motion page). Show mouse pointer trails (Motion page). Change other mouse settings (General page).
Date/Time	Adjust the internal clock's date and time.
Add/Remove Programs	Install new programs (Install/Uninstall page). Uninstall Windows 95 and its applications; remove old versions of DOS and Windows 3.1 (Install/Uninstall page). Add or remove certain Windows 95 components (Windows Setup page). Create a Startup diskette (Startup Disk page).
Fonts	View and print font samples. Add or remove fonts.

Review Exercises

Section 5.1

1. To start Control Panel, point at the ___________ option on the Start menu and then click on the Control Panel item.
2. To start a particular Control Panel utility, select it and choose the ___________ command from the File menu or the right-click pop-up menu.
3. True or false: The type and number of Control Panel functions available for your computer system depend on its configuration.
4. True or false: If you change a Control Panel setting, the original setting will be restored the next time you start Windows.
5. Which of the following Control Panel utilities can be used to change the properties of audio devices connected to your system?
   a. Modems
   b. Multimedia
   c. Sound
   d. Regional Settings
6. Which of the following Control Panel utilities can be used to change settings such as the format of numbers and currencies?
   a. Modems
   b. Multimedia
   c. Regional Settings
   d. System

Section 5.2

7. To place a patterned background on your Desktop, begin by opening Control Panel and double-clicking on the ___________ icon.
8. You can use Control Panel to place ___________, a graphic image, either tiled or centered on the Desktop.
9. A ___________ can be used to cause an animated image to appear on the screen after a specified period of inactivity.
10. True or false: To apply a new Desktop pattern or wallpaper to the Desktop, you must first close the Display Properties dialog box.
11. True or false: When wallpaper is centered (instead of tiled), it always completely covers the Desktop.
12. True or false: The delay time for a screen saver is how long the mouse and keyboard must be inactive before the screen saver appears.
13. To open the Display Properties dialog box without first opening Control Panel:
    a. Right-click on the Taskbar and then click on Properties.
    b. Right-click on the Desktop and then click on Properties.
    c. Double-click on the Taskbar and then click on Properties.
    d. Double-click on the Desktop and then click on Properties.
14. If your computer has been inactive for a while and a screen saver has been activated, to return to your work you must:
    a. Click the mouse.
    b. Move the mouse.
    c. Press a key.
    d. Perform any of the above actions.

Section 5.3

15. To change the colors of various objects in a window, use the ___________ page of the Display Properties dialog box.
16. To select a predefined window scheme, open the ___________ drop-down list in the Display Properties dialog box.
17. True or false: You can modify certain elements of a predefined window scheme by clicking on an element in the Item drop-down list and then making changes to it.
18. True or false: One-half inch is equivalent to 36 points.
19. From the Appearance page of the Display Properties dialog box, you *cannot* change the size of
    a. Scroll bars
    b. Title bars
    c. Menu entries
    d. The Desktop

20. From the Appearance page of the Display Properties dialog box, you cannot change the color of
    a. Scroll bars
    b. Title bars
    c. Menu entries
    d. The Desktop

Section 5.4

21. To change the keyboard repeat rate and delay, begin by double-clicking on the ___________ icon in Control Panel.
22. If it seems as if the functions of the left and right mouse buttons have been interchanged, you can switch them back by using the ___________ utility in Control Panel.
23. True or false: To change the cursor blink rate, use the Cursor utility in Control Panel.
24. True or false: Turning on mouse trails may be useful if you're having trouble following the movement of the mouse pointer.
25. The Mouse Properties dialog box:
    a. Cannot be used to change the double-click speed.
    b. Cannot be used to turn mouse pointer trails on or off.
    c. Cannot be used to change the mouse pointer speed.
    d. Can be used to perform all the above tasks.
26. The Keyboard option in Control Panel cannot be used to
    a. Swap the functions of certain keys on the keyboard.
    b. Change the cursor blink rate.
    c. Extend the time delay for repeating keys on the keyboard.
    d. Increase the repeat rate for repeating keys on the keyboard.

Section 5.5

27. If the Taskbar Clock is displaying the wrong time, you can correct it by using Control Panel's ___________ utility.
28. TrueType is a collection of ___________, some of which are included with the Windows software.
29. To add or remove certain Windows components, such as Accessories, use Control Panel's ___________ utility.
30. True or false: The system date and time must be set every time you start Windows.
31. True or false: Some programs that are distributed on CD-ROMs can be installed without starting Control Panel.
32. True or false: Every character in an 18-point font is roughly 1/4-inch wide.

33. The Fonts utility in Control Panel allows you to:
    a. Change the font used for icon titles.
    b. Change the font used in the active application.
    c. Set a default font for your printer.
    d. View the fonts on your hard disk.

34. Using the Add/Remove Programs utility in Control Panel,
    a. You can install programs on your hard disk.
    b. You can remove old versions of DOS from your hard disk.
    c. You can create a "startup disk".
    d. You can perform all of the above tasks.

Build Your Own Glossary

35. The following words and phrases are important terms that were introduced in this chapter. (They appear within the text in boldface type.) Use WordPad (see Section 2.2) to enter a definition for each term, preserving alphabetical order, into the Glossary file on the Student Disk.

Add/Remove Programs utility	Font	Scalable font
Control Panel	Fonts folder	Screen saver
Date/Time utility	Install software	TrueType font
Display utility	Keyboard utility	Wallpaper
	Mouse utility	Window scheme

Lab Exercises

Work each of the following exercises at your computer. Begin by turning the machine on (if necessary) to start Windows 95, closing any open windows, and starting Control Panel. If you want to produce a written record of your answers, review the material on WordPad and capturing screens in Sections 2.2 and 2.3.

Lab Exercise 1 (Section 5.2)

a. Start the Display utility from the Control Panel window, which opens the Display Properties dialog box. Which (tab) page of this dialog box is active?

b. Select the "50% Gray" repeating pattern from the Pattern List box. Based on its appearance in the preview window, how would you describe this pattern?

c. Choose the Edit Pattern command button. Based on its appearance in the left side of the Pattern Editor dialog box, what is a better name for the "50% Gray" pattern?

d. Close the Pattern Editor dialog box and return the Desktop pattern to its original setting.

e. Select the Center option button and select the wallpaper images one-by-one. Which, if any, of the wallpapers cover the entire preview window?

f. Select the Tile option button, select a wallpaper from the list box, and then choose the Apply command button. Does the wallpaper cover the entire visible Desktop?

g. Return the wallpaper to its original setting and close the Display Properties dialog box.

Lab Exercise 2 (Section 5.2)

a. Start the Display utility from the Control Panel window, which opens the Display Properties dialog box. Now, click on the Screen Saver tab. Which, if any, screen saver is in effect?

b. Select the Flying Windows screen saver from the Screen Saver drop-down list. Is this screen saver displayed in the preview window?

c. Set the delay time for ".5" minutes and choose the Preview command button. What time is displayed in the Wait text box after the preview is complete? What conclusion can you draw about the possible delay times?

d. Choose the Settings command button. Try various warp speeds and densities and observe the effect on the preview window. (You will have to choose OK in the Options for Flying Windows dialog box to see the effect of each change.) Describe the effect of changing warp speed and density.

e. In the Display Properties dialog box, choose the Apply button and wait for a minute or two. Did the screen saver become active? If it did, what action did you take to return to the dialog box?

f. Restore the previous screen saver, if any, and close the Display Properties dialog box.

Lab Exercise3 (Section 5.3)

a. Start the Display utility from the Control Panel window, which opens the Display Properties dialog box. Now, click on the Appearance tab. Which, if any, window scheme is named in the Scheme text box?

b. Select the Active Title Bar from the Item list. What font and font size are used for it?

c. Open the Scheme drop-down list. How many schemes are listed?

d. Select, in succession, the "Windows Standard", "Windows Standard (large)", and "Windows Standard (extra large)" schemes. What are the respective font sizes for the Active Title Bar? Is the same font (type style) used for all three schemes?

e. By selecting, one-by-one, all the available schemes, answer the following questions:

- Which schemes use no colors other than black and white (for the items displayed in the preview window)?
- Which schemes use the Times New Roman font for the Active Title Bar?

f. Select the Windows Standard scheme and 3D Objects (from the Item list). Change the font color to bright red. Which objects in the preview window are affected by the 3D Objects color?

g. Choose the Cancel button to close the Display Properties dialog box.

Lab Exercise 4 (Section 5.3)

a. Start the Display utility from the Control Panel window, which opens the Display Properties dialog box. Now, click on the Appearance tab. Which, if any, window scheme is named in the Scheme text box?

b. Select the High Contrast White scheme and change 3D Objects to light gray. Which objects in the preview window changed color?

c. Change:

- The Active Title Bar color to dark blue.
- The Desktop color to teal (blue-green).
- The Inactive Title Bar color to dark gray and its font color to light gray.
- Menu items to light gray.

How does the look of the resulting preview window differ from that of the Windows Standard scheme?

d. *Optional*: Capture the Display Properties window, paste it into WordPad, and print the resulting document. (Try this only if you've already read Sections 2.2 and 2.3.)

e. Choose the Cancel button to close the Display Properties dialog box.

Lab Exercise 5 (Section 5.4)

a. Start the Keyboard utility from the Control Panel window. Where are the Repeat Delay and Repeat Rate sliders positioned (relative to the "tick marks" that appear just below each slider)?

b. Set the repeat delay as short as possible and the repeat rate as fast as possible. In the test area, hold down a character key for about one second. How many characters were displayed?

c. Now set the repeat delay as long as possible and the repeat rate as slow as possible. In the test area, hold down a different character key, also for about one second. How many characters are displayed this time?

d. Set the cursor blink rate as slow as possible; then set it at the middle of the scale. In each case, with the aid of a watch with a second hand, determine how many "blinks" take place in ten seconds.

e. Click on the Language tab. What language and layout are used by your keyboard?

f. Click on the General tab. What is your keyboard type?

g. Choose the Cancel command button to close the Keyboard Properties dialog box.

Lab Exercise 6 (Section 5.4)

a. Start the Mouse utility from the Control Panel window.

b. Switch the button configuration from right-handed to left-handed (or vice-versa). What changes do you see in the dialog box?

c. Set the double-click speed to slow; then to fast. By trying each setting in the Test area, which one requires you to double-click more quickly?

d. Click on the Pointers tab. Make a list of all the available pointer schemes.

e. Click on the Motion tab. What options are available on the Motion page?

f. Set the pointer speed to slow; then, to fast. Do you notice any change in pointer speed?

g. Select the pointer trails check box (or deselect it, if it's currently selected). Do you notice any change in pointer trails?

h. Click on the General tab and choose the Options command button, if it is present. What options, not available elsewhere in the Mouse Properties dialog box, are displayed in the resulting dialog box?

i. Close the Options dialog box and choose the Cancel command button to close the Mouse Properties dialog box.

Lab Exercise 7 (Section 5.5)

a. Start the Date/Time utility from the Control Panel window. What is the name of the "current time zone"?

b. By using the up and down arrows, determine the earliest and latest years available for the calendar.

c. Choose the Cancel command button to close this dialog box.

d. Start the Fonts utility from the Control Panel window. How many fonts are available on your system? (Look on the status bar, at the bottom of the Fonts window.)

e. Use the View menu or Toolbar to switch to List view. How many columns are displayed?

f. Select the Times New Roman font; then, view (open) it and choose the Print command button in the dialog box. (Make sure that the printer connected to your computer is ready before issuing the Print command.)

g. Close the Times New Roman dialog box and the Fonts window.

If You Want to Learn More ...

The notes presented here allow you to delve more deeply into some of the topics covered in this chapter.

Having Control Panel running on Windows startup

If you find that you use the Control Panel utilities frequently, you can arrange to have Control Panel running when you start Windows.

- If Control Panel is minimized when you shut down Windows, it will appear as a Taskbar button the next time Windows starts up.
- If the Control Panel window is open when you shut down Windows, it will open automatically the next time Windows starts up.

You can also achieve these ends by placing a shortcut to Control Panel in the StartUp folder (see Sections 3.4 and 4.2 for information about shortcuts and the StartUp folder).

More colorful screens

Most computer systems are capable of simultaneously displaying at least 256 different colors on the screen. To see how many colors your computer's video adapter is currently set to display, open Control Panel's Display utility and click on the Settings tab in the Display Properties dialog box. The current mode is shown in the Color Palette drop-down list. To increase the number of colors, select a higher setting from this drop-down list and choose the OK command button. (You will probably have to restart Windows for the change to go into effect.)

The procedure just described will not change the current screen colors. To do so, you must open the Appearance page of the Display Properties dialog box and change the color of individual screen elements. However, clicking on the Color button for a particular element displays a palette of only 20 colors (see page 191). To display a broader color palette or define your own custom colors, choose the Other command button. (For information about creating custom colors, see the *If You Want to Learn More* section of Chapter 8.)

Icon spacing on the Desktop

After you've used Windows for a while and added a number of shortcuts to the Desktop (see Section 3.4), you'll probably want to arrange them neatly in ordered rows and columns. This can be accomplished by right-clicking on an empty part of the Desktop and, on the resulting pop-up menu

- Point at Arrange Icons and choose an option from the submenu to order the icons by their name, the type of file they represent, the size of that file, or the date it was created.

or

- Choose Line up Icons, which keeps the icons in the current order but arranges them within an invisible grid of rows and columns.

Each cell in the invisible Desktop grid has a certain default height and width, which determines how far apart the icons are spaced. To change this spacing (perhaps to move the icons closer together):

1. Open the Display utility and click on the Appearance tab.
2. Select *Icon Spacing (Horizontal)* from the Item drop-down list.
3. Enter a smaller figure in the Size text box to move the icons closer together in the horizontal direction, or a larger figure to spread them apart. (The number in the Size box is the width of each grid cell in *pixels* — the tiny dots of light that make up the screen image.)
4. Select *Icon Spacing (Vertical)* from the Item drop-down list to adjust the vertical spacing of the Desktop icons.
5. Choose the OK or Apply command button to put your changes into effect.

Note that if the icon spacing figures are too small, the reduced size of the grid cell may cut off some of an icon's text and/or picture. You'll probably have to experiment with these settings to get them "right".

Using the Date/Time utility as a calendar

The main function of the Date/Time utility is to adjust the date and time of the system's internal clock. However, it can also be used to provide monthly calendar views of the years 1980 through 2099. To view any month in this time span, just select the appropriate month and year from their drop-down lists. If you do use Date/Time for this purpose, be sure to close the Date/Time Properties dialog box by choosing the Cancel command button or clicking on the close button. If you choose the OK command button, the system clock will be reset to the currently selected date.

Loading missing Windows components

Depending on the way Windows has been set up on your computer, certain components may or may not be installed. These include wallpapers, screen savers, accessibility options (Section 6.4), accessories (Chapter 9), and communications components (Chapters 10 and 11). To install a missing component:

1. Open Control Panel's Add/Remove Programs utility.
2. Click on the Windows Setup tab to open the Add/Remove Programs Properties dialog box.
3. Select the component you wish to add from the list displayed.
4. Choose the Details command button to open another dialog box that lists all items within that component.
5. From this list, select the check box next to each of the items to be installed.
6. Choose the OK command button. You may be asked to insert the disk that contains the appropriate files. If so, follow the on-screen instructions.
7. When you are done, close the Add/Remove Programs Properties dialog box and Control Panel.

Note that the collections of wallpapers and screen savers are listed under "Accessories" on the Windows Setup page.

Where to go from here

In this chapter, we have only described a few of the utilities typically supplied by Control Panel. Many others will be discussed in Chapter 6. These include Printers, Add New Hardware, Sounds, Multimedia, Accessibility Options, Modems, System, and (briefly) Network, Passwords, and Regional Settings. The Network utility is discussed in more detail in Chapter 10.

The Registry provides another, very sophisticated, way to customize Windows. It will be discussed in Section 12.4.

CHAPTER 6

More About Control Panel

In Chapter 5 we discussed some basic Control Panel options and how you can use them to customize the Windows user interface. In this chapter we will continue this discussion, presenting additional information about Control Panel. The sections in this chapter are independent of one another and, consequently, need not be read in their given order. To be more specific:

- Section 6.1 describes how to change printer settings, manage print jobs, and set up a new printer.
- Section 6.2 discusses how to set up newly-installed hardware, such as a sound card or monitor.
- Section 6.3 describes how to change the sounds associated with certain system "events" (if your computer is equipped with a sound card) and how to change the settings for multimedia devices.
- Section 6.4 deals with the ways that Windows makes the computer more accessible to people with disabilities.
- Section 6.5 presents information about configuring a modem and fine-tuning your hardware, and contains brief descriptions of Control Panel's Network, Passwords, and Regional Settings utilities.

6.1 *Managing Printers*

In Section 2.2, we discussed how to print a document from within a Windows-based application. Recall that choosing Print from the File menu opens a Print dialog box, which allows you to select various print options, such as which pages to print and the number of copies of each. You can exert even more control over the printing process, changing the printer setup, managing the active print jobs, and adding new printers, using the Printers option in Control Panel.

The Printers Folder

Printers

Recall that to open the Control Panel window, you click on the Start button, point at the Settings option on the Start menu, and choose the Control Panel item from the resulting submenu. Then, double-clicking on the Printers icon opens the **Printers folder** window, which is shown in Figure 1. (Your window may look quite different from the one pictured here.)

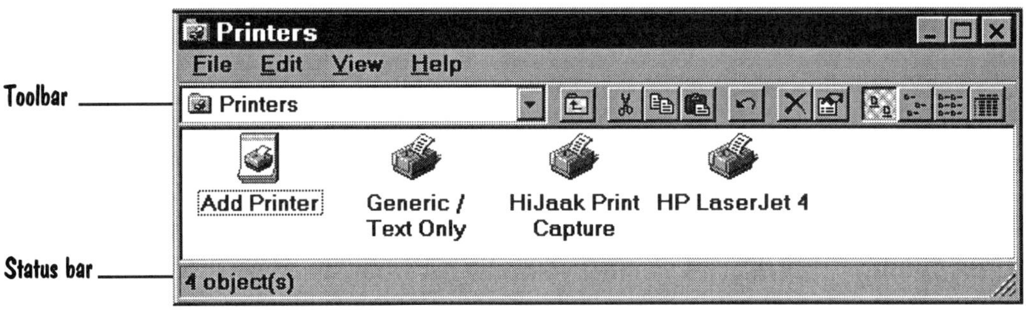

Figure 1 The Printers Folder Window

NOTE

You can also open the Printers folder window in the following ways:

- Click on the Start button, point at the Settings option on the Start menu, and choose the Printers item from the resulting submenu.
- Start My Computer (by double-clicking on its Desktop icon) and double-click on the Printers icon in the resulting window.
- Start Explorer from the Programs submenu of the Start menu and open the Printers folder — near the bottom of the folder tree pane (see Section 3.2).

If the Toolbar (or Status bar) is not visible in the Printers folder window (see Figure 1), it can be toggled on by choosing its name from the View menu. The last four icons on the Toolbar affect the way the printer names and icons are displayed in the window.

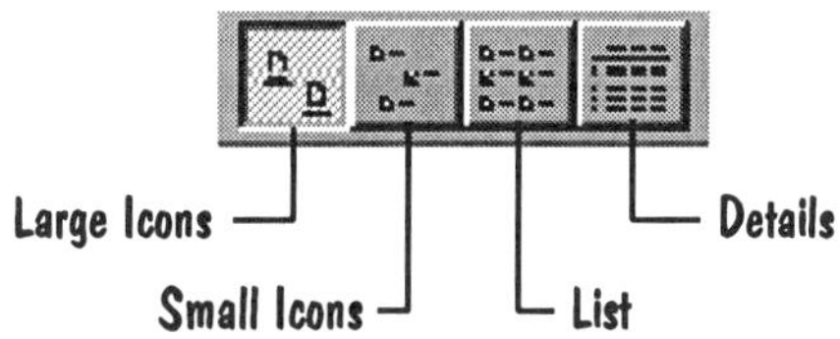

Figure 1 shows the Large Icons view. Clicking on another Toolbar button (or choosing the corresponding item from the View menu) arranges the names and icons differently. For example, Details view, which is shown in Figure 2, gives a little more information about each printer.

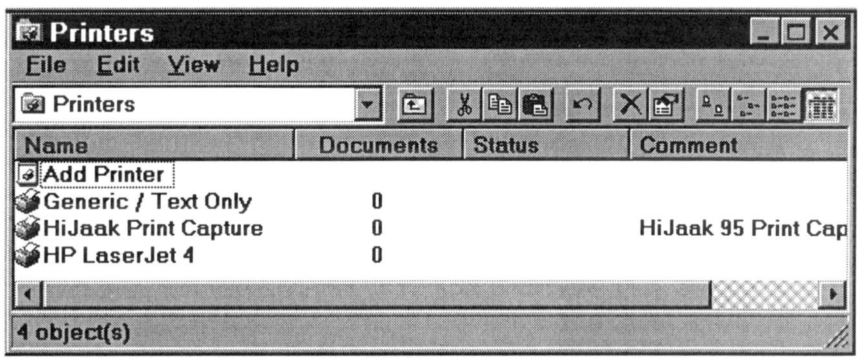

Figure 2 Details View of the Printers Folder Window

Changing the Printer Setup

From time to time, you may want to change certain printer settings, such as the print quality (resolution) or installed fonts. In Windows 95, printer settings are changed from within the Printer Properties dialog box. To display this dialog box:

1. Open the Printers folder, as described earlier in this section.
2. Right-click on the desired printer icon.
3. Choose the Properties item from the resulting pop-up menu.

The content of the Printer Properties dialog box varies considerably from printer to printer. A typical one is shown in Figure 3.

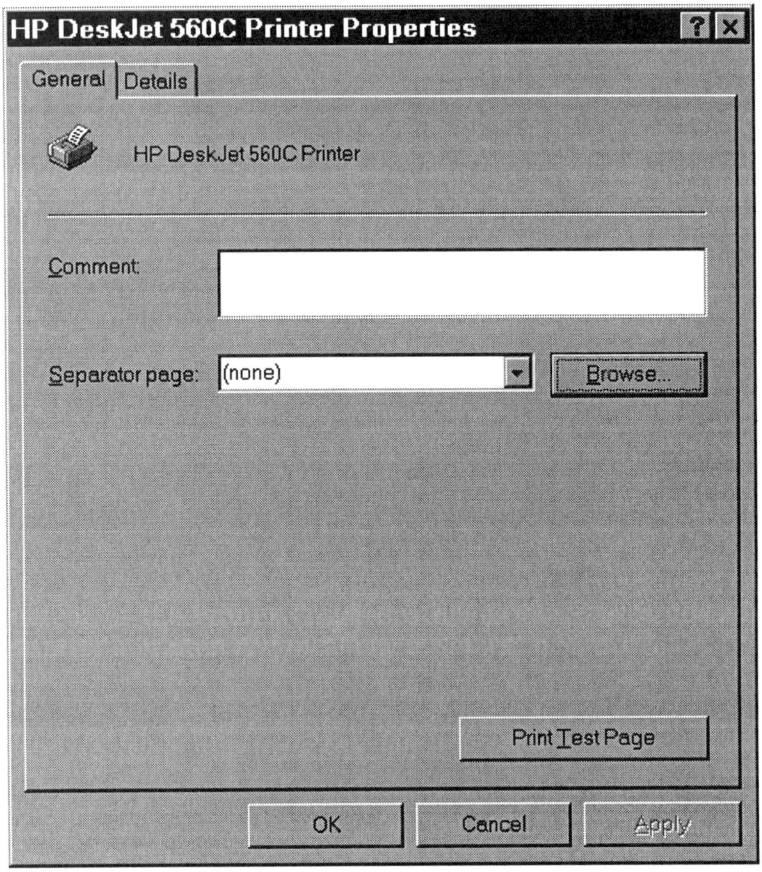

Figure 3 Printer Properties Dialog Box — *General* Page

The first page (the General page) of this dialog box gives the name of the printer and allows you to:

- Define a "comment" for this printer. The comment will appear in Details view of the Printers folder (see Figure 2).
- Specify a "separator page" — a page that will automatically be inserted between print jobs. It can be blank or be printed from a specified file.
- Print a "Test Page" to check that your printer is working properly.

The Details page (and other pages, if present) allows you to change the way the printer is configured. For example, clicking on the Details tab for the HP DeskJet 560C printer displays the page shown in Figure 4.

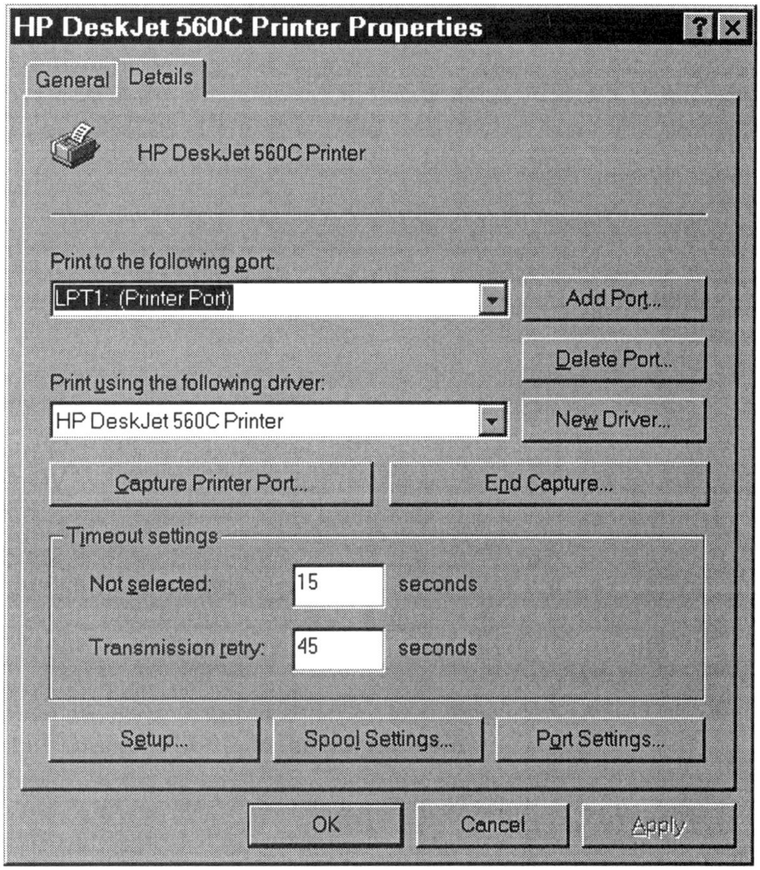

Figure 4 Printer Properties Dialog Box — *Details* Page

Much of the information on the Details page is fairly technical. Here is a quick rundown of the various options:

- The *Port* drop-down list and command buttons are used to change the settings for how your computer is physically or logically (in the case of a network printer) connected to the printer.
- The *Driver* drop-down-list and command button are used to install a different **printer driver** — a program that translates your document's text, graphics, and special codes into a language that

the printer can understand.

- The *Capture* command buttons are used in *mapping* (or removing the mapping of) a port to a network drive.
- The *Timeout* text boxes determine the amount of time Windows will wait for the printer to come online (*Not selected*) or to be ready to print (*Transmission retry*) before reporting an error.

Spooling print jobs

- The *Spool Settings* command button is used to change the manner in which a document is sent from the application to the printer. When a print job is **spooled**, it is temporarily stored on the hard disk (which is a rapid process) and then transferred to the printer at the leisurely pace required by these devices. With spooling in effect, you can use the computer for other tasks once the document has been sent to disk, instead of having to wait until the print job is complete. (You might want to turn spooling *off* if you have little free disk space or if you are encountering certain printing problems.)
- The *Setup* command button opens a dialog box with additional options. (For some printers, additional pages in the Properties dialog box take the place of the Setup button.)

Although the Setup options (or additional dialog box pages) vary from printer to printer, a few are common to virtually all printers. To illustrate these features, consider the Setup options for the HP Deskjet printer, which are shown in Figure 5.

Almost all printers allow you to adjust:

- *Print Quality* In the dialog box of Figure 5, the available print quality choices are labeled *Normal* (medium resolution), *Presentation* (high resolution), and *Fast* (low resolution). The higher the resolution, the nicer text and graphics will look on the page. Some printers refer to these settings using other terms, such as *Draft* for low resolution printing. Other printers (including lasers) use *dots per inch* (dpi) to describe resolution; here, the higher the number, the better-looking the output.
- *Paper Orientation* *Portrait* means that printing takes place parallel to the short side of the paper; the page you are reading is in portrait orientation. *Landscape* means that printing takes place parallel to the long side of the paper; for example, certificates and diplomas are printed in landscape orientation.
- *Media Size* The common 8½" by 11" paper is referred to as *letter size*. If you are about to print on a different size paper or on an envelope, you should let the printer know this by selecting the appropriate paper size.

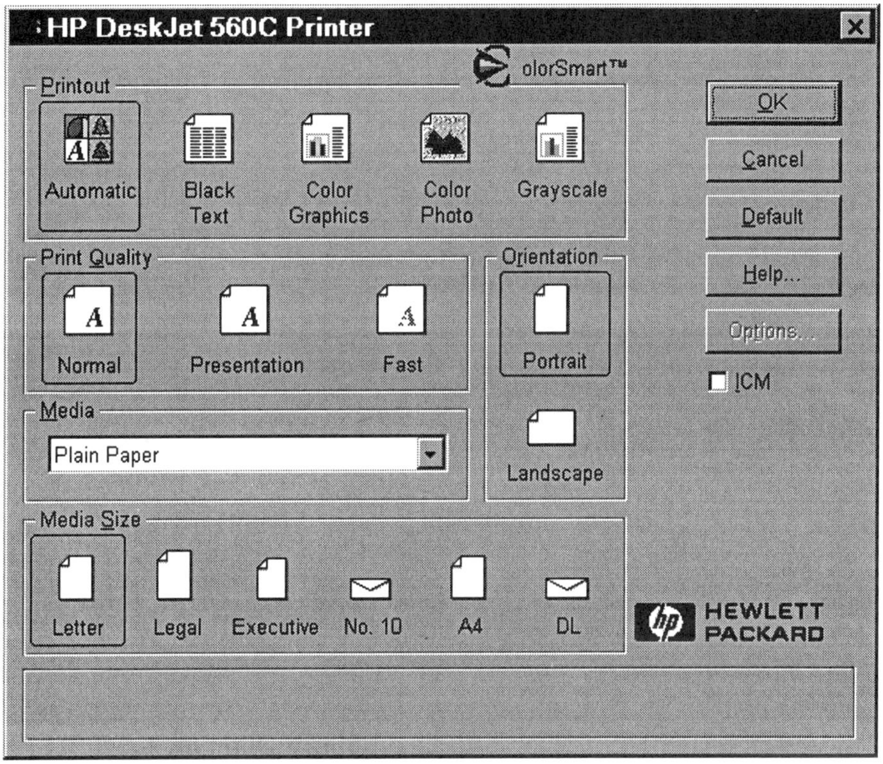

Figure 5 The Result of Choosing the Setup Command Button

NOTE

You can usually access some printer properties from within an application. For example, in WordPad, choosing Page Setup from the File menu opens a dialog box that contains options for paper size and orientation. Moreover, choosing the Printer command button and then the Properties button in the resulting dialog box provides access to additional setup options. In many other applications, you access printer properties by choosing Printer Setup from the File menu or by choosing the Properties command button in the Print dialog box.

Managing Print Jobs

If print spooling is in effect (see above), you can control various aspects of your print jobs while they are running or waiting to be printed. To do so, either:

- Open the Printers folder (as described earlier in this section) and double-click on the appropriate printer icon.

or

- While a document is printing, double-click on the printer icon to the left of the clock on the Taskbar.

In either case, a print manager window, like the one in Figure 6, will open[*]. The list of documents displayed in this window is called the **print queue**. The window in Figure 6 was captured during the printing process; it shows two documents in the queue. If you open the print manager window when the printer is idle, the queue will be empty.

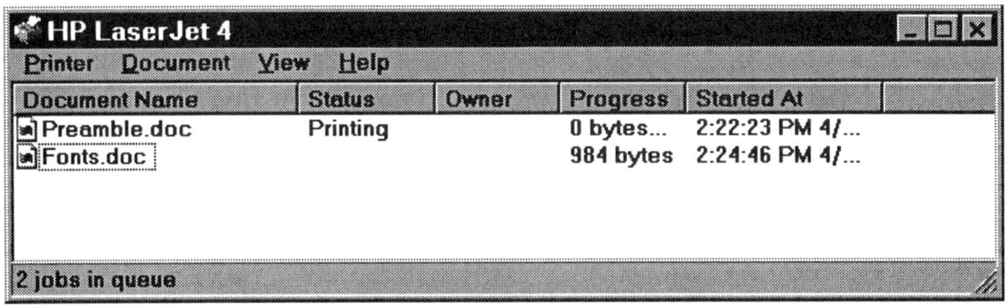

Figure 6 The "Print Manager" Window

Here's how to use the print manager window:

- To cancel printing of a document, select the desired document in the queue and choose Cancel Printing from the Document menu.
- To cancel all print jobs listed in the queue, choose Purge Print Jobs from the Printer menu. All documents will be removed from the queue.
- To pause the printing of a particular document, select the desired document in the print queue and choose Pause Printing from the Document menu. (A check mark will appear next to this menu item and the word *Paused* will appear next to the document name in the Status column.) To restart a paused print job, select the document and choose Pause Printing from the Document menu.
- To pause all print jobs, choose Pause Printing from the Printer menu. (A check mark will appear next to this menu item and the word *Paused* will appear on the title bar.) To restart a paused printer, choose Pause Printing from the Printer menu.

---

[*]This window, which has no official name, takes the place of the Windows 3.1 Print Manager. Most people still refer to it as "the print manager window".

- To change the order of the documents in the print queue, select the document you want to move and drag it to the desired position in the queue.

Adding a New Printer

If you want to use a new printer with your computer, you must first establish a physical connection between the two (say, via a cable) and also provide Windows with some information about the printer. Windows then installs the proper printer driver and sets up the proper pathway between computer and printer. To add a new printer:

1. Open the Printers folder, as described earlier in this section.
2. Double-click on the Add Printer icon (see Figure 1). The Add Printer Wizard will start, displaying an informational page.
3. Click the Next button. If you are connected to a network, you'll then be asked whether you want to install a local or network printer. To install a local printer (one that is directly connected to your computer), select Local and choose the Next button, which displays the dialog box shown in Figure 7.

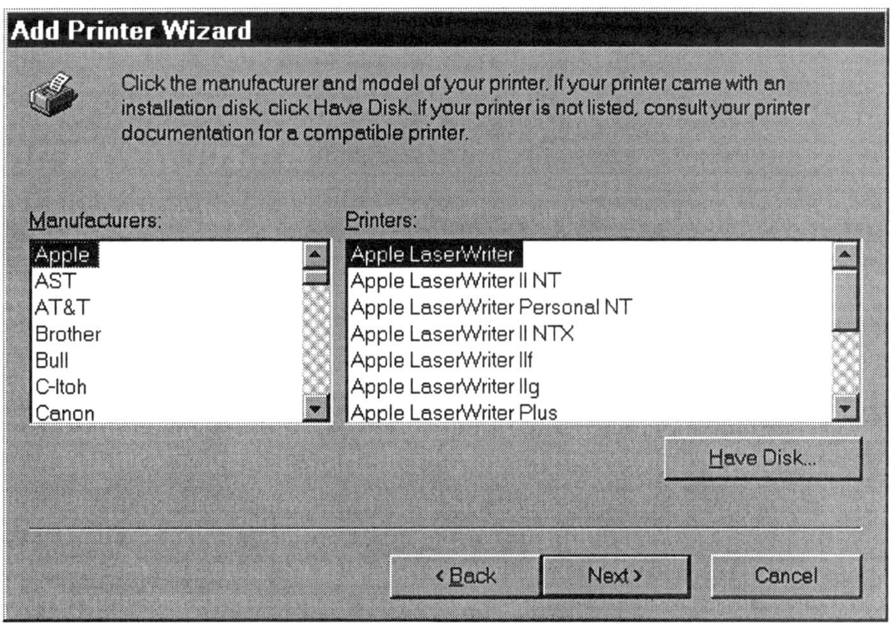

Figure 7 Choosing the Manufacturer and Model of Printer

4. Select the manufacturer and then the model of the new printer from their respective text boxes. If the manufacturer has supplied a printer driver on disk, insert this disk in its drive, choose the Have Disk command button, enter the appropriate drive in the resulting dialog box, and choose the OK button.
5. Choose the Next button. The Add Printer Wizard page shown in Figure 8 will be displayed.

Figure 8 Choosing a Printer Port for the New Printer

6. Check the printer's documentation to determine if it's a parallel or serial printer. In the former case, select LPT1; in the latter case, select COM1 if no other device is attached to the computer's primary serial port, otherwise select COM2.

   If the printer is of the serial variety, you may have to configure its port. In this case, choose the Configure Port command button, enter the requested information (as specified in the printer manual), and choose the OK button.

   Select the *File* option if the new printer cannot be accessed directly from your computer, but you would occasionally like to print files on it. In this case, when this printer is selected, the print job will be stored on disk and can be copied at a later time to the desired printer (via the computer connected to it).

7. Choose the Next button. The resulting dialog box allows you to select a name for the new printer (which will be listed in the Printers folder window). You can also make this printer the default printer, in which case it will automatically be used to print a document unless you specify otherwise at the time of printing.
8. Choose the Next button one more time. You are now asked if you want to print a test page. This is not necessary, but it is a good idea to see if the new printer is working properly.
9. Choose the Finish button. You may now be prompted to insert a diskette or CD-ROM in its drive. If so, insert it and choose the OK button. The appropriate printer driver files will be copied to the computer's hard disk and, if you requested that a test page be printed, printing will begin.
10. If a test page has been printed, a dialog box will open, asking if the page printed properly. Choose the Yes button, and the process is complete. (If you choose No, you will be led through some troubleshooting procedures.) The new printer will now be listed in the Printers folder window.

6-1 TUTORIAL

Try the following exercise on your own.

1. Turn on the computer (if necessary) to start Windows 95, and close any open windows.
2. Open the Printers folder: Click on the Start button, point at the Settings option, and choose Control Panel to start the latter; then, double-click on the Printers icon.
3. Right-click on the icon of one of the available printers and choose Properties from the pop-up menu.
4. In the Properties dialog box, click on the Details tab, choose the Spool Settings command button, then select the *Spool print jobs so that program finishes printing faster* option button (if it's not already selected), and choose the OK button.
5. Check out the function of the various options in the Printer Properties dialog box: Click on the question-mark button on the title bar and then click on the desired item. (To close the resulting window, click anywhere within the dialog box.)
6. Close the Properties dialog box.
7. In the Printers folder window, double-click on the icon of the selected printer. This opens the "print manager" window.

8. Pause the printer by choosing the Pause Printing command on the Printer menu. (Notice that the word *Paused* appears on the title bar.)
9. Insert the Student Disk in its drive and start WordPad by clicking on the WordPad item on the Accessories submenu of the Start menu's Programs option.
10. Open (from the File menu) the Fonts document on the Student Disk and send it to the printer (choose Print from the File menu and then choose OK in the resulting dialog box). Do the same for the Preamble document on the diskette.
11. Switch to the print manager window. The two print jobs will be listed in the "print queue" with the Fonts document first.
12. Change the order of the print jobs (so that Preamble will be printed first) by dragging the Fonts document to the bottom of the queue.
13. Cancel the Preamble print job: Select it and choose Cancel Printing from the Document menu.
14. Cancel the remaining print job by choosing Purge Print Jobs from the Printer menu.
15. "Unpause" the printer by choosing Pause Printing from the Printer menu. (The word *Paused* will disappear from the title bar.)
16. Close the print manager window, the Printers folder, and WordPad, and remove the diskette from its drive.

6.2 Installing New Hardware

One of the great things about personal computers is that they are "expandable" — you can install new hardware devices (such as more RAM or a CD-ROM drive) or replace existing components, to adapt the machine to your changing needs.

Installing a piece of hardware involves two fundamental steps:

1. You must physically connect the device to your computer, via either an external *port* (at the back of the system unit) or an internal connector (inside the system unit).
2. You must change certain settings and/or install special software so that the computer recognizes the device and makes full use of its capabilities.

The second step in this process may or may not involve Windows. For example, if you install additional RAM in your computer, the machine will recognize the change when it runs its start-up tests, and either automatically alter the necessary settings or instruct you to do so using a setup program. On the other hand, if you install a modem, Windows will probably detect the new hardware and either accommodate it automatically or guide you through the process.

In this section, we will discuss the way in which Windows deals with a piece of new hardware once the device has been physically connected to the computer. This process is also discussed to some extent in Section 6.1 (for printers), Section 6.3 (for multimedia devices), and Section 6.5 (for modems).

WARNING

Before installing a new piece of hardware, you should always read the instruction manual that accompanies it. The manual will include not only instructions for physically connecting the device to your computer system, but also information about configuring it correctly. If it suggests a procedure that is different than the ones described in this section, it is usually best to follow the manufacturer's recommendations.

Plug-and-Play

Plug-and-play is an industry-wide standard that makes the configuration of certain hardware devices particularly easy. To make full use of plug-and-play, both the device and your computer must support this standard. Generally speaking, plug-and-play works only with recently manufactured hardware.

Installing a plug-and-play device

To add a plug-and-play device to your system, all you have to do is:

1. Physically install the device (with the computer off), following the manufacturer's instructions.
2. Turn on the computer.

When Windows starts up, it will detect the new piece of hardware and inform you of this fact. If special software, such as a **device driver** (a program that translates signals from the device into a language that Windows can understand) is needed, Windows may request that you insert the appropriate disk or CD-ROM in its drive. In any case, Windows will determine the necessary settings and install the relevant software so that the device will run properly. Then, Windows may restart itself to put the changes into effect.

The Add New Hardware Utility

If you want to install a device that has not been designed to meet the plug-and-play standard, or if your computer does not support such devices, the process is more difficult. Once you have physically connected the new hardware to the system, turn on the computer and proceed as follows*:

1. Close all open windows and exit any running applications.
2. Start Control Panel. (Click on the Start button, point at the Settings option, and choose Control Panel from the resulting menu.)
3. Double-click on the **Add New Hardware** icon, which starts the Add New Hardware Wizard.

Add New Hardware

4. In the resulting dialog box, choose the Next command button, which displays the window shown in Figure 9.
5. You now have to decide whether or not to have Windows try to

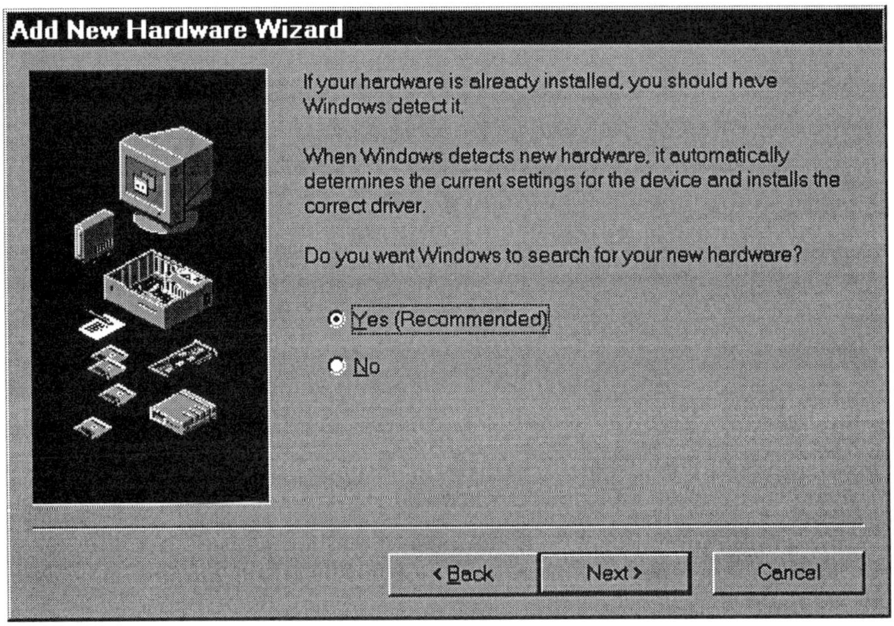

Figure 9 The Add New Hardware Wizard

*These procedures are generic in nature and do not apply to adding RAM, a disk drive, and certain other hardware. The installation of these devices proceeds quite differently; follow the instructions supplied by the manufacturer.

detect the new hardware. If you select the Yes option button and click on Next, a new dialog box will appear providing some information about the process. Then, choose the Next button and:

- Windows will search for the new hardware, and try to identify it and determine its proper settings.
- If the search is successful, Windows will display the results, asking you to confirm the listed information and perhaps supply a few more details. (The instruction manual may come in handy here.)
- You may then be asked to insert a certain diskette or CD-ROM in its drive so that the proper device driver can be copied to the hard disk.
- Windows may restart the computer to put the changes into effect. The installation process is now complete.

If Windows informs you that no new hardware was found, it will return you to the window shown in Figure 9.

6. If you select the No option button in Figure 9, you will have to complete all remaining steps in this procedure. Choose the Next command button, and the window shown in Figure 10 will appear.

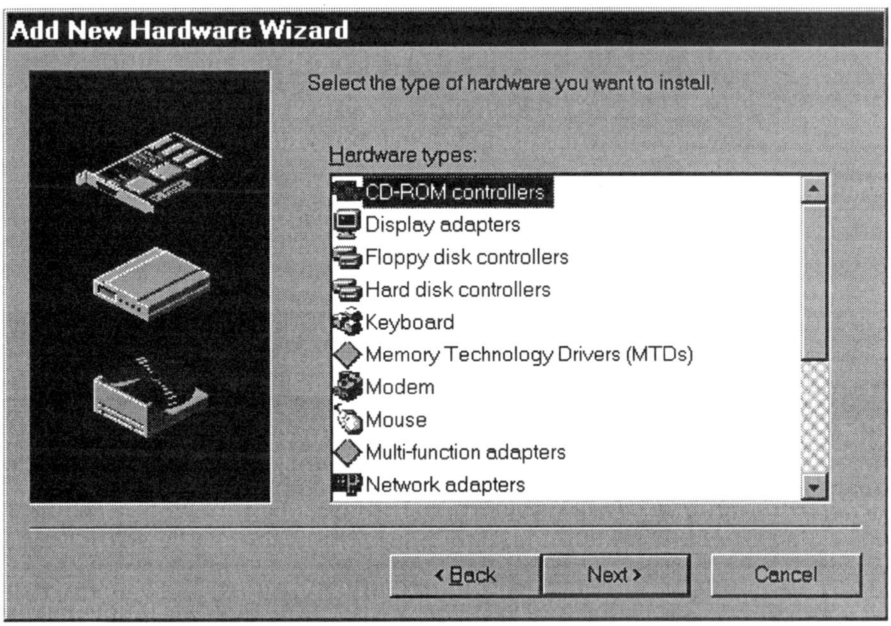

Figure 10 Selecting the Type of Hardware to be Installed

7. Select the type of hardware you are installing and choose the Next command button. The window shown in Figure 11 will be displayed.

TIP

If you are not sure what "type" of hardware you are installing, select *Other devices* from the list. This selection will display all available hardware choices in the next window, the one shown in Figure 11. (Contrary to the statement in this window, there is no "Unknown Hardware" selection.)

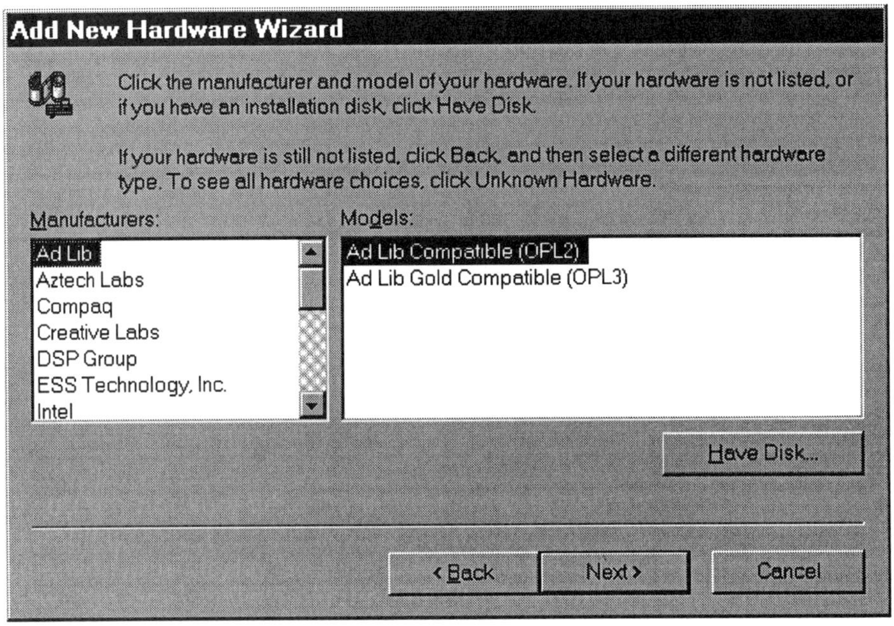

Figure 11 Selecting the Particular Piece of Hardware to be Installed

8. Select the manufacturer of the new hardware in the left box and a list of corresponding models will appear in the right box. Select the appropriate model from this list and choose the Next command button.

NOTE

If the manufacturer has supplied an installation disk, insert it in its drive, choose the Have Disk command button, enter the appropriate drive in the resulting dialog box, and choose OK.

9. Depending on the device you are installing:
   - Windows may now display a list of settings for the device to be installed and it may be necessary for you to set certain switches or jumpers on the device to match these settings. If so, make these changes after you are finished with the Add New Hardware Wizard and have turned off your computer.
   - Windows may now ask that you insert a certain diskette or CD-ROM in its drive in order to copy relevant files to your hard disk.
   - Windows may advise you that there is a conflict between the new device and another device. To proceed, choose the Next button, follow the instructions, and see if the *Conflict Troubleshooter* can help. If you have any doubts about your ability to handle this situation, choose the Cancel button instead and get help from someone who is more experienced in this area.
10. When the process is complete, choose the Finish button. You may be asked to restart your computer at this point to put the changes into effect.

6.2 TUTORIAL

Try the following exercise on your own. It simulates the configuration of a mouse that you have supposedly just connected to your computer.

1. Turn on the computer (if necessary) to start Windows, and close any open windows.
2. Open the Control Panel window (from the Settings option on the Start menu) and double-click on the Add New Hardware icon. This starts the Add New Hardware Wizard.
3. Read the information displayed and then choose the Next command button.
4. Select the No option button, telling Windows that you will enter the information about the new device instead of having the system detect it automatically. Then, choose the Next button. A list of hardware types will be displayed.
5. Select Mouse from the list and choose the Next button. Two lists, of manufacturers and models, will be displayed.
6. Select Microsoft from the list on the left and Microsoft Serial Mouse from the list on the right. (In practice, you would get this information from the device's instruction manual.) Choose the Next button. A dialog box is displayed informing you that Win-

dows knows how to install this software.

7. Choose the Cancel button to abort the installation process. The Add New Hardware Wizard will close, returning you to Control Panel. (In practice, you would click on Finish and follow the on-screen instructions to complete the process.)
8. Close the Control Panel window.

6.3 Sounds and Multimedia

What is multimedia?

Multimedia is a catch-all term that refers to the use of sound, animation, and video to enhance computer software. For example, a multimedia encyclopedia not only contains the usual text and pictures, but also audio and video clips about certain subjects. Multimedia applications currently represent the fastest growing area of software development.

In order to run multimedia applications, your computer must be equipped with at least a CD-ROM drive, sound card (occupying one of the slots within the system unit), and speakers. Most desktop PCs sold nowadays come equipped with these components; moreover, they can usually be added fairly easily to most older computers. (Installing new hardware is discussed in Section 6.2.)

Windows support for multimedia can be found in two places. Several "accessories" allow you to create or play back multimedia files (see Chapter 9) and two Control Panel utilities, Sounds and Multimedia, let you customize the use or configuration of multimedia devices. In this section, we will discuss these two utilities.

The Sounds Utility

If your computer is equipped with a sound card and speakers, you can specify that certain sounds be played at the occurrence of certain system "events", such as minimizing an application or exiting Windows. The assignment of a sound to a given event is made from within Control Panel's **Sounds utility**.

To start the Sounds utility:

1. Open the Control Panel window (by clicking on the Start button, pointing at the Settings option, and choosing the Control Panel item from the resulting submenu).

Sounds

2. Double-click on the Sounds icon. The Sounds Properties dialog box, shown in Figure 12, will open.

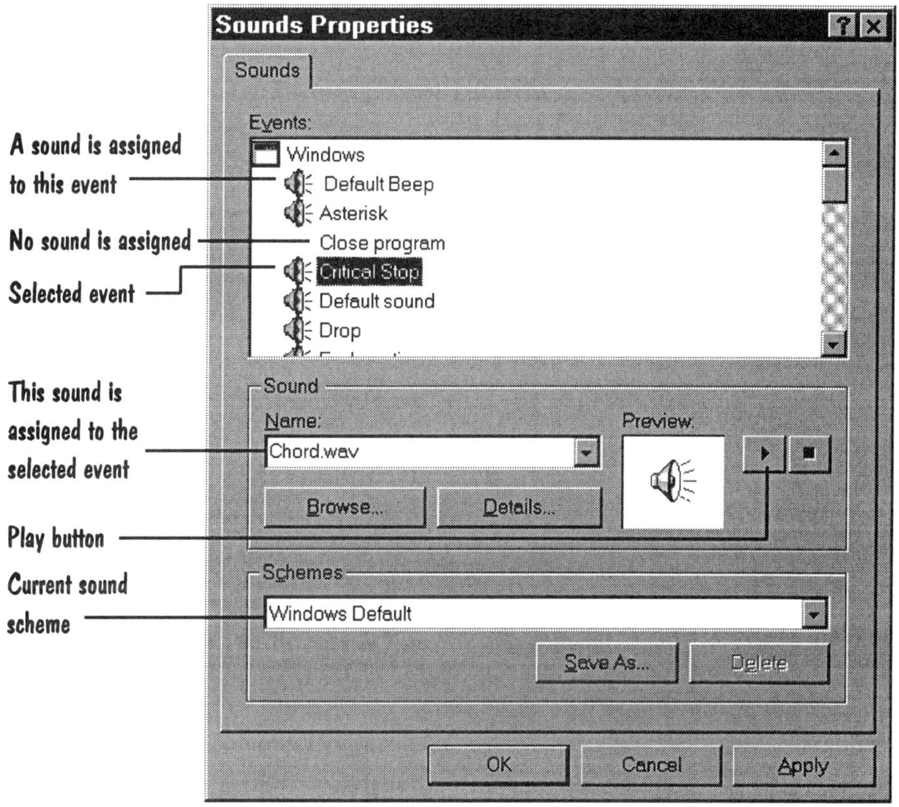

Figure 12 The Sounds Properties Dialog Box

Using the Sounds Properties dialog box, you can:

- Choose a built-in *sound scheme*, consisting of a collection of sounds pre-assigned to system events, or choose not to use sounds at all.
- Create a custom sound scheme by assigning particular sounds to specific events.

Selecting a Built-in Sound Scheme Windows comes equipped with several sound schemes. To select one of them:

1. Open the Sounds Properties dialog box, as described above.

2. Select a sound scheme from the Schemes drop-down list. Select "No Sounds" from the list if you do not want to hear sounds at system events.

Previewing sounds

3. To listen to (*preview*) an assigned sound, select the associated event from the Events list box and click on the Play button. To terminate a sound file before it has finished playing, click on the Stop button.

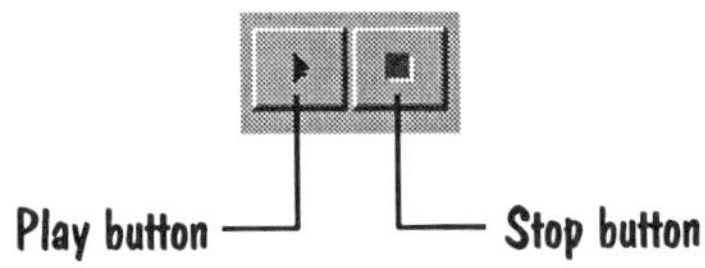

4. Choose the Apply command button, which puts the selected sound scheme into effect without closing the dialog box, or choose the OK button to put the scheme into effect and close the dialog box.

Creating a Custom Sound Scheme If you have the time and inclination, you can assign a sound of your choosing to each individual system event, creating a custom sound scheme. To do so:

1. Select a built-in sound scheme from the Schemes drop-down list that is similar to what you want.
2. Select a system event from the Events list box. (This box displays all events to which you can assign sounds; some events, such as Asterisk and Exclamation refer to dialog boxes of certain types.) The selected event will become highlighted.

   If the selected event is already associated with a sound, it will be preceded by the "speaker" symbol shown at the right, and the name of the corresponding sound file will be displayed in the Name text box. To preview the sound, click on the Play button.

3. To assign a new sound to the selected event, select another sound file from the Name drop-down list. (This list contains all files with extension *wav* in the default folder; to select a sound file from another folder, choose the Browse command button.)
4. Repeat steps 2 and 3 until your sound scheme is complete.
5. If you would like to save your new sound scheme (so that it will be added to the Schemes drop-down list), choose the Save As command button, enter a name for the scheme in the resulting dialog box, and choose the OK button.
6. Choose the Apply command button, which puts the new sound scheme into effect without closing the dialog box, or choose the OK button to put the scheme into effect and close the dialog box.

The Multimedia Utility

The **Multimedia utility** allows you to adjust certain settings for the multimedia devices connected to your system. These may include audio, video, and MIDI (musical instrument digital interface) devices.

To start the Multimedia utility:

Multimedia

1. Open the Control Panel window.
2. Double-click on the Multimedia icon. The Multimedia Properties dialog box, shown in Figure 13, will open.

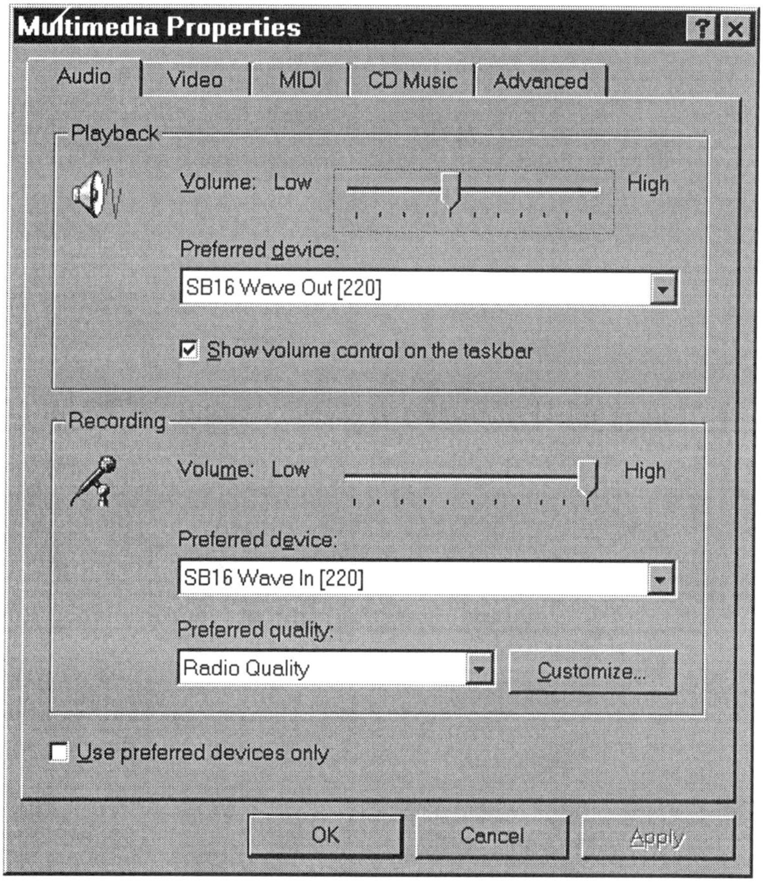

Figure 13 The Multimedia Dialog Box — Audio Page

As you can see, this dialog box contains several pages, each corresponding to some aspect of multimedia.

The Audio Page The audio page (Figure 13) is divided into two main areas: Playback and Recording.

The Playback section

In the Playback section, you can:

- Adjust the volume of sound coming from the computer's speakers by dragging the Volume *slider* to the left (to decrease the volume) or to the right (to increase it). Alternatively, you can click on the desired spot to the left or right of the slider.

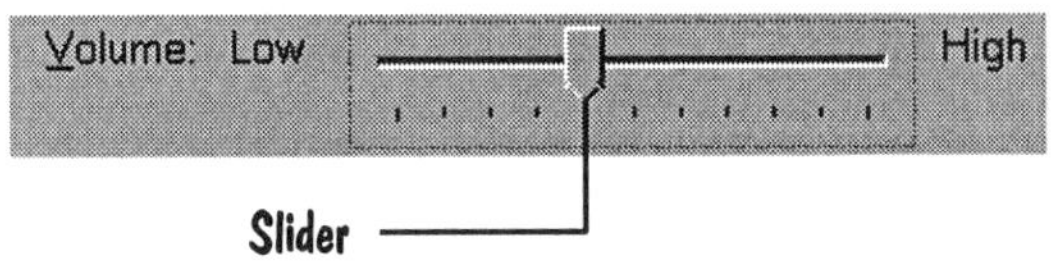

- Specify which of the audio devices connected to your computer will be the default device by selecting it from the *Preferred device* drop-down list.
- Choose to be able to access the volume control from the Taskbar by selecting the *Show volume control on the taskbar* check box. When this box is selected, a "speaker" symbol will appear next to the clock. Clicking on this symbol displays the volume control, as shown at the right.

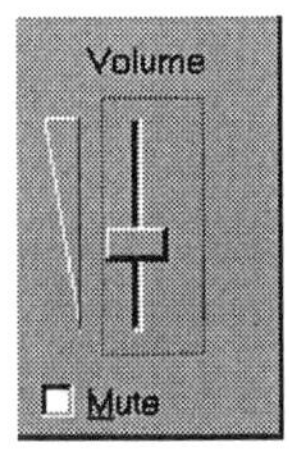

The Recording section

In the Recording section, you can:

- Adjust the microphone's sound level by using the Volume slider.
- Select the default audio recording device and the default quality at which it records by using the *Preferred device* and *Preferred quality* drop-down lists. (Typically, high, medium, and low quality settings are referred to as *CD*, *Radio*, and *Telephone* quality, respectively.) Be aware that high quality recordings may produce very large sound files.
- Change certain recording settings (such as whether a stereo or mono sound file is produced) by choosing the Customize command button.

The Other Dialog Box Pages Here is a brief rundown of the kinds of settings you can alter on the other Multimedia Properties dialog box pages.

- The *Video* page allows you to decide whether to run video clips full-screen or in a window and, if you select the latter, what size window to use. Be aware that video looks best when it is run in its original size window.

- The *MIDI* page lets you select the instrument on which Windows plays MIDI output. If several MIDI instruments are available, you can assign the instruments to different channels.
- The *CD Music* page lets you adjust the headphone volume setting for your CD-ROM drive.
- When you click on the *Advanced* tab, a list of multimedia categories is displayed on the corresponding page of the dialog box. Clicking on the "+" symbol to the left of a category (or double-clicking on the category name) displays all drivers installed for this type of device. (Recall that a *device driver* is a program that translates the various commands from the device into a language that Windows can understand.) Selecting a particular driver and choosing the Properties command button provides information about the driver and allows you to change some of its settings.

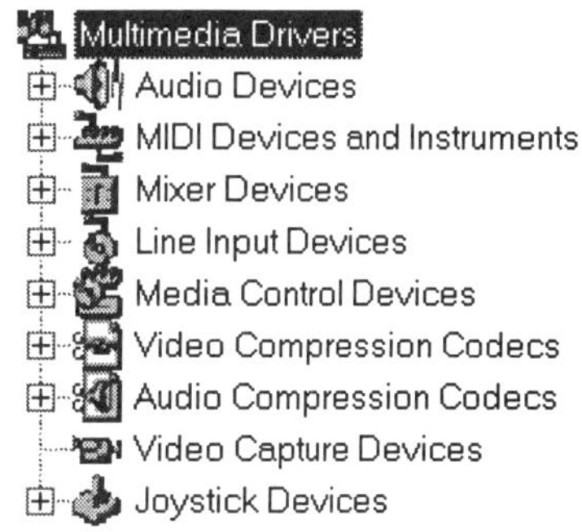

6.3 TUTORIAL

Try the following exercise on your own.

1. Turn on the computer (if necessary) to start Windows 95, and close any open windows.
2. Open the Control Panel window (from the Settings option on the Start menu) and double-click on the Sounds icon. The Sounds Properties dialog box will open.
3. Open the Schemes drop-down list and select the Windows Default sound scheme. (If a warning message box appears, choose No to close it.)
4. Play (preview) the sound associated with the Asterisk event by selecting it from the Events list and then clicking on the Play button (shown at the right). 
5. Change the sound assigned to the Asterisk event: With Asterisk still selected, open the Name drop-down list and click on *tada .wav*. Preview this sound.
6. Choose the Cancel command button to close the Sounds Properties dialog box without putting your change into effect.
7. In the Control Panel window, double-click on the Multimedia icon to open the Multimedia Properties dialog box.

8. Experiment with the Playback volume control on the Audio page: Drag its slider to several different positions and listen to the sounds emitted when you release the mouse button.
9. Successively click on the other tabs in the Multimedia Properties dialog box. Notice the options available on each page.
10. Close the Multimedia Properties dialog box by choosing the Cancel command button, and then close Control Panel.

6.4 *Accessibility Options*

Windows contains several features that make it easier for physically challenged people to use (or *access*) the computer. For example:

- For the visually impaired, text on the screen can be increased in size and given more contrast.
- For the hearing impaired, visual cues can be set up to accompany system sounds.
- For those who lack full dexterity, certain keystroke combinations can be made easier to manage and the keyboard can be set up to emulate mouse movements.

Most of these accessibility features are enabled from within Control Panel's **Accessibility Options utility**.

To start this utility:

1. Open the Control Panel window (by pointing at Settings on the Start menu and choosing Control Panel from the submenu).

Accessibility Options

2. Double-click on the Accessibility Options icon. The Accessibility Properties dialog box, shown in Figure 14, will be displayed.

As you can see this dialog box contains five tabs. In the remainder of this section, we will discuss the various options available on each of the corresponding pages. To put the options you select into effect, choose either the OK or the Apply command button. (The Apply command button leaves the dialog box open.)

Keyboard Options

This set of options makes the keyboard easier to manage for those who lack some dexterity or only have the use of one hand. The changes made here affect all Windows applications.

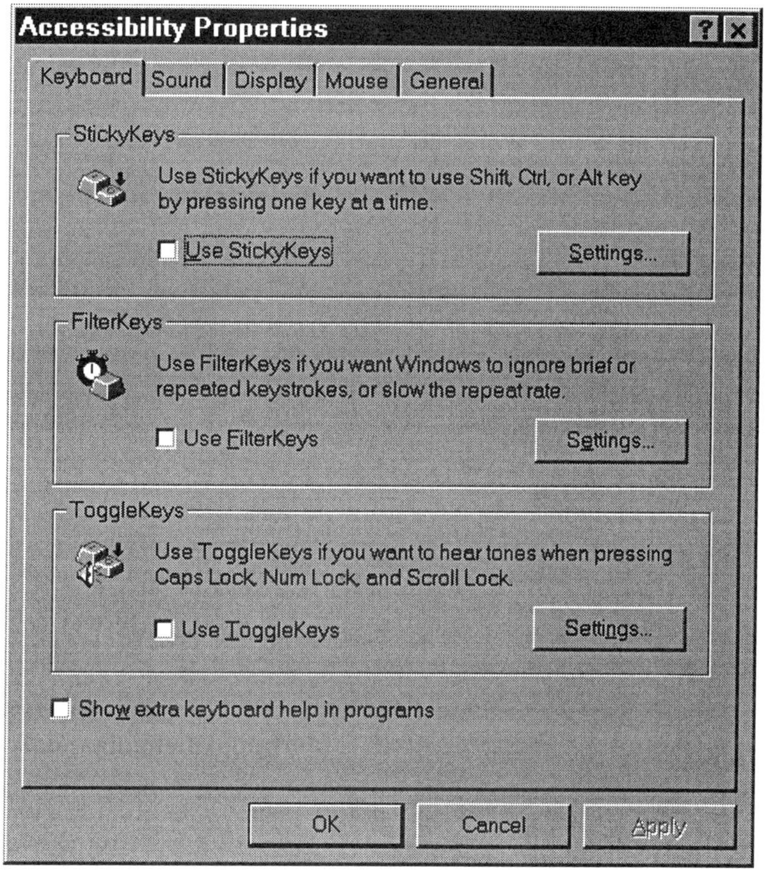

Figure 14 The Accessibility Properties Dialog Box

StickyKeys

As you know, many features of Windows and its applications can be accessed by means of keystroke combinations (such as Ctrl+Esc or Alt+Tab), which involve holding down one key while pressing another. Selecting the Use StickyKeys check box allows you to make these keystrokes one after the other, which is easier for some people to accomplish than pressing both keys simultaneously. For example, if StickyKeys is enabled, to open the Start menu, you would press (and release) the Ctrl key and then press (and release) the Esc key.

Choosing the Settings command button to the right of the check box allows you to select certain StickyKeys-related options, such as whether or not an icon appears on the Taskbar to show that StickyKeys has been enabled.

FilterKeys Selecting the Use FilterKeys check box instructs Windows to ignore quick keystrokes or ignore repeated keystrokes. (Enabling FilterKeys can help keep accidental keystrokes from being acted upon by Windows.) To select one of these options (and some others, as well), choose the Settings command button to the right of the check box.

ToggleKeys Many Windows users will find the ToggleKeys option useful. Selecting the Use ToggleKeys check box causes the speaker to emit a tone when one of the three "toggle keys" (Num Lock, Caps Lock, and Scroll Lock) is pressed. Enabling this option lets you know that you have (perhaps accidentally) pressed one of these keys.

Once you have selected the options you want to enable, choose the Apply or OK command buttons to put your selections into effect. (Choosing Apply leaves the dialog box open.)

NOTE Control Panel's Keyboard utility (see Section 5.4) also provides options for changing the action of the keyboard. In addition, some Windows applications supply extra help for using the keyboard. To display this help (if available), select the *Show extra keyboard help in programs* check box at the bottom of the Keyboard page.

TIP If you wish, any of the three keyboard accessibility options can be toggled on or off whenever Windows is running by using shortcut keys. To enable an option's shortcut key, choose the Settings command button for that option, select the *Use shortcut* check box in the resulting dialog box, and choose the OK button. The shortcut keys for these options are:

StickyKeys:	Press the Shift key five times
FilterKeys:	Hold down the right Shift key for eight seconds
ToggleKeys:	Hold down the Num Lock key for five seconds

Sound Options

The Sound page of the Accessibility Properties dialog box provides options that may be useful for the hearing impaired. These options are shown in Figure 15.

SoundSentry Enabling SoundSentry (by selecting its check box and choosing the Apply or OK command button) causes Windows to flash part of the screen whenever the speaker emits a sound. The Settings command button opens a dialog box that allows you to select which part of the screen (for example, the active title bar) will flash.

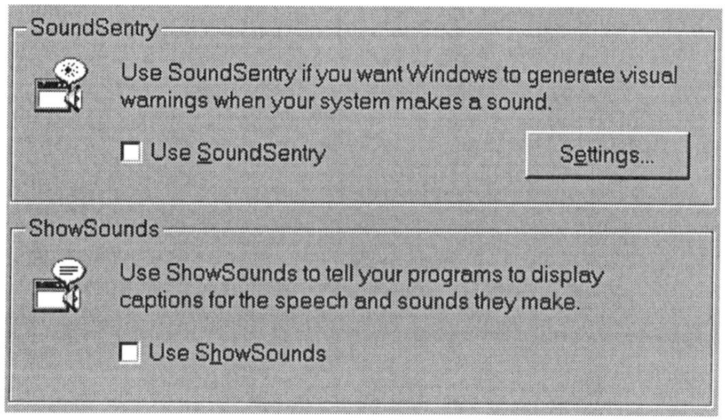

Figure 15 Options Available on the Sound Page

ShowSounds

SoundSentry informs a hearing impaired person that some kind of sound has been made. The ShowSounds option takes this idea a step further. When the Use ShowSounds check box is selected, certain applications will supply, usually by means of a message box on the screen, information related to the sound; for example, why it was made.

Display Options

The Display page of the Accessibility Properties dialog box only contains one option; it allows you to put a high contrast display scheme into effect. Figure 16 shows this option displayed in high contrast black-on-white. (Notice that the usual gray-colored dialog box background is now white.) By choosing the Settings command button, you can select white-on-black or a custom scheme, instead.

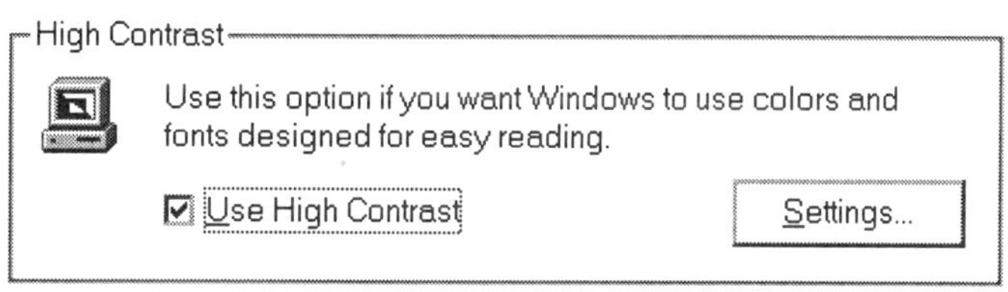

Figure 16 High Contrast Display Option

TIP: Control Panel's Display utility offers much more control over the size and appearance of text (see Section 5.3). If a visually impaired person is going to make extensive use of this computer, it's a better idea to use the Display utility to set up the screen resolution and a window scheme to his or her liking. The only advantage of the Display page of the Accessibility Options utility (other than its simplicity) is that you can use a shortcut key to toggle high contrast mode on and off. To do so, choose the Settings command button, select the *Use shortcut* check box in the resulting dialog box, and choose the OK button. The High Contrast shortcut key is Left Alt + Left Shift + Print Screen.

Mouse Options

The Mouse page of the Accessibility Properties dialog box only contains one option, MouseKeys (Figure 17). When the MouseKeys check box is selected, the numeric keypad can be used to move the mouse pointer around the screen and to simulate a mouse click, double-click, or drag:

- To move the mouse pointer horizontally or vertically, press the appropriate Arrow key (on the numeric keypad); to move the pointer diagonally, press the Home, End, PgUp, or PgDn key (on the numeric keypad).
- To simulate a mouse click, double-click, or right-click, on the numeric keypad press the 5 key, the + (plus) key, or the - (minus) key, respectively.
- To drag the mouse pointer to a new position, (on the numeric keypad) press the Ins key to start the drag operation, use the Arrow keys to move the pointer to the appropriate place, and then press the Del key to complete the operation.

Figure 17 The MouseKeys Mouse Option

Choose the Settings command button to open a dialog box offering various options to be used with MouseKeys. These include:

- Enabling the shortcut key Left Alt + Left Shift + Num Lock to toggle MouseKeys on or off.
- Adjusting the pointer speed.
- Specifying whether MouseKeys will respond to the numeric keypad when Num Lock is on or Num Lock is off.

NOTE

Control Panel's Mouse utility provides additional options for configuring the mouse (see Section 5.4). Some of these, such as selecting left-handed or right-handed operation and enabling mouse trails, may be of particular interest to a person with a physical disability.

TIP

Keep in mind that Windows provides many keyboard alternatives to using the mouse. For example, as we pointed out in Chapter 1, you can select menu items and dialog box options, and resize or move a window using just the keyboard. Windows and most applications also use shortcut keys to provide alternatives to mouse clicks. For a list of important Windows shortcut keys, see Appendix A.

Other Accessibility Options

The General page of the Accessibility Properties dialog box provides a few additional options. These are displayed in Figure 18.

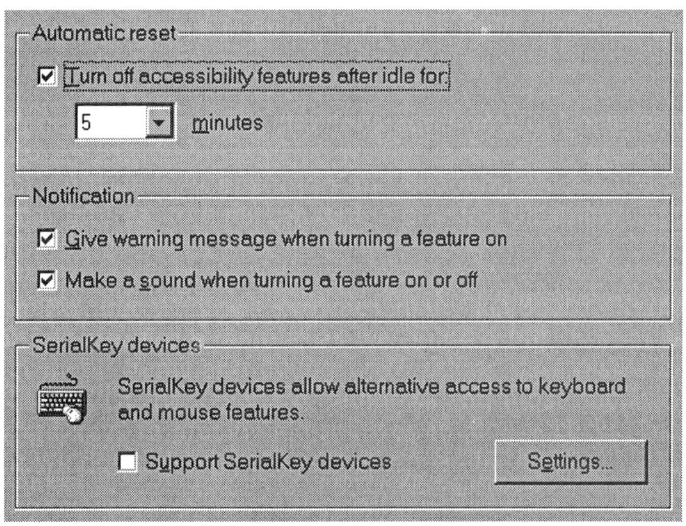

Figure 18 Options on the General Page

The first two sets of options in this dialog box, *Automatic reset* and *Notification*, are fairly self-explanatory. The third, *SerialKey devices*, is used to configure (by choosing the Settings button) an alternate input device attached to the computer's serial port. These devices are intended for people who are unable to use a standard keyboard or mouse.

6.4 TUTORIAL

Try the following exercise on your own.

1. Turn on the computer (if necessary) to start Windows 95, and close any open windows.
2. Open the Control Panel window (from the Settings option on the Start menu) and double-click on the Accessibility Options icon. The Accessibility Properties dialog box will open.
3. On the Keyboard page, select the Use StickyKeys and Use Toggle-Keys check boxes, and choose the Apply command buttons. Now:
   - Press (and release) the Alt key, then the Tab key. Notice that (because StickyKeys is enabled), this works like Alt+Tab to switch the active window to Control Panel. Switch back to the Accessibility Properties dialog box.
   - Press the Caps Lock, Num Lock, and Scroll Lock keys twice each. Notice that (because ToggleKeys is enabled), an audible tone is emitted each time.

   Deselect the check boxes and choose the Apply button again.
4. Choose the Settings command button next to the Use FilterKeys check box. A Settings dialog box will open.
5. In this dialog box, select each of the two Filter options buttons and type in the test box to see the effect. (You may have to adjust the corresponding Settings to see a difference!) Cancel this dialog box.
6. Click on the Display tab, then select the Use High Contrast check box and choose the Apply button. Notice the dramatic difference in the screen's appearance. Deselect the Use High Contrast check box and choose the Apply button again.
7. Click on the Mouse tab, then select the Use MouseKeys check box and choose the Apply command button. Now:
   - Hold down the Up Arrow key on the numeric keypad. If the mouse pointer doesn't move, turn on (or off) the Num Lock key and try again. Use the Arrow keys to move the mouse pointer over the Settings command button.

- Simulate a right-click by pressing the + (plus) key on the numeric keypad. The one-item *What's This?* menu will open.
- Use the Arrow keys to position the mouse pointer over the menu item, and press the 5 key on the numeric keypad to simulate a click. Close the resulting pop-up box by pressing the Esc key. (The minus key on the numeric keypad simulates a *double*-click.)

8. Deselect the Use MouseKeys check box and choose the Apply button again.
9. Explore the various other options and settings in the Accessibility Properties dialog box with the help of context-sensitive help.
10. Close the Accessibility Properties dialog box and Control Panel.

6.5 Other Control Panel Options

In this section, we will briefly discuss a few other common utilities housed within the Control Panel window. We will introduce the Modems and System utilities and then briefly describe the Network, Passwords, and Regional Settings options.

The Modems Utility

A **modem** is a device that translates computer-generated data into signals that can be sent (usually over phone lines) to another computer. If your computer is equipped with a modem and the proper *communications software*, you have the potential to access the vast quantities of information found on **online information services** (such as CompuServe and America Online) or the **Internet**, a world-wide system of interlinked computer networks.

Control Panel's **Modems utility** helps you to install and/or configure a modem. To start this utility:

Modems

1. Open the Control Panel window (from the Settings option on the Start menu).
2. Double-click on the Modems icon.

The Modems Properties dialog box, shown in Figure 19 on the next page, will open.

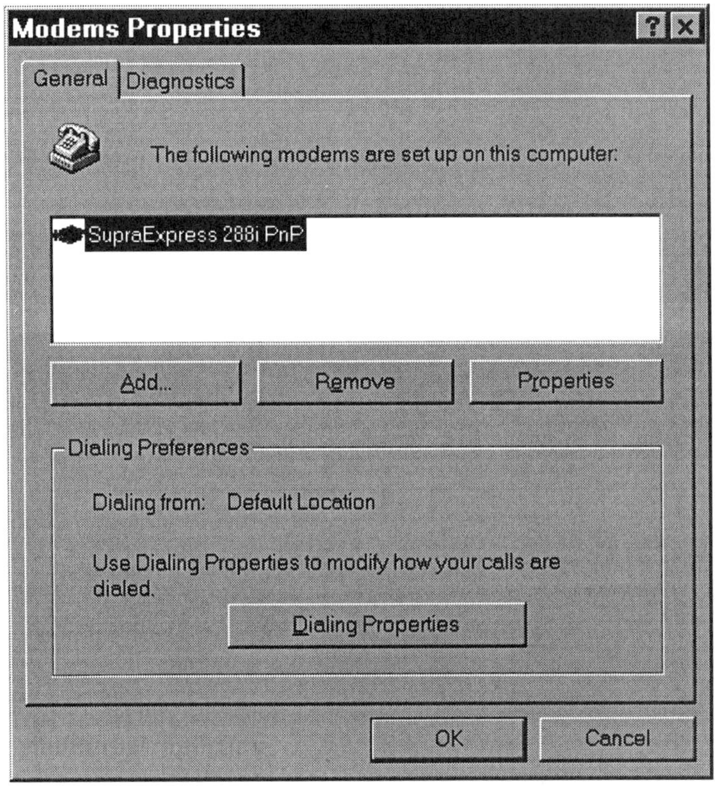

Figure 19 The Modems Properties Dialog Box

The Modems utility has two basic functions: installing a new modem and configuring an existing one.

Installing a Modem To use the Modems Properties dialog box to install a new modem:

1. With the computer off, connect the modem to the computer:
   - If the modem is an *internal* type, insert it in a free slot within the system unit.
   - If the modem is an *external* type, attach it to a serial computer port with the appropriate cable and turn it on.
2. Turn on the computer, starting Windows, and open the Modems Properties dialog box, as described above.
3. Choose the Add command button. This starts the Install New Modem wizard.

4. Typically, you would now let Windows detect the new modem by choosing the Next command button, and if all goes well, the installation will proceed with little or no additional input on your part.
5. If, in carrying out step 4, Windows encounters problems in the installation process, select the *Don't detect my modem; I will select it from a list* check box, and choose the Next button. This option requires some information about the modem, so keep its instruction manual handy.
6. Follow the instructions, making selections and choosing Next (or Finish), until the process is complete. (For a more detailed description of the installation process, see the procedure in Section 6.2 for installing new hardware.)

NOTE

If your modem and computer support the *plug-and-play* standard, installation may be a lot simpler. Just physically connect the modem to your system, turn on the modem if it's an external one, and then turn on the computer. During start-up, Windows should indicate that it has detected and installed the new modem. (At some point in the process, you may have to insert a certain disk in its drive.)

If your modem is not of the plug-and-play variety, you should read through the instruction manual before installing it. If the manufacturer's instructions differ from the process outlined above, use the former!

Configuring a Modem The installation process installs a universal *driver*, a program that can be used by any Windows application to communicate with the modem. The Modems utility provides a central location to configure this driver by setting various parameters for its operation. This information can be entered or changed from the Modems Properties dialog box by choosing either the Properties or Dialing Properties command button (see Figure 19).

The Properties command button

Choosing the Properties button opens a dialog box that allows you to change information about the modem itself. This includes:

- The volume level of the modem's speaker.
- The maximum speed, measured in bits per second (bps), at which the modem can connect to a remote computer.
- Default connection parameters — the parity, and number of data and stop bits. (The settings for these parameters must match the requirements of the remote computer and can be changed, if

necessary, using communications software when making a particular connection.)

- Certain default calling preferences, such as how much time is allowed to elapse (between dialing a number and making the connection) before the call is canceled.
- Settings for the serial port that the modem is using.

The Dialing Properties command button

Choosing the Dialing Properties button opens a dialog box that allows you to express preferences for the way a call is made. For example:

- You can specify that a certain country code and area code be used, whenever necessary, in dialing a phone number.
- You can specify that "call waiting" be disabled while a call is in progress to prevent the connection from being lost should an incoming call come through.
- You can specify whether *tone* or *pulse* dialing is used to make the call. (Specify pulse dialing only if tone dialing is not available on your phone line.)

Troubleshooting a Modem's Operation The Modems Properties dialog box also contains a Diagnostics page that can help you to resolve conflicts with other serial (communications) devices. The information supplied on this page is fairly technical and we won't discuss it further in this text.

The System Utility

The Windows **System utility** displays information about the various components of your computer and allows you to make changes in the way that some of them operate. To start this utility, either:

System

- Open the Control Panel window, as described earlier in this section, and double-click on the System icon.

or

- Right-click on the My Computer icon (on the Desktop) and choose the Properties item from the resulting pop-up menu.

In either case, the System Properties dialog box, similar to the one shown in Figure 20, will be displayed.

As you can see, the first page of this dialog box displays some general information about the computer system. The other three pages, which are discussed below, allow you to make changes to certain system parameters.

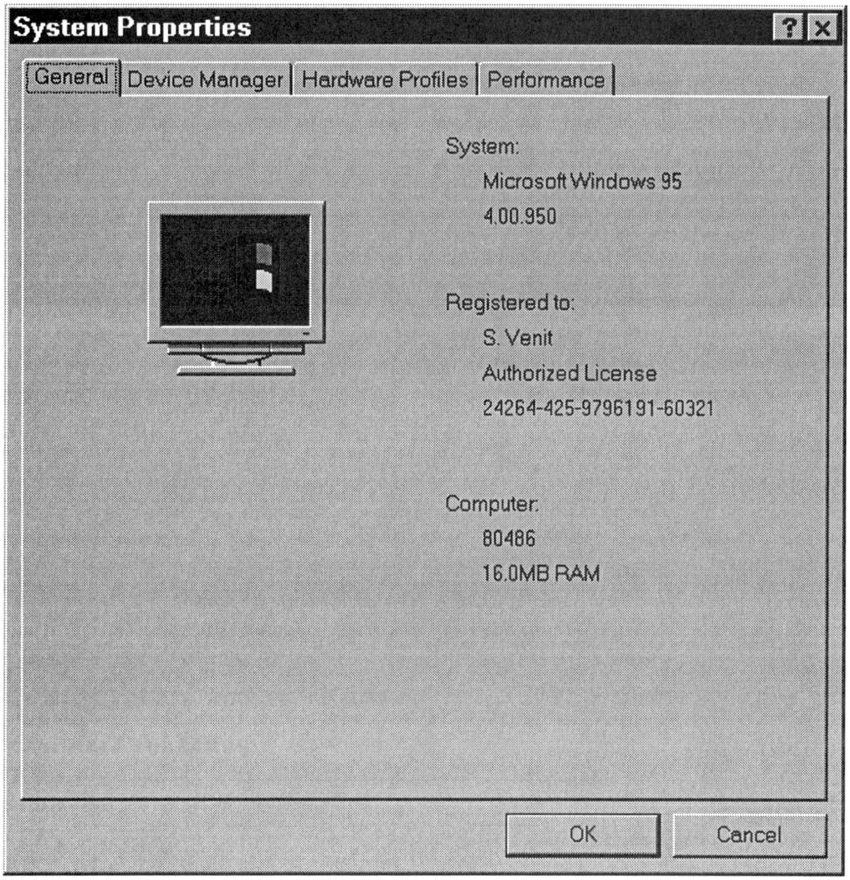

Figure 20 The System Properties Dialog Box

WARNING The System utility should be treated with respect. Changing certain settings in the System Properties dialog box can sometimes have unfortunate consequences. For example, after making a modification, a piece of hardware may stop working or Windows itself may fail to run. So, do not make any changes here unless you are sure of what you are doing.

Device Manager Clicking on the Device Manager tab in the System Properties dialog box displays a list of the types of hardware connected to your computer. If you want to see the hardware devices within a particular category, click on the plus sign next to the category name, or double-click on the latter. (The diagram at the right shows the result of clicking on the plus sign next to the CD-ROM icon.)

Now, if you double-click on a particular device (or select it and choose the Properties command button), a dialog box with information about that device will open. In most cases, you will also be given the opportunity to change certain settings for the given device.

Hardware Profiles A **hardware profile** consists of a set of *device drivers*, programs that help Windows communicate with the corresponding hardware devices. Normally, the hardware attached to a computer does not change from session to session, so only one hardware profile, created automatically by Windows, is necessary.

In certain special circumstances, however, you may want to use a couple of different hardware configurations on a regular basis. The most common case of this sort occurs with a portable computer. Most of the time, you will probably use the portable's built-in screen, keyboard, and pointing device. However, at times, you may find it more convenient to connect a regular monitor, keyboard, and mouse to the portable. In such a case, you would need different drivers for these components. This set of drivers can be set up as a hardware profile.

Creating a new hardware profile

To create a new hardware profile:

1. Open the System Properties dialog box, as described above, and click on the Hardware Profiles tab to display the corresponding page.
2. Select an existing profile that is close to the one you want, choose the Copy command button to copy its contents, type the new profile's name in the resulting dialog box, and choose OK.
3. To enable or disable a specific device for this profile, click on the Device Manager and:
   - Click on the plus sign next to the desired hardware type and then double-click on the device that you want to enable or disable.
   - In the Device Usage area of the resulting dialog box, select or deselect the new hardware profile, depending on whether you want to enable or disable the selected device.
   - Choose the OK command button to return to the System Properties dialog box.
4. Choose the OK button in the System Properties dialog box.

If more than one hardware profile has been set up for your computer, when Windows starts up, you will be asked which profile you want to use.

Improving System Performance When Windows 95 is installed or a new device is added, Windows tries to set up the hardware so that it operates in an optimal manner. The Performance page of the System Properties dialog box displays information about memory and hard disk use and allows you to change a few related settings to enhance performance "manually". However, in most cases, it is best not to make changes here; they are more likely to *adversely* affect performance.

File System Properties

Choosing the File System command button opens the File System Properties dialog box, which has three tabs:

- On the Hard Disk page, you can change the *read-ahead buffer* size allotted to the hard disk. When a hard disk read takes place, Windows will not only copy the requested information to RAM, but also *read-ahead* — transfer the data stored in the next disk sectors, as well. The amount of additional data sent to the hard disk — the read-ahead buffer size — is normally set to "Full", the largest available amount.
- On the CD-ROM page, you can change the *supplemental cache* size allotted to the CD-ROM drive. A *cache* is an area in RAM set aside to temporarily store information read from a hard disk or CD-ROM. Then, if this information is needed again, it can be quickly retrieved from RAM, instead of using the much slower process of reading again from the disk or CD. This setting is normally set to "Large".
- On the Troubleshooting page, you can disable certain performance-enhancing features if they appear to be causing trouble.

Graphics settings

Choosing the Graphics command button on the Performance page allows you to adjust the amount of *hardware acceleration* used by Windows. (*Acceleration* is accomplished through routines that speed up the display of new information on the screen.) This setting is normally set to "Full".

Virtual Memory settings

Virtual memory refers to Windows' practice of using the hard disk as if it were additional RAM. Windows 95 normally determines the amount of hard disk space to be used for this purpose, and it's best to accept this setting. If you want to change it (perhaps to use a different hard disk to hold the *swap file*), choose the Virtual Memory command button on the Performance page.

Other Control Panel Utilities

Here are brief descriptions of a few other Control Panel utilities.

Network

The Network Utility This utility installs Network drivers and sets up other network components. To be more specific:

- The Configuration page is used to add, remove, and set up network components (such as adapters, protocols, and devices) on your system. It also allows you to share your files and/or printer with other network users.
- The Identification page allows you to provide a name for your computer ("workstation") and the "workgroup" in which it is located.
- The Access Control page provides ways to restrict access to your computer's shared resources. There are two general types of access control:
  1. *Share-level* access control creates a password for each shared resource.
  2. *User-level* access control creates passwords that allow individual users to gain access to shared resources.

Passwords

The Passwords Utility Using this utility:

- You can change passwords for both starting Windows and logging onto a network.
- You can set up a password that allows someone at another (*remote*) computer to access your computer.
- You can set up *user profiles* — collections of user-specific preferences, such as the icons present on the Desktop or the fonts and colors in which various items are displayed. User profiles are useful when a machine is shared by several people.

Regional Settings

The Regional Settings Utility This utility customizes the way Windows displays numbers, currencies, dates, and times. Its settings affect Windows itself and those Windows applications that elect to make use of them. Although the primary use of Regional Settings is to customize Windows for use in another country, you might want to change the default formats for numbers, dates, or times, even if you live in the United States.

Chapter Summary

Managing Printers	To open the Printers folder	Double-click on the Printers icon in the Control Panel window or My Computer; *or* choose Printers from the Start menu's Settings option.
	To change a printer's settings	Open the Printers folder, right-click on the desired printer, and choose Properties from the pop-up menu; then, enter changes in the resulting dialog box.
	To manage print jobs	Open the Printers folder, double-click on the desired printer, and use the resulting "print manager" window to manipulate print jobs.
	To add a new printer	Open the Printers folder, double-click on the Add Printer icon, and use the resulting Add Printer Wizard.
Adding New Hardware	If it is plug-and-play compatible	Physically install the device, turn on the computer, and follow the on-screen instructions.
	Using the Add New Hardware utility	Physically install the device, double-click on Control Panel's Add New Hardware icon, and use the resulting Add New Hardware Wizard.
Multimedia-type Utilities	Sounds utility	Associates sounds with system events by using a built-in sound scheme or customizing an existing one.
	Multimedia utility	Places a speaker icon on the Taskbar, adjusts speaker volume, and changes recording settings (Audio page). Changes video settings (Video page). Changes the MIDI setup (MIDI page). Adjusts CD-ROM headphone volume (CD Music page). Changes multimedia device driver settings (Advanced page).
Accessibility Options	Keyboard page	Enables the StickyKeys, FilterKeys, and ToggleKeys options.
	Sound page	Enables the SoundSentry and ShowSounds options.
	Display page	Enables the High Contrast option.
	Mouse page	Enables the MouseKeys option.

Other Control Panel Utilities		
	Modems	Installs and configures a modem.
	System	Displays computer system information, changes device driver and performance settings, and creates hardware profiles.
	Network	Installs and configures network drivers.
	Passwords	Changes passwords used in starting Windows and logging onto a network.
	Regional Settings	Customizes the way Windows displays numbers, currencies, dates, and times.

Review Exercises

Section 6.1

1. To ___________ a print job means to have it temporarily stored on the hard disk before it is transferred to the printer.
2. A ___________ is a program that translates your document's text, graphics, and special codes into a language that the printer can understand.
3. The "print manager" window displays the current print jobs in a list that is known as the print ___________.
4. To start the Add Printer Wizard, double-click on the ___________ icon in the Printers folder window.
5. True or false: The Printers folder can be opened from the Start menu's Settings option without starting Control Panel.
6. True or false: A separator page is a page that Windows automatically inserts between print jobs.
7. True or false: If a document is printed in portrait orientation, its text runs parallel to the long side of the page.
8. True or false: To interchange the order in which the first two jobs in the print queue will be printed, drag the first document's name and icon just below that of the second document.
9. If a printer is "paused", as indicated on the title bar of the print manager window, you can restart it by choosing
   a. Pause Printing from the Printer window.
   b. Unpause Printing from the Printer menu.
   c. Pause Printing from the Document menu.
   d. Unpause Printing from the Document menu.

10. The computer's primary parallel port is referred to as
    a. COM1
    b. COM2
    c. LPT1
    d. File

Section 6.2

11. The term ____________ refers to an industry-wide standard that makes the configuration of certain hardware devices easier.
12. Configuring a new hardware device can be accomplished from Control Panel's ____________ utility.
13. True or false: A device driver is a program that translates the signals from the device into a language that Windows can understand.
14. True or false: When you use the Add New Hardware Wizard to configure a newly-installed device, it is recommended that you let Windows try to detect the new hardware.
15. Before you use the Add New Hardware utility to help install a new device, you should
    a. Physically connect the device to your computer.
    b. Open Control Panel and then restart Windows.
    c. Start the Add/Remove Programs utility.
    d. Make sure that the device's driver is installed.
16. The Add New Hardware Wizard
    a. Will always automatically appear when Windows starts if a new device has been installed in your computer.
    b. Must be used to install a plug-and-play device.
    c. Only works with plug-and-play devices.
    d. Will try to detect and configure a new device, if you instruct it to do so.

Section 6.3

17. To associate particular sounds with certain system events, open Control Panel and double-click on the ____________ icon.
18. To put a predefined sound scheme into effect, open the Sounds Properties dialog box, select the scheme from the ____________ drop-down list, and choose the OK or Apply button.
19. The term ____________ refers to the use of sound, animation, and video to enhance computer software.
20. True or false: If a sound is associated with an event, a "speaker" icon appears next to its name in the Sounds Properties dialog box.
21. True or false: To hear the sound you have just assigned to an event, you must first close the Sounds Properties dialog box.

22. True or false: You can use the Sounds utility to place a volume control icon on the Taskbar.

23. Which of the following tasks cannot be accomplished using the Sounds utility?

    a. Assigning a new sound to a system event.
    b. Removing an assigned sound from a system event.
    c. Creating a sound to be assigned to a system event.
    d. Previewing a sound that is assigned to a system event.

24. Which of the following tasks cannot be accomplished using the Multimedia utility?

    a. Increasing the volume level of the computer's speakers.
    b. Adjusting the bass and treble settings for the computer's speakers.
    c. Adjusting the sound level of the computer's microphone.
    d. Changing the size of the window that shows video clips.

Section 6.4

25. The Control Panel utility that can help some physically challenged people use the computer is called ____________.

26. If you want to open the Start menu by pressing Ctrl and Esc in sequence, select the ____________ option button in the Accessibility Properties dialog box.

27. The Use MouseKeys option in the Accessibility Properties dialog box allows you to use the Arrow keys on the ____________ area of the keyboard to move the mouse pointer.

28. True or false: The StickyKeys, FilterKeys, and ToggleKeys keyboard options can, if you want, be turned on and off using shortcut keys.

29. True or false: The Accessibility Properties dialog box allows you to specify the size of type used for text in dialog boxes.

30. True or false: The Accessibility Properties dialog box allows you to use the keyboard to move the mouse pointer, but not to simulate a mouse click or double-click.

31. If you want the computer to emit a sound when the Caps Lock, Num Lock, and Scroll Lock keys are pressed, in the Accessibility Properties dialog box, select the

    a. Use StickyKeys check box.
    b. Use FilterKeys check box.
    c. Use ToggleKeys check box.
    d. Use SoundSentry check box.

32. If you select the Use MouseKeys check box in the Accessibility Properties dialog box, you can use the keyboard to

a. Move the mouse pointer on the screen.
b. Simulate a mouse click.
c. Simulate a mouse drag.
d. Perform all of the above actions.

Section 6.5

33. A ____________ is a device that translates computer-generated data into signals that can be sent over phone lines to another computer.

34. If you frequently use your laptop computer with an auxiliary monitor, you should set up a ____________ that tells Windows, on your command, to load the proper driver for this device.

35. A ____________ is a portion of RAM set aside to temporarily store information read from a hard disk or CD-ROM so that, if the information is needed again, it can be quickly retrieved.

36. True or false: The term *virtual memory* refers to RAM that has been added to your computer after the initial purchase.

37. True or false: The Passwords utility allows you to set up passwords to limit access to your shared network resources.

38. True or false: The Regional Settings utility allows you to adjust the time on the Taskbar clock.

39. Which of the following tasks cannot be accomplished using the Modems utility?

    a. Install a driver for a newly-connected modem.
    b. Set the maximum connection speed for your modem.
    c. Set up an "address book" of phone numbers that can be dialed from your modem.
    d. Specify that pulse dialing be used by your modem.

40. You can fine-tune your computer's hard disk and CD-ROM performance using Control Panel's

    a. System utility.
    b. Network utility.
    c. Regional Settings utility.
    d. Hardware Profiles utility.

Build Your Own Glossary

35. The following words and phrases are important terms that were introduced in this chapter. (They appear within the text in boldface type.) Use WordPad (see Section 2.2) to enter a definition for each term, preserving alphabetical order, into the Glossary file on the Student Disk.

Accessibility Options	Device driver	Modem
Add New Hardware utility	Hardware profile	Modems utility
	Internet	Multimedia

Multimedia utility
Network utility
Online information service
Passwords utility
Plug-and-play utility
Printer driver
Printers folder
Print queue
Regional Settings utility
Sounds utility
Spool print jobs
System utility

Lab Exercises

Work each of the following exercises at your computer. Begin by turning the machine on (if necessary) to start Windows 95. If you want to produce a written record of your answers, review the material on WordPad and capturing screens in Sections 2.2 and 2.3.

Lab Exercise 1 (Section 6.1)

a. Open the Printers folder window. How many printers are listed there?

b. Open the Properties dialog box for the printer that you normally use. What is the name of this printer?

c. Print a test page. Did it print in portrait or landscape orientation?

d. Click on the Details tab. What is the name of the port to which this printer is connected?

e. By locating the appropriate feature in the Properties dialog box, answer each of the following questions and give the location (for example, "Details page" or "Setup dialog box") of the feature. If a feature cannot be located, answer "Not found".

- Is paper orientation set to portrait or landscape?
- What paper size is currently selected?
- What is the current printing resolution?
- Are any font cartridges installed?
- How much printer memory is installed?

f. Close the printer's Properties dialog box and the Printers folder.

Lab Exercise 2 (Section 6.1)

Note: You may not be able to do this exercise if you are using a network printer.

a. Open the Printers folder window and select the printer you normally use.

b. Open the "print manager" window for this printer (by double-clicking on it). What is the actual title of this window?

c. Pause the printer (so that it will accept print jobs, but not print them). How did you accomplish this?

d. Start the WordPad word processor (from the Accessories submenu of the Start menu's Programs option). Type your name, your class, and the date on separate lines.

e. Choose the Print command from the File menu, and in the resulting dialog box, choose the Properties command button. Is portrait or landscape orientation selected?

f. Close the Properties dialog box and choose the OK button in the Print dialog box to send the document to the printer. Was it printed?

g. Insert the Student Disk in its drive and open the Preamble document in WordPad. (Answer "No" to the warning message.) Now, send this document to the printer.

h. Switch to the "print manager" window. How many print jobs are in the queue? What is the first job called? *Optional*: Size the window so that it has no extra "white space" and capture it.

i. Cancel all print jobs and restart ("unpause") the printer. How did you accomplish these tasks?

j. Close the print manager window, the Printers folder, and WordPad, and remove the diskette from its drive.

Lab Exercise 3 (Section 6.2)

a. Open the Control Panel window and start the Add New Hardware utility. What is the name of the resulting dialog box?

b. Choose the Next command button. You are going to simulate setting up a printer that has just been connected to your computer, so select the No option button and then choose the Next button.

c. Select Printer from the hardware types list and choose the Next button. What is the dialog box called now?

d. Suppose that the Printer is made by Epson and its model designation is "LQ-850". Select the appropriate items from the Manufacturers and Printers lists. What is the exact name of the item in the Printers list?

e. Choose the Next button to display the "ports" page. Which computer port is highlighted?

f. Choose the Next button. Select, if necessary, the No option button so that the new printer does not become the default one. What *is* the name of your default printer?

g. Choose the Next button and then the Cancel button.

h. Close the Control Panel window.

Lab Exercise 4 (Section 6.3)

Note: This exercise requires that your computer be equipped with a sound card.

a. Open the Control Panel window and start the Sounds utility. What is the name of the resulting dialog box?

b. Select the Windows Default sound scheme. (If necessary, answer "No" to the warning message.) What event, if any, is highlighted in the Events list?

c. Preview the sounds for the Start Windows and Exit Windows events. Are they the same sound?

d. Assign the "Chimes" sound to the Maximize event. Did a speaker icon automatically appear next to Maximize when you did this?

e. Choose the Cancel command button to close the dialog box.

f. Start the Multimedia utility from Control Panel. Which page of the resulting dialog box is displayed?

g. On the Audio page, drag the volume slider to High, then to Low. Was a sound emitted in both cases when you released the mouse button?

h. Use the Multimedia Properties dialog box to help answer the following questions:

- How many choices are there for the size of the window in which video clips will be shown? Which size is highlighted?
- What drive letter is assigned to your CD-ROM drive?

i. Choose the Cancel command button to close the dialog box and then close the Control Panel window.

Lab Exercise 5 (Section 6.4)

a. Open the Control Panel window and start the Accessibility Options utility. What is the name of the resulting dialog box?

b. On the Keyboard page, enable (turn on) StickyKeys and choose the Settings button next to it. Using context-sensitive help, state the function of the *Show StickyKeys status on the screen* check box.

c. Select this check box, then the OK button, and finally, the Apply button. Describe the StickyKeys status icon.

d. Disable (turn off) StickyKeys. Choose the Settings button next to the FilterKeys check box. What is the shortcut key for FilterKeys?

e. Select the *Ignore repeated keystrokes* option button and choose the Settings button next to it. In the resulting dialog box, move the slider to Long. How much time must now elapse between keystrokes before the second keystroke is recognized by Windows? (Try it in the test box!)

f. Choose Cancel twice to return to the Keyboard page. Enable ToggleKeys and then choose the Apply button. Now, press the Caps Lock key twice. Is the same sound emitted both times? What other keys are affected by ToggleKeys?

g. Disable ToggleKeys and choose the OK button to close the dialog box.

h. Close the Control Panel window.

Lab Exercise 6 (Section 6.4)

a. Open the Control Panel window and start the Accessibility Options utility.

b. Click on the Display tab, enable (turn on) High Contrast, and then choose the Settings command button. Did the screen go into high contrast mode?

c. Select the *White on black* option, choose OK, and then Apply. What is the color of the dialog box background? Of its title bar?

d. Select the *Black on white* option, choose OK, and then Apply. What is the color of the dialog box background? Of its title bar?

e. Disable (turn off) High Contrast and choose the Apply button. Then, click on the Mouse tab.

f. Enable MouseKeys and choose the Settings button. What is the shortcut key for MouseKeys?

g. Select the Num Lock *On* option and elect to show MouseKey status on the screen. Choose OK to return to the Mouse page. Did the MouseKeys icon appear on the Taskbar?

h. Choose the Apply button and then use the numeric keypad to drag the dialog box to another part of the screen. Give the steps you took to accomplish this.

i. Use the numeric keypad to disable MouseKeys. How did you accomplish this?

j. Close the dialog box and the Control Panel window.

Lab Exercise 7 (Section 6.5)

a. Open the Control Panel window and start the Modems utility. How many pages are there in the resulting dialog box?

b. If your computer is equipped with a modem, use this utility to answer the following questions:

- What is the name and maximum speed for this modem?
- What are the current settings for data bits, parity, and stop bits?
- Is the modem using tone dialing or pulse dialing?

c. Close the Modems utility and start the System utility. Use the latter to answer the following questions:

- What kind of processor and how much RAM does your computer have?
- What type of display adapter and monitor does it have?
- What are the names of the available hardware profiles?
- Is the hard disk making use of disk compression?

d. Close the System utility and start the Regional Settings utility. Use the latter to show how Windows would display:

- The current time
- The current date in both short and long format

e. Close the Regional Settings utility and the Control Panel window.

If You Want to Learn More ...

The notes presented here allow you to delve more deeply into some of the topics covered in this chapter.

Accessibility Options for everyone

You may find a couple of the Accessibility Options features useful even if you're not physically challenged.

- Do you occasionally make typing errors because you've pressed the Caps Lock or Num Lock key without realizing it? To avoid this kind of mistake, select the Use ToggleKeys check box on the Keyboard page of the Accessibility Properties dialog box. With this feature enabled, you'll hear a tone whenever you press Caps Lock, Num Lock, or Scroll Lock.
- Do you sometimes find your mouse or laptop's pointing device frustrating to use? In this case, select the Use MouseKeys check box on the Mouse page of the Accessibility Properties dialog box. Then, you'll be able to use the numeric keypad keys to move the mouse pointer and click, double-click, or drag the mouse. To fully benefit from this feature, choose the Settings command button on

the Mouse page and customize MouseKeys to your liking. Enabling the shortcut key (Left Alt+Left Shift+Num Lock) is particularly useful, making it very easy to turn the feature on or off.

The CD-ROM AutoPlay feature

As you may have noticed, when you insert a CD-ROM into its drive, Windows sometimes automatically opens an application stored on it. This feature is known as *AutoPlay.* Although AutoPlay is convenient at times, it can also be annoying when you insert a CD without the intent of using it immediately. Fortunately, you can easily turn off this feature on either a case-by-case or long-term basis.

- To turn off the AutoPlay feature for the CD you are about to load, hold down the Shift key as you insert the disc into its drive.
- To turn off AutoPlay on a more permanent basis:
    1. Open Control Panel's System utility.
    2. Click on the Device Manager tab and then double-click on the CD-ROM drive icon.
    3. In the resulting dialog box, click on the settings tab.
    4. Deselect the *Auto insert notification* check box.
    5. Choose OK command buttons to close the current dialog box and the System utility.

Improving performance

As we mentioned in Section 6.5, it's usually best to leave the System utility's Performance settings at their defaults. Here are two special cases for which you might want to make a change:

- If your system has an older single- or double-speed CD-ROM drive, you might be able to improve its performance by telling Windows that it's a quad-speed drive. To do so:
    1. Click on the Performance tab in the System Properties dialog box and choose the File System command button.
    2. In the resulting dialog box, click on the CD-ROM tab and select *Quad-speed or higher* from the drop-down list.
    3. Choose the OK command button and close the System utility.

  Windows will now assign a larger amount of cache memory to the CD-ROM drive.
- If your system has two hard disk drives, you might improve performance by using the faster of these disks (especially if it has more free disk space) for the Windows swap file. To do so:

1. Click on the Performance tab in the System Properties dialog box and then choose the Virtual Memory command button.
2. In the resulting dialog box, select the *Let me specify my own virtual memory settings* option button and then select the faster drive from the *Hard disk* drop-down list.
3. Choose the OK command button (a warning message will appear; respond "No" if you're not sure what you're doing) and close the System utility.

Of course, if you experience any difficulties with a new setting, return it to the default.

Printing a system resource report

Control Panel's System utility allows you to print a "system resource report"; a comprehensive listing of your computer system's components and their settings. This report contains information about the computer's processor, its IRQ (interrupt request lines) and I/O (input/output) settings, memory usage, hardware devices, and installed device drivers. To print the report:

1. Open the System utility and click on the Device Manager tab.
2. Choose the Print command button and, in the Print dialog box, select the *All devices and system summary* check box.
3. Choose the OK command button.

Be aware that the report might be more than ten pages long.

Where to go from here

Here's where to find some more information about some of the topics discussed in this chapter:

- Instead of using the Printers folder, you can set up a printer from within an application, usually using a Page Setup dialog box. See Sections 7.3, 8.5, and 9.2.
- Several Windows "accessories" provide more control over multimedia devices than the Control Panel utilities discussed in Section 6.3. Some of these accessories are described in Section 9.5.
- More information about modems (and especially their uses) is provided in Chapters 10 and 11.
- The Network utility is discussed in more detail in Chapter 10, which contains a lot of information about networks, in general.

CHAPTER 7

Word Processing with WordPad

Windows supplies two applications whose primary purpose is to help you "process words"; that is, to create text-based documents. **Notepad** is little more than a *text editor*, with virtually no text formatting capability, and we will discuss it in Section 9.2. **WordPad**, which was introduced in Section 2.2, is more powerful and will be considered in depth in this chapter. To be more specific, you will learn:

1. Some additional ways to select and edit text in a WordPad document.
2. To change the typeface, font size, and font style of text.
3. To specify page margins and paper orientation for a WordPad document.
4. To format paragraphs by setting tabs and specifying text alignment and indentation.
5. To create a list of items automatically preceded by "bullets".
6. To insert graphics into a WordPad document.
7. To move, copy, resize, and delete graphics.
8. To use WordPad's Find and Replace utility.
9. To preview a document before printing it.
10. About the various file formats that WordPad can recognize.

7.1 WordPad Revisited

Using a word processor to create a document involves several steps. You have to:

1. Enter the text that makes up the document or open a previously created document.
2. Edit the document to correct errors, modify its content, or improve its style.
3. Format the document; for example, set margins and choose fonts.
4. Save the document to disk.
5. Print a copy of the document on paper.

In Section 2.2, we presented an introduction to the WordPad word processor that quickly covered a few of these points. In this section, we will review and expand upon some of this material.

The WordPad Window

To start WordPad:

1. Click on the Start button (or press Ctrl+Esc) to open the Start menu.
2. Point at the Programs option and then at Accessories on the resulting submenu.
3. Click on the WordPad item on the Accessories submenu.

A window, similar to the one in Figure 1, will open. The Toolbar, Format bar, Ruler, and Status bar can all be toggled on or off by selecting or deselecting the corresponding item on the View menu. If you don't use one of these features, you can increase the size of the document window slightly by removing that feature from the screen.

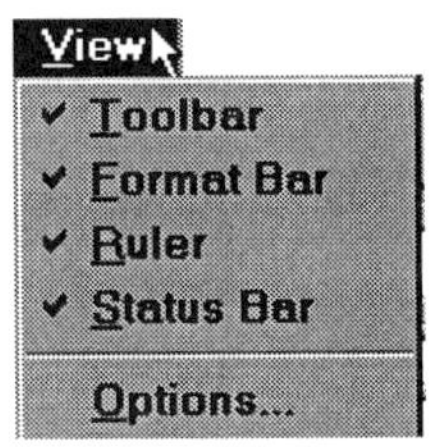

Recall that to create a document, you just begin typing. The text you type will appear in the *document window* and also be stored in the computer's internal memory, RAM. The *insertion point* moves to indicate where the next character you type will appear on the screen. When you reach the end of a line, just keep typing; WordPad automatically *wraps* the text to the beginning of the next line. Press the Enter key to start a new line only if you want to begin a new paragraph or skip a line. When you reach the bottom of the document window, continue typing; the window will scroll to accommodate the new text.

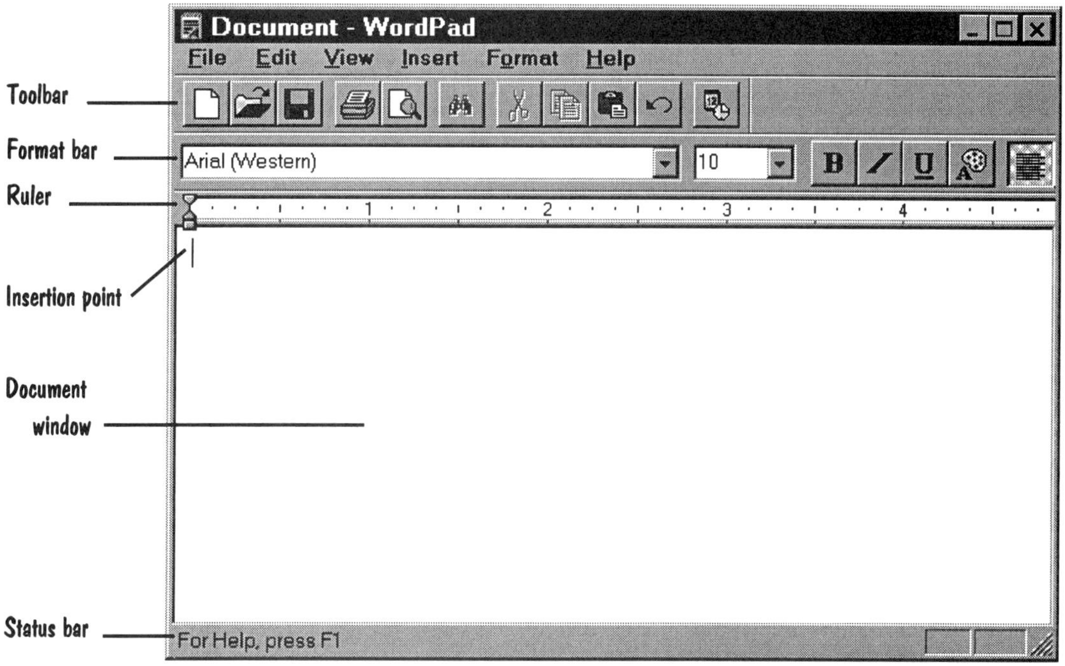

Figure 1 The WordPad Window

Editing a Document

It is inevitable that from time to time you will want to modify the content of the text you have typed. Making changes to existing text, for whatever reason, is called **editing** the document. To modify a piece (*block*) of text, you have to:

1. Move the insertion point to the text you are changing.
2. Delete the undesirable text and/or insert the new text.

In Section 2.2, we briefly discussed how to use the mouse or Arrow keys to move the insertion point within the document window or scroll the window. In some situations, using one of the keys or keystroke combinations given in the following table will move the insertion point more quickly to a desired location in the document.

Insertion point movement keys

Key	Moves the insertion point . . .
Home	To the beginning of the current line
End	To the end of the current line
Page Up	One window up
Page Down	One window down
Ctrl + Left Arrow	To the previous word
Ctrl + Right Arrow	To the next word
Ctrl + Home	To the beginning of the document
Ctrl + End	To the end of the document

Deleting and inserting text

Once you have moved the insertion point to the desired spot, you can:

- Delete the character to the *left* of the insertion point by pressing the Backspace key, or delete the character to the *right* of the insertion point by pressing the Delete key. If you want to delete a number of consecutive characters quickly, hold down the Backspace or Delete keys (as appropriate) until the block of text is erased from the screen.
- Insert text at the insertion point by typing it at the keyboard. If the new text just replaces (types over) existing characters, then WordPad is in *overwrite mode*. To return WordPad to the default *insert mode*, press the Insert key.

You can also delete or insert text by moving it from place to place within the document with the aid of the Windows Clipboard. In Section 2.3, we discussed how to select, cut, copy, and paste text. Recall that:

- To *select* a block of text, position the insertion point at the beginning of the block and then either hold down the Shift key while moving the insertion point to the end of the block or mouse-drag the insertion point to the end of the block. In either case, the selected block of text will become highlighted.

- To *cut* a block of text to the Clipboard, deleting it from its current location in the process, choose Cut from the Edit menu or click on the Toolbar's Cut button.

- To *copy* a selected block of text (which does not delete it from its current location), choose Copy from the Edit menu or click on the Toolbar's Copy button.

- To *paste* a block of text at the insertion point, choose Paste from the Edit menu or click on the Toolbar's Paste button.

These techniques work with every Windows-based application. In addition, WordPad provides some shortcuts for these procedures:

Other ways to select text

- To select a word, double-click on any letter in it.
- To select a paragraph, triple-click anywhere within it.

You can also select certain blocks of text by moving the mouse cursor (the I-beam) into the left margin. The cursor will become a right-facing pointer, called the *selection cursor* (see Figure 2). Then:

- To select the line of text at the cursor, click the mouse (see Figure 2). To select several consecutive lines of text, drag the mouse pointer down the left margin until all the desired lines have become highlighted.
- To select the paragraph at the cursor, double-click the mouse.
- To select the entire document, triple-click the mouse. (You can also select the entire document by choosing the Select All command from the Edit menu.)

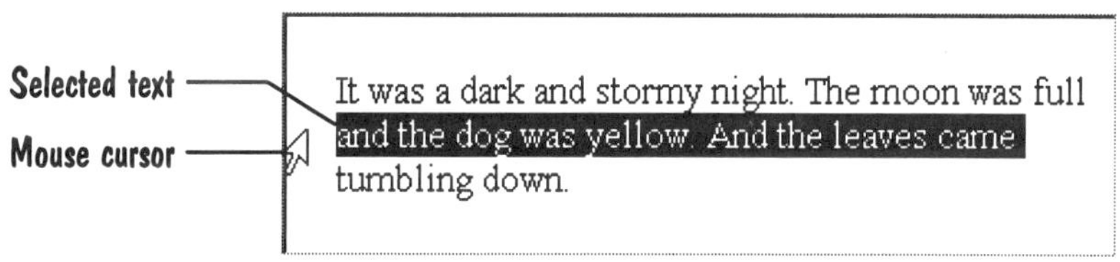

Figure 2 Selecting a Single Line of Text

Deselecting text

To *deselect* a block of text, click the mouse anywhere on the screen or press a cursor movement key, such as an Arrow key. (Do not press any other kind of key while a block of text is selected; the corresponding character will *replace* the selected text!)

Drag-and-drop move or copy

You can also move or copy text from one place in a WordPad document to another using the *drag-and-drop* technique. (In Section 3.3, we used this technique to move and copy files or folders.) Here's the way it works:

1. Select the block of text to be moved or copied.
2. Position the mouse pointer anywhere in the highlighted text (the cursor will become a left-facing pointer).
3. If you want:

- To *move* the selected text, press (but do not release) the left mouse button and reposition the mouse pointer at the selected text's new location.
- To *copy* the selected text, hold down the Ctrl key and press the left mouse button as you move the pointer to the selected text's new location. (In this case, the mouse pointer displays a small box containing a plus symbol.)

The insertion point moves with the mouse cursor and indicates the exact place the text will be positioned (see Figure 3).

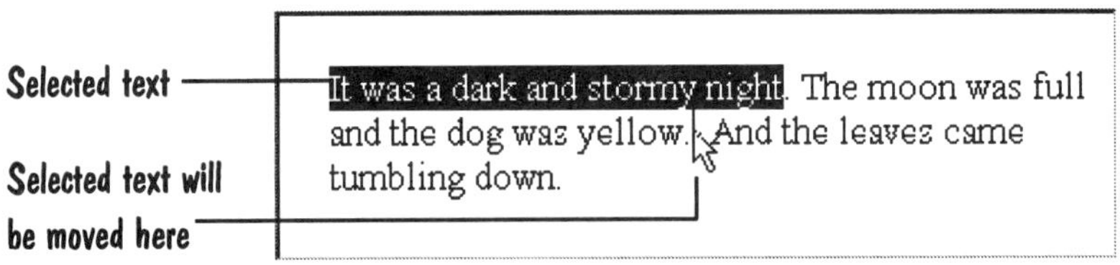

Figure 3 Moving Selected Text by Drag-and-Drop

4. When the insertion point is positioned properly, release the mouse button (and Ctrl key, if copying). The selected text will appear in the new location.

NOTE

Once you have selected a block of text, in addition to moving or copying it, you can:

- Delete the text by pressing the Delete or Backspace key.
- Change the text's font, as described in Section 7.2.

To *undo* your last edit (such as moving or deleting some text), either choose the Undo command from the Edit menu or click on the Toolbar's Undo button.

TIP

When using a word processor, you may find it more convenient to perform editing operations using the keyboard rather than by clicking on menu commands or Toolbar buttons. Here are some shortcut keys for the operations discussed in this section:

Ctrl+A selects the entire document.
Ctrl+X cuts a selected block of text to the Clipboard.
Ctrl+C copies a selected block of text to the Clipboard.
Ctrl+V pastes the text on the Clipboard at the insertion point.
Ctrl+Z undoes the last editing operation.

7.1 TUTORIAL

Try the following exercise on your own.

1. Turn on the computer (if necessary) to start Windows 95 and open WordPad by clicking on the WordPad item on the Accessories submenu of the Start menu's Programs option.
2. Begin a document by typing the sentences "It was a dark and stormy night. The dogs were barking.", and then pressing the Enter key.
3. Select the first line of this document by moving the mouse cursor into the left margin, where it becomes a right-facing arrow, and clicking. (Because the first line happens to be a paragraph, you can also select it by either double-clicking while the mouse cursor is in the left margin or triple-clicking while the cursor is in the paragraph itself.) The first line of text will become highlighted.
4. *Copy* the selected text to the end of the document by dragging it there: Hold down the Ctrl key (if you forget to do this, the text will be *moved*, not copied), position the mouse cursor within the selected text, press the left mouse button, reposition the cursor (and insertion point) at the end of the document, and release the mouse button and Ctrl key.
5. Select the entire document by either
   - Repositioning the mouse cursor in the left margin and triple-clicking.

   or
   - Choosing Select All from the Edit menu (or pressing Ctrl+A).
6. Copy the selected text to the end of the document: Copy it to the Clipboard (press Ctrl+C), reposition the insertion point at the end of the document (press Ctrl+End), and paste the text there (press Ctrl+V). There should now be four lines of stormy nights and barking dogs.
7. Undo the last action (step 6): Either choose the Undo command from the Edit menu, click on the Undo Toolbar button, or press Ctrl+Z.

8. Close WordPad, responding No to the "save changes?" message.

7.2 Using Fonts in WordPad

In Section 7.1, we discussed some of the basic capabilities of the WordPad word processor. In this section, we will describe how you can control the way text appears on the screen and the printed page.

Fonts Revisited

Nothing makes a bigger difference in the impact your words will have on the reader than the fonts you use to print them. In Section 5.5, we briefly discussed the nature of fonts; we will expand upon that material here and then show how fonts are implemented within a WordPad document.

Recall that a **font** is a collection of characters of a given design, size, and style.

- The *design* or **typeface** of a font refers to the general appearance of the characters, independent of their size, thickness, or other attributes. For example, Arial, `Courier New`, and Times New Roman are three of the typefaces supplied by Windows.
- The *size* of a font refers to its height, measured in **points**. There are 72 points per inch, so 18-point type, for example, is roughly 1/4-inch high on the printed page. Here are some examples of different sizes of the Arial typeface:

  8-point 12-point 18-point

- The *style* of a font is dictated by attributes such as **bold** or *italic*.

Some fonts are only supplied in discrete sizes, such as 10-point, 12-point, and so on. Others, called **scalable fonts**, can be scaled to any size. Microsoft includes several scalable typefaces, known as *TrueType fonts*, with the Windows 95 software. These fonts are available for use in any Windows-based application.

WYSIWYG When you type text in WordPad, the corresponding characters appear on the screen in the current font (which is displayed on the Format bar). If you print the document, the fonts that appear on the screen will also be used by the printer. We say that WordPad is a WYSIWYG (What You See Is What You Get, pronounced "whizzywig") word processor. WYSIWYG means that the appearance of the document on the screen, including fonts, graphics, spacing, and so on, previews the way it will appear on the printed page.

Changing the font There are several ways to change the current font in WordPad. With any of these techniques, the font change will apply to either:

- The currently selected block of text, if text is selected when the change is made.

or

- The text you type after the change is made, if no text is currently selected.

Using the Font Dialog Box

The most flexible way to change the current font is to make use of the Font dialog box, which allows you to change not only the typeface, style, and size of the font, but also other attributes such as underline (underline), strikeout (~~strikeout~~), and color. Here's how to use this dialog box:

1. If you want the new font to apply to existing text, select that block of text. (Otherwise, the new font will apply to the text you type after the change is made.)
2. Choose the Font command from the Format menu. The Font dialog box, shown in Figure 4, will be displayed. The current font's typeface, style, and size are shown in the Font, Font style, and Size text boxes, respectively; a sample of this font is displayed in the Sample box. As you make selections to change this font, the sample text changes accordingly.

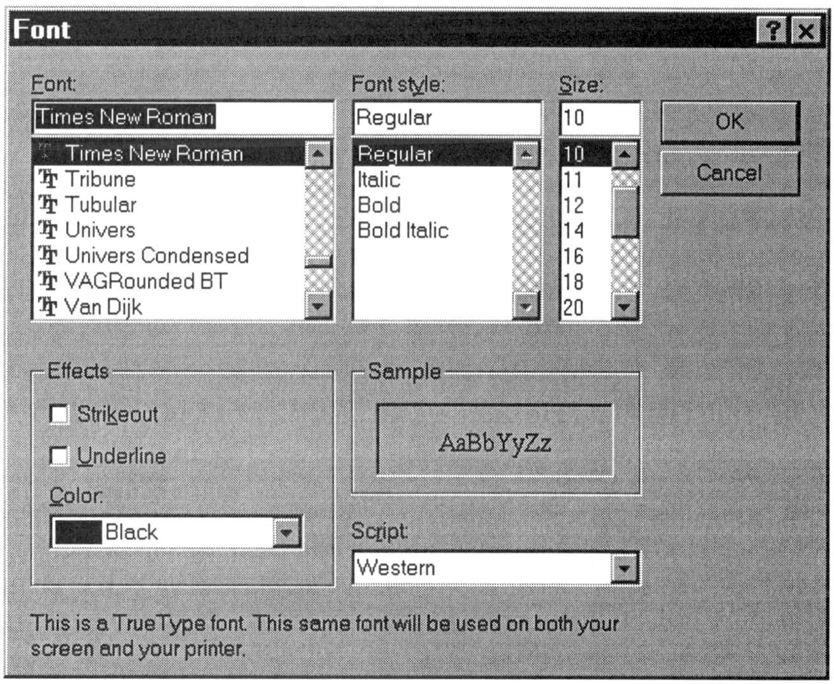

Figure 4 The Font Dialog Box

3. Select a typeface for the new font from the Font list box. Instead of scrolling to the desired name, you might save time by typing its

first few letters in the Font text box at the top of the list. For example, to change to Arial, type "ar" in the text box and the Font list box will scroll to display Arial and other "nearby" typefaces.

4. Select bold, italic, or bold italic, if you wish, from the Font style list. Selecting Regular turns off (cancels) a current style.
5. Select a font size (in points) from the Size list. You can select any (whole number) size that your printer can print, even if it doesn't appear in this list. Just click on the text box at the top of the Size list and enter the desired size.
6. If you want to add an underline and/or strikeout line to the text, select the appropriate check boxes.
7. You can select a text color from the Color drop-down list. Of course, to print the resulting text in this color, you need a color printer. (Some non-color printers print text colors in various shades of gray.)
8. The Script drop-down list is used to select an alternate character set for use with a language other than English. If Windows has not been configured for another language, you can ignore this feature.
9. To put your font changes into effect, choose the OK command button. To ignore these changes, choose Cancel.

Using the Format Bar

The **Format bar** provides a quicker, though less flexible, way of changing fonts and their attributes. (Remember: If the Format bar is not displayed in your WordPad window, choose the Format Bar item from the View menu to display it.) The functions of the Format bar buttons that alter the current font are identified in Figure 5. Notice that the typeface and font size of the current font are displayed on the Format bar; if the current font has bold, italic, or underline attributes, the corresponding buttons will appear to be "pressed in".

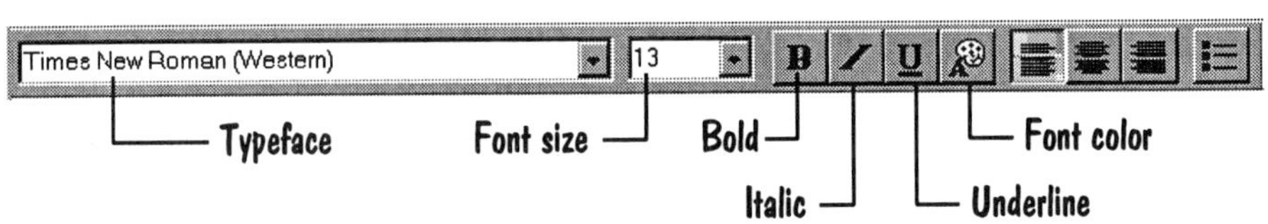

Figure 5 Font Attributes on the Format Bar

To use the Format bar to change the font of selected text or the text that you are about to type:

1. Select a new typeface or font size from the appropriate drop-down list.
2. Select or deselect bold, italics, or underline by clicking on the corresponding button.
3. Change the font color by clicking on the Font Color button and selecting the desired color from the drop-down list.

TIP

The easiest way to turn the bold, italics, or underline attribute on or off is to use the keystroke combinations Ctrl+B, Ctrl+I, or Ctrl+U, respectively. For example, to bold a word you are about to type, press Ctrl+B, type the word, and press Ctrl+B again. Or, to remove italics from a word you have already typed, select the word and press Ctrl+I.

7.2 TUTORIAL

Try the following exercise on your own.

1. Turn on the computer (if necessary) to start Windows 95.
2. Open WordPad from the Start button's Accessories submenu and maximize its window.
3. Insert the Student Disk in its drive and open the document named Preamble. (For information on opening documents, see Section 2.2.)
4. If the Format bar is turned off, display it by choosing the Format Bar command from the View menu. Notice (from the Format bar) that 14-point Arial type is used for the title of the document.
5. Change the title's font to 12-point bold italic Times New Roman:
   - Select the title (by, for example, clicking in the left margin).
   - Choose the Font command from the Format menu to open the Font dialog box.
   - In the dialog box, select Times New Roman from the Font list, Bold Italic from the Font style list, and 12 from the Size list.
   - Choose the OK command button.
6. Change the text for the preamble from 12-point Times New Roman to 11-point Arial:
   - Select the text of the preamble (by, for example, double-clicking in the left margin next to this paragraph).
   - Select "Arial (Western)" and "11" from the drop-down lists on the Format bar.

7. Deselect the selected text by clicking elsewhere in the WordPad window.
8. Italicize the words "United States of America":
   - Select these words.
   - Either press Ctrl+I or click on the Format bar's Italic button to italicize them.
   - Deselect these words.
9. Add the words THE END at the end of the document in bold type:
   - Reposition the cursor at the end of the document and press the Enter key twice.
   - Turn on boldface by clicking on the Format bar's Bold button (or pressing Ctrl+B).
   - Type the words THE END and turn off boldface by clicking on the Bold button (or pressing Ctrl+B) again.
10. Close WordPad (responding No to the "save changes?" message) and remove the Student Disk from its drive.

7.3 Formatting Text in WordPad

Formatting a document changes, in some manner, the way the text in that document is arranged on the page. In this section, we will discuss WordPad's formatting features.

Formatting the Document as a Whole

WordPad provides several formatting features that apply to the entire document. When one of these commands is issued, it doesn't matter where the insertion point is positioned; the command affects all text that has already been typed and will be typed in the current document. These features include:

Document-oriented features

- Placing text on the page in either portrait or landscape orientation.
- Specifying the size of the left, right, top, and bottom page margins.

To access either of these formatting features, choose Page Setup from the File menu. The Page Setup dialog box, shown in Figure 6, will be displayed.

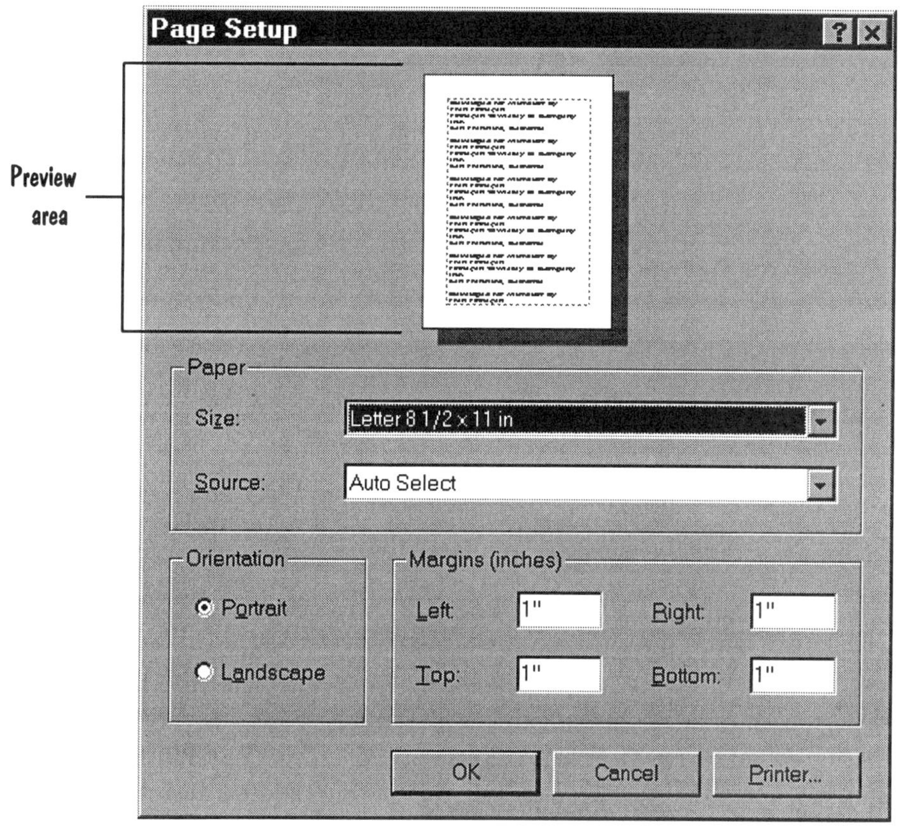

Figure 6 The Page Setup Dialog Box

Specifying Page Orientation You can choose to print your document in either portrait or landscape orientation. In **portrait** orientation, the document's text is printed parallel to the short side of the paper. For example, the page you are now reading is printed this way. In **landscape** orientation, the text is printed parallel to the long side of the paper. Landscape orientation is usually used for certificates and diplomas. The figures at the right further illustrate this concept.

To specify page orientation:

1. Open the Page Setup dialog box (Figure 6) from the File menu.
2. Select the Portrait or Landscape option button. (The "page" shown

in the preview area will appear in the selected orientation.)

3. Choose the OK command button.

Specifying Margins By default, WordPad leaves the margin settings for a new document the same as they were in the previous one. To specify different margins for the current document:

1. Open the Page Setup dialog box (Figure 6) from the File menu.
2. Enter the desired margins in the Left, Right, Top, and Bottom text boxes. (The "page" shown in the preview area will indicate the new margins.)
3. Choose the OK command button.

NOTE

The width and height of a page's text area depend not only on its margins and orientation, but also on the size of the paper being used. For example, suppose that all margins are set to one inch and the orientation is portrait. Then, on a standard 8½" × 11" ("letter size") piece of paper, all text is enclosed in an imaginary box that is 6½ inches wide and 9 inches high. However, for "legal size" paper (which is 8½" × 14"), our imaginary box becomes 6½ inches wide and 12 inches high. Thus, WordPad needs to know the size of paper you are using. This setting is also specified in the Page Setup dialog box, by selecting the appropriate item on the Paper Size drop-down list.

Formatting Paragraphs

When you press the Enter key while typing text in WordPad, a paragraph marker code, which is not visible on the screen, is placed in the document file. To WordPad, a *paragraph* is the text lying between two paragraph markers, or between a paragraph marker and the beginning or end of the document. In other words, every time you press the Enter key, WordPad interprets it as the beginning of a new paragraph.

WordPad has several formatting features that apply either to the paragraphs containing selected text, or (if no text is selected) to the paragraph that contains the insertion point. These features include:

Paragraph-oriented features

- Centering the text or aligning it with the left or right margin.
- Indenting a paragraph of text from the left and/or right margin, or the first line of a paragraph from the rest of the paragraph.
- Setting tabs to help create columns of text.
- Automatically placing a "bullet" before each item in a list.

NOTE

When you start typing a new paragraph, it automatically inherits all the formatting characteristics of the previous one. For example, suppose the current paragraph is centered between the margins. If you press the Enter key and start typing, you'll see that the new text is still centered.

Changing Text Alignment WordPad provides three options for aligning (or *justifying*) text relative to the left and right margins:

The text in this paragraph is *left-justified*. All lines in this paragraph align on the left margin.

This text is *centered*. All lines in this paragraph are centered between the margins.

The text in this paragraph is *right-justified*. All lines in this paragraph align on the right margin.

The default alignment option is left-justification. To change text alignment, place the insertion point in the desired paragraph or select the paragraphs to be aligned and:

1. Choose the Paragraph item from the Format menu.
2. Select the desired option (Left, Right, or Center) from the Alignment drop-down list.
3. Choose the OK command button.

TIP

It is a little easier to select an alignment option using the Format bar. To do so, place the insertion point in the desired paragraph or select the paragraphs to be aligned and click the appropriate Format bar button, as shown below:

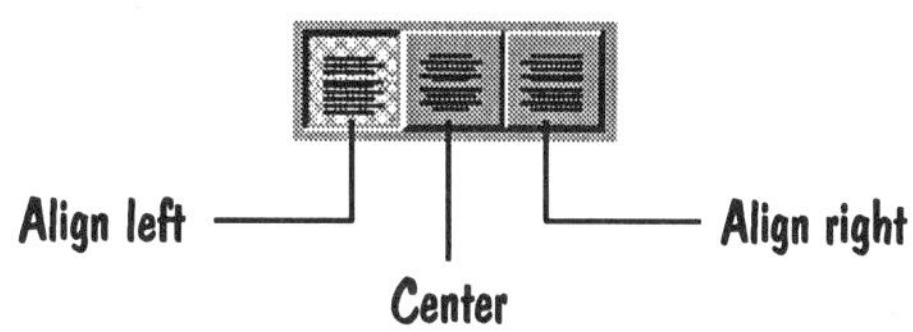

The button that appears to be "pressed in" (*Align left*, in the diagram above) indicates the justification of the current paragraph.

Changing Paragraph Indentation As you know, when you change the margins for a document, that change applies to the entire document. To change the left or right margin for a particular paragraph in WordPad, you change its *indentation* relative to the given margin. The indentation feature also allows you to indent the first line of the paragraph relative to the rest of the paragraph.

For example, in Figure 7:

- The first paragraph is not indented.
- The second paragraph is indented 1 inch on the left, 0.5 inches on the right, and the indent for the first line is 0 inches. Since the first line indent is measured relative to the rest of the paragraph, it is indented the same amount as the rest of the paragraph.
- The third paragraph is indented 1 inch on the left, 1.5 inches on the right, and has a first line indent of -0.5 inches. Since the indent for the first line is *negative* and is measured relative to the rest of the paragraph, it starts one-half inch to the *left* of the rest of the paragraph. (*Positive* first line indents start this line to the *right* of the rest of the paragraph.)

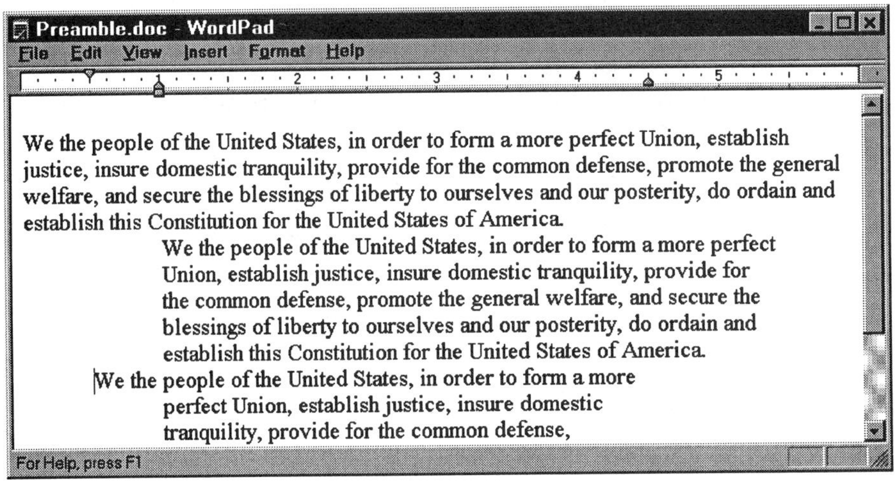

Figure 7 Examples of Indented Paragraphs

To change indentation, place the insertion point in the desired paragraph, or select text in the paragraphs to be changed, and:

1. Choose Paragraph from the Format menu. The Paragraph dialog box, shown in Figure 8, will open.
2. Type the desired numbers in the *Left*, *Right*, and *First line* indentation text boxes.
3. Choose the OK command button.

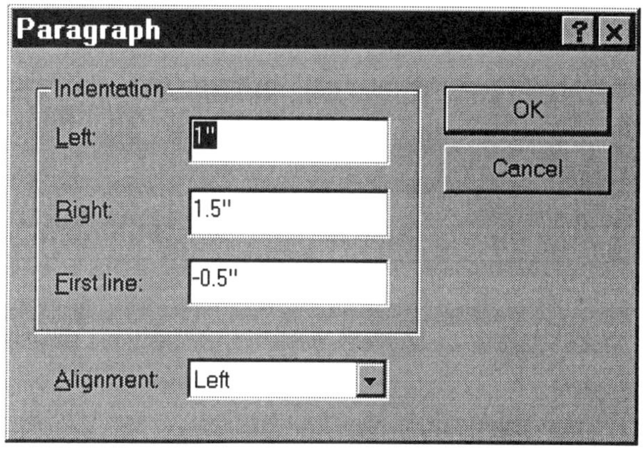

Figure 8 The Paragraph Dialog Box

TIP

You can also use the WordPad Ruler to change paragraph indenting. (Remember: If the Ruler is hidden, you can display it by choosing the Ruler item from the View menu.) To change indentation this way:

1. Place the insertion point in the desired paragraph, or select text in the paragraphs to be changed.
2. Use the mouse to drag the left-, right-, and/or first-line-indent markers to the appropriate positions on the Ruler.

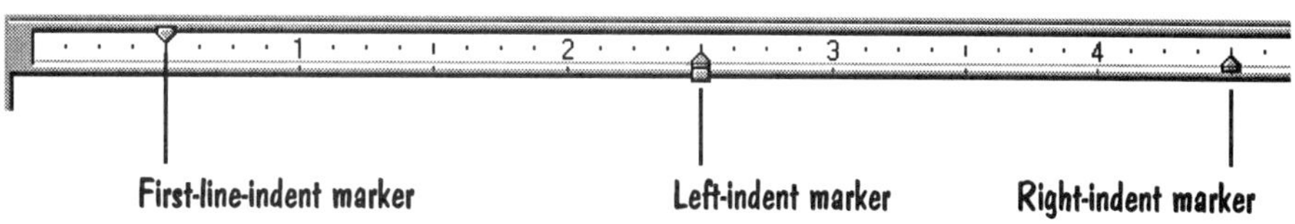

Figure 7 shows the markers set for the third paragraph's indentation.

Changing the Tab Settings When you press the Tab key while working in a WordPad document, the insertion point moves to the right and is positioned at the next tab setting (or *tab stop*). By default, the tab stops are set at half-inch intervals, beginning at the left margin. Thus, if you press the Tab key when the insertion point is 2.75" from the left margin (and the default tab stops are in effect), it will move to a position on the same line 3" from the margin.

Tab stops can be very useful in creating columns of text in a document. To add or remove tab stops for a given paragraph:

1. Place the insertion point in the desired paragraph, or select text in the desired paragraph.
2. Choose the Tabs item from the Format menu. The dialog box shown in Figure 9 will open.

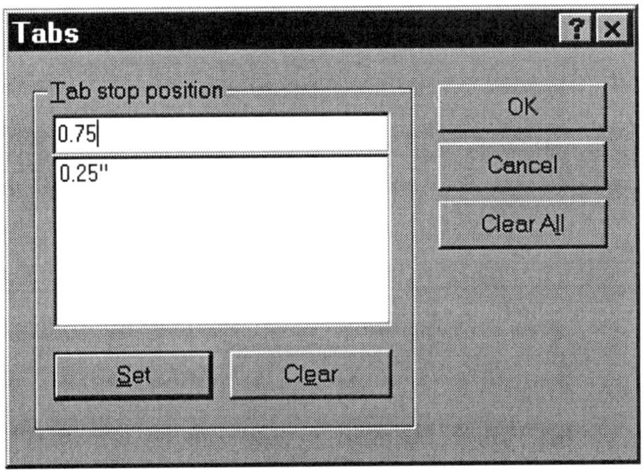

Figure 9 The Tabs Dialog Box

3. To add a new tab stop:
   - Enter its position (relative to the left margin) in the *Tab stop position* text box.
   - Choose the Set command button. The new tab stop will be displayed in the *Tab stop position* list box and all *default* tab stops to its left will be removed. For example, adding a tab setting of 0.75 removes the default tab stop at 0.5.
4. To remove all tab stops displayed in the *Tab stop position* list box, choose the Clear All command button. To remove one of the tab stops displayed in the list box, select it and choose the Clear command button.
5. Choose the OK command button to close the dialog box and put the new settings into effect. If the Ruler is currently displayed in the WordPad window, L symbols will appear on it in the appropriate positions.

TIP

The WordPad Ruler provides an easier way to add and remove tab stops. To use the Ruler for these purposes:

1. Position the insertion point (or select text) in the desired paragraph.
2. To add a tab stop, click on the appropriate location on the Ruler. An L symbol will appear there.

3. To remove an existing tab stop, drag that L symbol off the Ruler.

Creating a Bulleted List If your document contains a list of important points, you can add emphasis by preceding each item on the list by a "bullet". A **bullet** is a small symbol, often round or square, used for this purpose. Here are some examples of typical bullets: ● ■ ○ ☛ ✔

WordPad has a *bullet style* feature that allows you to easily create a bulleted list. When this feature is in effect, new paragraphs will begin with a solid round bullet followed by a tab. To turn the bullet style on, either

- Choose the Bullet Style item from the Format menu.

or

- Click on the Format bar's Bullets button, which is shown at the right.

Once you have completed your list, press the Enter key, moving the insertion point to the next line and inserting a new bullet. Then, either choose Bullet Style from the Format menu (it's a toggle) or click on the Toolbar's Bullets button. The last bullet will disappear.

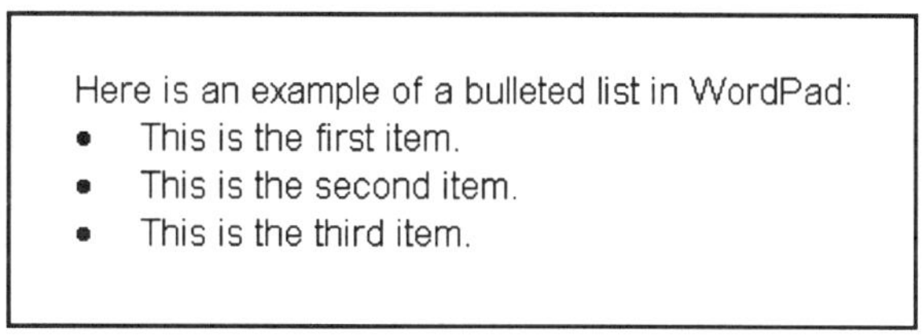

Here is an example of a bulleted list in WordPad:
- This is the first item.
- This is the second item.
- This is the third item.

TIP

The amount a bullet and the corresponding list item are indented is governed by the first-line-indent and left-indent, respectively, for that paragraph. Thus, to change the positions of the bullets and list items relative to the left margin, just change these indentation options (as described earlier in this section) for all lines of the list.

If you want to use another symbol for your bullets, you can do so with the help of the Character Map accessory, which is discussed in Section 9.5. However, with this technique, you will have to manually insert each bullet and then press the Tab key before typing the corresponding list item.

7-3 TUTORIAL

Try the following exercise on your own.

1. Turn on the computer (if necessary) to start Windows 95.
2. Open WordPad from the Start button's Accessories submenu and maximize its window.
3. Insert the Student Disk in its drive and open the document named History.
4. Display the Page Setup dialog box, by choosing this item from the File menu, and:
   - Set the margins for the History document to 1.5" on the left and right and 1.25" on the top and bottom by entering these numbers in the appropriate text boxes.
   - Select the Portrait option button (if necessary) so the document's text will print parallel to the short side of the page.

   Choose the OK button to put these changes into effect.
5. Center the title by positioning the insertion point within it and clicking on the appropriate button on the Format bar. In a similar way, right-align the first paragraph of the document. (This step can also be carried out by choosing Paragraph from the Format menu and selecting the proper option from the Alignment drop-down list.)

   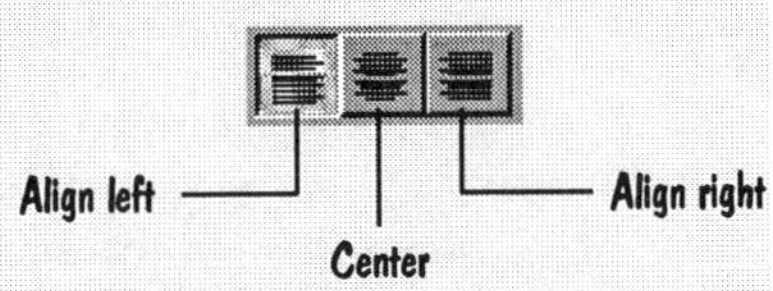

6. Indent the second and third paragraphs 1 inch on the left and right (relative to the margins), with a first-line-indent of 0.5 inches: Select both paragraphs, choose Paragraph from the Format menu, enter these figures in the Indentation text boxes, and choose OK. (These settings can also be made using the Ruler's indent markers; see the TIP on page 283.)
7. Remove all tabs for the second paragraph of the document and set a new tab stop at 2.25 inches for this paragraph:
   - Click the mouse within the second paragraph.
   - Choose Tabs from the Format menu to open this dialog box.
   - Choose the Clear All button to remove the existing tabs.
   - Enter 2.25 in the *Tab stop position* text box.
   - Choose the OK button.

   (An existing tab can also be removed by dragging the corresponding **L** symbol off the Ruler; similarly, a new tab can be set by clicking on the appropriate spot on the Ruler.)

8. To see the effect of your new tab stop, position the insertion point in front of the first letter in the second paragraph and press the Tab key.
9. Close WordPad (responding No to the "save changes?" message) and remove the diskette from its drive.

7.4 Using Graphics in a WordPad Document

WordPad lets you do more than just process words. It allows you to insert **graphics** (pictures) into a document and then, if you wish, to move or resize them. In this section, we will describe how to perform these operations.

Inserting a Graphic into a Document

Although WordPad itself cannot be used to create graphics, you can insert (or *import*) a graphic created by another application into a WordPad document. There are two ways to accomplish this task.

Using the Clipboard As we mentioned in Section 2.3, the Windows Clipboard can be used to transfer a graphic from one document to another. Here's the way the process works:

1. Use a graphics program (such as Paint, which is discussed in Chapter 8) to create the picture or to open an existing graphics file.
2. Select the graphic and copy it to the Clipboard.
3. Switch to WordPad.
4. Place the insertion point where you want the graphic to appear.
5. Choose Paste from the Edit menu or click on the Toolbar's Paste button. The graphic will be displayed in your document at the insertion point.

TIP

If the graphic does not display satisfactorily in WordPad when you issue the Paste command, delete the graphic (by pressing the Del key), and choose the Paste Special command from the Edit menu. A dialog box will open allowing you to choose from among several image formats. Now, try these one at a time (by selecting a format from the list box and choosing the OK button) to get the most satisfactory image. However, be aware that some formats will not let you edit the graphic (see below) after it has been imported into WordPad.

Using the Insert Object Command There is another way to import a graphic into a WordPad document. This method works especially well if the graphic is stored on disk, but it does require some familiarity with the Windows 95 file system (Chapter 3). To use this technique:

1. Place the insertion point in the WordPad document where you want the graphic to appear.
2. Choose the Object item from the Insert menu. The Insert Object dialog box, shown in Figure 10, will open.

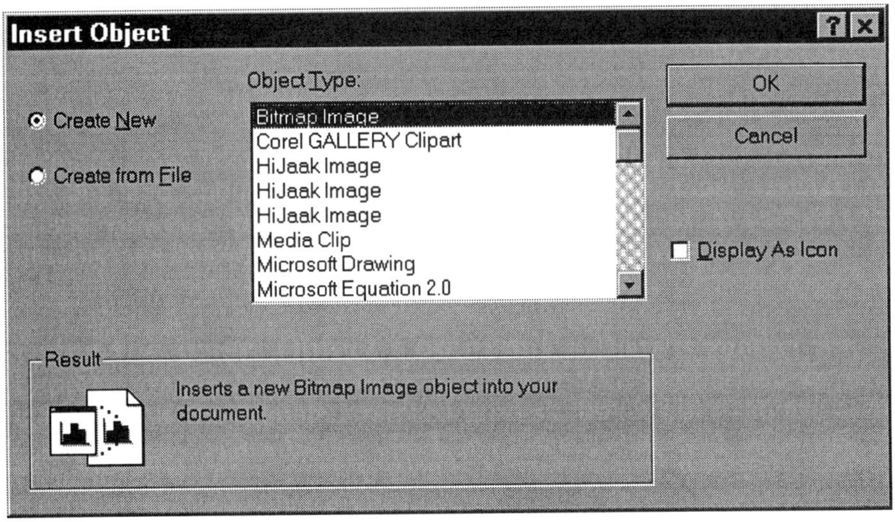

Figure 10 The Insert Object Dialog Box

3. If you want to create the graphic (using another application), select the Object Type corresponding to that application and then choose the OK command button. A box will open (at the insertion point) in the WordPad window, in which you can draw the graphic using the selected application's tools. When you are done, just click the mouse anywhere outside of the box.

   As an example, selecting Bitmap Image and choosing OK invokes the Paint application, and the WordPad window looks as pictured in Figure 11. (Although the title bar says "WordPad", the menus and available tools are those of Paint.)

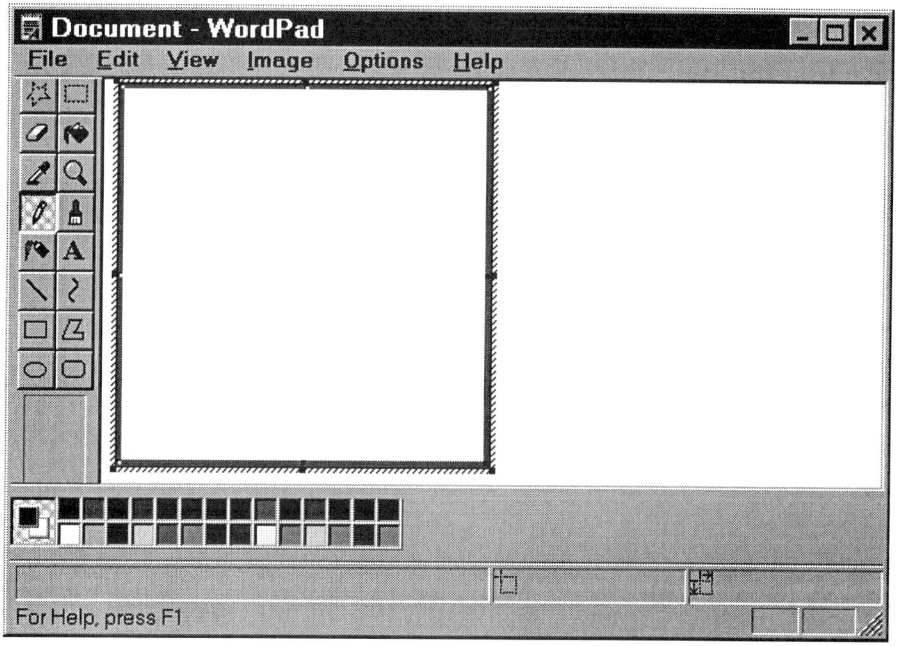

Figure 11 Working with Paint Inside the WordPad Window

4. If, instead of creating a graphic, you want to retrieve one from disk, select the *Create from File* option button. The Object Type list in the Insert Object dialog box will be replaced by the following display:

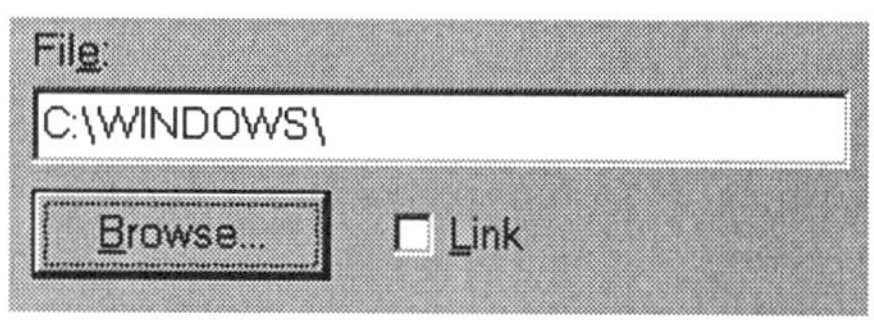

Now, either type the path name (see Section 3.1) for the desired file in the *File* text box or choose the Browse button to locate the desired file by browsing folders (see Section 3.5). Then, in either case, choose the OK command button in the Insert Object dialog box, and the graphic will be inserted into the WordPad document at the insertion point.

Editing a Graphic

When you *edit* a graphic, you modify the way it looks. WordPad has no graphics editing capabilities of its own. However, you may be able to edit a graphic contained in a WordPad document using a Windows feature known as **Object Linking and Embedding**, or **OLE**.

If the object was pasted or inserted into the document from an application that supports OLE (such as Paint), then it can be edited using that application's tools. To edit such a graphic:

1. Right-click on the graphic and point at the last item on the resulting pop-up menu. (This item has a name of the form *object-type* Object; for example, Bitmap Image Object.)
2. Choose either Edit or Open from the submenu:
   - If you choose Edit, the graphic will be enclosed in a box and the WordPad window will take on the look of the application that is being used to edit the image (see Figure 11).
   - If you choose Open, the application that is being used to edit the graphic will start and the graphic will open within it.

   (Double-clicking on a graphic achieves the same result as right-clicking on it, pointing at the "Object" item, and choosing Edit.)
3. Edit the graphic as you wish using the graphics application's tools.
4. When you are done, to return to WordPad:
   - If you chose Edit to begin the process, just click outside the graphic's box.
   - If you chose Open to begin, now choose Exit & Return to Document from the File menu.

OLE is discussed in more detail in Section 12.5.

Deleting, Moving, and Resizing a Graphic

Although you need to make use of another application to *edit* a graphic, WordPad can be used to delete, move, copy, or resize it.

TIP

If you are unhappy with the result of any of these operations, you can undo it: Either press Ctrl+Z, click on the Toolbar's Undo button (shown at the right), or choose the Undo command from the Edit menu.

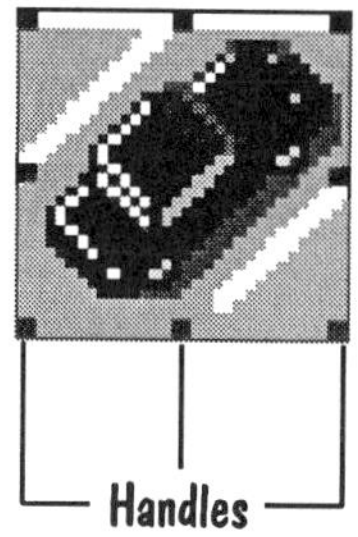

Selecting a Graphic In most cases, before you can delete, move, copy, or resize a graphic, you must first select it. To select a graphic, just click on it. The graphic will become enclosed in a box containing small squares, known as *sizing handles*, at each of its corners and at the midpoint of each side. (See the figure at the right.)

To deselect a graphic just click anywhere else in the document window.

Deleting a Graphic To delete a graphic from a WordPad document, either

- Select the graphic and press the Delete key.

or

- Position the insertion point just before or just after the graphic and press the Delete key or Backspace key, respectively.

Moving or Copying a Graphic To some extent, a graphic acts as if it were a character of text. (For example, as you have just seen, it can be deleted by positioning the insertion point just to the right of it and pressing the Backspace key.) This feature also provides a means for moving a graphic within a document.

Moving a graphic like a piece of text

- The graphic can be left-aligned, centered, or right-aligned (relative to the left and right margins) by selecting it and clicking on the appropriate button on the Format bar:

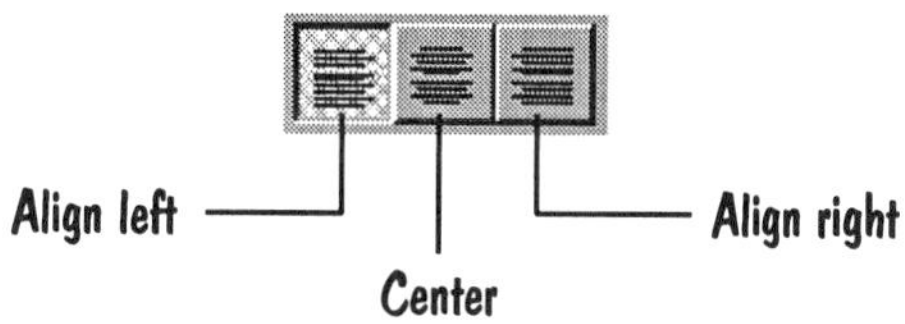

- The graphic can be "pushed" to the right or down the page by positioning the insertion point just to the left of the graphic and pressing the Spacebar, Tab key, or Enter key.
- You can select the graphic, cut or copy it to the Clipboard, and then paste it into another part of the document.

In addition to these text-oriented ways of moving a graphic, you can use the mouse to drag it to another part of the document. To be more specific:

Using drag-and-drop

1. Select the graphic.
2. Position the mouse pointer over the graphic, press and hold down

the mouse button, and reposition the pointer at the desired place within the document. (If you want to *copy* the graphic, instead of moving it, hold down the Ctrl key during this process.)

3. Release the mouse button (and, if necessary, the Ctrl key). The graphic will be displayed in the new location.

NOTE

If you use drag-and-drop to move or copy a graphic, be aware that the graphic must be dropped at some location *within* the existing document. For example, if the graphic is located at the end of the document and you try to move it down the page, you *will* be able to drag the mouse cursor downward, but when you release the button, the graphic will remain in its original position.

Resizing a Graphic To enlarge or reduce the size of a graphic within a WordPad document:

1. Select the graphic.
2. Position the mouse pointer over one of the eight handles:
   - Use the top side or bottom side midpoint handle to change the height of the graphic without changing its width.
   - Use the left side or right side midpoint handle to change the width of the graphic without changing its height.
   - Use a corner handle to change both height and width at the same time.
3. Drag the handle in the desired direction. An outline of the graphic's box will move with the cursor to show you the corresponding size, as shown below.

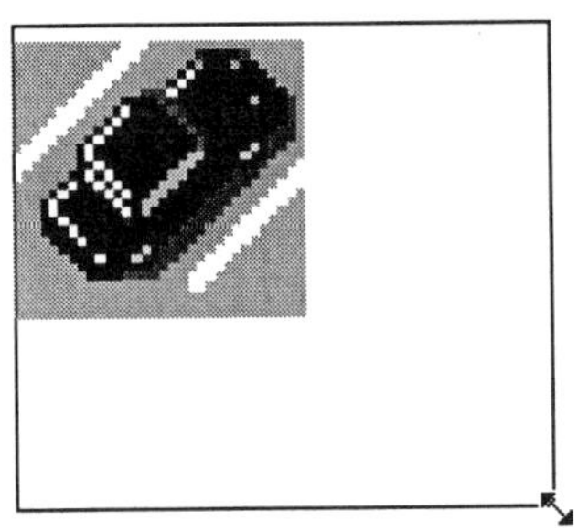

4. Release the mouse button when the graphic is the desired size. (To abort the process, press the Escape key before releasing the mouse button.)

7-4 TUTORIAL

Try the following exercise on your own.

1. Turn on the computer (if necessary) to start Windows 95.
2. Open WordPad from the Start button's Accessories submenu and maximize its window.
3. Insert the Student Disk in its drive.
4. Insert a graphic into the empty WordPad document:
   - Choose Object from the Insert menu.
   - Select the Create from File option button.
   - Erase the text in the *File* box and type: `A:\shapes`
   - Choose the OK command button. A graphic will be displayed in the document window.
   - Deselect the graphic by clicking elsewhere in the document window. The box around the graphic, together with its eight "sizing handles", will disappear.
5. Press Ctrl+Home to move the insertion point to the beginning of the document, just to the left of the graphic. Press the Enter key twice to "push" the graphic down two lines and then click on the Center Format bar button to center the graphic between the left and right margins.
6. Select the graphic by clicking on it; a box with "handles" will appear around the graphic. Now:
   - Reduce its size: Drag the handle in the lower-right corner of the selection box (the mouse pointer will become a two-headed arrow when it's positioned properly) about half-way toward the upper-left corner.

   - Increase its width without increasing its height: Drag the middle handle on the right side of the box to the right about one inch.
7. Add six blank lines to the bottom of the document by positioning the insertion point at the end of the document and then pressing the Enter key six times.
8. Create a copy the graphic at the bottom of the document:
   - Select the graphic.
   - Position the mouse pointer over the graphic and hold down the Ctrl key (for *copying*).
   - Drag the cursor to the end of the document, and release the mouse button and Ctrl key.
9. While the copy of the graphic is still selected, delete it by pressing the Delete key.

10. Right-click on the remaining graphic, point at Bitmap Image Object on the resulting submenu, and choose Open. The Paint graphics program will start, allowing you to edit the graphic.
11. Close Paint and WordPad (responding No to the "save changes?" message), and remove the diskette from its drive.

7.5 Other Features of WordPad

In the first four sections of this chapter, we have discussed how to create, edit, format, and add graphics to a WordPad document. In this section, we will introduce a few more assorted features of WordPad.

Find and Replace

Occasionally, you may want to locate an occurrence of a particular word in a given document, perhaps to replace it with another word. You can accomplish this in WordPad using the Find and Replace utility. As its name implies, this utility performs two functions:

- It can be used to locate a particular piece of text within a document.
- It can be used to automatically replace a particular piece of text with something else.

Finding text To locate a desired piece of text:

1. Choose Find from the Edit menu or click on the Toolbar's Find button. The Find dialog box, shown in Figure 12, will open.

2. Type the text you wish to locate in the *Find what* text box, and:

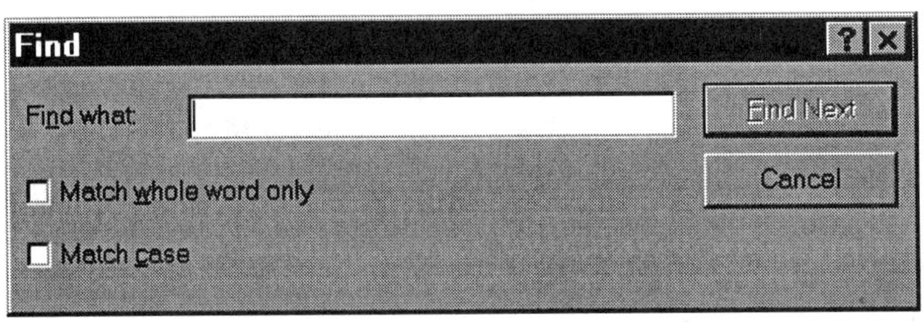

Figure 12 The Find Dialog Box

- Select the *Match whole word only* check box if you do not want the utility to search for longer words that contain the text you've typed. For example, suppose your document contains the words *all*, *small*, and *allow*, and you type *all* in the *Find what* text box. If the *Match whole word only* check box is selected, only the word *all* will be located. If it is not selected, all three words will be found.
- Select the *Match case* check box if you want to locate text that has the same combination of upper- and lower-case letters as the *Find what* text. For example, if this check box is selected and you type *all* in the *Find what* box, then *all* will be searched for, but not *All*; if this check box is not selected, both *all* and *All* (and, for that matter, *ALL*) will be sought.

3. Choose the Find Next command button. The next occurrence of the *Find what* text will be located and highlighted. (The search starts at the insertion point and, if the end of the document is reached before the text is found, the search continues at the beginning of the document.) If the *Find what* text is not found, a message to this effect will appear on the screen.

The Find dialog box will not close when the desired text is found, so that you can locate the next occurrence of the text, if so desired. To close this dialog box, choose the Cancel command button, press the Escape key, or click on the close button.

Replacing text The Find and Replace utility can also replace the next occurrence of a particular piece of text (or *all* occurrences, if you wish) with text that you specify. To perform this operation:

1. Choose the Replace command from the Edit menu. The Replace dialog box, shown in Figure 13, will be displayed.

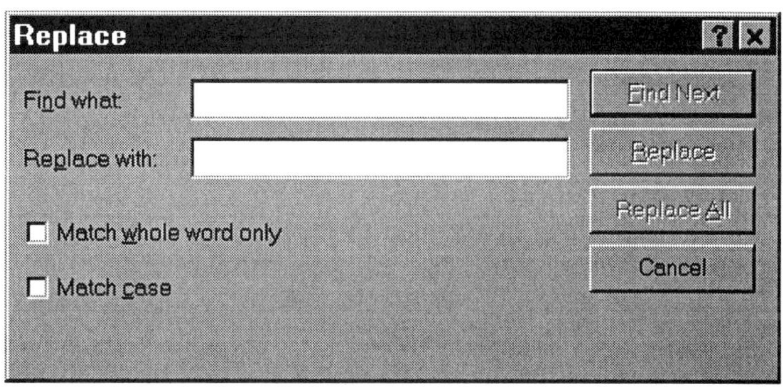

Figure 13 The Replace Dialog Box

2. Type the text you want to change in the *Find what* box and select the *Match whole word only* and/or *Match case* check boxes, if desired (their functions are described above).
3. Type the replacement text in the *Replace with* box.
4. Choose one of the command buttons:
   - Find Next locates the next occurrence of the *Find what* text and highlights it, but does not replace it.
   - Replace automatically replaces the highlighted word (if any) with the *Replace with* text, and then finds the next occurrence of the *Find what* text and highlights it.
   - Replace All automatically replaces every occurrence of the *Find what* text with the *Replace with* text.
   - Cancel terminates the find and replace operation and closes the dialog box.

TIP

You can use Find and Replace to speed up the entry of text into a document that has many occurrences of the same long word or phrase. For example, suppose you are writing a report on the Mediterranean region of Italy. Instead of typing the phrase *Mediterranean region of Italy* over and over again, simply type (say) *Med* each time. Then, when you're done, use Find and Replace to automatically replace all occurrences of *Med* with the longer phrase.

Print Preview

WordPad does not show certain formatting features, such as margins and page breaks, in the document window. However, it does provide a *print preview* feature to give you a better idea of what a document will look like when it's printed. This feature can sometimes save lots of time and paper.

To open the print preview window, either

- Choose the Print Preview command from the File menu.

or

- Click on the Toolbar's Print Preview button (as shown at the right).

In either case, the window shown in Figure 14 will open, displaying the first two pages of the document. (The page numbers are given on the status bar at the bottom of the window.) The margins are shown as "white space" outside the dashed lines that enclose the text.

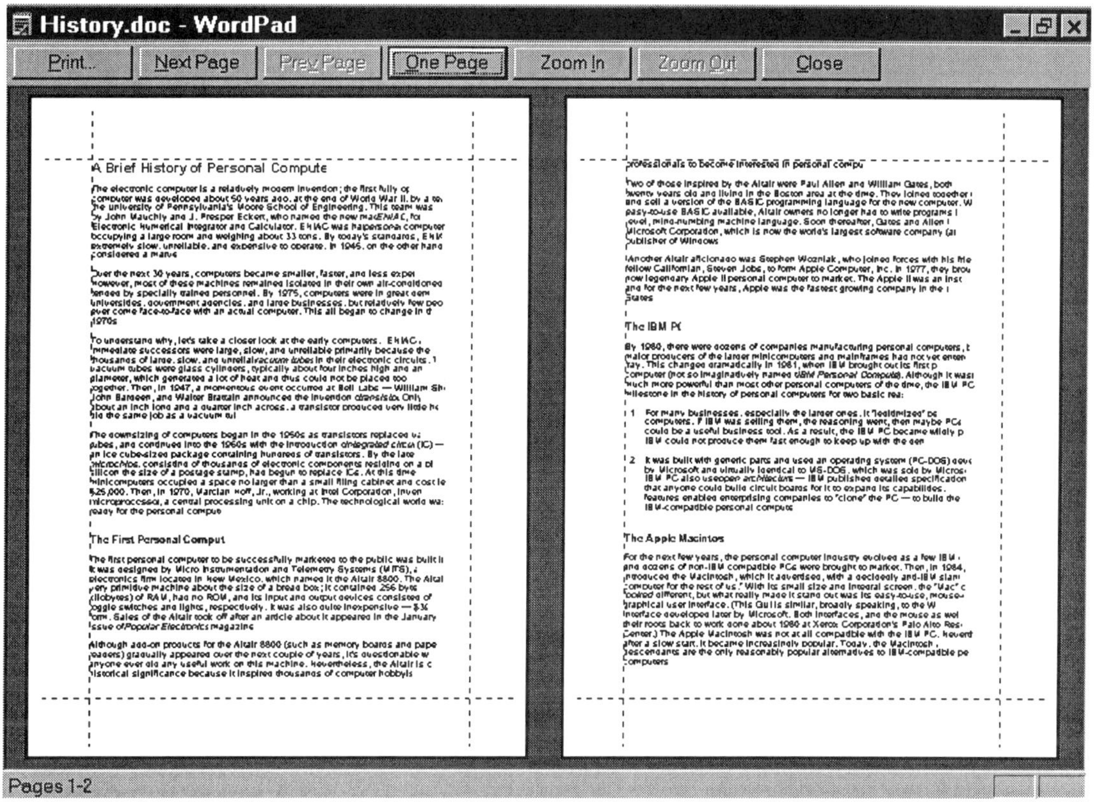

Figure 14 WordPad's Print Preview Window (Two-Page View)

Paging through the document

You can get an overall view of the appearance of the entire document by paging through it.

- To display one page at a time click on the One Page button at the top of the window. (It will be relabeled *Two Page*.)
- To display the next page, click on the Next Page button or press the Page Down key (on the keyboard).
- To display the previous page, click on the Prev Page button or press the Page Up key.

Zooming in and out

As you can see, it is difficult (sometimes, impossible) to read the text displayed in the preview window. (The situation does not improve if you switch to One Page view.) To deal with this problem, WordPad provides three levels of magnification, the default view and two "zoom" modes.

To *zoom in*, so that text appears larger (but with less of it displayed at once), either

- Click on the part of the page that you would like to enlarge. (In the preview window, the mouse cursor takes the shape of a magnifying glass, as shown at the right.)

or

- Click on the Zoom In button (at the top of the window). Then, use the scroll bars to display the desired part of the page.

In either case, the window will switch to One Page view (if necessary) and the text will be displayed in a larger font.

Clicking on the page or the Zoom In button again displays the second Zoom mode, increasing the magnification even more. At this point, the Zoom In button is dimmed, and clicking again on the page will return the display to the default magnification level. While in one of the two Zoom modes, clicking on the Zoom Out button changes the display to the next lower magnification level.

The relative magnification levels are shown below; each figure displays the same amount of screen area.

When you are done using the print preview window, either choose the Close button to return to the WordPad document window or choose the Print button to print the document.

Specifying a File Format

When a word processor (or, for that matter, any program) saves a document, it does so using a certain **file format** — a scheme for encoding the document's text, fonts, formatting symbols, and graphics, so that this information can be stored on disk. Unfortunately, every word processor uses a different file format for storing the documents it produces. Thus, if you want to be able to open a document created by WordPad in another word processor, or vice-versa, you may have to specify a particular file format when it is saved. WordPad recognizes (opens documents in) four different file formats, offers a different default view option for each such format, and saves files in three of these formats.

File formats recognized by WordPad

WordPad is able to open documents that were saved in the following file formats; the conversion process is done automatically:

- *Microsoft Word for Windows (version 6)* Because Word contains a greater number of formatting features than WordPad, some of a document's original formatting may be lost when it is saved in Word and then opened in WordPad.
- *Windows 3.1 Write* Again, some formatting may be lost.
- *Rich Text Format (RTF)* This is a common format, recognized by most word processors. If you are transferring a formatted document from a word processor other than Word for Windows or Write, save it (in that word processor) in RTF.
- *Text* WordPad opens any file whose format it does not recognize as a plain text file, consisting of letters, numbers, punctuation marks, and a few other symbols. If, in fact, the file was saved in a format other than Text, you will see a lot of strange characters on the screen.

File format view options

When WordPad opens a document, it displays the document in a certain way and makes certain "tool bars" available, depending on the format in which the file was saved. For example, by default, Text files are displayed in the Courier New typeface with no alignment choices other than left-justification, and the Ruler and Format bar are hidden. You can specify which view option defaults are used for each format in the following way:

1. Choose the Options item from the View menu, which displays the Options dialog box, shown in Figure 15 (on the next page).
2. Click on the tab corresponding to the file format for which you wish to set the default view. (The last tab, *Embedded*, is used for text that is exported to another document via Object Linking and Embedding; the first tab, *Options*, applies to all formats and will be discussed later in this section.)
3. Select a *Word wrap* option by clicking on the appropriate button:
   - If you select *No wrap*, the text you type will continue on the same line until you press the Enter key. This option is often used with Text files.
   - *Wrap to window* does just that; it starts a new line when the text reaches the right window border. This option is useful when viewing text in a small document window.

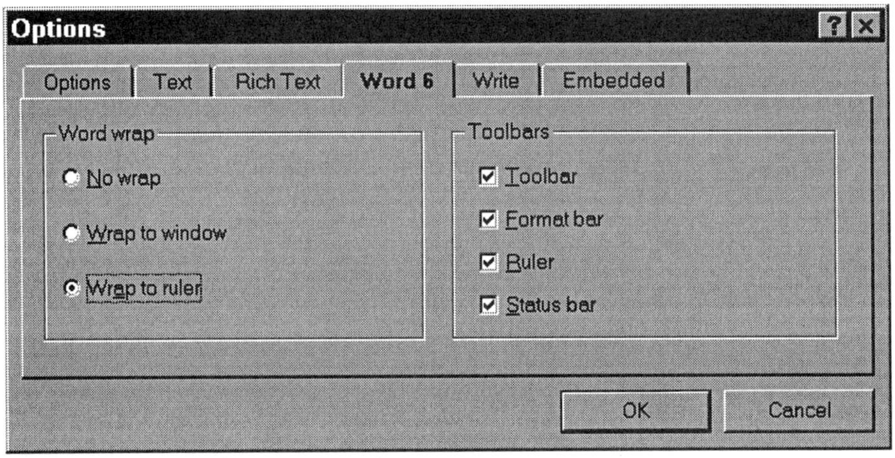

Figure 15 The (View) Options Dialog Box

- *Wrap to ruler* begins a new line as determined by the margins and indents specified for the document and paragraph.

Note that regardless of which word wrap option is in effect, when a document is printed, the specified margins and indents will be used to determine where lines are broken.

4. In the *Toolbars* area, select the check box of each "bar" that you want displayed in the WordPad window.
5. Choose the OK command button to close the dialog box and put the new defaults into effect.

NOTE

When you choose the New command from the File menu, a dialog box (pictured below) opens from which you can select a "document type".

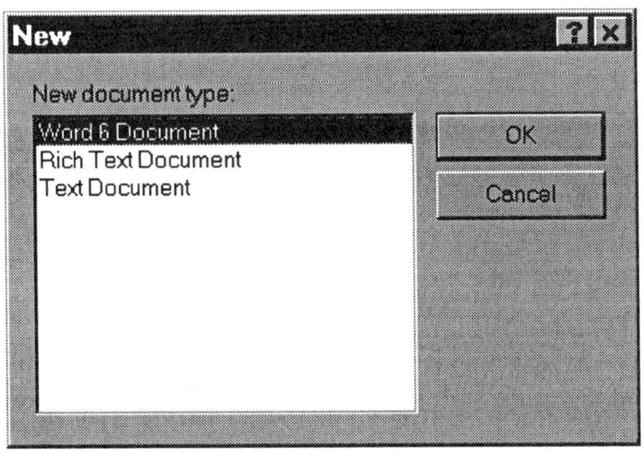

The type selected determines the way the document is displayed and the kinds of "bars" available (as specified in the Options dialog box), just as if the document were opened with that file format. It is a good idea to select *Word 6 Document* unless you have a particular reason to do otherwise.

File format save options

WordPad can *save* files in Word for Windows 6.0, RTF, or Text formats, regardless of which one was used to open or view the document. To save a document in one of these formats:

1. With the document displayed in the WordPad window, choose Save As from the File menu. The Save As dialog box will open, as shown in Figure 16.

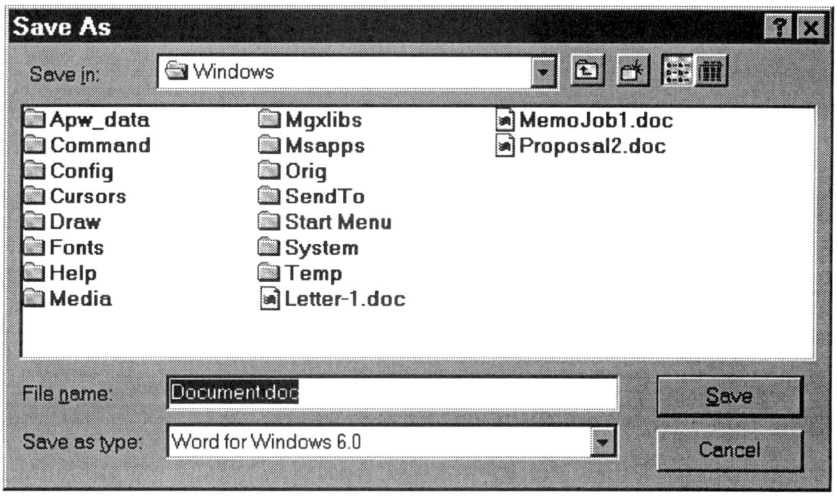

Figure 16 The Save As Dialog Box

2. Select a file format from the *Save as type* drop-down list.
3. Now, proceed as usual: Type a name for the document in the *File name* box, select a location (disk and folder) for the file, if necessary, and choose the Save command button.

And a Few Frills ...

We will close this section with a look at a few minor (but nice) WordPad features.

Inserting the Date or Time WordPad provides a very easy way to insert the current date or time into a document at the insertion point:

1. Choose the Date and Time item from the Insert menu or click on the Date/Time button, shown at the right, on the Toolbar. The Date and Time dialog box (Figure 17) will open.

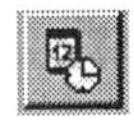

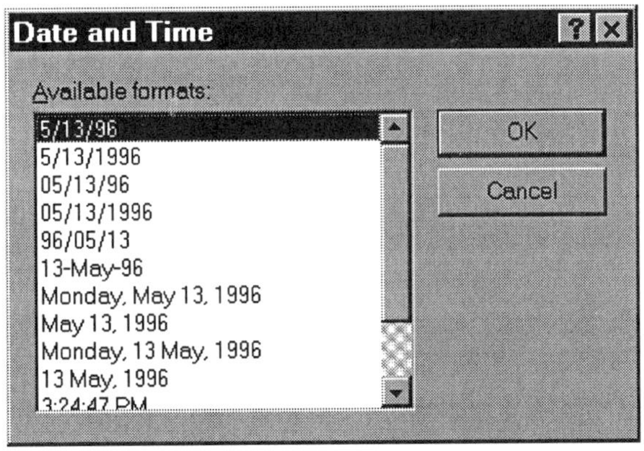

Figure 17 The Date and Time Dialog Box

2. Select the format you want for the date or time and either double-click on it or click on it and choose the OK command button. The date or time selected will be inserted into the document at the insertion point.

Opening Recently Saved Documents This is a very handy, time-saving feature: To open one of the last four documents saved by WordPad, just display the File menu and choose that document from the list at the bottom of the menu (see the figure at the right).

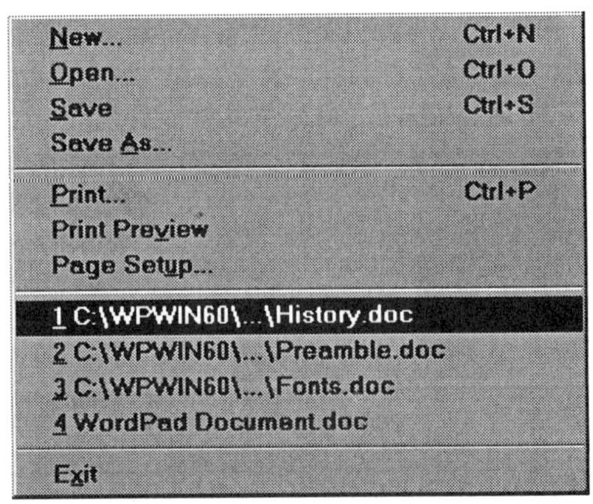

Specifying Units of Measurement By default, all measurements shown on the Ruler and in the Paragraph and Tabs dialog boxes are given in inches. If you want to use another unit of measurement:

1. Choose the Options command from the View menu. The Options dialog box will open.
2. Click on the Options tab in this dialog box and the page shown in Figure 18 will be displayed.

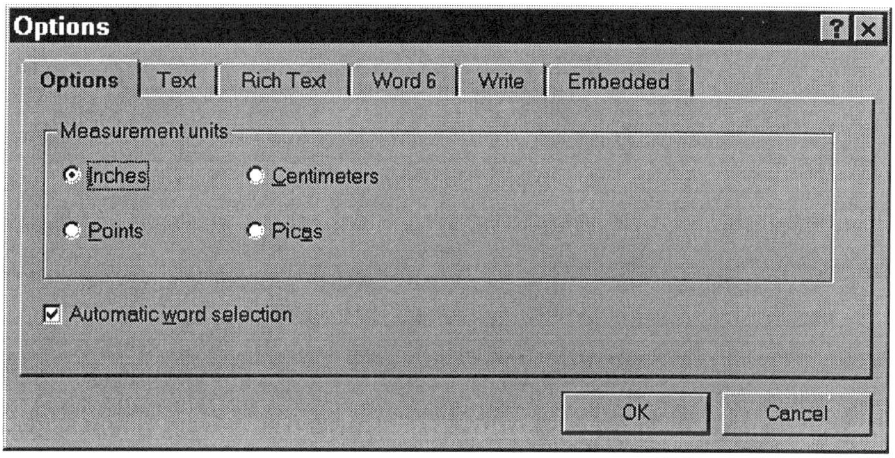

Figure 18 The Options Page of the (View) Options Dialog Box

3. Select the appropriate *Measurement units* option button. (In one inch, there are 2.54 centimeters, 72 points, and 6 picas.)
4. Deselect the *Automatic word selection* check box if you want to be able to select parts of words. Otherwise, leave it selected; it will be easier to use the mouse to select blocks of text.
5. Choose the OK command button to put your changes into effect and close the dialog box.

7.5 TUTORIAL

Try the following exercise on your own.

1. Turn on the computer (if necessary) to start Windows 95.
2. Open WordPad and maximize its window.
3. Insert the Student Disk in its drive and open the document named History.

4. Use the Find and Replace utility to locate the first occurrence of the word *chip* and replace it with *microchip*:
   - Choose the Replace command from the Edit menu.
   - In the *Find what* and *Replace with* boxes, enter *chip* and *microchip*, respectively.
   - Select the *Match whole word only* so you don't locate longer words that contain the letters *chip*, but leave *Match case* deselected so that you do find *Chip* or *chip*.
   - Choose the Find Next command button. The first occurrence of the word *chip* will be highlighted.
   - Choose the Replace command button. The replacement will be made and the next occurrence of *chip* will be highlighted.
   - Choose the Close command button to close the dialog box.
5. Choose the Print Preview item from the File menu and check out the features of this command:
   - Display a single page at a time by clicking on the One Page button. (Notice that its label changes to Two Page.)
   - Page through the document by clicking on the Next Page button twice. Now, page backwards by clicking on the Prev Page button twice.
   - Try the Zoom feature by observing what happens when you click on the Zoom In button twice, then click on the Zoom Out button twice, and finally click (slowly) on the displayed page three times.
   - Click on the Close button to return to the document window.
6. Choose the Options item from the View menu and then click on the Text tab. Click on the *No wrap* option button, deselect the *Format bar* check box, and select the *Ruler* check box. Then, choose the OK button.
7. Choose the New command from the File menu, select Text Document from the list, and choose the OK button. (Respond No to the "save changes?" message.) Notice that, due to the selections made in step 6, the Format bar is hidden and the Ruler is displayed.
8. Type something (without pressing the Enter key) until you see that the line continues past the right margin marker on the Ruler (because word wrap is off).
9. Close WordPad (responding No to the "save changes?" message) and remove the diskette from its drive.

Chapter Summary

Basic Operations in WordPad	To start WordPad	Choose the WordPad item on the Accessories submenu of the Start menu's Programs option.
	To select a word of text	Double-click on it.
	To select a line of text	Click in the left margin next to that line.
	To select a paragraph	Triple-click within it *or* double-click in the left margin next to it.
	To select the entire document	Triple-click in the left margin *or* choose Select All from the Edit menu *or* press Ctrl+A.
	To move/copy selected text	Choose Cut/Copy from the Edit menu or press Ctrl+X/Ctrl+C, then paste the text in another location. Or, drag-and-drop the text (holding down the Ctrl key for a copy).
	To undo a change	Choose Undo from the Edit menu *or* press Ctrl+Z.
Changing Fonts in WordPad	To change the typeface	Choose Font from the Format menu and select one from the Font list in the resulting dialog box; *or* select a new typeface from the Format bar's drop-down list.
	To change the font size	Choose Font from the Format menu and select a size from the Size list; *or* select a new size from the Format bar's drop-down list.
	To change the font style	Choose Font from the Format menu and select a style from the Font style list; *or* click on the Format bar's Bold, Italic, or Underline buttons.
	To change the font color	Choose Font from the Format menu and select a color from the Color drop-down list; *or* click on the Format bar's Font color button and then on a color.
Formatting a Document	To specify portrait or landscape orientation	Choose Page Setup from the File menu and select the appropriate option button.
	To set margins	Choose Page Setup from the File menu and enter the settings in the Margin text boxes.

	To change text alignment	Choose Paragraph from the Format menu and select Left, Right, or Center; *or* click on the appropriate Format bar button.
	To change paragraph indentation	Choose Paragraph from the Format menu and enter figures in the text boxes; *or* move the Ruler's indent markers.
	To change tab settings	Choose Tabs from the Format menu and enter desired tab stops; *or* click on the desired positions on the Ruler.
	To create a bulleted list	Choose Bullet Style from the Format menu; *or* click on the Format bar's Bullets button.
Using Graphics in WordPad	To insert a graphic	Paste it from the Clipboard *or* choose Object from the Insert menu.
	To edit a graphic	Double-click on it (if the graphic was created by an OLE-compatible application).
	To select a graphic	Click on it.
	To delete a graphic	Select it and press the Delete key.
	To move/copy a graphic	Move/copy it as if it were a character of text.
	To resize a graphic	Select it and drag a sizing handle.
Finding Text in WordPad	To find text	Choose Find from the Edit menu *or* click on the Toolbar's Find button, and use the resulting dialog box.
	To replace text	Choose Replace from the Edit menu and use the resulting dialog box.
Print Preview	To open the print preview window	Choose Print Preview from the File menu *or* click on the Toolbar's Print Preview button.
	To page through the document	Choose the Next Page or Prev Page command button.
	To zoom in or out	Choose the Zoom In or Zoom Out command button *or* click on a part of the displayed page.
WordPad File Formats	To specify view option defaults for a format	Choose Options from the View menu, click on the appropriate tab, and select the desired options.
	To use a desired file format option	Open a document saved in that file format; *or* choose New from the File menu and select the file format in the resulting dialog box.

To save a document in a desired file format	Choose Save As from the File menu and select a format from the *Save as type* drop-down list in the resulting dialog box.

Review Exercises

Section 7.1

1. In WordPad, to move the insertion point to the beginning of the current line, press the ____________ key.
2. To select a word in a WordPad document, ____________ the mouse on any letter within it.
3. To undo the last editing change in WordPad, choose Undo from the Edit menu or just press the ____________ keystroke combination.
4. True or false: To move the cursor to the end of a WordPad document, press the End key.
5. True or false: To select an entire WordPad document, move the insertion point into the left margin and double-click the mouse.
6. True or false: You can copy a selected block of text by dragging it to its new location while holding down the Ctrl key.
7. To paste a block of text into a WordPad document, click on the Toolbar button that looks like:

   a.  b.  c.  d. 

8. Which of the following keystroke combinations can be used to select an entire WordPad document?

   a. Ctrl+A
   b. Ctrl+V
   c. Ctrl+X
   d. Ctrl+Z

Section 7.2

9. To print type that is about one inch high, use a ____________ point font size.
10. To change the current typeface in WordPad, select one from the Format bar's drop-down list or choose the ____________ command from the Format menu.
11. True or false: If text is selected when you make a font change in WordPad, the font change applies only to the selected text.

12. True or false: The "strikeout" attribute (selected in the Font dialog box) causes the affected text to become unreadable.
13. Which of the following text formatting features is not accessible from WordPad's Format bar?
    a. Changing the font size.
    b. Changing the font color.
    c. Changing the font style to bold, italic, or underline.
    d. All the above features are accessible from the Format bar.
14. Which of the following keystroke combinations will not affect the style of currently selected text?
    a. Ctrl+A
    b. Ctrl+B
    c. Ctrl+I
    d. Ctrl+U

Section 7.3

15. When a document is printed with the text running parallel to the long side of the page, we say it is in ___________ orientation.
16. If the left-indent for a paragraph is 1.5" and the first-line-indent is 0.5", then the text on the first line of that paragraph will begin ___________ inch(es) to the right of the left margin.
17. The default tab stops for WordPad are set every ___________ inch(es) across the page.
18. You can select an alignment option in the dialog box that opens when you choose the ___________ command on the Format menu.
19. True or false: In WordPad, it is not possible to align text in a given paragraph with both the left and right margins.
20. True or false: If you set a tab stop at the beginning of a WordPad document, then (unless you remove it later on) this tab setting will apply to the entire document.
21. True or false: When using WordPad's bullet style feature, you can elect to use either round or square bullets.
22. Which formatting feature is not available in WordPad?
    a. Changing tab settings.
    b. Changing page margins.
    c. Changing line spacing.
    d. Changing page orientation.
23. Assuming that no text is currently selected, which of the following format changes applies to all text in a WordPad document?
    a. Changing the margins.
    b. Changing the tab settings.

c. Changing the text alignment.
d. Changing the paragraph indentation.

24. Which of the following WordPad format settings is not displayed on the Ruler?

    a. The right margin for the document.
    b. The left indent for the current paragraph.
    c. The alignment option for the current paragraph.
    d. Custom tab stops for the current paragraph.

Section 7.4

25. To insert a graphic from a disk file into a WordPad document, begin by choosing the ___________ item on the Insert menu.

26. The feature of Windows that allows you to edit a graphic from *within* a WordPad document is called ___________.

27. True or false: You can delete a graphic from a WordPad document by positioning the insertion point just to the right of the graphic and pressing the Backspace key.

28. True or false: Once you have inserted a graphic into a WordPad document, it cannot be resized.

29. Which of the following techniques cannot be used to reposition a graphic at the beginning of a WordPad document?

    a. Using the mouse to drag it there.
    b. Cutting it to the Clipboard and pasting it there.
    c. Choosing the Move command from the Edit menu and then moving the graphic there using the Arrow keys.
    d. All of the above actions can be used to move the graphic.

30. After a graphic is inserted into a WordPad document, you cannot

    a. Enlarge its size.
    b. Move it to another place in the document.
    c. Copy it to another place in the document.
    d. All of the above operations can be performed on a graphic.

Section 7.5

31. If you want to see where page breaks occur in a WordPad document, either print the document or choose the ___________ item from the File menu.

32. To change the units of measurement on the Ruler, begin by choosing the ___________ command from the View menu.

33. True or false: In the Find dialog box, if you type *the* in the *Find what* text box, select the *Match whole word only* check box, and choose the Find Next button, WordPad will search the current document for any word that contains the letters *the*.

34. True or false: To turn word wrap off for the current WordPad

document, begin by choosing Options from the View menu.

35. True or false: You can have WordPad automatically insert the current date in a document by clicking on the Toolbar's Date/Time button and making a selection in the resulting dialog box.

36. The Find command on WordPad's Edit menu can be used to

   a. Locate all occurrences of the word *rich* in a document.
   b. Automatically replace the first occurrence of *rich* with *poor* in a document.
   c. Automatically replace all occurrences of *rich* with *poor* in a document.
   d. Perform all of the above tasks.

37. In WordPad's print preview window, you can

   a. Type new text.
   b. Edit existing text.
   c. Format existing text.
   d. Perform none of the above tasks.

38. Which of the following file formats does not preserve any of the text formatting features of the document being saved?

   a. Word for Windows 6.0 format
   b. Rich Text Format
   c. Text format
   d. Windows 3.1 Write format

Build Your Own Glossary

39. The following words and phrases are important terms that were introduced in this chapter. (They appear within the text in boldface type.) Use WordPad to enter a definition for each term, preserving alphabetical order, into the Glossary file on the Student Disk.

Bullet (symbol)
Edit a document
File format
Font
Format a document
Format bar
Graphic
Landscape orientation
Notepad
Object linking and embedding (OLE)
Point (unit of measure)
Portrait orientation
Scalable font
Typeface
WordPad

Lab Exercises

Work each of the following exercises at your computer. Begin by turning the machine on (if necessary) to start Windows 95 and closing any open windows.

Lab Exercise 1 (Section 7.1)

a. Start WordPad and maximize its window.

b. Type your name and class on separate lines, and skip a line (by pressing the Enter key twice).

c. Type the sentence: This is a test of the copy and paste operations. Then, press the Spacebar to insert a blank space after the period.

d. Select the sentence and the space that follows it. Describe how you accomplished this.

e. Copy the selected text to the Clipboard. What menu command or mouse actions did you use?

f. Paste the text from the Clipboard onto the end of the document. What menu command or mouse actions did you use?

g. Repeat step *f* four times. Try pasting the text without reselecting and recopying it. Did this work?

h. Print the document. (See Section 2.2, if necessary, for information about printing a document.)

i. Save the document if you wish and exit WordPad.

Lab Exercise 2 (Section 7.2)

a. Start WordPad and maximize its window.

b. Insert the Student Disk in its drive and open the document on this disk named Preamble. (See Section 2.2 for information on opening a document.)

c. Display the Format bar (if it's not currently visible) and use it to help determine the two fonts used in the Preamble document. What are they?

d. Break the title into two lines (after "Constitution"), select both lines, and center them. Describe how you centered the lines.

e. Change the font for the entire title to 19-point Arial bold. Do you have to use the Font dialog box to do this?

f. Within the preamble itself:

- Bold the phrase *We the people.*
- Italicize the word *Constitution.*
- Underline the last four words, *United States of America.*

What keystroke combination can be used to accomplish each of these text enhancements?

g. Skip a line at the bottom of the document and type your name.

h. Print the revised document (see Section 2.2, if necessary).

i. Save the modified document under another name if you wish, exit WordPad, and remove the diskette from its drive.

Lab Exercise 3 (Section 7.2)

a. Start WordPad and maximize its window.

b. Insert the Student Disk in its drive and open the document on this disk named Fonts.

c. Follow the instructions on the screen.

d. Skip a line at the bottom of the document and type your name.

e. Print the revised document.

f. Save the modified document under another name if you wish, exit WordPad, and remove the diskette from its drive.

Lab Exercise 4 (Section 7.3)

a. Start WordPad and maximize its window.

b. Insert the Student Disk in its drive and open the document on this disk named History.

c. Set all margins to 1.25" and the page orientation to landscape.

d. Type your name at the top of the document and skip a line.

e. Center the document's title and right-align the first paragraph.

f. In the second paragraph, set all indents equal to 0.5".

g. In the third paragraph:

- Remove the existing tabs at 0.35" and 0.7".
- Set a tab stop at 1.25".
- Move the insertion point to the beginning of this paragraph and press the Tab key.

h. Print the *first page* of the revised document.

i. Save the modified document under another name if you wish, return the page orientation to portrait, exit WordPad, and remove the diskette from its drive.

Lab Exercise 5 (Section 7.3)

a. Start WordPad and maximize its window.

b. Create a document similar to the one in Figure 19:

- Set all margins to 1.5" and orientation to portrait.
- Center the title in 18-point bold Arial type.
- Use 12-point Arial type for everything else, with bold for the column headings.

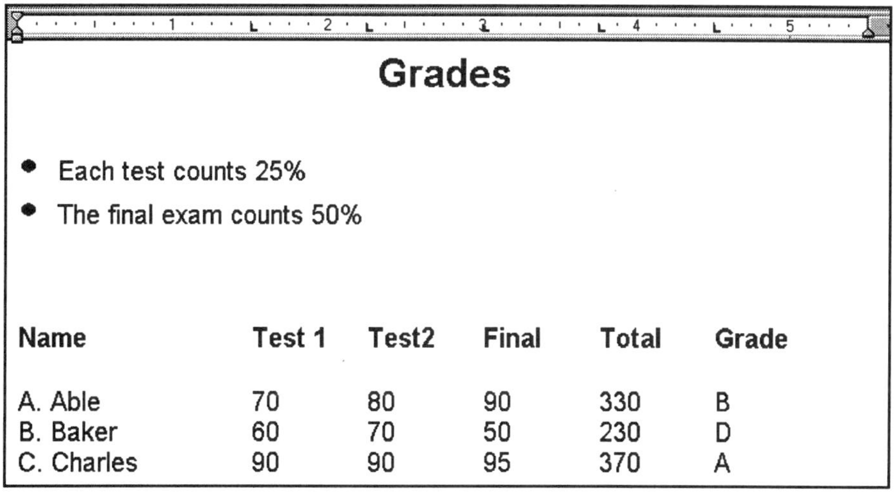

Grades

- Each test counts 25%
- The final exam counts 50%

Name	Test 1	Test2	Final	Total	Grade
A. Able	70	80	90	330	B
B. Baker	60	70	50	230	D
C. Charles	90	90	95	370	A

Figure 19 The Document for Lab Exercise 5

- Use the bullet style feature to create the list.
- Set tab stops to create the table columns at 1.5" and every 0.75" after that.

c. At the bottom, skip two lines and type your name.

d. Print the resulting document.

e. Save the document if you wish, exit WordPad, and remove the diskette from its drive.

Lab Exercise 6 (Section 7.4)

a. Start WordPad and maximize its window.

b. Insert the Student Disk in its drive and open the document on this disk named Title-3.

c. Set all margins to 1.25" and the page orientation to portrait, and display the Ruler if it's currently hidden.

d. Reduce the graphic's size so that the width of its "selection box" is about 1.5" (as measured on the Ruler).

e. Create a copy of this smaller graphic, positioned just to the right of the original (on the same line).

f. Position the insertion point between the two graphics and use the Spacebar to "push" the second graphic to the right about 1".

g. Center this configuration of graphics between the margins.

h. Center the document's title and replace the given name, class, and date by your name, your class, and the current date.

i. Skip a line and insert the Shapes graphic on the Student Disk into the document at the insertion point.

j. Print the revised document.

k. Save the modified document under another name if you wish, exit WordPad, and remove the diskette from its drive.

Lab Exercise 7 (Section 7.5)

a. Start WordPad and maximize its window.

b. Insert the Student Disk in its drive and open the document on this disk named History.

c. Set all margins to 1" and the page orientation to portrait.

d. Use the print preview feature to determine the last word on page one of this document. (You may have to zoom in!) What is it?

e. Use WordPad's Find command to locate all occurrences of the words *computer* and *computers*.

   - What word should you type in the *Find what* box so that both of these words will be searched for simultaneously?
   - How many occurrences of these words were there?
   - Were boldfaced words found? Were italicized words found?

f. Use the WordPad Replace command to replace (one-by-one) all occurrences of the word *chip* (but not *Chip*) with *microchip*. Which check boxes in the Replace dialog box did you select?

g. Now find all occurrences of the word *microchip*? How many are there?

h. Determine the file format of the History document. (Open the Options dialog box and note the active page.) What is this format?

i. Click on the Options tab. Which wrap option is in effect?

j. Exit WordPad (responding No to the "save changes?" message) and remove the diskette from its drive.

If You Want to Learn More ...

The notes presented here allow you to delve more deeply into some of the topics covered in this chapter.

Windows' other word processor

Windows also supplies a simple "word processor" called Notepad. This application doesn't have any text formatting capabilities (it is really a *text editor*) and the only file format it recognizes is *Text*. For this reason, Notepad is usually used for certain simple tasks, such as creating and/or editing notes, lists, programs, and system configuration files.

Notepad is discussed in Section 9.2. If you want to try it out, Notepad can be started from the Accessories submenu of the Start menu's Programs option.

What you see is not quite what you get

WordPad is technically *not* a WYSIWYG (what you see is what you get) word processor; for example, it does not show page breaks or margins in its document window. To view on-screen an accurate representation of the way the document will look when you print it, you must use the print preview feature (Section 7.5).

There is a more subtle WYSIWYG problem in WordPad. If the "wrap to ruler" setting is not turned on, line breaks (the right ends of lines on the printed page) will not be accurately shown on the screen. To ensure that this feature is turned on for the current document:

1. Choose Options from the View menu to display the Options dialog box.
2. Select (if necessary) the *Wrap to ruler* option button.
3. Choose the OK command button.

Importing files into WordPad

One of WordPad's new features is its ability to open documents that were saved in other file formats. Unfortunately, this is a mixed blessing. If a document was created in another word processor and saved in Word for Windows, Write, or RTF format, it may very well contain formatting codes (for example, for a header or double-line spacing) that WordPad does not support. In such a case, WordPad will ignore these codes, and the imported document may look quite different from the original.

WordPad should import correctly a document saved in the Text file format. To ensure that it does, check that word wrap is turned off for Text files before opening the document:

1. Choose Options from the View menu and click on the Text tab in the resulting dialog box.
2. Select the *No wrap* option button.
3. Choose the OK command button.

WordPad versus Write (Windows 3.1)

If you are familiar with Windows 3.1, you may have used its WordPad counterpart, which is known as *Write*. Generally speaking, Write has more powerful word processing capabilities than WordPad. In particular, Write contains the following features that are not present in WordPad:

- Paragraph alignment with both the left and right margins (*full justification*).
- Double-line spacing and 1½-line spacing, of text.
- Insertion of page breaks and "soft hyphens" (which appear only when needed for line breaks) wherever you want them.
- Subscript and superscript text styles.
- Headers and footers that are automatically placed on every page of a document. This feature also provides automatic page numbering.

On the other hand, the following features appear in WordPad, but not in Write:

- Choice of font color and a strikeout style for text.
- Automatic insertion of bullets and date and time.
- The ability to save and open files in several different formats.
- Print preview.

If you would like to use Write instead of WordPad, you *might* be able to do so if your copy of Windows 95 was upgraded from Windows 3.1. Use the Windows Find utility (Section 4.3) to search for the file Write .exe on your hard disk. If Find locates it, double-click on this file to see if it's really Write or just a shortcut to WordPad.

Where to go from here

Here's where to find some more information about some of the topics discussed in this chapter:

- The process of creating a graphic, selecting it, and copying it to the Clipboard is discussed (for the Paint application) in Chapter 8.
- More information about the subject of object linking and embedding (OLE) can be found in Section 12.5.

CHAPTER 8

Creating Graphics with Paint

Often, the best way to impart a large amount of information in a small amount of space is to use a **graphic** — a picture, diagram, graph, or other illustrative material. Windows supplies a drawing program called **Paint** to help you create graphics. In this chapter, we will describe how to use this application. You will learn:

1. How to start Paint and select the colors and tools needed to draw a graphic.
2. To use Paint's drawing tools to create lines, curves, and shapes.
3. To place text in a Paint graphic.
4. To erase portions of an existing graphic.
5. To magnify part of a graphic so that you can create or edit fine details.
6. To select part of a graphic and move, copy, flip, rotate, stretch, skew, or resize the resulting "cutout".
7. To set up the printed page and preview it before printing takes place.

8.1 An Introduction to Paint

Creating a *graphic* (a picture) using the Paint application is not unlike creating one using conventional artist's tools. (In fact, some Paint tools have familiar names, such as the Pencil, Brush, and Eraser.) Instead of using an artist's brush to apply paint to a canvas or other surface, Paint allows you to manipulate the tiny dots of light (*pixels*) that make up the screen image, coloring them as you wish to create various shapes. In this section, we will provide an introduction to the graphics-creation process.

The Paint Window

To start Paint:

1. Click on the Start button to open the Start menu.
2. Point at the Programs option on this menu and at Accessories on the resulting submenu.
3. On the Accessories submenu, click on the Paint item. The Paint window, shown in Figure 1, will open.

In addition to the usual components, such as title and menu bars, the Paint window is broken into three main parts:

1. The **Tool Box** contains icons that represent the tools you use to create the graphic. The names of these tools are given in Figure 2; we will describe their use later in this chapter. Below the icons is a box (see Figure 1) that displays the options, if any, available for the selected tool. For example, for the Line tool, the **Options Box** (shown at the right) displays the available line widths with the current width highlighted. To select another drawing width, click on it.

   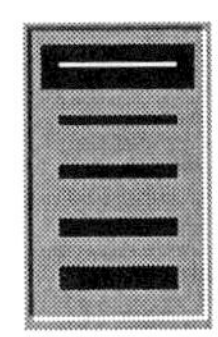

2. The **drawing area** (or *work area*) is the window in which you compose the graphic. Often, the graphic is larger than the drawing area, so only part of it is displayed. In such a case, you can view other parts of the graphic by scrolling the window. To minimize scrolling:
   - Maximize the Paint window.
   - Remove the Tool Box, Color Box, and/or Status Bar from the screen by choosing the corresponding command from the View menu. (Each command is a toggle; choosing it again returns the corresponding object to the screen.)

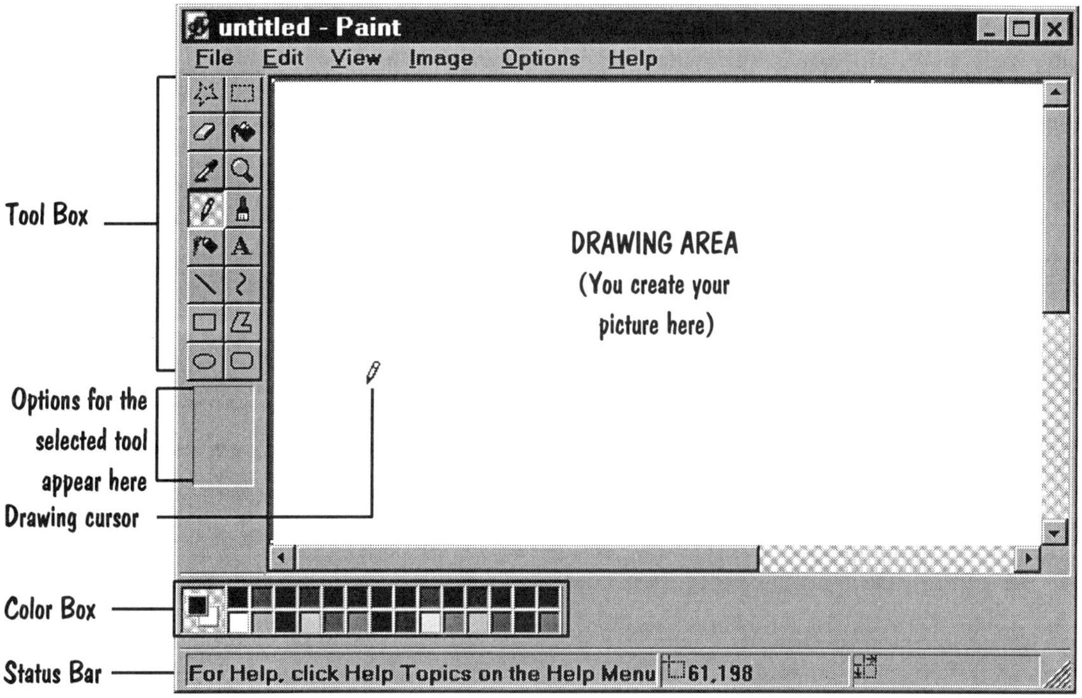

Figure 1 The Paint Window

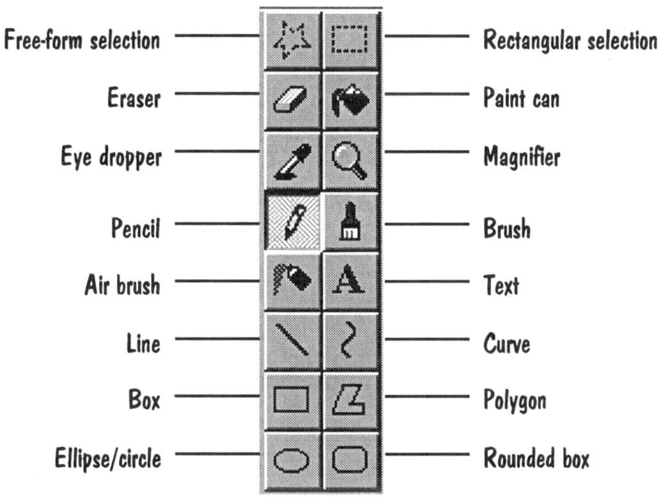

Figure 2 The Paint Tool Box

- To expand the graphic to fill the entire screen (whether or not the Paint window is maximized), choose the View Bitmap command from the View menu. (Unfortunately, you cannot work on your drawing while View Bitmap is in effect.) Clicking anywhere on the screen returns it to "normal".

3. The **Color Box** allows you to select the colors for the object you are about to draw (by clicking on them). It also displays the current foreground and background colors (Figure 3).

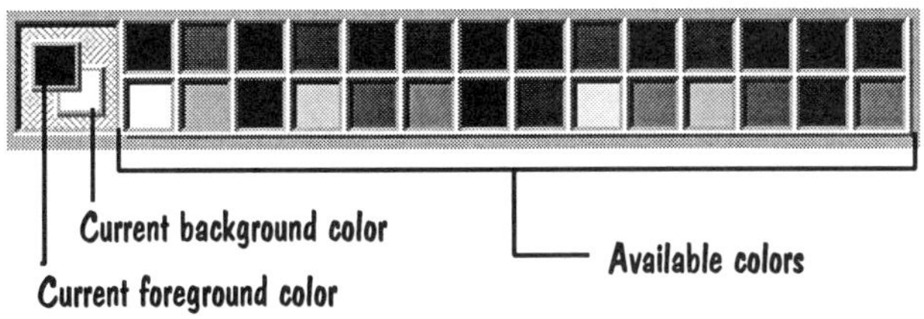

Figure 3 The Color Box

Drawing a Graphic

Using Paint to draw a graphic involves these general steps:

1. Select a **background color**, the color of the drawing area, by *right*-clicking on the desired color in the Color Box. Then, choose the New command from the File menu, which clears the drawing area and colors it as you specified.
2. For the object you are about to draw:
   - Select a drawing tool by clicking on its icon in the Tool Box. (The selected icon will appear to be "depressed".)
   - Select an option for this tool (when applicable) from the Options Box.
   - Select a **foreground color**, the color with which the object will be drawn, by *left*-clicking on the desired color in the Color Box. In some cases, you may also select a background color, which is used in different ways by different tools; this selection will not affect the color of the drawing area.

TIP

Paint makes it easy to select a foreground or background color that matches a color already present in your graphic. To do so, select the **Eye Dropper** tool from the Tool Box, position the mouse cursor (an "eye dropper") over an object that has the desired color, and select it as the foreground or background color by clicking the left or right button, respectively.

3. Draw the object:
   - Position the cursor at the location in the work area where you want to begin drawing.
   - Drag the cursor to draw the object; release the mouse button when you're done.
4. Repeat steps 2 and 3 until the drawing is complete.

An example To illustrate the drawing process, let's create the graphic image of a signature. (An example of the finished graphic is shown in Figure 4.)

- Leave the foreground and background colors at their default settings: black and white, respectively. 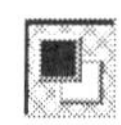
-  Select the Brush tool by clicking on its Tool Box icon. The options for Brush are various sizes and styles of "brush tips". Choose the smallest available tip from the Options Box; the one on the right end of the first row. 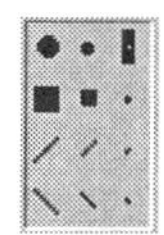
- Move the cursor (cross hairs) into the work area and position it where you want to begin drawing your first name.
- Drag the cursor to form your first and last names. (To move the

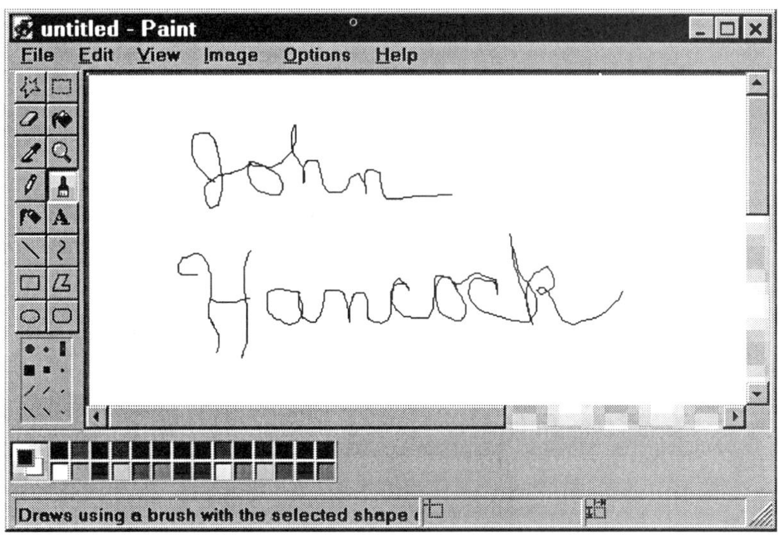

Figure 4 Graphic Image of a Signature

cursor from one place to another without drawing, just release the mouse button, reposition the cursor, and start dragging again.)

It takes some practice to use the Brush tool. If you want to delete the part of the graphic you just drew, choose Undo from the Edit menu or press Ctrl+Z.

NOTE

From Windows' point of view, the graphic you are creating is a "document". It is saved, opened, and printed in the same ways as a WordPad document (see Section 2.2). Moreover, as in WordPad, the last four graphics saved in Paint are displayed at the bottom of the File menu. To open one of these files, just click on it.

8-1 TUTORIAL

Try the following exercise on your own.

1. Turn on the computer (if necessary) to start Windows 95.
2. Start Paint by selecting it from the Accessories submenu of the Start button, and maximize its window.
3. If the Tool Box or Color Box (see Figure 1) is not visible on the screen, display it by choosing the corresponding item from the View menu.
4. Set the foreground color to red by left-clicking on the red square in the Color box; set the background color to yellow by right-clicking on the yellow square in the Color Box.
5. Color the entire drawing area in the background color by choosing the New command from the File menu.
6. Select the Brush tool from the Tool Box by clicking on its icon. The "brush tip" options will be displayed in the Options Box.
7. Select the smallest round brush tip by clicking on the right-most icon in the top row of the Options Box.
8. Position the mouse cursor inside the drawing area (it will become a pair of cross hairs) and draw a line across the screen by dragging the cursor horizontally to the right.
9. Delete the line you have just drawn by choosing the Undo command from the Edit menu (or by pressing Ctrl+Z).
10. Experiment with the Brush tool by choosing different brush tips to see their effect while drawing whatever you want. Select a different foreground color now and then. Note the following points:

- To clear the entire picture from the screen, choose the New command from the File menu.
- To print your graphic, choose the Print command from the File menu (see Section 2.2 for information about printing).
- To save your graphic, choose the Save command from the File menu (see Section 2.2 for information about saving a file).

11. Close the Paint window. Respond No to the "save changes?" message unless you want to save your graphic.

8.2 Using the Drawing Tools

Most of the tools in the Paint Tool Box (Figure 2) are used to create the curves, shapes, and text that make up your graphic. We will describe how to use these kinds of tools in this section. Tools that are used in modifying the graphic will be discussed in Section 8.3.

Creating Lines, Curves, and Other Strokes

The Pencil, Brush, Airbrush, Line, and Curve tools are used to form the lines, curves, and other "paint strokes" in the graphic. Each of these tools is used in the same basic way:

The basic technique

1. Select the tool by clicking on its icon in the Tool Box.
2. Select a drawing option (if available) from the Options Box.
3. Select a new foreground or background color, if you want.
4. Position the cursor in the drawing area where you want the paint stroke to begin. (The shape of the cursor depends on the tool selected; it may be cross hairs, a stylized pencil, or a tiny spray can.)
5. If you want to paint with the foreground color, press the left mouse button; to paint with the background color, press the right mouse button.
6. Continuing to depress the mouse button, create the stroke by dragging the cursor to another position in the drawing area.
7. When the stroke is complete, release the mouse button.

Of course, each tool has its own special capabilities; we will discuss them on the following pages.

To some extent, creating graphics with Paint is a trial-and-error process. Occasionally, while creating an object, it will become clear that you are not getting the desired effect. In such a case, to cancel the operation while you are still dragging the cursor, just tap the other mouse button or press the Escape key. Also, remember that you can undo an operation that you have just completed by choosing Undo from the Edit menu. (The last three changes can be undone in reverse order.)

The Pencil Tool The **Pencil** is a basic drawing tool. It is used to draw fine free-form curves, just as if you were using a pencil on paper. There are no options for this tool; all lines drawn with it are one pixel ("dot") wide. The Pencil does have a nice feature, though. If you hold down the Shift key while dragging the cursor, the result will be a straight line that is perfectly horizontal, vertical, or diagonal (inclined at a 45° angle), depending on the direction you move the mouse.

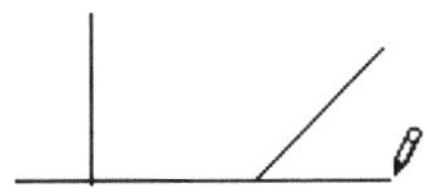

The Brush Tool The **Brush** tool is used like an artist's paint brush; it creates free-form curves using several different brush widths and styles, which are selected from the Options Box. The effect of selecting a particular option is shown in Figure 5.

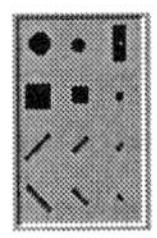

Figure 5 Brush Tip Effects for the Brush Tool

The Airbrush Tool The **Airbrush** tool draws a free-form figure made up of a spray of dots. The faster you move the Airbrush, the finer the spray, as illustrated below:

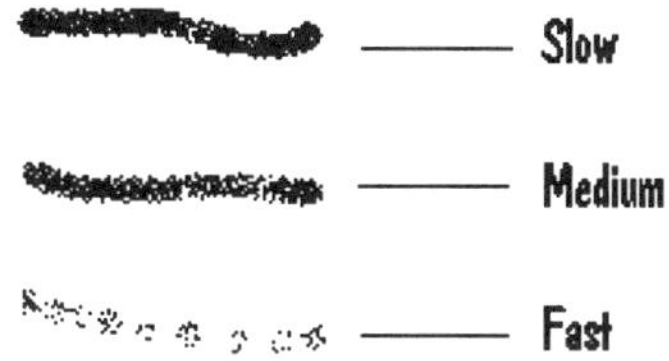

The Options Box for the Airbrush tool, which is shown at the right, allows you to select from among three different spray widths.

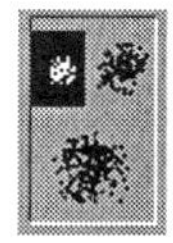

The Line Tool The **Line** tool is used to draw straight lines (it can *only* draw straight lines). Several line widths are available, and are selected in the Options Box (shown at the right). Holding down the Shift key while dragging the Line cursor creates perfectly horizontal, vertical, or diagonal (inclined at 45°) lines.

The Curve Tool Although the Pencil and Brush can draw curves, the result is a *free-form* curve. Unless you have a very steady hand, the result may not be as smooth as you might like. The **Curve** tool (which has the same available line widths as the Line tool) draws smooth, uniform curves, but is somewhat tricky to use.

In using the Curve tool, you first construct a line and then deform this line into the desired curve by "bending" the former once or twice with the aid of the mouse. To be more specific, after selecting the tool and the appropriate line width and drawing color:

1. Position the cursor (cross hairs) in the drawing area where you want the curve to begin, press the mouse button, drag the cursor to the other endpoint, and release the button. A straight line now connects the curve's two endpoints.
2. Drag the cursor away from the line in the direction you want it to bend. As you do, you will see a curve forming. Continue to drag the cursor around, until this part of the curve has the desired shape; then release the mouse button. If the curve's appearance is satisfactory, double-click the mouse to complete the operation.
3. If you want the curve to bend in a second direction, drag the cursor in this direction. When the curve has the desired appearance, release the mouse button. The curve is now anchored in place.

Let's try a specific example. Select the Curve tool from the Tool Box and the second thinnest line width from the Options Box. Now:

- Drag a vertical line that is about two inches in length (as shown in

Figure 6a).

- Position the cursor about one-half inch below the top of the line, drag it to the right as in Figure 6b, and release the mouse button. Notice that the curve bends to the right as you drag the cursor.
- Position the cursor about one-half inch above the bottom of the current curve, drag the cursor to the left as in Figure 6c, and release the mouse button. Notice that the curve has bent back to the left. When you release the button this time, the curve becomes anchored in place.

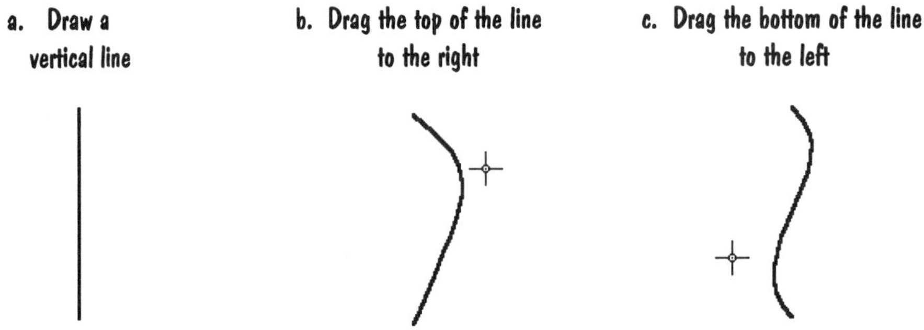

Figure 6 Using the Curve Tool

Creating Geometric Shapes

The Box, Rounded Box, Circle/Ellipse, and Polygon tools are used to create the corresponding geometric figures. To use one of these tools:

1. Select the tool by clicking on its icon in the Tool Box.
2. From the Options Box (shown at the right), select one of three border/fill options:

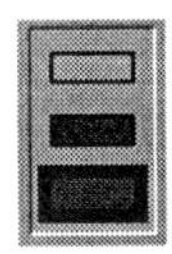

Border/fill options

   - *Hollow* — Only the border of the figure will be drawn (see the left box in Figure 7).
   - *Filled* — The border will be drawn and the figure will be filled with color (see the center box in Figure 7).
   - *Borderless* — The figure will be filled with color, but the border will not be drawn (see the right box in Figure 7).
3. Select new foreground and background colors (if you want) from the Color Box. These are used to color the figure, as follows:

Figure 7 Hollow, Filled, and Borderless Boxes

Drawing colors

- If you create the figure using the left mouse button, the current foreground color is used to draw the figure's border; the current background color is used to fill its interior.
- If you create the figure using the right mouse button, the current background color is used to draw the figure's border; the current foreground color is used to fill its interior.

Border width

4. If the figure is to have a border, select its width by clicking on the Line tool and selecting from among the five choices shown in the Options Box. (If you do this, you will have to reselect the tool you want to use to create the geometric shape.)
5. Position the cursor (cross hairs) in the drawing area and draw the figure. The way in which this is done varies a little from tool to tool and will be described below, when each tool is discussed.

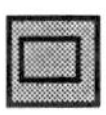

The Box Tool The **Box** tool draws rectangles and squares. (Examples of shapes drawn with the Box tool are shown in Figure 7.) To use this tool:

1. Select the Box icon from the Tool Box; then select a border/fill option, drawing colors, and a border width, as described earlier.
2. Position the mouse cursor at one corner of the box-to-be and drag the cursor toward the opposite corner. As you do, the corresponding rectangle will be displayed on the screen. To draw a perfectly square box, hold down the Shift key while dragging the cursor.
3. When the box is the correct size, release the mouse button.

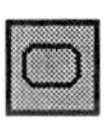

The Rounded Box Tool The **Rounded Box** tool draws a rectangle (or square, if you hold down the Shift key while dragging the cursor) with rounded corners. This tool is used in exactly the same way as the Box tool.

The Ellipse/Circle Tool The **Ellipse/Circle** tool is used to draw ellipses and circles. Here are a few examples:

To use the Ellipse/Circle tool:

1. Select the Ellipse/Circle icon from the Tool Box; then select a border/fill option, drawing colors, and a border width, as described earlier.
2. Picture the ellipse-to-be enclosed in an imaginary box. Now, position the mouse cursor at one corner of this box and drag the cursor toward the opposite corner. As you do, the corresponding ellipse will be displayed on the screen. To draw a circle, hold down the Shift key while dragging the cursor.
3. When the ellipse or circle is the correct size, release the mouse button.

The Polygon Tool The **Polygon** tool helps you draw a many-sided enclosed figure. Here are some examples of the kinds of figures you can draw using the Polygon tool:

Although the same border/fill options are available as for the Box tool, the Polygon tool is used in a very different way. Here's how it works:

1. Select the Polygon icon from the Tool Box; then select a border/fill option, drawing colors, and a border width, as described earlier.
2. Position the mouse cursor (cross hairs) at one of the polygon's vertices, drag the cursor to form the first side, and release the mouse button.
3. To construct the rest of the sides, except the last, click the mouse on each successive vertex. As you do, the side joining the previous vertex to the new one will be displayed.
4. To construct the last side of the polygon (the one that encloses the figure), double-click the mouse on the last vertex. It will automatically be joined to the first vertex by a straight line.

If you want to construct a side that is horizontal, vertical, or inclined at a 45° angle, hold down the Shift key while dragging or clicking.

The Paint Can Tool All the tools we have discussed so far draw objects on the screen. The **Paint Can** does not; it fills an existing enclosed figure with color or changes the color of a previously filled region. To use this tool:

1. Select the Paint Can icon from the Tool Box.
2. In the Color Box, set either the foreground or background color to the desired color.
3. Position the mouse cursor (a tiny paint can) anywhere within the figure to be colored. For small regions, make sure the tip of the "pouring paint" is inside the region.
4. Click a mouse button to color the region. If you click the left mouse button, the figure will be filled with the foreground color; if you click the right mouse button, the background color will be used.

TIP

Graphics programs like Paint are not usually used for precision work, such as technical drawing. Nevertheless, Paint supplies a very useful tool for aligning and correctly sizing objects. The Status bar at the bottom of the Paint window constantly displays *cursor coordinates,* (shown on the left in the figure below), which give the precise location of the mouse cursor relative to the upper-left corner of the drawing area. For example, the coordinates shown here indicate that the cursor is 416 pixels from the left border of the drawing area and 214 pixels down from the top border. (The use of cursor coordinates is demonstrated in the Tutorial at the end of this section.)

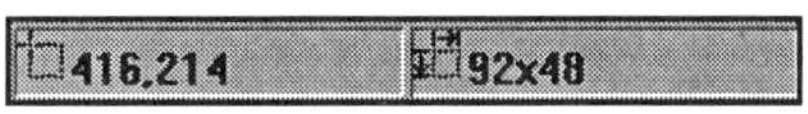

A second set of coordinates is displayed on the Status bar when you are creating a box, rounded box, ellipse/circle, or polygon. They give the width and height of the object being drawn. For example, in the figure above, the current width of the object is 92 pixels and its current height is 48 pixels.

Inserting Text into a Graphic

Although a graphic can often convey a thought without any explanatory text, it sometimes needs a few words to clarify the message. Through the use of the **Text** tool, Paint allows you to place text in a graphic in your choice of color, design, style, and size. To use this tool to insert text:

1. Select the Text icon from the Tool Box.
2. Select a foreground color from the Color Box (by clicking on it) for the color of the text to be inserted. (You should also select a background color from the Color Box if you want the new text displayed on a colored background.)
3. Drag the mouse cursor (cross hairs) to form a box in the drawing area within which you will place the text. Don't be overly concerned about sizing this window to fit the given text; its size (and position) can be adjusted later.
4. Release the mouse button. After a few moments, the Fonts window (which is usually referred to as the *Text Toolbar*) will open somewhere on the screen. (If it doesn't, choose the Text Toolbar item from the View menu.)

The text frame you have created will sprout eight "sizing handles" and an insertion point will appear in its upper-left corner.

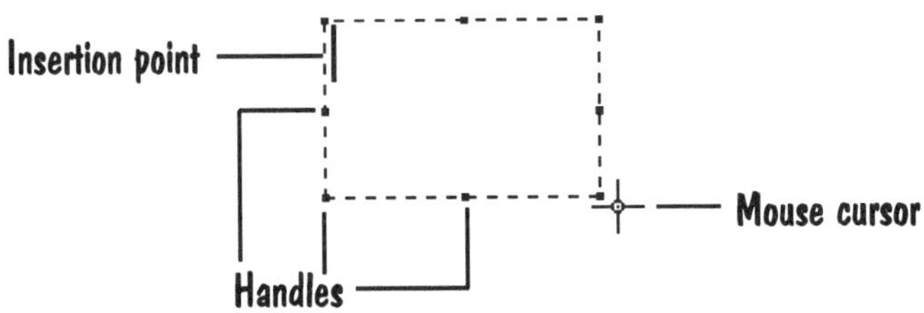

5. Using this Text Toolbar (Fonts window):
   - Select a *typeface* for the text from the first drop-down list. The typeface determines the overall design or "look" of the characters. (The typeface selected in the figure above is *Arial*.)
   - Select a *font size* for the text from the second drop-down list. The font size is (roughly) the height the characters will be on the printed page, measured in *points*, where 72 points equal one inch.

- Select *attributes* for the text (if you want) by clicking on one or more of the buttons. Here are examples of the resulting effects:

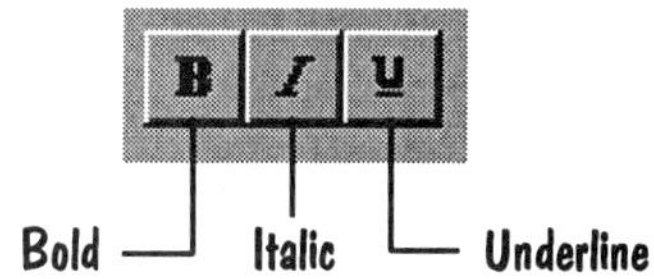

Bold *Italic*

Underline

6. From the Options Box, select either *opaque* mode, the top option, or *transparent* mode, which is the one selected in the figure at the right. (As an alternative, you can toggle between these modes by choosing the Draw Opaque command from the Options menu.)

   - If you use opaque mode, the text you type will appear within a frame that is colored in the current background color, as shown at the right.

   - In transparent mode, the text is displayed without the colored frame.

7. Click inside the text frame and type the desired text. When the text reaches the right frame border, it will wrap (possibly in the middle of a word) to the next line. (The text box will extend, if necessary, in the vertical direction to accommodate the text you are typing.) You can start a new line manually by pressing the Enter key.

8. To complete the text-insertion operation (to "paste down" the text), click anywhere outside the text frame.

TIP

Until you paste the text in place (that is, while the frame outline is still visible), it is possible to make changes to the text and its background. You can:

- Modify the text as you would in WordPad (see Section 2.2).
- Change the frame mode from transparent to opaque or vice-versa.
- Change the color of the text or its background (if any).
- Increase the size of the text frame by dragging one of its handles in the desired direction away from the existing "box". For example, to widen the box, position the mouse cursor over the middle handle on the right side of the frame (it will become a two-headed arrow when it's positioned properly), and drag it to the right. When you release the mouse button, the frame will redraw to the new size and the text that had been wrapped to a new line will rearrange itself accordingly within the new frame (see below).

- Move the text frame (and enclosed text) by positioning the mouse pointer over any part of the border that is not a handle and dragging the frame to its new location.

After the text-insertion operation is complete, the text (and its background, if applicable) becomes a single object in the graphic. At this point, the block of text can be moved (as described in Section 8.4), but none of the other operations listed above can be carried out.

8.2 TUTORIAL

Try the following exercise on your own, creating a drawing of the truck shown in Figure 8. Remember: To start over while creating an object, press the Escape key; to undo the last change to the graphic, press Ctrl+Z.

1. Start Windows 95 (if necessary) by turning on the computer.
2. Start Paint by selecting it from the Accessories submenu of the Start button, and maximize its window.
3. Draw the road:

   - Select the Line tool from the Tool Box (see Figure 2) by clicking on it and select the second smallest line thickness in the Options Box (see Figure 1) by clicking on it.
   - Position the Line cursor in the drawing area about one inch from the lower-left corner, hold down the Shift key (for a horizontal line), and drag the cursor to the right side of the drawing area.

   - Select the Airbrush tool from the Tool Box, and select a medium thickness from the Options Box.
   - Position the Airbrush cursor just under the left edge of the line you've just drawn and drag the cursor slowly across the screen under this line.
4. Draw the truck tires:

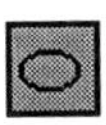

   - Select the Ellipse/Circle tool from the Tool Box and the hollow (top) option from the Options Box.
   - Draw the rear tire by positioning the cursor about one inch above the road, holding down the Shift key (for a circle), and dragging the cursor down and to the right until the circle touches the road.
   - Use the cursor coordinates on the Status bar to help create a

Figure 8 Truck Graphic for Tutorial 8.2

front tire of exactly the same size: Position the cursor at the top of the rear tire and note the second cursor coordinate. Then, for the front tire, position the cursor so that its second coordinate has this value, hold down the Shift key, and drag a circle until it touches the road.

5. Draw the truck's trailer:

   - Select the Box tool from the Tool Box and the "filled box with border" option (the middle one) from the Options Box.
   - Select a foreground of black (by clicking on this color in the Color Box) and a background of light gray (by *right*-clicking on this color in the Color Box).
   - Start near the rear wheel and drag a box that makes a rectangle about 2" high and 4" long.

6. Draw the lower (shaded) part of the cab of the truck:

   - Select a background color of white from the Color Box.

   - Select the Polygon tool from the Tool Box and the "hollow" option from the Options Box.
   - Hold down the Shift key (for horizontal, vertical, and diagonal lines) and drag the Polygon cursor from corner to corner of the polygon that makes up the lower cab. At each corner, click the mouse to end the previous line segment before dragging the next one. Double-click on the last corner to close the polygon.

   - Fill the polygon with color: Select a foreground color of dark gray from the Color Box, select the Paint Can tool, and click inside your polygon.

   - Select a foreground color of black, select the Line tool, hold down the Shift key, and draw the vertical line that forms the door.

7. Continuing to use the Line tool, draw the four lines that make up the window area of the cab.
8. Insert the text (Sam's Delivery Service) on the truck's trailer using 24-point, boldface type:

   - Select the Text tool from the Tool Box.
   - Drag the cursor to form a box (a text frame) just within the trailer rectangle. When you release the mouse button, the Fonts window will appear.
   - In the Fonts window, select Arial from the first drop-down list, "24" from the second, and click on the Bold button.
   - Click within the text frame and type *Sam's*, *Delivery*, and *Service*, pressing the Enter key after each of the first two words. (If the text doesn't fit, select a smaller font size from the Fonts window.) Now, center each word on the trailer by inserting spaces (using the Spacebar) before that word.
   - Click outside the text frame to complete the operation.
9. Save and/or print the graphic, just as you would in WordPad, and exit Paint.

8.3 Editing a Graphic

At some point in the process of creating a graphic, you will probably want to *edit* it — to alter the graphic to correct mistakes or improve its looks. We have already described one way to edit a graphic: You can use the Undo command on the Edit menu to undo the last three operation you have carried out. This section discusses other, more specialized editing features of Paint.

Erasing Mistakes

The **Eraser** is the editing tool you're likely to use the most. It works on your electronic graphic in the same general way that an ordinary eraser works on a penciled drawing. However, the Eraser tool is more powerful:

Basic operation of the Eraser tool

- If you left-drag the Eraser's cursor, it wipes out everything in its path; if you right-drag the cursor, it removes only the current foreground color.
- The area that is erased is replaced with the current background color, which need not be the color of the graphic's background.

More specifically, here's how to use this tool:

1. Select the Eraser tool from the Tool Box by clicking on its icon.
2. Select an eraser size from the Options Box (shown at the right) by clicking on it. The smaller sizes are best for fine work; the larger ones are best at erasing large areas.

3. Set the background color as desired by right-clicking on the corresponding square in the Color Box. (This color will replace the ones erased.)
4. If you only want to erase one specific color, set the foreground to this color by left-clicking on the corresponding square in the Color Box.
5. Position the mouse cursor (a small square) where you want to begin erasing, and drag it across the area to be erased. Remember:
   - Left-dragging the cursor replaces everything in its path with the current background color.
   - Right-dragging the cursor replaces only the current foreground color with the current background color.

An example Figure 9 shows the two ways the Eraser tool can be used. In both erasures, the background color was set to white and the foreground color was set to black. The left erasure was accomplished with a left-drag; it replaces everything with white. The right erasure is the result of a right-drag; only black is replaced with white.

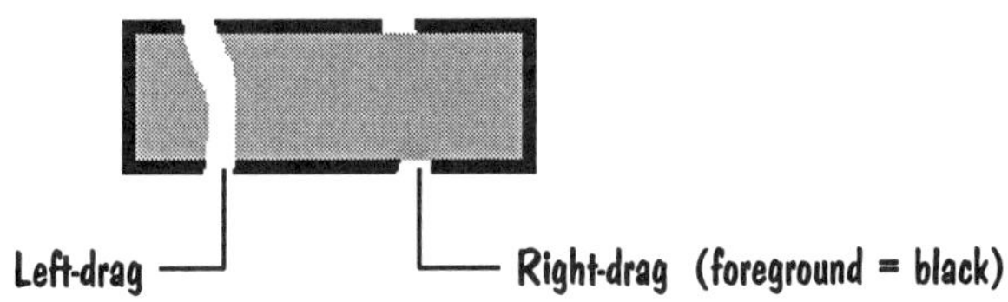

Figure 9 Using the Eraser Tool

Zooming In on the Graphic

At times, you may want to change small details in a graphic. For these occasions, Paint supplies the Zoom command, which allows you to magnify a small part of the graphic so that it fills the Paint window. Once the graphic is suitably enlarged, you can even edit it pixel by pixel. (Recall that *pixels* are the small dots of light that make up the screen image.)

To zoom in on a graphic, point at the Zoom command on the View menu. The resulting submenu has five options. Choosing:

Zoom menu options

- *Normal Size* returns the graphic to its original size if it currently magnified.
- *Large Size* magnifies the image by a factor of four (400 percent). When you choose Large Size, scroll bars may appear in the Paint window so that you can view the entire image. Figure 10b shows the result of applying the Large Size command to the graphic in Figure 10a and then scrolling to display the dog's nose.
- *Custom Size* opens the following dialog box:

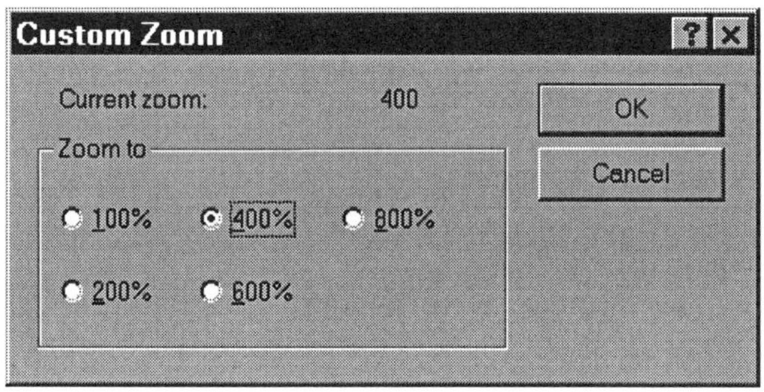

By selecting the appropriate option button and choosing the OK command button, you can magnify the original graphic one, two, four, six, or eight times. (Figure 11a shows the original dog graphic enlarged 600 percent.)

Figure 10a "Normal" Zoom Size

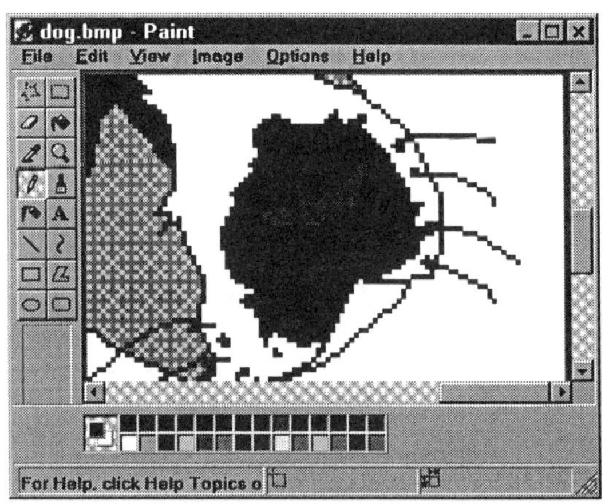

Figure 10b "Large" Zoom Size

- *Show Grid* is a toggle that turns the pixel grid on or off (Figure 11b shows the grid displayed). By magnifying to a relatively large size (600% or 800%) and turning on the grid, you can edit the graphic pixel by pixel, obtaining the finest detail possible.
- *Show Thumbnail* is also a toggle; it turns the Thumbnail window on and off. Displaying this window gives you an overall view of the normal-sized graphic as you work on the close-up. The Thumbnail window can be moved around the screen and resized, if so desired.

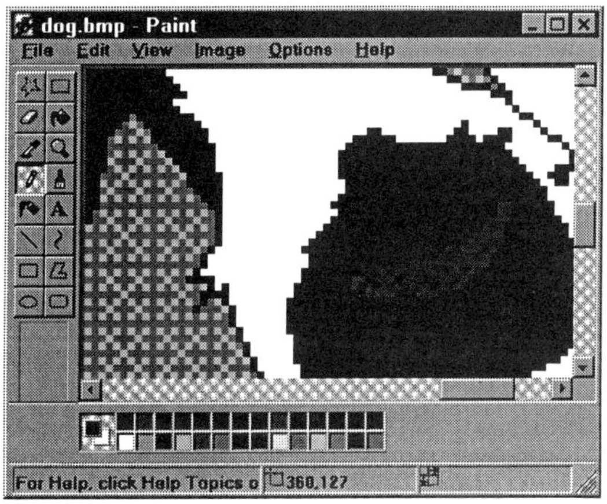

Figure 11a Custom Zoom — 600%

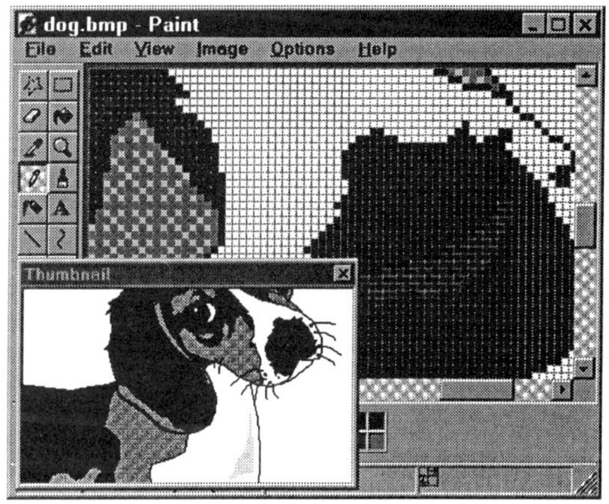

Figure 11b Grid and Thumbnail On

TIP

Here is perhaps the easiest way to edit individual pixels in a graphic:

1. Use the Custom Size option on the Zoom menu to magnify the image to 600 or 800 percent.
2. Scroll to the part of the image you wish to edit.
3. Select the Pencil tool from the Tool Box.
4. In the Color Box, set the foreground color to the color you want to paint in, set the background color to that of the background area in which you are working.
5. Then, using the Pencil cursor as a pointer, just left-click in any grid square that you want to add to the graphic, and right-click in a grid square if you want to erase it from the graphic.

To edit larger areas, involving a relatively large number of pixels, you may want to use other tools, such as the Brush, Eraser, or Paint Can.

Magnifier tool

The **Magnifier** tool provides another way to zoom in on your graphic. It is a little easier to use, but not as versatile as the Zoom command. To use this tool:

1. Click on the Magnifier icon in the Tool Box.
2. You now have two choices. Either

   - Click on the desired magnification factor in the Options Box (shown at the right). Notice that you can magnify the image two, six, or eight times (but not four times, as with the Zoom command).

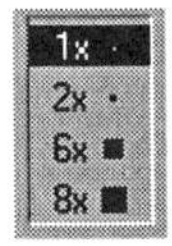

   or

   - Move the mouse cursor into the drawing area. A box containing a magnifying glass icon will appear. Position the box around the part of the graphic you wish to magnify and click the mouse button. (The size of the box and the degree of magnification depend on the last option button selected in the Custom Zoom dialog box.)

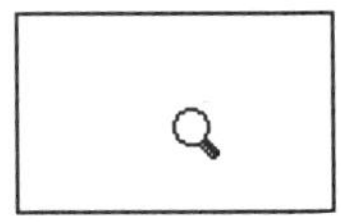

Selecting Part of a Graphic

One of the major advantages of Paint over conventional drawing is its ability to move, copy, and resize any object in the graphic. Before performing one of these operations, you must select the object to be manipulated; in Paint parlance, you must "define a cutout". A **cutout** is a region in the graphic that has been selected using one of Paint's two selection tools:

- The **Rectangular Selection** tool is the easier of the two to use, but it is less versatile. This tool is used when you can place a rectangular box around the object to be selected without including part of another object (see Figure 12a).
- The **Free-form Selection** tool is generally used in situations where

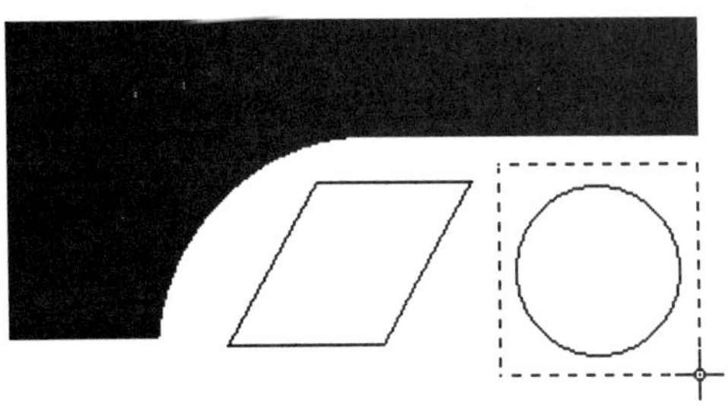

Figure 12a Rectangular Selection

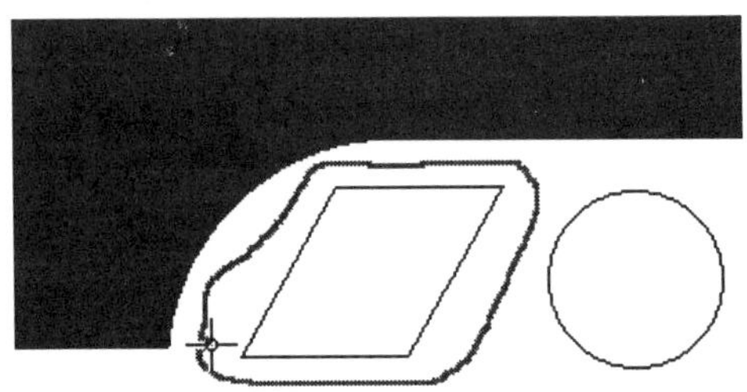

Figure 12b Free-form Selection

rectangular selection doesn't work; free-form selection creates an irregularly shaped cutout (Figure 12b).

Rectangular selection

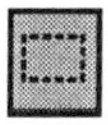

To use the Rectangular Selection tool:

1. Select its icon from the Tool Box.
2. From the Options Box, select either *opaque* mode, the top option, or *transparent* mode, which is the one selected in the figure at the right. (As an alternative, you can toggle between these modes by choosing the Draw Opaque command from the Options menu.)

   - If you use opaque mode, the resulting selection will consist of everything within the selected region, both foreground and background colors.
   - In transparent mode, the resulting selection does not include anything colored in the background color. This is the mode that is normally used with cutouts.

   We will provide examples of the two selection modes in Section 8.4, while discussing how cutouts are moved and copied.
3. Position the mouse cursor (cross hairs) at one corner of the cutout, the region that contains the object(s) to be selected.
4. Press the mouse button and drag the cursor to the opposite corner of the cutout. As you drag, a box will move with the cursor, indicating the selected region (see Figure 12a).
5. When the cutout is defined as you want, release the mouse button. A "dashed" rectangular box delineates the selected region.

Free-form selection

To use the Free-form Selection tool:

1. Select its icon from the Tool Box.
2. From the Options Box, select either *opaque* mode, the top option, or *transparent* mode, which is the one selected in the figure at the right. (See the description of the two modes under "rectangular selection".) The transparent mode is almost always used with free-form selection.

3. Position the mouse cursor in the drawing area where you want to start the cutout, the region that contains the object(s) to be manipulated.
4. Press the mouse button and drag the cursor, creating a free-form curve that defines the cutout (see Figure 12b).
5. Release the mouse button. A "dashed" rectangular box, like the one in rectangular selection, delineates the selected region.

NOTE

Whether you use rectangular or free-form selection:

- To abort the selection process while you are dragging the cursor to define the cutout, press the Escape key.
- To deselect the selected object, which causes the selection box to disappear, click anywhere outside the box.

Deleting a cutout

Here's a simple example of how cutouts are used. Suppose you want to delete an object from a graphic; say, the circle in Figure 12a. Usually the easiest way to do this is to select the circle (that is, define a cutout that includes the circle), as in Figure 12a, and then press the Delete key. The cutout and the object it contains will be replaced by the current background color, so be sure that this color is set properly before pressing the Delete key.

We will discuss many other ways in which cutouts can be manipulated in Section 8.4.

8-3 TUTORIAL

Try the following exercise on your own.

1. Start Windows 95 (if necessary) by turning on the computer.
2. Start Paint, maximize its window, and insert the Student Disk in its drive.
3. Open the Truck-2 bitmap image on this disk.
4. Use the Zoom submenu of the View menu to:
   - Choose the Large Size command.
   - Turn off (if necessary) the Show Grid option.
   - Turn on (if necessary) the Show Thumbnail option.
5. Scroll the Paint window so that the front end of the truck is visible.
6. Modify the slanted part of the hood, as follows:

   - Erase the slanted line: Select the Eraser tool from the Tool Box, select the smallest size in the Options Box, set the background color to white, and drag the cursor over the line.

   - Using the Curve tool with the second thinnest line option, put a curved line in its place. (See section 8.2.)
   - Turn on the Show Grid command on the Zoom submenu of the View menu.

   - Fill in the modified area with color: Set the foreground color to dark gray (top row, second from the left), select the Brush tool from the Tool Box and a medium brush tip from the

Options Box, and drag the cursor over the appropriate white squares in the grid to turn them gray.

7. Return the magnification to normal size: Select the Magnifier tool from the Tool Box and click on "1x" in the Options Box. (You can also do this by choosing Normal Size from the Zoom submenu of the View menu.) 
8. Delete the word *Sam's* from the side of the truck:
   - Set the background color to light gray.
   - Select the Rectangular Selection tool from the Tool Box. 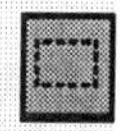
   - Use the mouse to drag a box around the word to be deleted and then release the mouse button.
   - Press the Delete key.
9. Exit Paint, responding No to the "save changes?" message.

8.4 Manipulating Cutouts

Once you have *defined a cutout* — selected an area in the graphic — using either the Free-form or Rectangular Selection tool (as described in Section 8.3) you can:

- Delete the cutout.
- Cut or copy the cutout to the Clipboard.
- Save the cutout in a graphic file on disk.
- Move, copy, or sweep the cutout to another part of the graphic.
- Resize the cutout.
- Flip, rotate, stretch, or tilt the cutout, or invert its colors.

In this section, we will describe how to perform these operations.

Basic Operations on Cutouts

Deleting a cutout As we mentioned in Section 8.3, a convenient way to remove objects from your graphic is to select them (using one of the selection tools), defining a cutout, and then delete the cutout. To delete a cutout, perform any of the following actions:

- Press the Delete key.
- Choose the Clear Selection command from the Edit menu.

- Right-click inside the cutout and choose the Clear Selection command from the resulting pop-up menu.

NOTE

When you "delete" a cutout, you actually replace it with the current background color, as indicated in the Color Box. Unless you're trying for some special effect, you'll want to make sure that the current background color matches the color behind the cutout. If you forget this fact, you may wonder why the rectangular cutout you just deleted was replaced by, say, a red box on the screen.

Cut, copy, and paste

A cutout, like any other selected information, can be cut or copied to the Clipboard, and then pasted into Paint or another Windows application (see Section 2.3). Recall that when information is *cut* to the Clipboard, it is deleted from the current document, but when it is *copied* to the Clipboard, the current document remains unchanged. Here's how these procedures work in Paint.

- To *cut* a cutout to the Clipboard, choose the Cut command from the Edit menu or right-click inside the cutout and choose the Cut command from the pop-up menu. The cutout will be deleted from the current graphic (and replaced by the current background color).
- To *copy* a cutout to the Clipboard, choose the Copy command from the Edit menu or the right-click pop-up menu.
- To *paste* a cutout from the Clipboard into a Paint graphic, choose the Paste command from the Edit menu or the right-click pop-up menu. The cutout is pasted into the upper-left corner of the drawing area and remains *active*, as indicated by the selection box enclosing it. An active cutout can continue to be manipulated; in particular, it can be moved (as described shortly) to another location in the drawing area.

TIP

Once it is selected, a cutout remains active, outlined by the selection box, until it is *pasted down* (anchored in place). To paste down a cutout, perform any of the following actions:

- Click the mouse outside the cutout.
- Define (select) a new cutout.
- Select any tool from the Tool Box.

When a cutout is anchored in place, its selection box disappears.

Saving and retrieving a cutout

Paint allows you to save a cutout as a separate file on disk. It can then be opened at a later time as a graphic of its own or as part of another graphic. In this way, you can create a *library* of graphic components. For example, if you frequently draw pictures of houses, you can create and save types of windows, doors, and other "house components" for use in all your drawings.

To save an active cutout to disk:

1. Choose the Copy To command from the Edit menu or right-click inside the cutout and choose the Copy To command from the pop-up menu. The Copy To dialog box, which is virtually identical to the Save As dialog box (Section 2.2), is displayed.
2. Proceed as you would to save any file to disk.

If you want to *retrieve* a graphic that is stored on disk and place it in your current drawing, you must use the Paste From command. If you use the Open command, the new graphic *replaces* the current one in the drawing area. To insert a graphic file into the current drawing:

1. Choose the Paste From command from the Edit menu. The Paste From dialog box, which is virtually identical to the Open dialog box (Section 2.2), is displayed.
2. Proceed as you would to open any file stored on disk.

The retrieved graphic will be pasted, as an active cutout, into the upper-left corner of the current graphic. You can then move it anywhere in the drawing area, as we will now demonstrate.

Moving, Copying, and Sweeping a Cutout

Paint makes it easy to transfer a cutout from one location in the drawing area to another. There are three types of "transfer" operations:

Move

- When you *move* a cutout, it is transferred to the new location and deleted from the original one. (The region occupied by the original cutout takes on the current background color.) To move an active cutout, position the cursor inside the selection box (it will become a four-headed arrow), press the mouse button, drag the cutout to the new location, and release the mouse button.

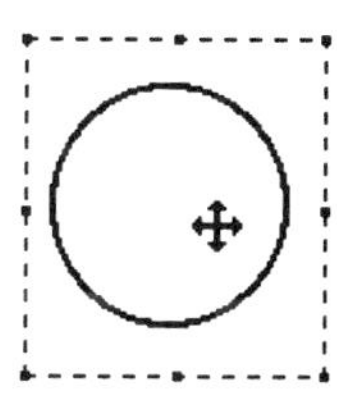

Copy

- When you *copy* a cutout, it is transferred to the new location without being deleted from the original one. To copy an active cutout, follow the *move* procedure, but hold down the Ctrl key as you drag the cutout.

Sweep

- When you *sweep* a cutout, it is transferred to the new location, leaving a series of copies in its path. To sweep an active cutout, follow the *move* procedure, but hold down the Shift key as you drag the cutout. Shown below is the result of sweeping a square (with a black border and gray interior) from one location to another:

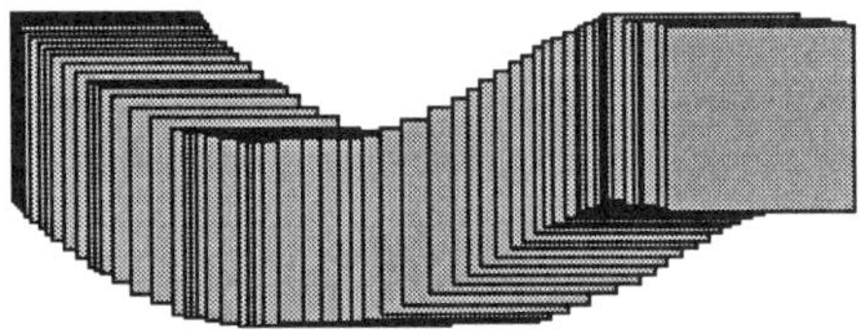

Opaque vs. transparent transfers

When you perform a transfer operation (move, copy, or sweep), the image of the cutout may obscure whatever is beneath it. This is called an *opaque* transfer. When the part of the graphic lying beneath the copy shows through, we call it a *transparent* transfer. Figure 13 illustrates the difference between the two types of transfers. The original figures, circles, are shown on the left. They were selected with the Rectangular Selection tool and copied over the picture of the car on the right. In Figure 13a, the copy is opaque — the copied cutout obscures the car; in Figure 13b, the copy is transparent — the car shows through the copied circle.

a. Opaque Copying **b. Transparent Copying**

Figure 13 Opaque versus Transparent Transfer

Selecting transparent or opaque mode

To transfer a cutout opaquely, select the top option from the Options Box before moving, copying, or sweeping the cutout. To transfer a cutout transparently, select the bottom option. Alternatively, you can turn on opaque mode by selecting (placing a check mark on) the Draw Opaque item on the Options menu; to turn on transparent mode, deselect Draw Opaque.

Resizing a Cutout

To change the size of a cutout (and all of the objects contained within it):

1. Position the mouse pointer over one of the eight *handles*. The pointer will become a two-headed arrow when positioned properly (Figure 14a).

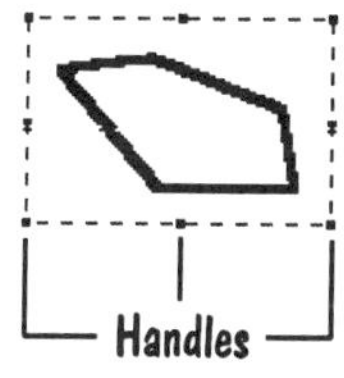

   - Use the middle handle on the top or bottom side to change the height of the cutout without changing its width.
   - Use the middle handle on the left or right side to change the width of the cutout without changing its height.
   - Use a corner handle to change both height and width at the same time.

2. Drag the handle away from the selection box to increase the size of the cutout, or drag it inside the box to decrease its size. An outline of the selection box will move with the cursor to show you the resulting effect (Figure 14b).
3. When the selection box is the desired size, release the mouse button. The cutout will be redrawn in the new size, as shown in Figure 14c. (To abort the process, press the Escape key before releasing the mouse button.)

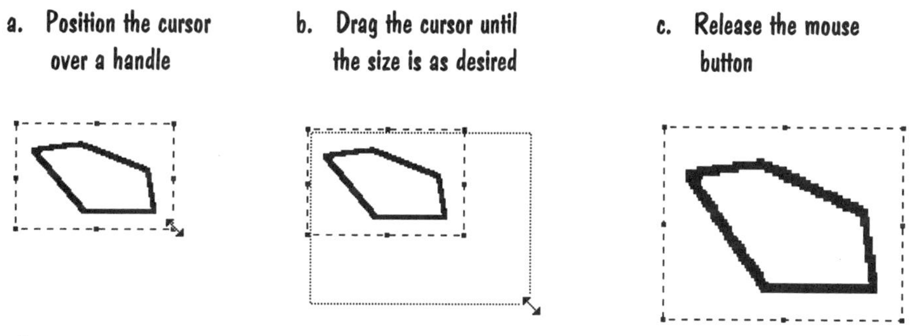

Figure 14 Resizing a Cutout

NOTE

When the cutout is resized, the original selection box may take on the current background color, so select an appropriate background color from the Color Box before starting the process.

When the cutout is made larger and opaque mode is in effect, part of the existing graphic may be obscured. If you don't want this to happen, be sure that transparent mode (the bottom option) is selected in the Options Box before beginning the process.

Other Operations on Cutouts

Paint provides several other ways to manipulate cutouts, all of which are accessible from the Image menu (as well as from the right-click pop-up menu).

Flips and Rotations You can *flip* an active cutout from left to right (a *horizontal flip*) or from top to bottom (a *vertical flip*). Here is an example of each type of flip; in an actual graphic, the triangle on the right would *replace* the one on the left.

Flipping a cutout

To flip an active cutout:

1. Choose the Flip/Rotate command from either the Image menu or the menu that pops up when you right-click inside the cutout. The Flip and Rotate dialog box, shown in Figure 15, will be displayed.

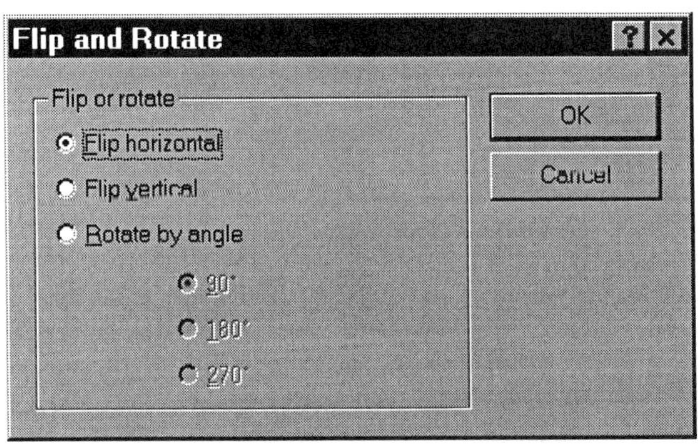

Figure 15 The Flip and Rotate Dialog Box

2. Select the *Flip horizontal* or *Flip vertical* option button, as appropriate.
3. Choose the OK command button.

Rotating a cutout

Paint provides the ability to *rotate* a cutout a quarter turn (90°), a half turn (180°), or a three-quarter turn (270°). Here's an example (as with a flip, the rotated cutout replaces the original):

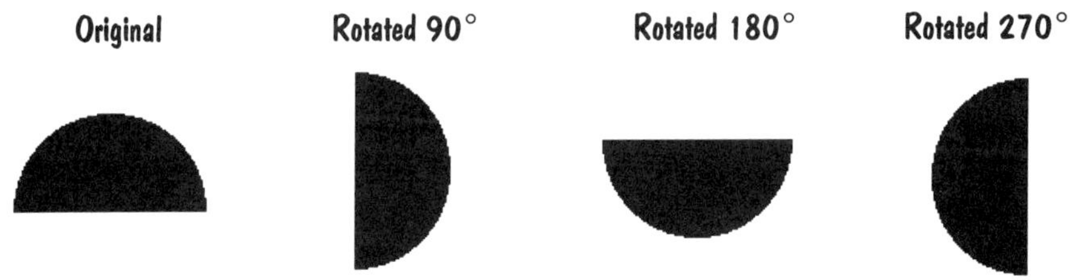

To rotate a cutout:

1. Choose the Flip/Rotate command from either the Image menu or the menu that pops up when you right-click inside the cutout. The Flip and Rotate dialog box, (see Figure 15) will be displayed.
2. Select the *Rotate by angle* option button and then select the option button that gives you the desired amount of rotation. (The rotation takes place in a clockwise direction.)
3. Choose the OK command button.

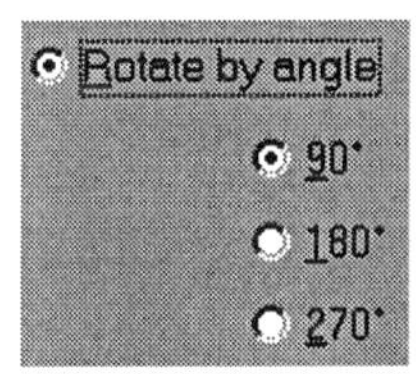

Stretching or Skewing a Cutout *Stretching* a cutout changes its size in either the horizonal or vertical direction. For example, stretching a circle creates an elliptical shape, as shown below:

Stretching a circle

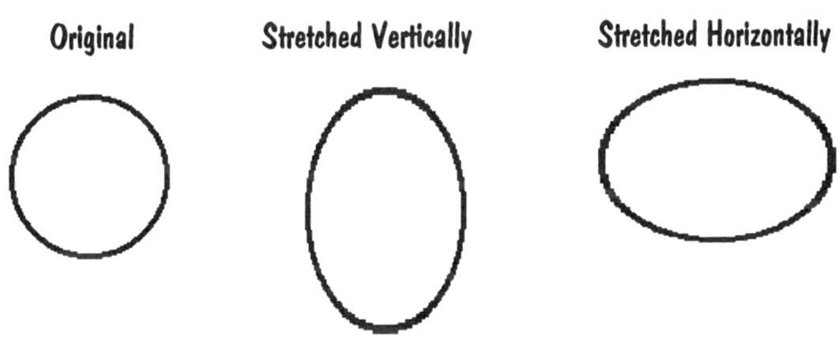

Skewing a cutout tilts it in a horizontal or vertical direction. For example, skewing a square creates a parallelogram, as shown in the figure below:

Skewing a square

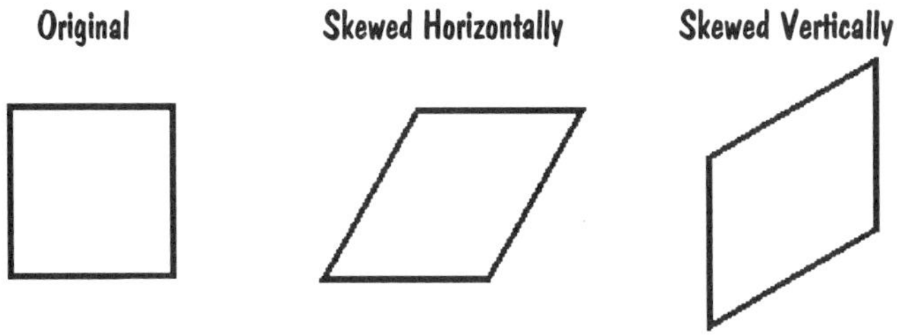

To stretch and/or skew an active cutout:

1. Choose the Stretch/Skew command from either the Image menu or the menu that pops up when you right-click inside the cutout. The dialog box shown in Figure 16 will open.

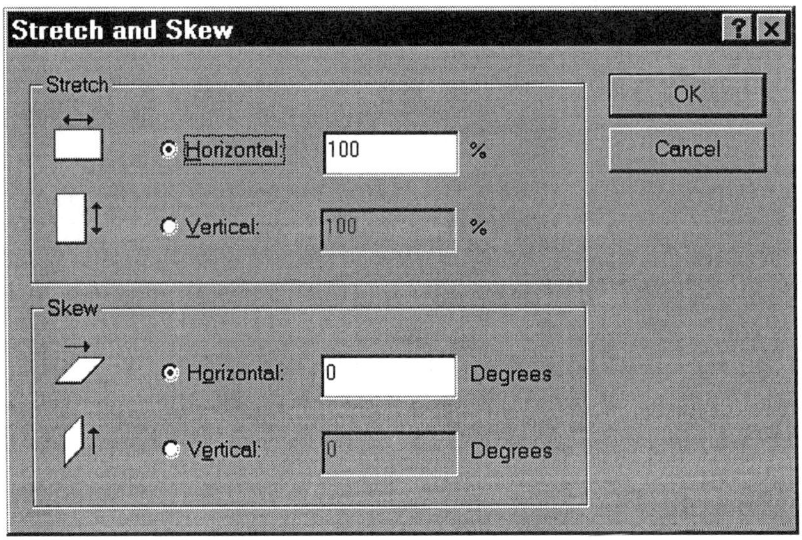

Figure 16 The Stretch and Skew Dialog Box

2. If you want to stretch the cutout, select the Horizontal or Vertical option button in this part of the dialog box and enter a percentage in the corresponding text box. For example, entering "200" in the Horizontal text box will double the cutout's size in that direction; entering "25" will reduce its size by a factor of four. (The circle on the previous page was stretched 150%.)

3. If you want to skew the cutout, select the Horizontal or Vertical option button in this part of the dialog box and enter a number of degrees in the corresponding text box. (You may have to experiment here to get the desired effect.) For example, the square on the previous page was skewed 30°.
4. Choose the OK command button to complete the process.

Inverting the Colors in a Cutout To *invert* the colors in a cutout means to replace each one by its *complement*, the opposite color on the color wheel. For example, whites are changed into blacks, blues into browns or yellows, and reds into greens (and vice-versa). As a specific example, the object shown below on the left has a blue border, black interior, and white stripes. When its colors are inverted, the object on the right (which has a brown border, white interior, and black stripes) replaces it.

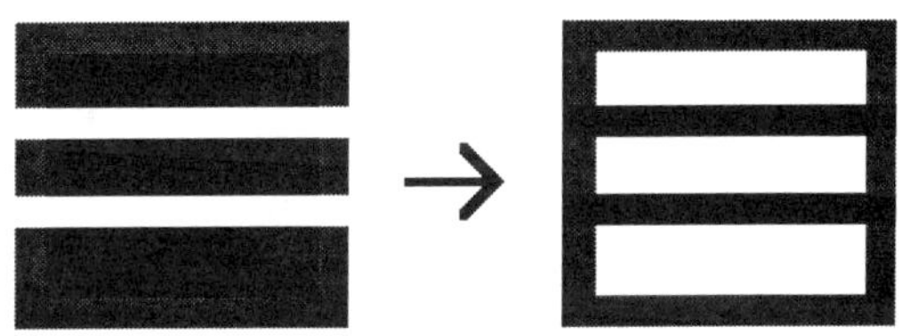

To invert the colors in the active cutout, choose the Invert Colors command from either the Image menu or the menu that pops up when you right-click inside the cutout.

TIP

You can issue the Flip/Rotate, Stretch/Skew, and Invert Colors commands even if no cutout is active. In this case, the operation applies to the entire graphic! However, be aware that the result of applying one of these operations to the entire graphic is sometimes difficult to predict. (If you don't like the effect, just choose the Undo command from the Edit menu to return the graphic to its former state.)

8 4 TUTORIAL

Try the following exercise on your own, creating a drawing of the factory shown in Figure 17 (on the next page).

1. Start Windows 95 (if necessary) by turning on the computer.
2. Set the line width by selecting the Line tool from the Tool Box and, in the Options Box, selecting the second option from the top.
3. Draw the factory building at the bottom of the drawing area: Use the Box tool and the "hollow" (top) option in the Options Box.

Figure 17 Graphic for Tutorial 8.4

4. Draw the smokestack with the Box tool, using the "borderless" (bottom) option and dragging with the *right* mouse button so that it is colored black.
5. Draw the right-most window: Use the Box tool with the hollow option for the outside and the Line tool for the crosspieces. (Remember that holding down the Shift key results in horizontal or vertical lines.)
6. Create the middle window:
   - Select the existing window using the Rectangular Selection tool, position the mouse cursor inside the resulting cutout, hold down the Ctrl key, and drag the cutout's outline to the left of the existing window.
   - Reduce the size of the copy by dragging one of the corner handles toward the center of the new window until it is the proper size; then release the mouse button.
   - Move the new, smaller window into position by placing the mouse cursor inside the cutout and (without holding down Ctrl), dragging it to the proper place.
7. Create the triangular piece above the middle window (the one that was just created) using the Line tool.
8. Copy the middle window and place it to the left of the original (see step 6).

9. With the left-most window still selected, flip it horizontally so that it faces in the proper direction: Choose the Flip/Rotate command from the Image menu (or from the menu that pops up when you right-click inside the cutout), select the Flip horizontal option button in the resulting dialog box, and choose the OK command button.
10. Select a light gray foreground color and paint the building this color: Choose the Paint Can tool and click on a part of the building that is not a window.
11. Draw the smoke — use the Airbrush tool, with a medium brush width selected from the Options Box.
12. Close Paint, saving the graphic if you want.

8.5 Other Features of Paint

In the first four sections of this chapter, we have discussed how to use the Paint application to create and edit a graphic. In this section, we will introduce a few additional features of Paint. These include:

- Setting page orientation and margins.
- Previewing the way the graphic will look on the printed page.
- Changing image attributes, such as the size of the drawing area.
- Using Paint to create Desktop wallpaper.

Setting Up the Page

Before printing your graphic, you should specify the size of the paper you are using, and its orientation and margins. These settings are entered in the Page Setup dialog box (Figure 18, on the next page). To open this dialog box, choose the Page Setup command from the File menu. Then, you can:

Paper size

- Specify the size of the paper on which you will be printing by selecting a size from the Paper Size drop-down list.

Margins

- Specify the top, bottom, left, and right page margins by entering the appropriate numbers in the Margins text boxes. The margin settings determine the size of the blank border around the graphic. By increasing the top and left margins, you can "push" the graphic down and to the right, perhaps to center it on the page.

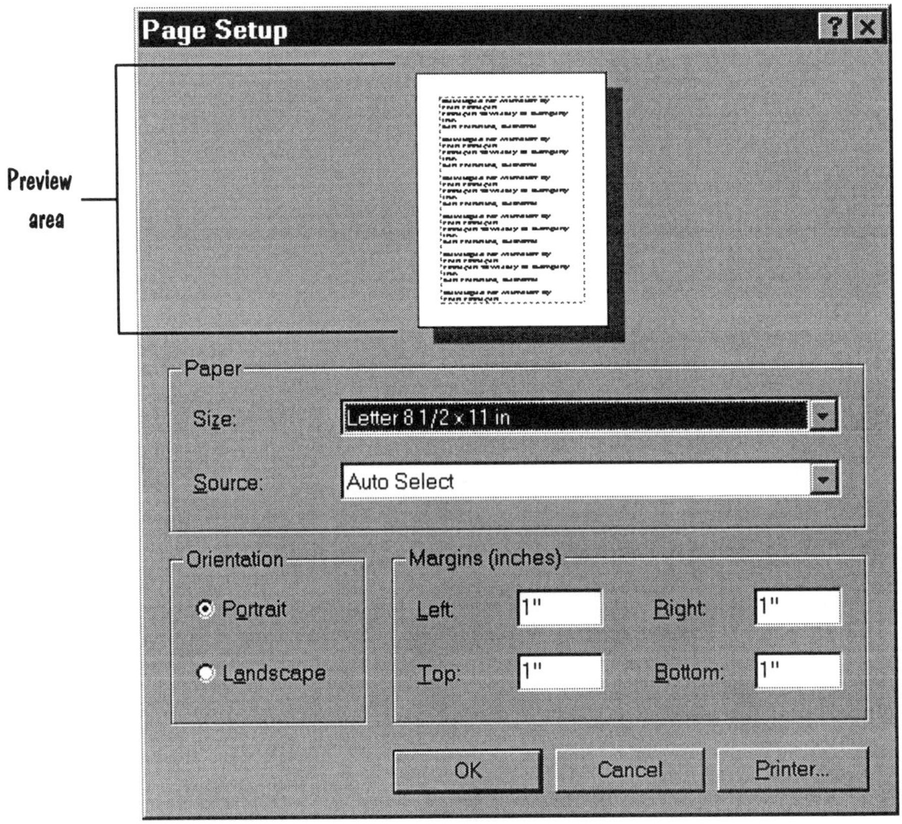

Figure 18 The Page Setup Dialog Box

Orientation

- Specify the paper's orientation, either *portrait* or *landscape*, by selecting the corresponding option button. In **portrait** orientation, the graphic is viewed holding the page so that the long side is vertical; in **landscape** orientation, the graphic is viewed with the long side horizontal. The following figures further illustrate this concept:

When you change a setting, the sample page in the preview area will also change to indicate the effect of the new setting. After you have entered all the needed information, choose the OK button to put the changes into effect.

Print Preview

If you would like to see how the graphic will appear on the printed page before it is actually printed, choose the Print Preview command from the File menu. The **print preview** window will open (Figure 19), not only displaying the graphic as it appears in the drawing area, but also taking into account paper size, orientation, and margins. For example, the graphic in Figure 19 was positioned in the upper-left corner of the drawing area and the page settings were 8½" × 11" paper size, landscape orientation, and margins of 2" left and right, 1" top and bottom.

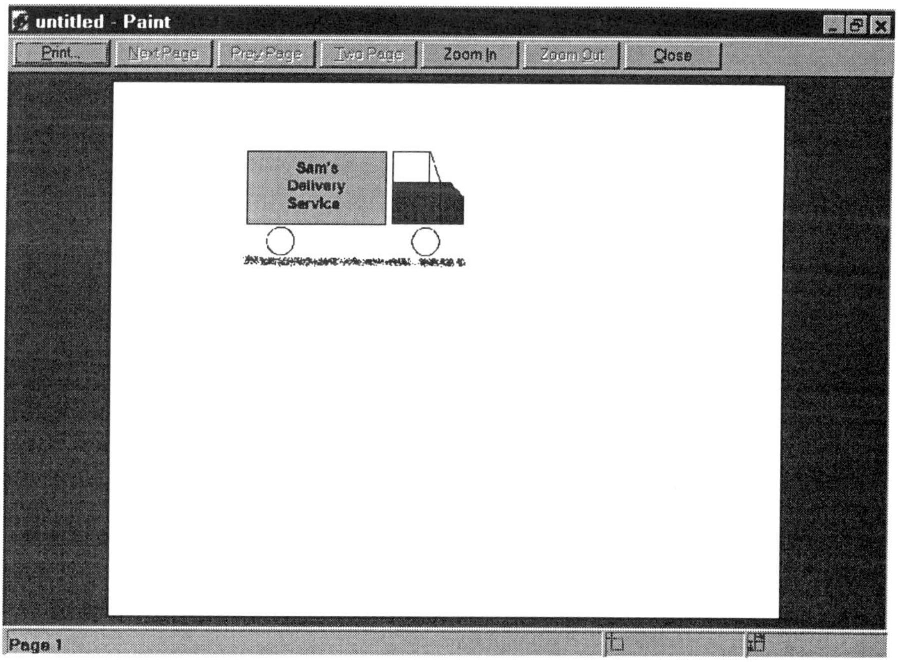

Figure 19 The Print Preview Window

Zooming in and out

Although you cannot edit the graphic while it is in the print preview window, you can magnify parts of it to see finer detail. In addition to the full-page view shown in Figure 19, there are two "zoom" modes. To *zoom in*, magnifying the graphic:

- Click on the part of the page that you would like to enlarge. (In the preview window, the mouse cursor takes the shape of a magnifying glass, as shown at the right.) 

or

- Click on the Zoom In button (at the top of the window). Then, use the scroll bars to display the desired part of the page.

Clicking on the page or the Zoom In button again displays the second Zoom mode, increasing the magnification even more. At this point, the Zoom In button is dimmed, and clicking again on the page will return the display to the default magnification level. While in one of the two Zoom modes, clicking on the Zoom Out button changes the display to the next lower magnification level.

The relative magnification of the full-page view (on the left) and the two zoom modes is shown below:

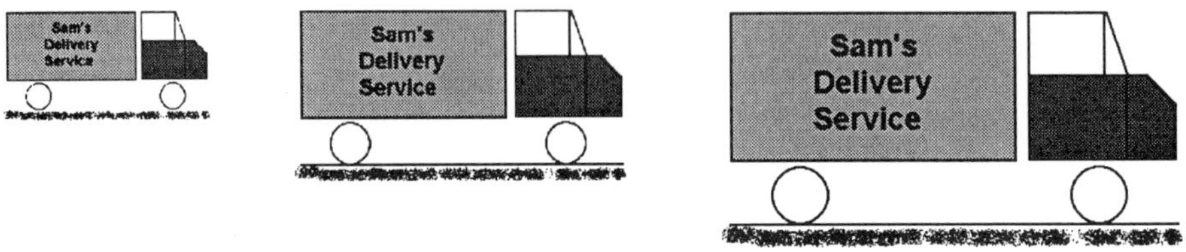

When you are done using the print preview window, either choose the Close button to return to the drawing window or choose the Print button to print the document.

Changing the Size of the Drawing Area

Paint uses a default drawing size that is 6.67" wide and 5" high (on the printed page). When you start Paint, however, the drawing area will be set to the same size it was when you last exited. To return to the default dimensions, or to change to another drawing size:

1. Choose the Attributes command from the Image menu. The dialog box pictured in Figure 20 will be displayed.
2. To return to the default drawing size, choose the Default command button.
3. To set another drawing size, enter the desired dimensions in the Width and Height text boxes. (The units of measurement are determined by which option button is currently selected.)
4. Choose the OK command button to close the dialog box and put the changes into effect.

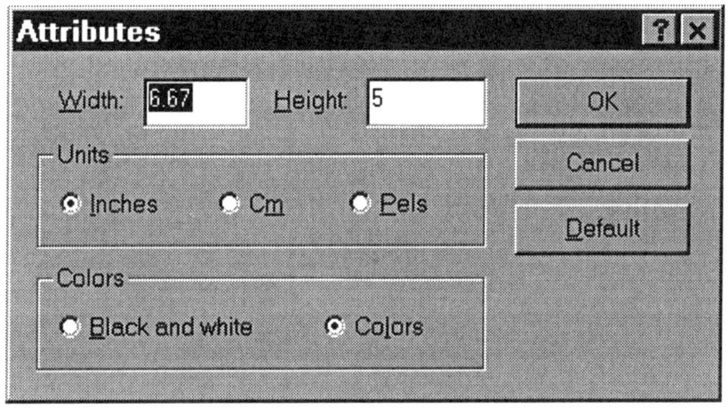

Figure 20 The Image Attributes Dialog Box

If the specified dimensions are *larger* than the Paint window can accommodate, scroll bars will appear. (A larger drawing size uses more RAM and it takes more disk space to store the graphic.) If the specified dimensions are *smaller* than the Paint window, a rectangular box will be displayed in its upper-left corner marking off the new drawing area.

NOTE

As you can see, the Image Attributes dialog box also allows you to:

- Specify units of measurement — inches, centimeters (cm), or pixels (pels) — for the drawing size.
- Elect to use patterns of black and white for your palette, instead of colors. Here's how the Color Box will look if you select the *Black and white* option button and choose the OK command button:

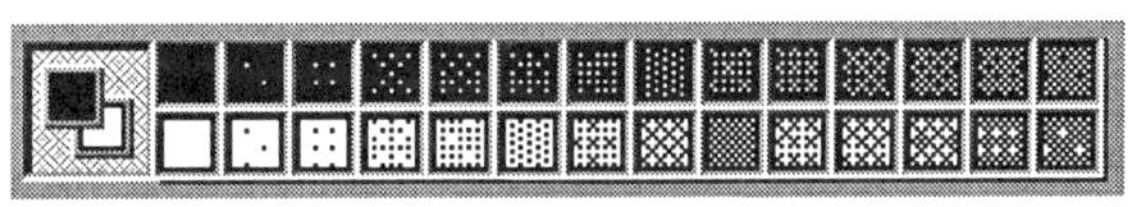

Be aware that if you switch to black and white while creating a graphic, all colors will be changed to patterns and you will not be able to restore its original colors!

Creating Wallpaper

Wallpaper is a graphic image that covers the Desktop. It acts as a background for the icons, windows, and other objects that occupy the Desktop during a typical Windows session. Although wallpaper is normally selected using Control Panel's Display utility (see Section 5.2), you can also set up a Paint graphic to be the current wallpaper. To do so:

1. Use Paint to create or open the graphic.
2. Save it to disk (if the latest version has not already been saved).
3. Choose one of the *Set as Wallpaper* commands from the File menu:
   - If you choose *Set as Wallpaper (Tiled)*, the graphic will be repeated as many times as necessary to cover the entire Desktop (see Figure 21a).
   - If you choose *Set as Wallpaper (Centered)*, a single copy of the graphic will be centered on the Desktop (see Figure 21b).

In order to see the new wallpaper, you may have to first minimize all windows.

a. Tiled Wallpaper **b. Centered Wallpaper**

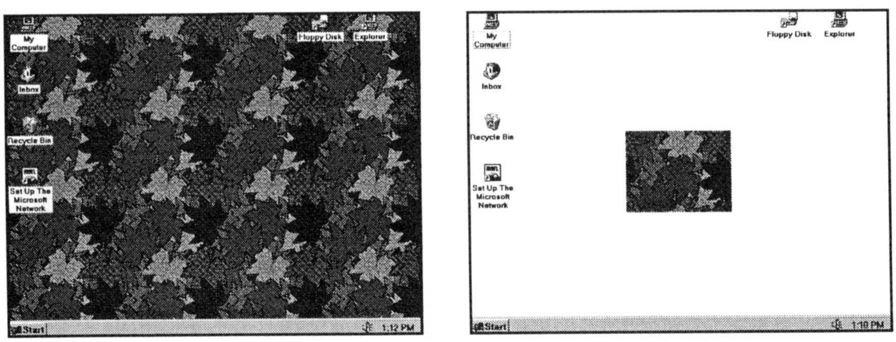

Figure 21 Examples of Wallpaper

NOTE

When you set a graphic as wallpaper, it not only becomes the current Desktop background, but its file name is also added to the list of wallpapers on the Background page of Control Panel's Display utility. Consequently, at any time in the future you can:

- Change this wallpaper from tiled to centered, or vice-versa.
- Reselect this wallpaper, if another one is currently in use.

For more information about wallpaper, see Section 5.2.

Chapter Summary

The Basics of Paint	To start Paint	Choose the Paint item from the Accessories submenu of the Start menu's Programs option.
	To select a foreground color	Click on it in the Color Box.
	To select a background color	Right-click on it in the Color Box.
	To select a Paint tool	Click on its icon in the Tool Box.
	To zoom in on the graphic	Point at Zoom on the View menu and choose a magnification level; *or* use the Magnifier tool to magnify part or all of the graphic.
	To select a part of the graphic	Define a cutout with the Rectangular Selection or Free-form Selection tool.
Paint Tools	Free-form Selection	Defines a cutout by selecting a free-form region.
	Rectangular Selection	Defines a cutout by selecting a box-shaped region.
	Eraser	Erases part of the graphic.
	Paint Can	Fills an enclosed region with color.
	Eye Dropper	Establishes a color in the graphic as the current foreground or background color.
	Magnifier	Magnifies part or all of the graphic.
	Pencil	Draws a free-form figure using a one-pixel-thick curve.
	Brush	Draws a free-form figure using your choice of brush tip.
	Airbrush	Draws a free-form figure made up of a spray of dots.
	Text	Inserts text into the graphic in your choice of font.
	Line	Draws a straight line.
	Curve	Draws a smooth curve.
	Box	Draws a filled or unfilled rectangle.
	Polygon	Draws a filled or unfilled polygon.

	Ellipse/Circle	Draws a filled or unfilled circle or ellipse.
	Rounded Box	Draws a filled or unfilled rectangle with rounded corners.
Operations on Cutouts	To define a cutout	Use the Free-form Selection or Rectangular Selection tool.
	To delete a cutout	Press the Delete key; *or* choose Clear Selection from the Edit or right-click menu.
	To cut, copy, or paste a cutout on the Clipboard	Choose Cut, Copy, or Paste from the Edit or right-click menu.
	To save/retrieve a cutout on disk	Choose Copy To/Paste From from the Edit menu.
	To move/copy/sweep a cutout	Drag the cutout to a new location; hold down the Ctrl key to copy, the Shift key to sweep.
	To resize a cutout	Drag one of the cutout's handles.
	To flip or rotate a cutout	Choose Flip/Rotate from the Image or right-click menu.
	To stretch or skew a cutout	Choose Stretch/Skew from the Image or right-click menu.
	To invert the colors of a cutout	Choose Invert Colors from the Image or right-click menu.
Other Features of Paint	To set up the printed page	Choose Page Setup from the File menu; then specify paper size, orientation, and margins in the resulting dialog box.
	To preview the printed page	Choose Print Preview from the File menu.
	To change the size of the drawing area	Choose Attributes from the Image menu and enter a width and height in the dialog box.

Review Exercises

Section 8.1

1. To select red as the foreground color in a Paint graphic, click the ___________ mouse button on that color in the Color Box.
2. To expand Paint's drawing area so that it fills the entire screen, choose the ___________ command from the View menu.
3. True or false: If you select a new background color from the Color

Box after drawing a graphic, the background of that graphic will change to the new color.

4. True or false: Paint's Eye Dropper tool can be used to change both the foreground and background colors.

5. To select blue as the foreground color in Paint:

   a. Click the left mouse button on blue in the Color Box.
   b. Double-click the left mouse button on blue in the Color Box.
   c. Click the right mouse button on blue in the Color Box.
   d. Double-click the right mouse button on blue in the Color Box.

6. Which of the following tools cannot be found in Paint's Tool Box?

   a. Eraser
   b. Pencil
   c. Pen
   d. Brush

Section 8.2

7. To draw a horizontal line with Paint's Line tool, hold down the ____________ key while dragging the cursor.

8. When you use Paint's __________ tool, a spray of dots is produced.

9. When you use Paint's Box tool to create a hollow box (using the left mouse button), it is drawn in the current ____________ color.

10. An existing polygon can be filled with color by using Paint's ____________ tool.

11. True or false: Paint's Brush tool can only produce curves of a single line thickness.

12. True or false: To draw a perfect circle with Paint's Ellipse/Circle tool, hold down the Ctrl key while dragging the cursor.

13. True or false: The Tool Box icon for Paint's Text tool is the capital letter "T".

14. True or false: Paint's Rounded Box tool is used to create a rectangular shape with rounded corners.

15. Which of the following Paint tools cannot draw an "L-shaped" pair of lines?

    a. The Polygon tool
    b. The Line tool
    c. The Pencil tool
    d. The Brush tool

16. To fill an irregularly shaped region in a Paint graphic with color

    a. Double-click on that color in the Color Box.
    b. Use the Filled Box tool.

   c. Use the Paint Can tool.
   d. Use the Airbrush tool.

17. To draw a square using Paint's Box tool, while dragging the cursor, hold down the

   a. Alt key.
   b. Ctrl key.
   c. Shift key.
   d. Spacebar.

18. In the Text tool's Fonts window, you cannot select

   a. The color for the current text.
   b. The typeface for the current text.
   c. The point size for the current text.
   d. A bold and italic style for the current text.

Section 8.3

19. To erase a green circle that is enclosed in a red square using Paint's Eraser tool, set the background color to ___________.

20. You can magnify a part of your graphic using Paint's ___________ tool.

21. True or false: To define an irregularly-shaped cutout, use Paint's Free-form Selection tool.

22. True or false: You can use the Custom Size command (on Paint's Zoom submenu) to magnify the current graphic by any factor you want.

23. To delete the current (active) cutout in Paint, you can

   a. Press the Delete key.
   b. Choose the Clear Selection command from the Edit menu.
   c. Right-click inside the cutout and choose Clear Selection from the resulting pop-up menu.
   d. Carry out any of the above actions.

24. You cannot use the Zoom command (on Paint's Edit menu) to:

   a. Magnify the graphic by 400%.
   b. Show the graphic as it will appear on the printed page.
   c. Turn the (pixel) grid on and off.
   d. Display a thumbnail view of the graphic.

Section 8.4

25. To *sweep* a cutout in Paint, hold down the ___________ key while dragging the cutout.

26. To flip a cutout in Paint from top to bottom, begin by choosing the ___________ command from the Image menu.

27. To save a cutout to disk, choose the Copy To command from Paint's ___________ menu.

28. True or false: To move a cutout transparently in Paint, select the bottom option in the Options Box.

29. True or false: Paint allows you to rotate a cutout by 90°, 180°, or 270°.

30. To paste down (anchor) a cutout in Paint:

    a. Choose Paste from the Edit menu.
    b. Choose Clear Selection from the Edit menu.
    c. Reposition the cursor.
    d. Click outside the cutout.

31. To copy a cutout from one location to another:

    a. Drag it to the new location.
    b. Drag it to the new location while holding down the Ctrl key.
    c. Drag it to the new location while holding down the Shift key.
    d. Drag it to the new location while holding down the Spacebar.

32. Which operation on cutouts is not performed by issuing a menu command?

    a. Resizing
    b. Flipping
    c. Rotating
    d. Skewing

Section 8.5

33. To see how your Paint graphic will look on the printed page before it is actually printed, choose the ___________ command from the File menu.

34. You can replace the colors in a Paint drawing by black-and-white patterns by choosing the ___________ item from the Image menu.

35. True or false: You can edit a Paint graphic that is displayed in the print preview window.

36. True or false: When you use one of the Set as Wallpaper commands on Paint's File menu, the resulting wallpaper is immediately put into effect.

37. Which of the following operations cannot be carried out using Paint's Page Setup dialog box?

    a. Setting the page margins.
    b. Setting the page orientation.
    c. Placing a header or footer on the page.
    d. Selecting a paper size.

38. Paint's Image Attributes dialog box can be used to specify the size of

    a. The page margins.

b. The text font.
c. The drawing area.
d. The screen resolution.

Build Your Own Glossary

39. The following words and phrases are important terms that were introduced in this chapter. (They appear within the text in boldface type.) Use WordPad (see Section 2.2) to enter a definition for each term, preserving alphabetical order, into the Glossary file on the Student Disk.

Airbrush tool
Background color
Box tool
Brush tool
Color Box
Curve tool
Cutout
Drawing area
Ellipse/Circle tool
Eraser tool
Eye Dropper tool
Foreground color
Free-form Selection tool
Graphic
Landscape orientation
Line tool
Magnifier tool
Options Box
Paint (application)
Paint Can tool
Pencil tool
Polygon tool
Portrait orientation
Print preview
Rectangular Selection tool
Rounded Box tool
Text tool
Tool Box

Lab Exercises

Work each of the following exercises at your computer. Begin by turning the machine on (if necessary) to start Windows 95 and closing any open windows.

Lab Exercise 1 (Section 8.2)

a. Start Paint and maximize its window.
b. Use the 24-point Arial Bold font to insert the words Greek Flag at the top of the drawing area.
c. Create a drawing that resembles the blue-and-white Greek flag pictured at the right.

d. Insert your name, your class, and the date under the drawing in your choice of font.
e. Save the graphic to a floppy disk under the name Flag and print the graphic.
f. Exit Paint and remove the diskette from its drive.

Lab Exercise 2 (Section 8.2)

a. Start Paint and maximize its window.

b. Create a drawing that resembles the 5¼" floppy disk pictured at the right. Make it as large as you can, yet ensuring that the entire disk can be viewed without scrolling.

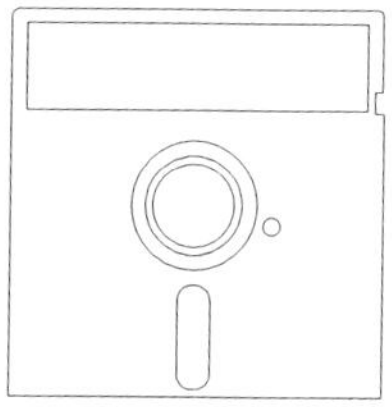

c. Insert your name, your class, and the date on the diskette's label (the rectangle at the top) in an appropriately-sized font.

d. Save the graphic to a floppy disk under the name Floppy and print the graphic.

e. Exit Paint and remove the diskette from its drive.

Lab Exercise 3 (Section 8.3)

a. Start Paint and maximize its window.

b. Insert the Student Disk in its drive and open the Graph1 graphic on this disk.

c. Edit the Graph1 graphic, so that the revised version resembles the one pictured at the right, using your class in the title. (Use the 10-point Arial font for all the text.)

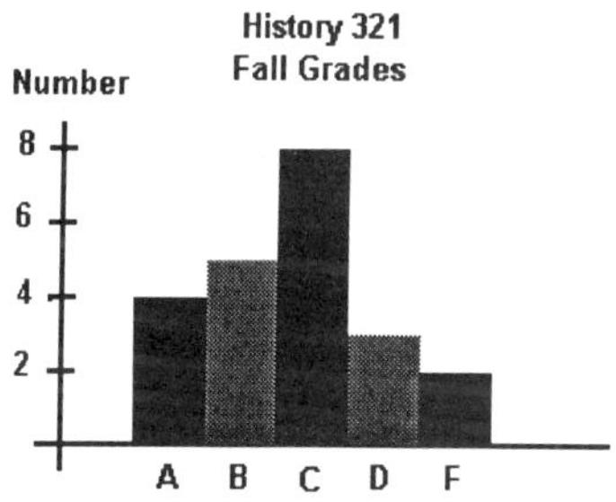

d. Insert your name and the date below the revised graphic in your choice of font.

e. Save the revised graphic to a floppy disk under the name Graph2 and print the graphic.

f. Exit Paint and remove the diskette from its drive.

Lab Exercise 4 (Section 8.3)

a. Start Paint and maximize its window.

b. Create the Palette graphic shown on the next page. Here are a couple of hints so that your graphic will look right:

- Use the cursor coordinates on the Status bar to help create even subdivisions in the palette.
- Zoom in at 800% magnification on the line intersections and "clean them up" so that the lines meet perfectly.
- Use the Paint Can tool to fill each compartment with a different color from the Color Box.

c. Insert your name, your class, and the date under the palette in your choice of font.

d. Save the graphic to a floppy disk under the name **Palette** and print the graphic.

e. Exit Paint and remove the diskette from its drive.

Lab Exercise 5 (Section 8.3)

a. Start Paint and maximize its window.

b. Insert the Student Disk in its drive and open the Factory1 graphic on this disk.

c. Edit the Factory1 graphic, so that the revised version resembles the one pictured in Figure 22, by:

- Using the Eraser tool to erase the triangular part of the two existing windows.
- Using the Box tool to create the new rectangular window and second smokestack.
- Using the Airbrush tool to create the new smoke.

Figure 22 Final Graphic for Lab Exercise 5

d. Insert your name, your class, and the date to the left of the smokestacks in your choice of font.

e. Save the revised graphic to a floppy disk under the name Factory2 and print the graphic.

f. Exit Paint and remove the diskette from its drive.

Lab Exercise 6 (Section 8.4)

a. Start Paint and maximize its window.

b. Create a drawing that resembles the house shown at the right. Make use of the copy and resize operations to simplify your work.

c. Insert your name, your class, and the date below the graphic in your choice of font.

d. Save the graphic to a floppy disk under the name House and print the graphic.

e. Exit Paint and remove the diskette from its drive.

Lab Exercise 7 (Section 8.4)

a. Start Paint and maximize its window.

b. Create a drawing that resembles the locomotive shown at the right. Make use of the copy and resize operations to simplify your work.

c. Insert your name, your class, and the date below the graphic in your choice of font.

d. Save the graphic to a floppy disk under the name Loco and print the graphic.

e. Exit Paint and remove the diskette from its drive.

If You Want to Learn More ...

The notes presented here allow you to delve more deeply into some of the topics covered in this chapter.

Editing the colors in the Color Box

As you know, Paint's Color Box displays a palette of 28 colors that can be used for either foreground or background. If you want to use a different color in your graphic, it's easy to replace an existing color with one of your choosing. Here's how:

1. Double-click on the Color Box color to be replaced (or click on it and choose Edit Colors from the Options menu). The Edit Colors dialog box will open, displaying 48 "basic colors" and any "custom colors" you have defined in the current Paint session. (We will discuss how to define a custom color in the next note.)
2. Click on the color of your choice; it will be enclosed in a box.
3. Choose the OK command button. The selected color will replace the original one in the Color Box.

Defining a custom color

If you want to use a certain color in your graphic and it does not appear in the Color Box or in the basic 48 colors displayed in the Edit Colors dialog box (see the note above), here's how you can create any *custom color* you wish:

1. Choose Edit Colors from the Options menu to open the Edit Colors dialog box.
2. Choose the Define Custom Colors command button. The Edit Colors dialog box will expand and look as shown below:

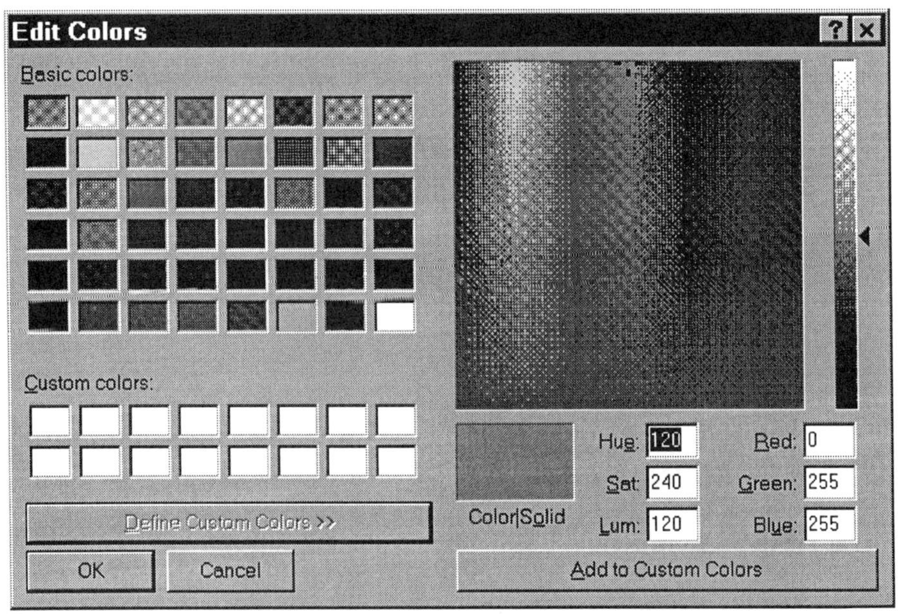

3. Click on the desired color in the color spectrum on the right side of the dialog box. The selected color will be displayed on the left side of the Color|Solid box. The right side of this box will display the nearest "solid" (pure) color to it.
4. You can make adjustments to the selected color by changing the entries in the Hue, Sat (saturation), Lum (luminosity), Red, Green, and Blue text boxes, or by dragging the pointer on the "luminosity bar" (on the far right of the dialog box) up or down. The best way to see how these parameters affect the selected color is to experiment with them!
5. If you prefer the nearest pure color (on the right side of the Color|Solid box) to the selected one, double-click on the Color|Solid box.
6. Choose the Add to Custom Colors command button. The new color will fill one of the *Custom colors* boxes on the left side of the dialog box.
7. Repeat steps 3 through 6 to create additional custom colors.
8. To place a custom color in the Color Box, replacing the current foreground color in the palette, click on the desired color and choose the OK command button. Otherwise, choose the Cancel command button.

Saving a color palette

If you like to create your own custom colors, it's important to know that they are only preserved for the current Paint session; the next time you start Paint, the palette of colors in the Color Box will be returned to the default set and no custom colors will appear in the Edit Colors dialog box. To save custom colors from one session to another, you must add them to the Color Box and then save the resulting palette. To do so:

1. Choose Save Colors from the Options menu. The Save Colors dialog box will open.
2. Enter a name for the new palette in the *File name* text box.
3. Choose the Save button.

To retrieve a saved palette for use in another Paint graphic:

1. Choose Get Colors from the Options menu. The Get Colors dialog box will open.
2. Select the desired palette from the list displayed.
3. Choose the Open command button. The Color Box will display the new set of colors.

Moving the Tool or Color Box

As you know, you can increase the size of the work area by removing the Tool Box and/or Color Box from the screen. Unfortunately, you can then no longer select tools and/or colors to be used in your graphic. A more practical way to expand the work area is to "tear off" the Tool Box or Color Box, creating a corresponding window that sits on top of your graphic and can be moved about the screen. To tear off either of these boxes, just drag it to a new location. To return the Tool or Color window to its original, fixed location, drag its title bar to the left edge or bottom edge of the screen, respectively.

Comparison of Paint and Paintbrush (Windows 3.1)

Paintbrush, the Windows 3.1 drawing program, is very similar to Paint. If you've used the former, you shouldn't have any trouble adapting to its Windows 95 variant. In fact, Paint is slightly easier to use due to the presence of several new features:

- There are two new tools, the Line and Eyedropper. (Paintbrush's Color Eraser has been incorporated into Paint's Eraser and its Paint Roller is now a Paint Can.)
- You can draw figures in either the foreground or background colors (depending on which mouse button you depress).
- Cutouts now have "handles", making it easier to resize them.
- Print preview allows you to see what the printed graphic will look like without actually printing it.

The only significant feature of Paintbrush that is not present in Paint is the former's ability to display headers and footers on the printed page.

CHAPTER 9

Using Other Windows Accessories

In Chapters 7 and 8, we discussed two of the applications, WordPad and Paint, included with the Windows 95 package. These applications are sometimes referred to as **accessories** because they appear on the Accessories submenu of the Start menu's Programs option. In this chapter we will describe how to use other Windows accessories. More specifically:

- Section 9.1 introduces a simple, but useful accessory called Calculator, which includes two types of on-screen calculators.
- Section 9.2 discusses the Notepad text editor.
- Section 9.3 describes how to back up your files using the Windows Backup utility.
- Section 9.4 discusses several tools (ScanDisk, Disk Defragmenter, and DriveSpace) that help maintain your hard disk.
- Section 9.5 briefly describes the Character Map utility and introduces Windows built-in multimedia and communications applications.

The topics in this chapter are independent of one another, so you can read them in any order, or skip any you want.

9.1 The Windows Calculators

Windows' **Calculator** accessory provides two types of on-screen calculators — a basic *standard* calculator and a more powerful *scientific* calculator. To start Calculator:

1. Click on the Start button to open the Start menu.
2. Point at the Start menu's Programs option and then at the Accessories item on the resulting submenu.
3. Click on the Calculator item on the Accessories submenu.

Switching between the calculator types

The Calculator window will open, displaying the calculator type (standard or scientific) that was active when you last exited this accessory. To switch from one type to the other, choose Standard or Scientific, as desired, from the View menu.

The Standard Calculator

If you know how to use a conventional calculator, then you'll be able to use Windows' Calculator; it works in a completely analogous way! In standard mode (Figure 1), Calculator contains all the keys usually found on a basic calculator, but instead of pressing a key with your finger, you click on it with the mouse. For example, to multiply 365 by 23:

1. Click on the 3, 6, and 5 buttons. As you do, the corresponding digits appear in the calculator's "display".

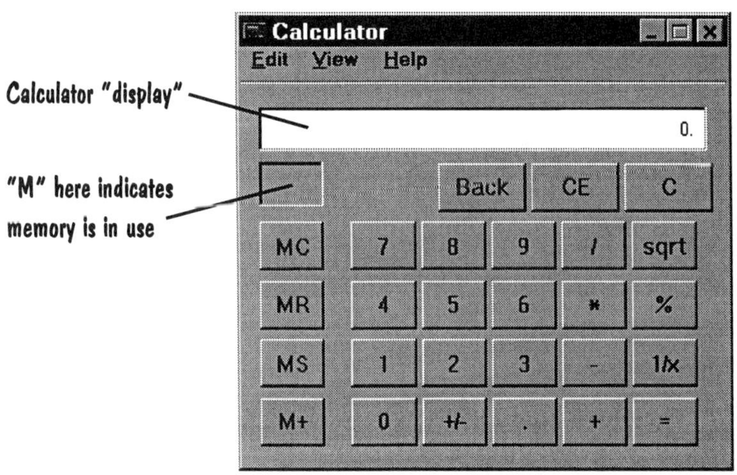

Figure 1 Standard Calculator

2. Click on the multiplication key (*).
3. Click on the 2 and 3 buttons; 23 appears in the display.
4. Click on the equals key (=). The product, 8395, appears in the display.

In addition to the number and operation (/, *, +, -, =) keys, the standard calculator contains all the keys usually found on a basic calculator (and one atypical key, *Back*). The following table provides a quick rundown of their functions.

Key	Symbol	Function
Back	Back	Deletes the last digit entered into the display.
Clear entry	CE	Clears the number in the display.
Clear	C	Clears the entire current computation.
Memory clear	MC	Clears the number stored in memory.
Memory recall	MR	Replaces the displayed number by the one in memory.
Memory store	MS	Stores the displayed number in memory, replacing the currently stored number.
Memory plus	M+	Adds the displayed number to the number in memory.
Plus/minus	+/-	Reverses the sign of the number in the display.
Reciprocal	1/x	Replaces the displayed number by its reciprocal.
Percentage	%	Multiplies the result of a multiplication by 100.
Square root	sqrt	Replaces the displayed number by its square root.

Table 1 Standard Calculator Keys

TIP

If you use Calculator a lot, you can speed up data entry by using *keyboard equivalents*. For example, the number keys and operation symbols can be activated by pressing the corresponding keys on the keyboard. (If you use the numeric keypad to do this, make sure the

Num Lock light is on; if it isn't, press the Num Lock key.) Here are a few other useful keyboard equivalents; instead of clicking on:

- The Back button — press the Backspace key.
- The CE button — press the Delete key.
- The C button — press the Escape key.

To discover the rest of the keyboard equivalents, right-click on the key in question and choose *What's This?* from the resulting pop-up menu.

Copy and paste with Calculator

You can transfer numbers between the Calculator display and another application with the aid of the Clipboard:

- To copy the displayed number to the Clipboard, choose the Copy command from the Edit menu.
- To transfer a number from the Clipboard to the Calculator display, choose Paste from the Edit menu.

The Scientific Calculator

In scientific mode (Figure 2), Calculator supplies an impressive array of advanced functions, in addition to the basic operations provided by standard mode.

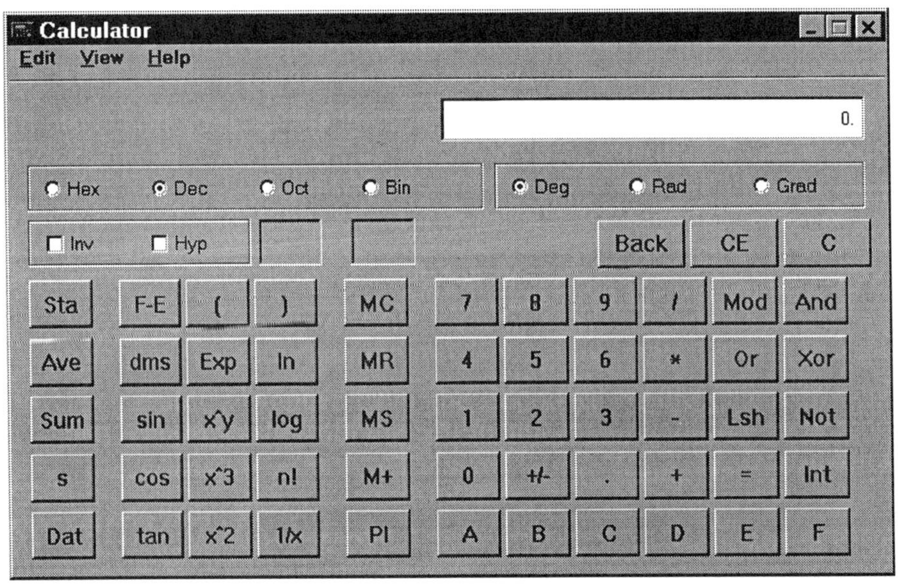

Figure 2 Scientific Calculator

Dealing with Numbers In scientific mode, you can choose to enter and manipulate numbers in four different number systems. Calculator defaults to our everyday *decimal* (base 10) number system. If you want to set Calculator to work in the *hexadecimal* (base 16), *octal* (base 8), or *binary* (base 2) system, select the corresponding option button:

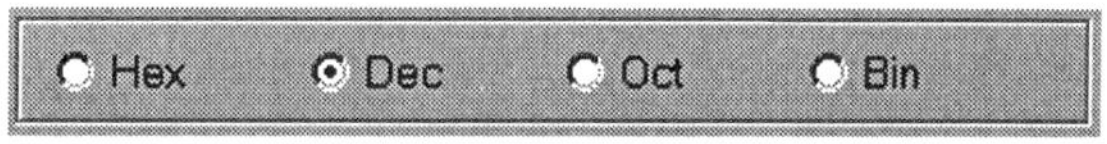

Calculator will only accept numbers that are valid for the selected system. For example, if *Bin* is selected and you try to enter anything but a 0 or 1 into the display, you will hear a "beep" and nothing will happen. At the other extreme, the hexadecimal system uses the digits 0, 1, ..., 9, A, B, C, D, E, and F and the additional "digits" are entered by using the corresponding calculator (or keyboard) keys:

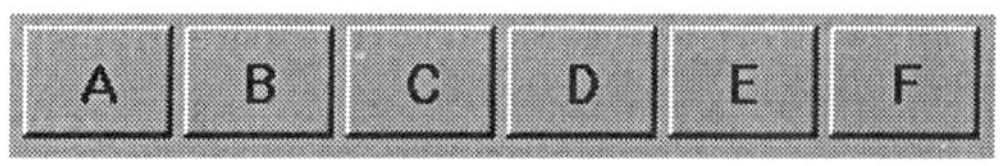

You can use the number system option buttons to convert a number from one system to another. To do so:

1. Select the option button for the system to be converted *from*.
2. Enter the desired number (actually, its representation in the current system) into the display.
3. Select the system to be converted *to*. The numeral in the display will change to the correct representation in the new system.

Performing Statistical Calculations Calculator can compute the sum, mean (average), and standard deviation of a given set of numbers. To perform one of these operations:

1. Click on the *Sta* button. The Statistics Box window will open.
2. Click on the RET (return) button in the Statistics Box to close this window.
3. Enter the data (the numbers with which you want to work) into the display one at a time, clicking on the *Dat* button after each number is entered. (Each time you click on Dat the displayed number is added to the list in

the Statistics Box, even though the latter is hidden from view.)

4. If you wish to review the numbers you have just entered, click on the *Sta* button again. The Statistics Box window will open, displaying the data and the total number (n =) of items.

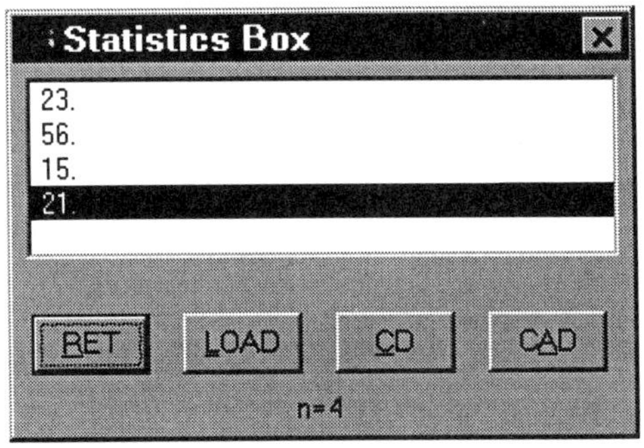

5. To delete a number, select it and click on CD. To clear the window, click on CAD. To replace the number in the Calculator display by the one currently selected in the Statistics Box, click on LOAD.
6. Click on RET to close the Statistics Box. Now, to display:
   - The mean of the data — click on the *Ave* button.
   - The sum of the data — click on the *Sum* button.
   - The standard deviation of the data — click on the *s* button.

Trigonometric Functions Calculator allows you to compute trigonometric and hyperbolic functions and their inverses. Moreover, in working with trig functions, you can elect to have the angle measured in degrees (*Deg*), radians (*Rad*), or gradients (*Grad*) by selecting the appropriate option button prior to the calculation:

Table 2 gives the functions of the trigonometric keys. Selecting the *Inv* (Inverse) and/or *Hyp* (Hyperbolic) check boxes prior to clicking on a trig button, modifies its function as described in the table. We will use the following notation with regard to these check boxes:

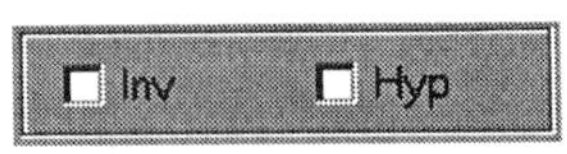

- Inv+*button* (or Hyp+*button*) means select the *Inv* check box (or *Hyp* check box), then click on the indicated button. For example, Inv+cos means select *Inv*, then click on *cos*.
- Inv+Hyp+*button* means select both check boxes, then click on the indicated button. For example, Inv+Hyp+cos means select *Inv*, select *Hyp*, then click on *cos*.

Key	Function
dms	Converts the displayed angle from decimal degree format to degree-minute-second format. Inv+dms does the reverse.
sin	Calculates the sine of the displayed angle. Inv+sin calculates the inverse sine (arcsin) of the displayed number. Hyp+sin and Inv+Hyp+sin calculate the hyperbolic sine (sinh) and its inverse, respectively.
cos	Calculates the cosine of the displayed angle. Inv+cos calculates the inverse cosine (arccos) of the displayed number. Hyp+cos and Inv+Hyp+cos calculate the hyperbolic cosine (cosh) and its inverse, respectively.
tan	Calculates the tangent of the displayed angle. Inv+tan calculates the inverse tangent (arctan) of the displayed number. Hyp+tan and Inv+Hyp+tan calculate the hyperbolic tangent (tanh) and its inverse, respectively.

Table 2 Calculator's Trig-related Functions

Other Scientific Calculator Functions We conclude this section by briefly discussing the other functions provided in scientific mode.

- *F-E* toggles the display between ordinary (floating point) and scientific (exponential) notation.
- *Exp* allows you to enter numbers using scientific notation.
- The keys, *(* and *)*, allow you to insert parentheses into a calculation.
- The keys *ln* and *log* calculate the logarithm (base *e* and 10, respectively) of the displayed number. (Inv+ln and Inv+log calculate e^x and 10^x, respectively, where *x* is the displayed number.)
- The key *n!* calculates the factorial of the displayed integer.
- The key *x^y* calculates the value of *x* raised to the *y* power. (Inv+ x^y calculates the yth root of *x*.)
- The keys *x^2* and *x^3* square and cube, respectively, the displayed number. (Inv+x^2 and Inv+x^3 calculate square and cube roots.)

- *Pi* inserts the value of π into the display.
- *Mod* calculates the remainder in an integer division.
- *Int* displays the integer part of a decimal number. (Inv+Int displays the decimal part.)
- *And*, *Or*, *Xor* (exclusive or), *Lsh* (left shift), and *Not* perform the corresponding logical operations on binary numbers.

9-1 TUTORIAL

Try the following exercise on your own.

1. Turn on the computer (if necessary) to start Windows 95 and display Calculator by clicking on the Calculator item on the Accessories submenu of the Start menu's Programs option.
2. Switch to the Standard calculator (if necessary) by choosing this item from the View menu.
3. Calculate the value of the expression 21(15 - 3.67):
   - Enter 15 into the calculator's display by clicking on the "1" and "5" calculator buttons.
   - Click on the minus (-) button.
   - Enter 3.67 by clicking on the appropriate buttons.
   - Click on the multiply (*) button.
   - Enter 21 by clicking on the appropriate buttons.
   - Click on the equals (=) button. The answer (237.93) will appear in the display.
4. Clear this calculation by clicking on the C (clear) button.
5. Perform the same calculation as in step 3, but this time use the keys on the computer's keyboard. (Hopefully, your answer will be the same as before.)
6. Clear this calculation.
7. Enter the number 2345. Now, click on the Back button to delete the last digit entered (5); then, click on the CE (clear entry) button to clear the resulting number from the display.
8. Determine the reciprocal of the square root of 10, $1/\sqrt{10}$:
   - Enter 10 into the display.
   - Take its square root by clicking on the *sqrt* button.
   - Take the reciprocal of the displayed number by clicking on the *1/x* button. (The answer, 0.316..., will appear in the display.)
9. Use the calculator's memory keys to add the integers from 1 to 5:

- Enter 1 into the display.
- Store the displayed number in memory by clicking on the MS button. (An "M" appears in the box above the memory buttons to indicate that the memory is in use.)
- Enter 2 into the display and add it to the number in memory by clicking on the M+ button.
- Repeat the previous step for the numbers 3, 4, and 5.
- Transfer the number currently in memory (the sum of 1, 2, 3, 4, and 5) to the display by clicking on the MR button.
- Clear the calculator's memory by clicking on the MC button. (The "M" disappears from the box above the memory buttons.)

10. Switch to scientific mode by choosing the Scientific item from the View menu. If you are familiar with the use of a conventional scientific calculator, explore this electronic version by performing various calculations. Remember: To get help with a particular button or feature, right-click on it and choose the *What's This?* item from the pop-up menu.
11. Close Calculator by clicking on its close button.

9.2 *The Notepad Text Editor*

Notepad is a very simple type of word processor called a **text editor** because its capabilities are limited to entering and editing (modifying) text. Unlike more sophisticated word processors, such as WordPad, Notepad cannot *format* text (you have no choice of fonts and no alignment or indentation options) or insert graphics into a document.

Advantages of Notepad

Notepad's major virtue is simplicity; it loads more quickly and takes up less memory than WordPad. Notepad is (arguably) more convenient than WordPad for taking quick notes and editing text files. A **text file**, which is also known as an **ASCII** (pronounced "askey") file, is the simplest and most universal format for storing text. A text file is made up solely of characters you can type on the keyboard; it does not contain any special symbols (such as £ or ©) or formatting codes. Some system files (such as autoexec.bat and config.sys) and program files are stored in ASCII format.

Starting Notepad

To start Notepad:

1. Click on the Start button to open the Start menu.
2. Point at the Start menu's Programs option and then at the Accessories item on the resulting submenu.

3. Click on the Notepad item on the Accessories submenu. Notepad will open and display its window, as shown in Figure 3.

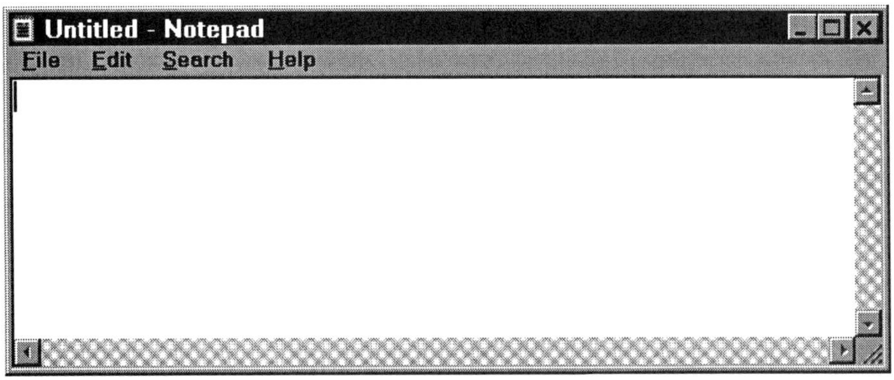

Figure 3 The Notepad Window

Basic Features

At a basic level, Notepad creates, edits, and operates on documents the way you would expect from any Windows-based word processor.

Entering text

You enter text into a Notepad document in the same general way as you would in WordPad — just type, and the words appear on the screen. However, when you start Notepad, **word wrap** is turned off, which means that the text you type continues on the same line until you press the Enter key. If you turn word wrap on (by choosing this item from the Edit menu), text will wrap to the beginning of the next line when it reaches the right edge of the Notepad window.

One of the Notepad's few frills gives you the ability to enter the current time and date into a document. To insert this text at the insertion point, choose the Time/Date command from the Edit menu or just press the F5 function key. (Unlike WordPad, you cannot select the format in which the time and date will be displayed.)

Editing text

Simple editing is done in much the same way as with WordPad; the Backspace and Delete keys work in exactly the same way, as does the Undo command on the Edit menu (see Section 2.2). Moreover, text is selected, cut or copied to the Clipboard, and pasted from the Clipboard in the usual Windows-compliant way (see Section 2.3). Notepad also supplies a quick way to select all the text in a document; just choose the Select All command from the Edit menu. (However, Notepad lacks the other, more sophisticated ways of selecting text that are available in WordPad, which were described in Section 7.1.)

Standard File menu commands

The New, Open, Save, Save As, Print and Exit commands on Notepad's File menu work in the same way as in most Windows applications (see Section 2.2) with one major exception: When you issue the Print command, printing begins immediately; the Print dialog box does not appear. As a result, you do not have access to some of the usual print features, such as specifying a range of pages to be printed.

Beyond the Basics

Notepad does provide two relatively advanced features: It can locate any specified piece of text within a document and has page layout options to enhance the look of the printed page.

Searching for Text One of Notepad's most useful features when editing a long or complicated document is its ability to search for a specified word or other sequence of characters. To search a Notepad document:

1. Choose the Find command from the Search menu. The Find dialog box (Figure 4) will open.

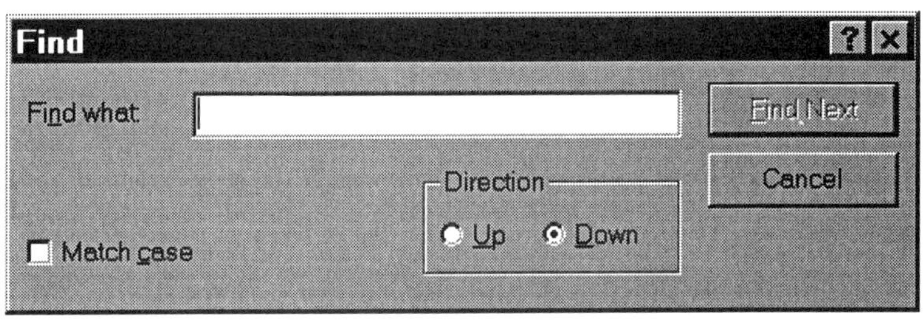

Figure 4 The Find Dialog Box

2. Type the text you are seeking in the *Find what* box. Notepad will search for this sequence of characters, whether or not it is part of a word, an entire word, or spans more than one word. For example, if you enter the win in the *Find what* box, Notepad may locate "the winner" or "the window", but not "a window".
3. Select the *Match case* check box if you want to search for text that

has the same combination of upper and lower case letters as that entered in the *Find what* box. For example, if you leave this box *de*selected and search for able, then "able", "Able", and "ABLE" will be located (if they appear in the document); if the box is selected, then only "able" will be located.

4. The search commences at the insertion point. Select the *Down* option button if you want the search to proceed forward through the document; select the *Up* button to proceed backward.
5. Choose the Find Now command button. Notepad will locate and highlight the next occurrence (in the specified direction) of the *Find what* text. If this text is not found, a message to this effect will be displayed.

TIP

You can use Find to locate the last text entered in the *Find what* box even if the Find dialog box is no longer on the screen. To do so, choose the Find Next command from the Search menu or press the F3 function key.

Setting Up the Page Although Notepad provides no choice of fonts, alignment, or indentation, it does allow you to specify certain page layout options prior to printing. These features are accessed from the Page Setup dialog box (Figure 5), which is opened by choosing the Page Setup command from the File menu.

In the Page Setup dialog box:

- You can specify the size of the paper on which you will be printing by selecting the appropriate item on the Paper Size drop-down list. (When you select a new size, the "page" shown in the Preview area will reflect the change.)
- You can specify the printer bin from which the blank paper will be fed by selecting an item from the Paper Source drop-down list.
- You can choose to print your document in either portrait or landscape orientation. In *portrait orientation*, the document's text is printed parallel to the short side of the paper; in *landscape orientation*, the text is printed parallel to its long side. The figures at the right illustrate this concept.

  To specify page orientation, select the Portrait or Landscape option button. The "page" shown in the Preview area will appear in the selected orientation.

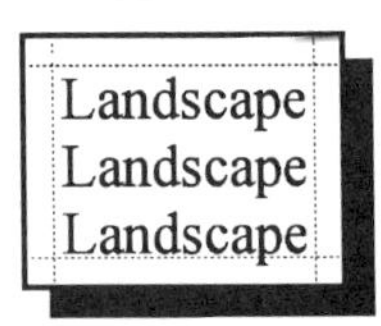

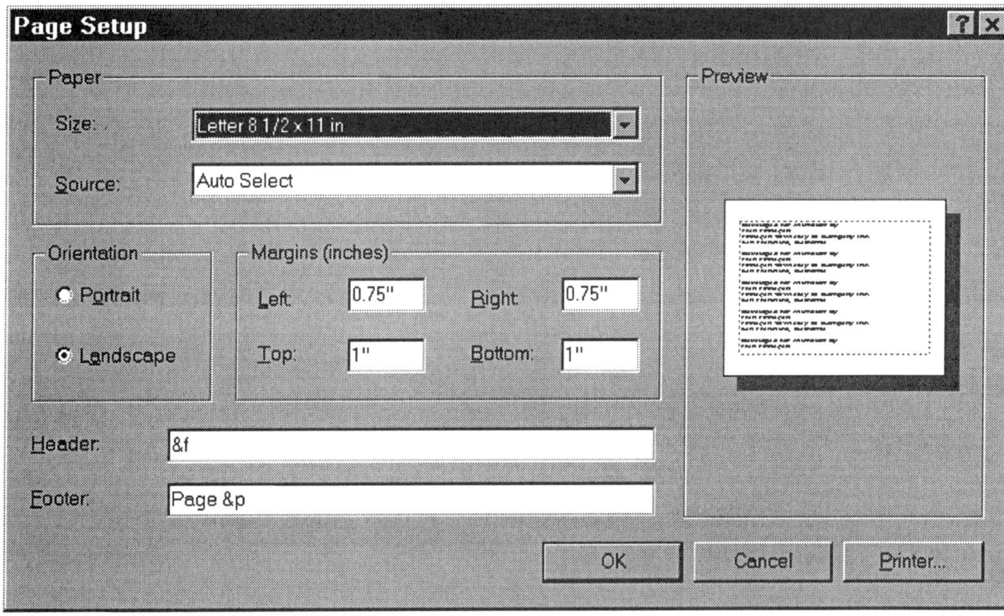

Figure 5 Notepad's Page Setup Dialog Box

- You can change the margins for the current document by entering the desired margins in the Left, Right, Top, and Bottom text boxes. (The "page" shown in the Preview area will indicate the new margins.)
- You can create headers and footers for the document. A **header** is text that is automatically placed in the top margin of every page of a document. Similarly, a **footer** appears in the bottom margin of every page. To create a header or footer for the current document, enter text in the Header or Footer boxes. The text is printed as entered except for letters that are preceded by an ampersand (&) symbol. These codes have the following meaning:

&c	centers the text that follows this code
&d	inserts the current date
&f	inserts the document's file name
&l	aligns the text that follows with the left margin
&p	inserts the current page number
&r	aligns the text that follows with the right margin
&t	inserts the current time

  If no alignment code is present, the header or footer text is centered on the line. Thus, in Figure 5: the text in the Header box (&f) will cause the document's file name to be printed at the top center of every page; the Footer text will print the current page number, preceded by the word Page and a blank space, at the bottom center of each page. As another example, the Header text &l&p&cWindows 95&r&d produces a header (when the document is printed) like the following one:

```
1                    Windows 95                    1\7\96
```

9.2 TUTORIAL

Try the following exercise on your own.

1. Turn on the computer (if necessary) to start Windows 95 and open Notepad by clicking on the Notepad item on the Accessories submenu of the Start menu's Programs option.
2. Insert the Student Disk in its drive and open the `History2` document on this diskette. (See Section 2.2 for more information about opening a document.)
3. Maximize the Notepad window.
4. Use Notepad's Find utility to search for all occurrences of the word *computer* in the History2 document:
   - Choose the Find command from the Search menu to open the Find dialog box.
   - Type the word *computer* in the *Find what* box, deselect the *Match case* check box (so that capitalized spellings of *computer* will be found), and select the *Down* option button (so that the search, which begins at the insertion point, will proceed in a forward direction).
   - Choose the Find Next command button. The first occurrence of *computer* will be located and highlighted.
   - Continue to search for additional occurrences of *computer* by repeatedly choosing the Find Next button. When the last occurrence is found, close the resulting message box and choose the Cancel command button to close the dialog box.
5. Prepare the document for printing:
   - Choose the Page Setup command from the File menu to open the corresponding dialog box.
   - Select (if necessary) "Letter 8 1/2 × 11 in" from the Paper Size drop-down list and the Portrait option button.
   - Set the page margins to 1" left and right and 1.5" top and bottom by entering these numbers in the corresponding text boxes. (Notice how the "page" in the Preview area reflects these changes.)
   - Place the following text and codes in the Header and Footer boxes so that the indicated text will appear at the top and

bottom, respectively, of each page of the printed document (a list of the available codes precedes this tutorial):

Header: `&lHistory &r&d`

(The word "History" aligned with the left margin; the current date aligned right.)

Footer: `&c&p`

(The current page number, centered.)

- Choose the OK command button.

6. Print the revised document by choosing the Print command from the File menu.
7. Exit Notepad and remove the diskette from its drive.

9.3 Backing Up Your Hard Disk

To **back up** a file on your hard disk simply means to copy it to another medium; for example, a floppy disk or tape. You should back up your newly created or just-modified data files at the end of every session at the computer. Then, if a file becomes inaccessible or you accidentally erase it at some time in the future, you can easily copy that file from your backup to the hard disk, instead of having to recreate it from scratch.

In addition to daily backups of individual files, many users also make more extensive backups, of key folders or even the entire disk, every once in a while. Then, should a major disaster occur and your hard disk (or a large part of it) become inaccessible, you can recreate its contents after it has been repaired or replaced.

Starting the Backup Utility

Simple backups can be made using the Copy or Send To commands in Explorer or My Computer (see Chapter 3). For more extensive backups, Windows supplies the **Backup utility**. To start Backup:

1. Click on the Start button to display the Start menu.
2. Point at Programs, then at Accessories, and finally at System Tools on each resulting submenu.
3. Click on Backup on the System Tools submenu, which starts the Backup utility and displays the window shown in Figure 6, on the next page. (You may first see one or two informational dialog

boxes. If one of them appears, choose its OK command button to clear it from the screen.)

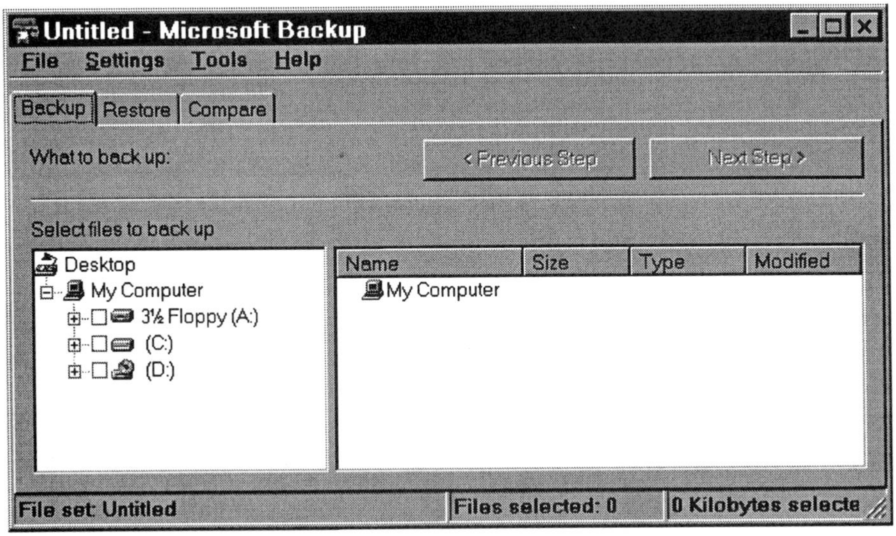

Figure 6 The Main Backup Window

The three tabs in the Backup window correspond to the three main functions of this utility:

- The Backup page allows you to back up the desired files.
- The Restore page enables you to copy files from the backup media (floppies or tapes) to their original location, when needed.
- The Compare page allows you to compare the original files with their backups.

The Backup Procedure

The basic backup procedure consists of three steps:

1. Select the files to be backed up.
2. Select a destination to which they will be backed up.
3. Start the copying process.

Carrying out these steps is easy if you're familiar with Explorer's way of navigating the Windows folder system (see Section 3.2). Here's a more detailed description of the backup process:

1. Start the Backup utility, as described above.
2. If you want to back up an entire folder, click on the little box to the left of the folder's icon. A check mark will be displayed indicating that this folder is selected. If you want to back up specific files in a given folder, open that folder (by clicking on its icon) and click on the boxes next to the desired files. (In either case, you may have to scroll and/or expand the folder tree in the left pane, just as you would in Explorer.)

   Figure 7 shows the result of clicking on the box to the left of the "Chap-2" icon in the folder tree. All files in the contents (right) pane were automatically selected when this was done. The shaded, checked box next to the parent folder (Win95Txt) indicates that part, but not all, of this folder has been selected. Notice that the status bar indicates the number of files that have been selected and the total number of kilobytes they contain.

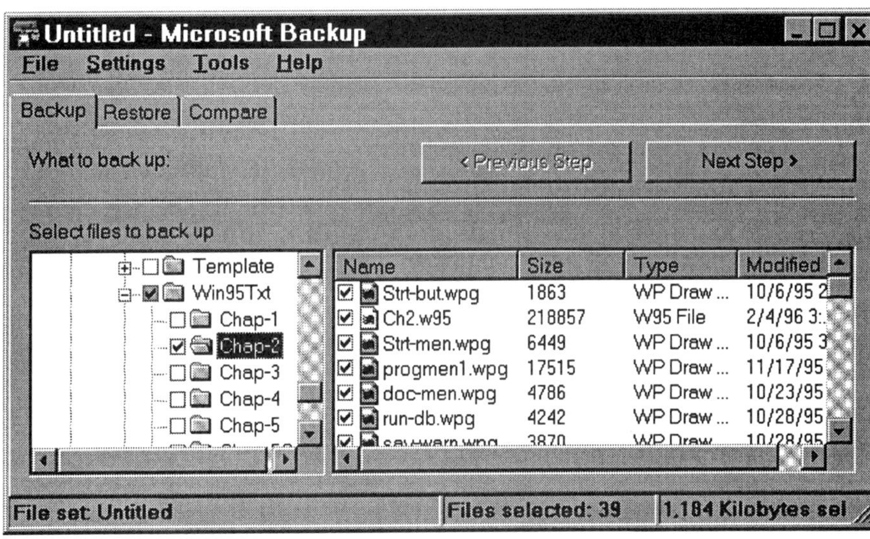

Figure 7 Selecting the "Chap-2" Folder in Backup

3. Click on the Next Step command button. The Backup window will take on the look shown in Figure 8, on the next page.
4. Select the destination to which the files are to be copied in the folder tree by clicking on the desired drive or folder name. It will become highlighted. In Figure 8, the selected destination is the disk in the 3½" floppy drive.

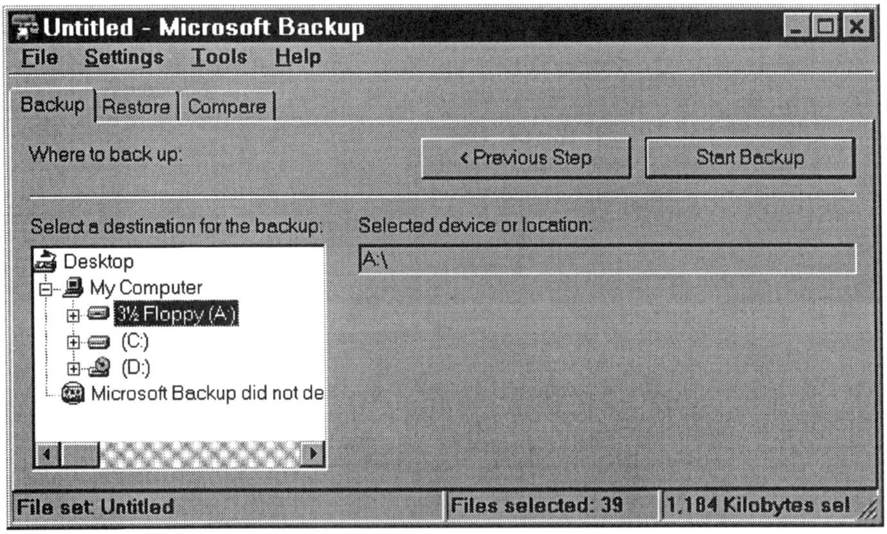

Figure 8 Selecting a Destination for the Backup

5. Insert a diskette or tape cartridge in the appropriate drive.
6. Now choose the Start Backup command button. The Backup Set Label dialog box will open:

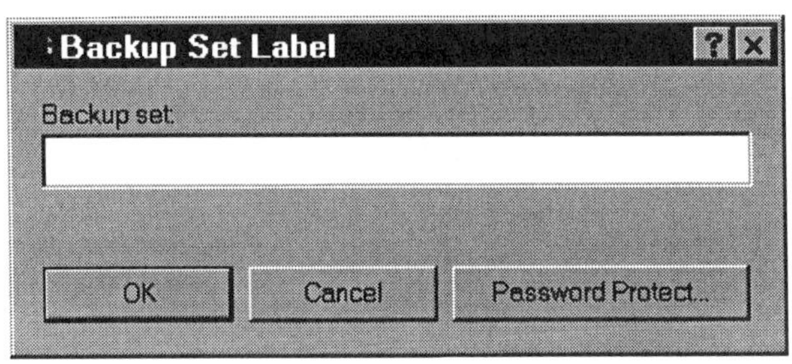

7. In the *Backup set* text box, type a name for the set of files you are backing up. Choose a meaningful name. For example, for the collection of files shown selected in Figure 7, the name "Chapter 2 of Win95 Text" would be appropriate. You should use the same name when you write a label on the actual disks or tape used in the backup.
8. Choose the OK command button and the copying process will begin. The animated Backup dialog box will show the progress of the backup. If a destination diskette becomes full, you will be prompted to insert another one. When the backup process is

complete, a message to this effect will appear on the screen.

NOTE

If you are backing up particularly important files and you want to be sure that the backups exactly match the originals, you can compare the two. To do so:

1. Click on the Compare tab in the Backup window.
2. Insert the disk or tape in its drive that contains the file set you want to compare.
3. Select that drive in the *Compare from* folder tree.
4. Select the backup set you want to compare in the right pane of the window and choose the Next Step command button.
5. In the *Select files* folder tree, select (by clicking on the appropriate boxes) the (original) files and folders you want to compare.
6. Choose the Start Compare command button. The animated Compare dialog box will indicate the progress of the operation. When the process is complete, a message to this effect will be displayed.

TIP

If you intend to back up the same files or folders in the future, you can save the *file set* — the set of selected objects together with the destination folder. To do so, after your selections have been made, choose Save As from the File menu. A Save As dialog box will open (see Section 2.2), allowing you to save the file set. Then, whenever you want to back up that set of files, start Backup, choose the Open File Set command from the File menu, and select the appropriate file set from the resulting Open dialog box.

To further simplify the process, you can place a shortcut to the saved file set on the Desktop, as described in Section 3.4. Then, double-clicking on this shortcut icon will start Backup, make the specified selections, and begin the copying process!

Restoring Backed Up Files

Backups are worth their weight in gold when something goes wrong and the original files become unusable. In such a case, it is an easy matter to *restore* the backups — copy them to their original locations. Here's how the process works:

1. Start Backup, as described earlier in this section, and click on the Restore tab. The resulting page of the Backup dialog box is shown in Figure 9.

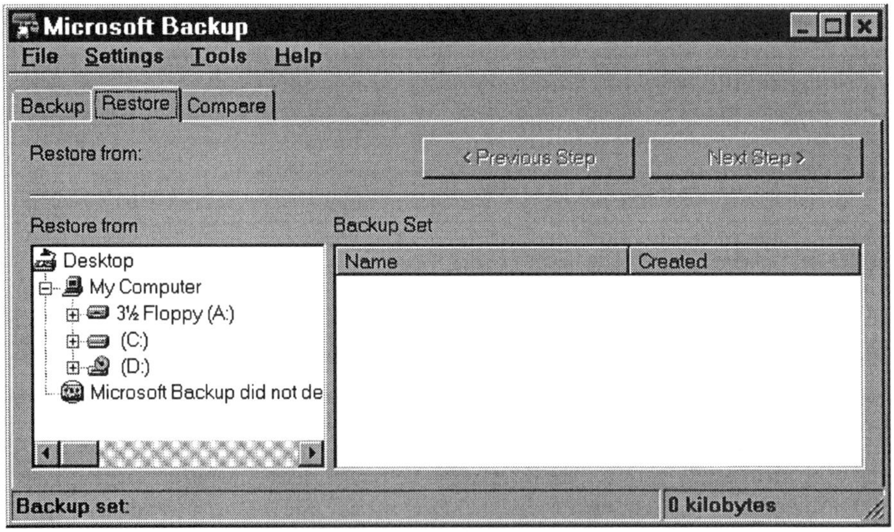

Figure 9 The Restore Page of the Backup Window

2. Insert the appropriate backup diskette or tape cartridge in its drive. (This is the point at which careful labeling pays off!)
3. Select this drive in the *Restore from* folder tree. The names of the backup sets on the disk or tape in this drive will appear in the right pane.
4. Select the desired backup set from the right pane.
5. Choose the Next Step command button.
6. Select the files and/or folders to be restored (by clicking on the corresponding boxes).
7. Choose the Start Restore command button, and the copying process will begin. The animated Restore dialog box will appear, indicating the progress of the operation. When the process is complete, a message to this effect will be displayed.

Some Options for the Backup Process

The Backup utility offers quite a few options for the way the backup, restore, and compare processes are carried out. These options are selected by choosing the Options command from the Settings menu. The dialog box that results has four tabs — one for general options and one for each of the three processes. We will only discuss the

Backup options page here. It is shown in Figure 10.

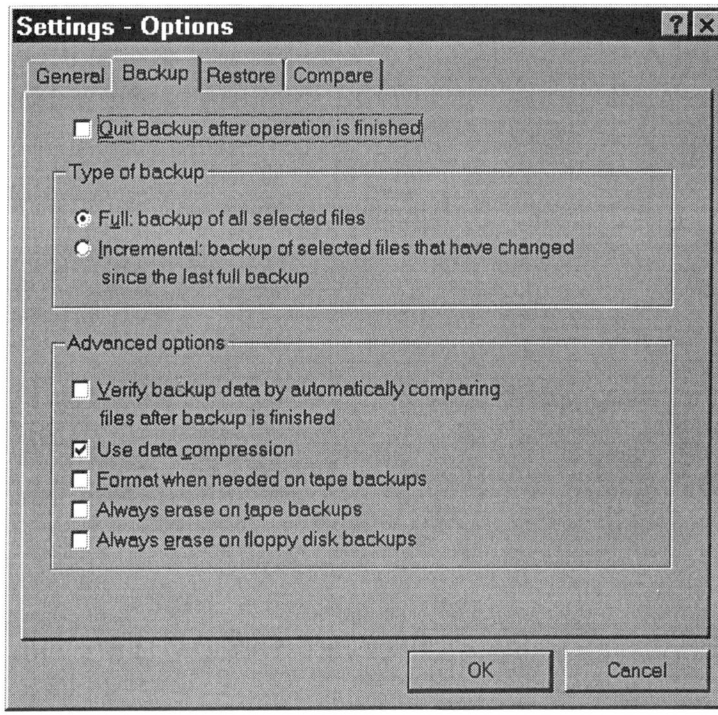

Figure 10 The Backup Page of the Options Dialog Box

- Select the *Quit Backup after operation is finished* check box at the top of the dialog box if you want the Backup utility to close when the current operation is complete.
- An *incremental backup* copies only those selected files that have been modified since the last backup. Thus, selecting this *Type of backup* option button may save time if the current file set has been backed up before.
- In the *Advanced options* section of the dialog box:

  Selecting *Verify backup data by automatically comparing files after backup is finished* does just that.

  Use data compression works with tapes only; when selected, this feature reduces the space used by the backed up files.

  Selecting *Format when needed on tape backups* will automatically format unformatted tapes before backup begins.

Selecting *Always erase on tape backups* erases the tape in the drive before backup begins. If not selected, the new files are added to those already on the tape.

Selecting *Always erase on floppy disk backups* erases the diskette in the drive before backup begins. If not selected, the new files are added to those already on the disk.

9-3 TUTORIAL

Try the following exercise on your own.

1. Turn on the computer (if necessary) to start Windows 95 and open the Backup utility: Click on the Start button, successively point at Programs, Accessories, and System Tools, and finally click on the Backup item on the last submenu.
2. Place a formatted diskette in its drive.
3. Select files to be backed up:
   - In the *Select files to back up* subwindow, open the Programs subfolder of the Start Menu folder: Successively click on the plus (+) symbols next to the C:, Windows, and Start Menu icons; then click on the Programs icon.
   - In the right-hand window, select the Accessories subfolder and the Windows Explorer and MS-DOS Prompt shortcuts by clicking on the box to the left of these icons.
4. Select a destination for the backup:
   - Choose the Next Step command button.
   - In the window, click on the icon for the floppy drive in which you inserted the diskette.
5. Start the backup:
   - Choose the Start Backup command button. The Backup Set Label dialog box will open.
   - Type a name for the set of backup files, say "My Backup", and choose the OK command button. The animated Backup dialog box will show the progress of the backup operation.
6. Complete the operation by clicking on the OK buttons to clear the "operation complete" and Backup dialog boxes from the screen.
7. Restore the backed up files to their original locations (which could be necessary if the originals became unusable):
   - Click on the Restore tab in the Backup window.
   - Select the floppy drive in the *Restore from* subwindow and the My Backup item in the *Backup Set* subwindow.
   - Choose the Next Step command button. The right-hand

window will display the contents of the My Backup set.

- Select (by clicking on the check box) all the listed items.

8. At this point, you would normally choose the Start Restore command button to begin the restoration. Here, however, close the Backup window and remove the diskette from its drive.

9.4 *Using Other System Tools*

In this section, we will discuss several accessories that help you to maintain and make more efficient use of your disks. Like Backup (which was introduced in Section 9.3), these utilities are located on the System Tools submenu of the Start button's Accessories menu. We will discuss:

- *ScanDisk*, which finds and repairs (when possible) certain disk problems.
- *Disk Defragmenter*, which rearranges the data on a disk so that its files occupy contiguous sectors.
- *DriveSpace*, which compresses the data stored in files so that they occupy less space on the disk.

ScanDisk

Considering their complexity, disk drives and disk drive controllers are amazingly reliable devices. Nevertheless, every once in a while, data are not stored properly and, as a result, become unusable or needlessly take up disk space. You should periodically use the **ScanDisk** accessory to detect and repair these problems.

Running ScanDisk To have ScanDisk check one of your disks:

1. Click on the Start button to display the Start menu.
2. Point at Programs, then at Accessories, and finally at System Tools on each resulting submenu.
3. Click on the ScanDisk item on the System Tools submenu. This utility will start and display the window shown in Figure 11, on the next page.
4. In the ScanDisk window, select the drive you want to check for errors.

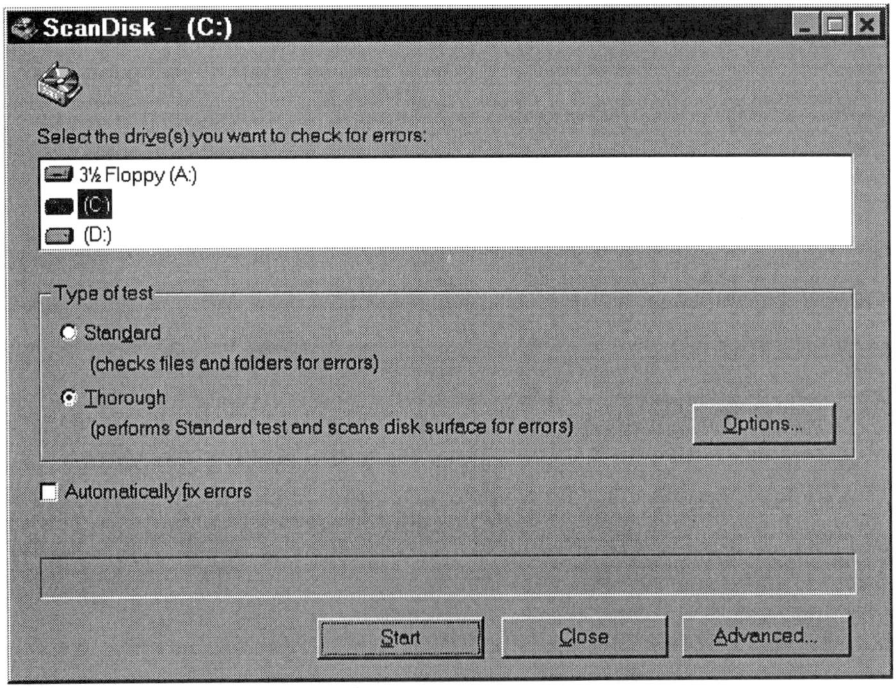

Figure 11 The ScanDisk Window

5. Select either the *Standard* or the *Thorough* option button. The Standard option checks for errors in the way files and folders have been stored on disk. The Thorough option not only runs these tests, but also checks the physical integrity of the selected disk. The Thorough option takes *much* longer and, as a practical matter, need not be run as frequently as the Standard one.
6. If you select the *Automatically fix errors* check box, ScanDisk will not only detect and report any errors, but also attempt to repair them. It is safer to deselect this box. You can always have ScanDisk try to fix the reported errors later.
7. You can select additional options for the ScanDisk run by choosing the Advanced button (for both Standard and Thorough test modes) and the Options button (which is available only if the Thorough mode is selected). There is normally little reason to change most of these options, and we will discuss them later.
8. Choose the Start command button to activate ScanDisk. The progress of the testing process will be indicated at the bottom of the ScanDisk window. (You can abort the process at any time by choosing the Cancel button.) When testing is complete, a message

to this effect or a report summarizing ScanDisk's findings will be displayed.

9. Choose the Close command button to exit ScanDisk.

ScanDisk Options As we mentioned earlier, you can select options for ScanDisk testing by choosing either the Advanced or Options (in Thorough test mode only) command buttons. You should be aware that the defaults chosen for these options tend to emphasize safety over speed; think twice before changing them.

Choosing the Advanced button

When you choose the Advanced command button in the ScanDisk window, the dialog box shown in Figure 12 is displayed.

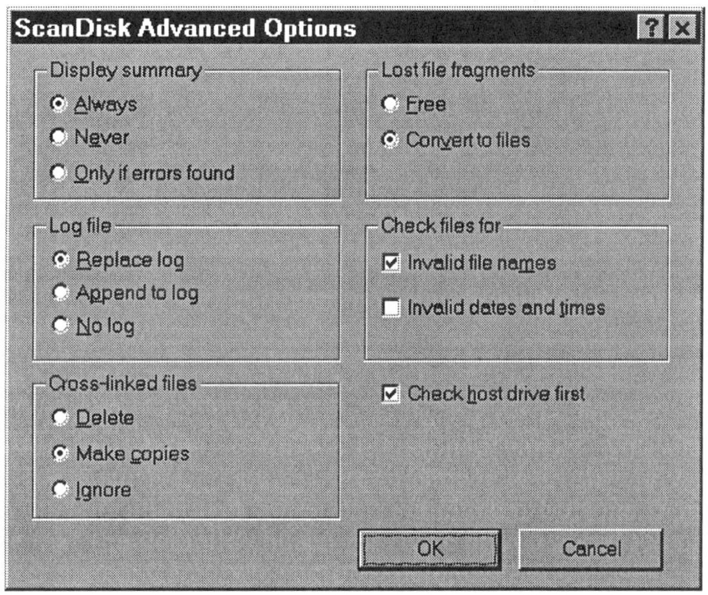

Figure 12 "Advanced" ScanDisk Options

Here's a description of some of these options:

- The *Log file* option buttons determine whether or not a report of the testing is stored on disk (in the Scandisk log file in the C:\ folder) and, if it is, whether it replaces or is appended (added) to the existing file.
- *Cross-linked files* are files that, according to the disk's file allocation table, share the same disk space. If you try to read a cross-linked file, you may be denied access or see "garbage" displayed

on the screen. Although cross-linked files can rarely be fixed without losing some data, ScanDisk gives you several options for dealing with them. *Delete* erases the cross-linked files; *Make copies* copies each cross-linked file to a new location (the "safe" alternative), and *Ignore* leaves the problem unfixed. (The last option is actually the best one *if* you have other, more advanced disk-repair software with which to attack this problem.)

- *Lost file fragments* (or *lost clusters*) are parts of the disk that, according to the disk's file allocation table, contain data which does not belong to any file. The *Free* option deletes these files; the *Convert to files* option is almost always the better choice — you can then try to view the resulting files (which are named File0000, File0001, etc.) to see if they contain useful information.

Choosing the Options button

The Options button in the ScanDisk window provides options for thorough testing only. Choosing this command button displays the dialog box shown in Figure 13.

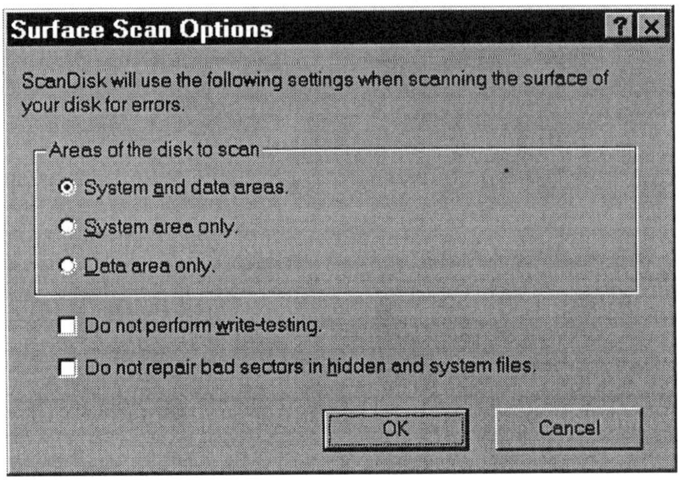

Figure 13 Options for Thorough Testing

Here's a description of these options. (The defaults are set for the most thorough, and most time-consuming, disk testing.)

- *Areas of the disk to scan:* In this context, the disk is divided into two parts — the system area (consisting of operating system files that control startup, file allocation, and the like) and the data area (everything else). Be aware that disk surface errors in the system area can rarely be fixed (at least by ScanDisk).

- By default, ScanDisk tests the surface of a disk by both reading from and writing to every disk location. If you want to speed up the testing process, using a less rigorous test, select the *Do not perform write-testing* check box.
- Hidden and system files are usually used for special purposes. Although it may be possible to move such a file to a new location if the disk area in which it is stored has become damaged, the file may not work in the new location. So, unless you observe problems in running Windows or an application that seem to be related to the file in question, it may be best to select the *Do not repair bad sectors in hidden and system files* check box.

Disk Defragmenter

When a file is stored on disk, Windows writes it to the first available location. If that area is not big enough to hold the entire file, the file becomes *fragmented* — parts of it are stored in noncontiguous locations. This occurs often and isn't as bad as it sounds. You won't have any trouble accessing the file (the operating system keeps track of where the various parts are stored); it may just take slightly longer to read the file into RAM.

However, if a disk has become highly fragmented, its performance may suffer. The **Disk Defragmenter** accessory tells you the degree to which a disk has become fragmented and, if you wish, you can use this utility to **defragment** the disk — rearrange its files so that each is stored as a single contiguous unit.

Running Disk Defragmenter To start the defragmenting process:

1. Click on the Start button to display the Start menu.
2. Point at Programs, then at Accessories, and finally at System Tools on each resulting submenu.
3. Click on the Disk Defragmenter item on the System Tools submenu. This action starts the utility and displays the small window shown in Figure 14, on the next page.
4. Select the drive to be analyzed for fragmentation (and possibly, to be defragmented) from the drop-down list and choose the OK command button.
5. Disk Defragmenter will determine the degree of fragmentation of the selected drive and display it (as a percentage) in another

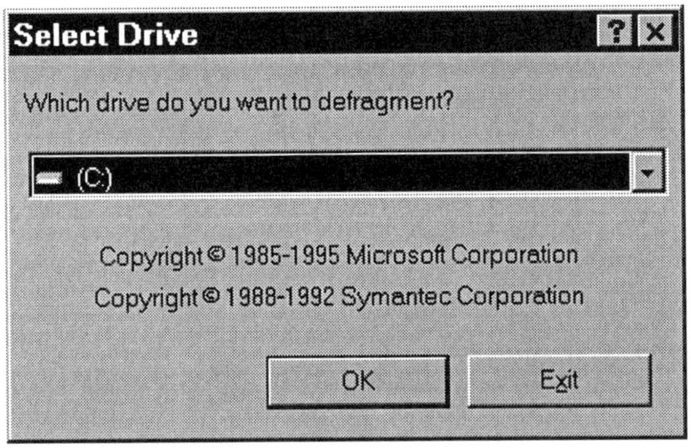

Figure 14 Initial Disk Defragmenter Window

window (Figure 15). It also makes a recommendation concerning whether or not defragmentation is desirable.

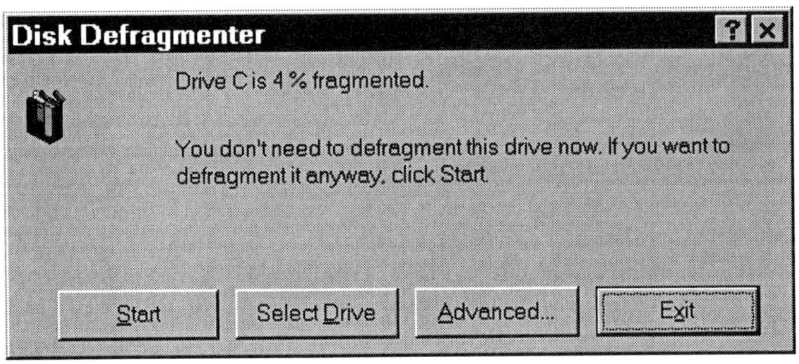

Figure 15 Assessing the Amount of Fragmentation

6. You now have four choices, as provided by the command buttons:
   - To close the Disk Defragmenter utility, chose *Exit.*
   - To select another drive for analysis and possible defragmentation, choose *Select Drive.* You will be returned to the dialog box of Figure 14.
   - To select certain defragmentation options, choose *Advanced.* We will discuss these options later in this section.
   - To begin the defragmentation process, choose *Start.* The following dialog box, which shows the progress of the defrag-

mentation, will be displayed:

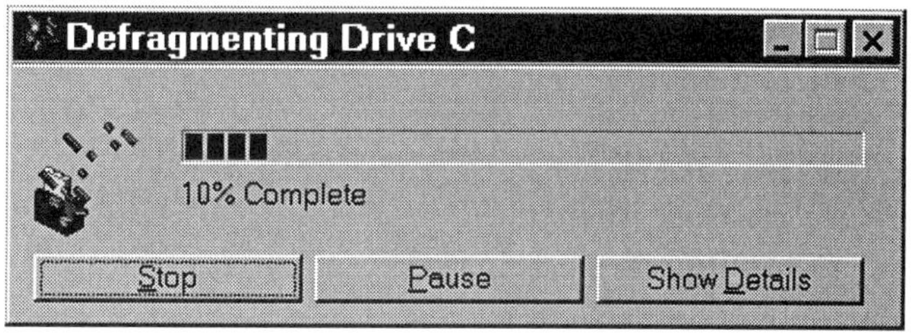

To halt the process at any time, choose the Stop button; to halt it temporarily, choose the Pause button. (The Show Details command button opens another dialog box that provides a graphical display of the defragmentation process.)

Disk Defragmenter Options Prior to beginning the defragmentation process, you can select options by choosing the Advanced command button (see Figure 15), which opens the dialog box shown in Figure 16. The default settings (which are shown in Figure 16) provide the most thorough (and most lengthy) defragmentation. Here is a rundown of the available options:

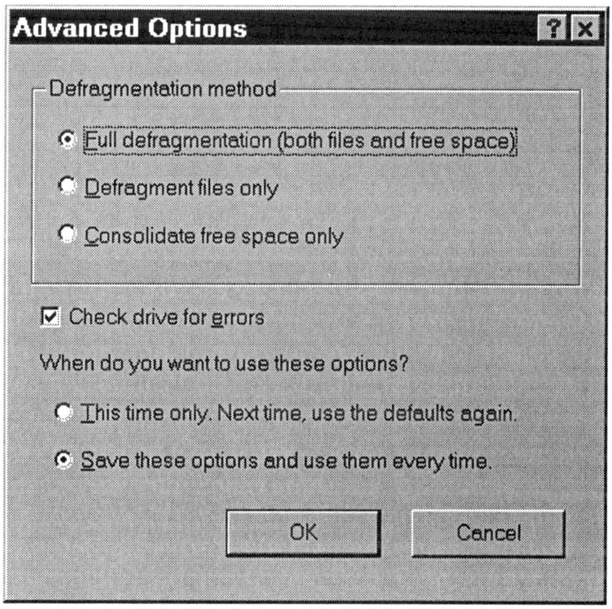

Figure 16 Defragmentation Options

- The first set of option buttons in the Advanced Options dialog box determines the extent of the defragmentation to be undertaken (and the amount of time it will take to complete the process). The top option does the most thorough job; *Defragment files only* consolidates each fragmented file into a single contiguous unit, but leaves existing free disk space spread across the disk; *Consolidate free space only* makes a single contiguous unit of your disk's free space but does not defragment files.
- Selecting the *Check drive for errors* box is equivalent to running ScanDisk's "Standard" test option prior to defragmentation. It takes extra time, but is a good idea unless you have just run ScanDisk.
- The last pair of option buttons determine whether or not the current settings will be used for just this run of Disk Defragmenter (the upper button) or will become the new default settings for future runs (the lower button).

DriveSpace

Modern hard disks have seemingly limitless capacities, at least when they're new. However, if you use audio, video, or complex graphics files, even the largest of disks will eventually fill up. At this point, you could buy a larger hard disk, but it's easier to increase the storage capacity of the existing one by **compressing** it — encoding the files on the disk in such a way that they take up much less space.

The **DriveSpace** accessory compresses and "uncompresses" both hard and floppy disks. It does this by creating a single large file on the disk to hold all the compressed files. The original disk that contains this *compressed volume* is called the *host drive*. When a file is written to a compressed disk, it is automatically compressed; when a file is read from a compressed volume, it is automatically decompressed. To the user performing a read or write operation, a compressed disk is indistinguishable from an uncompressed one.

WARNING

It takes a long time — often several hours — to compress a disk, especially if it already contains a lot of files. First, DriveSpace checks the disk for errors and defragments it (the compressed volume must occupy a single unbroken unit of disk apace). Then, an empty compressed volume is created. Finally, DriveSpace copies each file to this area, compressing it in the process and erasing it from its original location.

The compression process usually goes through without a hitch.

Nevertheless, with an operation of this scope and complexity, something may go wrong. To avoid the potential loss of valuable data, it's a very good idea to back up the entire disk (see Section 9.3) before proceeding.

Running DriveSpace To use DriveSpace to compress a disk:

1. Click on the Start button to display the Start menu.
2. Point at Programs, then at Accessories, and finally at System Tools on each resulting submenu.
3. Click on the DriveSpace item on the System Tools submenu. This action starts the utility and displays the window shown in Figure 17.

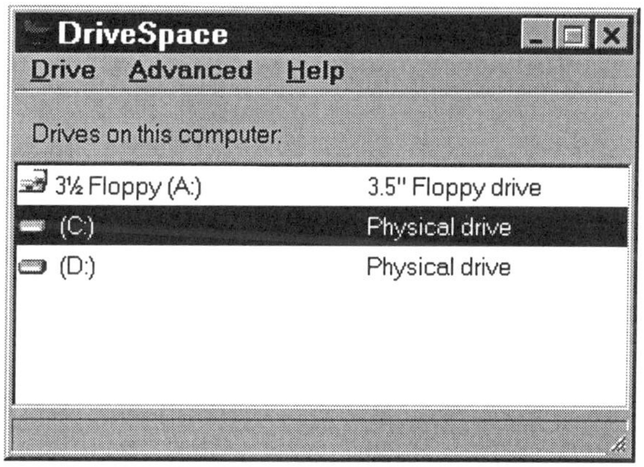

Figure 17 The DriveSpace Window

4. Select the drive to be compressed.
5. Choose the Compress command on the Drive menu. The Compress a Drive dialog box shown in Figure 18 (on the next page) will open.
6. Choose the Start command button. A dialog box will appear giving you the opportunity to back up your files. If you have not yet backed them up, do so now!
7. Chose the Compress Now command button to begin the compression process. A dialog box will open, showing the progress of the this procedure.

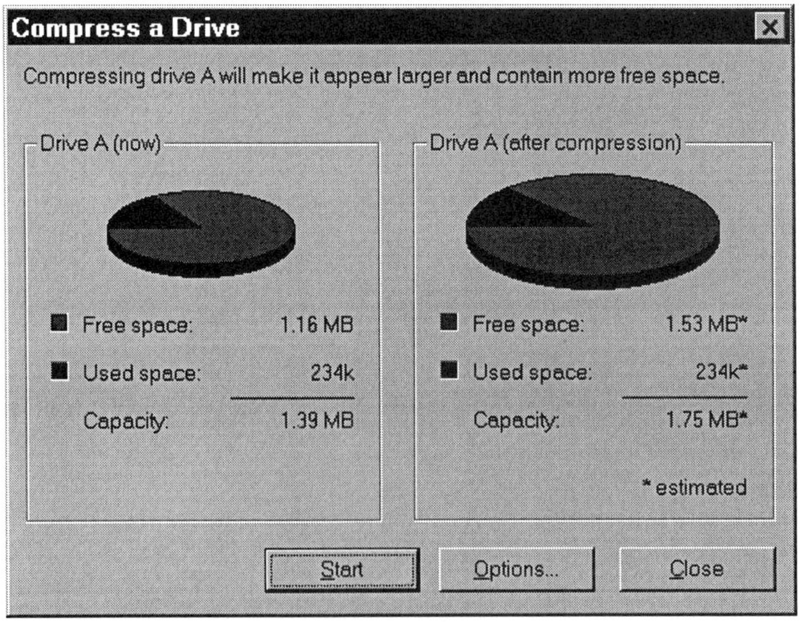

Figure 18 Compressing a Drive Begins Here

8. At the completion of the process, you may be prompted to restart Windows or you may have to close the Compress a Drive dialog box and the DriveSpace window.

NOTE

The compressed volume takes on the drive letter of the original drive and the host drive is assigned a new letter, such as H. By default, the entire disk is compressed, so that no "free" (uncompressed) space remains on the host drive. However, it is sometimes desirable to leave free space on a hard disk to store, for example, important disk utilities should something go wrong with that disk.

Prior to compression, you can specify the amount of "free" space on the compressed drive by choosing the Options command button in the Compress a Drive dialog box. After compression, you can accomplish this by selecting the drive in the DriveSpace window and choosing the Adjust Free Space command from the Drive menu.

Uncompressing a Disk If you want to, you can *uncompress* a compressed drive — decompress all files on it and delete the compressed volume. To do so:

1. Start DriveSpace, as described earlier. The DriveSpace window

(Figure 17) will be displayed.

2. Choose the Uncompress command from the Drive menu. The Uncompress a Drive dialog box (which is similar to the one in Figure 18) will open.
3. Choose the Start command button. The resulting dialog box will give you the opportunity to back up your files. If you have not done this already, do it now!
4. Choose the Uncompress Now command button to begin the process. Another dialog box will appear, showing the progress of the operation.
5. When the operation is complete, close the Uncompress a Drive dialog box and the DriveSpace window.

9-4 TUTORIAL

Try the following exercise on your own.

1. Insert the Student Disk in its drive.
2. Check the floppy disk for errors:
   - Start the ScanDisk utility from the System Tools submenu of the Start button's Accessories menu.
   - Select the relevant floppy drive in the ScanDisk window.
   - Select the Standard option button (which checks the disk for file and folder errors, but not for physical flaws). Leave all options (available from the Advanced command button) at their defaults.
   - Choose the Start command button.
   - When testing is complete, close the Summary window and the ScanDisk window.
3. Defragment the floppy disk:
   - Start the Disk Defragmenter utility from the System Tools submenu of the Start button's Accessories menu.
   - Select the relevant floppy drive from the Select Drive drop-down list and choose the OK command button.
   - In the Disk Defragmenter window, choose the Advanced (options) command button; then, select the *Full defragmentation* option button, deselect the *Check drive for errors* check box (because you have just used ScanDisk to do this), select the *This time only* option button, and choose the OK command button.
   - In the Disk Defragmenter window, choose the Start button.
   - When the defragmentation starts, choose the Show Details command button and then the Legend button to obtain a

graphical view of what is going on.
- When defragmentation is complete, choose the Yes command button in the message box to close Disk Defragmenter.

4. Compress the files on the floppy disk:
    - Start the DriveSpace utility from the System Tools submenu of the Start button's Accessories menu.
    - Select the relevant floppy drive in the DriveSpace window.
    - Choose the Compress command from the Drive menu.
    - Choose the Start command button in the Compress a Drive dialog box and then the Compress Now button in the resulting dialog box.
    - When the process is complete, close the Compress a Drive dialog box.
5. Uncompress the floppy disk:
    - Select the relevant floppy drive in the DriveSpace window.
    - Choose the Uncompress command from the Drive menu.
    - Choose the Start command button in the Uncompress a Drive dialog box and then the Uncompress Now button in the resulting dialog box. (If the Remove Compression dialog box appears, choose the Yes button.)
    - When the process is complete, close the Uncompress a Drive dialog box and the DriveSpace window.
6. Remove the diskette from its drive.

9.5 *Additional Accessories*

In this section, we will briefly discuss a few other Windows accessories: Character Map, and some multimedia and communications utilities.

Character Map

Character Map lets you insert special symbols into a document open in another Windows application. To use Character Map:

1. Click on the Start button, point at Programs, then at Accessories, and choose the Character Map item from the resulting submenu. The window shown in Figure 19 will open.

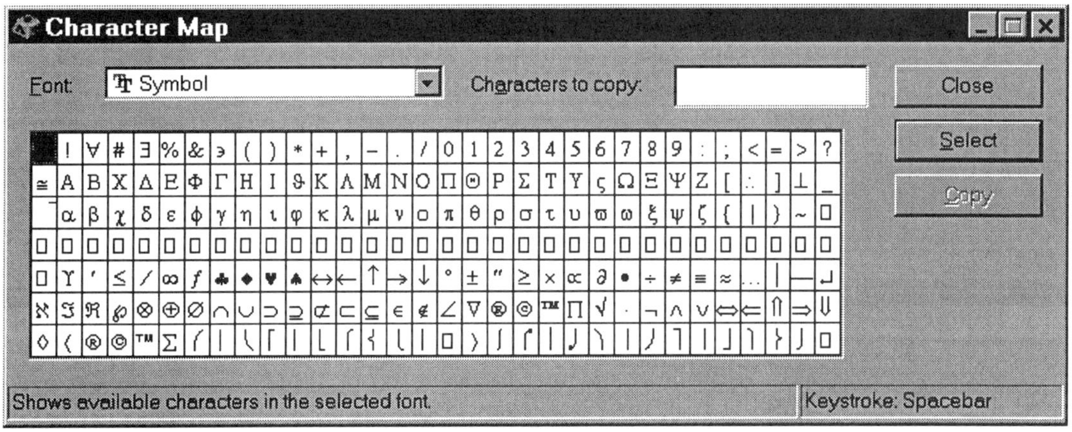

Figure 19 The Character Map Window

2. Select a typeface from the Font drop-down list. The *character set* for the selected font will be displayed in the window.
3. Select a character from those displayed by double-clicking on it (or by clicking on it and choosing the Select command button). The selected character will appear in the Characters to copy box.
4. If you want, repeat step 3 to select additional characters.
5. Choose the Copy command button to copy the selected characters to the Clipboard.
6. Switch to the application and document in which you want to insert the characters.
7. In this document, position the insertion point where you want the characters to be inserted, select the same typeface as the one used in Character Map, and choose the Paste command from the Edit menu.

Multimedia Accessories

Multimedia is a catch-all term that refers to the creation, recording, display, or playback of documents that contain sophisticated sound, graphics, and/or video components. If your computer is equipped with multimedia devices (such as a sound board or CD-ROM drive), the Multimedia item on the Accessories submenu provides access to programs that manipulate these devices. The particular multimedia accessories available to you depend on how your system is configured. They may include:

- **CD Player** allows you to play audio compact discs on your CD-ROM drive. Its interface resembles the control panel of the compact disc player connected to your stereo system. The music is transmitted by the computer's sound board and played through its speakers.
- **Media Player** allows you to play multimedia files of various kinds and control a variety of multimedia devices, including CD-ROM drives, sound boards, and MIDI (Musical Instrument Digital Interface) keyboards. Each available Media Player "device" corresponds to a separate set of files and controls. For example, if you choose the Sound command from the Device menu, a collection of sound files will be displayed. Double clicking on one of them "plays" the content of the file through the sound board and speakers.
- **Sound Recorder** allows you to record sound (input via a microphone or a line-in cable to the sound board), edit it, and store the result as a file on your hard disk. The Sound Recorder's interface resembles the controls on an audio tape player.
- **Volume Control** lets you adjust the volume, balance, and tone of the various sound devices connected to your computer system.

Communications Accessories

If your computer is equipped with a **modem**, a device that translates computer-generated data into signals that can be sent (usually over phone lines) to another computer, you can access information on other computer systems. Using computer-to-computer communication:

- You can access the vast quantities of data supplied by an **online information service**, such as CompuServe, America Online, or the Microsoft Network. With such a service, you will be able to receive *e-mail* (electronic mail), use encyclopedias, obtain stock market quotes, make airline reservations, and even "chat" with other subscribers.
- You can post messages on electronic *bulletin boards* and read messages posted there by others.
- You can make use of the **Internet** — a worldwide system of computer networks — to browse through the information posted by hundreds of thousands of organizations and individuals on the *World Wide Web*.
- You can connect to your campus computer network and access the software and data on it that have been authorized for public use.

- If your modem contains fax capabilities (as virtually all modems do, nowadays), you can send computer-generated faxes and receive any fax transmitted by others.

To take advantage of these communication possibilities, you not only need a modem and phone line, but also *communications software.* For this purpose, Windows supplies two key accessories:

- **HyperTerminal** is a communications software package that allows you to configure, dial, and pass commands to the modem from your keyboard. It ensures, with your input, that the signals sent by your computer, through its modem and the telephone lines, will be understandable to the hardware setup on the remote system.
- **Microsoft Fax** is a fax communications program; it helps you to send and receive faxes through your computer's fax modem. In order to use Microsoft Fax, the Microsoft Exchange software (also supplied with Windows) must be installed on your computer, as well. **Microsoft Exchange** acts as a clearinghouse for all electronically transmitted documents received by your computer, regardless of their source.

These accessories, and computer-to-computer communications in general, will be discussed at length in Chapters 10 and 11.

Chapter Summary

Calculator	To select a mode	Choose Standard or Scientific from the View menu.
	To activate a calculator key	Click on it.
	For the functions of the calculator keys	See Section 9.1.
Notepad	To turn word wrap on or off	Choose Word Wrap from the Edit menu.
	To enter and edit text	Proceed as in WordPad (see Section 2.2).
	To search for text	Choose Find from the Search menu.
	To set up the printed page	Choose Page Setup from the File menu and specify paper size, orientation, and margins in the resulting dialog box.

	To create a header or footer	Choose Page Setup from the File menu and enter text and codes in the Header and/or Footer text boxes.
Backup	To back up files	On the Backup page of the Backup window, select the files to be backed up, select a destination, and start the process.
	To restore backed up files	Click on the Restore tab in the Backup window, select the appropriate backup set and files, and start the process.
	To select Backup options	Choose Options from the Settings menu and select the desired options in the resulting dialog box.
ScanDisk	To test a disk for errors	Select the desired drive from the ScanDisk window, select options for the test, and start the process.
	To fix errors found in the disk test	Before the test, select the *Automatically fix errors* check box.
Disk Defragmenter	To analyze a disk for defragmentation	Select the desired drive in the initial Disk Defragmenter window and choose the OK command button.
	To defragment a disk	Select the desired drive and options, and choose the Start command button in the Disk Defragmenter window.
DriveSpace	To compress a disk	Choose Compress from DriveSpace's Drive menu, select the desired drive, and choose the Start and Compress Now buttons.
	To uncompress a disk	Choose Uncompress from DriveSpace's Drive menu, select the desired drive, and choose the Start and Uncompress Now buttons.
Character Map	To change the typeface	In the Character Map window, select a typeface from the Font drop-down list.
	To copy a character to the Clipboard	Double-click on the character in the Character Map window (or click on the character and choose the Select button) and choose the Copy button.
Multimedia Accessories	CD Player	Plays audio compact discs on your CD-ROM drive.
	Media Player	Plays multimedia files of various types.
	Sound Recorder	Records, edits, and saves sounds.

	Volume Control	Adjusts the volume, balance, and tone of sound devices.
Communications Accessories	HyperTerminal	Configures, dials, and passes commands to a modem for computer-to-computer communication.
	Microsoft Fax	Helps you to send and receive faxes through a fax modem.
	Microsoft Exchange	Acts as a clearinghouse for electronically-transmitted documents received by your computer.

Review Exercises

Section 9.1

1. In the Calculator accessory, you can display a standard or scientific calculator by choosing the corresponding item from the ____________ menu.
2. To clear Calculator's memory, click on the ____________ button.
3. In Scientific mode, to have Calculator find the mean and standard deviation of a collection of numbers, begin by clicking on the ____________ button.
4. True or false: Clicking on Calculator's Back button deletes the last digit entered into the display.
5. True or false: It is not possible to copy the number in Calculator's display to the Clipboard.
6. True or false: To calculate the sine of an angle using Calculator's Scientific mode, you must enter the angle in radian measure.
7. If you want to multiply 3.14 by the number in Calculator's memory, enter 3.14 into the display, click on the multiply symbol (*), and then

   a. Click on the MC button.
   b. Click on the MR button.
   c. Click on the MS button.
   d. Click on the M+ button.

8. The default number system used by Calculator when in Scientific mode is:

   a. Binary
   b. Octal

c. Decimal
d. Hexadecimal

Section 9.2

9. Notepad is a simple word processor that has no text formatting capabilities and is thus known as a ____________.

10. By default, ____________ is turned off in Notepad, so the text you type remains on the same line until you press the Enter key.

11. A ____________ for a document is text that is automatically placed at the top of every page.

12. True or false: Although Notepad can search a document for a specified word, it cannot automatically replace it with another word of your choice.

13. True or false: To read a page that is printed in portrait orientation, hold it so that the long side is vertical.

14. True or false: In Notepad, you can specify the number of copies to be printed before the printing process begins.

15. Which of the following operations can be performed by Notepad?

    a. Aligning text with the right margin.
    b. Setting top, bottom, right, and left margins.
    c. Changing the font displayed on the screen.
    d. Indenting the text in a given paragraph.

16. Which of the following sequences of symbols is used to create a Notepad footer that displays the current page number at the left margin and the current date at the right margin?

    a. &p &d
    b. &l &p &d
    c. &l &p &d &r
    d. &l &p &r &d

Section 9.3

17. The Backup utility is found on the ____________ submenu of the Start button's Accessories menu.

18. To ____________ a backed up file means to copy it from the backup medium to its original location.

19. True or false: In Backup, a shaded, checked box next to a folder icon in the *Select the files to back up* window means that some, but not all, of the files in that folder have been selected.

20. True or false: You can place a shortcut on the Desktop which, when double-clicked, not only starts the Backup utility, but also makes predefined selections and starts the backup process.

21. The Backup utility cannot back up a file on the hard disk to:
    a. A tape cartridge, even if your computer is equipped with a tape drive.
    b. A floppy disk.
    c. Another location on the hard disk.
    d. None of the above is correct.

22. The Backup utility cannot be used to:
    a. Back up files and folders from the hard disk to a floppy.
    b. Restore backed up files from a floppy to the hard disk.
    c. Move (copy and delete) files from the hard disk to a floppy.
    d. Compare a backed up file to the original.

Section 9.4

23. If you want to locate and delete lost file fragments, use the Windows ____________ utility.

24. A disk file is said to be ____________ if it is stored in two or more nonadjacent locations on disk.

25. When DriveSpace ____________ a file, the file takes up less space on disk than it did formerly.

26. True or false: The ScanDisk utility can be set up to detect errors without fixing them.

27. True or false: Disk Defragmenter tells you the degree to which the selected disk is fragmented before starting the defragmentation process.

28. True or false: DriveSpace can uncompress disks that it had previously compressed.

29. To use the ScanDisk utility to check for physical flaws on the surface of a disk:
    a. Choose the Advanced command button.
    b. Select the Standard option button.
    c. Select the Thorough option button.
    d. ScanDisk cannot perform this test.

30. When Disk Defragmenter does a full (complete) defragmentation:
    a. It defragments files, but does not consolidate free space.
    b. It consolidates free space, but does not defragment files.
    c. It defragments files and consolidates free space.
    d. It neither defragments files nor consolidates free space.

Section 9.5

31. The Windows ____________ accessory enables you to insert special symbols into documents open in another Windows application.

32. The term ____________ refers to applications that contain sophisticated graphics, sound, and video components.

33. True or false: To copy a character from the Character Map accessory to the Clipboard, choose the Copy command on the Edit menu.

34. True or false: To use ordinary telephone lines to access an online information service, your computer needs to be equipped with a modem.

35. Which of the following is not a multimedia device?

    a. A sound card
    b. A CD-ROM drive
    c. A modem
    d. A MIDI keyboard

36. Which of the following applications does not deal with computer-to-computer communications.

    a. Media Player
    b. HyperTerminal
    c. Microsoft Fax
    d. Microsoft Exchange

Build Your Own Glossary

37. The following words and phrases are important terms that were introduced in this chapter. (They appear within the text in boldface type.) Use WordPad (see Section 2.2) to enter a definition for each term, preserving alphabetical order, into the Glossary file on the Student Disk.

Accessories
ASCII
Back up files
Backup utility
Calculator accessory
CD Player accessory
Character Map accessory
Compress a disk
Defragment a disk
Disk Defragmenter utility
Footer
Header
HyperTerminal accessory
Internet
Media Player accessory
Microsoft Fax
Microsoft Exchange
Modem
Multimedia
Notepad accessory
Online information service
ScanDisk utility
Sound Recorder accessory
Text editor
Text file
Volume Control accessory
Word wrap

Lab Exercises

Work each of the following exercises at your computer. Begin by turning the machine on (if necessary) to start Windows 95 and closing any open windows.

Lab Exercise 1 (Section 9.1)

a. Start Windows Calculator and display the Standard calculator. Can you maximize the Calculator window?

b. What value would you expect for the expression 4 + 5 * 6, 34 or 54? Why? Use Calculator to find its value. What did you get?

c. Enter the number 13 into memory. Which memory key did you use? Did an "M" appear in the box above the memory keys?

d. Add 22 to the number in memory? What memory key did you use?

e. Now, find 6% of the current number in memory. What did you get?

f. Clear both memory and the current calculation. What two keys did you use to accomplish this?

g. Find $1/\sqrt{11}$ and $\sqrt{1/11}$. Did you get the same answer for both expressions?

h. Close Calculator.

Lab Exercise 2 (Section 9.2)

a. Start Notepad and maximize its window.

b. Type your name and class on separate lines, and skip a line (by pressing the Enter key twice).

c. Type the sentence: This is a test of the copy and paste operations. Then, press the Enter key.

d. Select this sentence. Describe how you accomplished this.

e. Copy the selected text to the Clipboard. What menu command or mouse actions did you use?

f. Paste the text from the Clipboard onto the end of the document. What menu command or mouse actions did you use?

g. Repeat step *f* four times. Try pasting the text without reselecting and recopying it. Did this work?

h. Print the document.

i. Save the document (see Section 2.2) if you wish and exit Notepad.

Lab Exercise 3 (Section 9.2)

a. Start Notepad and maximize its window.

b. Insert the Student Disk in its drive and open the History2 document (see Section 2.2, if necessary).

c. In the Page Setup dialog box:

- Set the orientation to *portrait* and all margins to one inch.

- Create a header that contains your name (left-aligned) and your class (right-aligned).
- Create a footer that displays the date, centered on the line.

d. Open the Find dialog box and enter the word *large* in the *Find what* box. Now, use this utility to determine the number of times the word *large* occurs in the document.

e. At the end of the document, type complete sentences stating the number of times the word *large* occurs and the number of times words containing *large* occur in the document.

f. Print the revised document.

g. Save the document if you wish, exit Notepad, and remove the diskette from its drive.

Lab Exercise 4 (Section 9.3)

a. Start the Backup utility and insert the Student Disk in its drive (we will assume this drive is A:).

b. Perform a partial backup of the Student Disk:

- In the left window, select the A: drive.
- In the right window, select the Paint folder and the Testfile and Memo files to be backed up. Does a check mark appear in the box next to the A: drive icon in the left window?
- Try to select A: as the destination for the backup. What message is displayed?
- Select the root folder of the C: drive (C:\) as the destination for the backup.
- Use Backup Test as the label for the backup set and start the backup. How long did it take?

c. Compare some of the backed up files with the originals:

- In the *Compare from* window, select the C: drive.
- For *Files to compare*, select the Testfile and Memo files "From drive A:".

How long did the comparison take?

d. Restore some of the backed up files:

- Restore from the C: drive and the Backup Test set.
- Select as the "Files to restore": Testfile and Memo "From drive A:".

Was an error message displayed? If so, what caused the error?

e. Start Explorer and locate the Backup Test file in the C:\ folder. What size is it? Delete the Backup Test file.

f. Close Explorer and Backup and remove the diskette from its drive.

Lab Exercise 5 (Section 9.4)

a. Start the ScanDisk utility.

b. Insert the Student Disk in its drive and select this drive in the ScanDisk window.

c. Select the Thorough test mode, but elect not to perform write-testing or repair bad sectors in hidden or system files. In which dialog box are the last two options found?

d. Elect not to print a "log file" but do check files for invalid dates and times. Also, make sure that a summary is displayed whether or not there are errors. In which dialog box did you select these options?

e. Start the ScanDisk tests. Were any errors found? If so, what are they?

f. Use the summary to answer the following questions:

   What is the total disk space for this disk?
   How many bytes of space are there in bad sectors?
   How many files are there are on this disk?

g. Close ScanDisk and remove the Student Disk from its drive.

Lab Exercise 6 (Section 9.4)

a. Start the Disk Defragmenter utility.

b. Insert the Student Disk in its drive, select this drive from the drop-down list, and choose the OK button. What is its degree of fragmentation (as a percentage)?

c. Elect to perform a full fragmentation, but not to check the disk for errors. In which dialog box did you select these options?

d. Start the defragmentation process and choose the Show Details button, then the Legend button. Use the Defrag Legend window to answer the following questions. (You can choose the Pause button to give yourself more time to find the answers.)

   What color is used to represent free disk space?
   Are any parts of the disk marked as "bad (damaged) area"?
   What does each box in the display represent?

e. Resume the defragmentation, if necessary. When defragmentation is complete, close Disk Defragmenter and remove the diskette from its drive.

Lab Exercise 7 (Section 9.5)

a. Start Notepad, WordPad, and the Character Map accessory.

b. In Character Map, choose the Symbol font from the drop-down list.

c. Position the mouse pointer over a character and hold down the mouse button. What happened?

d. Select several characters (of your choice), displaying them in the *Characters to copy* box.

e. Choose the Copy command button. What does this action accomplish?

f. Switch to WordPad and display the Format Bar, if necessary. What is the current font (as indicated on the Format Bar)?

g. Choose the Paste command from the Edit menu. Are the same characters displayed in the WordPad document window as were copied from Character Map? What is the current font now?

h. Switch to Notepad and choose the Paste command from the Edit menu. Are the same characters displayed in the Notepad window as were copied from Character Map?

i. Close Notepad, WordPad, and Character Map (responding No to the "save changes?" messages).

If You Want to Learn More ...

The notes presented here allow you to delve more deeply into some of the topics covered in this chapter.

Installing missing accessories

If a Windows accessory discussed in this chapter (or mentioned in the next note) does not appear on your Accessories menu, you can install it from the original Windows installation disks or CD-ROM. To do so:

1. Start Control Panel by choosing this item from the Start menu's Settings option.
2. In the Control Panel window, double-click on the Add/Remove Programs icon. The Add/Remove Programs Properties dialog box will open.
3. Click on the Windows Setup tab.
4. Select Accessories from the Components list.
5. Choose the Details command button. The Accessories dialog box

will open, displaying a list of all available accessories. (Those that are already installed have a check mark beside their name.)

6. Select the check box next to each of the accessories you want to add.
7. Choose the OK button in the Accessories dialog box; then the OK button in the Add/Remove Programs Properties dialog box. You will be prompted to insert a diskette or CD-ROM in its drive.
8. Insert the requested disk and choose the OK command button. The relevant files will be copied to the hard disk and the selected accessories will appear on the Accessories menu.

Other items on the Accessories menu

The content of the Accessories menu on a given computer depends on several factors: the configuration of the system, whether or not Windows 95 was installed as an upgrade to Windows 3.1, and which accessories were "manually" added after the original installation. Here are some items that may appear on your Accessories menu, but have not yet been discussed in the text:

- *Games*, as you might guess, supplies a few simple computer games for you to play. The content of the Games submenu depends on the same factors (described above) as that of the Accessories menu.
- *Briefcase* allows you to synchronize the files on your desktop and laptop computers so that the same versions are stored on both. This accessory is discussed in Chapter 10.
- *Dial-Up Networking* and *Direct Cable Connection* provide special networking features. They are also discussed in Chapter 10.
- *System Monitor*, which may appear on your System Tools submenu, provides up-to-the-moment information about your computer system's resources, such as memory and disk use.
- *Phone Dialer* uses your modem to dial a specified telephone number.
- *Calendar* and *Cardfile* are useful Windows 3.1 accessories. Calendar provides a daily appointment book, complete with alarms, and a month-by-month calendar. Cardfile is a simple *database manager*, which allows you to enter information (say, names and addresses) as if you were filling out a set of index cards.

A simple backup technique

As we mentioned in Section 9.3, it really is important to back up files, especially your data files. If a program file becomes inaccessible or is accidentally deleted, it can usually be reinstalled from the original distribution disks. But, documents (and all the hours of work you put into creating them) may be irretrievable if disaster strikes.

Unfortunately, the Windows Backup utility is somewhat cumbersome for small backups; enough so that it might discourage daily use. Here's an easier way to back up your data files. First, you need to do some one-time preparation:

1. Create a folder to hold the documents you generate from each application you use (see Section 3.4).
2. Create a Desktop shortcut for each of these folders and rename them appropriately (Section 3.4).
3. Use the shortcuts to successively open each folder's window. In the folder window, select the Details view option and order the files by date, with the most recent ones at the top (to do so, click on the *Modified* button).

Now, whenever you double-click on one of these shortcuts, the documents you've just created will appear at the top of the folder window. To back up these documents:

1. Insert an appropriately labeled diskette in its drive.
2. Select the files to be backed up.
3. Right-click on one of the selected files, point at the Send To command on the pop-up menu, and then choose the appropriate drive from the submenu. The selected files will be copied to the floppy.

Try to get in the habit of using this technique at the end of every session in which you create or modify documents.

Inserting special characters without using Character Map

If you insert certain special characters (such as Greek letters or a copyright or trademark symbol) into your documents frequently, there may be a way to do it without starting Character Map. In many applications, some special characters can be entered directly from the keyboard. To determine the appropriate keystroke:

1. Start Character Map and select the typeface (from the Font drop-down list) that contains the desired character.
2. Click on this character, highlighting it.
3. The keystroke that will create this character in most Windows applications is displayed in the lower-right corner of the Character Map window.

For example, suppose you want to use the Greek letter α (alpha) and the copyright symbol, ©, in a WordPad document. Both of these characters are contained in the Symbol font (see Figure 19 on page 403). Clicking on α and then © in the Character Map window, we see that the corresponding keystrokes are *a* and Alt+0211, respectively. Thus, in WordPad, to insert one of these characters at the insertion point:

1. Select the Symbol typeface.
2. Then,
   - to insert the character α, type the letter *a*;
   - to insert the character ©, turn on Num Lock, hold down the Alt key, type 0211 on the numeric keypad, and then release the Alt key.

Where to go from here

The HyperTerminal, Microsoft Fax, and Microsoft Exchange communications programs were described briefly in Section 9.5. These accessories are discussed in detail in the following sections:

HyperTerminal — Section 10.5
Microsoft Exchange — Section 10.3
Microsoft Fax — Section 10.4

Here is where you can find information about accessories other than those covered in this chapter:

Briefcase — Section 10.6
Clipboard Viewer — Section 2.3
Dial-Up Networking — Section 10.2
Direct Cable Connection — Section 10.6
Paint — Chapter 8
WordPad — Chapter 7

CHAPTER 10

Networking with Windows 95

Communication in our society is characterized by the electronic exchange of information. When this exchange happens by connecting more than one computer together, the connection is made possible, for the most part, by networking. A **network** is a communication system that moves information from one computer to another.

This chapter introduces the characteristics, concepts, and definitions of networking. Some network features will be explored, such as Dial-Up Networking, the Microsoft Exchange application, and the Briefcase utility. To be more specific, you will learn about:

1. Different types of networks and the equipment needed to establish a Local Area Network.
2. Establishing a Dial-Up Networking connection.
3. Using Microsoft Exchange to send, receive, and delete electronic mail.
4. Using Microsoft Exchange to send and receive faxes.
5. Computer communications with the HyperTerminal application.
6. Windows features specific to portable computing.
7. The use of the Briefcase to manage transported files.
8. The deferred printing option.

10.1 Networking

Networking can exist on a small scale or a large scale. In either case, a network enables users to communicate with each other and to share resources (such as files and printers). Different types of networks meet the varied needs of individuals, small or large businesses, and educational institutions.

Types of Networks

Some definitions are necessary before we can explore networking in more detail. First we will discuss different types of networks and how they function.

- A **Local Area Network** (or LAN) is a network on a small scale. A LAN might span one company site, a campus, or a small office. A LAN usually requires a **server**, which is a computer that manages the network, and a *scheduler*, which is server software that manages and allocates the network resources.
- A **peer-to-peer network** is a small LAN that allows individual computers to communicate and share resources on a single-task basis without a scheduler. The benefit of a peer-to-peer network is that a server is not required.
- As our society becomes a global community, more and more of us will be using networks to send and receive electronic mail and "surf" the Internet. These kinds of communication use a **Wide Area Network** (a WAN), which connects computers in distant locations, even across continents. With a WAN, people can, for example, use teleconferencing to conduct meetings in which all participants need not be present at the same location to communicate face-to-face.

Advantages of networking

By networking computers that perform similar functions, computer resources can be shared, maximizing the hardware investment. Physical hardware, such as a printer or mass storage for data files, is easy to share on a network. Information, such as software applications and commonly used files, can also be shared on a network. For example, client scheduling between two different offices can be shared, operating from the same database. This information sharing helps combat data duplication and redundancy. Likewise, both offices can use the same printer, providing a more cost-effective hardware setup.

Physical connections

The computers and other equipment in a network system are usually physically connected to one another by means of network cable or other wire. The cable can be used to connect individual computers or entire computer systems, enabling individuals to communicate electronically. Telephone lines are often used for connection since that wire is already installed in most buildings. Large capacity phone lines called *trunk lines*, or T1s, are used for high traffic areas, but are expensive. *ISDN* lines (Integrated Services Digital Network) allow high-speed access at a relatively low cost. Fiber optic lines are sometimes used instead of phone lines, because they enable a higher quality transmission of the network connection.

Two basic types of network transmissions are baseband and broadband. A *baseband* network provides a single avenue for data transfer, perhaps using telephone lines. The *broadband* network traditionally uses coaxial cable to transfer the multiple streams of data simultaneously.

As we transmit information on a network, the rate at which data are exchanged becomes important. Bits per second (bps) is the measurement unit used to express the data transfer rate, sometimes called the *baud rate.* The table below illustrates some different transfer rates for a block of data, and the time to transfer that data.

Rate in Bits Per Second	Time Necessary for Data Transfer
9,600 bps	9.6 hours
56,000 bps	1.6 hours
1,000,000 bps	6.87 minutes
(T1) 1,540,000 bps	3.6 minutes
10,000,000 bps	41.25 seconds
(T3) 45,000,000 bps	0.92 seconds
1,000,000,000 bps	0.4 seconds

Depending upon the hardware configuration, a local area network sends data at a rate ranging from 1 to 10 mps (megabits per second). Obviously the faster data are transmitted, the more effective that transmission is to the networking process.

Network Hardware

When the decision is made to share resources through networking, the following additional hardware is necessary:

- A **network server** is a designated computer that runs the network operating system. This network operating system controls the multitasking and scheduling of resources. **Multitasking** is the ability to do more than a single task concurrently; this ability allows the server to answer user requests while managing the network resources. A server is often a high performance machine, which is necessary to facilitate timely multitasking of events.

- Typically, the server is not used as a workstation. A **workstation** is a computer that can operate as a stand-alone unit or can be connected to the network; it is typically the computer on which a user performs tasks. A workstation must have *client* software installed to operate properly with the network. This software allows communication from the workstation to the server and other shared resources. The workstation is considered to be the *client.*
- **Network cabling** consists of cable and connectors. There is a wide variety of cable available. A few commonly used types are *coaxial* and *twisted pair*; cable price and data transfer rates vary considerably from type to type. A wireless network (or *virtual network*) works with infrared mini-transformers and receivers and does not require traditional cabling.
- A **network interface card (NIC)** is a *card* (a circuit board) that fits in the computer. The NIC connects to the network cabling and uses software to set up each workstation for network use.
- **Network hubs** function as network traffic controllers. Hubs assist in removing noise and strengthening the line signal, while controlling network traffic.

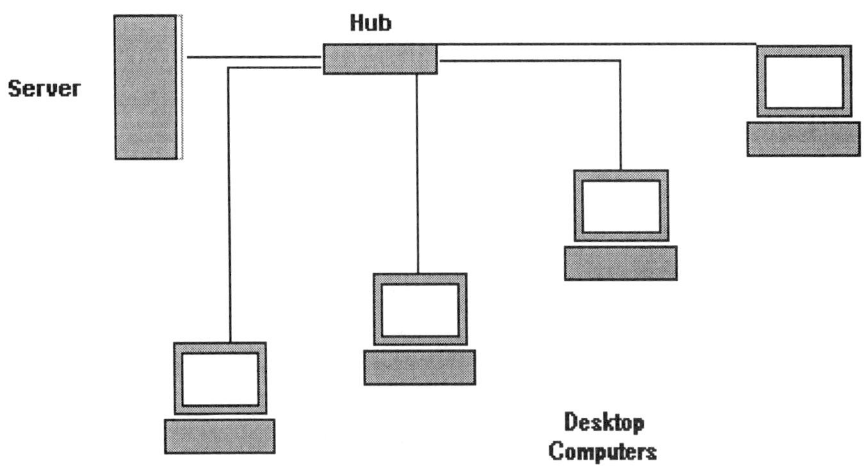

Accessing a Network

Windows 95 establishes network access to traditional networks with a server, as well as to peer-to-peer networks, with a login and a password. A *login* is a unique name given to an individual on the network; a *password* is a secret word or phrase that only the user knows. Both elements are required to gain access to the network system.

Most networks are set up to provide access to users only through the login and password system, which provides security for the network files against improper or illegal use. The network system administrator controls the user logins and passwords for the system. This information must be set up for specific users prior to their connecting to the network. Before turning off the computer, the user should *log out* of the system. The process for logging in and out of a particular network system can vary, depending upon what network software is being used.

An example of logging in

In the following procedure, we will look at how to use the Novell NetWare 4.1 software as the identified network software to log in to a network system. Be aware that your network system may work differently from this example, although entering the login and password will always be a part of the process.

To access the network:

1. Click on the Start button, point at the Programs option, and choose Novell from the resulting submenu. Now, click on NetWare Login on the Novell submenu. A dialog box similar to the one shown in Figure 1 will open.

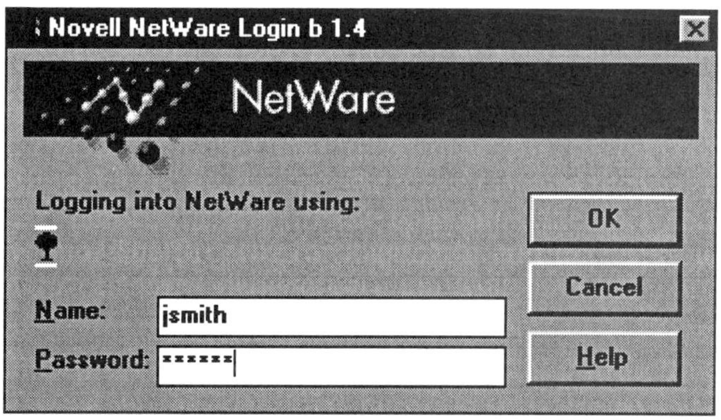

Figure 1 A Sample Login Dialog Box

2. Type your login name in the text box next to Name.
3. Press Tab or click in the Password text box and then type your password. The letters typed will not appear in the box for security reasons, but may display as asterisks. Press the Backspace key to correct a typing mistake.
4. Choose the OK command button. A window will open, as shown in Figure 2, indicating whether the attempt to log in was successful or not. Choose the Close command button to return to the Windows Desktop.

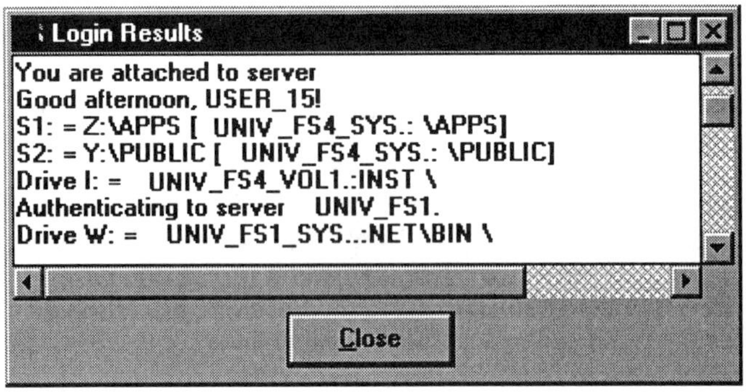

Figure 2 The Login Results

After using the network system, the log out procedure should always be executed. This procedure is a sequence of steps that may differ for each network type. Some networks require that you run a logout routine; other networks log you out of the system automatically when you shut down your Windows 95 session.

The Network Neighborhood

The **Network Neighborhood** is a built-in Windows application that is normally represented by an icon on the Desktop when the computer is connected to a network. This program provides you with an area in which to browse and access folders on the network, or on any of the network's resources.

Double-clicking on the Network Neighborhood icon displays all areas of the connected network within the resulting window. In fact, this window is very similar to a My Computer or Explorer display, except that only the network equipment and folders are visible. A sample window is pictured below; remember that each window displays only the items on the connected network, so this graphic just represents one particular network connection.

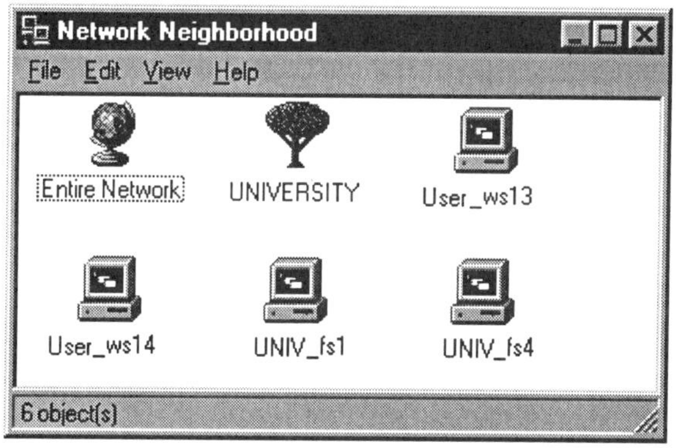

The Network Control Utility

The **network control utility** is a built-in Windows application that is used to identify network hardware and *driver* files (programs that allow Windows to communicate with various devices) for accessing network systems. (Usually the *network administrator*, the person in charge of setting up the network, configures these settings.) For instance, the network control utility defines the network driver you will use on a workstation so that the network knows how to communicate with your specific computer.

To start the network control utility double-click on the Network icon in the Control Panel window. A dialog box similar to the one shown in Figure 3 (on the next page) will be displayed.

There are three pages in the Network Control Utility dialog box that allow settings changes to be made.

- The first page, Configuration, adds or removes the network components that are needed for communications. This page also activates File and Print Sharing, which allows you to share files and printers with other users on the network.
- The Identification page contains text boxes (shown below) for naming and describing your computer and workgroup. These descriptions are how you (or your computer) will be known by other users on the network. For example, the name given a computer is how that computer can be identified and located using Network Neighborhood or the Windows Find utility (see Section 4.3).

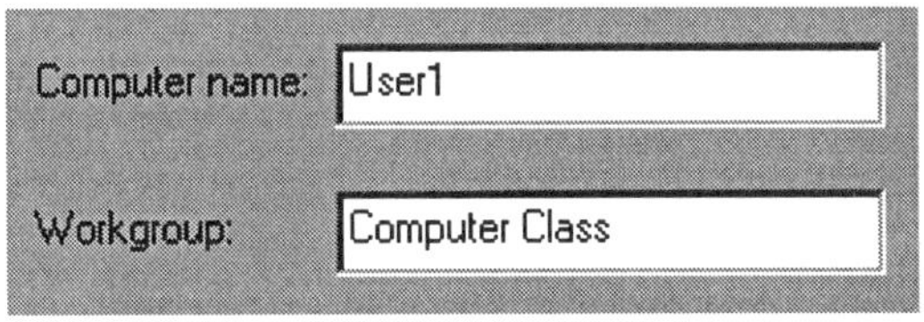

The workgroup with which a computer is identified limits the display of and access to files and other resources to users included in the workgroup.

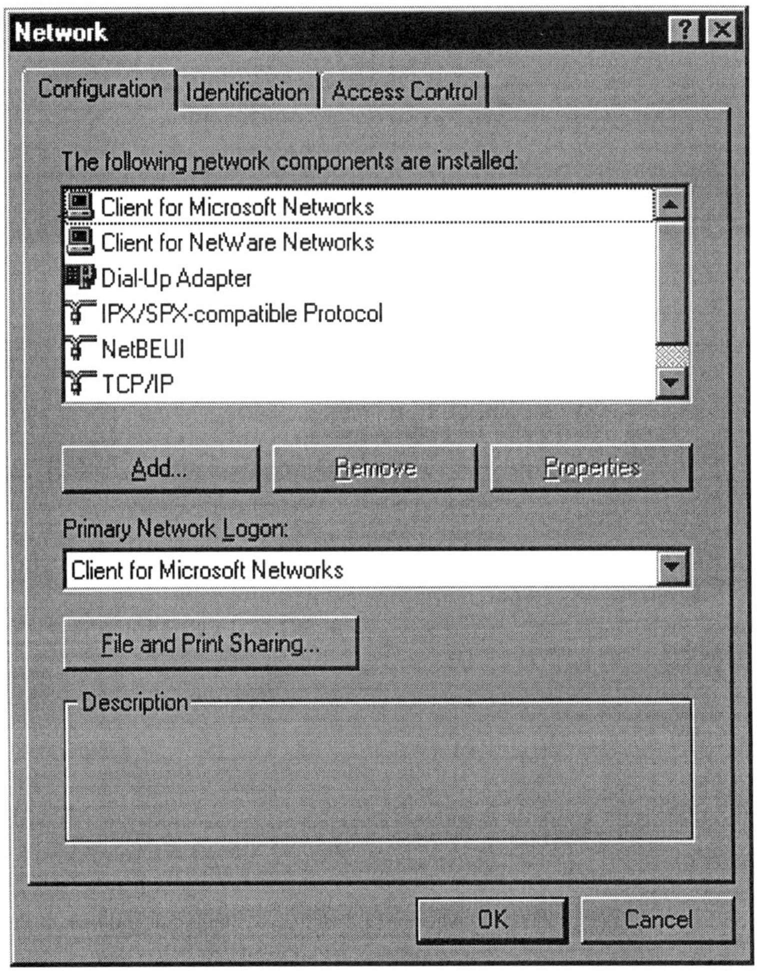

Figure 3 The Network Control Utility

- The Access Control page (Figure 4) provides two levels of access control that can be designated for files and/or printers on a network:

  Share-level access control lets you set a password for each shared printer or file, so that any other user on the network must supply that password before using that resource.

  User-level access control provides the ability to select specific users with whom your files and/or printer(s) will be shared; these specific users will not need a password to gain access to those resources.

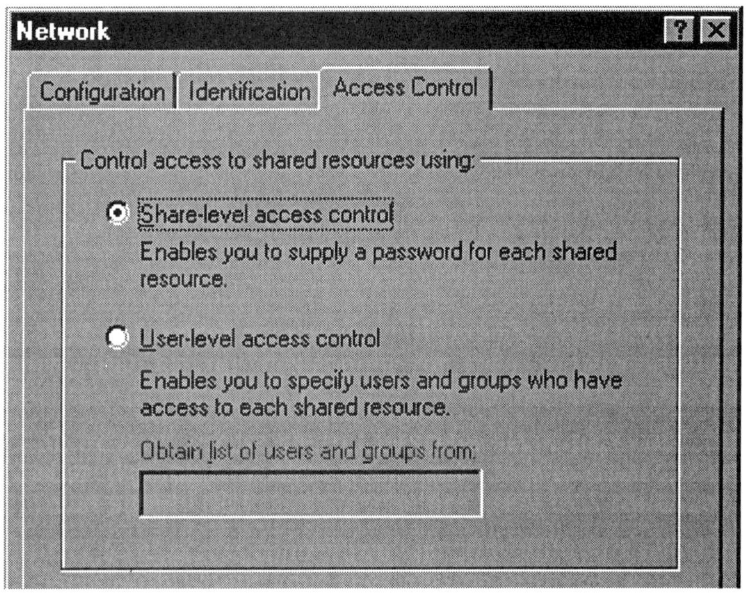

Figure 4 Network Control Utility — Access Control Page

10.2 Dial-Up Networking

Dial-Up Networking is a built-in Windows application that allows connection to another computer, a network system, or an online service. Dial-Up Networking provides **remote network access** to another computer system, using a modem and a telephone line, and without formally networking the two computers. The benefit of remote access is that the computers do not require traditional hardware and cabling, and they do not have to be located close together. The remote dial-up system functions as if it were a regular network connection, except that it does not process information as quickly.

With a dial-up connection, one computer must be configured as a network server for the other computer to use its shared resources. For example, a home computer can dial in and connect to an office computer. Both computers must have modems installed. The Dial-Up Networking program must be installed and configured on the home computer to communicate with the work computer. Once connected, you have complete network computing capabilities from home, such as printing to a network printer, accessing a customer database, or using shared files.

NOTE

Dial-Up server capabilities are available only if you have installed *Microsoft Plus!*, which is sold separately from the Windows 95 software.

When two computers are linked with a dial-up networking connection, one system is called the *host* and the other the *guest*. The host computer allows the guest to access its information.

Installing the Dial-Up Networking Files

You can easily determine if Dial-Up Networking has been installed on your system.

1. Click on the Start button, point to the Programs option, and then point to the Accessories option on the resulting submenu.
2. If Dial-Up Networking has been installed, it will be listed along with the other Accessory programs.

TIP

An alternative method to check if Dial-Up Networking has been installed is to look in the My Computer window for the Dial-Up Networking folder.

If it has not been installed, to use Dial-Up Networking, you must first install the appropriate files. To do so:

Installing Dial-Up Networking

1. Click on the Start button, point to the Settings option, and choose Control Panel from the resulting submenu; the Control Panel window will open.

2. In the Control Panel window, double-click on the Add/Remove Programs icon, which opens the Add/Remove Programs Properties dialog box.
3. Click on the Windows Setup tab, which displays the corresponding page of the dialog box.
4. Select the Communications item from the Components list box and choose the Details command button. A list of communications options will be displayed. If the Dial-Up Networking option is not selected, click on its check box to activate it.
5. Choose the OK command button. The Network dialog box (see Section 10.1) will open, displaying its Identification page. Enter a name for your computer and the workgroup to which it belongs in the appropriate text boxes. Then, choose the Close command button.
6. If the files for Dial-Up Networking are not installed on the computer, Windows will prompt for specific disks or the CD to be inserted. Follow the instructions until all of the necessary files have been installed.
7. When finished, Windows displays the final dialog box, advising you that the computer must be restarted to use the Dial-Up Networking application. Choose the OK command button and restart the computer (see Section 1.5) to enable Dial-Up Networking.

NOTE

To communicate and share resources through a Dial-Up Networking connection, your computer system must contain a modem. For information on installing a modem, see Section 6.5.

Using the New Connection Wizard

Now that the Dial-Up Networking files are installed, Windows needs to know about the computer (or computers) with which you want to connect. The setup process for a remote connection is initiated by the New Connection Wizard, which collects information for that connection. The Wizard then handles the process of setting up a Dial-Up Networking connection definition. After the New Connection Wizard has completed its sequence, the connections settings are saved as a specific file in the Dial-Up Networking folder. The settings are then activated when initiating the Dial-Up connection with a double-click.

In this procedure, we begin to set up a connection for remote access to a work computer. The steps for initiating new connection settings are:

1. Open the Dial-Up Networking folder. There are two ways do this:

   - Open the My Computer window, and you will see the Dial-Up Networking folder. Double-click on this icon (shown at the right) to display the window.

   or

   - Click on the Start button, point to the Programs option, point to the Accessories option, and click on the Dial-Up Networking item on the resulting submenu.

2. Double-click on Make New Connection, the icon shown at the right. The New Connection Wizard will start.

3. Place the cursor in the first text box and type the name of the computer you wish to access with the remote connection (for example, The Office Computer) as shown in Figure 5.
4. Choose the Next command button to display the screen shown in Figure 6.
5. Enter the phone number that will dial in to the remote computer. Do not include the area code unless it must be dialed to access the number. (In other words, if the number is a local one, skip the area code box.) Then, choose the Next command button to display the next Wizard dialog box.
6. This dialog box lets you know that you have successfully completed setting up the new connection. Choose the Finish command button; then choose the Close button. The connection you created will show up in the Dial-Up Networking window as an icon, shown at the right.

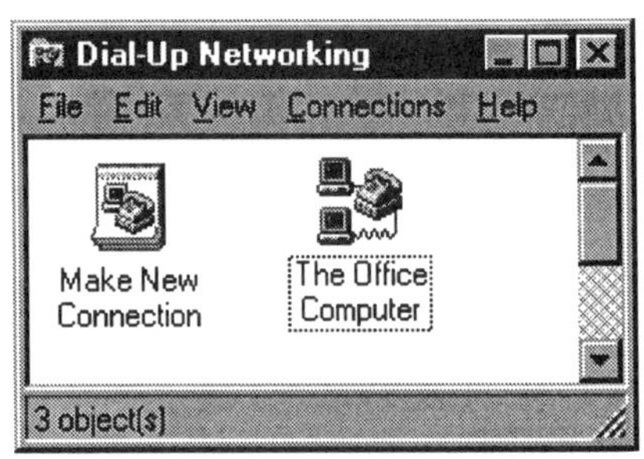

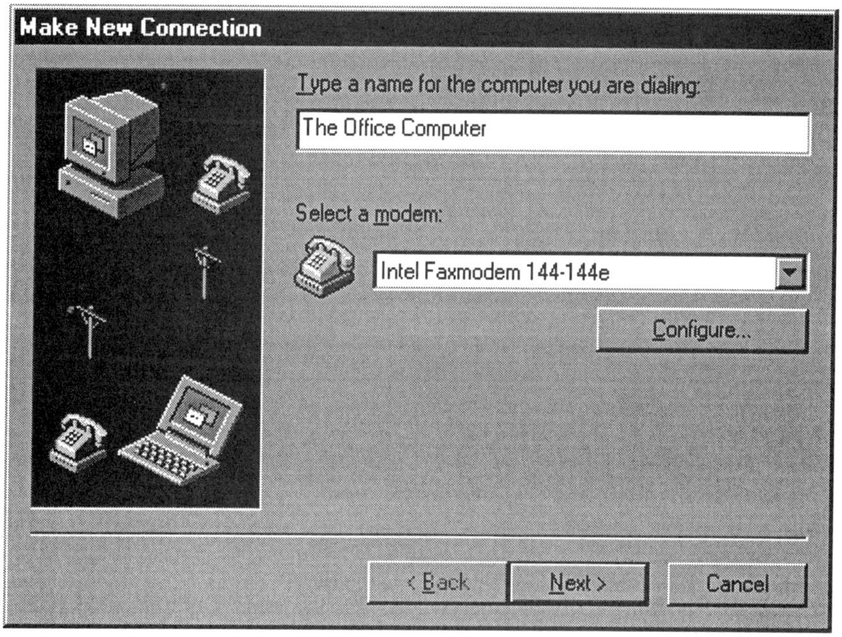

Figure 5 The Make New Connection Dialog Box

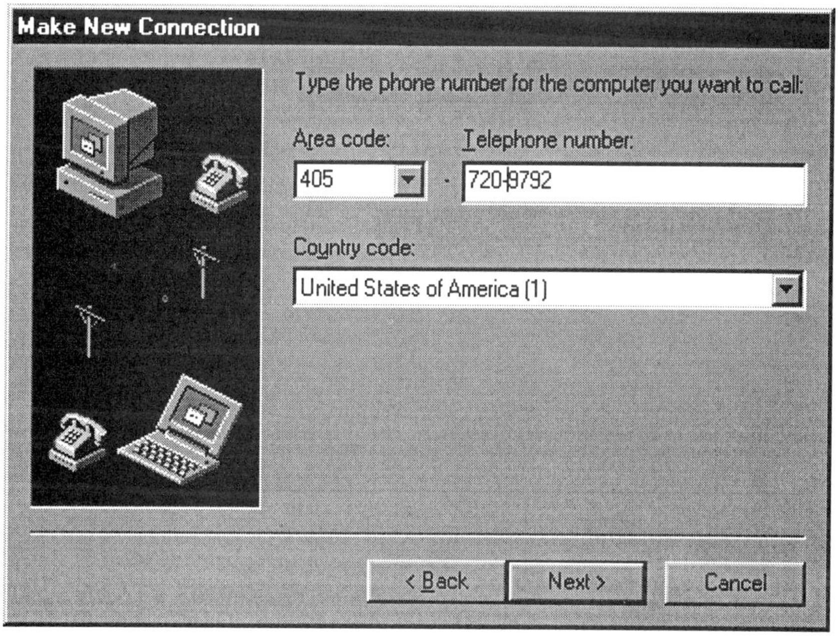

Figure 6 Entering the Remote Connection Telephone Number

NOTE

If you are connecting to a remote site that is networked with a file server, you need to let the connection know about the server type of that computer system. To do this, right-click on the icon for the connection and then click on Properties on the pop-up menu. The Properties dialog box for the connection icon will be displayed. Now, click on the Server Type command button to display a list of servers (see the dialog box below) and select the type of dial-up server that matches the operating system of the remote computer.

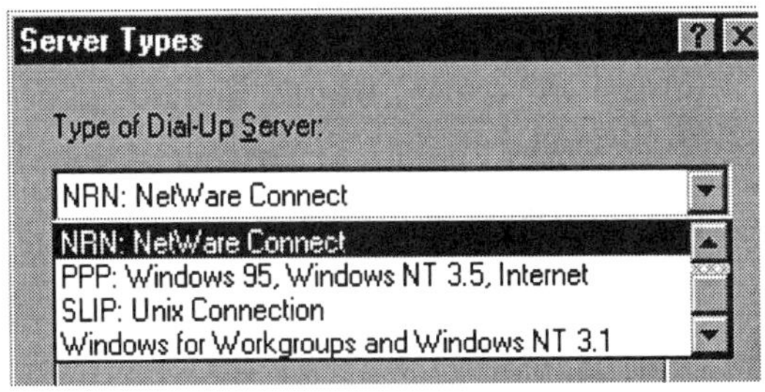

Then choose the OK command button to return to the Properties dialog box, and choose the OK command button again to accept the settings change.

10.3 Using Microsoft Exchange

Inbox

The **Microsoft Exchange** Inbox provides a central location for processing communications, such as electronic mail and fax. There are many different kinds of *messaging systems*, software for sending and receiving messages. Exchange works with these systems to:

- Connect to a LAN's electronic mail server to communicate with users on the network and on other connected networks.
- Transmit electronic mail via an online service, using a modem.
- Send and receive fax messages.

In this section, we will explore setting up the Exchange program and sending and receiving electronic mail. Section 10.4 will discuss sending and receiving fax messages.

How Exchange Works

Exchange works with most electronic mail or fax software, as long as the appropriate driver files are installed. It is easy for Exchange to utilize the Microsoft Mail and Microsoft Fax software because those drivers are available for installation when setting up the Exchange Inbox.

A **profile** is created when Exchange is installed. The profile is a group of settings defined for each user who needs to work within Exchange. These settings include the name and location of your Personal Folder File, your Personal Address Book, and configuration details for each mail service. The *Personal Folder File* is where all incoming and outgoing messages reside. Messages are kept in folders within the Personal Folder File; the default folders are Inbox, Outbox, and Sent Items. The *Personal Address Book* stores the names and addresses that you frequently use for electronic mail and/or faxing. Many profiles can exist, but usually one is enough for most users.

NOTE

A new version of the Exchange application may be installed on your computer if it was purchased after June, 1996. This update changes the name of the program to *Windows Messaging* and appears in the title bar of the window while open. Other enhancements are not significant enough to change the concepts and procedures explained here, regardless of the version you may be using. The examples used in this section and the resulting graphics displayed use the Exchange version of the program.

Installing Exchange

Exchange can be installed either when setting up Windows initially or after the fact. If Exchange has been installed, the Inbox displays as an icon on the Desktop, and Microsoft Exchange is listed as an item on the Programs submenu of the Start menu. Even if Exchange has already been installed, you may still need to set up the messaging services (e-mail program and fax program) you wish to use.

NOTE

When you install Windows or use Exchange for the first time, the Microsoft Exchange Setup Wizard will run. The Wizard is also run each time you add a new profile using the Mail And Fax icon in Control Panel.

Exchange requires a minimum of 6 megabytes of RAM. It is recommended that you have at least 8 megabytes of RAM and 10 megabytes of free hard disk space if you want to use Exchange.

If Exchange has not been installed, or if you have removed the Inbox from the Desktop, you must install it before setting up the messaging services. You can install Microsoft Exchange by using the Add/Remove Programs utility found in Control Panel.

To install Exchange:

Installing Exchange

1. Open the Control Panel window and choose the Add/Remove Programs option. The Add/Remove Programs Properties dialog box will be displayed.
2. Click on the Windows Setup tab to display that page of the dialog box. The components list will appear. Choose the messaging components you wish to install; for instance, Microsoft Exchange and/or Microsoft Fax. Then, choose the OK command button.
3. Choose the OK command button to begin the installation.
4. If the files for Microsoft Exchange are not present on the computer, Windows will prompt you to insert specific floppy disks or a CD. Follow the instructions until all of the necessary files have been copied.
5. After the appropriate files needed to run Microsoft Exchange are copied, a message box will appear advising you that the computer will need to be restarted for the new settings to take effect.

Setting up messaging services

To set up messaging services with the Inbox icon:

1. If you have never set up messaging services before, double-click on the Inbox icon on the Desktop; the Setup Wizard will start (Figure 7), assisting you in installation.
2. Choose the Mail Services you wish to add to Microsoft Exchange and choose the OK command button. The Inbox Setup Wizard asks you if you have used Exchange before; click the appropriate option button and choose the Next command button.
3. In the resulting Wizard screen, select the mail services you wish to install. The available options are based on the choices you made in the initial Wizard screen (Figure 7). After you have made the appropriate selections, choose the Next command button.
4. You will be asked for the path to the post office location. More than likely, you will want to use the Windows folder (on your main hard drive) as the location. Type this path name or choose the Browse command button to select a path. Choose the Next command button to continue.
5. Name the Mailbox where you will receive mail. You might give the mailbox the same name as your network user ID, if you have one. Enter the desired name in the Mailbox text box, as shown in Figure 8.

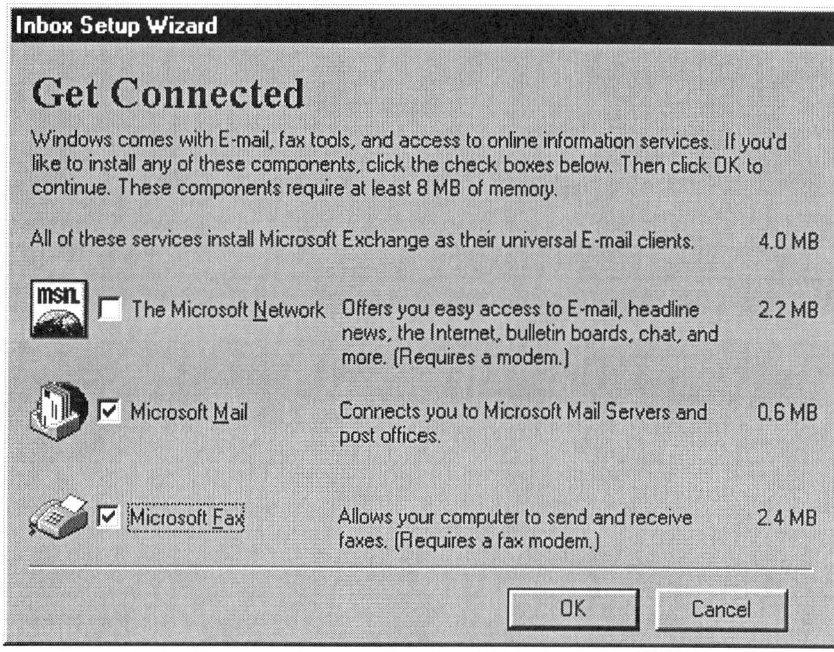

Figure 7 The Inbox Setup Wizard Dialog Box

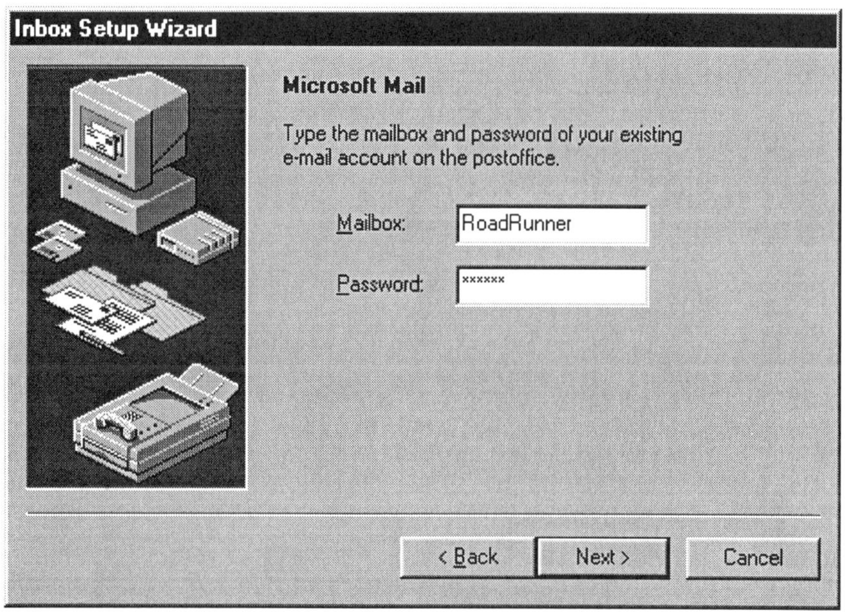

Figure 8 Naming the Mailbox

6. Next, you may type a password, if desired. As you type the password, asterisks will appear in the text box. Leave the password blank if you do not require one. Then choose the Next command button.
7. The Wizard screen displays a dialog box indicating the path to your personal folder file; choose the Next command button to accept this path, or choose the Browse command button to specify a different location.
8. The next dialog box indicates the path to your personal address book. Choose the Next command button to accept this path or choose the Browse command button to select a different location.
9. The next dialog box allows you to add Exchange to the Startup folder, which automatically runs Exchange when you start Windows. After making the desired selection, choose the Next command button.
10. When the process is complete, choose the Finish command button to exit the Setup Wizard.

WARNING

A folder named Wgpo0000 is created in the post office location you specified, and other folders are created in the Wgpo0000 folder. All folders created by this process are necessary for the post office to function correctly. Do not delete these files or folders.

Electronic Mail Terminology

When using Exchange for messaging services, the following terms apply:

Electronic mail, or **e-mail**, consists of electronic messages sent over a network between users in an office environment, or perhaps via the Internet or an online service. E-mail structure, concepts, and terms are similar to those used with a traditional paper mailing system. The e-mail must be created, addressed, and sent, and opened when received.

The basic unit of exchange in an electronic mail system is the **message**. A message can contain a number of different items, similar to that of paper communication — a cover letter, a form, a graphic, a memo, or any other document you can create on a computer. The contents of a message are called *message items*; existing files to be sent along with the message are called *attachments*, and can include up to 20 elements such as text, graphics, files, and fax pages. When attachments are used, the message becomes the cover letter to the correspondence.

The **Inbox** is the folder in which all new messages are delivered. When you start Exchange, any new mail is visible in the Inbox. The mail remains there until you delete it or move it to another folder.

The **Outbox** is the folder in which all messages ready for delivery are placed. Once the messages are delivered, they are placed in the Sent Items folder.

The **Sent Items folder** holds each message that has been delivered from the Outbox. The messages remain in this folder until you delete them or move them to another folder.

The Exchange post office operations are managed by the **Exchange Administrator.** The Exchange Administrator manages, maintains, and controls the mail and fax applications. If on a network, the Administrator can rename, add or delete users from the electronic mail system. On a single-user system, you are the Exchange Administrator.

Sending Electronic Mail

Once Exchange has been set up, you can use it to send and receive mail messages. To open Microsoft Exchange, click on the Start button, point to the Programs option, and then choose Microsoft Exchange; or just double-click on the Inbox icon on the Desktop. Either action results in the display of the Exchange window, which is called the Exchange Viewer (Figure 9). Key parts of this window are:

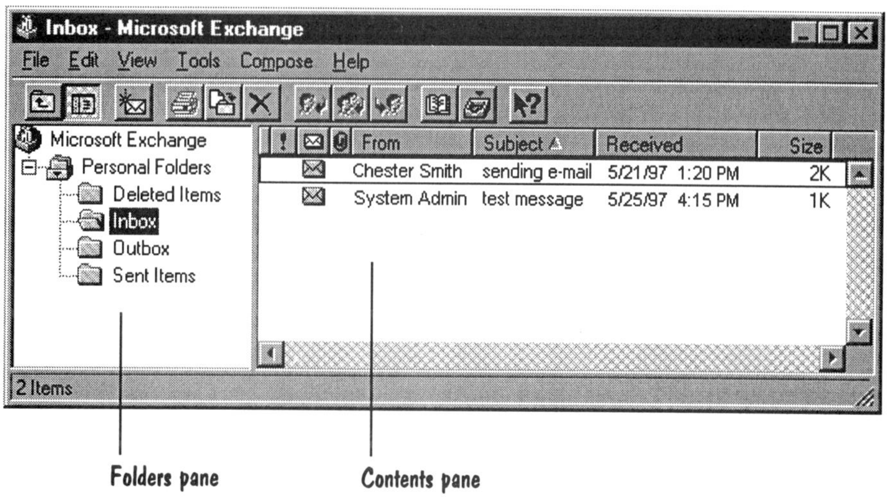

Figure 9 The Exchange Viewer Window

- The left (*folders*) pane of the Viewer lists your personal folders. These folders store e-mail messages, faxes, and messages from other messaging systems, such as online services. The right (*contents*) pane lists the contents of the selected folder.

NOTE

If you open Microsoft Exchange for the first time by double-clicking on the Inbox icon on the Desktop, the folder list will not be displayed automatically. Choose Folders from the View menu to display it. When you restart Exchange, the last view you selected is displayed.

- The Toolbar provides easy, single-click access to the most used commands in Exchange. The most frequently used icons are New Message, Print, and Delete.
- All incoming mail is placed in the Inbox. After reading the items in the Inbox, you can reply to, forward, delete, or file them in other folders. Select the Inbox by clicking on this folder in the folders pane; all messages that are in the Inbox are displayed in the contents pane.

To create a new message:

1. From within the Exchange window, click on the New Message icon on the Toolbar or choose New Message from the Compose menu. The New Message window will open, as shown in Figure 10.
2. In the To text box, type the address of the person(s) to receive the message; separate multiple names with a semicolon to send the message to more than one person. You must provide the correct e-mail address for the recipient(s), and different e-mail systems use different addressing formats.
3. Type the appropriate subject of the message in the Subject text box. This information is important, as it will appear in the recipient's Inbox, letting that person know what your message is about.
4. Enter the desired message by typing it in the large text box below the subject line. This text box behaves as a word processing text area, and the text in your message can be formatted with the commands found on the Format menu or on the Format bar. The Format bar commands in Exchange are identical to those in the WordPad (see Section 7.2), and they function in the same way. (Exchange also includes a spell-check program, found on the Tools menu.)

5. When you have finished entering the message, choose the Send command from the File menu or click on the Send icon on the

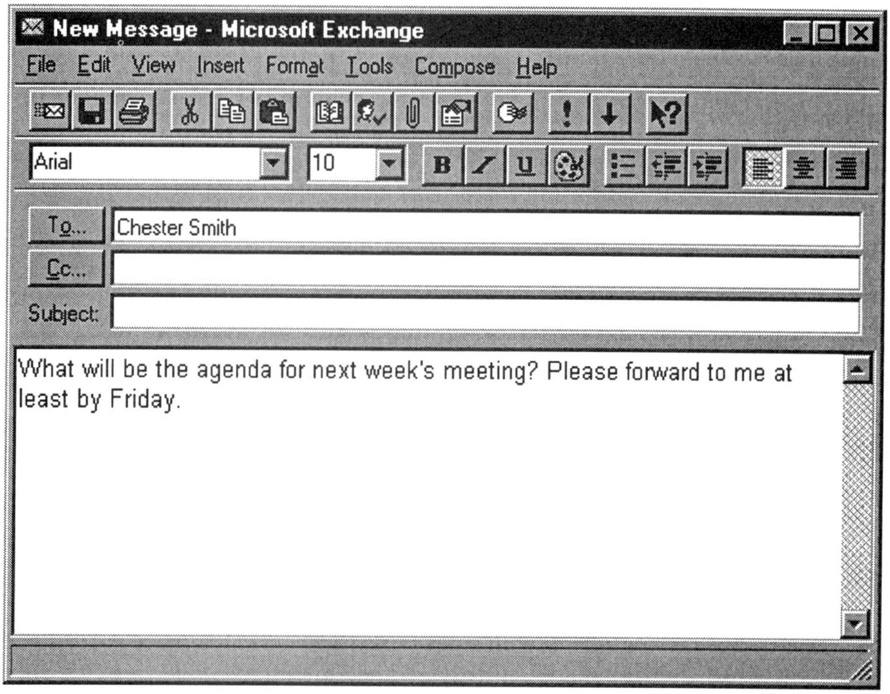

Figure 10 The New Message Dialog Box

Toolbar to place the message in the Outbox, awaiting delivery. The Exchange window will again be displayed; the folders that contain unprocessed information will appear bolded. When connected to a LAN, the message will be sent as soon as the network has *polled*, or checked, the mail system belonging to the recipient(s) of your message.

6. When the message has been delivered, Exchange moves that message to the Sent Items folder.

TIP

You can send a file as an e-mail message, even if Exchange is not open. From any folder window, right-click on the file. Then, point at the Send To item and choose Mail Recipient on the resulting submenu. Exchange will open and start a new mail message with the selected file as an attachment.

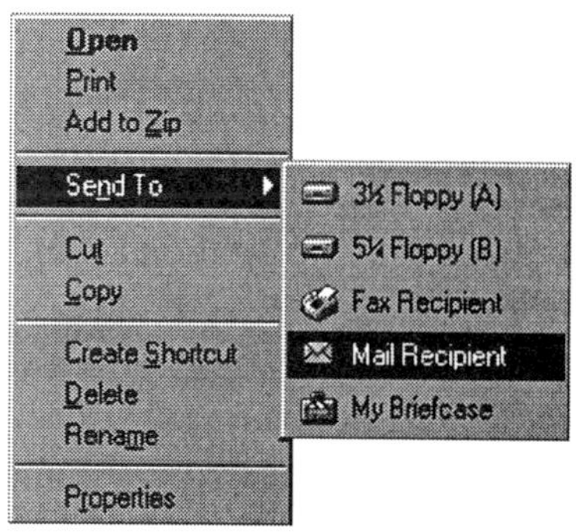

Receiving Electronic Mail

On a LAN, messages will be received when the network has polled your mail system. If Exchange is running, the program will notify you when new mail is received by displaying an envelope icon in the Taskbar notification area (to the left of the clock).

To open new mail:

1. If the Exchange program is not running, open it by double-clicking on the Inbox icon on the Desktop.

   If Exchange is open but minimized, and the envelope icon is displayed in the notification area on the Taskbar, double-click on the envelope icon. The Exchange window will be restored and display the contents of your Inbox, including the new messages.
2. The Inbox folder will appear bolded when new messages are in it. Select this folder (by clicking on it) to list new messages in the contents pane.
3. Any unread messages will appear in bold within the Inbox contents pane. To display a message, either double-click on it or select it (by clicking on it once) and then press the Enter key.
4. When you are finished reading a message, press the Escape key or click on the window's close button.

NOTE The messages you have read will remain in the Inbox until you delete them or move them (as described below).

Managing Mail Messages

Mail messages that you have sent remain in the Outbox and mail messages that you have read remain in the Inbox until you move or delete them. Over time, messages can accumulate in these folders, and mail message management becomes an important task.

Moving Messages Messages can easily be moved by dragging and dropping them into other folders. The only folders that appear in the folders pane are the default ones. Exchange gives you the ability to customize these folders, providing a logical and easy way to better organize your messages.

Before you can store messages in a different folder, you must create that folder. To do so:

1. The new folder will be the child of the currently selected folder, so select the parent folder first. Then choose the New Folder command from the File menu.
2. Type the name of the new folder and press the Enter key. The new folder will appear in the Folders list.

Moving a message is easy to do with drag-and-drop. To move a message into another folder:

1. Select the source folder, the one that contains the message you wish to move.
2. Drag that message across the pane divider and drop it onto the destination folder. That message now exists only in the destination folder.

Deleting Messages When you no longer want to keep a message, you need to delete it. Deleting messages you no longer need, together with moving messages when appropriate, helps to keep your mailbox organized.

To delete a message:

1. If the message is still open, click on the Delete icon on the Toolbar to delete that message. 

   Otherwise, select the folder that contains the message and click on the message in the contents pane. Then, choose the Delete command from the File menu or click on the Toolbar's Delete button.
2. Deleted messages are not removed from disk; they are moved into the Deleted Items folder, which allows you to restore a deleted message if you change your mind later on. To permanently delete a message, select the Deleted Items folder to view its contents. Then, select the message(s) to be permanently deleted and choose the Delete command from the File menu. You will be prompted to confirm the deletions; choose Yes to permanently delete the message(s).

Using Mail-Enabled Applications

A *mail-enabled application* is one that allows e-mail to be sent directly to others on a LAN-based mail system without using Exchange. Many of the new Windows 95-based applications have this ability. A program is mail-enabled if the File menu contains commands such as Send, Send File, Routing Slip, or other mail commands. Such applications are equipped with *MAPI* support, which is Microsoft's Mail Application Programming Interface.

From within a MAPI-supported program, choosing the Send command creates a new mail message using the Exchange new mail screen, and attaches the currently open file to that message. Exchange does not have to be running to send mail from a mail-enabled application.

10.4 *Just the Fax*

If your computer is equipped with a fax-capable modem, or if you are connected to a network that provides a shared fax, you can use Windows to send fax documents utilizing Microsoft Fax or other fax software. The fax program uses the modem and a telephone line to transmit a file to another fax machine or fax modem.

Ways to send a fax

Faxes can be sent in several ways:

- You can use the Compose New Fax Wizard; it is initiated from the Start menu, and assists you with the creation of the fax step-by-step.
- If the program you are using is mail-enabled, you can choose the Send command from the File menu, and specify a fax addressee.
- Using an application's Print command, you can print to the fax item (which is listed as one of the printers).
- You can use Exchange to address a message to a fax recipient and send a file from the message window, just as you send an e-mail message.

Faxes that you receive will appear in the Exchange Inbox, where you can view them or print them. To open Exchange to send or receive a fax, double-click on the Inbox icon on the Desktop.

NOTE If the Inbox icon does not appear on your Desktop, then Microsoft Exchange is not installed. You must install both Microsoft Exchange and Microsoft Fax to send and receive fax messages.

After installing the fax software, a fax item will appear within the Printers folder, as shown below. Printing a file using the fax item as the designated printer routes the file through the fax modem for transmission.

WARNING The fax item's printer should *not* be associated with a physical port connection, such as LPT1 or COM1. It should be listed, on the Details page of this printer's Properties dialog box, as "FAX: (Unknown local port)", as shown below.

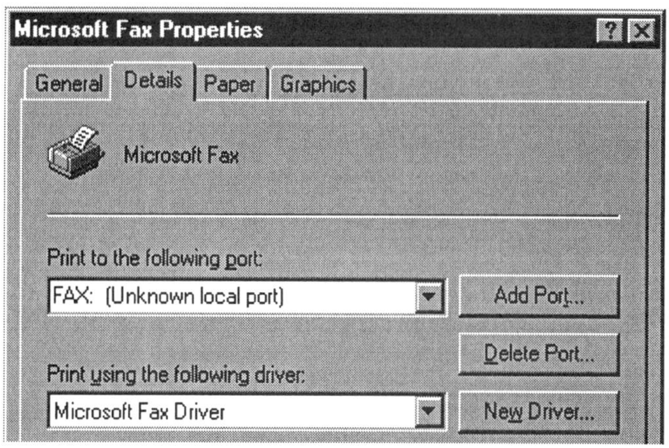

TIP If you create a Desktop shortcut to the fax item, a document can be faxed simply by dragging and dropping it onto the shortcut. To create the shortcut, drag the fax item from the Printers folder onto the Desktop (see Section 3.4).

Sending a Fax

You can send a fax transmission to another computer's fax modem or to a traditional fax machine. When creating a fax document, the Fax Wizard plays an important part in that process, assisting you with step-by-step instructions for building and creating the fax document. There are many ways to access the Fax Wizard:

Ways to access the Fax Wizard

- Exchange handles the fax program in the same way it does the mail service program. In particular, a fax message is initiated from within Exchange in a way similar to that of an e-mail message — choose New Fax from Exchange's Compose menu.
- Click on the Start button, point at the Programs option, and choose Accessories from the resulting submenu. Then, from the Accessories submenu, choose the Fax option.
- If you created a fax item shortcut on the Desktop, to send a file as a fax document, drag-and-drop that file onto the shortcut.
- From within Explorer or any folder window, right-click on a file, point at the Send To command, and then choose the Fax Recipient option from the resulting submenu.

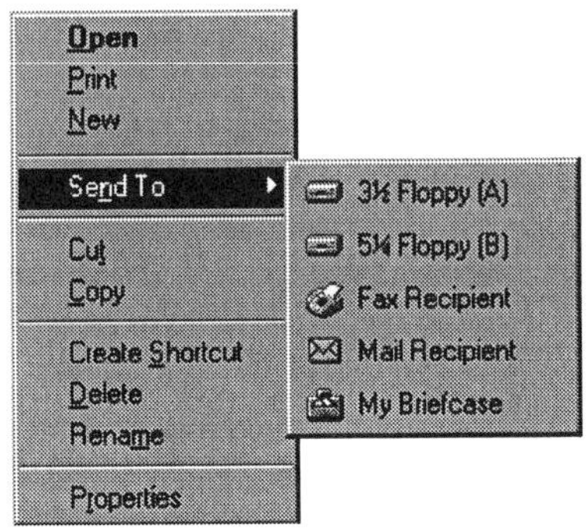

- From within a mail-enabled application, select Send from the File menu, and address the transmission to a fax recipient. The open document will be the attachment to the fax.
- Open the file to be sent as a fax, choose the Print command from the File menu, and specify the Fax as the designated printer. Then, choose the OK command button to "print" to the fax.

To finish creating a fax within the Fax Wizard:

1. Using any of the above methods, start the Fax Wizard.
2. In the first Wizard dialog box, make sure the number in the *I'm dialing from* text box is correct. This number is not going to change if you do not fax from a portable computer, so you may want to select the check box next to the *I'm not using a portable computer, so don't show this to me again* option.

   Choose the Next command button. The Wizard displays the next screen, which is shown in Figure 11.

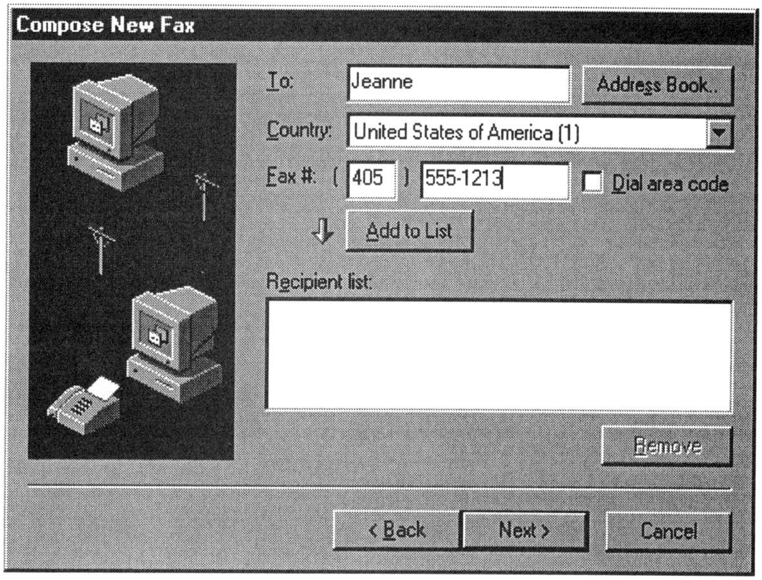

Figure 11 The Fax Wizard Dialog Box

3. Specify the addressees to which you want to send the fax. As you add new recipients, choose the Add to List command button to add that person to your personal address book.

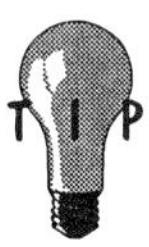

If you address the fax to users who are not fax recipients, but who are e-mail recipients, they will receive the transmission as an e-mail message. These recipients can be added by choosing the Address Book command button, which displays your personal address book.

4. Choose the Next command button to display the next Wizard dialog box, which is shown in Figure 12 on the next page.
5. If you do not want a cover page with the fax message, select the *No* option button. If you do want a cover page, select the *Yes. Send this one* option, and then select one of the styles of cover pages from the list box. Choose the Next command button to display the next Wizard screen (Figure 13 on the next page).
6. The Wizard screen in Figure 13 provides you with the ability to enter a subject and a note that will appear on the cover page of the fax. Type in the desired information, and choose the Next command button.

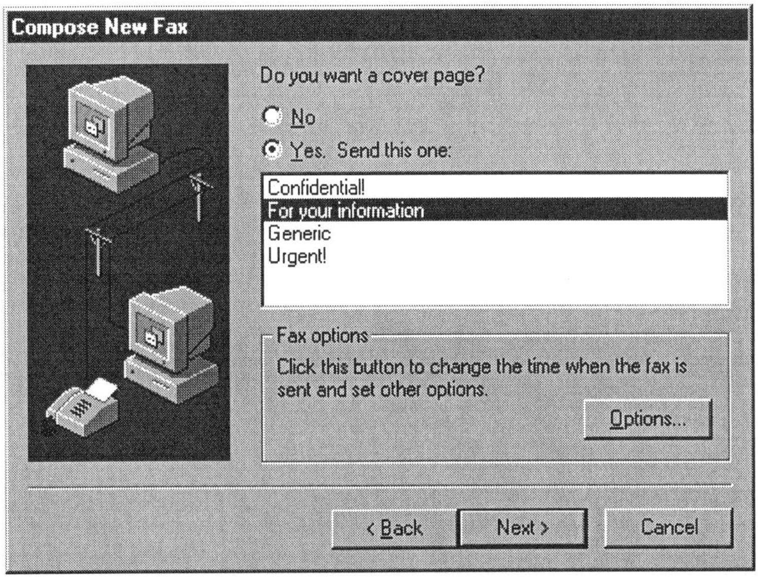

Figure 12 Choosing a Fax Cover Page

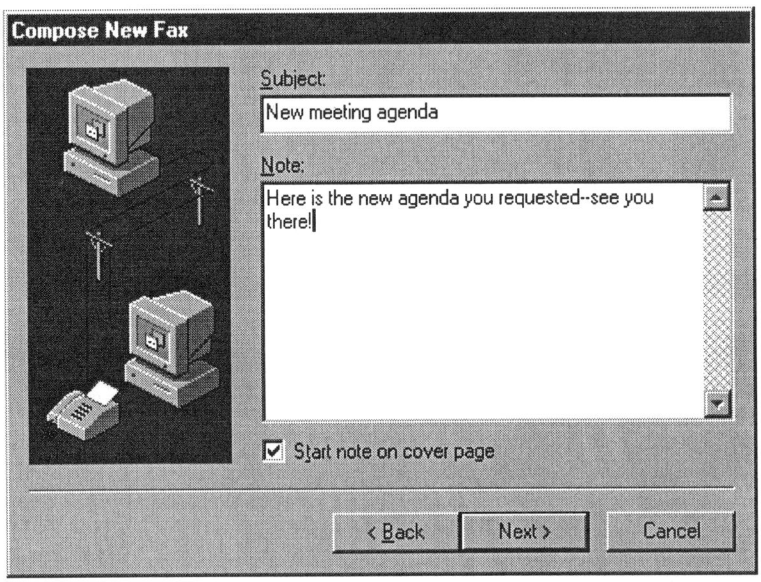

Figure 13 Adding a Subject and a Note to the Fax

7. The next Wizard screen lets you add files to the fax transmission. Choose the Add File command button to select any number of files you wish to transmit.
8. After selecting files to be transferred, choose the Finish command button to end the Wizard sequence. Your fax will be sent through the fax modem.

NOTE

If the recipient's system supports *binary file transfer*, (or BFT), the files will be send as embedded objects (see Section 12.5), which can be edited on the recipient's computer after transmission. If the recipient's system does not support BFT, the files will be translated into graphic images, and cannot be edited.

TIP

All of the standard Exchange tools that apply to e-mail messages apply to fax messages.

If the fax transmission is not successful, the fax dialog box will close automatically. Check the phone connections into and out of the modem. Then send the fax again; the creation of the fax must be started from the beginning.

Receiving a Fax

Fax answer modes

The Exchange application, when running, will automatically answer any incoming calls on the fax line and display a fax machine icon in the Taskbar's notification area (to the left of the clock). Mouse-pointing at this icon displays a tool tip that informs you of the current *answer mode*, which determines what action your modem takes if a call comes in on the line. There are three answer modes: Auto Answer, Manual Answer, or Don't Answer. The tool tip displays these modes as Auto Answer, Manual Answer, or Idle, respectively. (Auto Answer is the default mode.) These modes are described below.

To change the answer mode (and the fax modem properties, in general):

1. Double-click on the fax machine icon in the notification area to display the Fax Modem Properties dialog box, shown in Figure 14 on the next page.

   If the fax machine icon is not visible in the notification area, open the Control Panel window (from the Start menu's Settings option). Then, double-click on the Mail and Fax icon (if you use Messaging instead of Exchange, the icon is simply called Mail); the MS Exchange Settings Properties dialog box will be displayed. Select Microsoft Fax, choose the Properties command button, and the Microsoft Fax Properties dialog box will open. Click on the Modem tab to display the Modem page of the dialog box (Figure 14).

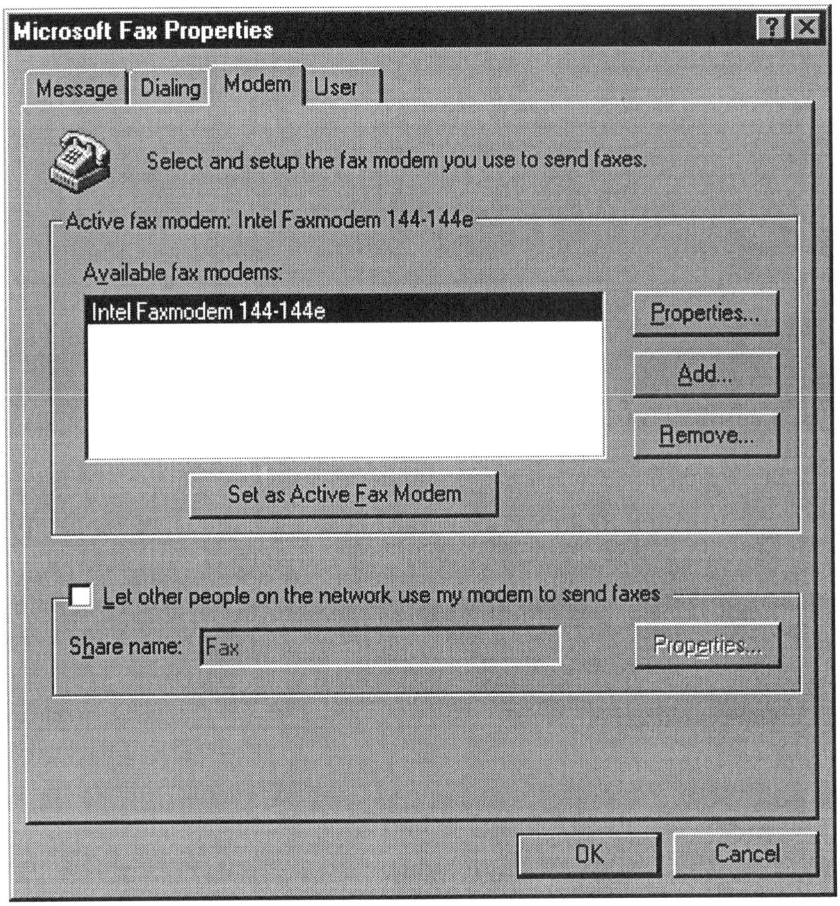

Figure 14 The Microsoft Fax Properties Dialog Box

2. With the appropriate modem selected in the list (there is usually only one), choose the Properties command button. The Fax Modem Properties dialog box opens (Figure 15) and the following options are available:

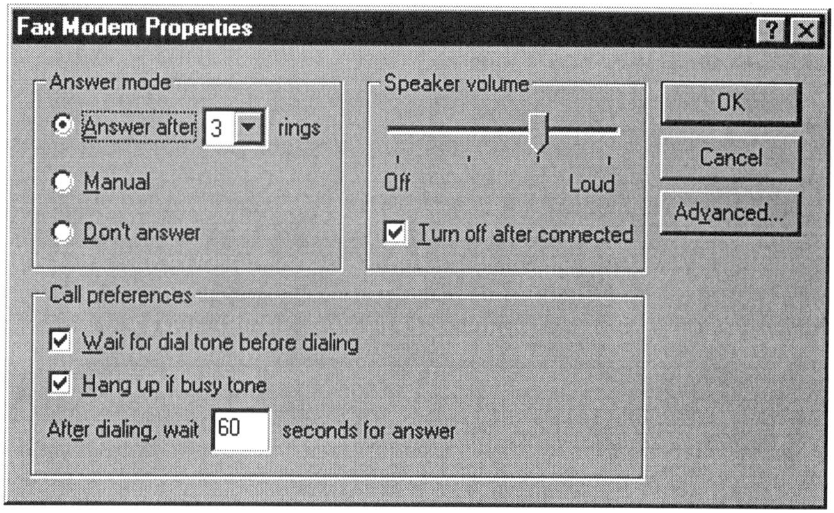

Figure 15 The Fax Modem Properties Dialog Box

- The Auto Answer option allows you to choose the number of rings before the fax modem will pick up an incoming call.
- Changing the fax modem to Manual requires that you instruct the modem to answer when a call is coming in. This is achieved by double-clicking on the fax modem icon in the notification area to display the Fax Modem Status window and then choosing the Answer Now command button.
- You can disable the Answer Mode to prevent the fax modem from answering the line by selecting Don't Answer. The fax modem icon will still display in the notification area, but the Fax program will not occupy the communications port, allowing its use for another application or device.

3. Choose the OK command button to accept any changes you have made. Continue choosing the OK command button in each dialog box to close them all and return you to the original starting point.

When the fax modem receives a fax transmission, a status dialog box will open on the Desktop, indicating the progress of the receipt of the new fax. When the transmission is complete, the fax message will appear within the Inbox of the Exchange program, just as an e-mail message does. (All of the standard Exchange tools that apply to e-mail messages apply to fax messages.)

The Fax Viewer Just as you can send both editable and graphic faxes, you can receive either kind as well. What makes the difference is how the sender transmits the fax to you. Incoming faxes will appear within the Exchange Inbox, just as e-mail messages do, and those that are editable will look and behave as e-mail messages. Microsoft Fax uses a Fax Viewer program to display graphic messages; its window is shown in Figure 16.

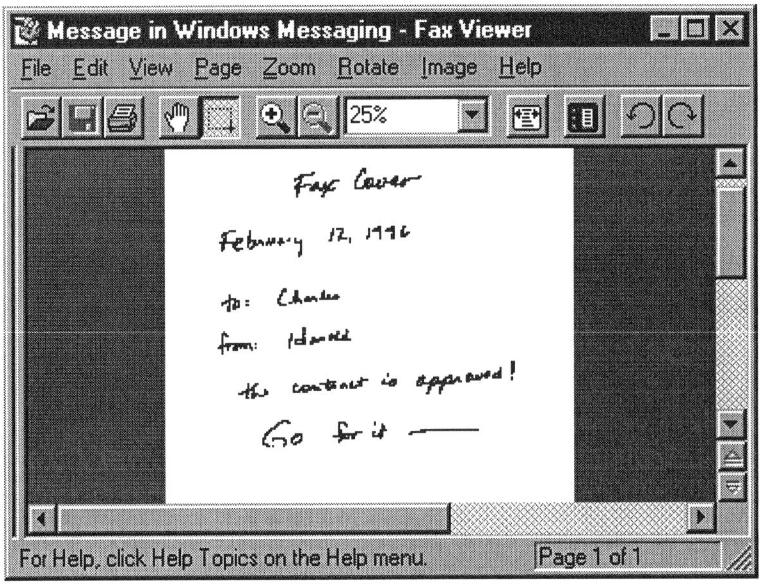

Figure 16 The Fax Viewer Program

The Fax Viewer displays the fax as a picture; the fax message cannot be edited.

10-4 TUTORIAL

Try the following exercise on your own.

1. Turn on the computer (if necessary) to start Windows 95 and start the Fax Wizard to create a fax:
   - Click on the Start button and point at Programs, then Accessories, and finally Fax.
   - Click on the Compose New Fax option on the resulting menu. The Compose New Fax Wizard will start.
2. Type your instructor's name as the recipient of the fax.

3. Enter a valid fax telephone number in the *fax#* text box. If you do not have access to a fax line, enter your home phone number. Then, click on the Next command button.
4. Select a cover page from the list of available styles and click on the Next command button.
5. Enter the subject as Fax Tutorial in the *Subject* text box.
6. Type a note in the large text box. Let the instructor (as the recipient) know that this is a test fax and that he or she should ignore the transmission. Then, choose the Next command button.
7. Choose the Next command button without selecting any files as part of the fax.
8. Click on the Finish command button to begin the fax transmission. If you do not have a fax modem or if the fax number used is not a real fax line, an error message will be displayed.

10.5 HyperTerminal

By now, you have worked with a personal computer long enough to appreciate how powerful and versatile it is. Its capabilities can be extended even further by using it to access information on other computer systems. Even though your computer is not connected to a local network:

- You can post messages on electronic *bulletin boards* and read messages posted there by others.
- You can transmit files to and from a bulletin board service, or another computer.
- You can connect to your campus mainframe, and use the software and data on it that has been authorized for public access.

Some Communication Basics

When you create a link between your computer and another system, the latter is known as the *host* computer. In order to "talk to" a host computer, your system must contain, or have access to, some special hardware and software. You need:

- A modem.
- A nearby telephone jack. The modem is connected to the tele-

phone lines by the same kind of wire and connectors as your telephone.

- **Communications software**, a program that allows you to establish a modem connection to the host computer at a remote site and exchange data with that computer. The communications software supplied with Windows is called **HyperTerminal**.

Using HyperTerminal

Hypertrm

To start HyperTerminal:

1. Click on the Start button, point at the Programs option, and then point at the Accessories item on the resulting submenu.
2. Click on the HyperTerminal item on the Accessories submenu, which opens the HyperTerminal folder (Figure 17).

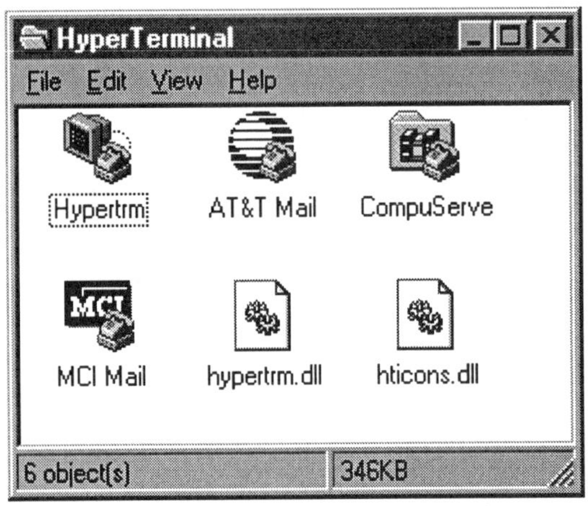

Figure 17 The HyperTerminal Folder

3. Choose the HyperTerminal icon (by double-clicking on it) to start this application.

You can now use HyperTerminal to establish a communications link with a host computer. This process involves two basic steps:

1. Create a connection and configure (set up) that connection properly, so that the host computer will "understand" the signals it is sent. This step entails specifying certain communications settings.
2. Connect to the host computer by dialing its modem's telephone

number and logging on to the system, providing any necessary identification codes.

Once the link is established, you can exchange information, view data, and/or transfer files between your computer and the host system.

Configuring HyperTerminal for the Connection

Before you can transmit data to another computer, you have to *configure* HyperTerminal — specify a few communications settings (or *parameters*). The proper settings depend mostly on the system with which you are trying to communicate, so you may have to specify different parameters for each remote computer with which you want to connect.

Fortunately, many parameters can be left at their *default* values — those suggested by Windows. The others are usually prominently listed in your modem's user guide or in documentation available from the organization that runs the host system. If this documentation is not available, you may be able to call the host system (at its voice, not data, phone number) to get the required information.

To configure a new connection:

1. Open the Connection Description dialog box in one of the following ways:
    - If HyperTerminal is not running, start it as described above. The HyperTerminal window will open and the dialog box in Figure 18 (on the next page) will be displayed.
    - If you are already in a HyperTerminal session, choose the New Connection command from the File menu. This, too, will display the dialog box shown in Figure 18.
2. In the Name text box, type the name you want to assign to the connection and select an icon to visually represent the connection.
3. Choose the OK command button. The dialog box in Figure 19 (on the next page) will open, prompting you to enter the first group of configuration settings.
4. Choose the Country code for the country from which you are calling. Then enter the area code, if necessary, in the Area code text box and the phone number for the remote computer in the Phone Number text box. (This is the number that HyperTerminal dials when you activate the connection.) Spaces, parentheses, and hyphens are ignored. Thus, (213) 555-1212 and 2135551212 will dial the same number.

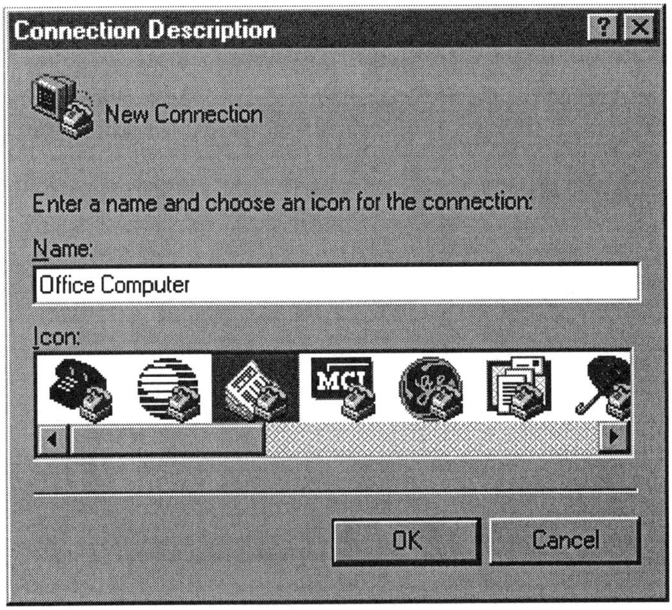

Figure 18 Naming the Connection

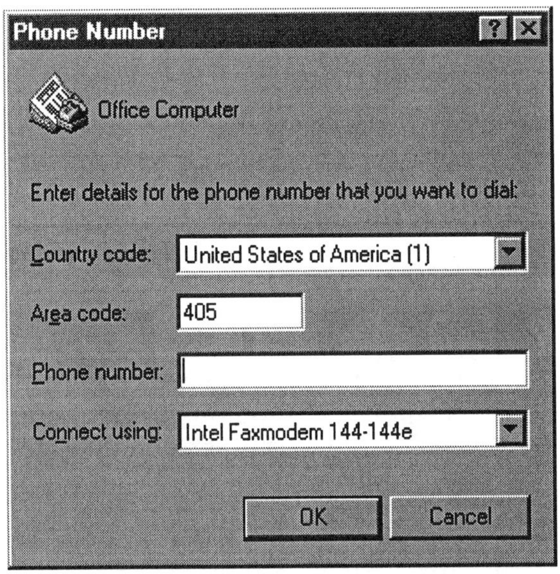

Figure 19 The Phone Number Dialog Box

5. If you want the modem to pause in the dialing process (perhaps to wait for the dial tone on an "outside line"), place a comma at this point in the phone number. Typically, each comma inserts a two-second pause. For example, 9,,5551212 inserts a four-second pause after the 9 is dialed.
6. After entering the phone number, make sure that the modem you are using is listed in the *Connect using* drop-down list. (The default setting will most likely be the modem that is installed on your computer.)
7. Choose the OK command button. The Connect dialog box (Figure 20) will open.

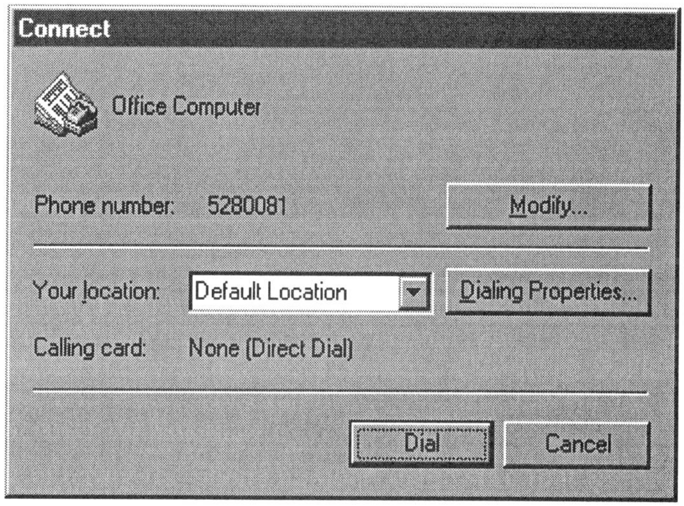

Figure 20 The Connect Dialog Box

8. Choose the Modify command button to display a two-page dialog box that allows you to change the Phone Number parameters or modify more advanced settings on the Settings page, which is shown in Figure 21 on the next page.

   The Settings page lets you change three aspects of the connection:

   - *Function, arrow, and ctrl keys act as* — Choose between using the host computer's function key set up (*Terminal keys*) or the usual Windows keys. (You should probably use the Terminal keys option so that your keyboard behaves as the remote connection expects.)

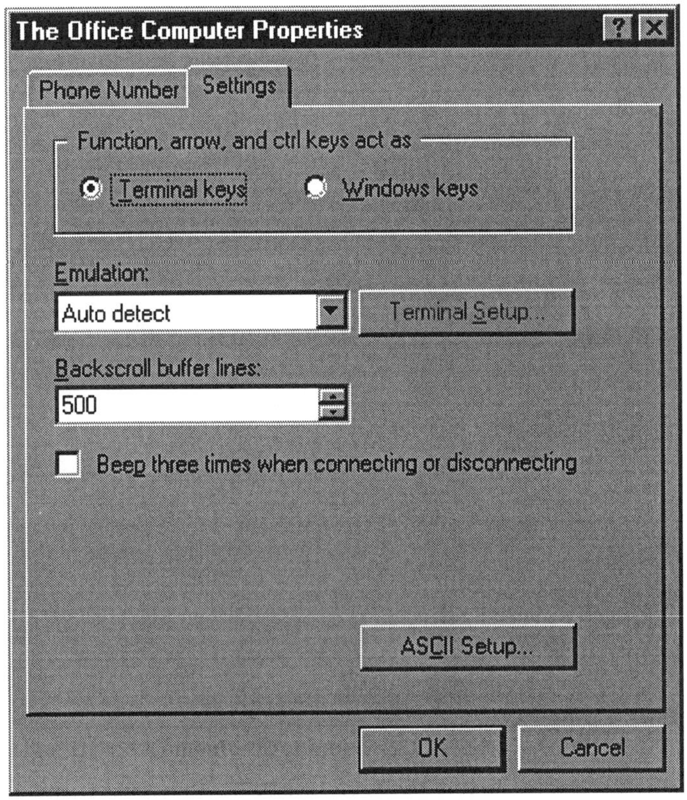

Figure 21 The Settings Page of the Modify Dialog Box

- *Emulation* — The remote system may expect your computer to act like (emulate) a specific type of terminal. Check the host's documentation for the proper emulation. Then, select the terminal type from the drop-down list. If you leave the selection as Auto Detect, HyperTerminal should automatically sense what emulation is needed upon connecting to the host system.
- *Back scroll buffer lines* — This setting determines the number of lines that are seen when scrolling with the PageUp key.

9. Choose the OK command button to accept all settings and close the dialog box. The Connect dialog box will reappear.
10. Choose the Dial command button to access the new connection or choose Cancel to return to HyperTerminal.

Saving the new connection After making settings changes, if you are planning to connect to the same host computer at some time in the future, you should save the set of parameters by choosing the Save command from the File menu. (Remember: The connection was named when it was created.) The connection file is saved by default in the HyperTerminal folder.

Opening a connection file The next time you want to call this host computer, choose the Open command from the File menu. The usual Open dialog box (see Section 2.2) will be displayed, allowing you to select the file that contains the proper settings for this connection.

Connecting to the Host Computer

After you have configured HyperTerminal to work with your modem and the host computer (as described above), establishing a communications link to a host computer is a simple process:

1. From within the HyperTerminal window, double-click on the appropriate connection file icon.

   or

   If the connection file is open and the HyperTerminal window is displayed, choose Connect from the Call menu or click the Connect button on the Toolbar.

   In either case, the Connect dialog box (Figure 22) will open.

2. Choose the Dial command button to begin the connection process.

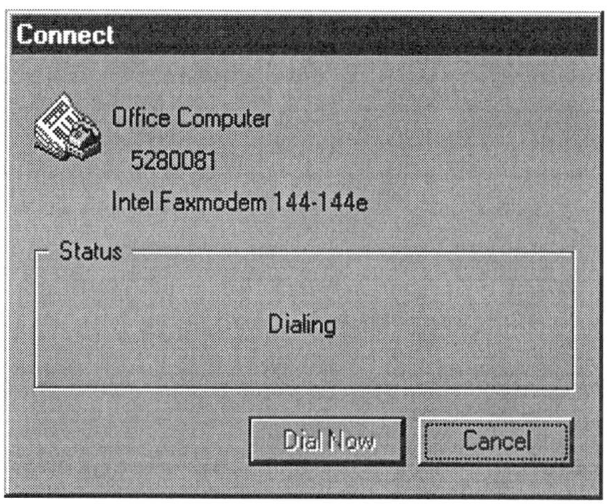

Figure 22 Making the Connection

3. When the host computer "answers", you may have to go through a login process, giving your account or identification number and perhaps a password. The text sent by the remote computer and your responses will appear in the HyperTerminal window.

TIP

Due to the number of parameters involved, setting up and establishing a link to a remote computer can be a tricky business. Here are a few trouble-shooting tips:

- If the modem doesn't dial when you choose the Dial command button, check the cable connections and, if you have an external modem, check that it's turned on. Also, make sure you've selected the proper model in the Modem list and specified the correct serial port in the Connections Properties dialog box. (Choose Properties from the File menu and then choose the Configure button to view the serial port setting.)
- If the modem dials and apparently connects with the host, but the text that appears in the window is garbled, check the Modem configuration settings. (From the Connection Properties dialog box, choose the Configure button.) If you don't have documentation from the host, try each of the following, one at a time, and try to connect again: select a lower baud rate (2400 almost always works); change the data bits setting from 7 to 8, or vice-versa; change the parity; and increase the stop bit number.

Using the Host Computer

After you have logged onto the host computer, you will have access to specific applications and/or data on this system. Access is often provided in the form of menus or queries sent by the host and displayed in the HyperTerminal window. Some systems also allow you to type commands to access information. These, too, appear in the window as you type them.

HyperTerminal stores all text sent and received in a special area of RAM called the *scroll buffer*. If you have sent and/or received more text than can fit in the window, you can review text that is not visible by using the scroll bars to move through the scroll buffer.

Printing text

Text can be *printed* in two ways:

- You can print incoming text as you receive it by choosing Capture to Printer from the Transfer menu. The Capture to Printer option remains in effect until you choose it again. A check mark next to this menu item indicates that it is in effect.

- You can print any or all text in the scroll buffer by copying it to the Clipboard, pasting it into a word processor such as WordPad, and then printing it from this application. (The Select All item on the Edit menu may be useful here; it selects all the text currently in the scroll buffer.)

Transferring Files

To transfer text, data, graphics, and programs between your computer and the host, you can *send* files to the host computer or *receive* files from it. HyperTerminal can send or receive two types of files:

- In a *text file transfer*, the file must consist entirely of *ASCII characters*; roughly speaking, those that can be typed at the keyboard. Text files cannot contain any other symbols or formatting commands, such as you might find in a spreadsheet or word processing file.
- In a *binary file transfer*, the symbols in the file are transmitted as a sequence of bits — zeros and ones. Any file, including a text file, can be transmitted as a binary file.

Sending a File Before sending a file, you must decide which of the two forms of file transfer to use. Since text file transmission is faster, you should use it whenever you can; for example, for electronic mail and word processing files in ASCII form (those with no special formatting codes). Non-ASCII data files and graphics must be sent in binary form. If you try to transmit a binary file using a text transfer method, an error message will be displayed or the transmission will be garbled.

To send a file to the host computer:

1. Prepare the host computer (usually by selecting an option from a menu) to receive your file. Sending a *text* file is usually treated the same way as typing the text at the keyboard, so this step may not be necessary for text files.
2. Choose either Send Text File or Send File (for binary files), as appropriate, from the Transfer menu. The corresponding dialog box will open. For example, if you choose Send Text File, the dialog box shown in Figure 23 (on the next page) is displayed. (The Send File dialog box looks almost the same.)
3. Sending a file is analogous to *opening* your file on the host computer, and the Send dialog boxes work the same way as the Open dialog box (discussed in Section 2.2). Select the drive and folder in

which the file is stored from the *Look in* drop-down list. Then, double-click on the appropriate file name or select it and choose the Open button to send the file.

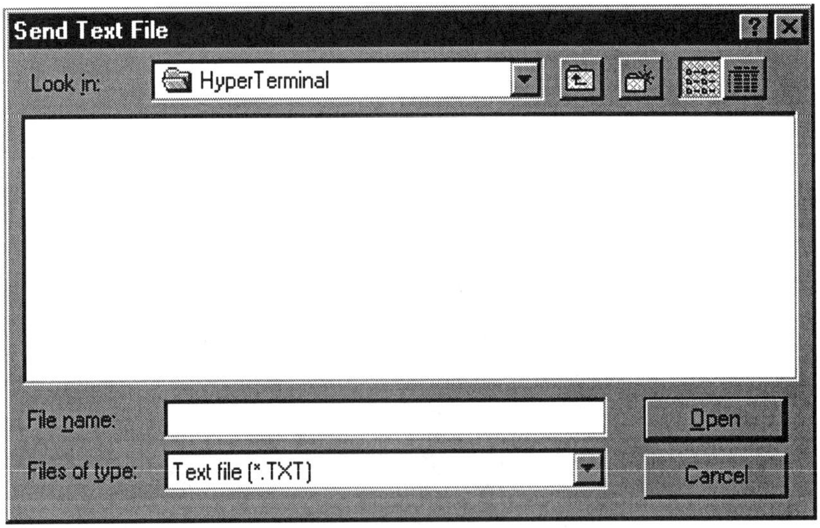

Figure 23 The Send Text File Dialog Box

Receiving a File To receive a file from the host computer:

1. Give the host computer the required command (it varies from host to host) to start transmission (to *download* the file).
2. Choose Receive File from the Transfer menu. The resulting dialog box, which is shown in Figure 24, will open.

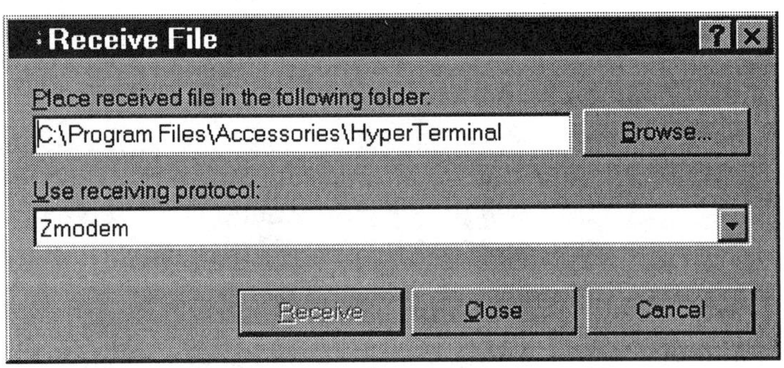

Figure 24 The Receive File Dialog Box

3. Select the drive and folder in which to save the incoming file and the *protocol* the host computer is using to send the file.
4. Choose the Receive command button.

Terminating Your Session

When you are done working with the host computer:

1. Execute the host's *log-off* procedure. This usually consists of choosing an exit command from the main menu or typing bye at a command prompt.
2. Break the connection by choosing Disconnect from the Call menu.
3. Exit HyperTerminal.

10.6 Portable Computing

Portable (or **laptop**) computers are smaller versions of the desktop models, providing powerful computing while away from the home or office. Using a laptop allows you to remotely access a network or another computer, thus taking advantage of full work-group functions; you can work on the remote connection just as if you were at your desk connected to the network or using the desktop computer. Windows has built-in user-friendly help and laptop tools, providing easy remote network access, electronic mail, and fax features that make laptop use easier than ever.

Windows delivers laptop support in several ways:

Windows' support for laptops

- Users get the most out of a portable's hardware with less hassle because Windows automatically loads necessary configuration files during installation.
- Communicating using the laptop is possible with electronic mail, fax, and remote network access.
- Windows tools provide assistance with the transfer of information between the desktop computer and the laptop computer.
- Dial-Up Networking can establish a connection to the LAN at a remote site, as long as the LAN has a terminal server enabled. When used in this way, Dial-Up Networking acts as the laptop's network card.

Laptop users tend to utilize their portable computers for the same tasks as they use a traditional desktop machine (word processing, spreadsheets, electronic mail, and so on). Although the computing tasks that these users want to accomplish are very much the same, the desktop and mobile computing environments are radically different.

Nonetheless, portable computer users can take advantage of most of the Windows features that we have discussed in this chapter. For example, laptop users can create a network connection using Dial-Up Networking (see Section 10.2) to access their desktop workstation while away from that location. Also, the Microsoft Exchange e-mail and fax systems (Sections 10.3 and 10.4) enable portable computer users to easily send and receive e-mail and faxes while mobile.

In this section, we will explore other Windows features that make portable computing easier. To be more specific, we will discuss the following topics:

- Docking detection
- The Direct Cable Connection utility
- The Briefcase utility
- Deferred printing

Docking Detection

A **docking station** connects a portable computer, through communications ports, to a network or *peripheral hardware*, such as a monitor, CD-ROM drive, or other storage device. Because the system hardware changes when a laptop is connected to a docking station, traditionally, users have had to spend a lot of time reconfiguring and rebooting their machines when they take them in and out of their docking stations. No more!

Windows 95 enables a user to perform docking and undocking operations without turning off the equipment, a process known as *hot docking*. Windows provides the flexibility of multiple *hardware profiles* (see Section 6.5), each defining a different hardware configuration. When more than one profile exists, Windows prompts the user, when booting the computer, to choose the desired profile. For example, the video resolution for the docked monitor on the desktop is different from the laptop's built-in LCD panel, and Windows adjusts for this change via the appropriate hardware profile.

Direct Cable Connection

The simplest way to connect a laptop to a desktop computer (or, for that matter, to connect *any* two computers) is with Windows' **Direct Cable Connection (DCC)** utility. (The machines are usually physically connected by a serial or high-speed parallel cable.) While connected, the laptop has access to the shared resources on the desktop computer and to any network to which that computer is connected. Transferring files between a desktop and a portable computer with DCC provides a reasonably fast transfer and is much less expensive than using a docking station.

When two computers are connected with Direct Cable Connection, one computer is labeled the *host*, and the other computer is the *guest*. The guest computer can access all folders on the host computer, but the host cannot access folders on the guest. The Direct Cable Connection must be set up first on the host computer; then on the guest computer.

Before setting up the Direct Cable Connection, you must first determine if this utility has been installed. To do so, click on the Start button, point at the Programs option, and choose Accessories from the resulting submenu. If Direct Cable Connection does not appear on the Accessories submenu, then it has not yet been installed.

To install the Direct Cable Connection utility:

Installing DCC

1. Click on the Start button, point at the Settings option, and choose the Control Panel item from the resulting submenu. The Control Panel window will open.
2. In the Control Panel window, select the Add/Remove Programs item by double-clicking on its icon. The Add/Remove Programs Properties dialog box will open.
3. Click on the Windows Setup tab to view that page of the dialog box.
4. Select Accessories from the Components list and then choose the Details command button.
5. Select Direct Cable Connection and choose the OK command button. Windows may prompt you to insert the original Windows disks or CD so that the appropriate files can be installed on your hard disk. If so, follow the on-screen instructions.

Connecting Two Computers When you are ready to connect two computers with Direct Cable Connection, physically join the computers with the proper cable connecting their parallel or serial ports and then follow this procedure:

1. Choose the Direct Cable Connection item from the Accessories submenu. The Direct Cable Connection Wizard will start and display its first dialog box, as shown in Figure 24.

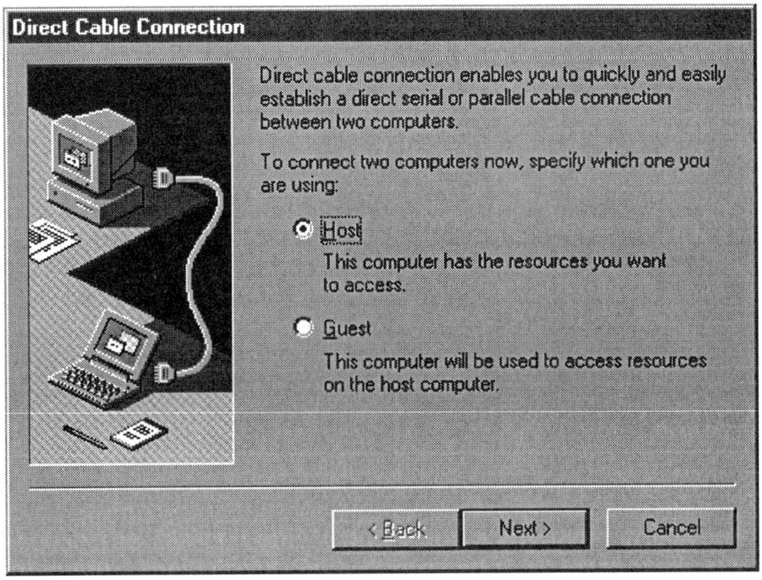

Figure 24 The Direct Cable Connection Wizard

2. Decide whether the computer you are using is to be the *host* or *guest* by selecting the appropriate option button. (Remember: The guest can make use of the host's files.) Then choose the Next command button; the Wizard checks the communications ports on your computer and then displays another screen.
3. Select the communications port you are using for the connection and choose the Next command button.
4. The next Wizard dialog box may prompt you to activate File and Print Sharing between the two computers. If so, click on the File and Print Sharing command button, which will open the Network Control utility dialog box.
5. Choose the File and Print Sharing command button from within the Network Control utility dialog box, shown in Figure 25. This will open the File and Print Sharing dialog box (Figure 26).

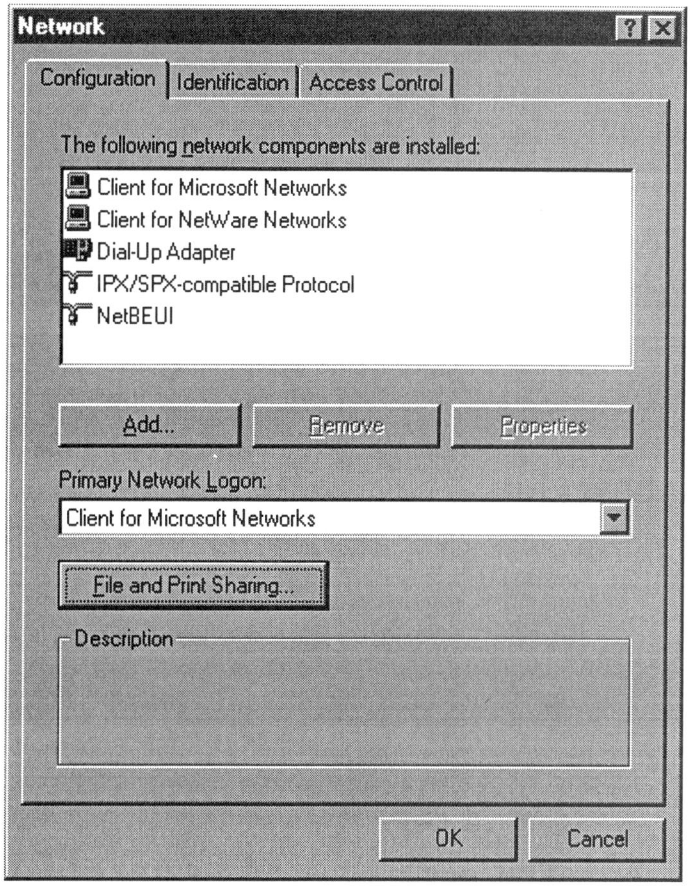

Figure 25 The Network Control Dialog Box

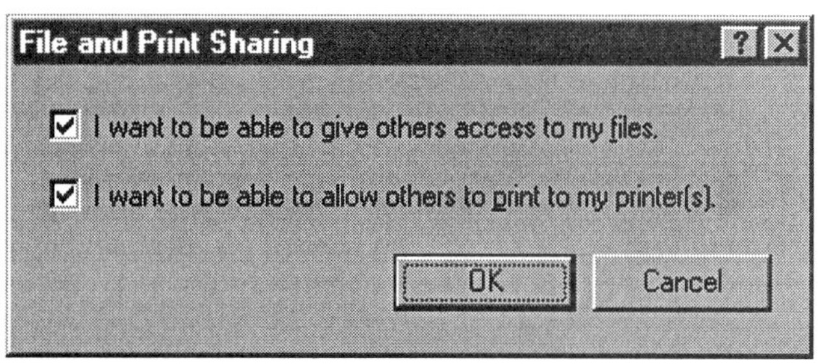

Figure 26 The File and Print Sharing Dialog Box

6. In this dialog box, select either or both of the options to allow file sharing and/or printer sharing between the two computers, then choose the OK command button. The Network Control dialog box will open again; choose the OK command button to close it.
7. From within the Direct Cable Connection Wizard dialog box, choose the Next command button. When configuring the host computer, a third Wizard screen is displayed. You can now select a password, if desired, by clicking on the Password Protection check box. Then choose the Set Password command button and type the desired password, confirming that password when prompted. This password can be used to restrict files and printers on the host computer to authorized users.

   After setting the password, or if you decide not to use a password, choose the Next command button.
8. Repeat the previous steps to set up the Direct Cable Connection on the guest computer, and the connection between the two computers is established.

The files and folders on the host computer can now be accessed by the guest computer. Printers can also be shared.

The Briefcase Utility

My Briefcase

When one person works with both a portable and desktop computer, typically there are copies of the same files on both machines. After working on the portable, some of the files may need to be updated to the desktop computer and vice-versa. Keeping that information organized is a difficult and on-going task. Moreover, if you lose data by inadvertently overwriting a new file with an old version, it can be an exasperating experience!

Windows built-in **Briefcase** utility takes care of updating the files, whether the newer files are on the laptop or desktop computer, with a process termed *synchronization*. Synchronization keeps track of the original locations of the files. The Briefcase identifies which files have been modified and which ones haven't, and older files are updated to the newest version. Briefcase will update the files on the desktop or laptop computer automatically, preventing confusion.

If the Briefcase icon appears on the Desktop, then this utility has already been installed. If the icon does not appear, it must be created before the program can be used.

If you think you have installed Briefcase, but its icon isn't on the Desktop, create the Briefcase folder using the following procedure:

1. Right-click on an empty area of the Desktop. The pop-up menu shown at the right will appear.
2. Point at the New option to open its submenu.
3. If the Briefcase item is listed on the submenu, then Briefcase has been installed.
4. Choose the Briefcase item. A new icon, called My Briefcase, will appear on the Desktop.

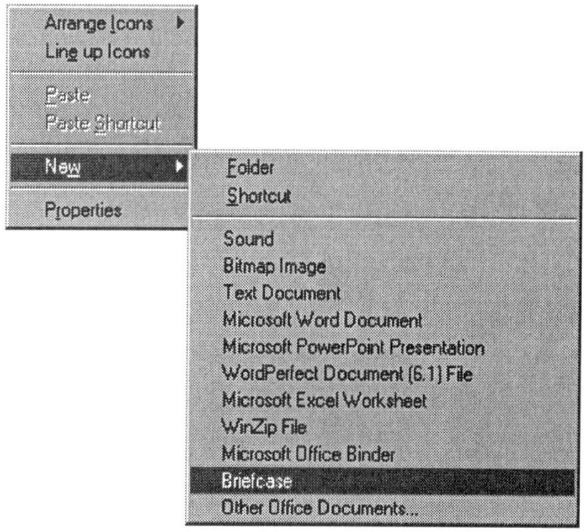

NOTE If there was no Briefcase option on the submenu in the previous procedure, you need to install the Briefcase utility. To do this, proceed as with Direct Cable Connection, described earlier in this section.

Once the Briefcase icon has been created on the Desktop, files to be used on the laptop must be copied into the Briefcase on the portable computer. While the portable computer is connected to the desktop computer by a Direct Cable Connection:

1. From the desktop computer, open a My Computer or Explorer window and locate the files to be copied.
2. Copy the files from the main computer to the Briefcase icon on the Desktop.
   - Right-click on a file you wish to copy to the Briefcase and point at the Send To command on the pop-up menu.
   - The My Briefcase option will appear on the resulting submenu; choose this command to copy the selected file(s) to the Briefcase on the Desktop.
3. Using the DCC, copy the Briefcase to the portable. Briefcase makes a copy of each file and records information about its original location on the desktop computer. The Briefcase file is called a *sync copy* (or synchronization copy).

NOTE

When you copy a folder into the Briefcase, a sync copy of the entire contents of the folder is made, including all files and any existing subfolders.

4. While working on the portable computer, do not copy the files out of the Briefcase; work with them from within the Briefcase by opening the Briefcase window (double-click on the icon). Open a file by double-clicking on that file.
5. When finished working on the files on the portable computer, reconnect to the main computer.
6. Open the Briefcase on the portable computer by double-clicking on its icon.
7. Choose the Update All command on the Briefcase menu to automatically replace the unmodified files on the main computer with the modified files in your Briefcase. To just update certain files, select those files in the Briefcase window and choose the Update Selection command from the Edit menu.
8. A dialog box will open, listing the files that Briefcase suggests be updated, including the file date and time of last modification and the file's original location. Figure 27 displays this window.
9. Choose the Update command button to revise the files.

TIP

Use the Briefcase to update files between a networked computer's local drive and the network drive. This is helpful, for example, if you want to work on the local desktop computer, but want to back up your files on the network.

WARNING

After copying files to Briefcase, take care not to move the original files on the desktop computer. The Briefcase keeps track of the original file location, but there is no built-in tracking system for moved files. If you *do* move a file on the desktop computer, the file is no longer associated with the sync copy of that file in the Briefcase. Even if you move the file back to its original location, the file will not be updated correctly. This problem must be corrected with manual synchronization.

Manual Synchronization If Briefcase cannot find the original files, and therefore is unable to update them, *manual file synchronization* may solve the problem. This procedure allows you to recreate a sync copy in the Briefcase by manually copying the most current file to the appropriate location, either the drive or the Briefcase.

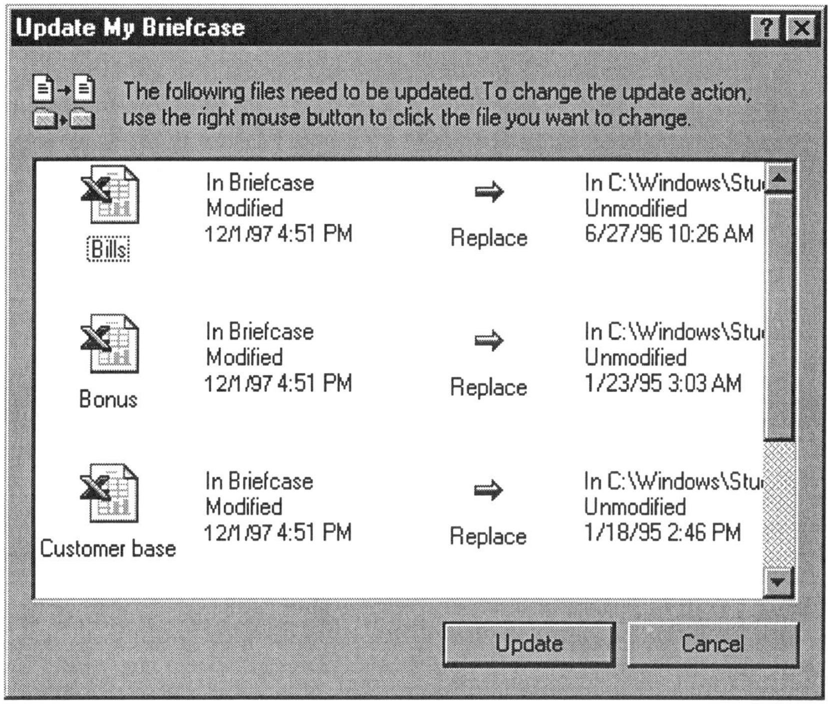

Figure 27 The Briefcase Update Dialog Box

To manually synchronize a file, decide if you want to use the original file on the desktop computer or the copy of the file in Briefcase as the most recently updated file. Then:

- If you choose to use the original file, delete the copy of that file in Briefcase and copy the original file to Briefcase.
- If you choose to use the copy of the file in Briefcase, move the file from the Briefcase to a new location on your hard disk and copy the file to Briefcase.

Deferred Printing

Deferred printing is a feature that manages and holds print jobs that you create while not connected to or not using a local or networked printer. Deferred printing establishes a *print queue* that saves print information until the printer is reconnected. You can therefore send print jobs to a printer even if you are not connected to that printer.

Upon reconnection to the printer, the deferred printing queue is activated and the jobs are printed.

The Deferred Printing utility is useful for portable, network, and desktop computers. For example, you can "print" documents while traveling with a laptop computer, queuing them to print all at once when you return. Upon connecting the laptop to a printer, the document will print automatically if the printer supports plug-and-play technology (see Section 6.2). Otherwise, you must manually start the printing process.

NOTE The automatic printing of queued jobs works only if the reconnected printer is the same as the one to which the documents were "printed" in the first place.

How to defer printing

To defer printing while using a portable computer or network printer:

1. Click on the Start button, point to the Settings option, and choose Printers from the resulting submenu. The Printers folder will open.
2. Select the printer that you want to use by clicking on its icon. It will appear highlighted.
3. Choose the Work Offline option on the File menu. This action adds a check mark by the menu option, indicating that the Work Offline feature is active (Figure 28, on the next page). The printer itself will remain inactive and the printer icon will appear dimmed, indicating that it is unavailable.

To defer printing with a local printer:

1. From within the Printers folder, select that printer's icon and choose the Pause Printing option from the File menu. (A check mark will appear there.)
2. Close the Printers folder.

How to reactivate deferred jobs

To reactivate deferred print jobs (if plug-and-play does not reactivate them automatically):

1. Click on the Start button, point to the Settings option, and choose Printers from the resulting submenu. The Printers folder will open.
2. Select the offline printer that you want to use. (Printers that are offline will be dimmed.)

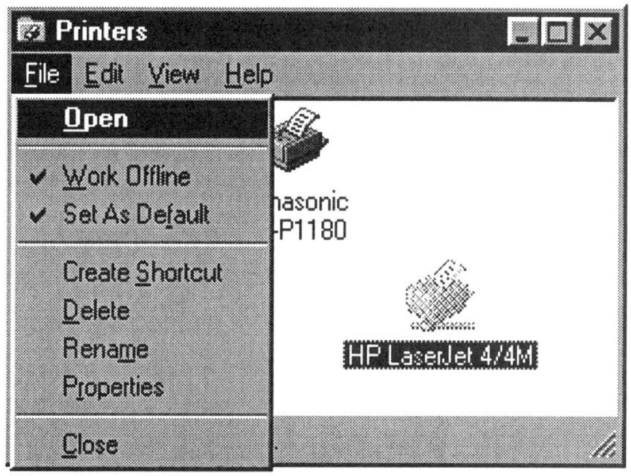

Figure 28 The Printer is Currently Working Offline

3. ■ When using a portable computer or network printer, choose the Work Offline option from the File menu to remove the check mark next to this item.

   ■ When using a local printer from a desktop computer, choose the Pause Printing option from the File menu to remove the check mark.

4. Close the Printers folder by choosing the Close button. The deferred print jobs will begin to print.

Chapter Summary

Networking	To access a network	Click on the Start button, point at the Programs option, and choose your network program (the name of the network option varies). Then, enter the login and password when prompted.
	To browse and access network resources	Open the Network Neighborhood program by double-clicking on its Desktop icon.
	To configure the network options	Open Control Panel and choose the Network icon; the network control utility will open, allowing you to change settings.

Using Dial-Up Networking	To create a Dial-Up Networking connection	Double-click on My Computer and open the Dial-Up Networking folder; *or* choose the Dial-Up Networking item from the Start button's Accessories submenu. Then, choose the Make New Connection icon and make use of the New Connection Wizard.
Using Microsoft Exchange	To start Microsoft Exchange	Double-click on the Inbox icon on the Desktop.
	To create a new mail message	Choose the New Message option from the Compose menu *or* click on the Toolbar's New Message button; enter the address of the recipient in the To text box; enter the subject in the Subject text box; type the message in the message area; and choose the Send item from the File menu *or* click on the Toolbar's Send button.
	To receive e-mail	Start Exchange. The new messages will appear in the Inbox folder. Double-click on a message to view it.
	To move a message	Select the folder that currently contains the message; then select the message and drag-and-drop it onto the desired folder.
	To delete a message	If the message is open, click on the Toolbar's Delete button. Otherwise, select the folder that contains the message, select the message, and choose Delete from the File menu or click on the Toolbar's Delete button. (Deleted messages are moved to the Deleted Items folder.)
	To send any file as e-mail	Open the file in a mail-enabled application and choose the Send item from the File menu.
Using Microsoft Fax	To send a fax	Choose Fax from the Start button's Accessories submenu; *or* in the Exchange program, choose the New Fax item from the Compose menu; *or* print an open file using the fax item listed in the printers list. Then, make use of the Fax Wizard.
	To receive a fax	Faxes that are text files will be received in the Exchange Inbox and are viewed like e-mail messages. To view graphic faxes (non-text files), double-click on the message in

		the Inbox folder; it will be displayed in the Fax Viewer window.
HyperTerminal	To start HyperTerminal	Choose the HyperTerminal item from the Start button's Accessories submenu.
	To configure a connection	Double-click on the HyperTerminal icon; then, name the connection, select an icon, and enter the phone number of the host computer.
	To connect to the host computer	Choose the connection icon from the HyperTerminal window; *or* if the HyperTerminal window is open, choose Open from the File menu and select the connection file name. Then, choose the Dial command button and login to the host computer.
	To transfer files	To send a file, choose the Send Text File or Send File option from the Transfer menu.
		To receive a file, choose the Receive File option from the Transfer menu. Select the file from the dialog box list and choose the OK command button to receive the file.
	To disconnect from the host computer	Execute the host computer's log off procedure and break the connection by choosing Disconnect from the Call menu.
Portable Computing	Direct Cable Connection	To connect two computers, choose the Direct Cable Connection item from the Start button's Accessories submenu; decide whether the computer will be the host or guest; identify the communications port to be used; and activate the desired File and Print Sharing options.
	The Briefcase	To create a Briefcase folder, right-click on the Desktop, point at the New option, and choose Briefcase.
		To work with files in the Briefcase, copy the files from the main computer to the Briefcase folder on the Desktop; then copy the Briefcase folder to the portable computer or to a floppy disk. Edit the files from within the Briefcase folder.
		To update the files from the Briefcase, copy the Briefcase back to the main computer *or*

connect to the main computer; then, open the Briefcase folder and choose the Update All option from the Briefcase menu and choose the Update command button.

Deferred printing	To defer printing, choose Printers from the Start button's Settings option, click on the desired printer icon, and select the Work Offline option from the File menu.
	To print the deferred jobs: If the printer supports plug-and-play, simply connect the printer to the computer; if not, open the Printers folder, select the desired (dimmed) printer, and choose Work Offline from the File menu.

Review Exercises

Section 10.1

1. A small scale network is called a ____________.
2. A large scale network is called a ____________.
3. A designated computer that runs the network operating system is a ____________.
4. NIC is a type of network hardware best described as
    a. A commonly used cable type.
    b. A hub that assists in removing noise, strengthening the line signal, and controlling the network traffic.
    c. A card that fits in the computer, connecting it to the network cabling, and which uses software to set up each workstation for network use.
    d. A wireless network (or *virtual network*) that works with infrared mini-transformers and receivers and does not require traditional cabling.
5. To establish a connection with the network, each user must initiate a(n)
    a. Logout procedure.
    b. Login procedure.
    c. Server procedure.
    d. Exit procedure.
6. The Network Neighborhood displays the resources to which you have access

a. On the network.
b. In My Computer.
c. In Explorer.
d. On the Desktop.

Section 10.2

7. Dial-Up Networking provides the user ____________ to another computer system, using a modem and a telephone line, without formally networking the computers.

8. The remote dial-up system functions as if it were a ____________, except that it does not process information as quickly.

9. Once connected via dial-up networking, you will have complete ____________ capabilities, such as printing to a network printer, accessing a customer database, or using shared files.

10. When you are using remote access and are connected to an office computer, the latter is called the

    a. Guest.
    b. Server.
    c. Host.
    d. Link.

11. When you are using remote access and are connected to an office computer, the computer you are dialing in on is called the

    a. Guest.
    b. Server.
    c. Host.
    d. Link.

12. The process of setting up a Dial-Up Networking connection definition is handled by

    a. Peripheral hardware.
    b. The New Connection Wizard.
    c. The Next command button.
    d. Direct Cable Connection.

13. The icon in the window shown on the right initiates

    a. The New Connection Wizard.
    b. The New Modem Wizard.
    c. The Direct Cable Connection Wizard.
    d. Dial-Up Networking.

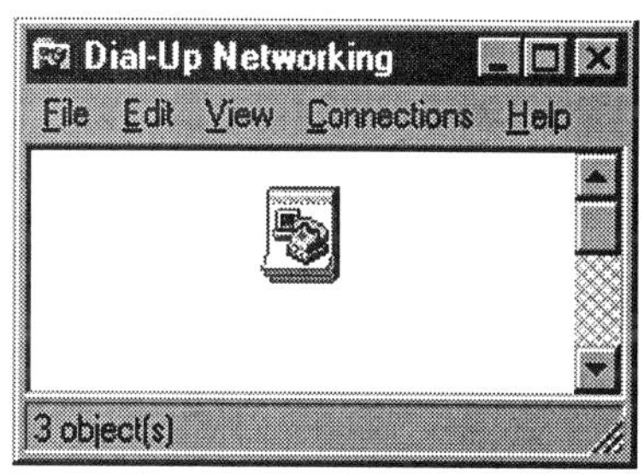

14. True or false: the New Connection Wizard can assist you in setting up a phone connection to a fax machine.

15. True or false: Dial-Up Networking provides remote access to another computer system, using a modem and a telephone line, only when the computers are formally networked.

16. True or false: A modem is a hardware device that sends and receives the appropriate codes through telephone lines from one computer to another.

Section 10.3

17. With Microsoft Exchange, you can send and receive
    a. Print based correspondence.
    b. Electronic mail or fax messages.
    c. Important air-mail documents.
    d. None of the above.

18. When choosing a Microsoft Mail Service, as an end user, you will define the following:
    a. Who will be the post office administrator
    b. The user ID and password
    c. Whether you have access to voice mail
    d. Which icon displays the program

19. The icon pictured at the right opens
    a. WordPad.
    b. My Computer.
    c. Microsoft Exchange.
    d. Notepad.

20. True or false: A profile is a group of settings defined for each user who needs to work within the Exchange.

21. True or false: When you use Exchange for the first time, the Exchange Setup Wizard will run.

22. True or false: Messages are automatically deleted by Exchange after you read them.

23. ____________ consists of electronic messages sent over a network between users.

24. The Microsoft Exchange post office operations are managed by the ____________.

Section 10.4

25. A fax program uses a ____________ and a telephone line to transmit a file to another fax machine or fax modem.

26. Faxes will appear in the Exchange ____________ folder, where they can be viewed or printed.

27. After installation of fax software, a fax icon will appear in the
    a. My Computer folder.

b. Inbox folder.
c. Printers folder.
d. Startup folder.

28. Which "wizard" takes you step-by-step through the process of creating a fax?
    a. Fax Wizard
    b. New Connection Wizard
    c. E-mail Wizard
    d. None of the above
29. True or false: Pointing at the fax icon in the Taskbar's notification area displays the fax status.
30. True or false: The Fax Viewer is used to display editable fax messages.

Section 10.5

31. With HyperTerminal, you can
    a. Post messages on electronic bulletin boards.
    b. Send and receive files.
    c. Connect to a campus mainframe.
    d. All of the above.
32. When entering the phone number for the host computer, which character inserts a "pause"?
    a. Period
    b. Comma
    c. Question mark
    d. Quotation mark
33. True or false: HyperTerminal stores all text sent and received in a special area of RAM called the scroll buffer.
34. True or false: In a text file transfer, the file can contain non-ASCII symbols and formatting commands.
35. The HyperTerminal application is found on the Start button's ____________ submenu.
36. Terminal ______________ sets up your computer to act like a type of computer with which the remote computer can communicate.

Section 10.6

37. A portable computer, also known as a ____________, is a small version of a desktop model.
38. A ____________ physically connects a portable computer, through its communication ports, to a network or peripheral hardware.
39. A portable and desktop computer that are physically connected to each other by a cable can be logically connected using the Windows ____________ utility.

40. The Briefcase program takes care of updating files with a process known as
    a. Synchronization.
    b. Annihilation.
    c. Transportation.
    d. Communication.
41. Deferred printing is a feature that holds print jobs in
    a. The Briefcase.
    b. The Exchange Inbox.
    c. A print queue.
    d. The Recycle Bin.
42. True or false: When a computer is reconnected to a printer that supports plug-and-play, deferred print jobs will automatically be sent to that printer.
43. True or false: The Windows deferred printing feature is available only for portable computers.

Build Your Own Glossary

44. The following words and phrases are important terms that were introduced in this chapter. (They appear within the text in boldface type.) Use WordPad (see Section 2.2) to enter a definition for each term, preserving alphabetical order, into the Glossary file on the Student Disk.

Briefcase utility
Communications software
Deferred printing
Dial-Up Networking
Direct Cable Connection
Docking station
Electronic mail
E-mail
E-mail administrator
Hub
HyperTerminal
Inbox
Local Area Network (LAN)
Message
Microsoft Exchange
Microsoft Fax
Multitasking
Network
Network cabling
Network control utility
Network interface card (NIC)
Network Neighborhood
Outbox
Peer-to-peer network
Portable computer
Profile
Remote network access
Server
Wide area network (WAN)
Workstation

Lab Exercises

Work each of the following exercises at your computer. Begin by turning the machine on (if necessary) to start Windows 95 and closing any open windows.

Lab Exercise 1 (Section 10.1)

a. Click on the Start button and point to the Programs option. On the resulting submenu, what network options are listed?

b. Click on an empty area of the Desktop to close the Start menu.

c. Start the Network Neighborhood program by double-clicking on its icon on the Desktop, which opens the Network Neighborhood window. What is visible in the window? Why don't you see different network drives and peripheral equipment? Close the Network Neighborhood window.

d. Open the Control Panel window and start the Network utility, which opens the Network Control dialog box. Which network options are installed?

e. Click on the Identification tab to display that page of the dialog box. Are the computer and workgroup named? If so, what are their names?

f. Choose the Cancel command button to close the Network Control dialog box.

g. Close the Control Panel window.

Lab Exercise 2 (Section 10.2)

(This exercise requires that Dial-Up Networking and a modem be installed on your computer.)

a. Start My Computer.

b. Open the Dial-Up Networking folder by double-clicking on the folder icon in the My Computer window. What icons appear in the Dial-Up Networking folder?

c. Start the New Connection Wizard by double-clicking on the Make New Connection icon. Use the following information to create the connection:

- Name your connection with "*your name's* Connection".
- Enter your home phone number as the dial-up number.

d. *Optional:* Capture the Dial-Up Networking window with your icon visible, and paste it into WordPad. Print the resulting document. (See Section 2.3 for the procedure for capturing screens.)

e. Delete your connection icon from the Dial-Up Networking folder and close all open windows.

Lab Exercise 3 (Section 10.4)

a. Double-click on the Inbox icon on the Desktop to start the Exchange program.

b. Look at the Taskbar's notification area; is a fax icon displayed?

- If so, double-click on the Fax icon in the notification area to display the Fax Modem Properties dialog box.
- If the icon is not visible, open the Control Panel window and double-click on the Mail and Fax icon. In the resulting MS Exchange Settings Properties dialog box, select Microsoft Fax and choose the Properties command button. The Fax Modem Properties dialog box will open; click on the Modem tab to display the Modem page of the dialog box.

c. With your modem selected in the list, choose the Properties command button to open the Modem Properties dialog box What are the current settings?

d. *Optional:* Capture the Modem Properties dialog box, paste it into WordPad, and print the resulting document. (See Section 2.3.)

e. Choose the OK command button to close the Modem Properties dialog box. Continue clicking on OK command buttons until all dialog boxes are closed.

f. Close the Exchange program.

Lab Exercise 4 (Section 10.5)

(You must have a modem installed on your computer system to complete the following exercise.)

a. Open the HyperTerminal window.

b. Turn on the Capture to Printer option. On which menu does it appear?

c. In the HyperTerminal window, double-click on the MCI Mail connection icon. (This connection is installed by default by Windows 95.) The Connect dialog box for MCI Mail will open in the window.

d. Choose the Dial command button to initiate the connection and open the Connection window. (Notice that the connection status is visible in the left corner of the status bar.)

e. If prompted to enter a user name, type your name and press Enter. For a password, any word will do. Since you do not have an account with MCI Mail, the sign-on information will be rejected. If you are not prompted for a login or the connection is not successful, continue with this exercise anyway.

f. Turn off Capture to Printer.

g. Click on HyperTerminal's close button. A HyperTerminal dialog box opens, informing you that you are still connected. Choose the Yes command button to terminate the connection.

h. Close the HyperTerminal window.

Lab Exercise 5 (Section 10.6)

a. Insert the Student Disk in its drive and open My Computer.

b. Display the contents of the Student Disk.

c. Right-click on the file called Preamble and point to the Send To option; then choose the My Briefcase item from the resulting submenu.

d. Open the Briefcase window. What is the status of the Preamble file?

e. Where does Briefcase indicate that the sync copy exists?

f. Open the Preamble file from the Briefcase window. Insert a blank line at the top of the document and type your name. Then, save and close the file.

g. In the Briefcase window, choose the Update All option from the Briefcase menu. Which file(s) are listed in the window? Update the Preamble document to your Student Disk.

h. Close the Briefcase and My Computer windows and remove the diskette from its drive.

Lab Exercise 6 (Section 10.6)

a. Open the Printers folder.

b. Select the printer that is connected to your computer; then open the File menu.

c. Which option is available for deferring printing on this printer? (The name of the option depends on whether the printer is local or on a network or laptop connection.) Choose this option.

d. Open the File menu again. What change occurs in the appearance of the option of step *c*?

e. Use the Escape key to deactivate the File menu without changing any options.

f. Start WordPad and maximize its window (if necessary).

g. Insert the Student Disk in its drive and open one of the text documents. Print this file and exit WordPad. Does the printer activate?

h. In the Printers window displayed on the Desktop, select the printer (if necessary). Open the File menu and activate printing by choosing either the Work Offline or the Pause Printing option. Close the Printers window. What happened when you did this?

i. Close all open windows and remove the Student Disk from its drive.

If You Want to Learn More ...

The notes presented here allow you to delve more deeply into some of the topics covered in this chapter.

Sharing files, folders, and printers

As you have seen in this chapter, one of the advantages of a network is that its resources can be shared among those connected to the network. To share resources, however, it is not enough to *designate* them for sharing with the Network Control Utility; you must tell Windows exactly which resources are to be shared. To do so:

1. Right-click on the icon of a file, folder, or printer to be shared and choose the Sharing item from the pop-up menu. The Properties dialog box for the selected object will open.
2. Click on the Share tab to display this page of the dialog box.
3. On the Share page, designate how you want to share this resource by providing it with a network name and deciding whether others have read-only rights, full rights, or must use a password to use the resource. For example, sharing printers or project folders within a project workgroup on the network allows just those workgroup members to use those resources.

Using the network drives for backup locations

To protect your data from loss due to hardware failure, you can use the network drive as a location for your backups. Network drives are usually backed up frequently by the network administrator. Take advantage of this routine by copying your critical files to your designated area on the network drive. Then, if your computer fails or if you lose data for any other reason, the relevant files can be retrieved from the network drive.

Be aware that if you keep critical files on the network drive, you should also keep copies of these files on your own computer. Then, if the network server goes down (out of service), you can continue working even though you can't access the network.

CHAPTER 11

Windows and the Internet

In Chapter 10, we introduced basic networking concepts and some network-related features of Windows 95. In this chapter, we will discuss the **Internet**, a world-wide network that joins together thousands of smaller, local networks.

The Internet gives us access — from our homes, schools, and offices — to a wide assortment of information and resources. This chapter shows you how to connect to the Internet and how to use *browser* software to access these resources. To be more specific, you will learn:

1. About the structure and origins of the Internet.
2. About Internet names and addresses.
3. To connect to the Internet in several different ways.
4. To use Microsoft's Internet Explorer to browse the Internet.
5. To search for, print, and download information on the Internet.
6. To configure a Dial-Up Networking connection that accesses the Internet through an Internet Service Provider.

11.1 The Internet

The Internet is the largest network in the world and has many capabilities. It can transmit text, graphics, sounds, video and data; it can carry real-time interaction among numerous people over long distances; and it can be used by people around the world. Access to the Internet is also relatively inexpensive.

Internet–related software

The most commonly used method to access information on this "information superhighway" is through a software application called a *browser.* As the name implies, this software facilitates quick and easy access to many parts of the Internet.

Today's browser applications incorporate a variety of services. These include:

- The **World Wide Web** (the *Web*) — a hypertext/multimedia-based system for finding and accessing Internet resources.
- **Usenet** — the structure for transfer and maintenance of *news groups*, a group of systems that allow for online discussion and transfer of data between individuals with related interests.
- **E-mail**, or electronic mail — allows for the sending of messages to anyone connected to the Internet.
- **FTP**, or File Transfer Protocol — allows for the transfer of files between computers.

In addition to browsers, other software is used on the Internet for various purposes:

- **Telnet**, a communications application, allows one computer to log onto other computers on the Internet.
- **Internet Relay Chat** (IRC), allows for online real-time discussion between users by typing, reading, and responding.
- **Internet Phone** is like IRC, except that it uses an audio card and microphone with special software to enable you to talk across the Internet connection instead of over a telephone.
- **Gopher** is a menu-based system for exploring the Internet resources.

Ways to access the Internet

There are three ways to connect to the Internet:

- Through a dedicated connection to the Internet via a local network, such as might be established at an educational or government institution.
- Through an *online information service*, such as America Online,

which supplies you with a phone number and software to access the World Wide Web, specialized news groups, "chat rooms", and certain other online services.

- Through an account with an *Internet Service Provider* (ISP), which also supplies a phone number and software to access the World Wide Web, but provides no other online services. There are many ISPs providing an Internet connection, both locally and nationally, including Microsoft's service, The Microsoft Network.

A Brief History of the Internet

Currently "the Internet" is the generic catch-all name for a wide-variety of interconnected networks and programs providing information and resources to computers all over the world. The Internet is growing in popularity for all types of activities, including conducting business, performing research, and occupying leisure time.

In the late 1950s, the United States Department of Defense established the *Advanced Research Projects Agency Network* (ARPANET) for the purpose of sharing research information within the scientific community. Another major reason for the government's original interest in this network was that in case of nuclear attack, the network's multi-point connections guaranteed the continued transmission of information. If one pathway were destroyed, the data could still travel over a different route; communications would not be completely lost.

For the next twenty-five years, universities, government agencies, and government contractors were the primary groups to be connected to this rapidly growing *wide area network*. In 1983, APRANET was split, creating MILNET to exclusively serve the military. Then, in 1987, the National Science Foundation (NSF) entered the picture, greatly expanding the existing network. As the emerging "internet" grew, it became increasingly more common for businesses of all sizes, and even individuals (through a local network), to connect to it. Currently, thousands of new users are added daily to the Internet, which now extends to virtually all parts of the world.

Internet Names and Addresses

Every computer or site on the Internet has a unique and specific location, called an **Internet address**. The address defines the user name, the service provider, and the organization or country hosting the connection. The Internet address of a computer (workstation) is identified in two ways: with either a word-like *domain name* or a numeric *IP (Internet Protocol) address.* Of course, the name is easier to remember than the numeric address, but both are important in communicating on the Internet.

IP Addresses The IP (Internet Protocol) address is commonly represented as four numbers separated by periods, sometimes also called a *dotted quad.* The ARPANET (the predecessor of today's Internet) originally had the capacity to assign numbers to a maximum of 256 systems because of the way each system was addressed. In the early 1980s, when it became clear that requests for numbers would quickly exceed that limit, the dotted quad addressing method was created, making thousands of host numbers available for assignment.

Each part of an Internet address represents one set of the four sets of numbers that are required to properly address the location. The first two or three sets of numbers (for instance, 205.228.216) represent the network to which a system is connected, called its *subnet.* For example, all of the computers for one networked site might be in the subnet 205.228. Individual workstations at that site may then have numbers like 205.228.216.10 or 205.228.225.19, with up to 65 thousand possible combinations, and that many possible workstation locations.

Your computer has either a permanently assigned (static) IP address or a changing (dynamic) IP address assigned by the system each time you connect to the Internet.

Domain Names Names are easier to remember than numbers, and Internet users can also be referred to by their complete *domain name.* The complete domain name for each host is linked to its IP address.

Most domain names contain three parts, but some have four or even more. Each part of the name is separated by a period. There are three basic components of a domain name:

- The user name or machine name
- The service provider
- The organization or country

The right-most component of the domain name is called the top-level domain and identifies the country or organization part of the address. There were six original top-level domain names:

edu — an educational institution
com — a commercial site
net — network resources

gov — government, non-military, organizations
mil — a military site
org — other organizations

The next (middle) component of the domain name indicates the service provider. The first (left-most) section identifies the user or machine name, followed by the @ symbol when identifying a user or a period (.) when it is a machine name. For example, in the Internet address genemeister@service.com, *com* represents a commercial domain, *service* represents the service provider, and *genemeister* is the individual's user name.

NOTE When an address identifies a site and not a specific user or machine, the first section of the address, the part that normally precedes the @ symbol, is not used.

When contacting genemeister@service.com, the network system for this address is asked if that domain name really exists. Then, *service .com* (the Internet Service Provider) will reply to the network system with genemeister@service.com's IP address for identification. You, as a user, never see this transaction as it happens, and rarely will you need to know the IP address of a site. The network system takes care of it for you!

Connecting to the Internet

Since there are three ways to access the Internet, the method of establishing a connection differs slightly from case to case.

- If you can access the Internet with a dedicated connection, the program used to connect will have been set up for you. It will appear as an icon on the Desktop, or on the Programs submenu of the Start menu. Start that program to connect to the Internet.
- If you are using an online service, that service will send you the proper software to be installed on your computer. After setting up this software (follow the instructions — it differs from service to service), an item will be added to the Programs submenu of the Start menu. Start that program to initiate the connection.
- When using an Internet Service Provider, there are several steps that must be completed to configure the connection; see Section 11.3 for these procedures.

Once the connection to the Internet has been established, you will use special software, called a *browser*, to interact with the Internet. The software allows users to move from place to place in the Internet environment, much like browsing through books in a library. We will use Microsoft's **Internet Explorer** (version 3.0) in this text. Internet Explorer can be obtained from Microsoft or through the Internet, free of charge. (Another popular browser program is Netscape Navigator.) Browser versions change rapidly, so some of the screens displayed in this text may be slightly different from what you see on your system.

To start Internet Explorer, either

The Internet

- Double-click on the Internet Explorer icon on the Desktop.

or

- Click on the Start button, point at the Programs option, and choose the Internet Explorer item on the resulting menu.

In either case, the Internet Explorer window will open (Figure 1).

Figure 1 Internet Explorer's Start Page

We will discuss how to use Internet Explorer in Section 11.2.

11.2 Using Internet Explorer

Microsoft's Internet Explorer is one of the most popular browsing software applications available. It acts as your guide to finding information on the Internet and displays that information in an understandable way.

In Section 11.1, we showed how to start Internet Explorer. This section will examine its use. To be more specific, we will discuss how to use Internet Explorer to

- Navigate the Internet.
- Perform searches on the Internet.
- Print Internet pages.
- Send and receive Internet mail.
- Download a file from the Internet.
- Disconnect from the Internet.

Navigating with Internet Explorer

To access the Internet with Internet Explorer, you work from within the Explorer screen. All interaction with the Internet begins with the Start page, which is always the first screen you see after starting Internet Explorer. (The Start page is sometimes referred to as the home page.) The Start page, like every page on the Internet, displays *links* to other Internet pages.

Links A **link** on an Internet screen is a connection between pages. Links appear on the screen as one or more words highlighted with color, underlining, or both, in the content area of a page. Images and icons with colored borders also serve as links. When the mouse pointer rests on a link, the pointer appears as a hand and the location of the link appears in the status bar at the bottom of the page.

You can bring a linked page to the screen by clicking once on the highlighted text, image, or icon. Clicking on a link transfers page content from a server location to your location.

An *unfollowed link* is a connection to a page that has not yet been viewed; a *followed link* is one that has been viewed. By default, unfollowed links are blue and followed links are purple. If you have a black and white monitor, unfollowed and followed links are highlighted only with underlining and are not differentiated.

The Internet Explorer Screen Internet Explorer's Toolbar, displayed in Figure 2, provides single-click access to the most frequently used commands. These commands are also found on the menus, but using the Toolbar is quicker.

Figure 2 The Internet Explorer Toolbar

Here are descriptions of the Toolbar commands:

Back Returns you to a previously-viewed screen. This button will appear ghosted, or dim, if there are no previous pages to be viewed; for example, if you haven't left the initial, or *home*, page.

Forward Moves you to the next screen.

Stop Stops a request in progress.

Refresh Reloads the current document to the screen; can sometimes push the transmission through a bottleneck.

Home Returns you to the home page.

Search Displays Microsoft's page that provides access to all of the search utility programs.

Favorites Lists pages you have previously marked as interesting sites.

Print Prints the displayed page.

Font Increases or decreases the size of the display font for the page.

The Address Box The **Address box** (Figure 3) identifies the complete Internet location of the currently viewed page. Just as you have a street address that identifies where you live, every location on the Internet has an address, too.

Figure 3 Internet Explorer's Address Box

URLs Web Internet addresses begin with http:// (for *hypertext transmission protocol*) in the **Universal Resource Locator**, which is the address of the page's location, commonly called its **URL**. Internet Explorer or other graphical browsers can be used to access locations by typing the URL in an address text box and pressing the Enter key. Be aware that URLs must be typed exactly as they appear; case (upper or lower) and punctuation are important.

The Address box drop-down list displays previously-entered URLs. It provides a quick way to return to a previous site.

TIP

Internet Explorer assumes the "http://" part of the URL when you are entering an address in the Address text box, so it is not necessary to type this part of the address.

11-2a TUTORIAL

Try the following exercise on your own.

1. Start Internet Explorer by double-clicking on its Desktop icon. The Start page will be displayed.
2. Scroll down the Start page to locate the first text link on the page. The text will appear in blue, because it is an *unfollowed link*, and may also be underlined.
3. Click once on the text link to display that page.
4. Now, the Back button on the Toolbar is available; click on the Back button to return to the previous page. Notice that the link is now red because it has been used; it is a *followed link*.
5. Now, the Forward button on the Toolbar is available. Click on the Forward button to view the previously-accessed page.
6. Notice that the Forward button is now dim because no pages have been viewed after this one.
7. Click on the Back button until it appears dim. The Start page will now be visible again.
8. From the Start page, scroll up or down to find another link. Click on the link to display that information.
9. Click on the Toolbar's Home button to return to the Start page.
10. Click in the Address text box to place the text cursor there. The existing address appears highlighted.
11. Type *www.enews.com* in the Address text box.
12. Press the Enter key to display the site. The page displayed will be

entitled *The Electronic Newsstand.*

13. Scroll down the page to see what is displayed there. Pass the mouse pointer over any special text items to determine which are links.
14. Click on the Magazines link to display that page.
15. Click in the text box that allows you to search the archives for an article.
16. Enter a topic of your choice, or choose from one of the general topic links further down the page.
17. Using the links on the page, explore different sites, as desired. Use the Toolbar's Back and Forward buttons.
18. Click on the Home button to return to the Start page.

Using Favorites A **Favorite** is an electronic place holder that identifies your favorite pages. Using Favorites to mark interesting pages on the Internet makes navigating to those sites in the future a quick and easy process.

To create a Favorite:

1. Display the desired page.
2. Choose Add to Favorites from the Favorites menu. Then, choose the OK command button to accept the name of the Favorite as suggested, or type a name of your own and choose OK. The new Favorite now appears on the list on the Favorites menu.

Favorites are quick to accumulate, and can become cumbersome to manage. Deleting old Favorites that are no longer appealing is important to do from time to time.

To delete a Favorite:

1. Choose the Organize Favorites item from the Favorites menu.
2. Highlight the desired page within the resulting window.
3. Press the Delete key on the keyboard or choose the Delete command button. Confirm the deletion by choosing the Yes command button to send the item to the Recycle Bin. Continue selecting Favorites and deleting them, as desired.
4. Choose the Close command button to return to Internet Explorer.

The Go Command The Go menu (Figure 4) lists commands that are otherwise available as Toolbar buttons and, at the bottom, lists pages you have previously viewed. Whether the pages you have previously visited are your "favorites" or not, using the Go menu lets you quickly navigate through Internet pages.

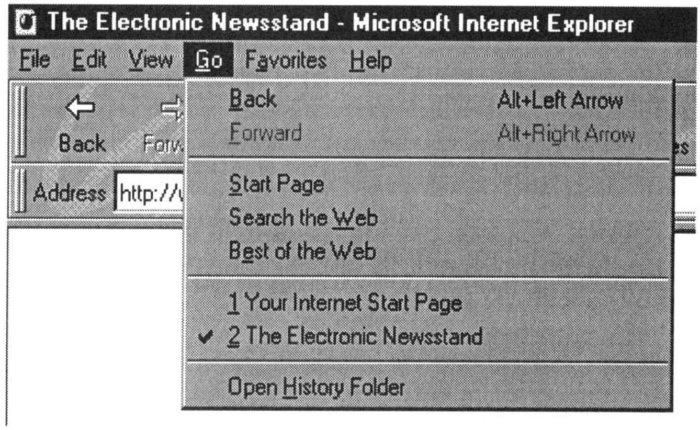

Figure 4 The Go Menu

To use the Go commands:

1. Open the Go menu.
2. Choose Back, Forward, Start Page, Search the Web, or Best of the Web as an alternative to using the Toolbar buttons.
3. Choose a previously viewed page from the list at the bottom of the menu to return to that page.

11-2b TUTORIAL

Try the following exercise on your own.

1. Start Internet Explorer, if necessary.
2. In the Address box, open the drop-down list to display previously accessed sites.
3. Select the *enews.com* location to return to this site.
4. Choose the Add to Favorites item from the Favorites menu; then choose the OK command button to accept the creation of a shortcut with the name The Electronic Newsstand.
5. Click on the Toolbar's Home button to return to the Start page.
6. Open the Favorites menu and select the newly-listed Favorite from the list to return to The Electronic Newsstand.

7. Click in the Address text box to place the cursor there. The existing address will automatically be selected.
8. Type *www.newslink.org* in the Address text box and press the Enter key. (This site lists local and national newspapers, magazines, radio stations, TV information, etc.)
9. Add this page to the list of Favorites by clicking on the Toolbar's Favorites button, then on Add to Favorites. Accept the shortcut name by clicking the OK command button when prompted.
10. Explore different links from this page.
11. Go to *www.xplore.com* and add it to the list of Favorites. (This site lists reference sources.)
12. Explore different linked pages and add any that are of particular interest to you to the Favorites list.
13. Open the Address box drop-down list to see the locations that were just typed in the Address box. Click on the *newslink.org* address to return to that page.
14. Open the Go menu and select the Electronic Newsstand page to return to that location.

Using the Links Toolbar The Internet Explorer Links Toolbar (Figure 5) provides a method of choosing different Internet sites by general topics.

Figure 5 The Links Toolbar

The Links Toolbar can be displayed instead of the page's address by clicking on the Links item to the right of the Address text box. When the Links buttons are displayed, the Address text box is temporarily hidden from view. Clicking on the Address item hides the Links buttons and redisplays the Address text box.

The Links Toolbar buttons provide easy access to certain locations in Internet Explorer. (These commands may differ slightly between versions of the software.) Here are the functions of the Toolbar buttons:

Best of the Web Lists the newest sites on and features of the Internet.

Today's Links	Today's hot topics.
Web Gallery	Provides links to resources for Web page developers.
Product News	Provides the latest information on Internet Explorer and other Microsoft products.
Microsoft	Displays the Microsoft Home page.
Status Indicator	The Internet Explorer logo becomes animated when transfers of data are in progress. Click on the logo to go to Internet Explorer's Home page.

NOTE

The progress bar, displayed at the right side of the status bar in the Internet Explorer window, becomes animated to show the progress of the current operation. Specifically, the bar shows the percentage done as a page loads.

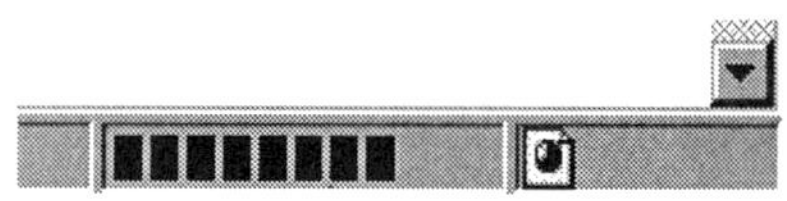

11-2c TUTORIAL

Try the following exercise on your own.

1. Start Internet Explorer, if necessary.
2. Choose the Links button to the right of the Address text box to display the Links Toolbar.
3. Click on the Best of the Web link to display that page. Choose additional links from that page, as desired.
4. Click on the Today's Links link button to view the current and new topics. Choose additional links, as desired.
5. Choose the Internet Explorer logo button to go to Internet Explorer's Home page.

Performing Searches

Once the browser is open, you can use search software to locate specific sites and information. There are several ways to search for information available on the Internet.

An easy way to display the search screen is to click on the Search button on the Internet Explorer Toolbar. This action takes you to Microsoft's Search Index page (Figure 6), from which you can access several search engines. A **search engine** is a program that seeks out information defined by the search criteria. Search engines allow specific information searches in many different ways — some engines search titles or headers of documents on the Internet, others search the documents themselves, and still others search indexes or directories. The type of information you need and your preferences in requesting that information will determine which search engine you decide to use. We will describe some of these engines later in this section.

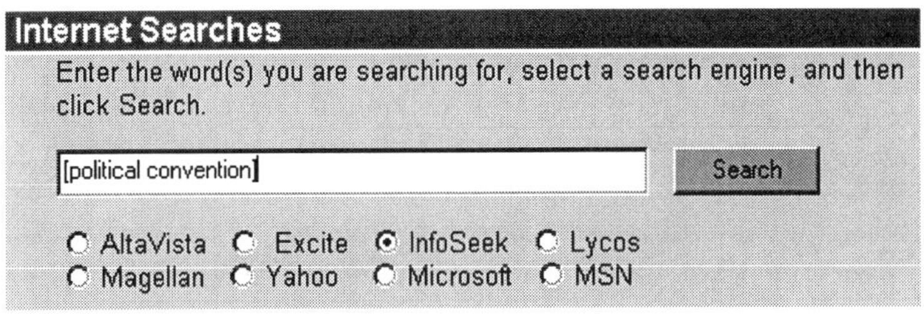

Figure 6 The Search Index Page

TIP

Unfortunately, the Search Index page is a busy site; frequent bottlenecks may occur when trying to access this page. Another way to display one of the search sites is to enter the address of the specific search screen. We will provide the URLs for some of these pages later in this section.

The general search procedure

To perform a search, follow this general procedure:

1. Click on the Internet Explorer Search button to display the Microsoft Search Index page (Figure 6), and select a search engine to use by clicking on its option button.

   or

   Enter the address of the desired search engine in the Address box and press the Enter key.

   In either case the search engine's home page will be displayed.

2. Click in the text entry search box to place the cursor there, and type the search criteria.

3. Choose the appropriate search command button to perform the search. The results of the search will be displayed on the screen.

Guidelines for the search

Some general guidelines when entering search text (step 2 of the previous procedure) are:

- Capitalize names of people and places, and use a comma to separate lists of names.
- Use lower case letters when case is not a factor.
- To identify a group of words that must appear together in order, use double quotation marks around them, or hyphenate them; for example, "Abraham Lincoln" or world-wide.

Most search engines provide a list of categories to allow you to search by subject. Each engine also has its own Help program to assist you. Listed below are brief descriptions of some of the available search engines.

Infoseek This fast search tool combines the qualities of a search engine and a listing service. Infoseek searches not only on the Web, but also the text of Usenet news groups, Web users' FAQ's (Frequently Asked Questions), e-mail addresses, current news, and company listings. The Infoseek location address is www.infoseek.com.

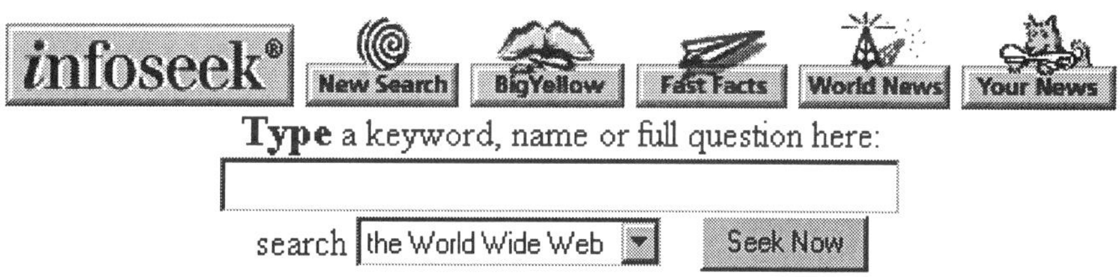

AltaVista AltaVista is a fast search tool. It searches 30 million pages found on 275,600 servers and four million articles from 14,000 Usenet news groups. It is accessed over 18 million times per weekday. The AltaVista address is www.altavista.com.

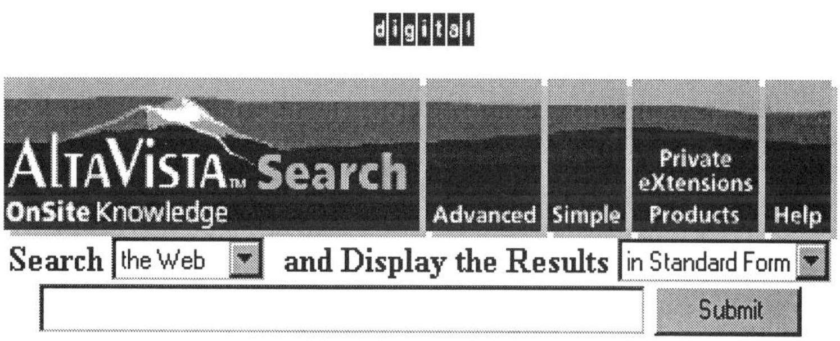

Yahoo! Yahoo! is a searchable, browsable hierarchical index of the Internet. It is primarily a directory, a list of Web sites that users have submitted for listing.

If you know exactly what you're looking for, use Yahoo! Select Search and specify a keyword or set of keywords, and Yahoo! will search its entire database to find listings that match the keys you provide. Or choose any of the links on the page to browse through screens by topic or category.

The Yahoo! location address is www.yahoo.com.

Excite Excite has a unique concept-based navigation technology that can help you find information when you are not sure how to ask for it. The software attempts to determine dominant *themes* or terms on a page, and then selects the items for the summary that best fit these terms. The themes are then used as search terms or keywords for you to work with while looking for the site. This process can produce a more accurate summary and keyword relationship than just selecting the first few lines of text from a document, as most other search engines do. Excite is found at www.excite.com.

After the Search The search results screen displays all the *hits,* or links found, on a subject, even if there are hundreds or thousands of sites. At the top of the screen is the search engine header, followed by the search criteria that you entered, along with the total number of hits. Below that is usually an advertisement, followed by the first ten (or twenty, depending upon the search engine that is being used) links to sites found.

To view the next ten (or twenty) hits, choose the text link Next 10 Results (Next 20 Results) found at the end of the list. Sometimes the search engine will list the results as page numbers at the bottom of the screen, allowing you to "page" back and forth by clicking on the number. The displayed screen will present the next set of results.

A new search link also appears at the bottom of the list that allows you to return to the original, clear search screen. But, if you want to modify your search, perhaps to narrow it, edit the existing criteria that appear at the bottom of the list and choose the Search command button to search again.

11-2d TUTORIAL

Try the following exercise on your own, which uses AltaVista to search for a few topics.

1. Start Internet Explorer, if necessary.
2. Display AltaVista's page by typing its URL, *www.altavista.com*, in the Address text box and pressing the Enter key.
3. Press the Enter key to display the search screen.
4. Click in the search text box and type *financial aid.*
5. Choose the Submit command button to perform the search. How many matches are found by AltaVista?
6. Add double-quote marks around the words *financial aid* in the search text box and choose the Submit command button to search again. How many matches are found this time?
7. Choose any links that seem interesting to you.
8. Return to AltaVista's page by choosing its URL from the Go menu.
9. Add your educational institution's name after the word *aid*, but inside the quote marks, and "submit" the search.
10. Perform a new search for *Yale University.*
11. Find the Yale Hand Page link and view the page by choosing this link.
12. Perform a new search for *dinosaur.*
13. Follow two or more links from the search results list.
14. Return to Internet Explorer's Start page.

Disconnecting from the Internet

When finished with your Internet session, you should exit the browser and terminate the connection. Staying online when not using the Internet occupies a connection that someone else could be using, and these days, the Internet is a busy place.

To exit Internet Explorer and disconnect from the Internet:

1. From within Internet Explorer, choose the Exit command from the File menu or click on the close button to close the window.
2. To disconnect from the Internet itself.
   - For dedicated network users, exiting Internet Explorer terminates the connection.
   - For online service users, exiting Internet Explorer returns you to the online service. To disconnect from it, execute the log-off procedure (which varies from service to service).
   - For ISP users, terminate the Dial-Up Networking connection by choosing the Disconnect command button in the Connected dialog box.

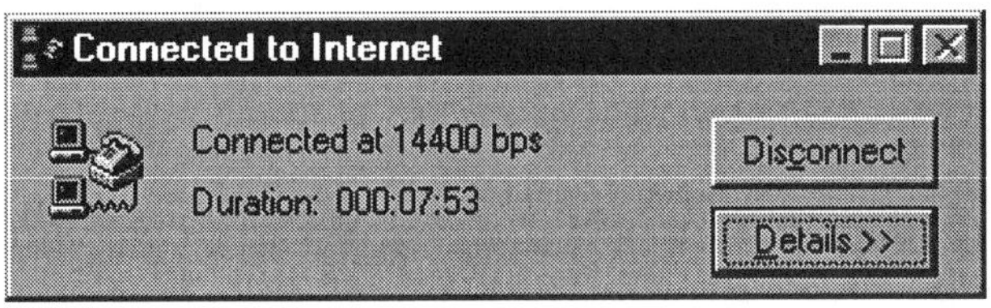

Printing Internet Pages

With all the information that is available on the Internet, it is inevitable that from time to time you will want to make a hard copy of some of it. Fortunately, it is possible to print any Internet page. To do so:

1. Use Internet Explorer to display the desired page.
2. Choose the Toolbar's Print button, or choose Print from the File menu.
3. Choose the OK command button from within the Print dialog box to send the page to the printer.

WARNING

Be aware that Internet pages are often copyrighted. Copyright laws apply to information on Internet pages in the same way they apply to conventional printed material.

11-2e TUTORIAL

Try the following exercise on your own.

1. Start Internet Explorer, if necessary, click in the Address text box, and type the URL for Infoseek: www.infoseek.com
2. Press the Enter key to go to that site and display the Infoseek screen.
3. Enter the search word *philharmonic* in the text box. Choose the Seek command button to perform the search. Notice the total number of matches for the search.
4. Scroll down the page to view the "philharmonic" results, and choose the link to view the Next 10 Results.
5. Scroll down the new list and modify the existing search text. Click to place the cursor in the text box and add the word *society* after *philharmonic*. Choose the Seek command button to perform the search. Notice the difference in total results found; this criteria broadens the search.
6. To narrow the search, modify the existing criteria by typing *"philharmonic society"* (including the quotes) and perform the search. How many sites are found?
7. Limit the search again. Modify the criteria by typing *New York* in the search text box and perform the search.
8. Choose one of the links to view its page.
9. Open the Go menu and choose the Infoseek page.
10. Perform a new search, looking for items of interest to you. If you want, add pages to the Favorites list.
11. Display Infoseek's main search screen by choosing it from the Go menu.
12. Find the Tips link and choose it.
13. Choose the How To Search link to display the How To Search information.
14. Scroll down to the Search Tips link and choose it.
15. Print the Search Tips page, if you wish, by choosing the Toolbar's Print button.
16. Choose the Toolbar's Home button to return to the Start page.
17. Exit Internet Explorer by clicking on the close button.
18. If you are using an online service or ISP, terminate the connection by exiting from that service.

Sending and Receiving Internet Mail

You can send e-mail messages through Microsoft Exchange to anyone on the Internet. (See Section 10.3 for information about Microsoft Exchange.) However, to do so, an Internet Mail utility must be installed on your system. The setup and configuration of the Internet Mail utility is achieved using the Microsoft Internet Mail Wizard. Your system has access to this software if any of the following conditions apply:

- You are using a computer that came with the non-retail version of Windows 95 pre-installed.
- Microsoft Plus! has been installed on your computer.
- Internet Explorer has been installed on your computer.

NOTE

If you don't have the required software components, a Microsoft Exchange Update for Windows 95 can be copied from the Internet. This update, which includes the Internet Mail utility, also converts your Exchange program to the Windows Messaging program. If you have Netscape Navigator version 1.2 or later, you can also use its Internet Mail program.

The Exchange utility for Internet Mail is installed with the Internet Mail Setup Wizard. To start the Wizard:

1. From within the Microsoft Exchange window (see Section 10.3), choose the Services option from the Tools menu. The list of currently installed messaging services is listed within this dialog box.
2. choose the Add command button to display the Add Services dialog box.

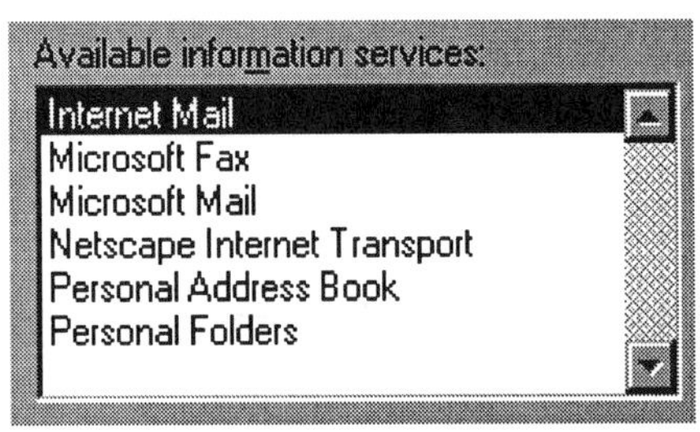

3. You should see Internet Mail as one of the choices. Select that option and choose the OK command button to start the Internet

Mail Wizard. The Internet Mail dialog box, shown in Figure 7, will be displayed.

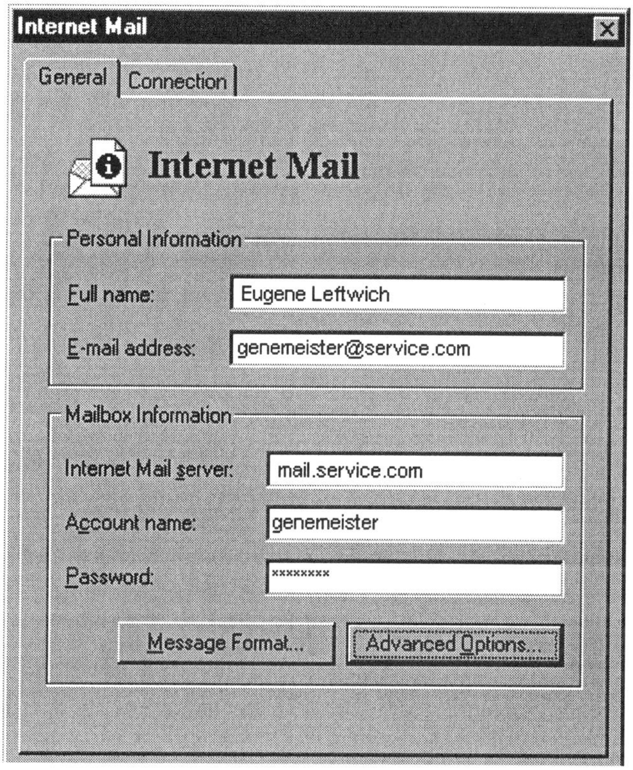

Figure 7 The Internet Mail Setup Dialog Box

4. Enter your name in the Full name text box. Then enter your complete Internet address in the E-mail address box.
5. Enter the Internet provider name, preceded by your mailbox name (this was added in the Exchange Wizard), and your Account name (which is your individual user name).
6. Enter your password.
7. This dialog box is now complete, but we still have to tell Exchange how we connect with this Internet account. Click on the Connection tab to display that page of the dialog box, shown in Figure 8 on the next page.

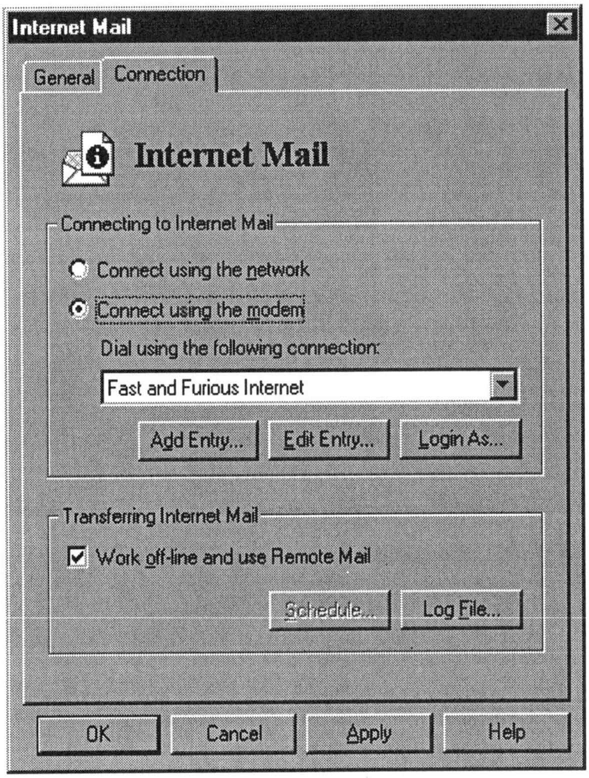

Figure 8 Setting up the Internet Mail Connection

8. If you are connecting to the Internet through a network, select the *Connect using the network* option button. Otherwise, you should select *Connect using the modem.*
9. Next, select the Dial-Up Networking option that you will be using from the drop-down list. If you have already created this option, it will appear on the list. If you haven't, choose the Add Entry command button to create the connection. (These steps are the same as those discussed in Section 10.2.)
10. If you wish to create mail messages before connecting to the Internet (and most of us do), select the *Work off-line and use Remote Mail* check box.
11. Choose the OK command button to end the Wizard and return to the Exchange window.

Sending mail To send Internet mail:

1. Start Exchange by either double-clicking on the Desktop's Inbox icon or choosing Microsoft Exchange from the Start menu's Programs submenu.
2. Choose the New Message command from the Compose menu and create your mail message in the resulting window.
3. Enter the Internet mail address of the recipient in the To text box and enter a title in the Subject box.
4. Open the Tools menu, point at the Deliver Now item, and choose the Internet Mail option from the submenu. Exchange will send the mail message and disconnect when through.

Receiving mail When receiving mail over the Internet, you must connect to the Internet and *poll for* your messages from within Exchange. To do so:

1. Start Exchange (as described above).
2. Open the Tools menu, point at the Deliver Now item, and choose the Internet Mail option from the submenu. Exchange will check for any messages to be sent, as well as for new mail to be delivered. (The connection to the Internet will be initiated and terminated automatically.)
3. The Inbox folder, displayed in the Exchange window, will contain the new messages; double-click on a new message to read it.

Downloading Files

Frequently, you may find files on the Internet that you would like to copy to disk. These files might include software updates or fixes, or *shareware* or *freeware*, which is software that is developed by individuals and not available on the mass market. Freeware is, as you might guess, software that does not cost anything to use. Shareware is not free, but you can usually try it before buying it, and the price is generally very reasonable.

The process of copying files from the Internet to a disk is called **downloading**. Copying files to the Internet is called **uploading**.

If a site contains software that you can download, there will be links within the page text of that site that pertain to this software. Usually, the linked word *download* will also appear within the related area. Sometimes, just choosing the software link will begin the download process; or, if the linked word *download* appears, choosing it will begin the process of transferring the files to your computer.

To download a file from the Internet:

1. Display the desired Internet page.
2. Choose the link to the software or the linked word *download*, if the latter is displayed.
3. Follow the prompts displayed on the screen. Eventually, you will need to identify the folder on your computer to be the destination for the downloaded file.
4. After downloading the file, which is usually in a compressed format, double-click on the file to start the decompression process (if any) and install the software (if applicable). If the software does not automatically install, double-click on the setup or installation file that was downloaded with it.

11.3 Configuring an ISP Internet Connection

In this section, we will discuss the process of configuring an Internet Service Provider (ISP) connection.

When using an Internet Service Provider, connecting to the Internet is most commonly done with Windows' Dial-Up Networking feature (see Section 10.2). Dial-Up Networking uses **TCP/IP** (Transmission Control Protocol/Internet Protocol) to communicate with the Internet.

TCP/IP Transmission

TCP/IP is a standard set of *protocols*, or rules, which provides the ability for computers with many different hardware and software configurations to interface with the same network without conflicts. TCP/IP is the standard data transfer protocol for the Internet.

TCP/IP transmission is made possible by networks that send data as chunks of information called *data packets*. These packets are created by breaking data into 1,024 byte (or character) units and sending them across the network from one point to another. Just as telephone calls may traverse a different route each time they are made, so it is with each data packet. Packets are reassembled by software at the destination to complete the message.

The TCP/IP software must be installed in Windows before connecting to the Internet via an ISP. Windows will automatically allow, or *bind*,

TCP/IP to work with the Dial-Up adapter or a network adapter, so that it can be used on a stand-alone computer system or as part of a local network. With TCP/IP as the indicated protocol, applications like Microsoft's Internet Explorer (called *Internet clients*, in this context) can be run to interface with the Internet connection.

You must be sure that TCP/IP has been installed on your system before configuring the ISP connection. To do so:

1. Click on the Start button, point to the Settings option, and choose Control Panel from the resulting submenu. The Control Panel window will open.
2. Choose the Network option by double-clicking on its icon. The Network dialog box will open.
3. On the Configuration page, TCP/IP will appear in the list of installed components if it has already been installed. If so, skip the rest of this procedure.
4. If TCP/IP does not appear on the list, choose the Add command button. The Select Network Component Type dialog box will open.
5. Choose the Protocol item from the Select Network Component Type list, and choose the OK command button.
6. In the Select Network Protocol dialog box, choose Microsoft from the Manufacturers list and choose TCP/IP from the Network Protocols list.
7. Choose the OK command button. The installation process will begin. Insert the requested diskettes or CD as prompted by the dialog box message. Follow the prompts until the installation is complete.

You are now ready to set up an ISP connection to the Internet.

Configuring the Connection

After the Dial-Up connection has been created, the modem installed, and TCP/IP is on the system, connecting to the Internet requires some specific information.

The following check list will guide you through the process of connecting to the Internet through an Internet Service Provider (ISP):

1. Obtain an Internet account with an ISP. Let them know that you will be using a Windows 95 Internet connection. The service provider will give you the following information:

- Your user name
- Your password
- The phone number to access the provider
- Your host and domain name
- The type of dial up server needed
- The Domain Name Server (DNS) address of the provider
- An IP address, if your provider assigns one

2. Check to ensure that your communications hardware (your modem and its connections) is set up properly.
3. Make sure that Dial-Up Networking (Section 10.2) is installed.
4. Create a connection to the provider in Dial-Up Networking using the phone number they have provided.
5. After creating this Dial-Up Networking connection, from within the Dial-Up Networking folder, select the Internet connection icon (by clicking once on it) so that it is highlighted.
6. Choose the Properties option from the File menu, or right-click on the connection icon and choose the Properties option. The Connection Properties dialog box will be displayed.
7. Choose the Server Type command button, and the Server Types dialog box will appear.
8. Select the Type of Dial-Up Server your provider uses from the drop-down list. Most Internet connections use PPP (Point to Point Protocol).
9. Choose the network protocol, also provided by your service; this entry is usually TCP/IP. Then, choose the TCP/IP Settings command button to display that dialog box, as shown in Figure 9.
10. If your provider has given you an IP address number, select the *Specify an IP address* option button and enter the numbers in the space provided. (Most providers do not assign a specific IP address.)
11. Select the *Specify name server addresses* option button and then enter the primary DNS numbers, exactly as your provider has designated, in that text box. If your provider has given you a secondary DNS, enter that number also.
12. Choose the OK command button. The Server Types dialog box will reopen.
13. Choose the OK command button to exit the Server Types dialog box. The Connection Properties dialog box will appear; choose the OK command button to accept all entries and return to the Dial-Up Networking folder.

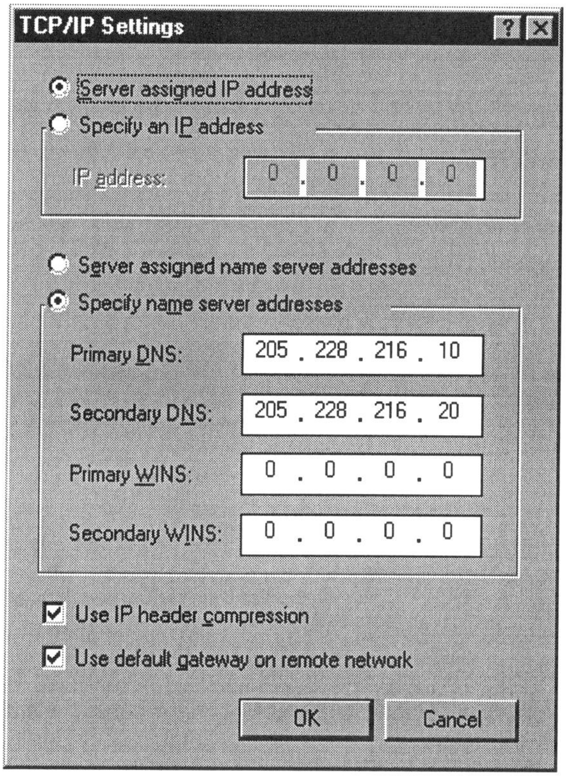

Figure 9 The TCP/IP Settings Dialog Box

14. Activate the Dial-Up Networking connection by double-clicking on the icon. Enter your name and password as prompted to connect to the service.

Chapter Summary

Connecting to the Internet	To access the Internet	Use a dedicated connection through a local network or an educational institution; *or* an online information service; *or* an Internet Service Provider (ISP).
	To start Internet Explorer	Choose Internet Explorer from the Start menu's Programs submenu; *or* double-click on the Internet icon on the Desktop.

	To disconnect from the Internet	For dedicated users, exit Internet Explorer; for online service users, exit Internet Explorer and exit the service; for ISP users, exit Internet Explorer and choose the Disconnect button in the Connected dialog box.
Using Internet Explorer	The Explorer Toolbar buttons	Back displays the previous page. Forward displays the next page. Stop halts a page display that is in progress. Refresh reloads a page. Home returns you to the Start page. Search displays Microsoft's Search screen. Favorites lists your Favorites. Print prints the displayed page. Font increases or decreases the size of the displayed typeface.
	Using the Address box	Click in the Address box and type the address of the Internet page you wish to display *or* select a previously-typed address from the drop-down list. Then, press the Enter key.
	Using the Favorites menu	Add to the Favorites list, go to a Favorite page, or delete from the Favorites list.
	Using the Go menu	Choose Back, Forward, Start Page, Search the Web, or Best of the Web, *or* go to a previously-viewed page.
	To perform a search	Choose the Toolbar's Search button to display Microsoft's Search Index page, select a search engine, and on the resulting page, type the keywords to search for and choose the search command button.
	To print an Internet page	Display the page and choose the Toolbar's Print button *or* choose the Print command from the File menu; then, choose OK.
	To download a file	Choose the download link or follow screen instructions to initiate the download, identify the folder on your computer where the file is to be copied, and choose the OK command button. Follow the prompts to complete the download.
Using an ISP	To configure the connection	Create the Dial-Up Networking connection, right-click on the connection icon, and

	choose Properties. Choose the Server Type command button and select PPP. Select TCP/IP as the protocol and choose the TCP/IP Settings command button. Enter the server addresses provided by the ISP.
To connect to the Internet	Double-click on the connection icon to connect to the Internet; then enter your login and password, when prompted.

Review Exercises

Section 11.1

1. The three avenues for connecting to the Internet are through a ____________, a ____________, or a ____________.
2. The ____________is the largest network in the world.
3. The most commonly used method to access information on the Internet is through software called a ____________.
4. Which of the following services is available on the Internet?
   a. FTP
   b. Telnet
   c. Internet Phone
   d. All of the above
5. Every computer on the Internet has a unique location, called
   a. A dynamic address.
   b. An Internet address.
   c. A subnet.
   d. A dotted quad.
6. If your computer has a permanently-assigned IP address, it is called
   a. A Terminate Stay Resident (TSR) address.
   b. A perpetual address.
   c. A static address.
   d. A dotted quad.
7. Which browsing application is started by the icon pictured at the right?

The Internet

   a. Mosaic
   b. Internet Explorer
   c. Netscape Navigator
   d. America Online

8. True or false: There are established standards for domain names.
9. True or false: The right part of the domain name is the user's name.
10. True or false: The middle part of the domain name usually identifies the service provider.

Section 11.2

11. Which Internet Explorer Toolbar button reloads a Web page to the screen?
    a. Refresh
    b. Stop
    c. Forward
    d. Back
12. Which screen is always displayed when you open the browser?
    a. Search screen
    b. Start (or Home) page
    c. Link
    d. Favorite
13. A search engine available on the Internet is:
    a. AltaVista
    b. Excite
    c. Infoseek
    d. All of the above
14. An unfollowed link appears ____________ in color, by default.
15. In Internet Explorer, a ____________ is an electronic place holder.
16. True or false: After an Internet search, eighty hits are immediately displayed on the screen.
17. True or false: Choosing the Print command prints every page you have viewed in the current Internet session.
18. True or false: Downloading is the process of copying files from the Internet to a disk.

Section 11.3

19. ____________ is the official data transfer protocol for the Internet.
20. Which File menu command configures the Dial-Up Networking connection?
    a. Close
    b. Print
    c. Properties
    d. Open

21. Some of the information needed to configure an ISP Internet connection consists of
    a. The phone number needed to access the provider.
    b. A password.
    c. A user name.
    d. All of the above.
22. True or false: TCP/IP uses data packets to send information from one point to another.
23. True or false: Most Internet connections use PPP (Point to Point Protocol).

Build Your Own Glossary

24. The following words and phrases are important terms that were introduced in this chapter. (They appear within the text in boldface type.) Use WordPad (see Section 2.2) to enter a definition for each term, preserving alphabetical order, into the Glossary file on the Student Disk.

Address box	Internet address	TCP/IP
Downloading	Internet Explorer	Telnet
FTP (File Transfer Protocol)	Internet Phone	Uploading
Gopher	Internet Relay Chat (IRC)	URL (Universal Resource Locator)
http	Link	Usenet
Internet	Search engine	World Wide Web

Lab Exercises

Work each of the following exercises at your computer. Begin by turning the machine on (if necessary) to start Windows 95 and closing any open windows.

Lab Exercise 1 (Section 11.2)

a. Connect to the Internet if you are using an ISP or an online service. If not, proceed to the next step.
b. Start Internet Explorer. What is the name of its Desktop icon?
c. Display Microsoft's Search Index page and select the AltaVista search engine. How did you accomplish this?
d. Search for the topic *National Geographic*. What is the name of the command button that initiates the search?
e. Choose a link of interest to you and print the page or article.

f. Perform a search using either AltaVista or Infoseek, searching for *Claude Monet.*

g. Once you have found a page or article of interest, print it.

h. Perform searches for the following topics, and follow links as desired: cave paintings, Beethoven, Mark Twain, Civil War, Emily Dickenson, Edgar Allen Poe, Astronomy, Recipes, Psychology, Sphinx, weather, "Aztec culture".

i. Exit Internet Explorer, and (if you are using an ISP or online service) disconnect from the Internet.

Lab Exercise 2 (Section 11.2)

This exercise takes you through the process of downloading the most recent copy of Winzip, which is a file compression utility. The software will be an evaluation copy, which means it can be used for a trial period and, if you desire, can be purchased.

a. Connect to the Internet if you are using an ISP or an online service and start Internet Explorer. Insert a formatted floppy disk in its drive.

b. Go to the Winzip site. Its address is *www.winzip.com.*

c. Scroll until you see the linked words *Download Evaluation Version.* Choose the link to begin the process.

d. Select Windows 95 as the version of the software.

e. Select the floppy disk drive as the destination for the file and choose the Save command button.

f. Exit Internet Explorer and disconnect from the Internet if you are using an ISP or online service.

Lab Exercise 3 (Section 11.2)

a. Connect to the Internet if you are using an ISP or an online service and start Internet Explorer.

b. Enter the address of the Yahoo! search page in the Address box and access the page. What is the address?

c. Choose a link on the Yahoo! page that is of interest of you. Continue choosing links until an article or page is displayed. Describe this page.

d. Add the page to the Favorites list. How did you do this?

e. Use the Go menu to return to Yahoo! What item did you choose from this menu?

f. Select a different topic from the list.

g. Use the Back button to return to the previous page. What is it?

h. Use the Forward button to return to the next page.

i. Go to the following sites and follow any links you wish:

www.si.edu	Smithsonian Institute
www.kodak.com	Eastman Kodak's page
www.nbew.com	National Business Employment Weekly magazine
www.parentsoup.com	Guides and services for families and parents
www.worldvillage.com	Family-oriented information, education, and entertainment
www.delorme.com	Map makers
www.ericir.syr.edu	Reference information
www.rs.internic.net	Net Scout services for reference information
www.nara.gov	Government databases
www.nypl.org	New York Public Library and other information

j. Choose the Organize Favorites item from the Favorites menu and capture the resulting dialog box to the Clipboard (see Section 2.3).

k. Open WordPad and paste the captured graphic into the document.

l. Add your name and date at the top of the document and print it. Exit WordPad without saving the document.

m. Return to Internet Explorer and delete the Favorites that you created by selecting these items in the dialog box and choosing the Delete command button.

n. Exit Internet Explorer and disconnect from the Internet if you are using an ISP or online service.

Lab Exercise 4 (Section 11.3)

(This lab exercise will not work if Dial-Up Networking and a modem are not installed on your computer.)

a. Use the New Connection Wizard in the Dial-Up Networking folder to create a connection. (Enter any connection name you like and your phone number.)

b. Right-click on the new connection icon and choose the Properties option to open the Properties dialog box.

c. Choose the Server Type command button. Which options are active?

d. Choose the TCP/IP command button. What numbers, if any, are listed there? When are these numbers necessary?

e. Choose the Cancel command button to return to the Server Type dialog box. Then, choose the Cancel command button to return to the Properties dialog box.

f. Choose the OK command button to close the Properties dialog box and return to the Dial-Up Networking window.

g. *Optional:* Capture the Dial-Up Networking window with your icon visible and paste it into WordPad. Print the resulting document.

h. Delete your connection icon from the Dial-Up Networking window.

If You Want to Learn More ...

The notes presented here allow you to delve more deeply into some of the topics covered in this chapter.

Choose your own default pages in Internet Explorer

In Internet Explorer, you can choose a specific location for the Start page, the Search page, and the links that appear on the Links Toolbar. To do so:

1. In Internet Explorer, display the page that is to be the new page.
2. Choose the Options item from the View menu and select the Navigation page in the resulting dialog box.
3. In the Customize section, with Start page visible in the Page box, choose the Use Current command button. The URL for the displayed page will appear in the Address text box.
4. If you are not viewing the desired page, type the URL in the Address text box.
5. Click on the down-triangle button in the Page box and select the Search page item.
6. Define a new Search page as the one that will display when choosing the Toolbar's Search button. For example, if you prefer to use AltaVista, you can avoid Microsoft's Search Index screen by entering AltaVista's URL in the Address text box.
7. Click on the down-triangle button in the Page box to select one of the Quick Link items (there are five to choose from). Each link represents one of the Link buttons displayed on the Links Toolbar.

8. Assign a name for the link in the Name text box; this name will appear on the Link button on the Toolbar.
9. Type, in the Address box, the URL for each link to be changed.
10. For any of the page choices, you can return the page to the default URL by choosing the Default command button.
11. Choose the OK command button to put the changes into effect.

Organizing Favorites

Once you start accumulating Favorites, the list can get quite lengthy. To deal with this situation, you can organize the Favorites into folders, shortening the list and grouping the Favorites by category.

1. In Internet Explorer, choose the Organize Favorites item from the Favorites menu; *or* choose the Toolbar's Favorites button, then Organize Favorites. The Organize Favorites dialog box will be displayed.
2. Create a new folder to contain Favorites by choosing the Create New Folder button. Type the name of the new folder and press the Enter key. The new folder will appear in the list box.
3. Select the Favorites to be placed in the new folder. Then, choose the Move command button, and identify the new folder by selecting it in the dialog box. Choose the OK command button. (You can also drag-and-drop the Favorites onto the folder in the list box.)
4. A Favorite can be renamed in the same way as any other file: select the Favorite, choose the Rename command button, type the new name, and choose the OK command button; *or* click on the Favorite name once to select it, again to activate the rename function, type the new name, and press the Enter key.
5. Choose the Close command button when finished. The new folder will appear on the Favorites list as a main folder with a cascading submenu listing the categorized Favorites.

Copy Internet page text or graphics

Any text or graphic on an Internet page can be copied to your word processor. Here's how:

1. Display the Internet page.
2. If copying text, select the text and then either
    - Right-click on the selected text and choose the Copy item from the pop-up menu.

    or
    - Choose the Copy item from the Edit menu.

3. If copying a graphic, right-click on it and choose the Copy item from the pop-up menu.
4. Open the destination application, such as WordPad.
5. Position the insertion point where you want and choose the Paste item from the Edit menu to insert the copied text or graphic.

CHAPTER 12

Additional Topics

This chapter contains an assortment of Windows 95 topics. Some, such as those dealing with DOS and OLE, expand on material that was briefly covered earlier in the text. Others, for example the section on the Windows Registry, contain information of a relatively advanced nature. To be more specific:

- Section 12.1 discusses certain special aspects of running DOS programs, such as the mark/copy/paste operation, changing the display font, and running a DOS session using MS-DOS Prompt.
- Section 12.2 continues the discussion of DOS applications, concentrating on a DOS program's property sheets.
- Section 12.3 describes various options that affect the way Windows starts up, including those available in special configuration files.
- Section 12.4 introduces the Registry and discusses how it can be used to further customize Windows.
- Section 12.5 covers object linking and embedding (OLE), which allows you to easily create and edit documents that contain information produced by multiple applications.

The first three sections in this chapter contain DOS-related material and should be covered in the order presented, but Sections 12.4 and 12.5 are independent of this material and of each other.

12.1 Running DOS Programs

A program that was designed to run under the DOS operating system, but not under Windows, is known as a **DOS application**. Although Windows-based software has many advantages over DOS programs (see the Introduction), the latter often run faster and make more efficient use of computer resources. For this reason, contemporary computer games and other graphics-intensive software are sometimes designed as DOS applications.

DOS programs are normally started in the same manner as Windows applications (see Section 2.1). You can run several DOS and Windows applications at the same time and switch among them using the techniques described in Section 2.3. In addition, Windows 95 provides special features for DOS applications that make them easier to use. We will discuss these features in this section.

Running DOS Applications under Windows

Unlike Windows applications, which always run inside a window on the Desktop, DOS programs can be run in two modes — in a window or *full-screen*; in the latter case the application occupies the entire Desktop, as shown in Figure 1.

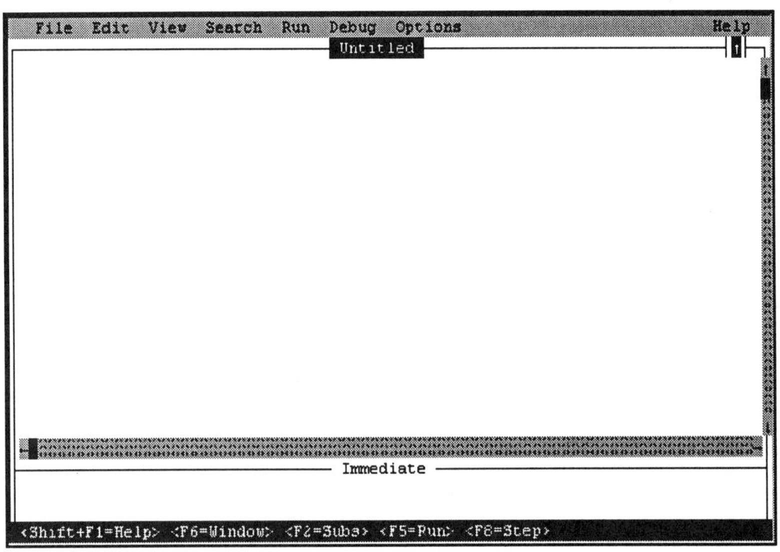

Figure 1 A DOS Application Running Full-screen

Switching screen modes

To switch from one mode to the other, press the Alt+Enter keystroke combination. When the program of Figure 1 is switched to window mode, the result is shown in Figure 2. Notice that the application window contains a title bar (complete with minimize, maximize, and close buttons) and a Toolbar. (The Toolbar can be toggled on and off by clicking on the Control icon, which opens the Control menu, and then choosing the Toolbar command.) We will only consider window mode in the remainder of this section because the special features described below cannot be accessed in full-screen mode.

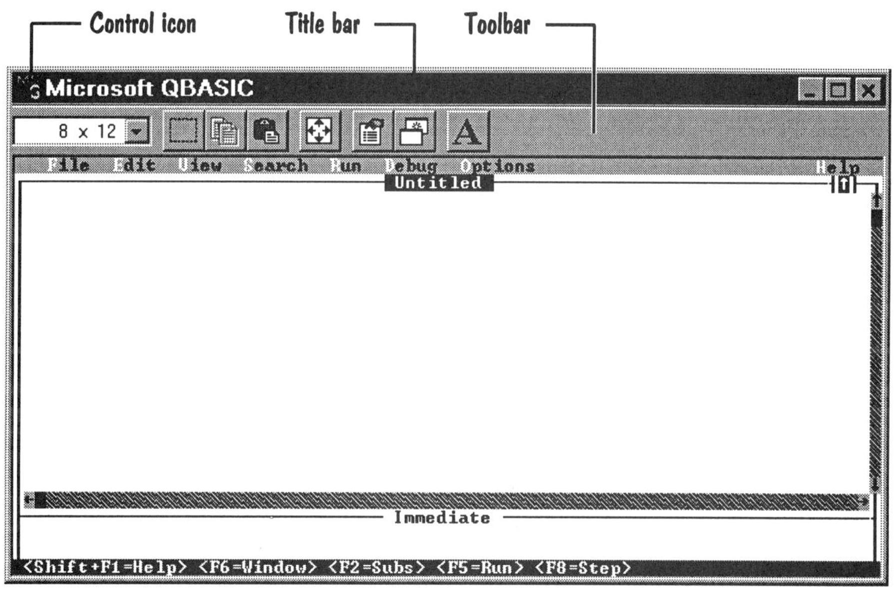

Figure 2 A DOS Application Running in a Window

Mark, Copy, and Paste Text in a DOS window can be selected and copied to the Windows Clipboard, and information on the Clipboard can be pasted into the current document. (See Section 2.3 for general information about these operations.)

Selecting text

To select (or *mark*) text in a document in a DOS window:

1. Click on the Toolbar's Mark button (see the figure at the right).
   or
   Click on the Control icon (or right-click on the title bar) to display the Control menu, point at the Edit

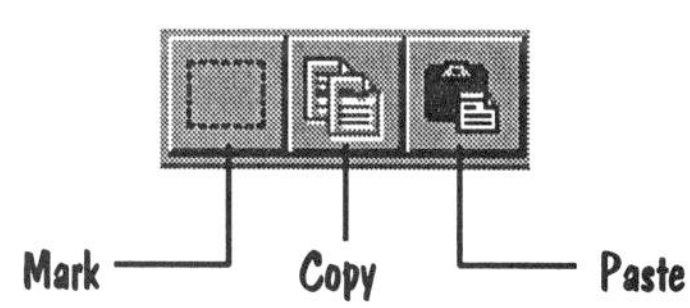

item, and choose the Mark command on the resulting submenu.

2. Use the mouse or keyboard to position the cursor at the beginning of the block of text to be selected and either mouse-drag the cursor to the end of the block, or hold down the Shift key and move the cursor to the end of the block.

The selected block of text will become highlighted.

Copying text To copy a selected block of text to the Clipboard, take any of the following actions:

- Press the Enter key.
- Click on the Toolbar's Copy button.
- Click on the Control icon to display the Control menu, point at Edit, and choose the Copy command from the resulting submenu.

Pasting text To paste text from the Clipboard into a document:

1. Position the cursor where you want to paste the text.
2. Click on the Toolbar's Paste button.

   or

   Click on the Control icon (or right-click on the title bar) to display the Control menu, point at Edit, and choose the Paste command from the resulting submenu.

Selecting a Font You can change the size of the font used to display the text in a DOS window by:

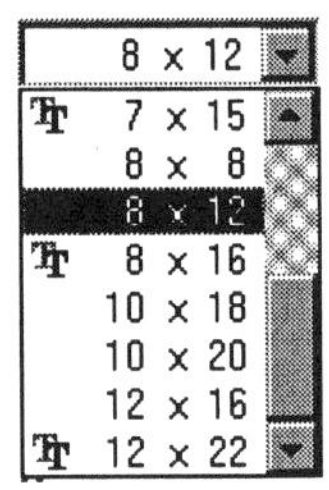

1. Opening the drop-down list on the Toolbar (the result is shown at the right).
2. Selecting (clicking on) one of the listed sizes.

The various font sizes are given in *pixels*; for example, the current font in Figure 2 is 8 pixels wide and 12 pixels high. Be aware that:

- Selecting a larger font size means that the text will be easier to read, but less text will fit in a given window. Selecting a smaller font has the opposite effect.
- Selecting the Auto item from the top of the list sizes the text so that a full DOS "screen" automatically fits the current window. If you resize the window, the font will resize accordingly.

NOTE You can also change the size of the display font by clicking on the Toolbar's Font button (shown at the right). Doing so opens the Font page of the Properties dialog box. The same

font choices are available here as on the Toolbar drop-down list, but when you select a font in this dialog box, its preview windows show the resulting window size and font size.

Other Toolbar Buttons Three other buttons reside on the Toolbar (Figure 3). Here are their functions:

- Clicking on the Full Screen button switches the DOS application from the current window mode to full-screen mode.
- Clicking on the Properties button displays the application's Properties dialog box. This dialog box allows you to fine-tune the way the application runs under Windows. We will discuss its options in Section 12.2.
- The Background button determines whether or not the DOS program will continue to process data when you switch to another application. If the button appears to be "depressed" (indented), background processing will take place.

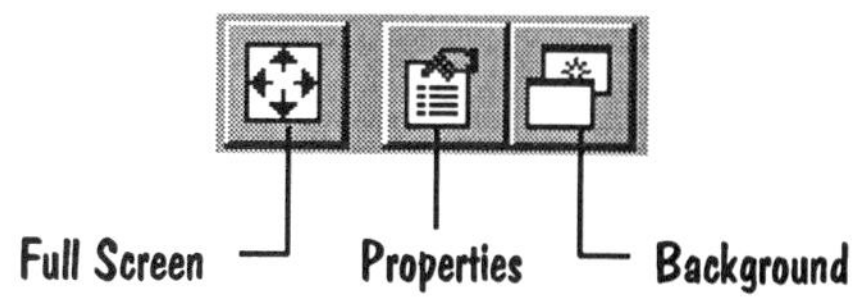

Figure 3 Other Toolbar Buttons

Running a DOS Session

If you are familiar with the DOS operating system, you may want to issue commands or run programs from the DOS prompt from time to time. You can do this — run a **DOS session** — without shutting down Windows 95 by starting the MS-DOS Prompt program. **MS-DOS Prompt** allows you to view directories, copy files, start programs, and so on, just as if you were actually running DOS.

Starting MS-DOS Prompt

To start MS-DOS Prompt:

1. Click on the Start button to display the Start menu.
2. Point at the Programs option to open its submenu.
3. Click on the MS-DOS Prompt item on this submenu. The window shown in Figure 4 on the next page, sometimes referred to as a *DOS box*, will open.

The DOS box provides all the features (described in the first part of this section) afforded to any DOS program running in a window. Using the Toolbar or Control menu, you can mark, copy, and paste text within the window, change the display font, switch between window and full-screen mode, and change certain properties. Moreover, from

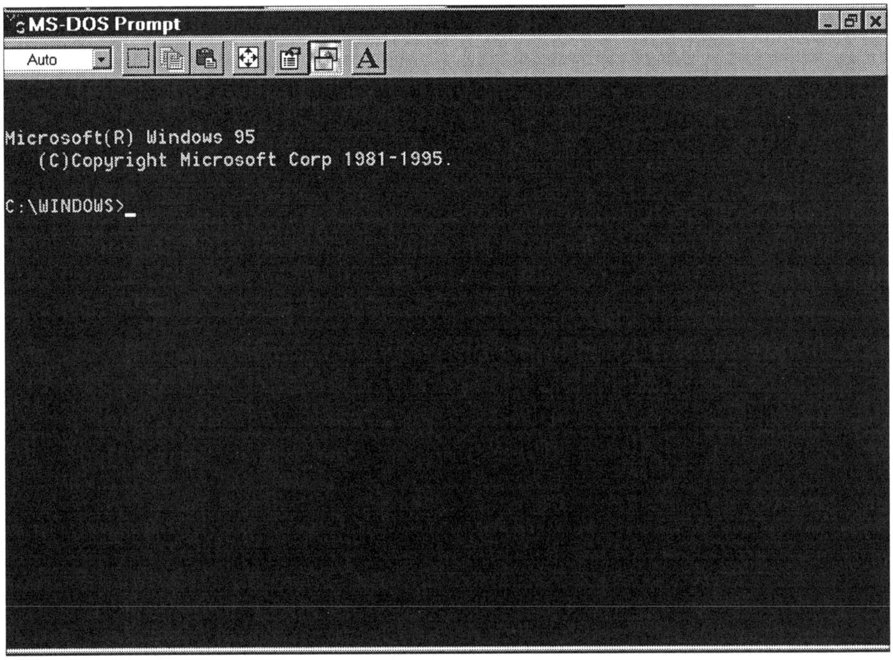

Figure 4 The MS-DOS Prompt Window

the DOS prompt, which is `C:\WINDOWS>` in Figure 4, you can issue any available DOS command (see Appendix B).

Exiting MS-DOS Prompt

To exit MS-DOS Prompt, close the program that's running (if necessary), and then take any of the following actions:

- Type `exit` at the DOS prompt and press the Enter key.
- Click on the close button.
- Double-click on the Control icon.
- Click on the Control icon to open the Control menu and choose the Close command.

NOTE

Here are two basic ways to run DOS by itself, outside of Windows 95 — before startup and after shut down.

- To run DOS before Windows starts up, turn on your computer and press the F8 function key when you see the message "Starting Windows 95". Now, select the menu item entitled "Safe mode command prompt only" and press the Enter key. DOS 7 (a version of DOS packaged with Windows 95) will start, but you may not have access to certain hardware devices and software enhancements. This technique should only be used in special cases; for example, if Windows 95 refuses to load and you would like to use diagnostic software that runs under DOS.

- To run DOS after Windows shuts down, while in Windows, choose the Shut Down command from the Start menu. Then, select the *Restart the computer in MS-DOS mode?* option button in the resulting dialog box, and choose the Yes command button. DOS will start after the computer reboots. This technique for running DOS may be useful if one of your DOS applications will not run under Windows; it may run in **MS-DOS mode** — after Windows has shut down.

There are a few other ways to run DOS outside of windows, which are a little more complicated to set up. We will discuss them in Section 12.3 and at the very end of this chapter.

12-1 TUTORIAL

Try the following exercise on your own.

1. Turn on the computer (if necessary) to start Windows 95 and insert the Student Disk in its drive.
2. Start the Dosprog application on this diskette by choosing the Run option from the Start menu, typing `a:dosprog` in the resulting dialog box, and choosing the OK command button.
3. Dosprog will open, and should be running in a window. Press Alt+Enter to run it full screen and then Alt+Enter again to return it to window mode.
4. Maximize the program's window, if necessary. If the Toolbar is not displayed near the top of the window, display it by clicking on the Control icon to the left of the word *Dosprog* on the menu bar and selecting the Toolbar item from the resulting Control menu.
5. Successively select fonts from the drop-down list on the left end of the Toolbar or from the dialog box that opens when you click on the Toolbar's Font button. Note the effect of your selections on the Dosprog window. Then, return to the Auto font.
6. Exit Dosprog by following the on-screen instructions and then close its window, if necessary, by clicking on its close button.
7. Start a DOS session by opening the MS-DOS Prompt window: Choose the MS-DOS Prompt item from the Programs submenu of the Start menu.

8. Maximize the MS-DOS Prompt window, if necessary.
9. At the DOS prompt, probably `C:\Windows>`, type `dir` to get a listing of the Windows directory (folder).
10. Select (mark) the words *Windows 95* on the screen:
    - Open the Control menu (see step 4), point at the Edit item, and choose Mark from the submenu; *or*, click on the Toolbar's Mark button.

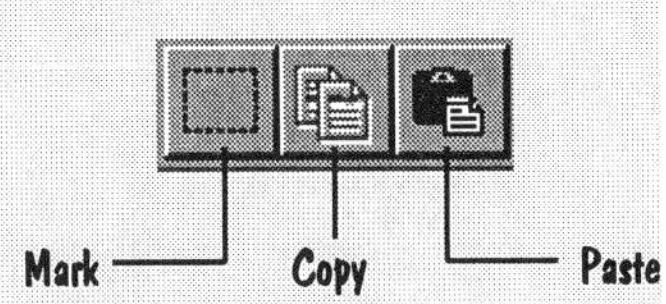

    - Highlight *Windows 95* by dragging the cursor (a white square) over it or by positioning the cursor at the beginning of the phrase, holding down the Shift key, and moving the cursor to the end of the phrase.
11. Copy the selected words to the Clipboard by pressing Enter, choosing Copy from the Edit submenu of the Control menu, or by clicking on the Toolbar's Copy button.
12. Paste the phrase *Window 95* at the DOS prompt by choosing Paste from the Edit submenu of the Control menu or by clicking on the Toolbar's Paste button.
13. Exit MS-DOS Prompt by clicking on its close button or by typing `exit` at the DOS prompt. Remove the diskette from its drive.

12.2 Property Settings for DOS Programs

Windows applications, by definition, follow certain rules governing their peaceful coexistence with other programs sharing the Desktop. A DOS program, on the other hand, assumes that it has sole possession of the computer's resources (its memory, display, hard disk, etc.). Most of the time, this doesn't cause problems; most DOS applications run well under Windows. However, on occasion, you may have to change the way a DOS program uses system resources in order for that program to run more efficiently or even run at all under Windows. This section discusses how you can make such changes.

Displaying a DOS Program's Property Sheets

As you have probably realized by now, just about everything in Windows or controlled by Windows has properties: files, folders, shortcuts, printers, the display, the mouse, and so on. A DOS application has properties as well. These properties help determine the way it runs under Windows.

You can view a DOS program's properties in two ways:

Viewing a DOS program's properties

- Run the DOS program in a window and display its Toolbar, if necessary (see Section 12.1); then, click on the Toolbar's Properties button (shown at the right).

or

- Right-click on the DOS program's icon (in Explorer or a folder window) or its shortcut's icon, and choose Properties from the pop-up menu.

In either case, the program's Properties dialog box* (or, its *property sheets*), will be displayed (Figure 5).

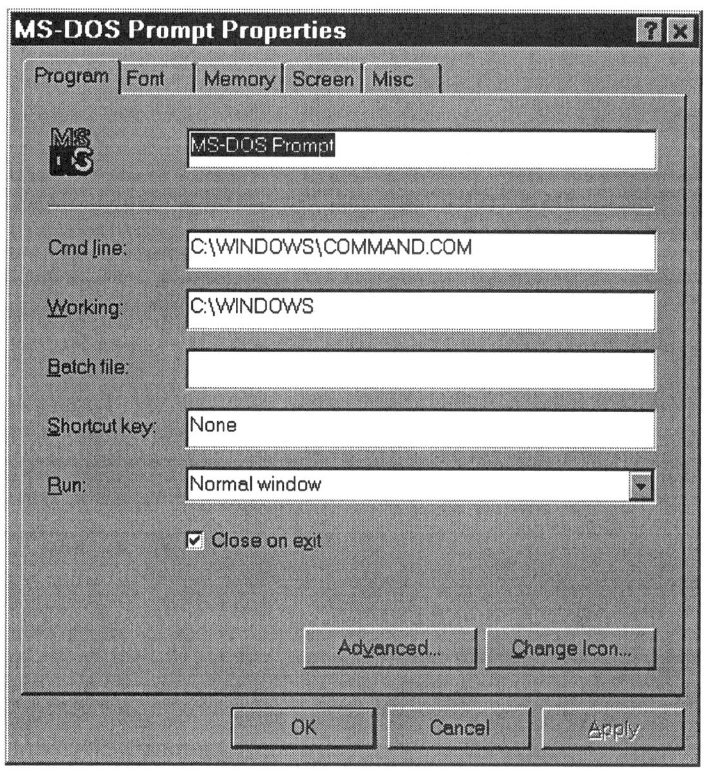

Figure 5 A Typical DOS Properties Dialog Box

*In Windows 3.1, the function of the Properties dialog box was carried out by the PIF Editor utility.

NOTE

The dialog box shown in Figure 5 was displayed by starting MS-DOS Prompt and clicking on its Toolbar's Properties button. If you display the Properties dialog box by using a program or shortcut icon's right-click menu, that dialog box will contain one additional page. This page gives general information about the program or shortcut.

TIP

The easiest way to locate a program or shortcut icon is to start the Windows Find utility (see Section 4.3). This technique will be the *only* way in some cases, because certain DOS icon's are hidden in Explorer, My Computer, and folder windows. (For example, try to find a shortcut to MS-DOS Prompt, which resides in the C:\Windows\Start Menu\Programs folder.) To aid your search, be aware that DOS program shortcuts usually have a *pif* extension (for "program information file").

Basic Properties

Some of the DOS program settings in the Properties dialog box affect the program in a fundamental way. We will discuss these settings here; others are more advanced, and will be discussed later.

On the Program Page The Program page of the Properties dialog box (see Figure 5) contains most of the basic properties. (It is similar to a shortcut's property sheet, which is discussed in Section 4.5.) Here's how you can make use of this page:

- If your DOS program usually saves and opens files in a folder other than the one from which it is started, enter this folder path name in the *Working* text box. This folder will become the default for save, open, and certain other commands.
- To make it easier to start the program, you can place a shortcut to it on one of the Start button menus (see Section 4.2) and then define a *shortcut key* for it. Once you do, pressing this keystroke combination anywhere in Windows will start (or switch to) the application.

  To define a shortcut key, click in the *Shortcut key* text box; then type the keystroke combination you want to use to start the program. The shortcut key will take precedence over the keystroke's normal function in the active program, so choose a shortcut key that is not likely to be used in applications. Typically, a shortcut key begins with some combination of Ctrl, Alt, and Shift; for example, Ctrl+Alt+D. To enter this keystroke into the *Shortcut key* text box, hold down the Ctrl and Alt keys and type D.

- The *Run* drop-down list determines how the window will look when the program is started — minimized, maximized, or "normal" (the way it looked at the last exit).
- Select the *Close on exit* check box if you want the program's window to close when you execute the exit command. If this check box is not selected, exiting the program will terminate it, but its window will remain on the screen and the word *Finished* will be displayed on the title bar. In this case, to remove the program's window from the screen, click on the close button or press Alt+F4.
- Choose the Change Icon command button to change the icon that represents this program. A dialog box will open, allowing you to select a new icon.

On the Screen Page If you click on the Screen tab, the DOS program's Properties dialog box will look as shown in Figure 6. Here are some features found on this page:

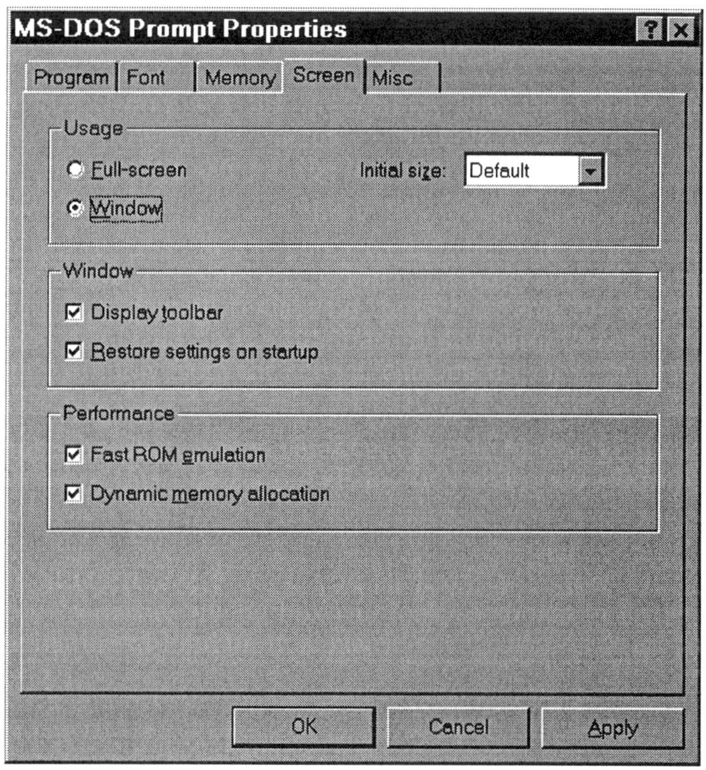

Figure 6 DOS Properties Dialog Box — Screen Page

- As you know, a DOS program can be run in a window or full-screen. To set the startup mode, select the appropriate option button. The program may run slightly faster full-screen, but the special features described in Section 12.1 can only be accessed in window mode.
- The *Display toolbar* check box allows you to specify whether or not the Toolbar will be displayed on program startup.
- The *Restore settings on startup* check box determines the startup settings for such parameters as display font and window size. If the box is selected, the default settings are used; if not, the settings in effect when the program was last exited are used.

On the Font Page You can use this page of a DOS program's Properties dialog box to set the default display font for the program. (See Section 12.1 for information about DOS display fonts.)

On the Misc Page The Misc (Miscellaneous) page of a DOS program's Properties dialog box is shown in Figure 7. Here are the basic features found on this page:

- If you want your screen saver to work while running the DOS program, be sure the corresponding check box is selected. If the screen saver seems to cause a problem, deselect this check box.
- If certain shortcut keys used by your DOS program don't seem to be working, you can probably correct the situation by deselecting a check box in the *Windows shortcut keys* area. For example, say that the Alt+Tab keystroke combination in your DOS program invokes a paragraph indent. To enable this function, the Alt+Tab check box must be deselected on the Misc page. If it isn't, pressing this keystroke combination will switch to another application. (See Appendix A for a list of Windows shortcuts and their functions.)

Types of Memory Used by DOS Programs

Recall that memory (RAM, ROM, or disk-based) is measured in *bytes*, where each byte can hold one character of information. One *kilobyte* (KB) is 1,024 bytes and one *megabyte* (MB) is 1,024 KB, or about one million bytes. (See the Introduction for more information about this topic.) To access memory, each byte is assigned an *address* — a number designating its storage location. (An address is really the "logical" location of a byte; physically, it resides on chips on the motherboard or on a circuit board plugged into the motherboard.)

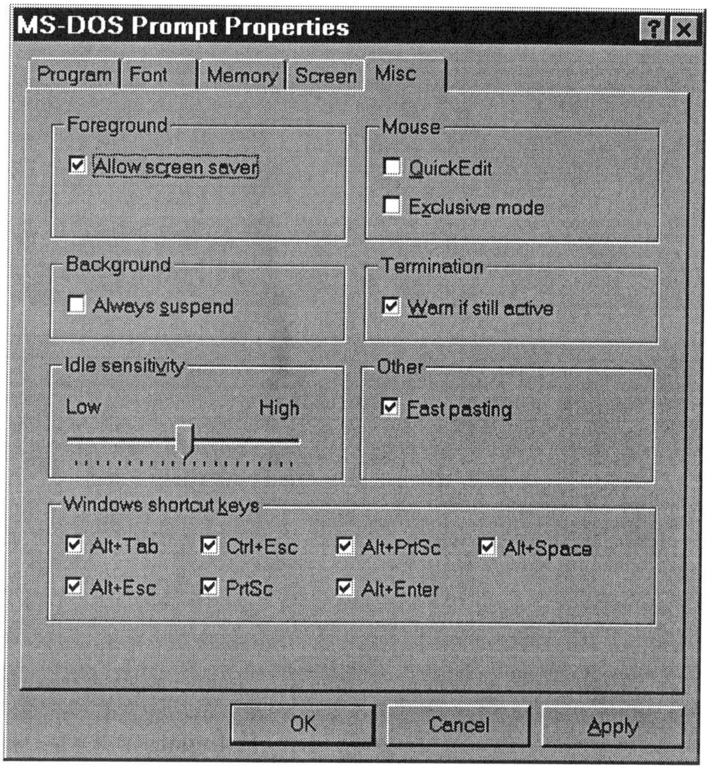

Figure 7 DOS Properties Dialog Box — Misc Page

Memory is sometimes classified according to its storage location or the way it is used. (Figure 8, on the next page, illustrates this in a pictorial fashion.)

- **Conventional memory** refers to the first 640 KB of RAM. This is the memory used by DOS and its applications. All programs running under DOS must reside partly or wholly in this address space.
- **Upper memory** has addresses ranging from 640 KB to one MB. This region was originally reserved for memory used by hardware devices (such as the video adapter) and ROM. Nowadays, a piece of system software called a *memory manager* can make use of unused portions of upper memory to store small programs, such as device drivers, and for other special purposes.
- **Extended memory (XMS)** is the term used to describe all memory in locations above one MB. An *extended memory manager* allows

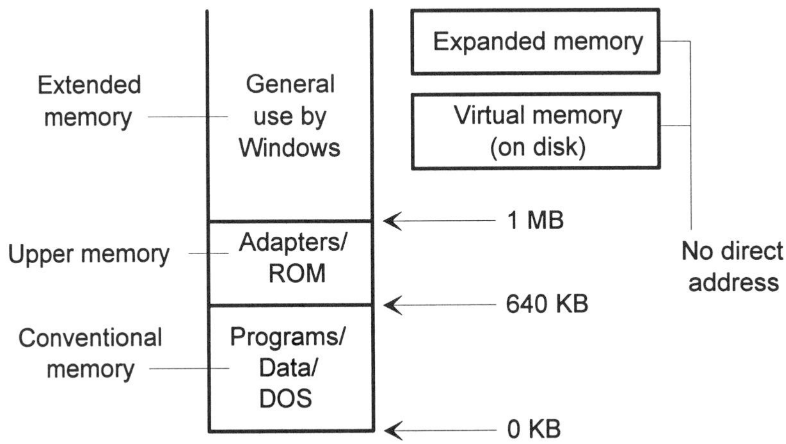

Figure 8 Types of Memory

programs to use this memory without conflicting with one another. Windows makes extensive use of extended memory with the help of its built-in extended memory manager.

- **Expanded memory (EMS),** unlike the types just described, does not refer to memory in a specific location. Rather, it is a system of memory management, developed before Windows became popular, that allows DOS programs to access more RAM than found in conventional memory. Windows and Windows-based applications do not use expanded memory, but Windows can provide expanded memory to DOS programs through a built-in expanded memory manager.
- **Virtual memory** is hard disk space that is used by the computer system as if it were additional RAM. Windows makes use of virtual memory through the use of a *swap file,* which allows it to run more applications simultaneously than the amount of available RAM would otherwise permit (see Section 6.5).

The Memory page

The Memory Page of a DOS program's Properties dialog box (Figure 9) allows you to control to some extent the way Windows supplies conventional, extended, and expanded memory for the program. The *Auto* entry on the various drop-down lists, the default selection, usually means that Windows will supply as much memory of each type as the DOS program requests.

- There is little reason to change the default *Auto* selection for *Conventional memory.* Even if the full 640 KB is allotted to a DOS program, conventional memory can still be supplied to other

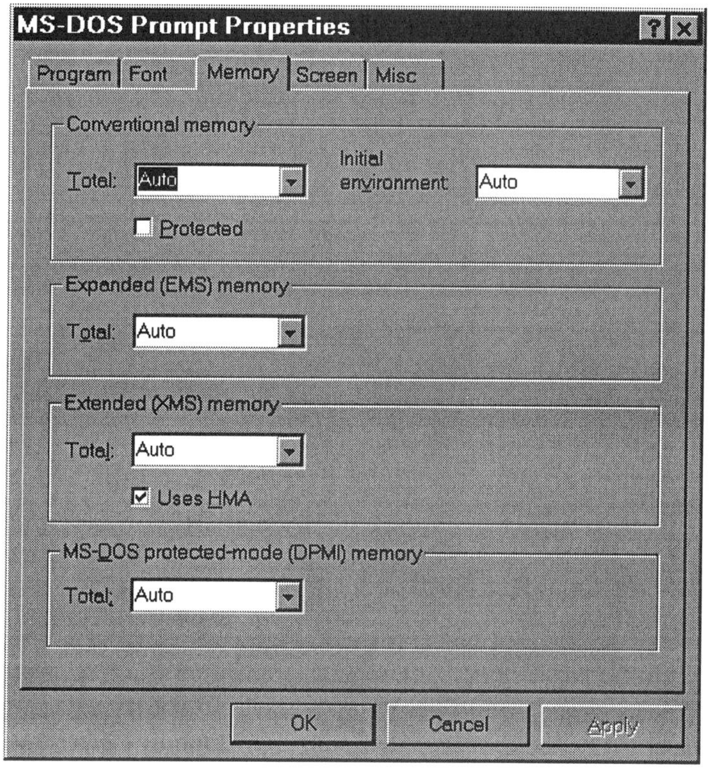

Figure 9 DOS Properties Dialog Box — Memory Page

applications because each DOS program runs in its own "virtual machine", as if it alone had control of the entire computer.

- It's usually a good idea to select the *Protected* check box to reduce the possibility that Windows will crash if the DOS program performs an "illegal" operation. (This selection may slow down the program a little, however.)
- In the *Initial environment* box, *Auto* supplies the amount of memory specified in the Config.sys system file (see Section 12.3). If the program will not start, check its user guide to see how much memory is required for environmental variables. Then, select this figure from the *Initial environment* drop-down list. (The numbers here are bytes, not kilobytes!)
- Some DOS programs will take all available RAM for use as expanded memory. In this case, set the *Expanded (EMS) memory* selection to a fixed figure; check the program's user guide. (The EMS setting will not be available if there is an entry in Config.sys

that prevents programs from using this type of memory.)

- The *Uses HMA* check box determines whether or not the **High Memory Area**, the first 64 KB of extended memory, can be used by the program. If the HMA is being used by Windows for other purposes, or if the DOS program cannot make use of the HMA, this selection will be ignored.
- DPMI, *DOS Protected Mode Interface*, is a relatively new Microsoft specification concerning the use of extended memory. Leave this setting on Auto. If the program cannot use DPM memory, this setting will be ignored.

NOTE

The DOS Properties dialog box contains a few additional settings that we have not discussed in this section. You can use Windows' context-sensitive help to determine their functions: Just right-click on the setting's label (in the DOS Properties dialog box) and choose *What's This?* from the pop-up menu.

12-2 TUTORIAL

Try the following exercise on your own.

1. Turn on the computer (if necessary) to start Windows 95.
2. Start MS-DOS Prompt from the Start menu's Programs submenu and switch to window mode, if necessary, by pressing Alt+Enter.
3. Click on the Properties icon on the Toolbar to open the Properties dialog box.
4. Note the current settings for the following parameters:
   - *Shortcut key* and *Run* on the Program page
   - *Usage* and *Display toolbar* on the Screen page
   - *Alt+Enter* shortcut key on the Misc page
5. Specify the settings shown for the indicated parameters:
   - *Shortcut key* (Program page) — Ctrl+Alt+D (Hold down Ctrl and Alt while typing D in the text box.)
   - *Run* (Program page) — Maximized
   - *Usage* (Screen page) — Window
   - *Display toolbar* (Screen page) — set (Select its check box.)
   - *Alt+Enter* (Misc page) — clear (Deselect its check box.)
6. Choose the OK command button to put the changes into effect.
7. Close MS-DOS Prompt by clicking on its close button.
8. Start MS-DOS Prompt by pressing Ctrl+Alt+D, which is possible due to its *shortcut key* setting. Notice that on startup, MS-DOS

Prompt is running in a maximized window with its Toolbar displayed because of the settings specified in step 5.

9. Press Alt+Enter. Notice that nothing happens. This shortcut key should have caused a switch to full-screen mode, but it was disabled in step 5.
10. Open the Properties dialog box by clicking on its Toolbar button.
11. Choose the Change Icon button on the Program page. Scroll through the available icons in the resulting dialog box; then, choose the Cancel button to close it.
12. In the Properties dialog box, return all parameters to their original settings as noted in step 4. (If the original setting for *Shortcut key* was "None", click in this text box on the Program page and press the Backspace key to reset it.
13. Choose the OK command button to close the Properties dialog box and then close MS-DOS Prompt.

12.3 Startup Options and Configuration Files

Normally, when you turn on your computer, you sit back, wait for a minute or so, and the Windows Desktop appears on your screen. However, in that "minute or so", a lot is going on behind the scenes. Moreover, if so desired, Windows makes it possible for you to change not only some of the things that occur during this period of time, but also the end result (for example, whether a Windows or a DOS startup screen is displayed). In this section, we will discuss the startup process (or **boot process**) in detail, including the configuration files that are accessed at this time.

The Boot Process

With the default settings in place (the way Windows is normally installed), this is what happens after you turn on your computer:

1. The computer's read-only memory (ROM) performs a few quick self-tests and starts a small program called Io.sys, whose main job is to start Windows 95. At this time, your screen display may show the results of the testing process and then the message "Starting Windows 95 ...".

2. Windows* now reads the commands located in three **configuration files**, in the order indicated here:
   - **Msdos.sys** determines the startup configuration for Windows 95 (such as whether Windows starts, DOS starts, or a menu of options is displayed), loads a memory manager that is needed to start Windows, and sets defaults for certain system parameters.
   - **Config.sys** contains commands that configure your system's hardware so that Windows and other software can use it.
   - **Autoexec.bat** contains commands that store startup information for DOS, establish the automatic search path, and perform other tasks that are to be carried out when the system starts up.

   (We will discuss the functions of these files in more detail, as well as how to edit them, later in this section.)
3. The Windows 95 logo screen (white clouds in a blue sky), and possibly the contents of Config.sys and Autoexec.bat, are displayed on the screen and then the Windows Desktop appears.

Startup Options

The scenario described above is the default boot process. You can alter this process:

- For just the current session, by pressing certain keys when the message "Stating Windows 95..." appears on the screen.

or

- For future sessions, by editing the Msdos.sys file while running Windows 95.

We will discuss each of these techniques below.

Using Startup Hotkeys When the message "Starting Windows 95..." appears on the screen (soon after you turn on the machine), pressing one of the keys (a *hotkey*) listed in Table 1 has the effect indicated there.

*Some say that DOS is actually in control of the computer at this point, but since DOS is now an integral part of Windows, rather than a separate operating system, this is really a moot point.

Keystroke	Effect on Startup
F4	Starts the "previous version of DOS"; the one that was running when Windows 95 was installed.
F5	Starts Windows 95 in *safe mode* — a basic configuration in which only certain device drivers are loaded.
Shift+F5	Starts "DOS 7", the version that comes with Windows 95, in safe mode.
Ctrl+F5	Starts DOS 7, but without compressed drives (see Section 9.4).
F6	Same effect as F5, but loads network drivers so that you can use your local network.
F8	Displays the Windows 95 Startup Menu (see Table 2, later in this section).
Shift+F8	Performs an "interactive startup" — allows the user to specify the details of the startup configuration, which includes whether or not to execute each command in Autoexec.bat and Config.sys.
Shift	Normal startup, but ignores the Autoexec.bat and Config.sys files.

Table 1 Startup Hotkeys

Editing the Msdos.sys File To alter the Windows 95 boot process on a more permanent basis, you will have to edit the Msdos .sys configuration file.

WARNING

It is not difficult to edit Msdos.sys, but you should do so with care because a misstep here could prevent your system from booting up. Thus, before you edit Msdos.sys:

- Be sure you have an emergency startup disk, a diskette that can be used to boot the system should something go wrong (see the part of Section 5.5 dealing with the Add/Remove Programs utility).
- Copy the current Msdos.sys file and rename the copy (say, Msdos .old) before editing the original.

To edit the Msdos.sys file to provide a customized boot process:

1. Msdos.sys is a hidden file, so "unhide it" if necessary: Start Explorer or My Computer, choose Options from the View menu, select the *Show all files* option button, and choose the OK command button.
2. Open Notepad (Section 9.2) from the Accessories submenu of the Start menu's Programs option.
3. Choose the Open command from Notepad's File menu, select All Files from the *Files of type* drop-down list, open the root folder of the boot drive (probably C:), and double-click on the Msdos.sys file. Figure 10 shows the result of these actions.

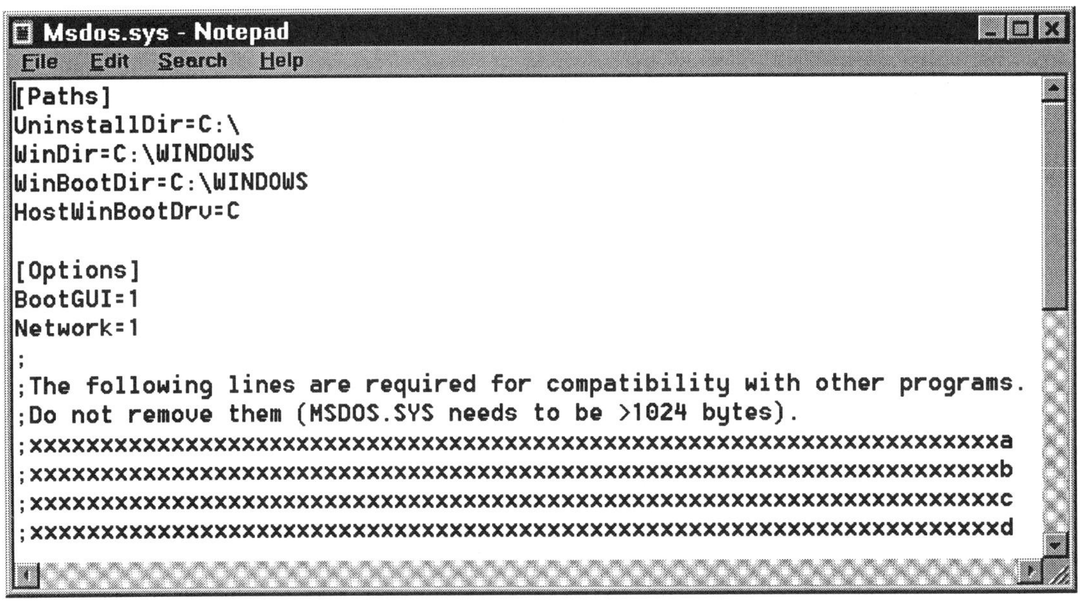

Figure 10 The Msdos.sys File Open in Notepad

4. In the [Options] section of Msdos.sys, change, delete, or insert lines to get the desired effect on the boot process. If an available option does not appear in the file, then the default value is used. Here are some examples:
   - BootGUI=1 (the default value) boots Windows 95; BootGUI=0 boots DOS 7.
   - BootMenu=0 (the default value) boots without displaying the Startup Menu.

BootMenu=1 displays the Startup Menu (see below).

- BootKeys=1 (the default value) enables (allows the use of) the startup hotkeys.
  BootKeys=0 disables the startup hotkeys.

5. Choose Save from the File menu to save your changes; or, if you don't want to save them, exit Notepad, responding "No" to the warning message.

WARNING

In the procedure above, we used Notepad to edit Msdos.sys. Other text editors, such as DOS's Edit and Windows 3.1's Sysedit, could be used instead. However, you must remember that Msdos.sys, Config .sys, and Autoexec.bat are *text files* and may not include any characters or codes that can't be typed at the keyboard. So, if you use another program to edit one of these files, make sure it saves files in Text format. Otherwise, the file will probably become unreadable, which in turn could cause major problems.

The [Paths] section of the Msdos.sys file tells Windows which folders contain certain key information. Editing one of these lines could have disastrous consequences.

The Startup Menu If you press F8 when the message "Starting Windows 95..." appears on the screen or place the appropriate command in the Msdos.sys file, the menu of options listed in Table 2 will be displayed on startup:

	Option	Effect on Startup
1	Normal	Starts Windows 95 (or DOS 7, if BootGUI = 0).
2	Logged	Same as Option 1, but creates a file (Bootlog .txt, in the root folder) that supplies details of the boot process.
3	Safe mode	Starts Windows 95 (or DOS 7, if BootGUI = 0) in safe mode (see the F5 and Shift+F5 hotkeys in Table 1).
4	Safe mode with network support	Same as Option 3, but allows use of your local network (see the F6 hotkey in Table 1).
5	Step-by-step configuration	Starts Windows 95 (or DOS 7, if BootGUI = 0) interactively (see Shift+F8 hotkey in Table 1).

6	Command prompt only	Starts DOS 7.
7	Safe mode command prompt	Starts DOS 7 in safe mode (see the Shift+F5 hotkey in Table 1).
8	Previous version of MS-DOS	Starts the previous version of DOS (see the F4 hotkey in Table 1).

Table 2 The Windows 95 Startup Menu

The Config.sys and Autoexec.bat Files

The Config.sys and Autoexec.bat files date back to the first version of DOS and are included in Windows 95 to ensure compatibility with older versions of DOS and Windows, and their applications. Both files are stored in the root folder of the boot drive (probably C:). If your version of Windows 95 was the first operating system installed on your computer, neither Config.sys nor Autoexec.bat may be present. If, on the other hand, Windows 95 was installed as an upgrade, both files will exist and are probably pretty complicated.

Config.sys and Autoexec.bat, like Msdos.sys, are text files. They consist of a series of lines, each of which represents a command to be executed on system startup, and are edited in the same way as Msdos .sys; the technique was described earlier in this section.

The Config.sys File Config.sys is short for *configure system*, which describes, in a nutshell, the purpose of this file. Here are a few of the more common commands found in the Config.sys file:

- The DEVICE and DEVICEHIGH commands load device drivers into RAM. (The latter command loads into upper memory, the region between 640 KB and 1 MB — see Section 12.2.) A **device driver** is a program that controls the workings of a hardware device, such as a mouse, keyboard, monitor, or disk drive.
- The FILES command determines how many files an application can have open at one time. (Msdos.sys sets a default value of 30.)
- The DOS command specifies whether DOS will use the *high memory area* (HMA) — the first 64 KB of extended memory (see Section 12.2) — and whether or not DOS will allow access to *upper memory blocks*, 64 KB sections of RAM in upper memory.

Figure 11 shows the content of a typical Config.sys file.

```
DEVICE=C:\WINDOWS\HIMEM.SYS
DEVICE=C:\WINDOWS\EMM386.EXE RAM HIGHSCAN
FILES=50
DOS=UMB
DEVICEHIGH /L:1,26928 =C:\SB16\DRV\CTSB16.SYS /UNIT=0
DEVICEHIGH /L:1,10416 =C:\SB16\DRV\CTMMSYS.SYS
DOS=HIGH
DEVICE=C:\CDROM\NEC_IDE.SYS /D:MSCD001 /V
```

Figure 11 A Typical Config.sys File

Annotation of Figure 11

Here's an explanation of the Config.sys commands displayed in Figure 11:

- The first two lines of Figure 11 load the memory managers HIMEM and EMM386 into RAM. HIMEM provides extended memory for Windows and other software; EMM386 supplies expanded memory for those DOS programs that can use it and also allows device drivers and certain other small programs to use upper memory.
- The command FILES=50 allows up to 50 files to be open at the same time.
- DOS=UMB and DOS=HIGH allow DOS to provide access to upper memory blocks and to load most of itself into the high memory area, respectively.
- The DEVICEHIGH commands ask EMM386 to load, if possible, certain sound drivers into upper memory, and the last DEVICE command loads a CD-ROM driver into conventional memory.

NOTE

In looking at Figure 11, you might notice that Config.sys does not load any mouse, keyboard, monitor, or other drivers. Efficient "32-bit" versions of these drivers are all loaded by Windows into extended memory. As a result, they do not take up any valuable conventional or upper memory.

TIP

Although some DOS programs can make use of expanded or extended memory, all DOS programs must run, whether in a DOS session or in MS-DOS mode, in conventional memory. It is thus sometimes necessary to make every possible scrap of conventional memory available to certain DOS programs.

For DOS programs running under Windows (in a DOS session) available conventional memory is usually maximized automatically.

However, for DOS programs running after Windows has shut down (in MS-DOS mode), you have to use Config.sys to optimize conventional memory. To do so, as many drivers and *memory resident programs* (TSRs) as possible must be loaded into upper memory. Fortunately, this can be done for you, relatively easily, by running MemMaker, which is supplied with Windows, or another optimization program.

The Autoexec.bat File Autoexec.bat is short for *automatically-executed batch.* A **batch file** is a program that contains a list of commands that are executed when it is run. Autoexec.bat is a batch file that is run at system startup unless you specify otherwise (by, for example, holding down the Shift key as Windows starts up).

Autoexec.bat may contain almost any command that can be typed at the DOS prompt. Usually, it contains commands similar to the ones shown in Figure 12. Here's an explanation of some of these commands:

Annotation of Figure 12

- The SET command defines an *environmental variable,* which acts as an alias for a directory (folder) or collection of parameters. For example, the first line of Figure 12 allows the Sound Blaster driver to refer to the variable SOUND when it wants to access a certain directory, which on this system happens to be C:\SB16.
- The command C:\SB16\DIAGNOSE/S (fourth line) runs the program DIAGNOSE, which can be found in the C:\SB16 directory. (The command on the fifth line also runs a program.)

```
SET SOUND=C:\SB16
SET BLASTER=A220 I5 D1 H5 P330 T6
SET MIDI=SYNTH:1 MAP:E
C:\SB16\DIAGNOSE /S
C:\SB16\SB16SET /P /Q
rem - By Windows Setup - C:\WINDOWS\COMMAND\mscdex /d:MSCD001
@ECHO OFF
LH /L:1,1664 c:\quality
PROMPT $P$G
SET MOUSE=C:\MSMOUSE
rem - By Windows Setup - LH /L:0;1,25424 /S C:\MSMOUSE\MOUSE
PATH=C:\WINDOWS;C:\WINDOWS\COMMAND;C:\;C:\DOS;C:\MACH32;
PATH C:\WINDOWS;C:\WINDOWS\COMMAND;C:\NU;%PATH%
SET SYMANTEC=C:\SYMANTEC
SET NU=C:\NU
SET TEMP=C:\WINDOWS\TEMP
```

Figure 12 A Typical Autoexec.bat File

- When a line begins with the letters *rem* (for "remark"), it is not executed by the computer. ("Remming out" a line is a good way to delete a command from a batch file; it makes it easy to restore it if you change your mind later on.)
- The ECHO OFF command suppresses the display of the commands that follow it. An @ symbol at the beginning of a line suppresses the display of just that line. (Thus, in Figure 12, all commands preceding ECHO OFF will be displayed on the screen as Windows starts, but this command and those that follow it won't be displayed.)
- The PROMPT command determines the way the DOS prompt will be displayed. Here, "$P" causes the current drive and directory to be displayed and "$G" displays a greater than (>) symbol, as in `C:\WINDOWS>`. (This type of prompt is actually set as the default by Msdos.sys.)
- The PATH command tells DOS where to search for a program whose name is typed at the DOS prompt. The search begins with the current directory and then continues, if necessary, with the directories listed in PATH commands, in the order listed. (Msdos .sys also contains PATH commands.)

TIP

For quick, detailed help with any Config.sys or Autoexec.bat command, type the word *help* followed by the command name at a DOS prompt. For example, for help with the SET command, just type `help set` at a DOS prompt.

NOTE

Windows 3.1 used two additional configuration files, Win.ini and System.ini. Both files are present in Windows 95, mostly for compatibility purposes. At installation, all relevant information in these files was placed in the Registry database (see Section 12.4). As a result, Windows 95 ignores almost all the information that appears in Win.ini and System.ini.

12.4 The Windows Registry

Windows 3.1 uses special files (such as System.ini and Win.ini) to store information about the hardware and software configuration of the computer system, and about user-specified preferences for the look and feel of its interface. These files are still present in Windows 95, but their main function here is to provide compatibility with older applications. Almost all the configuration information needed by Windows 95 is stored in files that are collectively known as the **Registry**.

The Structure of the Registry

The Registry consists primarily of two files located in the Windows folder on your hard disk:

Registry files

- The file System.dat contains information about the hardware and software present on your computer: the installed devices, drivers, ports, applications, and so on.
- The file User.dat contains information about user preferences such as Desktop icons, Start button menu items, wallpaper, screen colors, and the like.

Keys and value entries

When you view the Registry (as described later in this section), it is represented as a single object with a tree-like structure. This structure is analogous to that of the Windows file system. However, instead of folders, there are *keys*, and instead of files, there are *value entries.* A **key** describes the settings present in that section of the Registry; a **value entry** gives the name and value of a setting. As in the Windows file system, an entry in the Registry is located by means of a path name. For example, the entry that determines the size of Desktop icons is My Computer\HKEY_CURRENT_USER\Control Panel\Desktop\WindowMetrics\Shell Icon Size. Here, Shell Icon Size is the value entry and all the rest of the names are keys; each key (except My Computer) is a subkey of the ones to its left.

The root of the Registry tree is called My Computer. There are six main keys (sometimes called *root keys*) that appear as subkeys of it. (See Figure 13 for a pictorial representation of the relationship.) Here is a general description of the content of each root key:

- HKEY_USERS contains information about user-specific preferences for the "default user" (as defined in the User Profiles section of the Passwords utility; see Section 6.5), the "current user" (the one currently logged on), and possibly other users. (If no users were added by means of User Profiles, then the default user is the only subkey here.) This data is obtained from the User.dat configuration file and includes information about Control Panel settings, the Desktop setup, network connections, installed applications, and many other user-specified preferences.
- HKEY_CURRENT_USER is identical to a subkey of HKEY_USERS. It

contains the part of this key that applies to the user that is currently logged on to the computer.

- HKEY_LOCAL_MACHINE contains all information about the hardware and software present on your computer (except for the preference selections made by its users). This data is obtained from the System.dat configuration file.
- HKEY_CURRENT_CONFIG is identical to a subkey of HKEY_LOCAL_MACHINE; it contains information pertaining to the currently selected *hardware profile*. Hardware profiles are established in Control Panel's System utility (see Section 6.5); they create different hardware configurations for a single computer so that, for example, it can be easily switched from use as a standalone laptop to one that is connected to a network or docking station.
- HKEY_DYN_DATA contains current information about the status of devices and software that have been loaded during the current Windows session. (DYN stands for *dynamic*.) This key is the same as a subkey of HKEY_LOCAL_MACHINE and has an important role in the workings of plug-and-play devices (see Section 6.2).
- HKEY_CLASSES_ROOT primarily contains information about file associations (see Section 4.4) and object linking and embedding (see Section 12.5). This key is identical to a subkey of HKEY_LOCAL_MACHINE.

Editing the Registry

Whenever you make changes to settings in Control Panel, on a property sheet, or in certain other Windows locations, these modifications are reflected in the Registry. Thus, when you make such changes, you are, in effect, editing the Registry. It is also possible, and sometimes necessary, to edit the Registry directly. However, the Registry files, System.dat and User.dat, are not text files and cannot therefore be modified using Notepad or another text editor. To edit these files, you must use the Windows 95 Registry Editor.

WARNING Using the Registry Editor improperly can have unfortunate consequences; Windows may not load when you restart your computer, or if it does load, it may not work properly. For this reason, you should understand how the Registry is backed up and restored, and also exercise care when modifying it. We will discuss backing up and restoring the Registry later in this section.

The Registry Editor is a program with file name Regedit.exe that resides in the Windows folder. To start the Registry Editor, either

- Double-click on its icon in Explorer or a folder window.

or

- Choose the Run option from the Start menu, type Regedit in the resulting dialog box, and choose the OK command button.

In either case, the window shown in Figure 13 will open.

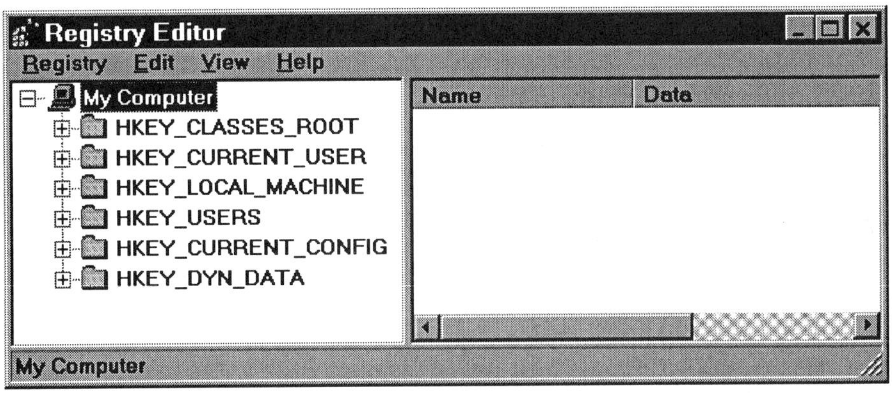

Figure 13 The Registry Window Showing the Six Main Keys

NOTE

If you are running Windows 95 in a computer lab and/or on a network, you may not be able to start the Registry Editor. It may have been removed by the lab coordinator or system administrator to protect the integrity of the system.

The general Registry editing procedure

Here is an outline of the general procedure for editing an entry in the Registry:

1. Start the Registry Editor, as described above.
2. Expand branches of the Registry tree (by clicking on the plus symbol next to certain keys in the left pane) until the desired key appears.
3. Click on this key to display its contents (all the value entries contained within it) in the right pane.
4. Double-click on the desired entry's name and enter its new value in the resulting dialog box.

5. Close the Registry Editor by choosing Exit from the File menu.

Some changes to the Registry are put into effect when you restart Windows; others take place immediately.

An example As you can see, the procedure just given is not very specific. We can better illustrate how to use the Registry Editor by walking through an example: Suppose you want to change the color of the text used to represent "dimmed" or "grayed-out" menu entries. Proceeding in what seems to be a logical way (once you've read Section 5.3), you open Control Panel's Display utility and click on the Appearance tab. However (as you can see if you work this example), there is no selection in the Item drop-down list for grayed-out items and clicking on *Disabled* in the sample window's menu bar has no effect. In other words, the color of grayed-out text cannot be changed from Control Panel.

Nevertheless, you *can* change the color of grayed-out text using the Registry. First, you have to determine the red-green-blue (RGB) composition of the color you want to use. This can be done by using the Display utility:

1. Click on the Color button on the Appearance page and, when the color palette is displayed, choose the *Other* command button. This action opens the Color dialog box.
2. In the color spectrum area of this dialog box, click on the desired color and make a note of the values displayed in the Red, Green, and Blue text boxes. (If these values don't change when you click in the color spectrum, first click on the vertical luminosity bar, then in the color spectrum.)

Now close the Display utility and start the Registry Editor, as described earlier in this section, and proceed as follows:

1. Since the entry you want to change is a user preference, click on the plus symbol next to HKEY_CURRENT_USER to display its subkeys.
2. Notice (in Figure 14, on the next page) that one of the subkeys of HKEY_CURRENT_USER is Control Panel, so expand this branch (by clicking on its plus symbol).
3. Finally, a Colors subkey appears; click on its name or icon to display its value entries. The result is shown in Figure 14. (Notice that the Status bar, at the bottom of the Registry window, contains the path for the Colors key.)

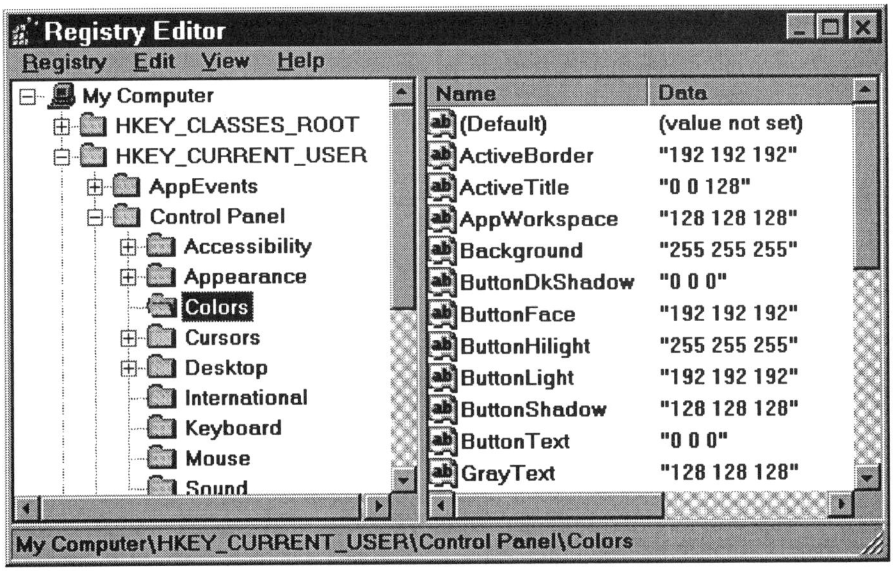

Figure 14 The Registry Window after Clicking on the Colors Key

4. Double-click, in the right pane, on the value entry named Gray Text. (Notice that its current value, its RGB composition, is "128 128 128".) A dialog box will open, as shown in Figure 15, allowing you to modify the value of this entry.

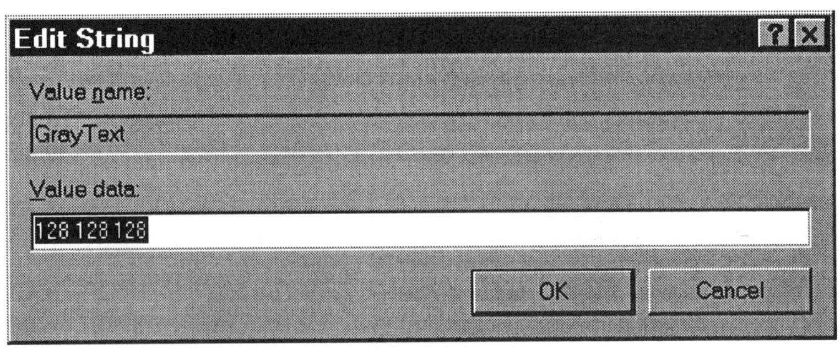

Figure 15 The Editing Dialog Box

5. Enter the desired red, green, and blue figures in the *Value data* text box and choose the OK command button.
6. Close the Registry Editor.

Regedit's Find utility

Often the hardest part of using the Registry Editor is locating the desired key or value entry. Fortunately, Regedit supplies a *Find utility* to help you in this respect. We will use another example to illustrate the use of the Find utility.

Suppose you would like to rename the Recycle Bin. But, when you right-click on its icon, the resulting pop-up menu has no Rename command. Obviously, Microsoft does not really want you to rename the Recycle Bin, but you can do so using the Registry Editor. The problem here is that it could take hours to locate the appropriate key in the Registry Editor window. Using Find, however, it's a snap:

1. In the Registry Editor, choose the Find command from the Edit menu. The Find window, shown in Figure 16, will open.

Figure 16 The Registry Editor's Find Window

2. Enter the words Recycle Bin in the *Find what* text box. (There is usually little point in changing the default status of the four check boxes.)
3. Choose the Find Next command button. When the words Recycle Bin are found, the Registry Editor will locate and open the appropriate key. The result of the search is shown in Figure 17, on the next page.
4. Now, double-click on the word *Default* in the right-pane, enter a new name in the resulting dialog box, choose the OK button, and exit the Registry Editor.

NOTE

The long strings of characters in the left pane of Figure 17 are known as *Class IDs*. Every object in Windows has a unique Class ID number, or CLSID. (The reason why a CLSID is so long is that it is assigned

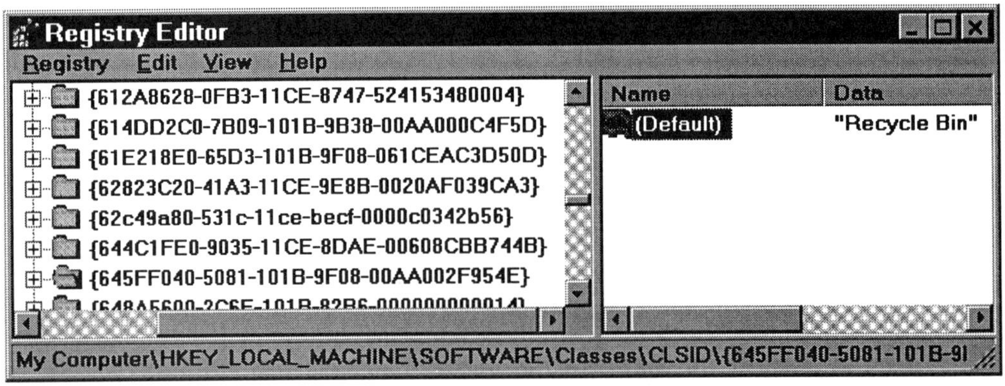

Figure 17 The Result of the Search for *Recycle Bin*

randomly and the length of the string virtually assures its uniqueness.) A good way to find the CLSID for a particular object is to use Regedit's Find utility, just as we did here.

Backing Up and Restoring the Registry

As we mentioned earlier in this section, if you're going to use the Registry Editor, then it is important to know how the Registry is backed up and restored.

Restoring the Automatic Backups It is not difficult to make a real mess of things while using the Registry Editor. Fortunately, Windows automatically backs up the System.dat and User.dat files every time it successfully starts. Then, if the Registry becomes corrupted, even to the extent that Windows will not start, you can replace the Registry files by their backups and start Windows again.

The backup files that Windows creates are named System.da0 and User.da0 (they both end with the number zero), and are located in the Windows folder of your boot drive, probably C:\Windows. Assuming that this is the case, to copy the backup files over the current System .dat and User.dat:

Restoring the backup files

1. Get to a DOS prompt (either C:\> or A:\>):
   - If you are in Windows, restart the computer in MS-DOS mode from the Shut Down dialog box.

   or

   - Turn on the computer and press Shift+F5 when you see the message "Starting Windows 95..." to start DOS in safe mode (or press F8 and choose this option from the resulting menu).

or

- Place a bootable diskette (see Section 3.6 or 5.5) in drive A: and turn on the computer.

2. At the DOS prompt, type the following lines, pressing the Enter key at the end of each one:

```
cd c:\windows
attrib -h -r -s system.dat
attrib -h -r -s system.da0
attrib -h -r -s user.dat
attrib -h -r -s user.da0
copy system.da0 system.dat
copy user.da0 user.dat
```

(The first line changes the current directory to C:\Windows. The next four lines clear the hidden, read-only, and system attributes — see Section 4.5 — from all four files to permit copying to take place. The last two lines copy the backup files over System.dat and User.dat.)

3. If there is a disk in the floppy drive, remove it, and restart the computer by pressing Ctrl+Alt+Del.

TIP

Although Windows automatically backs up copies of the System.dat and User.dat files to your hard disk, it's a good idea to copy them, every once and a while, to a floppy disk, as well. To do so, just copy these files, as you would any files, from the Windows folder to the floppy drive. (You may have to first unhide the files by choosing Options from Explorer's View menu and selecting the *Show all files* option button in the resulting dialog box.)

Exporting and Importing the Registry As you know, the Registry files System.dat and User.dat are not text files. However, if you want, you can create a text version of all or part of either file. This process is called **exporting the Registry**. The exported files can be modified using an ordinary text editor, such as Notepad, and then *imported* into the Registry — their data can be incorporated into System.dat and User.dat.

Exporting the Registry

To export the Registry:

1. Start the Registry Editor, as described earlier in this section.
2. Choose the Export Registry File command from the File menu; the corresponding dialog box, shown in Figure 18, will open.

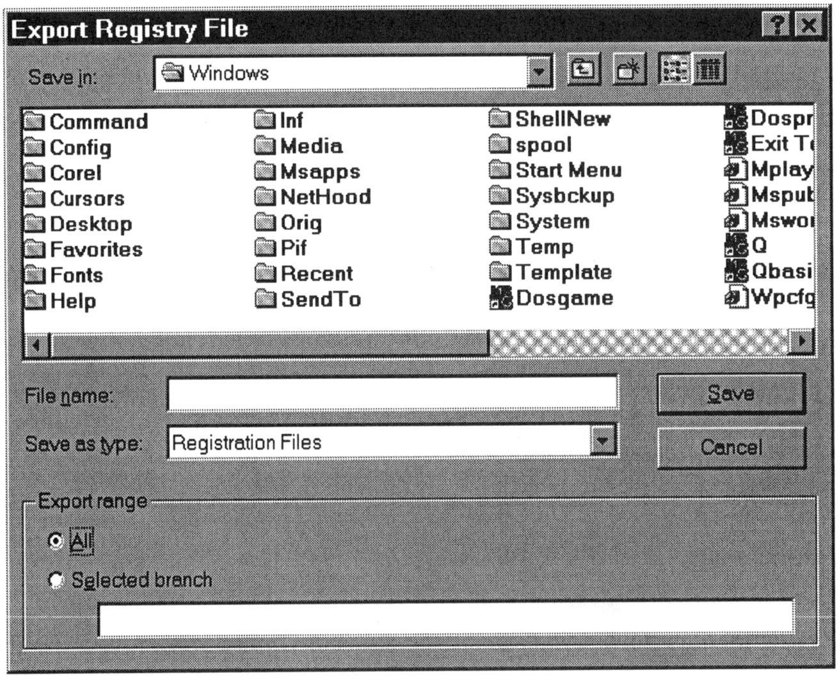

Figure 18 The Export Registry File Dialog Box

3. Select a folder in which to save the exported text file, just as if you were working in My Computer.
4. If you only want to export a branch of the Registry, click on the *Selected branch* option button and enter the path name that defines this branch in the text box.
5. Enter a file name for the exported Registry file in the *File name* text box. (Windows will automatically add a *reg* extension to your name.)
6. Choose the Save command button.

NOTE

An exported Registry file may be too large to open in Notepad. (The size of the entire Registry, converted to a text file, will probably exceed one megabyte.) In that case, you can use WordPad to edit it. A *reg* file is automatically opened and saved by WordPad as a text file.

The Registry looks quite different when viewed as a text file. Figure 19 shows a small portion of an exported Registry file opened in WordPad. Notice that:

- Registry keys are described by enclosing their path name in square brackets.
- Entry names are enclosed in double-quotes.
- Entry data values are either enclosed in double-quotes (if they are strings) or preceded by *dword* or *hex* (if they are decimal or binary values).

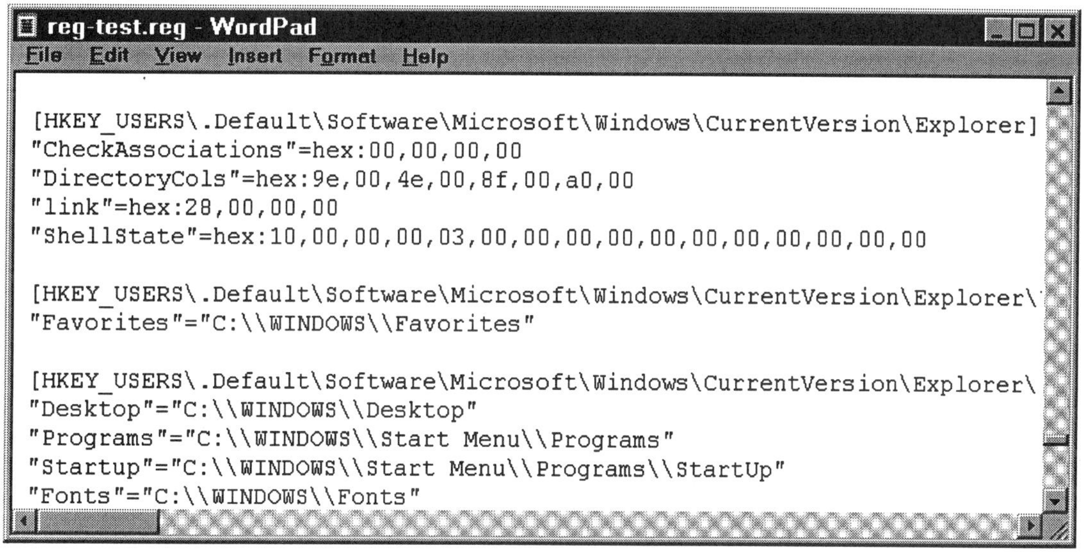


```
[HKEY_USERS\.Default\Software\Microsoft\Windows\CurrentVersion\Explorer]
"CheckAssociations"=hex:00,00,00,00
"DirectoryCols"=hex:9e,00,4e,00,8f,00,a0,00
"link"=hex:28,00,00,00
"ShellState"=hex:10,00,00,00,03,00,00,00,00,00,00,00,00,00,00,00

[HKEY_USERS\.Default\Software\Microsoft\Windows\CurrentVersion\Explorer\
"Favorites"="C:\\WINDOWS\\Favorites"

[HKEY_USERS\.Default\Software\Microsoft\Windows\CurrentVersion\Explorer\
"Desktop"="C:\\WINDOWS\\Desktop"
"Programs"="C:\\WINDOWS\\Start Menu\\Programs"
"Startup"="C:\\WINDOWS\\Start Menu\\Programs\\StartUp"
"Fonts"="C:\\WINDOWS\\Fonts"
```

Figure 19 An Exported Registry File Opened in WordPad

Importing the Registry

If you want to copy an exported (text) Registry file over the corresponding portion of the Registry, replacing the latter in the process, you must **import the Registry**. To do so:

1. Start the Registry Editor.
2. Choose Import Registry File from the File menu, which displays the corresponding dialog box (Figure 20, on the next page).
3. Select the appropriate *reg* file in the resulting dialog box or type its name in the *File name* text box.
4. Choose the Open command button.

Notice that the export/import procedures provide another way to back up and restore the Registry. However, this technique requires the use of the Registry Editor, which would not be accessible if Windows refused to start.

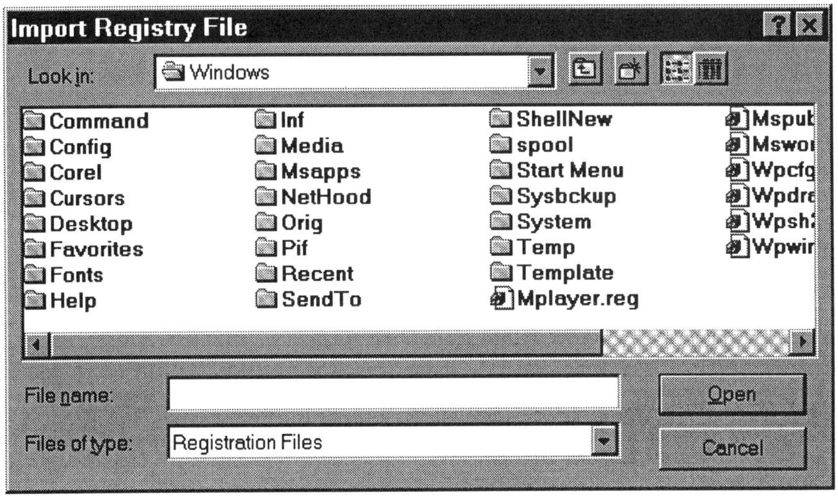

Figure 20 The Import Registry File Dialog Box

TIP

If you want, you can import the Registry from Explorer or My Computer. To do so, start either one and:

1. Open the folder that contains the appropriate *reg* file.
2. Right-click on the file's icon and choose Merge from the resulting pop-up menu. (Here, *Merge* has the same meaning as *Import*.)

Help! As you must realize by now, the Registry is large and complex. Fortunately, Microsoft has seen to it that you can make almost all the modifications you'd want to Windows 95 without having to use the Registry Editor. On the other hand, if you would like more information about this subject, see the help files located in the Admin\Reskit \Helpfile folder of the Windows 95 CD-ROM or pages 1017 - 1038 of the *Windows 95 Resource Kit*, published by Microsoft Press. (The Registry Editor's own help files, accessed from the Help menu, contain little information about the Registry.)

12-4 TUTORIAL

Try the following exercise on your own. It simulates making changes to a couple of entries in the Registry.

1. Turn on the computer (if necessary) to start Windows 95.

2. Start the Registry Editor: Either

   - Choose the Run option from the Start menu, enter Regedit in the Open text box, and choose the OK command button.

   or

   - Start Explorer or My Computer and double-click on the Regedit file name in the Windows folder.

3. Use the Registry Editor to change the active window's title bar color to black:

   - In the left pane, click on the plus symbols next to HKEY_CURRENT_USER and Control Panel to expand this key and subkey.
   - Click on the Colors icon (in the left pane) to display, in the right pane, the value entries for this key.
   - In the right pane, select the Active Title entry name and then change its value to "0 0 0", the red-green-blue values for black: Double-click on the entry name, enter the text "0 0 0", without the quotation marks, in the resulting dialog box, and choose the OK command button.

4. Use the Registry Editor to change the name of the object currently called *Inbox* to *Messages*:

   - Find a reference to the Inbox object by using the Find dialog box: Choose the Find command from the Edit menu, enter *Inbox* in the *Find what* text box, and choose the Find Next command button.
   - Windows will eventfully display the value entry for the Inbox in the right pane. Notice, from the status bar, that it is contained in the \SOFTWARE\Classes\CLSID subkey of HKEY_LOCAL_MACHINE. The long number at the end of the path name is the class ID number for the Windows object currently named *Inbox*.
   - Double-click (in the right pane) on the word *Default*, enter *Messages* in the resulting dialog box, and choose the OK command button.

5. Close the Registry Editor window without putting your changes into effect by clicking on the close button. (Had you wanted to put the changes into effect, you would have chosen Exit from the File menu and then restarted Windows.)

12.5 Object Linking and Embedding

The Windows Clipboard (Section 2.3) provides an easy way to transfer information from one document to another. However, once that information has been placed in the target document, it may not be so easy to edit it. For example, if changes have to be made to a picture pasted into a WordPad document, you might have to delete the picture, open the application that created it, make the desired changes, and reinsert the modified picture. Windows' *object linking and embedding* feature provides a more versatile way to transfer information — one that allows it to be easily edited should the need arise. In this section, we will discuss the embedding, linking, and editing processes.

What is OLE?

Object linking and embedding (or **OLE**, pronounced "oh-lay") allows you to transfer information, which in this context is called an **object**, from one document (the *source*) to another (the *destination*) in such a way that the transferred object retains a link with the application that created it. Using OLE, you can produce a **compound document** — one that contains pieces of information created using diverse applications — and then, if necessary, easily modify the document's various components. For example, you can create a letter within a word processor that contains easy-to-edit graphics, spreadsheet data, and even sound or video clips produced by other applications.

Not all Windows applications can make use of linking and embedding. If an application can *create* embeddable and linkable objects, it is called an **OLE server**. If it can *receive* these objects, it is called an **OLE client** or **container**. For example, Paint (Chapter 8) is an OLE server; WordPad (Chapter 7) is an OLE client. Some sophisticated Windows applications, such as WordPerfect and Microsoft Word, can act as both servers and clients.

The difference between linking and embedding

Although embedding and linking are usually mentioned together, they are actually two different processes:

- When you **embed** an object, a copy of it is inserted into the destination document. Then, if you edit the embedded object, the copy is modified, not the original; in other words, the editing process does not change the source document.
- To **link** an object, it must first be saved as a separate file. Then, when you link it to a destination document, an image of the object and information about it (for example, in which file it can be found) is inserted into the destination document. If you edit a linked object, the original file in which the object resides (the

source file) is modified, and when the link is *updated*, so is the image of the object in the destination document.

TIP

Embedding and linking have the same end: they both transfer an object from one document to another and provide easy editing of the image. So, which should you use? Broadly speaking:

- If an object is likely to be used in just one destination document, you should *embed* it there. An embedded object is a little easier to edit than a linked one and the resulting file is a little smaller.
- If you plan to use the same object in several documents, you should *link* it to them. Then, to edit the object's image in all the destination documents, you need only modify it once — in the source file.

Note that embedding is the more common process and is usually the default for the insertion operation.

NOTE

Microsoft introduced OLE (version 1.0) in conjunction with Windows 3.1. Since then, an improved version (OLE 2.0) has been developed. Even under Windows 95, older "OLE-aware" applications may only be able to handle version 1.0. In this section, we will primarily discuss the newer version, but when there are differences, we will point them out.

How to Embed or Link an Object

There are several ways to embed and/or link an object. You can:

- Select the object in the OLE server, copy it to the Clipboard, and paste it into the destination document. This method only works for embedding the object, unless the object is a file.
- Copy a file to the Clipboard (say, from Explorer) and paste it into the destination document. This method works for both linking and embedding.
- Use the Insert Object command in the OLE client to embed or link an object created by another application.
- Drag-and-drop the object from the OLE server into the destination document as an embedded object.

We will now explain how each of these methods works.

Embedding an Object using Select, Copy, and Paste The procedure described in Section 2.3 for using the Clipboard to transfer information between documents will often *embed* an object created in an OLE server into a client document. Here's how it works:

1. In the OLE server application, select the object in the source document that you want to embed.
2. Choose Copy from the Edit menu to place the object on the Clipboard.
3. Switch to the OLE client application and position the cursor in the destination document where you want to insert the object.
4. Now, either
   - Choose Paste from the Edit menu. This action will normally embed the object, displaying it at the cursor, and you can skip the rest of this procedure.

   or
   - Choose the Paste Special command from the Edit menu if you want more control over the insertion process. A dialog box, like the one shown in Figure 21, will be displayed and you must complete the rest of this procedure.

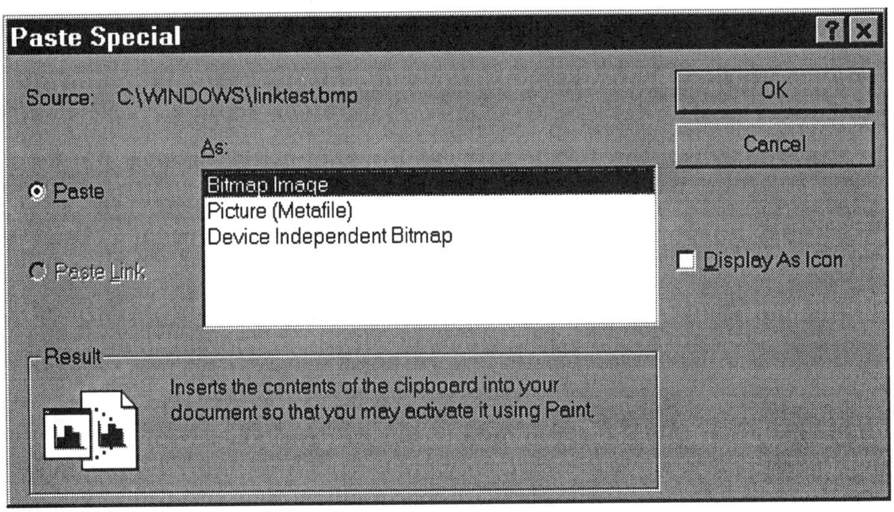

Figure 21 A Typical Paste Special Dialog Box

5. Select the *Paste* option button (if it's not already selected).
6. In the *As* window, select a format in which to embed the object. It is usually best to use the default (highlighted) option. Other formats, such as *Picture* and *Device Independent Bitmap* in Figure 21, will insert the object without embedding it. The text in the

Result area of the dialog box provides a short explanation of the consequences of choosing the currently selected format.

7. Select the Display As Icon check box if you want to insert an icon representing the object, instead of the image of the object, into the destination document. (Double-clicking on the icon in the document will then display the object.)
8. Choose the OK command button to embed the object, displaying it at the cursor.

Inserting a File using Copy and Paste You can use the procedure just described to embed *or* link an object saved in a separate file into an OLE client document. To be more specific:

1. Select the desired file in Explorer, My Computer, or a folder window.
2. Copy the selected file to the Clipboard by choosing Copy from the File menu or the right-click pop-up menu.
3. Switch to the OLE client application and position the cursor in the destination document where you want to insert the object.
4. Now, either
   - Choose the Paste command from the Edit menu, which normally embeds the object.

   or
   - Choose the Paste Special command from the Edit menu to open a dialog box like the one shown in Figure 21, select the *Paste* option button (for embedding) or the *Paste Link* option button*, and choose the OK command button. (In this situation, the Paste Link option will not be grayed out, as it is in Figure 21.)
5. The object contained in the file will be inserted into the client document and its image, or an icon representing it, will be displayed at the cursor.

Using the Insert Menu to Embed or Link When you embed or link an object using the copy and paste technique, as described above, the process begins in the server application. It is also usually

*Some OLE clients have a separate *Paste Link* command on their Edit menu to be used to insert a linked object. If this is the case, and you want to link the object, choose this command instead of Paste Special.

possible to initiate the process from within the OLE client through the use of an Insert Object command. This method is especially easy if the object is stored on disk. Here's how it works:

1. Place the cursor in the destination document (of the OLE client) where you want the object to appear.
2. Choose the Object item from the Insert menu. The Insert Object dialog box, shown in Figure 22, will open.

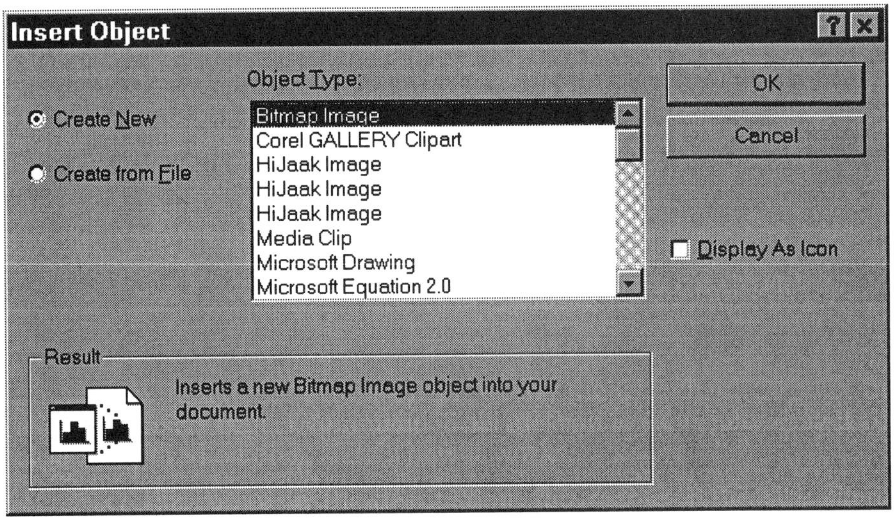

Figure 22 The Insert Object Dialog Box

3. If you want to create the object (using another application), select the Object Type corresponding to that application and then choose the OK command button. A box will open (at the cursor) in the destination document, in which you can create the object using the selected application's tools. When you are done, click the mouse anywhere outside of the box and the object will be *embedded* in the document.

   As an example, if you open the Insert Object dialog box in WordPad, select Bitmap Image, and choose OK, the Paint application will open, and the WordPad window will look as pictured in Figure 23. (Although the title bar says "WordPad", the menus and available tools are those of Paint.)

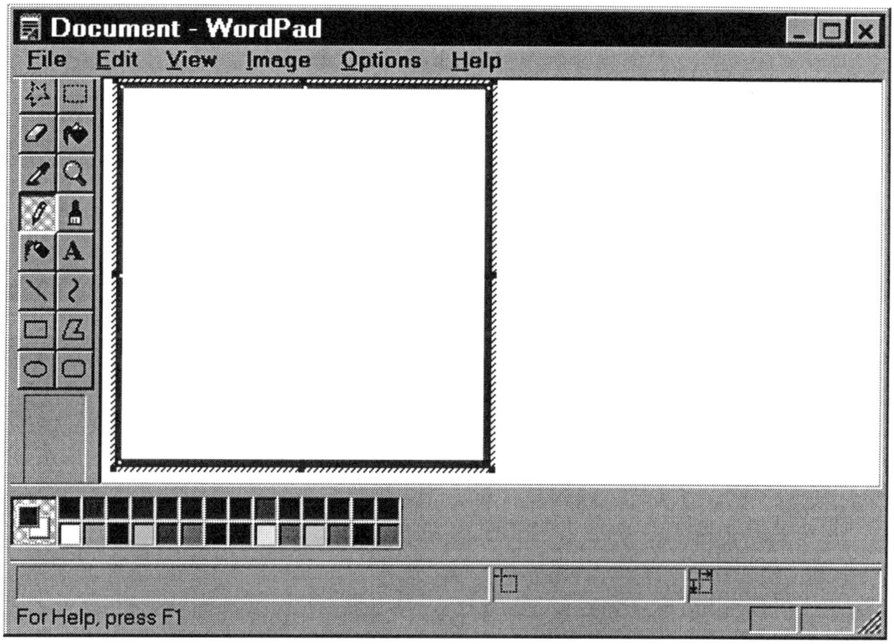

Figure 23 Working with Paint Inside the WordPad Window

4. If, instead of creating an object, you want to retrieve one from disk, select the *Create from File* option button. The Object Type list in the Insert Object dialog box will be replaced by the following display:

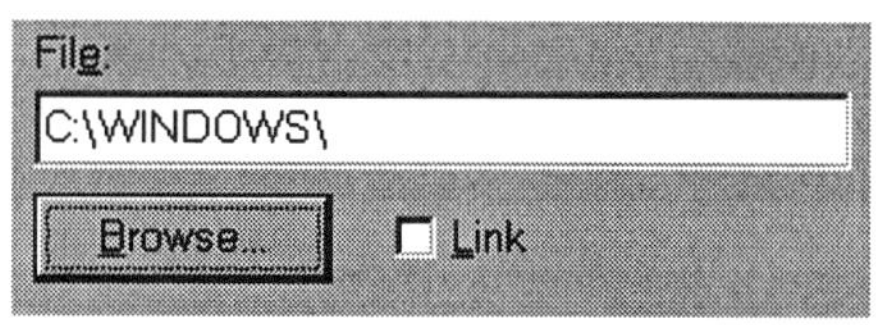

Now, either type the path name for the desired file in the *File* text box or choose the Browse button to locate the desired file by browsing folders. Then, choose the OK command button, and the object will be *embedded* in the client document at the cursor. If you want to *link* the object to the document, select the Link check box before choosing OK.

Using Drag-and-Drop This technique can only be used to embed an object and only works for applications that support version 2.0 of

OLE. All you need to do to carry out this technique is:

1. In the OLE server, select the object to be embedded.
2. Drag the object to the destination document and drop it (release the mouse button) where you want it inserted.

As an example, here's how you can insert a sound effect into a WordPad document. Start Explorer and arrange its window so that it and the WordPad window are both visible on the screen. Now, open the Windows folder, select the Chimes file, and drag it into the document; it will be displayed there as a icon, as shown at the right. The sound file is now embedded in the document. If you want to play the sound associated with the icon, just double-click on it.

Editing an Embedded or Linked Object

Once an object is embedded in or linked to a document, it can be edited from within that document. Linked objects can also be edited from within the OLE server, which can change the corresponding images in all linked documents.

Editing an Embedded Object If an object has been embedded in a OLE client document, the editing process starts within the client application and the changes made affect only that document, not the source material. To edit an embedded object:

1. Within the OLE client, open the document, if necessary, and select the object to be edited.
2. Double-click on the selected object. The server application will open within the client's window; the window size will remain the same, but a "box" will frame the object and the menus, menu items, and toolbars will change to reflect those of the server application.

   As an example, Figure 24b shows the effect of double-clicking on the bitmap graphic embedded in the WordPad document shown in Figure 24a. Notice that the content of the document window has not changed, but that Paint's Tool Box, Color Box, menu bar, and status bar are now displayed.
3. Use the server application to modify the object.
4. Click anywhere outside the framed box (but within the client window) to complete the process.

Figure 24a An Embedded Object

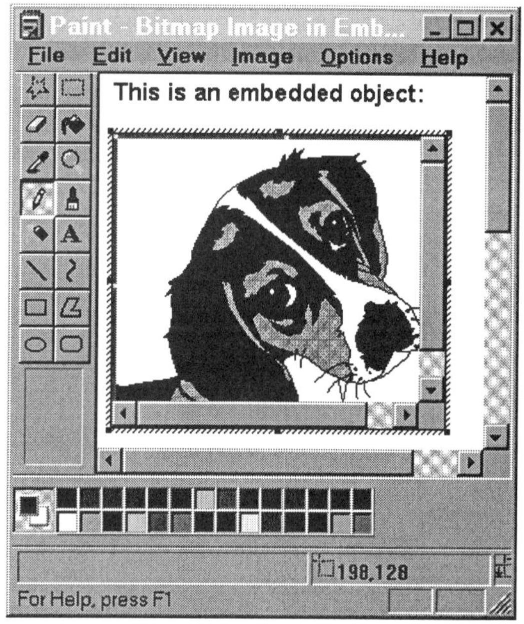

Figure 24b Double-clicking the Object

NOTE

Double-clicking on an embedded object will not always have the effect described in the procedure above.

- The "in-place" editing described above is a feature of OLE 2.0. In Windows applications that only support version 1.0, the server application will open in a separate window and, once the object has been edited, you must choose a command from the File menu to transfer the changes to the client document.
- Double-clicking on an icon that represents a sound file or video clip will play the corresponding sound or video. To edit these objects, you must use the technique described in the TIP below.

TIP

Because the image and window sizes do not change when you double-click an embedded object (see Figure 24), it may be awkward to modify the object. If you prefer, you can edit the selected embedded object in a separate server window. To do so:

1. Either right-click on the object or display the Edit menu.
2. Point at the last item on this menu (for example, "Bitmap Image Object") and choose the Open command from the resulting pop-up menu. (Choosing the Edit command from this menu has the

same effect as double-clicking on the object.)

3. Modify the object.
4. Choose the Exit and Return command from the server's File menu to complete the process.

This technique also gives you the opportunity to save the modified object in a separate file. To do so, choose the Save Copy As command from the server's File menu before returning to the client application.

Editing a Linked Object The process for editing a linked object differs slightly from the one described above for embedded objects. To edit a linked object:

1. Within the OLE client, open the document, if necessary, and select the object to be edited.
2. Either
   - Double-click on the selected object.

   or
   - Open the Edit menu or the right-click menu, point at the last item on it, and choose either Edit or Open from the resulting submenu.

   In either case, the server application will open in its own window.
3. Modify the object.
4. Save the modified file by choosing the Save command from the server's File menu.
5. Close the server application and save the changes in the client application.

The Links dialog box

If you carry out the procedure just described for editing a linked object, the linked document will, by default, be updated automatically to reflect these changes. However, you can change this default and control the linking process in other ways by choosing the Links command on the client's Edit menu, which opens the dialog box shown in Figure 25.

In the Links dialog box, you can perform the following actions:

- You can elect to update the client document when you want to, not necessarily whenever the source file changes. To do so, select the *Manual Update* option button.
- When manual updating is in effect, changes to the source file can be transferred to the client document by choosing the Update Now command button. (The Update Now button has another

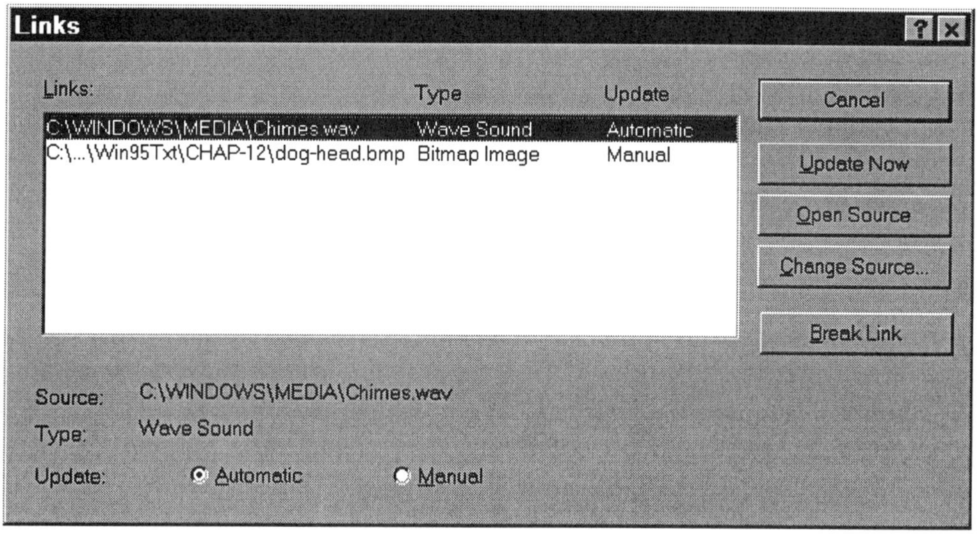

Figure 25 The Links Dialog Box

function — see the TIP given below.)

- Choosing the Open Source command button will open the source file within the application that created it. Choosing the Change Source command button will display a dialog box that allows you to link the selected object to another file.
- To end the association between the image of the object in the client document and the source file, choose the Break Link command. If you do, changes to the source file will no longer affect the object in the client document.

TIP

A linked object can be edited without first opening the client application. This technique is especially useful when several documents contain a link to a given source file. Here's how it works:

1. Open the server application and the source file.
2. Make the desired modifications, save the source file under the same name, and close the server application.
3. Open the client application and the linked document.
4. Choose Links from the Edit menu, which opens the Links dialog box, and select the appropriate linked object from the displayed list.
5. Choose the Update Now command button and then the Close button. The changes made to the source file will now be reflected in the linked document.

6. From the client's File menu, save the changes to the linked document.

12-5 TUTORIAL

Try the following exercise on your own.

1. Turn on the computer (if necessary) to start Windows 95.
2. Open WordPad and Paint (both reside on the Accessories submenu of the Start menu's Programs option) and insert the Student Disk into its drive.
3. In Paint, an OLE server application, open the Dog-head file on the Student Disk.
4. Choose the Select All command from the Edit menu and then choose Copy from the Edit menu to place the graphic on the Clipboard. Then, close Paint.
5. In WordPad (an OLE client), *embed* the object currently on the Clipboard in the WordPad document: Choose Paste Special from the Edit menu, select the Paste option button and the Bitmap Image type (if necessary), and choose the OK command button.
6. In WordPad, deselect the graphic by clicking to the right of it, and press the Enter key twice to move the insertion point.
7. Now link the Dog-head graphic to the WordPad document using another insertion technique: Choose the Object command from the Insert menu and, in the resulting dialog box, select the Create from File option button and the Link check box. Then, type `A:\dog-head` in the *File* text box and choose the OK command button.
8. Edit the linked graphic: Double-click on it to start Paint (the OLE server), make any changes you like to the dog's head, and save the resulting graphic in Paint. Then, close Paint. The changes you made will be reflected in the WordPad document.
9. In WordPad, deselect the linked graphic and select the embedded one by clicking on the latter.
10. Edit the embedded graphic: Double-click on it (which starts Paint within the WordPad window and frames the graphic in a "box"), make any changes you wish, and then click anywhere (in the document window) outside of the box to return to WordPad's menus and toolbars.
11. Close WordPad, responding No to the "Save Changes?" message, and remove the diskette from its drive.

Chapter Summary

Running DOS Programs in a Window	To switch between window and full-screen modes	Press Alt+Enter; *or*, in window mode, click on the Toolbar's Full Screen button.
	To open the Control menu	Click on the Control menu icon or press Alt+Spacebar.
	To select, copy, or paste text	Click on the Mark, Copy, or Paste Toolbar button; *or* open the Control menu's Edit submenu and choose the Mark, Copy, or Paste command.
	To change the display font	Select a font from the Toolbar's drop-down menu or click on the Toolbar's Font button.
Running a DOS Session	To start MS-DOS Prompt	Choose the MS-DOS Prompt item from the Programs submenu of the Start menu.
	To exit MS-DOS Prompt	Type `exit` at a DOS prompt and press Enter; *or* click on the close button.
DOS Program Property Sheets	To open a DOS program's Properties dialog box	Right-click on the program's icon or shortcut and choose Properties from the pop-up menu; *or* click on the program's Properties Toolbar button.
	Program page options	Specify the default startup folder, define a shortcut key, and specify the type of window used at startup and whether the window closes when exiting from the program.
	Font page options	Specify the font used on program startup.
	Memory page options	Specify the amount of conventional, extended, and expanded memory made available to the program.
	Screen page options	Specify whether the program starts in a window or full-screen, and whether the Toolbar is displayed on startup.
	Misc page options	Specify whether a screen saver and certain shortcut keys can be used with the program.
Types of Memory	Conventional memory (0 KB - 640 KB)	Stores programs and data while they are in use.
	Upper memory (640 KB - 1 MB)	Stores ROM and adapter memory; also used by memory managers to provide additional RAM and expanded memory.

	Extended memory (Above 1 MB)	Used by Windows to provide additional memory for programs and DOS.
	Expanded memory	Used by an expanded memory manager to provide additional RAM fro DOS programs.
	Virtual memory	Hard disk space used by Windows as if it were additional RAM.
Startup Options	To change the default Windows 95 startup	Press a hotkey while Windows 95 is starting or edit the Msdos.sys file.
	Available hotkeys	See Table 1 in Section 12.3.
	To access the Windows 95 Startup Menu	Press F8 while Windows 95 is starting or edit the Msdos.sys file.
	Startup Menu options	See Table 2 in Section 12.3.
	To start up DOS instead of Windows	Press F4 while Windows 95 is starting or edit the Msdos.sys file.
Configuration Files	Msdos.sys	Determines the startup configuration for Windows 95, loads a memory manager necessary for startup, and sets various system parameters.
	Config.sys	Contains commands that load memory managers and device drivers which configure the system's memory and hardware.
	Autoexec.bat	Contains commands that store startup information, establish the automatic search path, and perform other tasks to be carried out at system startup.
The Registry	Purpose of the Registry	Stores all the configuration information (concerning system hardware and user preferences) needed by Windows 95.
	Structure of the Registry	Contained primarily in the System.dat and User.dat files, which when viewed by the user, appear as a tree-like structure with six main branches (keys) containing subkeys and value entries.
	To edit the Registry	Make changes in Control Panel, a property sheet, or certain other Windows folders; *or* use the Registry Editor.
	To start the Registry Editor	Open the Regedit file from the Start Menu's Run option, Explorer, or My Computer.

	To use the Registry Editor	Locate the required subkey in the left pane, double-click on the desired entry name in the right pane, and make the change in the resulting dialog box.
	To back up/restore the Registry	Copy the System.dat and User.dat files/replace the originals by the copies.
	To import/export the Registry (as a text file)	Choose the Import Registry File/Export Registry File command from the Registry Editor's File menu.
Object Linking and Embedding	Embedded objects vs. linked objects	Embedded objects are copies of the source material; editing them does not affect the latter. Linked objects contain pointers to the source *file*; to edit them, you edit the latter.
	To embed an object	Copy the object or object's file to the Clipboard and paste it into the desired document; *or* use the Object command on the Insert menu; *or* drag-and-drop the object from source to destination.
	To edit an embedded object	Double-click on the object, make the changes in the resulting "box", and click outside that box.
	To link an object	Copy the object's file to the Clipboard and paste it into the desired document; *or* use the Object command on the Insert menu.
	To edit a linked object	Double-click on the object, make the changes in the new window, and save the source document to disk.

Review Exercises

Section 12.1

1. Under Windows, DOS applications can be run in a window or ____________.
2. To display the Control menu for a DOS program that is running in a window, click on the ____________, which appears on the title bar.
3. You can change the display font for a DOS program that is running in a window by selecting a new one from the drop-down list that appears on the ____________.
4. True or false: You can switch a DOS program between window and

full-screen modes, by pressing the Alt+Tab key.

5. True or false: Text displayed in a DOS program document cannot be copied to the Windows Clipboard.
6. True or false: To start a DOS session, choose the MS-DOS Prompt item from the Programs submenu of the Start menu.
7. To end a DOS session, you should close any open DOS programs, and then
   a. Turn off the computer.
   b. Type `exit` at the DOS prompt.
   c. Close Explorer.
   d. Restart the computer in MS-DOS mode.
8. You can run a DOS application by
   a. Double-clicking on its program file in Explorer.
   b. Starting a DOS session, typing its program file's name at the DOS prompt, and pressing the Enter key.
   c. Restarting the computer in MS-DOS mode, typing its program file's name at the DOS prompt, and pressing the Enter key.
   d. Performing any of the above actions.

Section 12.2

9. You can display a DOS program's property sheets by clicking on the Properties button on its ___________.
10. If you want a DOS program's window to close when you exit that program, select the *Close on exit* check box on the ___________ page of its Properties dialog box.
11. ___________ memory, or XMS, is the term used to describe all memory in locations above one MB.
12. True or false: Using a DOS program's Properties dialog box, you can set that program to open in full-screen mode, if you want.
13. True or false: A shortcut key used to start a DOS program must begin with Ctrl or Ctrl+Alt.
14. True or false: Virtual memory is hard disk space that is used by the computer system as if it were additional RAM.
15. The type of memory that occupies addresses from 0 to 640 KB is called
   a. Conventional memory
   b. Upper memory
   c. Expanded memory
   d. Extended memory
16. You cannot use the Memory page of the Properties dialog box to limit the amount of

a. Conventional memory used by a DOS program.
b. Expanded memory used by a DOS program.
c. Extended memory used by a DOS program.
d. Virtual memory used by a DOS program.

Section 12.3

17. The actions that a computer takes when starting up are collectively called the startup, or ____________, process.

18. If you want to alter your computer's default startup process, press a hotkey when the message ____________ appears on the screen.

19. The two DOS configuration files that are no longer required by Windows 95, but which are usually accessed during startup, are ____________ and ____________.

20. True or false: By pressing the appropriate hotkey during startup, you can display a menu of startup options.

21. True or false: You can specify whether the computer will start in DOS or start in Windows in future sessions by placing the appropriate command in the Config.sys file.

22. True or false: The PATH command tells DOS where to search for a program whose name is typed at the DOS prompt.

23. The command DOS=HIGH in a Config.sys file

    a. Allows DOS to provide access to upper memory blocks.
    b. Loads device drivers into upper memory.
    c. Loads DOS into upper memory.
    d. Loads DOS into the HMA (in extended memory).

24. If you don't want a particular command in an Autoexec.bat file to be executed when the file is accessed

    a. Begin the line with the @ symbol.
    b. Begin the line with *ECHO OFF.*
    c. Begin the line with *rem.*
    d. Begin the line with *SET.*

Section 12.4

25. The Registry consists of the files ____________ and ____________.

26. To edit the Registry "manually", you must start the Registry Editor, which has the file name ____________.

27. The left pane of the Registry Editor window resembles Explorer's folder tree pane, but the items listed there are called ____________, not folders.

28. True or false: When you make changes to Control Panel settings, these changes are entered in the Registry.

29. True or false: Registry keys, entry names, and entry data can all be located using the Registry Editor's Find utility.

30. True or false: The Registry files are automatically backed up every time Windows starts successfully.

31. The root key of the Registry that contains information about your Desktop color preferences is called:

    a. HKEY_USERS
    b. HKEY_CLASSES_ROOT
    c. HKEY_LOCAL_MACHINE
    d. HKEY_CURRENT_CONFIG

32. Using the Registry Editor to create a text file containing the contents of the Registry is called

    a. Saving the Registry.
    b. Importing the Registry.
    c. Exporting the Registry.
    d. None of the above.

Section 12.5

33. The application that creates an embeddable or linkable object is called the OLE ___________.

34. When you edit a(n) ___________ object, only the copy of that object in the client document is changed, not the original.

35. You can link an object to an OLE client document by choosing the ___________ command from the client's Insert menu.

36. You can embed the object currently on the Clipboard in an OLE client document by choosing the Paste or ___________ command from the client's Edit menu.

37. True or false: If an object has been linked to a source file, modifying and saving the source file will never affect the object in the client document.

38. True or false: The "in-place editing" feature of OLE 2.0 applies to embedded objects, ,but not to linked objects.

39. True or false: If you drag-and-drop a sound file from Explorer to WordPad, that file becomes linked to the WordPad document.

40. True or false: The Links dialog box allows you to end the association of a linked object with its source file.

41. In editing a linked object

    a. The process must be started within the client application.
    b. The original source file need not be changed.
    c. The source file is opened in a separate window.
    d. The object can be transformed into an embedded one.

42. In editing an embedded object
    a. The process must be started within the client application.
    b. The original source material must be modified.
    c. The OLE server cannot be opened in a separate window.
    d. The object can be transformed into a linked one.

Build Your Own Glossary

43. The following words and phrases are important terms that were introduced in this chapter. (They appear within the text in boldface type.) Use WordPad (see Section 2.2) to enter a definition for each term, preserving alphabetical order, into the Glossary file on the Student Disk.

Autoexec.bat file	Expanded memory (EMS)	Msdos.sys file
Batch file	Export the Registry	Object (in OLE)
Boot process	Extended memory (XMS)	Object linking and embedding (OLE)
Compound document	High memory area (HMA)	OLE client
Configuration file	Import the Registry	OLE container
Config.sys file	Key (in Registry)	OLE server
Conventional memory	Link an object	Registry
Device driver	MS-DOS mode	Upper memory
DOS application	MS-DOS Prompt	Value entry (in Registry)
DOS session		Virtual memory
Embed an object		

Lab Exercises

Work each of the following exercises at your computer. Begin by turning the machine on (if necessary) to start Windows 95 and closing any open windows.

Lab Exercise 1 (Section 12.1)

a. Start the DOS program called Edit by using the Run command on the Start Menu. What is the name of this program according to its title bar?

b. Switch to window mode, if necessary, maximize the window, and select the "8 × 12" display font. Does the Edit window occupy the entire screen (except, of course, for the Taskbar)?

c. Select the Auto font and maximize the window. Does it occupy the entire screen now?

d. Type your name and class on the first line and press the Enter key. Then, mark your name, copy it to the Clipboard, and paste it onto the second line. What shape did the cursor become when you clicked on the Mark command or button?

e. Restore the Edit window. Did the text shrink in size? *Optional*: Resize the window so that it is as small as possible and copy it to your homework document.

f. Close Edit, responding No to the "Save" message. What actions did you have to take to exit this application?

g. Start MS-DOS Prompt, type Edit at the DOS prompt, and press the Enter key to open this program again.

h. Try to exit MS-DOS Prompt by clicking on its close button. What message appeared?

i. Close the message box (by clicking on No), close the Edit program, and exit MS-DOS Prompt. How did you accomplish the latter?

Lab Exercise 2 (Section 12.2)

a. Start Explorer and open the \Windows\Command folder.

b. Locate the Edit program and open its Properties dialog box without starting the program. Which dialog box page is active?

c. In the Properties dialog box, note the current settings for the following properties and change each (if necessary) as indicated:

- Select a maximized window.
- Deselect *Close on exit.*
- Select the "8 × 12" font.
- Select window mode on startup.
- Deselect *Display toolbar.*

Choose the OK command button to put your changes into effect.

c. Start Edit from the Explorer window. When Edit starts:

- Is the window maximized? (Is there a restore button?)
- What display font is being used?

d. Display the Toolbar. How did you do this?

e. Open Edit's Properties dialog box without leaving the program. How did you do this?

f. Return all properties except "close on exit" to their original settings and choose the OK command button.

g. Exit the Edit program. Did its window close automatically? If not, click on its close button.

h. Close Explorer.

Lab Exercise 3 (Section 12.3)

a. Display the Windows 95 Startup Menu by restarting your computer and pressing the appropriate hotkey on startup. What hotkey did you press?

b. On the Startup Menu, select the "Start DOS in safe mode" option. What text is displayed for the DOS prompt?

c. Type `ver` (for *version*) at the DOS prompt and press the Enter key. What version of DOS is running?

d. Press the Ctrl+Alt+Del keystroke combination to restart the computer, and when the startup message appears, press Shift+F8 for an interactive startup. What's the first question you are asked? (Answer "yes" to all questions.)

e. From the Shut Down dialog box, restart the computer in MS-DOS mode.

f. At the DOS prompt, type `ver` and press the Enter key. What version of DOS is running now?

g. Type `win` and press the Enter key to return to Windows.

Lab Exercise 4 (Section 12.3)

a. Open the Notepad application from the Accessories submenu of the Start menu's Programs option and maximize its window.

b. Successively open and close the following files, all of which reside in the root directory of your computer's boot drive (probably, C:). For each file, explain as many of the commands as you can.

- Msdos.sys
- Config.sys
- Autoexec.bat

c. Close Notepad when you are done.

Lab Exercise 5 (Section 12.4)

a. Start the Registry Editor. How did you do this?

b. Expand the HKEY_USERS branch (by clicking on its plus symbol). What are its subkeys?

c. Expand branches of HKEY_USERS until you reach the Desktop subkey; then, click on it. What is its path name (as stated on the status bar)? Describe three of its value entries.

d. Open the HKEY_CURRENT_USER\Control Panel\Colors key. Note the current value of the Active Title entry and then change it to "0 0 0" (black). What is the name of the dialog box in which the change is actually made?

e. Press the F5 function key to refresh the Registry. Did its title bar color change to black?

f. Return the Active Title entry to its original setting.

g. Use the Find utility to search for Recycle Bin. Use the results of the search to determine its class ID number. What is it?

h. Close the Registry Editor.

Lab Exercise 6 (Section 12.5)

a. Start WordPad.

b. Insert the Student Disk in its drive and *embed* the Shapes graphic on this diskette into the WordPad document. What command did you use to do this? Click to the right of the graphic to deselect it and press the Enter key.

c. Start Explorer, open the Windows\Media folder, and drag-and-drop the Tada sound file at the insertion point in the WordPad document. Has the sound file been embedded in, or linked to, this document?

d. Double-click on the Shapes graphic to edit it. What application has control of the editing process? (Hint: Open the Help menu.)

e. Terminate the editing process, returning control to WordPad. How did you do this?

f. Double-click on the icon in the WordPad document that represents the Tada file. What happened?

g. Right-click on the Tada icon to edit it. What application is started? Did it open in a separate window?

h. Close WordPad, responding No to the "Save changes?" message, close Explorer, and remove the diskette from its drive.

Lab Exercise 7 (Section 12.5)

a. Start WordPad.

b. Insert the Student Disk in its drive and *link* the Shapes graphic on this diskette to the WordPad document. What command did you use to do this? Click to the right of the graphic to deselect it and press the Enter key.

c. Start Explorer, open the Windows\Media folder, and use the Clipboard to "paste link" the Tada sound file at the insertion point in the WordPad document. What WordPad command did you use to perform this task?

d. Double-click on the Shapes graphic to edit it. What application was started to carry out the editing process? Did a separate window open for this application?

e. Terminate the editing process, returning to WordPad. How did you do this?

f. Double-click on the icon in the WordPad document that represents the Tada file. What happened?

g. Right-click on the Tada icon to edit it. What application is started? Did it open in a separate window?

h. Close WordPad, responding No to the "Save changes?" message, close Explorer, and remove the diskette from its drive.

If You Want to Learn More ...

The notes presented here allow you to delve more deeply into some of the topics covered in this chapter.

Running DOS Programs in MS-DOS Mode

Most DOS programs will run just fine under Windows. However, occasionally, a DOS program will run only if it actually has sole control of the computer. In this case, you should run the program, after Windows has shut down — in *MS-DOS mode.*

As you know from Section 12.1, you can enter MS-DOS mode from the Shut Down dialog box by selecting the *Restart the computer in MS-DOS mode?* option button. In addition, you can give a *particular* DOS program sole control of the computer whenever it is run (and automatically return control to Windows when it is exited) using the following technique:

1. Open the DOS program's Properties dialog box (as described in Section 12.2).
2. On the Program page, choose the Advanced command button.
3. In the resulting dialog box, select the *MS-DOS mode* check box. (It's also a good idea to select the *Warn before entering MS-DOS mode* check box, which gives you a chance to change your mind about shutting down Windows.)
4. Choose the OK command button to close this dialog box; then choose the OK button again to close the Properties dialog box.

Now, when this program is started, Windows will shut down all open applications, shut itself down, and relinquish control to DOS, which starts the DOS program.

More on MS-DOS mode

When you specify, via its property sheets, that a particular program is to run in MS-DOS mode (see the note above), you can set up a system configuration that will be used with this program alone. To do so:

1. Open the program's Properties dialog box, click (if necessary) on the Program tab, and choose the Advanced command button to open the Advanced Program Settings dialog box.
2. Select the *Specify a new MS-DOS configuration* option button. (This option becomes available when the *MS-DOS mode* check box is selected.)
3. Enter the commands in the CONFIG.SYS and AUTOEXEC.BAT list boxes that this program will need at startup to successfully run in MS-DOS mode. (Windows displays, in these check boxes, the commands that *it* believes the program will need.)
4. Choose the OK command button to exit the Advanced Program Settings dialog box and choose it again to close the Properties dialog box.

When running a recalcitrant DOS program in MS-DOS mode, it is often necessary to maximize the amount of conventional memory available to this program. The following commands, placed in the CONFIG.SYS list box in the Advanced Program Settings dialog box, should help in this respect:

```
DEVICE=C:\WINDOWS\HIMEM.SYS /TESTMEM:OFF
DEVICE=C:\WINDOWS\EMM386.EXE NOEMS
DOS=HIGH
DOS=UMB
DEVICEHIGH= . . .
        .
        .
        .
```

(The last few lines represent DEVICEHIGH commands that load needed device drivers into upper memory.)

More about Msdos.sys options

In Section 12.3, we discussed a few of the commands that you can place (using a text editor like Notepad) in the [Options] part of the Msdos.sys configuration file to modify the way Windows 95 starts up. Here's a more complete list:

- `BootMulti=1` allows you to boot the previous version of DOS or Windows (if any) by pressing the proper hotkey on startup or selecting the appropriate Startup Menu option.
- `BootWin=0` boots the previous version of DOS (and possibly, Windows 3.1) unless the user presses a hotkey during startup.

- `BootGUI=0` together with `BootWin=1` (the default) automatically boots DOS 7.
- `BootMenu=1` automatically displays the Startup Menu on startup.
- `BootKeys=0` disables the startup hotkeys.
- `BootDelay=`*n* specifies the number of seconds, *n*, during which the system will respond to a hotkey, after the message "Starting Windows 95 ..." is displayed.
- `BootMenuDelay=`*n* specifies the number of seconds, *n*, the Start-up Menu will remain on the screen before the first menu option is automatically put into effect.
- `Logo=0` turns off the display of the Windows 95 logo screen (white clouds, blue sky) during startup.

Playing with the Registry Editor

In Section 12.4, we demonstrated a couple of changes you can make using the Registry Editor that can't be made from anywhere else in Windows. Here are a few more:

- You can change the size of the icons on your Desktop by opening the HKEY_CURRENT_USER\Control Panel\Desktop\WindowMetrics key and double-clicking on Shell Icon Size in the right pane. This entry's value gives the height and width of the Desktop icons in pixels.
- As you have surely noticed, when a window is minimized to its Taskbar button or is restored from the button, it seems to zoom in or out in the process. This dubious feature can be turned off. To do so:

  1. Open the HKEY_CURRENT_USER\Control Panel\Desktop\WindowMetrics key.
  2. If there is a MinAnimate value entry, change its value to "0". Otherwise, carry out the rest of this procedure.
  3. Right-click on an empty part of the right pane, point at the New item on the pop-up menu, and choose String Value from the submenu. A new value entry will appear in the right pane.
  4. Rename the new value entry *MinAnimate* and press the Enter key.
  5. In the resulting dialog box, enter the number 0 and choose the OK command button.

  To turn on the zooming effect, set MinAnimate equal to "1".

- When you create a Desktop shortcut, its icon contains a small arrow in the lower-left corner to indicate that it's a shortcut. To eliminate these arrows:

  1. Open the HKEY_CLASSES_ROOT\lnkfile key.
  2. Right-click on the IsShortcut item and choose Rename from the pop-up menu.
  3. Rename the IsShortcut item anything else; for example, No-ArrowShortcut.

  To eliminate the small arrow of a Desktop icon that represents a shortcut to a DOS program, you will have to repeat this procedure, but this time, begin by opening the HKEY_CLASSES_ROOT\piffile key.

APPENDIX A

General Shortcut Keys

As befits software running under a graphical user interface, Windows and its applications make extensive use of the mouse. Nevertheless, some operations can be performed more quickly using keystrokes (or keystroke combinations), which Windows refers to as *shortcut keys.* In this appendix, we will list some important shortcut keys and their functions. Other shortcut keys (for example, those for WordPad) are described at the appropriate place in the text.

On the Desktop

Alt+Enter	Displays the properties sheet for the selected item.
Alt+Esc	Cycles through the Taskbar buttons.
Alt+Print Screen	Copies the active window to the Clipboard (anywhere in Windows).
Arrow key	Selects the closest icon to the highlighted one in the specified direction.
Ctrl+Esc	Displays the Start menu.
Del	Sends the selected item to the Recycle Bin.
Enter	Opens the selected item.
F1	Starts Windows Help.

F2	Prepares the selected item for renaming.
F3	Opens the Find dialog box.
Print Screen	Copies the entire screen to the Clipboard (anywhere in Windows).
Shift+Del	Deletes the selected item without sending it to the Recycle Bin.
Shift+F10	Opens the selected item's right-click menu.
Tab	Moves the focus to the Start button.

In a Dialog Box

Alt+Down Arrow	Opens a drop-down list (if it has the focus).
Alt+F4	Closes the dialog box, putting all changes into effect.
Alt+Spacebar	Opens the Control menu.
Arrow keys	Cycles through a group of option buttons (if one of them has the focus).
Ctrl+Tab	Cycles forward through the dialog box tabs.
Ctrl+Shift+Tab	Cycles backward through the dialog box tabs.
Escape	Closes the dialog box, canceling all changes.
Tab	Moves the selection cursor (focus) from item to item.
Shift+Tab	Moves the selection cursor from item to item in the reverse direction.
Spacebar	Selects or deselects a check box (if it has the focus).

In Most Windows Applications

Alt	Activates the application's menu bar. (Or, closes all open menus and deactivates the menu bar.)
Alt+*underlined letter*	Opens the corresponding menu.
Alt+F4	Closes the application.
Alt+Spacebar	Opens the Control menu.

Alt+Tab	Switches among the running applications.
Ctrl+C	Copies the selected data to the Clipboard.
Ctrl+V	Pastes the contents of the Clipboard.
Ctrl+X	Cuts the selected data to the Clipboard.
Escape	Closes an open menu or dialog box.
F1	Starts Help for the application.
F10	Activates the application's menu bar. (Or, closes all open menus and deactivates the menu bar.)
Shift+F10	Opens the selected item's right-click menu.

In Explorer and My Computer

Alt+Enter	Displays the properties sheet for the selected object.
Backspace	Opens the parent folder.
Ctrl+A	Selects all objects.
Ctrl+Z	Undoes the last action.
Del	Sends the selected objects to the Recycle Bin.
Right/Left Arrow	Expands/collapses the selected folder (Explorer only).
Plus/Minus (on numeric keypad)	Expands/collapses the selected folder (Explorer only).
Asterisk (on numeric keypad)	Expands all folders (Explorer only).
F2	Prepares the selected object for renaming.
F3	Opens the Find dialog box.
F4	Displays the Go To drop-down list.
F5	Refreshes the display.
F6	Switches between the left and right panes (Explorer only).
Shift+Del	Deletes the selected objects without sending them to the Recycle Bin.
Shift+F10	Opens the right-click menu for the selected object.

When Starting Up The following keys apply when the message "Starting Windows 95 ..." appears on the screen.

F4	Starts the previously installed version of DOS (if possible).
F5	Starts Windows 95 in safe mode (a very basic configuration).
F6	Starts Windows 95 in safe mode, with network support.
F8	Displays a menu of startup options.

For "Windows 95 Keyboards" The following shortcut keys only apply to keyboards (such as the Microsoft *Natural Keyboard*) that contain a "Windows key", which we designate by Win.

Win+E	Starts Explorer.
Win+F	Opens the Find dialog box to search for files.
Win+Ctrl+F	Opens the Find dialog box to search for computers.
Win+F1	Starts Windows Help.
Win+M	Minimizes all open windows.
Win+Shift+M	Undoes the Minimize All command.
Win+R	Opens the Run dialog box.
Win+Tab	Cycles through the Taskbar buttons.

APPENDIX B

Some Useful DOS Commands

One of the major advantages of Windows over DOS is that you don't have to memorize esoteric commands to start programs, to copy, rename, or delete files, or to perform other routine tasks. However, there are a few situations in which DOS commands will do a job better than Windows. For example, DOS is superior for:

- Copying, renaming, deleting, or changing the attributes of certain *sets* of files, such as those with the same extension.
- Printing a listing of the files within a given folder.
- Creating a *batch file*, one made up of a sequence of commands that is executed when the file is run.

In this appendix, we will discuss DOS commands and how they can help you perform tasks like those listed above.

DOS Commands

Table 1 lists some of the commands recognized by DOS 7, the version that is supplied with Windows 95. To execute one of these commands, type it at a DOS prompt and press the Enter key. (You can display the DOS prompt before Windows starts, while it is running, or after it has shut down — see Section 12.1.)

Command	Function
ATTRIB	To set or clear file attributes.
CD	To change the default directory (folder).
CHKDSK	To check a disk and display a status report (see also SCANDISK).
COPY	To copy files (see also XCOPY, XCOPY32).
DATE	To display and/or change the date on the computer's internal clock.
DELTREE	To delete a directory and its subdirectories (folder/subfolders).
DEL	To delete files.
DIR	To display information about the contents of a directory (folder).
DISKCOMP	To compare the content of two floppy disks.
DISKCOPY	To copy an entire floppy disk.
DOSKEY	To reuse or edit previously-issued DOS commands.
EDIT	To edit text files.
FC	To compare the content of two files.
FDISK	To partition a disk.
FORMAT	To format a hard or floppy disk.
HELP	To start the DOS help system or display help for a given command.
MD	To create a directory (folder).
MEM	To display information about current memory use.
PATH	To specify or display the path for executable files.
PRINT	To print the contents of a text file on a printer.
PROMPT	To specify the form of the DOS prompt.
RD	To delete a directory (folder).
REN	To rename files.

SCANDISK	To analyze and repair certain disk problems (supersedes CHKDSK).
START	To run a Windows application from the DOS prompt.
TIME	To display and/or change the time on the computer's internal clock.
TREE	To display the structure of the directories (folders) on a disk.
TYPE	To display the contents of a text file on the screen.
UNDELETE	To restore a deleted file.
UNFORMAT	To recover from an accidental format.
VER	To display the version number of DOS or Windows.
VOL	To display a disk's volume label.
XCOPY	To copy files (an extended version of COPY).
XCOPY32	To copy files (a version of XCOPY for use with long file names).

Table 1 Some DOS Commands

Parameters and switches

Every DOS command has a specific form, or *syntax*, which must be followed exactly or the command will not be processed. The syntax for most commands includes optional parameters and/or switches.

- A command *parameter* generally gives the name of the file, directory*, or drive to which the command applies.
- A command *switch*, which is preceded by a slash (/) symbol, specifies that a certain option will or will not be in effect when the command is executed.

For example, when the DIR command is issued without any parameters or switches, the contents of the current directory are displayed. Here are some examples of how this command is modified by adding parameters and/or switches:

`DIR a:` (with parameter "a:")

Displays the contents of the (root directory of the) disk in the

*In this appendix, we will use the word *directory*, the DOS terminology, instead of its Windows 95 alias, *folder*.

a: drive; the listing will scroll until the end is reached.

`DIR c:\dos /p` (with parameter "c:\dos" and switch "/p")

Displays the contents of the c:\dos directory, pausing after each full screen until you press a key.

`DIR /w /p` (with switches "/p" and "/w")

Displays the contents of the current directory in "wide" format (which allows you to see more files at once), pausing after each full screen until you press a key.

DOS Help Due to their complexity and the need for exact syntax, DOS commands are not easy to master. Fortunately, help is always just a few keystrokes away. To obtain online help, at the DOS prompt type any of the following commands and press the Enter key:

- **`Help`** This command starts MS-DOS Help and displays a list of all available commands. To access information about a particular command, scroll until that command is displayed, and then click on it or press the Enter key. The resulting help screen displays the function of the command, its syntax, and the available parameters and switches.
- **`Help`** ***`command`*** (For example: `Help DIR`) This command displays the help entry for the specified command directly, without going through general Help. The information supplied is the same as that obtained via general Help (above).
- ***`command /?`*** (For example: `DIR /?`) This command supplies more concise help about the specified command than do those above.

Using Wildcards with DOS Commands

In Section 4.3, we discussed the use of *wildcards* — symbols that represent one or more characters of any kind — with the Windows Find utility. In fact, wildcards have limited range in Windows 95; they can only be used in the Find window and the Save and Open dialog boxes. In DOS, however, they are an important factor in increasing the power of many commands and sometimes allow you to perform certain tasks more efficiently than in Windows.

DOS wildcards DOS (like Windows) uses two wildcards:

? represents any single character.

* represents any combination of any number of characters.

For example, in the current directory:

.	represents all files, with or without an extension.
*.ltr	represents all files with extension *ltr*.
S*	represents all files beginning with *S* and having no extension.
S?m	represents all files with a three-character filename beginning with *S*, ending with *m*, and having no extension.
?d*.*	represents all files with second character *d*.

Using wildcards

Used with certain DOS commands, wildcards allow you to process sets of files, all at once. For example, here are some things that DOS does, with the aid of wildcards, more easily than Windows:

- To display only those files in the current directory with extension *bak*, use:

```
DIR *.bak
```

- To rename all files in the current directory, changing their existing extension *bak* to the extension *old*, use:

```
REN *.bak *.old
```

- To set read-only and hidden attributes for all files in the current directory with filename *outline* (regardless of their extension), use:

```
ATTRIB +r +h outline.*
```

Wildcards are also useful with the DEL command in deleting sets of files and with the COPY, XCOPY, and XCOPY32 commands in copying sets of files.

Special DOS Commands

As you have just seen, with the help of wildcards, DOS can perform certain tasks more efficiently than Windows. There are also certain DOS commands that can perform tasks that Windows cannot do at all! For example:

Printing a directory listing

- You can print a hard copy of the contents of a directory by "redirecting" the output of the DIR command to the printer. For example, the command

```
DIR > PRN
```

sends a listing of all files in the current directory to the printer; and the command

```
DIR \windows\*.bak > PRN
```

prints all files in the windows directory with extension *bak*.

Creating a file containing a directory listing

- You can create a text file that contains all files in a specified directory (or all files satisfying a wildcard string) by redirecting the output of the DIR command to a file. For example,

  ```
  DIR > DIR.TXT
  ```

  creates a text file (in the current directory) that contains a listing of the current directory.

Recovering a deleted file

- You can recover files that have been deleted from a hard or floppy disk by using the UNDELETE command. This is especially important when using DOS because files deleted from the DOS prompt are not sent to the Recycle Bin. Nonetheless, the UNDELETE command works with files deleted from disk by any means, including those removed from the Recycle Bin. Issuing the UNDELETE command starts the Undelete utility, which provides instructions for its use. (This command must be run in MS-DOS mode — after Windows is shut down.)

Comparing files

- You can compare the content of two files by using the FC command. For example,

  ```
  FC study.dat study.bak
  ```

  compares the data in the files study.dat and study.bak and issues a report.

Batch Files

A *batch file* is a program that consists of DOS commands. A batch file is usually created in a text editor, such as Windows' Notepad or DOS' Edit, and must be saved as a text (ASCII) file with a *bat* extension. As an example, Autoexec.bat is a batch file that is normally executed automatically when Windows or DOS is started.

Executing a batch file

You can execute a batch file in the same ways you would start any DOS program; for example:

- Type its filename (without the extension) at the DOS prompt.
- Double-click on its icon in Explorer or any folder window.
- Double-click on a shortcut to the batch file.
- Use the Run option on the start menu.

Batch files can also be executed from within many applications, but the way this is accomplished varies considerably; check the application's documentation.

Batch files are often used to automate oft-repeated tasks such as logging on to a network or setting up a modem link to another computer. As an example, the batch file

```
CD \DATA
\WP60\WP
CD \
```

changes the default directory to DATA, starts the program in the WP60 directory named WP and, after this application terminates, changes the default to the root directory.

Most DOS commands may be used in a batch file. Table 2 lists those whose primary use is in creating batch files.

Command	Function
CALL	To execute another batch file and then return to the current one.
ECHO	To turn the display of commands ON or OFF during execution.
FOR...IN...DO	To create a loop that repeats a set of commands.
GOTO	To cause a specific labeled command to be executed next.
IF	To cause a branch to a specific block of code.
REM	To insert a remark, ignored by the computer, into the code.
@	To turn off the display of the current line during execution.

Table 2 DOS Commands Primarily Intended for Use in Batch Files

APPENDIX C

Answers to Odd-Numbered Review Exercises

Introduction

1. hardware
3. eight
5. tape *or* CD-ROM
7. true
9. false
11. false
13. false
15. d
17. a
19. operating system
21. graphical user interface
23. false
25. true
27. c
29. ENIAC
31. 1975
33. Apple Macintosh
35. false
37. false
39. d

Chapter 1

1. icon
3. false
5. left mouse button
7. dialog box
9. false
11. c
13. title bar
15. right border / left border
17. true
19. a
21. A: Control icon   B: Title bar
    C: Minimize button   D: Maximize button
23. OK *or* Close

25. check box
27. true
29. c
31. Start
33. true
35. c

Chapter 2

1. Ctrl+Esc
3. Close (*or* Exit)
5. true
7. c
9. Accessories
11. open
13. true
15. true
17. a
19. Taskbar
21. Clipboard
23. true
25. c
27. Start
29. book
31. true
33. true
35. c

Chapter 3

1. file
3. true
5. b
7. contents (*or* right)
9. Details
11. true
13. d
15. Ctrl (Control)
17. Send To
19. true
21. a
23. Recycle Bin (*or* Recycled)
25. box
27. false
29. d
31. double-click
33. true
35. d
37. right-clicking
39. true
41. b

Chapter 4

1. top
3. tiled
5. true
7. d
9. shortcut
11. Start Menu Programs
13. false
15. d
17. Named
19. double-click
21. true
23. c
25. registered
27. false
29. d
31. sheet
33. true
35. a

Chapter 5

1. Settings
3. true
5. b
7. Display
9. screen saver
11. false
13. b
15. Appearance
17. true
19. d
21. Keyboard
23. false
25. d
27. Date/Time
29. Add/Remove Programs
31. true
33. d

Chapter 6

1. spool
3. queue
5. true
7. false
9. a
11. plug-and-play
13. true
15. a
17. Sounds
19. multimedia
21. false
23. c
25. Accessibility Options
27. numeric keypad
29. false
31. c
33. modem
35. cache
37. true
39. c

Chapter 7

1. Home
3. Ctrl+Z
5. false
7. c
9. 72
11. true
13. d
15. landscape
17. one-half
19. true
21. false
23. a
25. Object
27. true
29. c
31. Print Preview
33. false
35. true
37. d

Chapter 8

1. left
3. false
5. a
7. Shift
9. foreground
11. false

13. false
15. a
17. c
19. red
21. true
23. d
25. Shift
27. Edit
29. true
31. b
33. Print Preview
35. false
37. c

Chapter 9

1. View
3. Sta
5. false
7. b
9. text editor
11. header
13. true
15. b
17. System Tools
19. true
21. d
23. ScanDisk
25. compresses
27. true
29. c
31. Character Map
33. false
35. c

Chapter 10

1. Local Area Network (LAN)
3. (network) server
5. b
7. remote access
9. networking computing
11. a
13. a
15. false
17. b
19. c
21. true
23. E-mail
25. modem
27. c
29. true
31. d
33. true
35. Accessories
37. laptop
39. Direct Cable Connection
41. c
43. false

Chapter 11

1. network/online service/ISP
3. browser
5. b
7. b
9. false
11. a
13. d
15. Favorite
17. false
19. TCP/IP
21. d
23. true

Chapter 12

1. full-screen
3. Toolbar
5. false
7. b
9. Toolbar
11. Extended
13. false
15. a
17. boot
19. Config.sys/Autoexec.bat
21. false
23. d
25. System.dat/User.dat
27. keys
29. true
31. a
33. server
35. Object
37. false
39. false
41. c

Index

A

Accessibility Options, 180, 240, 264
  display options, 243, 244
  keyboard options, 240 - 242
  mouse options, 244, 245
  sound options, 242, 243
Accessories, 369
  adding, 414
  removing, 202
Active application, 52
Active cutout, 342
Add New Hardware (Control Panel), 180, 230 - 233
Address box (Internet Explorer), 490
Add Printer Wizard, 225 - 227
Add/Remove Programs (Control Panel), 180
  adding Windows accessories with, 414
  creating a startup disk with, 202
  installing programs with, 199, 202
  removing Windows components with, 202
  uninstalling programs with, 202
Airbrush tool (Paint), 319, 324, 325
Aligning text (WordPad), 281
Allen, Paul, I-15
Altair 8800, I-15
AltaVista (Internet site), 497
Always on Top option, 63, 75, 130, 131
America Online, 247, 404, 484
Apple II, I-15
Apple Computer, I-15
Apple Macintosh, *see* Macintosh
Applet, 41
Applications, I-9
  closing (exiting), 39, 40
  opening (starting), 36 - 39, 84, 148
  shortcut keys for, A-2, A-3
  switching among, 52, 53
  transferring data between, 53 - 56
  types of, I-9
Applications software, I-9
  see also Applications
APRANET, 485, 486
Archive attribute, 160
Arrow keys, I-6
ASCII file, 377, 459
Association (file type with application), 150 - 158
Attachment (mail), 436
ATTRIB (DOS) command, 551, A-9
Attribute, 160
Attributes command (Paint), 354, 355
Audio settings, 238
Autoexec.bat file, 536, 539, 540, 542, 543
Auto Hide option, 75, 130, 131
AutoPlay (CD-ROM), 265

B

Background color (Paint), 320, 321
Back up, I-5, 383, 415, 416, 482
Backup utility, 383
  options for, 388 - 390
  starting, 383
  using to back up files, 384 - 387
  using to compare files, 387
  using to restore files, 387, 388
  window, 384
Bardeen, John, I-14
Baseband network, 421
BASIC programming language, I-15
Batch file, 542, A-10, A-11
Bell Labs, I-14
Binary file transfer
  in HyperTerminal, 459
  in Microsoft Fax, 447
Bit, I-3
Bold text, 189, 276
  in Paint, 331
  in WordPad, 276, 277
Bootable diskette, 112, 202
Boot process, 535, 536
Border/fill options (Paint), 326
Box tool (Paint), 319, 327
Brattain, Walter, I-14
Briefcase utility, 415, 466
  installing, 466, 467
  using to synchronize files, 467 - 469
Broadband network, 421
Browse folders, 104 - 107
Browser software, 484
  see also Internet Explorer
Browse the Internet, 489 - 495
Brush tool (Paint), 319, 321, 324
Bulletin board (electronic), 404
Bullet symbol, 285
Byte, I-4

C

Cache, 253
Calculator (accessory), 64, 65, 370
  scientific mode, 370, 372 - 376
  standard mode, 370 - 372
Calendar accessory (Windows 3.1), 415
Capturing screens and windows, 54
Cardfile accessory (Windows 3.1), 415
Cascading windows, 132
CD music settings, 239
CD player (accessory), 404
CD-ROM, I-6
  AutoPlay feature, 265
  installing programs from, 200 - 202
CD-ROM drive, I-6, 234
  improving performance of, 265
Central processing unit, I-3
Character, I-4
Character Map, 285, 402, 403, 416
Check box, 19
Child folder, 78
Class ID (Registry), 549, 550
Click the mouse, I-7, 3
Clipboard, 53
  capturing screens to, 54
  copying data to, 53, 63, 270, 342, 372, 403
  copying objects to, 92, 94, 106, 107, 148
  cutting data to, 53, 270, 342
  cutting objects to, 93, 94, 106, 148
  pasting data from, 54, 271, 342, 372
  pasting objects from, 93, 94, 106, 107
  using to embed an object, 557 - 559
  using to insert graphics, 287
  using to link an object, 559
  viewing contents of, 53
Clipboard Viewer, 53
Clipbook Viewer, 53
Clock, 2, 3, 33, 199
  adjusting time of, 199, 200
  removing from Taskbar, 131
Close button, 11, 12
Closing
  applications, 39, 40
  documents, 46
  DOS applications, 40, 529
  windows, 10, 12
Collapsing the folder tree, 83
Color Box (Paint), 318 - 320, 355, 366, 368
COM1 port, 226
COM2 port, 226
Command button, 17
Command line interface, I-10
Communications software, 405, 452
Components of a computer, I-2, I-3
  central processing unit, I-3
  input devices, I-6
  internal memory, I-4
  mass storage devices, I-4
  output devices, I-7
Compound document (OLE), 556

Compressed volume, 398
Compressing files, 398 - 400
CompuServe, 247, 404
Computer, I-2
Computer literacy, I-1
Config.sys file, 536, 539, 540 - 542
Configuration files, 536 - 543
Contents pane
  in Explorer, 82 - 85
  in Exchange, 437, 438
  view options for, 85 - 87
Context-sensitive help, 63, 64
Control menu, 12
Control Panel, 178
  choosing a function, 181
  closing, 181
  starting, 178
  summary of functions, 180, 181
  using to add a modem, 248, 249
  using to add a printer, 225 - 227
  using to add hardware, 230 - 233
  using to adjust clock, 199, 200
  using to change display appearance, 190 - 192
  using to change keyboard properties, 193 -195
  using to change modem settings, 248, 249
  using to change mouse properties, 195 - 197
  using to change multimedia settings, 237 - 239
  using to change network settings, 254
  using to change passwords, 254
  using to change printer properties, 219 - 223
  using to change regional settings, 254
  using to change system settings, 250 - 253
  using to change system sounds, 234 - 236
  using to install software, 200 - 202
  using to manage printers, 223 - 225
  using to provide accessibility options, 240 - 246
  using to select a Desktop pattern, 182 - 184
  using to select a screen saver, 185 - 187
  using to select wallpaper, 184, 185
  using to view fonts, 202 - 205
  view options for, 179
Conventional memory, 531, 532
Copying cutouts, 343
Copying files and folders
  undoing, 94
  using drag-and-drop, 91 - 93, 107 - 109, 148
  using the Clipboard, 93, 94, 106, 107, 148
  using the Send To command, 92, 93
Copying floppy disks, 112, 113
Copying graphics, 291, 292
Copying Internet page data, 517, 518
Copying text, 53, 270, 522
Copying to the Clipboard, 53
  in Calculator, 372
  in Character Map, 403
  in DOS application, 522
  in Explorer, 93, 94
  in Find, 148
  in Help, 63
  in My Computer, 106, 107
  in Paint, 342
  in WordPad, 270, 291
Copy To command (Paint), 343
CPU, I-3
Crash
  hard disk, I-6
  program, 22
Create Shortcut wizard, 102, 138
Cross-linked files, 393
Cursor, I-6
Cursor blink rate, 195
Cursor control keys, I-6
Cursor coordinates (Paint), 329
Curve tool (Paint), 319, 325, 326
Custom colors (Paint), 366, 367
Customizing Windows, *see* Control Panel, Registry
Cutout, 338
  copying, 343
  defining, 338, 339
  deleting, 340 - 342
  flipping, 346, 347
  inverting colors of, 349
  moving, 343
  pasting down, 342
  resizing, 345
  retrieving from disk, 343
  rotating, 347
  saving, 343
  skewing, 348, 349

stretching, 347, 348
sweeping, 344
Cutting to the Clipboard, 53
in Explorer, 93, 94
in Find, 148
in Paint, 342
in WordPad, 270

D

Database manager, I-9
Date and Time (WordPad), 302
Date/Time (Control Panel), 180, 199, 200, 215
Deferred printing, 469 - 471
Defragment a disk, 395 - 398
Deleting cutouts, 340 - 342
Deleting graphics (in WordPad), 291
Deleting objects (in Explorer), 96 - 98
Deleting text, 43, 270
Deselecting
graphics, 291
objects (Explorer), 90
text, 53, 271
Desktop, 2
accessing from Start menu or Taskbar, 174
changing background of, 182 - 185
pattern, 182
shortcut keys for, A-1, A-2
shortcuts, I-12, 101
wallpaper, 184
Details view option
in Control Panel, 179
in Explorer, 86, 87
in Fonts window, 205
in Printers folder window, 219
Device driver, 229, 252, 540
see also Driver
Device manager, 252
Dialog box, 7, 16
shortcut keys for, A-2
types of objects in, 17 - 20
Dial-up Networking, 415, 427
creating a connection with, 429 - 432
installing, 428, 429
Dimmed option, 8
DIR (DOS) command, A-7 - A-10
Direct Cable Connection utility, 415, 463
installing, 463
using to connect computers, 463 - 466
Directory, *see* Folder
Disconnecting from the Internet, 499, 500
Disk, I-4, I-5
see also Floppy disk, Hard disk
compressing, 398 - 400
defragmenting, 395 - 398
repairing problems, 391 - 395
uncompressing, 400, 401
Disk Defragmenter utility, 391, 395 - 398
Disk drive, I-4
Diskette, *see* Floppy disk
Display accessibility options, 243, 244
Display Properties dialog box, 182, 183
Appearance page, 188 - 192
Background page, 182 - 185
Screen Saver page, 185 - 187
Settings page, 192
Display utility (Control Panel), 180
changing display settings, 192
modifying a window scheme, 190 - 192
selecting a Desktop pattern, 182 - 184
selecting a screen saver, 185 - 187
selecting wallpaper, 184, 185
selecting a window scheme, 189
Docking detection, 462
Docking station, 462
Documents, 35, 42
closing, 46
opening, 47, 48, 84
printing, 48 - 50
saving, 44, 45
Documents option (on Start menu), 37, 48
removing menu items from, 141, 142
Document window, 42, 268, 269
Domain name (Internet), 486, 487
DOS, I-10, 23
running without Windows, 22, 524, 525
uninstalling, 202
DOS application, I-12
changing display font in, 522, 523
closing (exiting), 40, 529
copying text in, 522
marking text in, 521, 522
memory use in, 530 - 534
pasting text into, 522
properties for, 526 -534, 577
running full-screen, 520, 523, 530
running in a DOS session, 523, 524
running in MS-DOS mode, 525, 577, 578
running in a window, 520 - 523, 530
running in the background, 523

selecting text in, 521, 522
shortcut key for, 528
DOS box, 523
DOS commands
batch files of, A-10, A-11
executing, A-5
help for, A-8
list of, A-5, A-6, A-11
parameters for, A-7
switches for, A-7
wildcards in, A-8, A-9
DOS file name, 79, 80
DOS prompt, I-10
DOS session, 523, 524
Dot matrix printer, I-8
Dotted quad, 486
Double-click the mouse, 4
Download files, 505, 506
Drag-and-drop
in Explorer, 91 - 93
in Find, 148
in My Computer, 107 - 108
in WordPad, 271, 272, 291
to add items to Start menu, 136
to embed an object, 561, 562
Drag the mouse, 4
Drawing area (Paint), 318, 319
changing size of, 354, 355
Drawing program, I-9
Draw Opaque command (Paint), 331, 339, 344
Driver, 229
device, 229, 252, 540
modem, 249
printer, 229
DriveSpace utility, 391, 398 - 401
Drop-down list box, 19, 20

E

Eckert, J. Presper, I-14
Edit, 43
configuration file, 537 - 543
document, 269
embedded object, 562 - 564
graphic, 290, 334
linked object, 564 - 566
Registry, 546 - 550
Electronic mail, *see* E-mail
Ellipse/Circle tool (Paint), 319, 327, 328
Embedded object, 556
creating, 557 - 562
editing, 562 - 564
E-mail, 404, 436, 484
managing, 440, 441
receiving, 440, 505
sending, 437 - 439, 442, 505
Emptying the Recycle Bin, 98
EMS, *see* Expanded memory
End Task command, 40
ENIAC, I-14
Environment variables, 533, 542
Eraser tool (Paint), 319, 334, 335
Exchange, *see* Microsoft Exchange
Excite (Internet site), 498
Exit
applications, 39, 40
DOS applications, 40, 529
Windows 95, 21, 23
Expanded memory, 532, 533
Expanding the folder tree, 83
Explorer, 81
font used for, 192
selecting objects in, 89, 90
shortcut keys for, 124, A-3
starting, 81
using to add or remove items from a Start button menu, 141
using to copy floppy disks, 112, 113
using to copy objects, 91 - 95
using to create files and folders, 99, 100
using to create shortcuts, 101, 102
using to delete objects, 96 - 98
using to format floppy disks, 110 - 111
using to move objects, 91 - 94
using to rename objects, 98, 99
window, 82 - 87
Export the Registry, 551 - 553
Extended memory, 531
Extension (for file name), 79, 150 - 152, 175
Eye Dropper tool (Paint), 319 - 321

F

Favorite (Internet Explorer), 492, 517
Fax, 405
receiving, 447 - 450
sending, 442 - 447
Fax Viewer, 450
FC (DOS) command, A-10
File, 78
backing up, 383 - 387

compressing, 398 - 401
copying, 91 - 95, 106 - 109
creating, 99, 100
deleting, 96 - 98
moving, 91 - 94, 106 - 109
naming, 79, 80
property sheet for, 159, 160
renaming, 98, 99, 148
searching for, 144 - 148
File attribute, 160
File format, 298
in WordPad, 298 - 301, 315
File name
DOS, 79, 80
Windows 95 (long), 80
Filename, 79
File set (Backup), 387
File type, 150, 175
FilterKeys option, 242
Finding text
in Notepad, 379, 380
in Registry Editor, 549
in WordPad, 304, 305
using the Find utility, 147
Find option (on Start menu), 143
Find utility, 84, 136, 143
starting, 84, 143
using search results, 148
using to search for files or folders, 144 - 148
using to search for text, 147
window, 144 - 147
Flipping cutouts, 346, 347
Floppy disk, I-4, I-5
bootable, 112, 202
copying, 112, 113
formatting, 110 - 112
installing programs from, 200, 202
startup, 202
write-protecting, I-5
Floppy disk drive, I-4
Folder, 78
copying, 91 - 95, 106 - 109
creating (new), 99, 100
deleting, 96 - 98
moving, 91 - 94, 106 - 109
naming, 80
property sheet for, 159, 160
renaming, 98, 99, 148
searching for, 144 - 148
Folders pane (Exchange), 437, 438
Folder tree pane (Explorer), 82, 83
Font, 188, 202, 274
choosing for screen element, 190 - 192
in DOS screen, 522, 523, 530
Postscript, 203
scalable, 203, 274
TrueType, 203, 274
using in Paint, 330, 331
using in WordPad, 273 - 277
viewing, 201 - 205
Font color, 190, 191, 276, 277
Font dialog box, 275, 276
Font size, 190, 191, 203, 274
in DOS application, 522, 523, 530
in Help window, 63
in Paint, 330
in WordPad, 275 - 277
Font style, 190, 191, 274
in WordPad, 275 - 277
Fonts window (Paint), 330, 331
Fonts utility (Control Panel), 180
using to view fonts, 203 - 205
Footer (Notepad), 381, 382
Foreground color (Paint), 320, 321
Format bar (WordPad), 268, 269, 276, 277, 279, 281, 285
Format floppy disk, 110 - 112
Fragmented file, 395
Free-form Selection tool (Paint), 319, 338, 339
FTP (File Transfer Protocol), 484
Full-screen mode (DOS program), 520, 523, 530
Function keys, I-6

G

Games (submenu of Start button), 415
Gates, William, I-15
Gigabyte, I-5
Go To command (Explorer), 84
Go to Folder drop-down list, 105
Graphic, I-9, 287, 317
in Paint, 317 - 356
in WordPad, 287 - 292
Graphical user interface, I-10
Grid (Paint), 337
Guest computer, 463
GUI, I-10

H

Handles, *see* Sizing Handles
Hard disk, I-4, I-5
Hard disk drive, I-4, I-5
Hardware, I-1, I-3
Hardware acceleration, 253
Hardware profile, 252, 462
Header (Notepad), 381, 382
Help, *see* Online help
Help option (on Start menu), 57
Help Topics dialog box, 58
  Contents page, 58, 59, 62
  Find page, 60 - 62
  Index page, 59, 60, 62
Help window, 62
  options in, 63
Hidden attribute, 160
High contrast display option, 243
High density diskette, I-5, 111
High memory area (HMA), 534, 540
Hoff, Ted, I-14
Home page, 489
Horizontal scroll bar, 13, 14
Host computer, 451, 463
Hot spot, 63
HTTP (Hypertext Transfer Protocol), 490
HyperTerminal, 404, 452
  ending a session, 461
  printing in, 458, 459
  starting, 452
  using to configure a connection, 453 - 457
  using to connect to a remote computer, 457, 458
  using to transfer files, 459 - 461

I

IBM-compatible computer, I-3, I-16
IBM, Inc., I-15
IBM Personal Computer (PC), I-10, I-15, I-16
Icon, I-10, 2
  changing size of, 579
  font for, 192
  spacing on Desktop, 214
Import the Registry, 553, 554
Inbox (Exchange), 432, 437, 442
  using to set up messaging services, 434 - 436
Indentation (WordPad), 281 - 283
Infoseek (Internet site), 497
Ink jet printer, I-8
Input devices, I-6
  keyboard, I-6, I-7
  mouse, I-7
Insert mode (WordPad), 270
Insertion point, 42, 268, 269
Insertion point movement keys, 270
Installing
  Briefcase utility, 466, 467
  Dial-Up Networking, 428, 429
  Direct Cable Connection utility, 463
  hardware, 229 - 233
  Internet Mail, 502 - 504
  Microsoft Exchange, 433 - 436
  modems, 248, 249
  plug-and-play devices, 229
  printers, 225 - 227
  software, I-9, 201, 202
  TCP/IP protocol, 507
Integrated circuit, I-14
Intel Corporation, I-14, I-16
Interface, I-10
  command line, I-10
  graphical user (GUI), I-10
Internal memory, I-4
Internet, 247, 404, 463
  addresses, 484 - 487
  browsing, 489 - 495
  connecting to, 487, 488, 506 - 509
  disconnecting from, 499, 500
  downloading files from, 505, 506
  history of, 485
  performing searches of, 495 - 499
  printing pages of, 500
  transmitting mail through, 502 - 505
  types of services on, 484
  ways to connect to, 484, 485
Internet address, 485 - 487
Internet Explorer, 488
  Address box, 490
  Favorites, 492
  Go menu, 492, 493
  Links Toolbar, 494, 495
  progress bar, 495
  starting, 488
  Start page, 488, 489, 516
  Toolbar, 490
  using to browse the Internet, 489 - 495
  using to download files, 505, 506
  using to perform searches, 495 - 499
  using to print Internet pages, 500

using to transmit e-mail, 502 - 505
Internet Mail
installing, 502 - 504
receiving, 505
sending, 505
Internet Phone, 484
Internet Relay Chat, 484
Internet Service Provider, 485
connecting to Internet with, 506 - 509
Inverting colors of a cutout, 349
Io.sys file, 535
IP address, 486
ISDN, 421
ISP, *see* Internet Service Provider
Italic text, 170, 171, 274
in WordPad, 276, 277

J

Jobs, Steven, I-15
Joystick utility (Control Panel), 180
Justifying text, 281

K

KB, I-4
Key (Registry), 544
Keyboard, I-6, I-7
repeat feature, 193 - 195
Windows 95, A-4
Keyboard accessibility options, 240 - 242
Keyboard utility (Control Panel), 180
using to change cursor blink rate, 195
using to change repeat characteristics, 194, 195
Kilobyte, I-4

L

LAN, *see* Local area network
Landscape orientation, 222, 279, 352, 380
Laptop, *see* Portable computer
Large Icons view option
in Control Panel, 179
in Explorer, 85, 87
in Fonts utility, 204, 205
in My Computer, 106
in Printers folder window, 219
Laser printer, I-8
LCD panel, I-7
Line tool (Paint), 319, 325
Lining up Icons command, 86
Link (Internet), 489
Linked object, 556
creating, 559 - 561
editing, 564 - 566
Links Toolbar (Internet Explorer), 494, 495
List box, 17, 18
List view option
in Control Panel, 179
in Explorer, 86, 87
in Fonts utility, 205
in My Computer, 106
in Printers folder window, 219
Local area network, 420
Login (to network), 423
Long file name, 80
Lost clusters (file fragments), 394
Low density diskette, I-5
LPT1 port, 226

M

Macintosh computer, I-10, I-16
Magnifier tool (Paint), 319, 338
Mainframe computer, I-2
Margins, 280, 351, 381
Marking text (in DOS application), 521, 522
Mass storage device, I-4
CD-ROM drive, I-6
floppy disk drive, I-4
hard drive, I-4
tape drive, I-6
Mauchly, John, I-14
Maximize button, 11, 12
Maximizing a window, 10, 12
MB, I-4
Media Player (accessory), 404
Megabyte, I-4
Memory I-4
types of, 530 - 532
use in DOS application, 530 - 534
Menu, I-10, 5
color and font of, 192
symbols on, 6 - 8
using, 5 - 8
Menu bar, 5
Message (mail), 436
Messaging system, 432
Microchip, I-14
Microcomputer, I-2
Micro Instrumentation and Telemetry Systems (MITS), I-14

Microprocessor, I-14
Microsoft Backup, *see* Backup utility
Microsoft Corporation, I-10, I-11, I-15
Microsoft Exchange, 405, 432
  installing, 433, 434
  installing messaging services in, 434 - 436
  starting, 437
  using to manage e-mail, 440, 441
  using to receive e-mail, 440
  using to send e-mail, 437 - 439
  using with Microsoft Fax, 442
Microsoft Fax, 405, 442
  answer modes in, 447 - 449
  property sheets, 447 - 449
  using to receive a fax, 447 - 450
  using to send a fax, 444 - 447
  Viewer, 450
Microsoft Network, 404
Microsoft Plus! software, 502
Microsoft Windows, *see* Windows
Microsoft Word, 48, 160, 299
MIDI, 180, 239, 404
MILNET, 485
Minicomputer, I-2, I-14
Minimize button, 11, 12
Minimizing a window, 10, 12, 132, 133, 579
Modem, 247, 404, 452
Modems utility (Control Panel), 180, 247
  using to configure a modem, 249, 250
  using to install a modem, 248, 249
Monitor, I-7, I-8
Motherboard, I-3
Mouse, I-7
  changing properties of, 195 - 197
  using, 3, 4
Mouse accessibility options, 244, 245
MouseKeys, 244, 245
Mouse pointer, 3
  changing look of, 196
  changing speed of, 197
  creating trails for, 197
Mouse utility (Control Panel), 180
  using to add mouse trails, 197
  using to change double-click speed, 196
  using to change pointers, 196
  using to swap mouse buttons, 195
Moving cutouts, 343
Moving files and folders
  undoing, 94
  using drag-and-drop, 91 - 93, 107 - 109
  using the Clipboard, 93, 94, 106
Moving graphics (in WordPad), 281, 282
Moving text, 53, 270
Moving windows, 10, 12
MS-DOS, I-15
  see also DOS
MS-DOS mode, 525, 577, 578
MS-DOS Prompt, 523, 524
Msdos.sys file, 536 - 539, 578, 579
Multimedia, I-9, 234, 403
Multimedia utility (Control Panel), 180, 237
  changing audio settings, 238
  changing other settings, 239
Multitasking, I-12, 442
Musical Instrument Digital Interface, *see* MIDI
My Computer, 3, 103
  shortcut keys for, A-3
  starting, 103, 104
  using to browse folders, 104 - 107
  using to copy floppy disks, 112, 113
  using to format floppy disks, 110 - 113
  using to move/copy objects, 106 - 109
  using to open Printers folder, 218

N

National Science Foundation (NSF), 485
Network, 419
  accessing, 423, 424
  hardware, 421, 422
  LAN, 420
  peer-to-peer, 420
  server, 420, 421
  sharing resources, 427, 482
  types of, 420, 421
  WAN, 420
Network administrator, 425
Network cabling, 422
Network control utility, 425 - 427
  see also Network utility
Network hub, 422
Network interface card, 422
Network Neighborhood, 424, 425
Network server, 421
Network utility (Control Panel), 180, 254
New command
  in Explorer, 100
  in Paint, 320
  in WordPad, 46, 300
New Connection Wizard, 429, 430

News groups, 484
Notepad, 54, 267, 315, 377
  editing text in, 378, 379
  entering text in, 378
  headers/footers in, 381, 382
  page setup in, 380, 381
  printing in, 379
  searching for text in, 379, 380
  starting, 377, 378
  word wrap in, 378
Novell Netware, 423
Numeric keypad, I-6
Num Lock key, I-7
Num Lock light, I-6

O

Object (OLE), 556
Object linking and embedding, 290, 556
  editing an embedded object, 562 - 564
  editing a linked object, 564 - 566
  embedding an object, 557 - 562
  embedding vs. linking, 556, 557
  linking an object, 559 - 561
  terminology, 556
OLE, *see* Object linking and embedding
OLE client, 556
OLE container, 556
OLE server, 556
Online help
  context sensitive, 63, 64
  for DOS commands, A-8, A-9
  for Registry Editor, 554
  for Windows 95, 57 - 63, 76
Online information service, 247, 404, 484
Opaque mode (Paint), 331, 339, 344
Open
  application, 36 - 39, 84, 248
  document, 47, 48, 84, 148, 302
  file set, 387
  folder, 82 - 84, 148
Open architecture, I-15
Open command, 47
Open With dialog box, 84, 155
Operating system, I-9, I-10
  DOS, I-10
  Windows 95, I-11 - I-13
Option button, 17, 18
Options Box (Paint), 318 - 320
Outbox (Exchange), 437
Output device, I-7
  monitor, I-7, I-8
  printer, I-8
Overwrite mode (WordPad), 270

P

Page (in dialog box), 18, 19
Page orientation, 222, 279, 352, 380
Page Setup dialog box
  in Notepad, 380 - 382
  in Paint, 351 - 353
  in WordPad, 279, 280
Paint, 317
  changing size of drawing area, 354, 355
  custom colors in, 366, 367
  erasing in, 334, 335
  manipulating cutouts in, 340 - 349
  print preview, 353, 354
  selecting part of a graphic in, 338 - 340
  setting margins in, 351
  specifying page orientation, 352
  starting, 318
  using drawing tools, 323 - 329
  using text in, 329 - 332
  using to create wallpaper, 355, 356
  using to draw a graphic, 320 - 322
  using with WordPad, 289
  window components, 318 - 320
  zooming in, 335 - 338
Paintbrush (Windows 3.1), 368
Paint Can tool (Paint), 319, 329
Painting program, I-9
Palette
  for screen elements, 191, 213, 214
  for screen fonts, 191
  in Paint, 366, 367
Paragraph (in WordPad), 280
Paragraph formatting (WordPad), 280 - 286
Parent folder, 78, 105
Password, 187, 423
Passwords utility (Control Panel), 180, 254
Paste From command (Paint), 343
Pasting down a cutout, 342
Pasting from the Clipboard, 54
  in Calculator, 372
  in DOS application, 522
  in Explorer, 93, 94
  in My Computer, 106, 107
  in Paint, 342
  in WordPad, 271
Path name, 80, 81

Pattern (Desktop), 182 - 184
PC, I-2
PC-DOS, I-15
  see also DOS
Pencil tool (Paint), 319, 314
Peripherals, I-3
Personal computer, I-2
  components of, I-2 - I-8
Phone Dialer accessory, 62, 415
PIF Editor, 527
Pixel, I-8, 318, 335
Plug-and-play, I-13, 229, 249, 470
Point (unit of measure), 191, 203, 274, 330
Point at (with mouse), 3
Pointer, *see* Mouse pointer
Pointer trails, 197
Polygon tool (Paint), 319, 328
Port (printer), 221, 226
Portable computer, 461
Portable computing features
  Briefcase utility, 466 - 469
  Deferred printing, 469 - 471
  Direct Cable Connection utility, 463 - 466
  Docking detection, 462
Portrait orientation, 222, 279, 352, 380
Postscript font, 203
Primary mouse button, 195
Print command, 49
  in Help, 59, 63
Printer, I-8
Printer driver, 221
Printer settings, 219 - 223
Printers folder, 180, 218
  using to add new printer, 225 - 227
  using to change printer settings, 219 - 223
  using to manage print jobs, 223 - 225
Printing
  a document, 48 - 50, 148
  Internet pages, 500
Print jobs
  canceling, 224
  changing order of, 225
  deferring, 469 - 471
  pausing, 224
Print Manager (Windows 3.1), 224
Print manager window, 224
Print preview
  in Paint, 353, 354
  in WordPad, 296 - 298
Print quality, 222
Print queue, 224, 469
Profile
  hardware, 252, 462
  in Microsoft Exchange, 433
  user, 254
Program, I-2
  see also Application
Programs option (on Start menu), 36
  adding menu items to, 135, 137 - 141
  removing menu items from, 140, 141
Progress bar (Internet Explorer), 495
Project folder, 162 - 164
Property sheet, 159, 176
  for accessibility options, 240 - 246
  for computer system, 250 - 253
  for display, 182 - 192
  for file or folder, 159, 160
  for DOS application, 526 - 534, 577
  for hardware, 194 - 197, 219 - 223, 237 - 239, 247 - 250
  for Microsoft Fax, 447 - 449
  for shortcut, 160 - 162
Protocol, 506
  FTP, 484
  HTTP, 490
  TCP/IP, 506, 507
Pull-down menu, 5

Q

Question-mark (help) button, 63
Quick View option, 154

R

Radio button, 18
RAM, I-4
Random access memory, I-4
Read-ahead buffer, 253
Read-only attribute, 160
Read-only memory, I-4
Receive
  a fax, 447 - 450
  a file (HyperTerminal), 460, 461
  e-mail, 440
  Internet Mail, 505
Recent folder, 142
Rectangular Selection tool (Paint), 319, 338, 339
Recycle Bin, 96 - 98, 124, A-10
  emptying, 98

restoring objects from, 98
Refresh command (Explorer), 83
Regional Settings utility (Control Panel), 181, 254
Registered file type, 150 - 152
creating, 152 - 156
modifying, 156 - 158
removing, 156
Registry, 544
backing up, 550 - 554
editing, 545 - 550
exporting, 551 - 553
importing, 553, 554
root (main) keys, 544, 545
structure of, 544, 545
Registry Editor, 545, 546
finding entries, 549
starting, 546
using to edit the Registry, 546 - 550, 579, 580
using to export the Registry, 551, 552
using to import the Registry, 553
Regular font style, 276
Remote network access, 427
see also Dial-Up Networking
REN (DOS) command, A-9
Renaming objects, 98, 99, 148
Repeat delay, 192, 195
Repeat feature of keyboard, 193
Repeat rate, 194, 195
Replacing text (WordPad), 295, 296
Resizing cutouts, 345
Resizing graphics (in WordPad), 292
Resizing windows, 11, 12
Resolution (printer), I-8, 222
Restarting Windows 95, 22, 33
from a DOS prompt, 23
in MS-DOS mode, 23, 525
Restore button, 12
Restoring windows, 12
Retrieving a cutout, 343
Rich Text Format, 299
Right-click the mouse, 4
Right-drag the mouse, 4
ROM, I-4
Root folder, 78
Rotating a cutout, 347
Rounded Box tool (Paint), 319, 327
Ruler (WordPad), 268, 269, 283 - 285
Run option (on Start menu), 37

S

Save As command, 46, 387
Save command, 40
Saving a cutout, 343
Saving a document, 44 - 46
Scalable font, 203, 276
ScanDisk utility, 391 - 395
Scheduler, 420
Scientific mode (Calculator), 370, 372 - 376
Screen saver, 185, 187
Scroll, 13, 14
Scroll arrow, 14
Scroll bar, 13
Scroll box, 14
Scroll buffer (HyperTerminal), 458
Search engine, 496
examples of, 497, 498
Search Index page (Internet Explorer), 497
Searching for
files and folders, 144, 148
Internet pages, 495 - 499
Registry entries, 549
text in a file, 147
text in a Notepad document, 379, 380
text in a WordPad document, 294 - 296
Search Results window (Find), 145, 148
Selecting graphics (in WordPad), 291
Selecting objects (Explorer), 89, 90
Selecting part of a graphic (in Paint), 338 - 340
Selecting text, 53
in DOS application, 520, 521
in WordPad, 270, 271
Selection cursor (WordPad), 271
Send
a fax, 442 - 447
a file (HyperTerminal), 459, 460
e-mail, 437 - 439
Internet Mail, 505
Send To command, 94, 95, 416
Sent Items folder, 437
Separator page, 220
SerialKey devices, 246
Server (network), 420
Settings option (on Start menu), 130, 178, 218
Share-level access, 427
Sharing network resources, 427, 482
Shockley, William, I-14
Shortcut, I-12, 101

creating, 101, 148
eliminating arrow in icon for, 580
on Start button menus, 135
property sheets for, 160 - 162
renaming, 102
Shortcut key, 8, 33, 75, 124, 142, 528, 530, A-1 - A-4
ShowSounds option, 243
Shutting down Windows 95, 21 - 23
Similarity view option, 205
Sizing handles, 291, 330
Skewing a cutout, 348, 349
Slider, 194, 196
Small Icons option
in Control Panel, 179
in Explorer, 85, 87
in My Computer, 106
in Printers folder window, 219
Software, I-1, I-8
applications software, *see* Applications
system software, I-9
Sound accessibility options, 242, 243
Sound card, 234
Sound Recorder (accessory), 404
Sound scheme, 235
built-in, 235
custom, 236
SoundSentry option, 242
Sounds utility (Control Panel), 181, 234 - 236
Spool (print jobs), 222
Spreadsheet program, I-9
Standard mode (Calculator), 370 - 372
Start button, I-12, 2, 3
Start button menus, 135
adding items to, 136 - 139, 141
removing items from, 140, 141
Starting applications
using Desktop shortcuts, 39
using Explorer, 84
using the Find utility, 148
using the Start menu, 36 - 38
Starting Windows 95, 2
options, 524, 536 - 540, A-4
Start menu, 21
adding items to, 136 - 139, 141, 174
color and font for, 192
Documents option, 37, 48, 141, 142
Find option, 143
Help option, 57
Programs option, 36, 135, 137 - 141
removing items from, 140, 141
Run option, 37
Settings option, 130, 178, 218
Shut Down option, 21
Start Menu folder, 135, 138, 139, 141
Start page (Internet), 488, 489, 516
Startup disk, 202
see also Bootable disk
StartUp folder, 139, 140, 213
Startup hotkeys, 536, 537
Startup menu, 539, 540
Startup options, 524, 536 - 540
Startup process, 535, 536
Start-up screen, I-10
Windows 3.1, I-11
Windows 95, I-13, 2
Status bar
in Explorer, 82
in Find, 145
in Paint, 318
in WordPad, 42, 268, 269
StickyKeys option, 241
Stretching a cutout, 347, 348
Strikeout text, 276
Subfolder, 78
Submenu, 7
Supercomputer, I-2
Surf the Internet, *see* Browse the Internet
Swap file, 253, 532
Sweeping a cutout, 344
Switching among applications, 52, 53
Synchronization (of files), 466
System attribute, 160
System.dat file, 544
System file, 160
System.ini file, 543
System Monitor accessory, 415
System utility (Control Panel), 181, 250 - 253, 265, 266

T

Tab (in a dialog box), 17, 18
Tab (WordPad), 283 - 285
Tape drive, I-6
Taskbar, I-12, 2, 3, 52, 75, 128, 174
changing location of, 129
font for, 129, 192
hiding, 130, 131
hiding the clock on, 131
increasing size of, 128, 129

keyboard shortcuts for, 76
Taskbar Properties dialog box, 130, 131, 140, 141, 237
TCP/IP protocol, 506, 507
Telnet, 484
Test page (for printer), 220, 227
Text box, 19, 20
Text editor, 54, 267, 377
Text file, 377, 459
Text file format, 299
Text file transfer (HyperTerminal), 459, 460
Text tool (Paint), 319, 329 - 331
Text Toolbar (Paint), 330, 331
Thumbnail (Paint), 337
Tiling windows, 132, 133
Timeout setting (for printer), 222
Title bar, 4, 5
Toggle, 7
ToggleKeys option, 242
Toolbar
in Control Panel, 179
in DOS application, 521 - 523, 530
in Explorer, 82, 87
in Fonts utility, 205
in Internet Explorer, 490
in My Computer, 105
in Printers folder window, 219
in WordPad, 45, 268, 269
Tool Box (Paint), 318, 319, 368
Tool tip, 45, 179
Transparent mode (Paint), 331, 339, 344
TrueType font, 203, 274
Trunk line, 421
Typeface, 202, 274
selecting in WordPad, 275 - 277

U

UNDELETE (DOS) command, A-10
Underline text, 276, 277, 331
Undo command
in Explorer, 94
in Paint, 322, 324
in WordPad, 270, 290
Uninstalling
DOS, 202
Windows 3.1, 202
Windows 95, 202
Windows 95 components, 202
Upper memory, 531
Upper memory block (UMB), 540
Uploading files, 505
Up One Level button, 105
URL (Universal Resource Locator), 490
Usenet, 484
User.dat file, 544
User-friendly, I-10
User-level access, 427
User profile, 254

V

Vacuum tube, I-14
Value entry (Registry), 544
Vertical scroll bar, 13, 14
Video adapter, I-7, 213
Video settings, 238
View Bitmap command (Paint), 320
Virtual memory, 253, 532
Volume Control (accessory), 404
Volume label, 112

W

Wallpaper, 180, 184, 185, 355, 356
WAN, *see* Wide area network
Web, *see* World Wide Web
What's This? command, 64
Wide area network, 420, 485
Wildcard, 145, 175, A-8, A-9
Window, 4
cascading, 132
changing the appearance of, 188 - 192
closing, 10, 12
maximizing, 10, 12
minimizing, 10, 12, 132, 133
moving, 10 - 12
resizing, 11, 12
restoring, 12
tiling, 132, 133
Windows (Microsoft), I-11, I-17
advantages of, I-11 - I-13
Windows 3.1, I-11, I-17
start-up screen, I-11
uninstalling, 202
Windows 95, I-11, I-17
advantages of, I-12, I-13
components (removing/adding), 202, 215
start-up options, 524, 536 - 540, A-4
start-up screen, I-13, 2
uninstalling, 202
Windows 95 keyboard, A-4

Windows application, I-12
Windows Messaging, *see* Microsoft Exchange
Window scheme
  custom, 190 - 192
  predefined, 189
Windows Explorer, *see* Explorer
WordPad, 41, 75, 76, 267
  aligning text in, 281
  copying text in, 270 - 272
  editing graphics in, 290
  editing text in, 43, 268 - 272
  entering text in, 42, 268
  file formats in, 298 - 301, 315
  finding/replacing text in, 294 - 296
  formatting text in, 278 - 286
  indentation in, 281 - 283
  inserting date/time in, 302
  inserting graphics in, 287 - 289
  manipulating graphics in, 290 - 292
  moving text in, 270 - 272
  print preview, 296 - 298
  selecting text in, 270, 271
  selecting units of measurement for, 303
  setting margins in, 280
  setting page orientation in, 279
  setting tabs in, 283 - 285
  specifying file formats in, 298 - 301
  starting, 42, 268
  using fonts in, 273 - 277
  word wrap in, 42, 268, 299, 300, 315
Word processor, I-9, 41
Word wrap
  in Notepad, 378
  in WordPad, 42, 268, 299, 300, 315
Work area (Paint), 318
Workstation, 422
World Wide Web, 404, 484
Wozniak, Stephen, I-15
Write (Windows 3.1), 299, 316
Write-protect a floppy disk, I-5
WYSIWYG, 274, 315

X

Xerox Corporation, I-16

Z

Zoom command (Paint), 336, 337